Conservative Parties and the Birth of Democracy

How do democracies form and what makes them die? Daniel Ziblatt revisits this timely and classic question in a wide-ranging historical narrative that traces the evolution of modern political democracy in Europe from its modest beginnings in 1830s Britain to Adolf Hitler's 1933 seizure of power in Weimar Germany. Based on rich historical and quantitative evidence, the book offers a major reinterpretation of European history and the question of how stable political democracy is achieved. The barriers to inclusive political rule, Ziblatt finds, were not inevitably overcome by unstoppable tides of socioeconomic change, a simple triumph of a growing middle class, or even by working class collective action. Instead, political democracy's fate surprisingly hinged on how conservative political parties – the historical defenders of power, wealth, and privilege – recast themselves and coped with the rise of their own radical right. With striking modern parallels, the book has vital implications for today's new and old democracies under siege.

Daniel Ziblatt is Professor of Government at Harvard University where he is also a resident fellow of the Minda de Gunzburg Center for European Studies. He is also currently Fernand Braudel Senior Fellow at the European University Institute. His first book, *Structuring the State: The Formation of Italy and Germany and the Puzzle of Federalism* (2006) received several prizes from the American Political Science Association. He has written extensively on the emergence of democracy in European political history, publishing in journals such as *American Political Science Review, Journal of Economic History,* and *World Politics.* Ziblatt has held visiting fellowships and professorships at Sciences Po (Paris), the Max Planck Institute for the Study of Societies (Cologne, Germany), Stanford University, the Radcliffe Institute (Harvard), and the Center for Advanced Studies (Munich, Germany).

Cambridge Studies in Comparative Politics

General Editor

Margaret Levi *University of Washington, Seattle*

Assistant General Editors

Kathleen Thelen *Massachusetts Institute of Technology*
Erik Wibbels *Duke University*

Associate Editors

Robert H. Bates *Harvard University*
Stephen Hanson *University of Washington, Seattle*
Torben Iversen *Harvard University*
Stathis Kalyvas *Yale University*
Peter Lange *Duke University*
Helen Milner *Princeton University*
Frances Rosenbluth *Yale University*
Susan Stokes *Yale University*
Sidney Tarrow *Cornell University*

Other Books in the Series

Continued after the index

Conservative Parties and the Birth of Democracy

DANIEL ZIBLATT

Harvard University

CAMBRIDGE
UNIVERSITY PRESS

CAMBRIDGE
UNIVERSITY PRESS

University Printing House, Cambridge CB2 8BS, United Kingdom

One Liberty Plaza, 20th Floor, New York, NY 10006, USA

477 Williamstown Road, Port Melbourne, VIC 3207, Australia

314-321, 3rd Floor, Plot 3, Splendor Forum, Jasola District Centre, New Delhi-110025, India

79 Anson Road, #06-04/06, Singapore 079906

Cambridge University Press is part of the University of Cambridge.

It furthers the University's mission by disseminating knowledge in the pursuit of education, learning and research at the highest international levels of excellence.

www.cambridge.org
Information on this title: www.cambridge.org/9780521172998
DOI: 10.1017/9781139030335

© Daniel Ziblatt 2017

First published 2017

A catalogue record for this publication is available from the British Library

Library of Congress Cataloging in Publication data
NAMES: Ziblatt, Daniel, 1972– author.
TITLE: Conservative parties and the birth of democracy / Daniel Ziblatt.
DESCRIPTION: New York, NY : Cambridge University Press, 2017. | Series: Cambridge studies in comparative politics
IDENTIFIERS: LCCN 2016056471 | ISBN 9781107001626 (hardback)
SUBJECTS: LCSH: Political parties – Europe. | Conservatism – Europe. | Democracy – Europe. | Europe – Politics and government. | BISAC: POLITICAL SCIENCE / General.
CLASSIFICATION: LCC JN94.A979 Z54 2017 | DDC 320.94–dc23
LC record available at https://lccn.loc.gov/2016056471

ISBN 978-1-107-00162-6 Hardback
ISBN 978-0-521-17299-8 Paperback

Contents

Figures

Tables

Preface

There is often a moment when a scholar's perspective is shocked into a new awareness of the problem he is working on. That moment struck me when I found myself on a detour from the basement archives of Hatfield House, a grand Jacobean-era home in Hertfordshire. I wandered down a long hallway with marble floors and high ceilings, the walls lined with oversized oil portraits depicting four centuries of ancestors. These were the Cecils, who had helped rule England since at least the reign of Queen Elizabeth I. There, standing amid the trappings of immense social power, I asked myself: How did the historical owners of this home and others like them, who had so much to lose and so much power at their disposal, ever come to terms with political democracy without fatally preventing its birth in the first place?

This question has absorbed me ever since. I became convinced that if I could answer it – if I could understand how and why powerful old-regime elites hand over political power with so much at stake – then I could begin to unscramble a great historical puzzle that bears far-reaching implications: how European societies themselves democratized over the course of the nineteenth and twentieth centuries. I have sifted through a century of archival and quantitative historical evidence in two countries, Germany and Britain, and analyzed the histories of a wide range of other European countries. Along the way, I have discovered the narrative of one of the most critical political phenomena in the contemporary world: how political institutions of accountability and representation are created and what makes them endure even through periods of uncertainty and crisis.

The answer I have arrived at is that the historical stabilization of European democracies required a long-run shift, spanning the mid-1800s to the mid-1900s, in the type of political parties representing *conservative social forces*. This finding may come as a surprise, as there is little doubt old-regime groups represented by conservative political parties were the most recalcitrant opponents of mass democracy. Yet, this is exactly why it is important to concentrate on the sources of their reluctant acquiescence to a new political order that they had initially resisted. European democracy's birth and its survival relied on an underappreciated earlier political rupture in the mid-nineteenth century: conservatives discovered the mobilizing power of modern political parties, which allowed them to protect their own interests, in turn ironically smoothing the way for a more stable path of democratization. Political systems endured when conservatives organized their own political parties and embraced the virtues of pragmatic political action – what nineteenth-century critics decried as "political wirepulling." By contrast, in the many countries where conservatives delayed this transition, the resulting legacy of rightist weakness and fragmentation was devastating in two ways. First, it left governments repeatedly susceptible to extreme right-wing groundswells that were chronically destabilizing; second, it meant there was little to rein in institutional strongholds, such as the military, Church, and powerful economic interests. These groups felt freer to insert themselves into politics directly, with gravely disruptive consequences.

Today, political democracies, new and old alike, are under siege, and Europe's past seems freshly relevant. For new, democratizing countries, Europe's experience reveals that old-regime elite party organization can help alleviate a key obstacle of democratic transitions, no matter whether old regimes elites are aristocrats, single-party rulers, or modern-day tyrants. Durable democratic transitions depend on the buy-in of groups opposed to democratic changes. And, robust political parties representing old regime successors can serve this role, easing democracy's opponents into new political regimes.

By the same token, Europe's past offers insight into the sources of resilience and decline in today's older democracies as well. Many contemporary advanced democracies – including my own – face a ferocious right-wing populist politics, which threatens to swallow older, self-identified conservative political parties. A historical view makes clear that this development is ominous. As I argue in this book, democracy required a long tradition of robust, organized and pragmatic conservative parties in order to be viable. If this type of conservative political party fails to develop, or falters, a key buttress supporting democracy is undermined, making it more fragile. The age of democracy's birth may serve as a vital and cautionary warning for our current age of democratic crisis.

Acknowledgments

While researching and writing this book, I have benefited from the assistance and feedback of individuals and the support of generous institutions. Harvard University, including its Department of Government, the Minda de Gunzburg Center for European Studies, the Weatherhead Center, and the Institute for Quantitative Social Science, has provided an intellectually vibrant and inspiring home for my work. Additionally, large portions of the book were written at Stanford University's Center for Advanced Study in the Behavioral Sciences and the Radcliffe Institute for Advanced Study at Harvard University. Several other institutions have been critical to this book's research and writing: the Alexander von Humboldt Foundation, which supported several years of research for me in Germany as well as the Max Planck Institute in Cologne and University of Konstanz; also, at a critical point, Sciences Po (Paris, France) provided facilities for research and writing. Additionally, the following archives and libraries in Britain and Germany have provided indispensable sources for me: the Conservative Party Archive at Oxford University, Special Collections at the Bodleian Libraries (Oxford), Hatfield House archives, Kent History and Library Centre (Kent County Archive, Maidstone), and the British Library; and, in Germany, the *Bundesarchiv* (Berlin-Lichterfelde), Geheimes Staatsarchiv Preussischer Kulturbesitz (Berlin), the Bavarian State Library (Munich), and the *Hauptstaatsarchiv* in Stuttgart.

But above all this book reflects input, criticism, and conversation with friends, colleagues, and students. One individual who provided initial encouragement before I even knew exactly where my findings would lead me, and always insightful feedback on my manuscript at every stage, was my mentor and colleague, Peter Hall. Several outstanding historians – experts on Germany, Britain, and France – read the manuscript at key stages to give absolutely critical input, including some at a book workshop sponsored by the "Eric M. Mindich Encounters with Authors" series at the Institute for Quantitative Social Science at Harvard. These historians are Barry Jackisch, Larry Eugene Jones, Thomas

Kühne, Charles Maier, Philip Nord, Hans-Jürgen Puhle, Matthew Roberts, Thomas Weber, and Philip Williamson. Iain McLean of Oxford University has provided feedback from an early stage as well as detailed feedback on the book manuscript. At an earlier book workshop held at University of Washington, I received very useful input from colleagues including Margaret Levi and Steve Pfaff. I also would like to thank Karl Kaiser for a careful reading of my manuscript at an event sponsored by Beth Simmons at the Weatherhead Center.

I have also presented versions of the manuscript at many institutions around the world, receiving useful feedback from Francis Fukuyama, Larry Diamond, and Stephen Krasner at Stanford University; Cornelia Woll and Jan Rovny at Sciences Po (Paris); Jan Teorell and his colleagues at Lund University (Sweden); Svend Erik Skaaning and Joergen Moeller at Aarhus University (Denmark); and Nancy Bermeo and Giovanni Capoccia at Oxford University. Additionally, I thank participants at workshops where I have presented my work at Arizona State University, University of British Columbia, Columbia University, George Washington University, Harvard University (The State and Capitalism Seminar), the Institute of Political Economy and Governance (Barcelona), Johns Hopkins University, Princeton University, Stanford University, and Yale University.

In addition to direct feedback on the manuscript, there are several colleagues and friends at Harvard University who, in ongoing conversation, often over lunch, provided enduring inspiration and encouragement: Noam Gidron, Patrice Higonnet, Torben Iversen, Steve Levitsky, Eric Nelson, James Robinson, and Nancy Rosenblum. Other colleagues and friends at other institutions have been a source of insight and assistance at key moments: David Art, Laia Balcells, Sheri Berman, Nancy Bermeo, Michael Bernhard, Deborah Boucoyannis, Giovanni Capoccia, Carles Boix, John Hall, Stephen Hanson, Ken Jowitt, Herbert Kitschelt, Jeff Kopstein, Marcus Kreuzer, Evan Lieberman, Paul Pierson, Jonathan Rodden, Dan Slater, John Stephens, David Stasavage, Kathy Thelen, and Joseph Wong.

My graduate and undergraduate students have been a critical part of this project from the beginning, providing ideas and research assistance. I have worked closely with seventeen Harvard undergraduate and graduate students on this project. In its beginning stages, two students, Eric Nguyen and Meike Schallert, formed a formidable and talented research team to which I am very grateful. I also received assistance from Theu Dinh, Didi Kuo, Roumiana Theunissen, and Charles Wells, and at later stages in the project from Elizabeth Auritt, Laura Bronner, Joan Cho, Aditya Dasgupta, Christian Garcia, Johannes Gerschewski, Konstantin Kashin, Christine Legros, Martin Liby Alonso, Brendan McElroy, and Manuel Melendez. Critical assistance in the last stages of the project was provided by Colleen Driscoll, Aizhan Shorman, and Patricia Martin-Sanchez. I also thank Tom Willkens and Susan Karani for outstanding editorial input, as well as Lew Bateman and Robert Dreesen at Cambridge University Press for their interest and support of the book.

Parts of different chapters of this book were first published in the *American Political Science Review* (2009), *World Politics* (2008), and the *Journal of Economic History* (2015). Special recognition goes to Aditya Dasgupta, who coauthored the *Journal of Economic History* article with me, and whose thinking on bond markets and political history has shaped my own, as reflected in Chapter 3 of the book.

A word of personal thanks to my parents, David and Susan Ziblatt, who in long, late-night phone calls from California and beautiful summers under the redwoods have provided more inspiration for my work than anyone can imagine. And finally, to my wife Suriya and two beautiful daughters, Talia and Lilah, who were born after the book was already underway – I thank you.

I

Two Patterns of Democratization

On November 9, 1918, after weeks of violent confrontations with armed internal security forces in German cities, thousands of protestors – on factory floors, in naval shipyards, and in city centers – heard the rumor that Kaiser Wilhelm was abdicating. Workers abandoned their factories, flowing into the streets of Berlin; troops disobeyed orders prohibiting fraternizing with protestors; and a red republican flag was hoisted on the Royal Palace. As socialist leader Philipp Scheidemann proclaimed the republic from the Reichstag balcony later that afternoon, the fragile coalition of democratic opposition, which included socialists, Catholics, and communists, could be excused for thinking that these were the first unstoppable steps on the road to political democracy.[1]

The sequence of events immediately leading up to Scheidemann's speech – the protests, the negotiations, the scrambling concessions by the regime – was reminiscent of many democratic transitions. So were the events immediately following: the flight of the Kaiser, the forming of a constitutional assembly, the writing of electoral rules, and the first elections. Seventy years earlier in Vienna, in the spring of 1848, during Europe's first wildfire diffusion of revolution, intense protests against the Austrian monarch Ferdinand I led the conservative Chancellor Prince Metternich to flee, ending the Hapsburg Empire's absolutist regime. In Moscow, 143 years later, in the summer of 1991, at the high point of the European "third wave" of democratization, Boris Yeltsin seized the moment, bolstered by a massive groundswell of protest against Soviet rule, and climbed atop a tank to deliver a speech that helped bring the previously imposing regime to its knees. Twenty years after that, in Cairo, Egypt, on February 11, 2011, after days of violent confrontation, protestors in Tahrir Square triggered President Mubarak's resignation.

[1] See Sebastian Haffner, *Die verratene Revolution: Deutschland 1918/1919* (Bern: Scherz Verlag, 1969), 73–86.

Historic showdowns and the upsetting of authoritarian regimes capture our political imagination. But despite the appeal of these scenes, democracy is not built in the dramatic but fleeting moments of authoritarian collapse. In all of these instances, what seemed to be a democratic transformation was actually short-lived. In Austria in 1848, the "springtime of the people" famously collapsed in the "counterrevolutionary autumn." In Germany after 1918, the exhilaration of democratic optimism soon began to wane, as it also did in Russia after 1991 and Egypt even more quickly after 2011. Events occurring both long *before* and *after* any jubilant episode of transition can derail a process of democratization, despite the genuine hopes and aspirations of citizens who believe they have taken history into their own hands. But not every democratic breakthrough ends in disappointment; there are also examples of sustained democratic breakthroughs.

To gain a better understanding of these unexpected twists in history, we must shift our perspective and place the thresholds of a country's democratic transition within a longer time frame. If we analyze breakthrough moments within the context of a particular long trajectory of democratization, two important and revealing patterns come into view. We see that in some countries, a flash of democratic breakthrough is actually part of a relatively settled path of democratization. Punctuated moments of democratic change, once unleashed, accumulate over time and become self-reinforcing, making *and* meeting the demand for further such moments. In the process, democratization becomes harder and harder to dislodge.

In other countries, however, these breakthrough moments, if they occur at all, are part of what can best be characterized as unsettled paths of democratization: paths marked by a "failure to institutionalize." Breakthroughs are frequently preceded and followed by either outright democratic breakdown or subtle authoritarian backsliding, regime oscillations that make enduring democratic change both unstable and elusive. In the past and today, these two recognizable patterns of long-run democratization – settled and unsettled – reappear again and again. But we know little about what leads to these patterns. Why do some countries, in the long run, find themselves on one path and other countries on the other? What can we say about the causes of settled and unsettled democratization?

A BEGINNING: THE CASE FOR A LONG-RUN VIEW

In the dry farming plains of northern Mesopotamia, for millennia, patches of weeds and slight indentations in the ground hardly ever attracted notice from passersby, let alone the archaeologists who frequently traveled through the region. However, aerial photography, beginning in the 1930s, and, more recently, sophisticated satellite imagery have allowed archaeologists to discover that these barely noticeable indentations were more than just accidental, or merely part of the natural landscape.[2] Images taken from above – in what archaeologists dubbed "remote sensing projects" – demonstrated conclusively that these shallow linear depressions were in fact at the heart of an intricate and sophisticated 6,000 km roadway system from the Early Bronze Age (2600–2000 BC), providing the outlines of civilizational settlements previously undetectable to archaeologists working on the ground.[3]

Greater physical distance can expose patterns that were once invisible, or simply mysterious. In analogous fashion, *temporal* distance – moving out from single events and placing them within a longer time frame – can also expose previously undetectable social patterns. The study of how countries become democratic illustrates the advantages of a long-run view. Like archaeologists working too close to the ground, scholars of democratization have often failed to take sufficient temporal distance from their subject.[4] The consequence is a type of deeply disjointed short-run analysis that fails to discern important patterns. Scholars often try to identify all the factors that make a particular case of democratization – for example, Russia or Egypt *before* their transitions in 1991 and 2011 – "impossible"; then, once democratic change occurs, why such changes were "inevitable"; then later, as democracy derails, why enduring democracy must have been "implausible" all along.

Chasing ever-changing facts with ever-changing explanations is an ad hoc and ultimately unsatisfactory method of understanding the world. Adopting a long-run view is a corrective in two ways. First, like contemporary archaeologists looking down from above, we can also detect previously invisible or underappreciated patterns that matter *more* for specific outcomes than any democracy "score" in a single given year. Second, we can identify and elaborate new explanations for those patterns. If we only analyze democracy's causes and consequences, as scholars sometimes do, in terms of the level of democracy or authoritarianism at a single moment in time, then we miss the critical patterns that unfold over time.[5] Since democracies, like most institutions, require time to develop, it is important to study the cumulative

---

[2] See Jason A. Ur, "CORONA Satellite Photography and Ancient Road Networks: A Northern Mesopotamian Case Study," *Antiquity* 77 (2003): 102–15; Jason A. Ur, "Spying on the Past: Declassified Intelligence Satellite Photographs and Near Eastern Landscapes," *Near Eastern Archaeology* 76 (2013): 28–36.

[3] Ur, "Spying on the Past" (2013): 31.

[4] For an alternative elaboration of the benefits of "long-run" analysis in history, see Jo Guldi and David Armitage, *The History Manifesto* (Cambridge: Cambridge University Press, 2014).

[5] In addition to the gripping nature of regime transitions, long-term dynamics often get missed because analysts have not taken full advantage of the available systematic cross-national datasets that social scientists typically use in their cross-national analyses (e.g., Polity IV, Freedom House). Usually, analysts conduct time series cross-sectional analyses of countries, estimating probabilities of democratic transitions; for example, within a given year or, at the most, a decade-long time frame.

stock of democracy over longer periods.[6] Just as economists have discovered that the causes of short-run business cycles and long-run patterns of economic growth do not automatically coincide, political scientists face an analogous paradox: that the determinants of year-to-year fluctuations in annual democracy scores are not necessarily the same as the determinants of long-term patterns of democratization.

As democracy itself becomes a widely proclaimed value, the puzzling bimodal clustering of long-term patterns into settled and unsettled democratization has significant consequences. Recent empirical work has demonstrated that the accumulated stock of democratic experience may have even greater consequences for economic growth and global social welfare than annual levels of democracy.[7] Further, the cumulative history of democracy is a better predictor of a democracy's chances of surviving at any given moment in time than many contemporary correlates.[8]

This shift in perspective also provides an opportunity to rethink the dominant modes of social scientific explanations for regime outcomes in the modern world. Consider again two of our descriptions from the outset: neither Germany's apparent 1918 democratic breakthrough nor Egypt's in 2011 endured as settled pathways of democratization. Why? International factors certainly were important for both. Yet, that democracy failed so vividly in these particular instances but not in many of their neighboring countries in the same periods – Sweden in the 1930s or Tunisia immediately after 2011 – indicates that domestic sources of regime development loom large. Thus, we ask, was the problem for both, economic backwardness? Or, was the ultimate source of democratic weakness in Egypt and Germany an unassertive and disorganized civil society? Is it possible that an overly quiescent middle class or absent liberal force is chiefly to blame? Or was the problem in Egypt in 2011 or Germany after 1918 that old regime elites in both countries had insufficient safeguards to guarantee their interests, leading them to embrace counterrevolution?

While economic and class-based explanations (e.g., the role of the middle class, the role of the working class) for democratic development have been the object of decades of research, the last idea that incumbent elites "must feel secure" and "buy-in" to democracy for it be created and to endure is a more

---

[6] The concept "cumulative stock of democracy" draws on John Gerring, Phillip J. Bond, William T. Barndt, and Carola Moreno, "Democracy and Economic Growth: A Historical Perspective," *World Politics* 57, no. 3 (2005): 323–64.

[7] Gerring, Bond, Barndt, and Moreno, "Democracy and Economic Growth" (2005): 356. These authors have illustrated this point by demonstrating that a country's level of democracy in a single year has no measurable impact on its rate of economic growth in the subsequent year, while its democratic experience over the course of the twentieth century is positively associated with growth in subsequent years.

[8] Torsten Persson and Guido Tabellini, "Democratic Capital: The Nexus of Political and Economic Change," *American Economic Journal: Macroeconomics* 1, no. 2 (2009): 88–126.

recent discovery.[9] The importance of upper-class *opponents* of democratization, as paradoxically both facilitating as well as opposing it, has rarely been elaborated theoretically, much less evaluated empirically. That task will be a central preoccupation of this book. To study these issues over the long run, we turn to the past and to Europe, a region with both "settled" and "unsettled" experiences of democratization.

THE ERA OF MODERN DEMOCRACY'S BIRTH?

The years 1848 to 1950 represent a critical window in the history of democracy. The "long nineteenth century" has been described by political scientist Samuel Huntington as "democracy's first wave," when Europe, Latin America, and North America began to converge upon a common set of modern democratic institutions, including universal male suffrage, civil liberties, and constrained executives.[10] While the concept of political democracy itself is constantly evolving, during this period these institutions that occupy our attention first appeared in the modern world, sometimes in conjunction with each other and sometimes separately, but always transforming the structure of political rule.[11] Though its precise dates and main contours are easily disputed, this era's shared experiences and connections surely qualify it as an age defined not only by democratization but also by organized conservative countermovements. Beginning in the mid-nineteenth century, steamships, underwater ocean telegraph wires, and railroads provided new "lines of force" that knit Europe, Latin America, and North America into one increasingly integrated socioeconomic space.[12] And, within the Atlantic world, increasingly crisscrossed with trade routes and new lines of communication, a variety of progressive political ideas and doctrines – including the rise of modern social policy, economic regulation, city planning, progressive income taxation, and

---

[9] Guillermo A. O'Donnell and Philippe C. Schmitter, *Transitions from Authoritarian Rule. Tentative Conclusions about Uncertain Democracies* (Baltimore: Johns Hopkins University Press, 2013 [1986]).

[10] Samuel Huntington, *The Third Wave: Democratization in the Late Twentieth Century* (Norman: University of Oklahoma Press, 1991).

[11] For the purposes of this book, these three institutional domains – an expanded suffrage, civil liberties, and an executive accountable to elections via parliamentary rule or direct election – constituted the core arena of democratization. Any movement that expanded the scope of these institutions counts as democratization; de-democratization entails movement that undermined them. For elaboration, see Charles Tilly, *Democracy* (New York: Cambridge University Press, 2007); Robert Dahl, *Polyarchy: Participation and Opposition* (New Haven: Yale University Press, 1971).

[12] Charles S. Maier, "Consigning the Twentieth Century to History: Alternative Narratives for the Modern Era," *The American Historical Review* 105, no. 3 (2000): 807–31; Kevin H. O'Rourke and Jeffrey G. Williamson, *Globalization and History: The Evolution of a Nineteenth-Century Atlantic Economy* (Cambridge, Mass: MIT Press, 1999); Jeffry A. Frieden, *Global Capitalism: Its Fall and Rise in the Twentieth Century*, 1st ed. (New York: Norton, 2006).

democracy – made "Atlantic crossings," profoundly reshaping domestic politics.[13]

However, this period was not marked by only a single unidirectional "rise of democracy." There was no straight line, no single wave of democracy but rather two waves: one of democracy, the other of authoritarianism, moving in opposite directions and frequently colliding. In fact, it is precisely the coexistence of these two contradictory trends that make this era such rich terrain for contemporary scholars. Like today, the world was rocked by highly kinetic transnational political bursts of democratic opening but also by regressive retrenchments in which old autocratic regimes were reinstated, new forms of authoritarianism were invented, and efforts to democratize were defeated. Many political regimes experienced many openings and contractions, often in short succession.

For example, beginning in the two decades before 1848, a short first modest burst of democratization spread across the North Atlantic world. The states of the United States began a step-by-step process of eliminating property requirements to vote for white males in places such as Massachusetts in 1821, against the opposition of prominent figures such as John Adams and Daniel Webster, yet spreading to nearly all states by the 1850s.[14] In France, in the summer of 1830, after Charles X's restrictive July Ordinances prompted protests and barricades in the streets of Paris, the king was unseated and French democrats demanded universal suffrage.[15] And, in Britain, the Reform Act of 1832 was in part a response to social unrest while the radical Chartist movement in the late 1830s began its push for universal male suffrage.[16]

---

[13] Daniel T. Rodgers, *Atlantic Crossings: Social Politics in a Progressive Age* (Cambridge, Mass: Belknap Press of Harvard University Press, 1998); James T. Kloppenberg, *Uncertain Victory: Social Democracy and Progressivism in European and American Thought, 1870–1920* (New York: Oxford University Press, 1986).

[14] Alexander Keyssar, *The Right to Vote: The Contested History of Democracy in the United States* (New York: Basic Books, 2000), 29; Sean Wilentz, *The Rise of American Democracy: Jefferson to Lincoln*, 1st ed. (New York: Norton, 2005). Though other very significant restrictions that deserve not to be underestimated continued to exist and were newly implemented, property requirements for voting for white males had been eliminated in nearly every state by the 1850s.

[15] Pierre Rosanvallon, *Le Sacre du citoyen: Histoire du suffrage universel en France* (Paris: Gallimard, 1992).

[16] The most recent literature on the 1832 Reform Act is summarized in Matthew Roberts, *Political Movements in Urban England, 1832–1914* (London: Palgrave Macmillan, 2009). It was incidentally the unfolding of all of these events before the perceptive eyes of Alexis de Tocqueville in 1830 that in large part prompted his trip to America, and his increasingly firm belief that the central tendency of the age was egalitarianism and democracy. Also undoubtedly informing this view was de Tocqueville's attendance of regular lectures by a leading *Doctrinaire* of the time, Professor Guizot, between April 11, 1829 and May 29, 1830. Guizot's lectures are summarized in Francois Guizot, *The History of Civilization in Europe*, trans. William Hazlitt (London: Penguin Books, [1832] 1997). The lectures were animated by the idea that history was governed by inexorable laws of progress and an

But, another convulsion, this time larger, soon reverberated across the transatlantic world. Sparked by global economic turmoil, the Revolutions of 1848 ended King Louis Philippe's rule in France, triggered the short-run demise of autocratic regimes in central and southern Europe, prompted major reforms in Belgium and Scandinavia, and, across the Atlantic, led to rebellions in northeastern Brazil and in Chile.[17] In this instance, however, hopeful moments of democratization were quickly followed in 1849 and 1850 by the reinstating of many repressive regimes, giving rise to a newly robust authoritarianism that persisted for decades.

The late 1860s and early 1870s found a new twist in the transatlantic history of democracy. First, in the wake of many civil wars that led to the building of modern nation-states, it was not revolutionaries but rather statesmen, such as Lincoln and his successors, Bismarck, Napoleon III, and Disraeli, who reforged their societies by carrying out dramatic suffrage reforms. By granting manhood or near-universal manhood suffrage, these politicians facilitated the national integration of fragile nation-states wracked by sectional divisions.[18] In some instances, such as in France and Germany, such moves were intended quite explicitly to bolster nondemocratic regimes, not to weaken them. Unintentionally, such "top-down" maneuvers nonetheless helped launch the age of mass politics.[19]

Beginning in the 1870s, just as Emile Vandervelde and his embryonic socialist party gave rise to reform movements in Belgium that culminated in universal male suffrage in 1893, and left-liberals pushed for universal male suffrage in Sweden (where it was achieved after 1906), old commercial elites moved to *restrict* the franchise. In global cities such as New York, Dresden, and Hamburg, business leaders reacted to urbanization, immigration, and the perception that universal male suffrage and "machine politics" were corrupting influences.[20] The *New York Times'* editors viewed the Paris Commune of 1871,

---

inevitable forward march. See George Pierson, *Tocqueville and Beaumont in America* (New York: Oxford University Press, 1938), 23.

[17] Michael Rapport, *1848: Year of Revolution* (New York: Basic Books, 2009); Kurt Weyland, "The Diffusion of Revolution: '1848' in Europe and Latin America," *International Organization* 63 (2009): 391–423.

[18] Maier, "Consigning the Twentieth Century to History" (2000); Robert C. Binkley, *Realism and Nationalism, 1852–1871* (New York: Harper & Row, 1935).

[19] These reforms coincided with parallel Conservative-led suffrage expansion in Chile in 1874. See J. Samuel Valenzuela, *Democratización vía reforma: La expansión del sufragio en Chile* (Buenos Aires: Ediciones del IDES, 1985).

[20] On Belgium, see Claude Renard, *La Conquête du suffrage universel en Belgique* (Brussels: Éditions de la Fondation J. Jacquemotte, 1966). On Sweden, Leif Lewin, *Ideology and Strategy: A Century of Swedish Politics* (Cambridge: Cambridge University Press, 1988). On this episode in New York, see Sven Beckert, "Democracy and Its Discontents: Contesting Suffrage Rights in Gilded Age New York," *Past and Present* 174, no. 1 (2002): 116–57. On Dresden, and Saxony more broadly, see Simone Lässig, *Wahlrechtskampf und Wahlreform in Sachsen, 1895–1909* (Weimar: Böhlau, 1996). On Hamburg, see

led by Parisian workers and the Paris National Guard, as an attack on civilization. This reflected the widespread upper-class sentiment of prominent New Yorkers such as railroad attorney Simon Sterne, who organized a movement for New York's Governor Tilden to restrict voting rights in New York City to property holders only.[21] After the end of Reconstruction in 1876, but even more so beginning in the 1880s and 1890s, there were even more pernicious and successful efforts to roll back the suffrage on racial grounds. Figures such as South Carolina Governor Ben Tillman initiated a series of statutory changes and state constitutional conventions that transformed the political landscape of the U.S. South, creating single-party rule for the next sixty years.[22]

Finally, into the twentieth century, just as some moves were being made to restrict democracy, other reformers were also pushing ahead with limited democratic reforms in the last days before the First World War. For example, universal male suffrage did come to Sweden between 1907 and 1909, though its parliament remained weak; the House of Lords' veto power was diminished in Britain in 1911 but suffrage was still restricted; and in Argentina in 1912, the passage of Sáenz Peña Law assured universal and secret voting, but only for *men*.[23]

It was not until the end of the First World War and the simultaneous collapse of the Ottoman, Russian, Austro-Hungarian, and German empires that the fully transformative breakthroughs of mass democracy took hold. Before 1918, there had been only three republics in Europe and now were thirteen. In 1922, the influential British observer James Bryce, counting the number of new democracies in the world, concluded that he was witnessing "the universal acceptance of democracy as the normal and natural form of government."[24] In the wake of the Soviet Revolution and the Versailles Peace Treaty, it suddenly appeared the choice everywhere was, in the words of Weimar-era German jurist Hugo Preuss, a stark one — "Wilson or Lenin."[25] However, very quickly, as

Richard Evans, "Red Wednesday' in Hamburg: Social Democrats, Police and Lumpenproletariat in the Suffrage Disturbances of January 17, 1906," *Social History* 4, no. 1 (1979): 1–31.
[21] Sven Beckert, *The Monied Metropolis: New York City and the Consolidation of the American Bourgeoisie, 1850–1896* (Cambridge, UK and New York: Cambridge University Press, 2001), 180.
[22] J. Morgan Kousser, *The Shaping of Southern Politics: Suffrage Restriction and the Establishment of the One-Party South, 1880–1910* (New Haven: Yale University Press, 1974); Robert G. Mickey, *Paths Out of Dixie: The Democratization of Authoritarian Enclaves in America's Deep South, 1944–1972* (Princeton: Princeton University Press, 2015).
[23] On each, see Lewin, *Ideology and Strategy: A Century of Swedish Politics* (1988); Philip Norton, "Resisting the Inevitable? The Parliament Act of 1911," *Parliamentary History* 31, no. 3 (2012): 444–59; Ruth Berins Collier, *Paths Towards Democracy: The Working Class and Elites in Western Europe and South America* (Cambridge: Cambridge University Press, 1999), 46.
[24] James Bryce, *Modern Democracies* (New York: The Macmillan Company, 1921), 4.
[25] Ellen Kennedy, *Constitutional Failure: Carl Schmitt in Weimar* (Durham: Duke University Press, 2004), 111.

economic crisis wracked the globe, democracies quickly unraveled; parliaments became the object of derision; vitriolic right-wing and left-wing critiques of parliaments diffused; and democracies fell, first in Poland, Portugal, Italy, and Spain, and then, after 1928, even in one of the world's richest countries, Germany, and across the globe.

Thus, though democracy may have been *the* theme of the age, this era attracts our attention because it followed cycles of rapid expansion and contraction that mark all democratic ages, including our own. Just as the economic world became increasingly integrated and interconnected, so too did politics. Fluctuations in the price of grain at the Chicago futures market could increasingly affect the economic fate of East Prussian Junkers; consumption patterns of new middle-class citizens in locations as distant as Chile and Romania were set in their breathless emulation of the British and French middle classes.[26] Politics too were now more interlinked and the dual forces of democratization and de-democratization sat side by side, making this period a critical one not only for understanding the birth of modern democracy in Europe but also for analysts trying to comprehend the causes of long-run democratic development more generally.

INSIDE EUROPE: TWO PATTERNS OF DEMOCRATIZATION

Western Europe offers a particularly revealing vantage point. First, in Europe, there was a layer of historical burden that makes it a useful empirical subject for the contemporary study of democratization. Sociologist John Markoff has noted that it was ironically not in the world economy's "core" (i.e., Europe) where democracy came easiest. Rather, small-scale democratic experiments went furthest earliest (in the early nineteenth century) in egalitarian agrarian settler societies on the global "periphery," far from the seat of global power, in such distant locations as New Zealand, Australia, and North America.[27] The idea of democratizing Europe's often repressive states, usually sitting atop concentrated landholding structures and highly stratified societies, bolstered by nondemocratic church institutions, represented a different and more challenging prospect altogether. What Arno Mayer calls Europe's "old regime" in this sense actually resembled contemporary authoritarian regimes more than one might first imagine.[28] In light of the contemporary durability of authoritarianism across the globe, the question of how Europe's democracies

---

[26] Andrew C. Janos, "The Politics of Backwardness in Continental Europe, 1780–1945," *World Politics* 41, no. 3 (1989), 332.

[27] John Markoff, "Where and When Was Democracy Invented?" *Comparative Studies in Society and History* 41, no. 4 (1999): 660–90. The situation of democracy in the United States, in Markoff's view, was challenged only after the United States increasingly became a global power in the 1890s.

[28] Arno J. Mayer, *The Persistence of the Old Regime: Europe to the Great War* (New York: Pantheon Books, 1981).

themselves democratized, when placed in a historical context, becomes even more puzzling.

But more than this, we must consider the bewildering divergence that characterized democracy's development within Europe during this hundred-year window between 1848 and 1950: a trait that also mirrors broader patterns in other places and historical periods. For example, scholars often note that suffrage reform came *early* to France, Germany, and Spain, but *late* to Britain, Belgium, and Sweden, while parliamentary sovereignty came *early* to Britain and Belgium, but *late* to Sweden, Germany, and only unevenly to France.[29] Despite the difficulty of disentangling the sequencing, timing, and coalitions underpinning these reforms, by taking a long-run view – the *temporal* equivalent of the archeologist's "remote sensing project" – we can clearly decipher two broad patterns of settled and unsettled democratization in Europe.

The first path of *settled democratization* was found in Britain, Belgium, the Netherlands, Norway, Sweden, and Denmark. Between 1848 and 1950, democracy in these countries was gradually constructed via a relatively direct path, absent high-profile moments of backsliding, authoritarian detours, or disruptive coups. Though democratization inevitably faced resistance and was always precarious, in these countries, political rights and institutional constraints on executives expanded over time *without* confronting complete constitutional breakdown or any serious retrenchment.

The second pattern, the mode of *unsettled democratization*, was apparent during the same period in Spain, Portugal, Italy, Germany, and in France before 1879. In these countries, democratic development was stalled for longer periods in time (as in Germany before 1918) and, once initiated, often subject to more severe antidemocratic threats and actual coups. This particular pattern of regime cycling revealed itself in these countries not only infamously in the years between the two world wars, but in the late nineteenth century as well.[30] Democracy was eventually achieved in these "unsettled" cases after the Second World War, and still later in Spain and Portugal, but most striking was that the pathway was marked by far greater institutional volatility.[31] At key moments, constitutional instability, regime breakdown, and even military coups marked these countries' unsettled histories. Thus, analyzing these two

---

[29] Stein Rokkan, *Citizens, Elections, Parties: Approaches to the Comparative Study of the Processes of Development* (New York: McKay, 1970); Collier, *Paths Towards Democracy* (1999); Dahl, *Polyarchy* (1971).

[30] For an incisive elaboration of the theoretical problems this type of "chronic instability" poses for traditional institutional analysis, see Michael Bernhard, "Chronic Instability and the Limits of Path Dependence," *Perspectives on Politics* 13, no. 4 (2015): 1–16.

[31] Giving us further confidence in the clustering of these countries into these two groups, it is worth noting that the only country in the *settled democratizers* with a single year of "backsliding" over the entire period, where the Polity IV score declined from the previous year, was Denmark in the 1860s. In the second cluster (*unsettled democratizers*), every single country experienced multiple years of democratic backsliding in which the Polity IV score declined over a previous year.

groups of countries, settled and unsettled democratizers, within this distinct window of time allows us to explore the barriers to stable democratization in Europe, shedding light on the long-run causes of these two broader patterns.

At the outset, it is crucial to clarify what I am *not* explaining. Most social scientific work on European democratization has been starkly bifurcated, either explaining the inauguration of specific formal democratic rules at certain "thresholds" of democratization in the nineteenth century and early twentieth century, or, on the other hand, explaining moments of democratic breakdown in the twentieth century.[32] The deep links between these two high-profile moments of change have not been fully analyzed.[33] The first set of writings focuses on episodes of suffrage expansion and those moments of "democratic transition" when democracy was formally achieved. The second set instead seeks to explain the demise of democracy in the interwar period, either analyzing the short-term political dynamics surrounding regime collapse or tracing the deep historical roots (e.g., back to feudalism, the nature of agricultural commercialization) of various interwar regime outcomes.[34]

Though each body of literature is powerful on its own terms, when juxtaposed they appear as near mirror images, revealing their respective limitations. Focusing on "democratic transitions" offers great insight into the formal adoption of democratic rules but tells us very little about long-term patterns *after* the adoption of formal rules. Scholarship on the "breakdown of democracy," by contrast, usually pivots around a particular historical endpoint and divulges very little about earlier moments of democratization, reducing all

---

[32] On the former, see, for example, Collier, *Paths Towards Democracy* (1999). Gertrude Himmelfarb, "The Politics of Democracy: The English Reform Act of 1867," *Journal of British Studies* 6, no. 1 (1966): 97–138; Collier, *Paths Towards Democracy* (1999). On the latter, see Juan J. Linz and Alfred C. Stepan, *The Breakdown of Democratic Regimes: Crisis, Breakdown and Reequilibration* (Baltimore: Johns Hopkins University Press, 1978); Gregory M. Luebbert, *Liberalism, Fascism, or Social Democracy: Social Classes and the Political Origins of Regimes in Interwar Europe* (New York: Oxford University Press, 1991); Nancy Bermeo, *Ordinary People in Extraordinary Times: The Citizenry and the Breakdown of Democracy* (Princeton: Princeton University Press, 2003); Giovanni Capoccia, *Defending Democracy: Reactions to Extremism in Interwar Europe* (Baltimore: Johns Hopkins University Press, 2005).

[33] A partial exception to this is Barrington Moore (1966), whose sweeping analysis of patterns of modernization is intended, in part, to explain interwar outcomes. However, his empirical analysis, especially of European cases, focuses more on early patterns of agricultural commercialization and early modern fights over absolutism and for Europe, largely ending in the eighteenth century and not actually encompassing specific battles over democratic reform in the nineteenth and twentieth centuries. See Barrington Moore, *The Social Origins of Dictatorship and Democracy: Lord and Peasant in the Making of the Modern World* (Boston: Beacon Press, 1966).

[34] See, e.g., the major works of Luebbert, *Liberalism, Fascism, or Social Democracy* (1991); Moore, *Social Origins of Dictatorship and Democracy* (1966); Dietrich Rueschemeyer, Evelyne Huber Stephens, and John D. Stephens, *Capitalist Development and Democracy* (Chicago: University of Chicago Press, 1992).

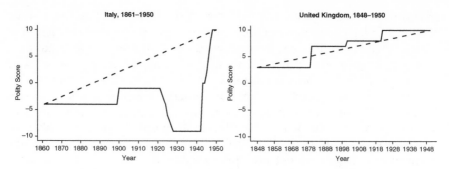

FIGURE 1.1: Two Paradigmatic Cases (Italy and Great Britain): Unsettled vs. Settled
Trajectories of Democratization in Europe, 1848–1950
Data Source: Polity IV

history to mere prologue to the "big events" of twentieth-century democratic
survival or collapse.[35]

This book conceptualizes democratization neither as singular moments of
"democratic breakthrough" nor as definable periods of "democratic
breakdown." Instead, taking the view from above, we account for a longer
time frame that encompasses *both* democratic breakthroughs and subsequent
regime cycling. In this way, we can elucidate broader patterns of regime
development.[36] In so doing, the two patterns of settled and unsettled
democratization within Europe come into clear view. Consider Figure 1.1,
which uses the cross-national dataset Polity IV to track the paths of
democratic development of two particularly well-known European historical
cases that also display the two patterns vividly: the United Kingdom and Italy.

[35] This risk of ex post retrospective bias certainty of these approaches is seen, for example, when we
consider how specific institutional democratizing reforms such as the early adoption of the secret
ballot, early universal suffrage, and other democratizing electoral reforms are dropped from the
sweeping accounts of countries that ended up fascist, for example, Luebbert, *Liberalism,
Fascism, or Social Democracy* (1991); Moore, *Social Origins of Dictatorship and Democracy*
(1966). See critique in Margaret Lavinia Anderson, *Practicing Democracy: Elections and
Political Culture in Imperial Germany* (Princeton, NJ: Princeton University Press, 2000).
Similarly, consider how all pre-1914 defeats of democratic reform are glossed over in democratic
states that ended up surviving in the interwar period.

[36] I follow Tilly, *Democracy* (2007), who considers any moves toward greater institutional
contestation and inclusion as *democratization* and moves away from them as *de-
democratization*. This corresponds to what Paul Pierson (2004) dubs a "moving pictures"
approach vs. a "snapshot" approach to social science, where outcomes themselves vary in
how they unfold over time. In studies of democratization, such an approach is implicit in the
recent work of Tilly (2007) and Acemoğlu and Robinson (2006), who distinguish between
different patterns of democratic stability as their main outcomes. See Paul Pierson, *Politics in
Time: History, Institutions, and Social Analysis* (Princeton: Princeton University Press, 2004);
Tilly, *Democracy* (2007); Daron Acemoglu and James A. Robinson, *Economic Origins of
Dictatorship and Democracy* (Cambridge: Cambridge University Press, 2006).

Figure 1.1 reports each country's annual "regime score," contrasting Great Britain's low starting point and settled path of gradual democratization with Italy's much less direct path, represented by the visually crooked line in the Polity IV data.[37] The dashed line connects each country's Polity IV score in the first year for which data is available to its Polity IV score in 1950, showing what would have been the most direct route to democracy given each country's starting point.

Had Italy's democratization experience been analyzed at any single moment – for example, after the upheaval and change that preceded its well-studied suffrage extension in 1912 – we might have suspected Italy was following a path not unlike Britain's.[38] Yet, as Figure 1.1 shows, Britain in the long run ultimately followed a more settled path than Italy. While no two countries' paths to democracy were exactly alike, Italy's and Britain's are exemplary of the two types of unsettled and settled democratization in Europe over this period more generally.

Some countries' paths looked more like Italy's – Germany, Portugal, Spain, and France before 1879 – in which history traced a circuitous route involving frequent breakthroughs (France in 1848 and 1870; Spain in 1873 and 1931; Portugal in 1910; Germany in 1918) often quickly followed by complete democratic breakdowns or coups d'etat (France in 1852; Spain in 1874 and 1936; Portugal in 1926; and Germany in 1933). By contrast, countries like Great Britain, Sweden, Belgium, the Netherlands, and France after 1879 moved in a relatively straight line toward democratic stability, overcoming intense moments of contention yet not suffering major regime interruptions into the post–Second World War era.

While a deep reading of the comparative and historical literature makes these different patterns self-evident, one way of summarizing them concisely is to draw again on the Polity IV annual democracy data to rank a selection of western European countries' political regime volatility over time. There are many ways of assessing levels of political volatility in a given time period, including counting the number of regime reversals or the number of years a country "counts" as a full-blown democracy.[39]

In contrast to some other accounts that rely on more complex assumptions, we can show how unsettled or settled a democratization process was over a particular time frame by constructing a simple ratio comprised of a numerator and denominator drawing on Polity IV values presented in the figures above.

---

[37] Italy's score begins in 1861, the first year data are available in Polity IV because of Italy's unification that year.

[38] On Italy's 1912 reform, see Collier, *Paths Towards Democracy* (1999), 68–72.

[39] For a variety of other valuable efforts to measure a similar idea, see Edward L. Gibson, *Class and Conservative Parties: Argentina in Comparative Perspective* (Baltimore: Johns Hopkins University Press, 1996); Gerring, Bond, Barndt, and Moreno, "Democracy and Economic Growth" (2005); Persson and Tabellini, "Democratic Capital: The Nexus of Political and Economic Change" (2009).

The numerator is the statistical distance that a country's Polity IV score traveled as it democratized between two points in time (in this case, 1848 and 1950, represented in the examples above by the solid line). The denominator is the distance of what would have been a country's most "efficient" or direct path from its actual starting point to its actual end value (again, in this instance 1848 and 1950, represented in Figure 1.1 by the dashed line).[40] The more crooked the line over the time period – the longer and more circuitous the route to democracy – the higher the volatility score. The shorter the relative length of the line, the more direct the route to democracy and the lower the volatility score (i.e., the closer to the value of 1/1).[41] Using this method, Figure 1.2 ranks European countries' regime volatility between 1848 and 1950.

At the left end of Figure 1.2 are countries with a volatility score near 1, which followed relatively steady and nearly linear paths (found in Britain, Belgium, the Netherlands, and Scandinavia) marked by a slow-moving and largely unidirectional process of democratization over the course of the late nineteenth century and first half of the twentieth century. In these countries, there were few if any instances of authoritarian backsliding, and the process of democratization appeared increasingly institutionalized. These countries' actual paths of democratization approximate the most direct possible paths of democracy possible, given their respective starting points in 1848, suggesting that history sometimes actually does move efficiently.

However, as the experiences of the countries at the right end of Figure 1.2 make clear, this is not always the case. Here, we see Europe's unsettled national paths of democratization (found in Germany, Italy, Portugal, Spain, and France). In these countries with higher volatility scores, democratization did occur, but bursts of democratization were often followed by equally rapid authoritarian detours, including stalled democratic reform (e.g., Germany), a pattern of lurching between regime types (e.g., Spain and France), threats of coups (e.g., Germany and France), democratic backsliding (e.g., Spain, France, Portugal, and Germany), and most famously the complete breakdown of democracy in the interwar period (e.g., Spain, Portugal, Germany, and

---

[40] This ratio measure captures the concept of "regime volatility" experienced by each country between 1848 and 1950. If the actual path matched the most efficient path, the ratio would be 1. To take one example: Italy's actual path covers approximately 109 units, while its most efficient path would have covered 90 units. The ratio is 109:90, or 1.21. The most efficient distance is calculated as the length of the hypotenuse of a right triangle, with legs composed of the change in years (e.g., 109 units from 1861 to 1950) and the change in polity score (e.g., 9 units for a country whose score goes from 1 to 10). The actual distance repeats the procedure but draws triangles for each annual change. For example, if a country's polity score dropped one unit over one year, the length of the line segment between the two years is $\sqrt{((1)^2 + (1)^2)}$ or $\sqrt{2}$. The total distance of the actual path is the sum of these annual changes.

[41] By definition, the score has a minimum possible value of 1 (lowest volatility), with no theoretical maximum value of volatility.

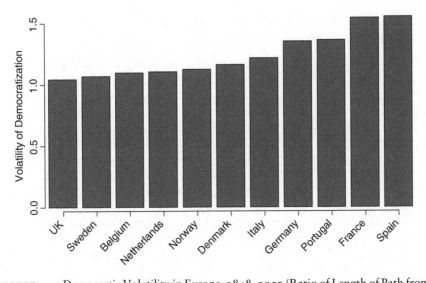

FIGURE I.2: Democratic Volatility in Europe, 1848–1950 (Ratio of Length of Path from Polity Score in 1848 to 1950/Length of Shortest Possible Line)
Note: These scores rank the stability of democracy between 1848 and 1950; lower scores indicate more stable democratization.
Data Source: Polity IV

Italy).[42] Here, in short, the actual paths of democracy's history more closely approximated a crooked line, reminding us of Bertolt Brecht's insight: "If there are obstacles in the way, the shortest path between two points may be a crooked line."[43]

[42] France's high volatility score primarily reflects the "breakthrough" and breakdown of 1848–51 period that lasted until 1871. Despite some threats of coups after 1878, the French Third Republic experienced no breakdowns after 1878 until the rise of the Vichy Regime in 1940. France certainly in this sense experienced a nearly full democratic transition after 1878. Critical for our purposes is its unsettled nature. (See, for example, Stephen E. Hanson, *Post-Imperial Democracies: Ideology and Party Formation in Third Republic France, Weimar Germany, and Post-Soviet Russia* (Cambridge: Cambridge University Press, 2010).) While surviving the nineteenth century intact, the democratic political order over the whole period was subject to more instability than other more "settled" cases – it is thus a hybrid case with a democratic transition combined with consistent threats of revanchist monarchists in the 1880s and a strong radical right throughout. See, for example, William D. Irvine, *The Boulanger Affair Reconsidered: Royalism, Boulangism, and the Origins of the Radical Right in France* (New York: Oxford University Press, 1989). We return to this case in Chapter 10.

[43] Bertolt Brecht, "The Life of Galileo," in *Plays*, ed. Bertolt Brecht (London: Methuen, 1960). Brecht's line is used in the title of the semiautobiographical work by Geoff Eley, *A Crooked Line: From Cultural History to the History of Society* (Ann Arbor: University of Michigan Press, 2005).

UNSETTLED AND SETTLED DEMOCRATIZATION: THE LIMITS OF EXISTING THEORY

Why, to continue with Brecht's metaphor, does democracy follow a "crooked line" in some instances but run in a "straight line" in others? And, which obstacles *twist* the shape of democratic development, pushing it either toward a linear or crooked path? The task of understanding European democratization from the middle of the nineteenth century thus presents two analytical challenges: first, to explain the convergent tendencies of democratization; and second, to account for the stark divergence in the character of democratic development among European states. Tackling this two-pronged challenge not only helps us understand the European experience but also helps reveal the causes of democratization more generally.

While analysts after the Cold War initially often directed their attention exclusively to the causes of "democratic transitions" with the expectation that democracy might triumph everywhere, we make the opposite mistake if we exclusively focus on the determinants of authoritarian durability and give little consideration to forces pushing for democratization. Both dynamics are often present and democratic institutional reform has typically left the world with a bimodal distribution of political regimes.

Upon what factors does existing theory instruct us to focus in order to explain these patterns? European democratization, and democratization as a general phenomenon, is typically analyzed in one of four ways: as an agentless "bottom up" outgrowth of Europe's status as the world's pioneer of industrialization and creator of national socioeconomic wealth; as the reflection of a triumphant middle-class or urban bourgeoisie as the historical carriers of democratic demands; as the victorious achievement of a working-class movement whose threat of redistribution and revolution won a series of concessions from elites that were essential for democratization. Finally, a fourth and more recent account of democratization emphasizes the response of elites themselves as decisive for democratic success or failure.[44] If elites can be made secure with regard to their future wealth, status, and power as democratization unfolds, this account holds, rather than supporting counter-revolutions, critical portions of the elite will become reluctant but essential democrats. On the other hand, if elites remain insecure, politically fragmented, and fearful of major loses in their future, then they will support and even lead counterrevolution, creating a historic record of unsettled democratization.

Each of these four perspectives presents unresolved theoretical problems and empirical anomalies, some of which have already been mentioned. For example, an "agentless" frame of modernization that emphasizes growing national

---

[44] O'Donnell and Schmitter, *Transitions from Authoritarian Rule. Tentative Conclusions about Uncertain Democracies* (2013 [1986]).

wealth and higher median income is effective at identifying broad cross-national patterns.[45] But it cannot account for specific and important anomalies. Contrast Germany and Sweden, two late-industrializing countries in the semiperiphery of Europe in the 1870s. Germany was a classic instance of unsettled democratization, with stalled and tragically interrupted development before 1950, whereas Sweden was an exemplar of settled democratization, with a gradual and stable path after 1866. Very similar levels of GDP per capita and industrial-sector employment throughout the period certainly cannot explain the vast long-run political differences between the two countries.[46] Indeed, after 1890, Germany had an increasingly labor- and capital-intensive economy that provided the ripest of conditions for a pro-democratic "liberal–labor" ("lib–lab") coalition of the British model; yet, something left Germany, unlike Sweden, with an unreformable political system until the destruction of the First World War.[47] Even after 1918, the triumph of the "lib–lab" Weimar coalition, while electorally dominant, was not enough to guarantee German an enduring democracy. In short, *a country's political regime is not simply a mirror of its economy.*

A perspective that accounts for successful democratization as the product of a rising urban-based commercial middle class correctly identifies a critical protagonist of democratic changes.[48] At the same time, it struggles to make sense of the fact that liberal political parties that spoke for the middle class, and were indeed defenders of early parliamentary sovereignty and partial suffrage extension, were at best ambivalent about mass democratization or universal male suffrage. In fact, such elite social groups and their political parties, as well as their social theorists, valued citizen "capacity" and had a view best summarized by the slogan: "votes should be weighed, not counted"; they could hardly be called upon to provide the mass mobilization for universal male suffrage or the foundations of mass democracy.[49]

---

[45] See Seymour Martin Lipset, "Some Social Requisites of Democracy: Economic Development and Political Legitimacy," *American Political Science Review* 53 (1959): 69–105; Carles Boix, *Democracy and Redistribution*, Cambridge Studies in Comparative Politics (Cambridge: Cambridge University Press, 2003); Carles Boix, "Democracy, Development, and the International System," *American Political Science Review* 105 (2011): 809–28.

[46] In fact, according to Maddison's (2007) estimates, Germany's GDP per capita *outpaced* Sweden's in 1870 ($1,839 vs. $1,662 in 1990 dollars) as well as in 1913 ($3,648 vs. $3,096). See Angus Maddison, *Contours of the World Economy* (Oxford: Oxford University Press, 2007), Table A7, 382.

[47] Ronald Rogowski, *Commerce and Coalitions: How Trade Affects Domestic Political Alignments* (Princeton: Princeton University Press, 1989).

[48] See, e.g., Barrington Moore (1966); most recently, see the important work by Ben Ansell and David Samuels, *Inequality and Democratization: An Elite-Competition Approach* (Cambridge: Cambridge University Press, 2014).

[49] See, e.g., Andrew Gould, *Origins of Liberal Dominance: State, Church, and Party in Nineteenth Century Europe*, Interests, Identities, and Institutions in Comparative Politics (Ann Arbor:

A third perspective emphasizes the critical role played by working-class socialist parties and the labor movement as "torchbearers of democracy."[50] This account has also been recast by contemporary political economists who argue that even the latent threat of revolution triggers democratic concessions.[51] While certainly correct in identifying critical protagonists pushing for democratic change, once again, anomalies are not accounted for. For example, if an organized working class was so critical to the process of democratization, why was Germany's political system, with by far the largest and best organized working class in Europe, among the least reformable in Europe into the twentieth century? Why also did it possess a remarkably inegalitarian three-class voting system, and why was its parliamentary sovereignty slow to develop until after the end of the First World War?[52] Conversely, if the organized working class was the most important agent for democratization and concentrated landed wealth its main barrier, why did Great Britain's democratization proceed in a settled fashion when its working class was comparatively moderate and its landed elites endowed with a higher concentration of land than elites anywhere else in western Europe – including eastern Prussia, the territory dominated by the fabled Junkers?[53]

The failures captured in these questions compel us to consider the fourth perspective: a perspective that highlights the response of established elites with the most to lose as democratization unfolds.[54] To receive the critical support required to generate a democratic transition, as well as to prevent a destabilizing counterrevolutionary backlash movement from emerging, authoritarian incumbents and their allies must be reassured that their interests in the end will be protected by trading countermajoritarian institutions for their support.[55] Political institutions such as unelected upper chambers, unelected

University of Michigan Press, 1999); Alan S. Kahan, *Liberalism in Nineteenth-Century Europe: The Political Culture of Limited Suffrage* (New York: Palgrave Macmillan, 2003), 5–6.

[50] The term "torchbearer of democracy" is from Geoff Eley, *Forging Democracy: The History of the Left in Europe, 1850–2000* (Oxford: Oxford University Press, 2002), 109. See, more generally, Rueschemeyer, Stephens, and Stephens, *Capitalist Development and Democracy* (1992).

[51] See, e.g., Acemoglu and Robinson, *Economic Origins of Dictatorship and Democracy* (2006).

[52] See Thomas Kühne, *Dreiklassenwahlrecht und Wahlkultur in Preussen 1867–1914: Landtagswahlen Zwischen Korporativer Tradition und Politischem Massenmarkt, Beiträge zur Geschichte des Parlamentarismus und der Politischen Parteien* (Düsseldorf: Droste, 1994).

[53] A highly coherent network of landed elites dominated all levels of British politics very late into the nineteenth century, occupying a majority of parliamentary seats and cabinet seats. For elaboration, see the next chapter. For data, see David Cannadine, *The Decline and Fall of the British Aristocracy* (New York: Vintage, [1990] 1999).

[54] O'Donnell and Schmitter, *Transitions from Authoritarian Rule. Tentative Conclusions about Uncertain Democracies* (2013 [1986]).

[55] Barry Weingast, Susan Alberts, and Chris Warshaw, "Democratization and Countermajoritarian Institutions: The Role of Power and Constitutional Design In Self-Enforcing Democracy," in *Comparative Constitutional Design*, ed. Tom Ginsburg (New York: Cambridge University Press, 2012), 69–100.

councils, or even federalism and an insulated military, all "beyond the reach of majorities," are regarded as critical mechanisms for assuaging elites and reassuring them of their control.[56] Thus, a democratic transition can be "crafted" by the agents of democratization, provided they are able to secure elite support, and, in so doing, limit egalitarian democracy. The choice both groups face is either accommodation or democratic breakdown.

That the majoritarian impulses of democracy need to be tempered by countermajoritarian institutions so that former authoritarian elites comply with democratic rules appears compelling at first glance, given a number of recent democratization experiences. For example, Portugal's post-transition Constitution in 1976 gave the Council of the Revolution (predominated by the military) the power to pass their own laws and the right to judge the constitutionality of all parliamentary laws; Spain's 1978 constitution guaranteed a special status for the Catholic Church; Poland's transition constitution of 1989 left only 35 percent of parliamentary (*Sejm*) seats contested; Chile's post-Pinochet transition in 1989 included restrictions on the ability of the President to appoint and remove heads of the military services leaving an insulated National Security Council dominated by the military, as well as a significant number of unelected Senate seats.[57] And finally, in an east Asian case such as the "archetypal" one of Taiwan, democratic transition after 1990 was driven, in the words of one important account, by the "victory confidence" of Taiwan's overwhelmingly dominant Kuomintang (KMT) who conceded free and fair elections, confident *they would not lose them*.[58]

Similar dynamics also seem to be on display in democracy's first wave. The "safeguard" of Britain's unelected House of Lords' veto power is sometimes attributed to having assuaged the fears of elites, allowing the peaceful passage of Britain's Third Reform Act of 1884; Germany's adoption of universal male suffrage in 1871 was accompanied by a weak national parliament which diminished the former's impact, leaving most taxing power out of the electorate's reach; the adoption of universal male suffrage in Belgium 1893 was achieved in part in exchange for the adoption of plural voting that gave the wealthy more votes; and, Sweden's turn to universal male suffrage in 1907–1909 was limited by a system of proportional representation that protected incumbent interests.

---

[56] See, e.g., Barry Weingast, Susan Alberts, and Chris Warshaw, "Democratization and Countermajoritarian Institutions: The Role of Power and Constitutional Design In Self-Enforcing Democracy," in *Comparative Constitutional Design*, ed. Tom Ginsburg (New York: Cambridge University Press, 2012), 69–100; James Fearon, "Self-enforcing Democracy," *The Quarterly Journal of Economics* 126, no. 4 (2011): 1661–708.

[57] This list of examples draws on Weingast, Alberts, and Warshaw, "Democratization and Countermajoritarian Institutions" (2012): 74.

[58] Dan Slater and Joseph Wong, "The Strength to Concede: Ruling Parties and Democratization in Development Asia," *Perspectives on Politics* 11, no. 3 (2013): 717–33.

Yet, the idea that settled and unsettled paths of democratization in Europe after 1848 rested on the presence or absence of "crafted" countermajoritarian concessions turns out to be a dubious proposition. First, the same counter-majoritarian institutions that in some cases appeared capable of compelling a democratic transition failed to do so in others. Consider again the British House of Lords: while the House of Lords might have eased Britain's smooth process of democratization, an equivalent body in Prussia, the Prussian upper chamber, its own unelected House of Lords, did little to defuse the fears of Prussia's conservative elites, and arguably blocked even more modest democratizing reforms between 1848 and 1914 in Prussia.[59] In fact, Germany's federal Imperial system, with its weak and decentralized parliament and restricted suffrage at the state level, contained within it far more countermajoritarian veto-players than Britain's highly centralized unitary parliamentary regime.[60] Yet, in Germany, reform was more difficult, pointing to the problem that counter-majoritarian political institutions rather than only making elites feel secure, sometimes simply close off avenues of democratic competition making full democratization less likely.

A second problem with accounts that place elite response at the center of analysis is the tendency to conflate economic interests with political interests.[61] Conflicting interests of upper-class and lower-class groups certainly provide much of the driving force behind processes of democratization and de-democratization. However, "upper-class" and "lower-class" groups are not the only relevant actors, and it is certainly incorrect to treat economic groups as if they themselves were *directly* fighting over democracy. Who is it, precisely, that needs to be "bought off" by countermajoritarian institutions? What is missing is a theoretical account that comes to terms with the fact that it was often *political parties* that only partially represented societal and political elites who were the key players in fights over democratization. And since political parties are not perfect "agents" for societal interests, we need an account that explicitly addresses political parties that represent the most powerful forces in society, both as advocates and opponents of democratization.

In short, it is crucial to elevate political parties, the "political carriers" of organized interests, to the status of a variable that shapes democratization. And, of all parties, those parties that originated as defenders of the old order, usually

---

[59] Hartwin Spenkuch, *Das Preussische Herrenhaus: Adel und Bürgertum in der ersten Kammer des Landtags 1854–1918* (Düsseldorf: Droste Verlag, 1998).

[60] Michael Koss, "The Legitimate Secret: The Institutionalization of Parliamentary Agenda Control in the United Kingdom and Germany," in *ECPR General Conference* (Bordeaux: 2013).

[61] Indeed, multiple actors with their own corporate interests may be relevant in a democratization episode, including high-ranking military officers who may or may not have overlapping member-ship with an old regime's economic elites. In the European context, they often did, but there were exceptions. See Nancy Bermeo, "Interests, Inequality, and Illusion in the Choice for Fair Elections. (The Historical Turn in Democratization Studies)," *Comparative Political Studies* 43, no. 8–9 (2010): 1119–47.

the most powerful socioeconomic and political collective actors in a democratizing society, deserve to sit at the center of analysis. If we focus on these types of political parties, a different proposition emerges – a proposition that will guide the rest of this book: no matter the level of socioeconomic development or the structure of the institutions of any state, *conservative political parties* that originated representing old regime elites are key shapers of the process of democratization. Whether or not economic and political elites could overcome the enormous collective action problems of forging effective and strong political parties to defend their interests shaped democracy's long-run evolution. Well-organized and highly institutionalized partisan defenders of old regime interests provided a way of "lowering the costs of toleration," and thus making democracy safe for key segments of old regime elites. Conversely, the absence of a well-organized and highly institutionalized party created to effectively defend the most recalcitrant old regime interests made democracy more difficult to construct and less settled and enduring.

CONSERVATIVE POLITICAL PARTIES AND THE BIRTH OF DEMOCRACY: LOOKING AHEAD

It may seem paradoxical to argue that old regime elites need to be well organized politically for democracy to be created and to be stable. Yet, precisely this claim will underpin the discussion that follows. Two questions structure my analysis. Under what conditions do such well-institutionalized or strong political parties representing old regime interests emerge? And, how do political parties make old regime former incumbents and their allies more secure so that democracy can develop in a settled fashion? I answer these two questions by explaining how democracy emerged in Europe's old democracies, beginning in the nineteenth century.

Each chapter of the book provides a key step in the story of two contrasting and paradigmatic paths of democratization: those of Great Britain and Germany, from the mid-nineteenth to the mid-twentieth centuries. Motivated by Karl Deutsch's maxim that truth lies at the confluence of independent and multiple streams of evidence, I draw upon a diverse range of source material: historical international bond market data, documents from official state archives, the collected papers and correspondence of well-known conservative party politicians in Germany and Britain, and the collected private papers and correspondence of their lesser-known political party operatives. I also use historical government statistical sources, parliamentary records, political party archives, memoirs, and the archival and unpublished papers, the letters and publications of important interest groups, as well as secondary sources. If the initial move to identify broad patterns is like the archaeologist looking from high above using "remote sensing technology," then this part of the project is analogous to the traditional fieldwork of an archaeologist, who follows up his initial view with his eye much closer to the ground uncovering and sifting through multiple layers of political history, formulating hypotheses, generating inferences, and reformulating hypotheses all with the aim of reconstructing broader patterns of political development. Well aware of the biases of any single source as well as the possibilities of spurious findings with any single research design, I draw on as many sources and formulate multiple tests of my main propositions.

Chapter 2 defines *conservative political parties* and develops a theory of conservative political party formation and identifies conservative parties' roles in democratization; the theory I present here structures my analysis of Great Britain and Germany, but aims to apply to other contexts as well. Chapter 3 explores how, beginning in 1832, British Conservative Party politicians, along with their inventive and highly talented "wire-puller" party operatives and the leaders of popular organizations, discovered the remarkable power of party organization and overcame the formidable collective action problems of party-building to create a tightly coupled robust party organization that could flourish in the face of rising electoral competition. Then in Chapters 4 and 5 we turn to several key thresholds of British democratization: the 1884 Reform Act; the counterrevolutionary events of 1910–1914 in Britain triggered by Irish Home Rule that came very close to sending Britain into a constitutional crisis; the creation of mass democracy in 1918; and the subsequent rise of the British Labour Party. Through this arc of events, often not sufficiently incorporated into political scientists' understanding of British democratization, several consistent themes emerge: first, until the mid-nineteenth century, the development of the political institutions we today associate with Britain's nineteenth- and early-twentieth-century pathway of democratization was much less secure, let alone predetermined for survival than traditional political science portrayals have suggested; second, the legacy of a well-developed party organization in the form of the British Conservative Party, a historical opponent of democratization, played a key role in easing the way to a more settled democratic transition and consolidation in Britain.

To consider Great Britain's settled path against an unsettled one, Chapters 6, 7, 8, and 9 follow the contrasting fate of organized conservatism and democracy in Germany. First, I explore how German conservatives "discovered" party organization in the aftermath of the 1848 Revolution, but repeatedly stumbled in their effort to build territorially encompassing party structures, instead relying on manipulative interventions of state officialdom and local government prefect (*Landrat*) as well as collusive bargains with other establishment parties to survive competitive elections and Germany's early universal male suffrage in 1871. I also show how "substituting" state officialdom and elite collusive bargains stalled the organizational development of the German Conservative Party and opened up opportunities for highly-mobilized and radical pressure groups and interest groups to infiltrate, capture, and ultimately radicalize German conservative political parties later in the century (Chapter 6).

Chapter 7 further investigates this pattern of conservative party malformation and how it led to a promising but ultimately stalled and unreformable nondemocratic political system in Germany before 1914, in which an increasingly "hardline" Conservative Party dominated by one radical faction provided traditional landed elites greater political influence than their objective position in the Germany economy alone would lead one to expect. In Imperial Germany, I explore the paradox of why a strong working-class movement and powerful socialist party, as well as a liberal–labor push for democratization, were not enough to break the narrow domination of a single organizationally *weak* political party.

Finally, in Chapters 8 and 9, I follow German political development through the promise of the early Weimar years and its tragic demise beginning in 1928. Here I show that a critical failing of the Weimar political system was not the weakness of Weimar's pro-democratic founding coalition, but rather was the absence of a constitutional center-right party that could have alternated in power with the pro-democratic Weimar coalition. At each stage of Weimar Germany's political life, battles within what, broadly speaking, were the successor groupings of the German Conservative Party, shaped by its legacy of organizational factionalism, made the long-run path of German democratization more difficult.

In sum, the German and British experiences of democratization are the centerpiece of a more general story of how settled and stable routes to democracy were achieved in Europe; a theme we explore comparatively in Chapter 10. It is not the now-familiar story of how the "outs," the working class and the bourgeoisie, successfully stripped power away from the "ins," landed elites, aristocrats, and monarchs, in a series of heroic struggles. Nor is it the story of how the "outs," carried on the unstoppable tides of societal change, inevitably took power away from the "ins," who stood on the losing side of history. Rather, I present a different, much more paradoxical story of how some of the "ins," Europe's nineteenth-century conservative parties, facing elections, remade themselves, built party organization, and accommodated themselves to democratic political competition while other conservative parties simply were not able to do so. Democracy's long-run stability, in short, hinged not on whether power could be taken away from elites but rather on just how elites themselves were able to organizationally change and survive.

2

The Old Regime and the Conservative Dilemma

The industrialization of nineteenth-century Europe did not wipe away all traces of the preindustrial world leading to the immediate triumph of the middle class and democracy. Rather, until the first decade of the twentieth century, wealth, status, and political power remained in the grip of collective actors at the heart of Europe's pre-democratic *ancien régime*: traditional landed elites, monarchs, high civil servants, military officers, and establishment church clergy.[1] The particular configuration of old regime persistence varied from country to country. And, different variations of "new" and "old" emerged within and between countries. But, a commonality was that the influence of old regime groups endured much later into the "age of capital" than standard accounts would lead us to believe.

In fact, in countries that industrialized earlier, traditional landed elites' hold on political power appeared paradoxically to wane most slowly. This was visible in the northern heartland of Europe's industrialization, in Britain and Germany into the twentieth century, where not only did monarchies remain the linchpins of power, but landed elites also continued to occupy a greater portion of high-ranking state positions than anywhere else in western Europe. In Britain, for example, in 1880, 325 of 652 members of the House of Commons were nobles, baronets, or landed gentry.[2] Until 1900, the majority of new recruits in the British Foreign Service came from a landed background, as did the Civil Service, even after introduction of Civil Service exams.[3] The armed forces, local government, and the House of Lords were thoroughly dominated by this same small social network. In the late 1870s, half of the establishment Church of England's 13,000 clerical hierarchy consisted of landowners, many of them the younger sons of peers.[4] In Germany, despite significant regional

---

[1] For a provocative elaboration of this thesis, see Mayer, *The Persistence of the Old Regime* (1981).
[2] Cannadine, *Decline and Fall of the British Aristocracy* (1999), 184. [3] Ibid., 280–81; 42.
[4] Ibid., 255.

variations, we see similar patterns at the apex of political power: the bureaucracy, the Reichstag, the executive, not to mention the upper chambers of nearly all German states, were also constituted by landed elites at levels far beyond their presence in society.[5] Finally, even in Belgium, where nobles had never been as politically dominant, their status, economic centrality, and political influence persisted into the late nineteenth century.[6]

In the northern and southern peripheries of Europe, as well as in late-industrializing France, similar patterns – though perhaps not as obvious – were still visible. Before Sweden's full twentieth-century parliamentarization, a potent conservative alliance of bishops, barons, and bureaucrats dominated political life via monarchy and an oligarchic upper chamber.[7] And in still predominantly agrarian Italy, Spain, and Portugal, monarchic rule persisted (until 1910 in Portugal). And, while national ministerial, parliamentary, and bureaucratic office holders in southern Europe began to reflect the decline of nobility, small circles of military officers remained central to national and local governments, and rural oligarchs dominated local government positions, especially in the *latifundia* regions of Alentejo in southwestern Portugal, in Andalusia in Spain, and in southern Italy.[8] There were some notable exceptions where nobility had formally lost their protected legal status early – namely, in the Netherlands and France.[9] But even among these countries, such as the Netherlands, recent scholarship clarifies that a small circle of old

---

[5] On Prussia, see Tibor Süle, *Preussische Bürokratietradition: zur Entwicklung von Verwaltung und Beamtenschaft in Deutschland, 1871–1918* (Göttingen: Vandenhoeck & Ruprecht, 1988).

[6] Samuel Clark, "Nobility, Bourgeoisie and the Industrial Revolution in Belgium," *Past & Present*, no. 105 (1984): 140–75.

[7] For a description of the oligarchic tendencies of the upper chamber and occupational background of upper chamber members after 1866, see sources cited in Dankwart A. Rustow, *The Politics of Compromise: A Study of Parties and Cabinet Government in Sweden* (Princeton: Princeton University Press, 1955), 23.

[8] For data on the position of landed elites, nobles, military officers, and other occupations in parliamentary ministerial positions in Portugal, see Pedro Tavares de Almeida and Antonio Costa Pinto, "Portuguese Ministers, 1851–1999: Social Background and Paths to Power," in *Who Governs Southern Europe? Regime Change and Ministerial Recruitment, 1850–2000*, ed. Pedro Tavares de Almeida, et al. (London: Frank Cass, 2003), 5–40.; on Spain, see Juan Linz, Miguel Jerez, and Susana Corzo, "Ministers and Regimes in Spain: From the First to the Second Restoration, 1874–2002," *South European Society and Politics* 7, no. 2 (2002): 41–116. On Italy, see Jens Petersen, "Der italienische Adel von 1861 bis 1946," *Geschichte und Gesellschaft. Sonderheft* 13 (1990): 243–59. Portugal stood out as a case of early decline of nobles, but military officers continued to possess outsized roles in government offices (the largest single group) before the First Republic in 1910.

[9] Indeed, France is arguably the most important exception to the patterns described here. While old notables continued to dominate local politics and elections through the 1870s, during the Third Republic a transformation of elites began, though even here, old elites still dominated certain rural regions (e.g., Brittany, Franche-Comté, south of the Massif Central) and the diplomatic corps and upper ranks of military. See Christophe Charle, "The Specificities of French Elites at the End of the Nineteenth Century: France Compared to Britain and Germany," *Historical Reflections* 36, no. 3 (2010): 7–18.

aristocratic families continued to hold disproportionate wealth and political power deep into the "age of capital," and even into the twentieth century.[10]

The old regime may still have been intact between 1848 and 1914, but it was also under assault. Everywhere industrialization began to shake the underpinnings of traditional power and the early stirrings of electoral competition and parliamentarization began to inject increased uncertainty into the process of selecting political leaders. This period, up to 1918, characterized Europe's *transitional* pre-democratic stage. It was only after 1918 that the effects of the First World War and its associated social mobilization were felt, shattering the institutional scaffolding supporting the old regime. In 1918–1919, many remaining monarchies crumbled, old elites were further sidelined, bourgeois Europe finally took the stage as the dominant collective actor of the age, and democratic transitions, even if not enduring, rose all across western Europe.[11] These two time periods, Europe's pre-democratic age (1848–1914) and the era of mass democracy (1918–1933), set the scope of our study.

To understand the pivotal role of conservative parties in the democratization of western Europe, we begin with Europe's pre-democratic age, as the organizational response of that era's first *preindustrial* opponents set the terms for how subsequent opponents of democracy would behave and how democracy would itself evolve. Table 2.1 provides an overview of the timing of two major institutional changes, parliamentarization and suffrage reform, during this pre-democratic period (1848–1918). Though in many cases universal male suffrage had not yet been achieved, these institutional changes began to alter the balance of power in European societies.

The two reforms came in different sequences in different countries: in Denmark, Sweden, Germany, Italy, Portugal, and Spain, universal male suffrage came *before* parliamentarization; elsewhere the opposite was the case. But, despite the order in which the reforms occurred, both represented a genuine threat to old regime interests, setting the terms for the politics of the successive century. The idea that such institutional reforms would threaten Europe's old socioeconomic elites, particularly its landed elites sitting atop highly concentrated wealth, and particularly its landed elites, is not merely an elaborate invention of contemporary political economists looking backwards.[12]

---

[10] For illustration of this thesis in the Netherlands that relies on extensive systematic data, see Jaap Moes, *Onder aristocraten: over hegemonie, welstand en aanzien van adel, patriciaat en andere notabelen in Nederland, 1848–1914* (Hilvershum: Verloren, 2012). For other evidence, see Huibert Schijf, Jaap Dronkers, and Jennifer van den Broeke-George, "Recruitment of Members of Dutch noble and High Bourgeois Families to Elite Positions in the 20th Century," *Information sur les Sciences Sociales* 43, no. 3 (2004): 435–75.

[11] Charles S. Maier, *Recasting Bourgeois Europe: Stabilization in France, Germany and Italy in the Decade after World War I* (Princeton: Princeton University Press, 1975).

[12] cf. Ansell and Samuels, *Inequality and Democratization: An Elite-Competition Approach* (2014); Boix, *Democracy and Redistribution* (2003); Acemoglu and Robinson, *Economic Origins of Dictatorship and Democracy* (2006).

TABLE 2.1: *Timing of Pre-Democratic Institutional Reforms in Europe, 1832–1919*

Country	Parliamentarization?	Suffrage for Lower House Exceeds 10 Percent of Males	Universal Male Suffrage
Britain	1832	1869	1918
Denmark	1901	1849	1849
Germany	1919	1871	1871
Portugal	1910	1865	1918
Belgium	1831	1894	1894
Spain	1931	1876	1890
Netherlands	1868	1888	1918
France	1876	1848	1919
Sweden	1917	1875	1911
Italy	1861	1882	1913/1919

Source: Scarrow 2005, 18. Nohlen and Stöver 2010

Increased parliamentary power and the expansion of the right to vote, even in a pre-democratic context, meant that the concentrated holders of wealth, in particular landowners, would come under assault in several specific ways.[13]

First, incremental suffrage reform and parliamentary reform challenged the very terms of landlord–tenant relations that still governed the lives of the vast majority of citizens in the nineteenth century. Reformers in contexts as diverse as Ireland and eastern Prussia vilified landed elites. Armed with new agricultural census data in the 1880s that exposed the extent of landholding concentrations and inspired by a new critique of the "unearned increment," liberal thinkers and political agitators challenged the basic structure of agrarian life, calling for fair rents, fixed tenures, and free sale of land.[14] Likewise, the push for land reform was accompanied by pressure from an increasingly "predatory" state to tax land and wealth at higher rates and electorally motivated efforts to eliminate agricultural protection that kept prices high for consumers.[15] By giving the vote to the "unwashed masses," who were often urban and unsympathetic to rural life, those with conservative rural interests feared economic ruin.

[13] For accounts of how constitutional changes challenged the privileges of old regime elites in Britain, see Cannadine, *Decline and Fall of the British Aristocracy* (1999). And in the Netherlands, see Moes, *Onder aristocraten: over hegemonie, welstand en aanzien van adel, patriciaat en andere notabelen in Nederland, 1848–1914* (2012).

[14] On "unearned increment," see Avner Offer, *Property and Politics, 1870–1914: Landownership, Law, Ideology, and Urban Development in England* (Cambridge: Cambridge University Press, 1981), 36, 152; Cannadine, *Decline and Fall of the British Aristocracy* (1999), 57.

[15] Cannadine, *Decline and Fall of the British Aristocracy* (1999), 61. See also Ansell and Samuels, *Inequality and Democratization: An Elite-Competition Approach* (2014).

Some scholars argue parliamentary and suffrage reforms were motivated by a demand for redistribution from working class groups.[16] Others regard these institutional reforms as efforts to protect middle-class groups from nondemocratic incumbent elites' expropriating tendencies.[17] In any case, the old regime was embattled socioeconomically. Lord Robert Cecil, a future British Conservative Party leader and Prime Minister as well as landowner himself, in a provocative essay written early in his career, pointedly put the perspective this way: "[Suffrage expansion] means that the whole community shall be governed by an ignorant multitude, the creature of a vast and powerful organization, of which a few half-taught and cunning agitators are the head ... it means, in short, that the rich shall pay all the taxes, and the poor shall make all the laws."[18] Even where landed wealth was no longer the primary form of capital (e.g., the Netherlands), conservative notables resisted the liberal goal of 1848 of expanding the power of parliament, loyally defending the prerogatives of the monarchy under the House of Orange.[19]

In addition to this socioeconomic challenge, the emerging outlines of electoral contestation, even before the arrival of mass democracy, had another face. It threatened a political order, resting on a particular *moral economy* in which political elites, whether local officials, elite bureaucrats, high-level clergy, military officials, or factions of conservative parliamentary politicians themselves, did not depend on "agitators" and "political organization" (the hallmarks of democracy from their view) to gain power. Instead, they relied on a familiar, informal, and localized pre-existing order in which their status and power as "natural authorities," predominated.[20]

Following the 1848 Revolutions, conservative party politicians chiefly represented propertied interests, who were typically closely aligned with, if not themselves, occupants of local offices; they relied on a longstanding fusion of traditional authority based on landowners' own moral and political status as employers, landlords, and local officials.[21] The result was an informal "politics of notability" (*Honoratiorenpolitik*) embedded in the old social order that made use of traditional social power.[22] Notability politics applied not only to

---

[16] See, e.g., Acemoglu and Robinson, *Economic Origins of Dictatorship and Democracy* (2006).

[17] Ansell and Samuels, *Inequality and Democratization: An Elite-Competition Approach* (2014).

[18] As cited by Paul Smith, ed., *Lord Salisbury on Politics; A Selection from His Articles in the Quarterly Review, 1860–1883* (Cambridge: Cambridge University Press, 1972), 155. For a nuanced take on Salisbury in his time, see Michael Bentley, *Lord Salisbury's World: Conservative Environments in Late-Victorian Britain* (Cambridge: Cambridge University Press, 2001).

[19] Hermann von der Dunk, "Conservatism in the Netherlands," *Journal of Contemporary History* 13, no. 4 (1978): 741–63.

[20] See description, for example, in Hellmut von Gerlach, *Erinnerungen eines Junkers [Memoir of a Junker]* (Berlin: Die Welt am Montag, 1925), 23.

[21] David Cresap Moore, *The Politics of Deference: A Study of the Mid-Nineteenth Century English Political System* (Hassocks: Harvester Press, 1976).

[22] Daniel Ziblatt, "Shaping Democratic Practice and the Causes of Electoral Fraud: The Case of Nineteenth-Century Germany," *American Political Science Review* 103, no. 1 (2009): 1–21.

"late industrializing" or the so-called backward rural regions of Europe, such as eastern Prussia or southern Italy, but also to the countryside of "early industrializers" such as England and in urban Belgium.[23]

Thus, old-regime economic and political interests faced several challenges: a well-documented challenge to socioeconomic elites; and an underappreciated threat to an older form of politics in which deep networks of informal authority trumped political party organization. In both instances, the old regime was eroding and risked collapse.

WHO WERE EUROPE'S CONSERVATIVE PARTIES?

However, old-regime elites were not passive objects of political events as they are depicted in many theories of democratization. Rather, they defended their interests and their world-views in the period between 1848 and 1914 through their participation in, support, and control of conservative political parties. These old-regime groups cast a long shadow over the structure of politics throughout the nineteenth and twentieth centuries, not only because they often dominated appointive high political office but also through the *conservative political parties* that represented them.

What counts as a conservative political party? Some analysts identify political parties by their ideologies.[24] Others identify them by the societal groups they primarily represent.[25] Both understandings confront similar challenges for purposes of long-run empirical analysis. Over extended periods of time, political parties often changed their ideological profiles as well as which groups they represented and even which groups can be considered their "core constituencies."[26] The British Tory Party, in one prominent example, actually predated its adoption of the label "Conservative."

For some analytical purposes, this shifting over time may not be problematic. But if our aim is to trace the evolution of how old-regime forces adapted to and shaped the rise of modern politics, an alternative way of identifying which of the myriad contenders count as conservative political parties is to identify *which societal groups a political party represented at its founding moment.* The significance of a party's (or any organization's) "founding coalition" rests on the fact that it leaves a decisive, in some ways indelible, imprint on its

---

[23] On Prussia, see Patrick Wagner, *Bauern, Junker und Beamte: Lokale Herrschaft und Partizipation im Ostelbien des 19. Jahrhunderts*, vol. 9, Moderne Zeit (Göttingen: Wallstein, 2005). And on England, see Moore, *The Politics of Deference* (1976). On Belgium, see Clark, "Nobility, Bourgeoisie and the Industrial Revolution in Belgium" (1984).

[24] Samuel Huntington, "Conservatism as an Ideology," *American Political Science Review* 51, no. 2 (1957): 454–73.

[25] Gibson, *Class and Conservative Parties* (1996), 7–8.

[26] David Karol, *Party Position Change in American Politics: Coalition Management* (Cambridge: Cambridge University Press, 2009).

subsequent evolution.[27] Further, such an approach allows us to trace why some political parties over time successfully shifted or expanded upon their core constituency. And finally, it allows us to get beyond the fact that in some contexts – for example, Italy, the Netherlands, and France – the "conservative political party" label was formally abandoned, as it was briefly in Britain in the twentieth century, though the same underlying political constellations continued to exist.

Thus, in this study, I define conservative political parties as those parties with a "core constituency" at their founding of upper-class propertied economic elites or political elites, the latter of whom were defined by their *institutional* ties to the upper echelons of Europe's pre-democratic "old regime."[28] Conservative political parties are the "partisan carriers" of ruling-class interests and are in this sense analogous, though not identical to the former ruling parties of authoritarian regimes.[29] In the context of nineteenth-century Europe, "conservative political parties" can also be conceived of as "old regime legacy" parties.

While I identify a conservative party by its founding coalition, European conservatism in general also possessed an identifiable stable core of ideas.[30] These included the rejection of egalitarianism, secularism, commercialism, as well as a liberal-rationalistic image of man while embracing an organic conception of society, political inegalitarianism, hierarchy, and a defense of landed elites as well as clerical and monarchical authority.[31] Conservatives

---

[27] See, e.g., Angelo Panebianco, *Political Parties: Organization and Power* (Cambridge: Cambridge University Press, 1988), 50; Arthur Stinchcombe, "Social Structure and Organizations," in *Handbook of Organizations*, ed. James March (Chicago: Rand McNally & Co., 1965), 142–93.

[28] Some clarifications: "old regime" in this context refers to the national political systems that were in existence before mass democracy, in most cases before 1918. See Mayer, *The Persistence of the Old Regime*, for elaboration. The notion of "core constituency" borrows from Gibson, *Class and Conservative Parties* (1996). And the "sociological" definition of conservatism builds on several sources including Gibson, Class and Conservative Parties (1996); and James Loxton, "Authoritarian Inheritance and Conservative Party-Building in Latin America" (Harvard University, 2014). I make the distinction here, however, that conservative parties represent in this context not only socioeconomic elites but political elites, including establishment clergy, bureaucracy, economic elites, and the military defined by their *institutional* ties to the pre-1918 political system.

[29] For an account that elaborates this point, see Daniel Ziblatt, "Reluctant Democrats: Old Regime Conservative Parties in Democracy's First Wave," in *Life after Dictatorship: Authoritarian Successor Parties Worldwide*, ed. James Loxton and Scott Mainwaring (N. D.).

[30] See Jan-Werner Müller, "Comprehending Conservatism: A New Framework for Analysis," *Journal of Political Ideologies* 11, no. 3 (2006): 359–65.

[31] I make this observation despite Leo Kofler's quip that "the essence of conservatism is continual treason unto itself" (Cited by James Retallack, *The German Right, 1860–1920: The Limits of the Authoritarian Imagination* German and European Studies (Toronto: University Press, 2006), 38. This "ideological core" is often associated with figures such as Edmund Burke (who ironically identified himself as a Whig), the German Justus Möser, and the Savoyard Joseph de Maistre. See discussion in Dunk, "Conservatism in the Netherlands" (1978); Eugen Weber, "Ambiguous Victories," *Journal of Contemporary History* 13, no. 4 (1978): 819–27. Underpinning

often deployed identifiable and reoccurring modes of argumentation against political and social change at important thresholds of political development; including, for example, when civil liberties and voting rights were in contention.[32] Table 2.2 presents a list of conservative parties, noting the date of the founding (and, sometimes, the re-founding) of the major conservative political parties in each national context.[33]

Many of these conservative groupings had a two-step path of formation: they originated in the first half of the century as socially elitist parliamentary factions of conservative politicians inside parliaments seeking to repel surges of social and political change, and to defend the prerogatives of monarchy, the power of aristocracy, or the role of established church institutions against liberal efforts to expand parliamentary power. For example, in Britain, Denmark, Prussia, Belgium, and the Netherlands, embryonic conservative parliamentary factions assembled as loose parliamentary groups in the wake of Europe-wide revolutionary turmoil in 1830 and 1848. But in each case, these parties declined, were re-founded or combined, often reluctantly, with ideologically conservative popular organizations in the 1870s and 1880s.[34]

Other parties of the electoral right sprang up at the outset as conservative parties in reaction to national moments of political unrest independent of Europe-

conservative ideology is a more fundamental conception of the world in which a "major abyss" divided "two modalities of existence": one a sacred world in which statesmanship, conviction, stability, and moral purity triumphed; the other a profane world in which narrow, vulgar, and petty interests only disrupted the natural order of things (Mircea Eliade, *The Sacred and the Profane: The Nature of Religion*, 1st American ed. (New York: Harcourt Brace, 1959).

[32] Albert O. Hirschman, *The Rhetoric of Reaction: Perversity, Futility, and Jeopardy* (Cambridge, MA: Harvard University Press, 1991).

[33] An alternative definition of the conservative *families spirituelles* is available in Klaus von Beyme, *Parteien im westlichen Demokratien* (Munich: Piper, 1984).

[34] For example, Belgium's parliamentary conservatives formed in opposition to Liberal forces in 1848 and later joined and helped found the Belgium Catholic Party. As Clark writes, "most nobles and the bulk of the rural population supported the Catholics" (Clark, "Nobility, Bourgeoisie and the Industrial Revolution in Belgium" (1984): 166. In a similar fashion, the anti-elitist Dutch Anti-Revolutionary Party in 1879 absorbed some of the elites of the conservative parliamentary faction that began to disintegrate in the 1860s, forging an ideologically conservative party of religious self-defense as a party opposed to the principles of the French Revolution. A key figure aiding party founder Abraham Kuyper was a nobleman, Jonkheer Alexander Frederik de Savornin Lohman. And later in the 1890s, the conservative aristocratic elements abandoned the ARP to found the Christelijk-Historische Unie (CHU) that shaped Dutch politics for generations. A similar dynamic was found in Denmark, where the Danish Conservatives of 1848 went into decline but were re-founded by conservative landowner and future Højre Party Prime Minister Jacob Estrup in 1881 out of a merger of traditional landed elites and right-wing national liberals fueled by their opposition to parliamentary government. See Jens Wendel-Hansen, "Landed Aristocracy and Danish Democratization, 1848–1940," in *Seminar on the Historical Democratization of Northern Europe* (Aarhus University: 2013). Finally, as we will elaborate in Chapter 6, the Prussian Conservative Party founded in the 1848 Revolution recast itself as the "German Conservative Party" for Germany's newly unified national parliament in 1876.

TABLE 2.2: *Conservative Political Parties in Europe before 1914*

Country	Party	Founded
Great Britain	British Conservative Party	1834
Denmark	Højre	1848/1881
Germany	Deutsch–Konservative Partei	1848/1876
Portugal	Partido Regenerador	1851
Belgium	Union Constitutionnelle et Conservatrice	1852
Belgium	Partido Catholique Belge	1878
Spain	Partido Conservador	1876
Netherlands	Anti-Revolutionaire Partij	1879
Netherlands	Christelijk-Historische Unie	1908
France	Action libérale	1901
France	Alliance démocratique	1901
France	Fédération républicaine	1903
Sweden	Allmänna valmansförbundet	1904
Italy*	NA	NA

*Note: Italy did not possess a self-identified conservative political party, despite significant efforts after 1897 by future prime minister Sidney Sonnino and others. See, Roland Sarti, "Italian Fascism: Radical Politics and Conservative Goals," in *Fascists and Conservatives: The Radical Right and the Establishment in Twentieth Century Europe*, ed. Martin Blinkhorn (Abingdon: Routledge, 1990), 14–30.

wide events. In Portugal, for example, the conservative-leaning *Partido Regenerador* formed in the wake of Portugal's 1851 regime change; in Sweden, the substitution of two chambers for four estates in 1866 triggered party formation among the groups that by 1904 would collectively establish conservative *Allmänna valmansförbundet*; in France, the Republican parliamentary victory in 1876, which weakened royalist grip on local courts and prefectures, had the same result, though effective party-building on the right did not come until 1901 in the form of the *Action libérale, Alliance démocratique*, and *Fédération républicaine*; in Spain, the restoration of constitutional monarchy in 1876 sparked conservative self-defense, the *Partido Conservador* in the new regime; and in Italy, conservative forces started to organize the historical "Right" (*destra*) in Piedmont as early as the 1850s, but party building on the right simply stalled, despite repeated efforts into the twentieth century, for reasons we will explore later.[35]

[35] Briefly, the "right" existed in Piedmont and post-unification Italian parliamentary politics. And despite a successful election campaign in 1857, Cavour's strategy of "*connubio*" that fused right and left halted party development, which in turn was exacerbated by church–state conflict, which fractured the right. See Anthony L. Cardoza, *Aristocrats in Bourgeois Italy:*

Despite these subtle differences, after 1848, conservative parties everywhere shared a common challenge: they conceived of themselves as running against the *self-perceived* tides of political and economic change. As defenders of the old order, whatever shape it took, they increasingly confronted a world in which their ascriptive bonds of obligation were loosening; mobility and economic exchange were increasing; and in which traditional systems of social power were melting away.[36] Not only were their political and economic interests being challenged, but a breakup of their entire political order in which their interests were embedded had begun.

THE CONSERVATIVE PARTY DILEMMA

Conservative parties faced a dilemma in the post-1848 world. To gain power meant reaching across the great abyss of voters deploying electoral strategies to win "the numbers game." By making appeals to voters in such a way, these politicians, however, would alter the very inegalitarian and hierarchical world that mid-century conservatives sought to preserve. At times nostalgic and at times simply resigned to inexorable change, conservative sentiment was captured by a leading British conservative in 1882, following Disraeli's death the year before; he described the descent of the old order as the "passing away of an epoch" and identified himself among "the last of the Conservatives."[37] To survive required adaptation, but too much adaptation was precisely what conservatives sought to avoid. How to preserve their world, their interests, and power while participating in politics was the essence of the "conservative dilemma" after 1848. While it is well-known that the left's use of "ballots" to obtain power posed the dilemma of whether a "party of workers" could maintain its identity if it tried to maximize votes by appealing to "non-workers," less frequently noted is that conservatives faced their own analogous dilemma even earlier.[38]

Political novelists of the age vividly capture the dilemma and the perceived need for new techniques of survival. Anthony Trollope's fictional Prime Minister, the Duke of Omnium, in *The Prime Minister* (1876) rejects his wife's pleas to use "influence" in a local parliamentary race, with the

The Piedmontese Nobility, 1861–1930 (New York: Cambridge University Press, 1997), 59–60. We will discuss this case further below.

[36] Ziblatt, "Shaping Democratic Practice" (2009); Peter Flora and Jens Alber, "Modernization, Democratization, and the Development of Welfare States in Western Europe," in *The Development of Welfare States in Europe and America*, ed. Peter Flora and Arnold J. Heidenheimer (New Brunswick, NJ: Transaction Books, 1981), 38.

[37] Robert G. Taylor, *Lord Salisbury* (London: Lane, 1975), 73.

[38] See, e.g., Adam Przeworski and John Sprague, *Paper Stones: A History of Electoral Socialism* (Chicago: University of Chicago Press, 1986), 45; Robert Michels, *A Sociological Study of the Oligarchical Tendencies of Modern Democracy* (New York: Hearsts International Library, Co., 1915).

revealing confession that "the influence which owners of property may have in boroughs is decreasing every day, and there arises the question whether a conscientious man will any longer use such influence."[39] And, it was not only in the "industrial pioneer" of Great Britain that the disintegration of traditional social power was felt. In Theodore Fontane's 1895–97 novel *The Stechlin*, the narrator reports on election day in economically less-developed East Prussia, where a local landed elite, Dubslav von Stechlin, realizes,

The Conservatives had grown accustomed to viewing Rheinsberg-Wutz as a citadel which could not be lost to their party. This belief was an error ... the whole business of perpetual personal favoritism had come to an end sometime ago ... the opposition parties were springing into action ... a Progressive, in fact, *even* a Social Democrat could be elected.[40]

In the face of the political uncertainty, a paradox became apparent: to keep things the same (i.e., to stay in power) required change.[41] There were, it turned out, *two possible solutions*, or strategies of "conservative electoral defense," for resolving the conservative dilemma. Both of these paths were novel organizational responses to the same challenge.

The first was to develop new informal techniques of electoral fraud, manipulation, clientelism and corruption that *substituted* for the "old corruption" of deference and coercion. Practices such as electoral fraud and party pacts went by different names in different countries, such as *el turno pacífico* in Spain, *trasformismo* in Italy, *Wahlbeeinflussung* in Germany, and *rotativismo* in Portugal.[42] These practices were not simple carry-overs from the past. They were deeply recast forms of manipulation: newly invented and hence highly innovative practices designed to respond to the forces of change that incumbent political parties faced. At their heart, these practices were anti-competitive strategies of containing new forms of electoral uncertainty. In Spain, for example, what came to be called *el turno pacífico*, invented after the Restoration of 1876, was a system in which voting occurred but its chief purpose was to support already-determined election outcomes: once the

---

[39] Anthony Trollope, *The Prime Minister*, Oxford World's Classics (Oxford: Oxford University Press, [1876] 2008), 194–95.

[40] Theodore Fontane, *The Stechlin* (Columbia, South Carolina: Camden House, [1899] 1995), 136.

[41] This is the dilemma facing the nineteenth-century Sicilian aristocrat in Giuseppe Tomasi di Lampedusa, *Il Gattopardo [The Leopard]* (New York: Pantheon, [1958] 2007), 28.

[42] Some comprehensive works on Spain and Portugal in this period are José Varela Ortega, ed., *El poder de la influencia: Geografía del caciquismo en España (1875–1923)* (Madrid: Centro de Estudios Políticos y Constitucionales, 2001); Pedro Tavares de Almeida, *Eleições e caciquismo no Portugal Oitocentista (1868–1890)*, Memória E Sociedade (Lisboa: Difel, 1991). On Germany, see Robert Arsenschek, *Die Kampf um die Wahlfreiheit im Kaiserreich. Zur parlamentarischen Wahlprüfung und politischen Realität der Reichstagswahlen, 1871–1914* (Düsseldorf: Droste Verlag, 2003).

monarch had selected the prime minister, the Interior Ministry assured the balance of power in parliament to support the outcome, in turn relying on local power-brokers, *caciques* to "deliver" the votes.[43] A similar system (*rotativismo*) hinged on local notables in Portugal in the 1850s and the local typically conservative-leaning landowning *Landrat* (prefect) in eastern Prussia after 1848 as well as in Italy after the 1852 the *connubio* [marriage] of Right and Left under Cavour, which launched Italy's *trasformismo*, a system of constantly negotiated majorities, not competing teams of politicians.[44] In each of these instances, innovative but collusive arrangements supported by a state prevented new political actors from gaining power and helped sustain the loosely organized old-regime parties in place.

However, in addition to this strategy, a second response, equally as innovative, was available to conservative parties before the First World War. That response was to build the machinery of hierarchical and mass competitive *political parties* and to win "clean" elections.[45] The scope of this organizational innovation was captured by James Bryce in his 1888 work, *The American Commonwealth*, in which he wrote with admiration,

The greatest discovery ever made in the art of war was when men began to perceive that organization and discipline count for more than numbers. This gave the Spartan infantry a long career of victory in Greece ...The Americans made a similar discovery in politics some fifty or sixty years ago ... It was perceived that the victories of the ballot box, no less than of the sword, must be won by the cohesion and disciplined docility of the troops, and that these merits can only be secured by skillful organization and long-continued training.[46]

---

[43] For a review of recent literature, see Javier Moreno-Luzon, "Political Clientelism, Elites, and Caciquismo in Restoration Spain, 1875–1923," *European History Quarterly* 37, no. 3 (2007): 417–41.

[44] See Pedro Tavares de Almeida; Tavares de Almeida, *Eleições e caciquismo* (1991).

[45] There was arguably, still, a third option facing incumbent actors to cope with electoral uncertainty, "institutional engineering" (e.g., proportional representation, plural voting). But this strategy emerged later, chiefly at the turn of the twentieth century (Rokkan, *Citizens, Elections, Parties*, 1970). Further, I will argue in Chapter 4, that this strategy is actually endogenous to the type of party "professionalism" that came with party building. Thus we focus on what for the entire period were the two key strategic options facing incumbents in everyday politics: electoral fraud and collusion, on the one hand, and party organization, on the other.

[46] James Bryce, *The American Commonwealth*, vol. II (New York: The Commonwealth Publishing Company, [1888] 1908), 78–79. Bryce was only one of many observers of the arrival of party organization in Europe. Others, including Ostrogorski, were interested in extraparliamentary party organizations spread out across national territory because he viewed them as a pernicious means of gaining control over MPs' behavior in national parliaments (Moisei Ostrogorski, *Democracy and the Organization of Political Parties*, vol. 1 (London: Macmillan and Co., 1902)). Recent scholarship (Cox, *The Efficient Secret*, 1987) has demonstrated the limits of the Ostrogorski thesis. However, our interest in party organization here follows a different line that regards it as a crucial mechanism of mobilizing voters during and between elections (E. E. Schattschneider, *Party Government* (New York: Farrar and Rinehart, 1942); John Aldrich, *Why Parties? The Origin and Formation of Party Politics in America* (Chicago:

Ironically, the innovation of mass "party organization" developed first in the United States in the early 1830s, but was perfected in Europe.[47] And, when it made its way to Europe, it was not always the electoral left that introduced this path-breaking organizational change. Rather, it was sometimes the electoral right – for example, the Dutch Anti-Revolutionary Party beginning in the late 1870s, the Danish Right (*Højre*) in the 1880s, and the British Tory Party – that was at the vanguard of this innovation, long before socialist parties were a genuine threat. The Dutch Calvinist Anti-Revolutionary Party, a critic of secularizing liberalism and defender of the House of Orange monarchy, entered onto the political stage as "the first mass political party in the Netherlands."[48] Likewise, one scholar of the Danish Conservative Party has noted that in 1880s Europe, only a single political party, the British Conservative Party, could match the Danish Conservative Party's precocious drive to create local associations and cross-class party clubs, but in this case, with the aim of "fostering conservative beliefs among men over the age of 18."[49]

Therefore, European conservative parties did not automatically and uniformly move through a single reactive path in sequential stages from cadre elite parliamentary factions to mass party organizations only under pressure from universal male suffrage and socialist "left contagion," as has long been argued.[50] Rather, some conservative parties gradually developed the novel response of an organizational infrastructure for political parties *before* universal male suffrage, absent a "contagion from the left." A second group of countries' parties, facing expanded suffrage, followed another path altogether using new techniques of electoral manipulation and collusion, and continued to use outdated "suboptimal" forms even in some cases *after* universal male suffrage and the rise of socialist political parties. Table 2.3 summarizes the responses of conservative parties to pre-democratic electoral competition, noting that in Britain, Denmark, Belgium, the Netherlands, and at a slightly later date, in Sweden, conservative parties were organizationally innovative, developing the organizational infrastructure of mass parties before their left-

---

University of Chicago Press, 1995)). It is the importance of party organization in mobilizing voters that is our concern here.

[47] As Samuel Huntington writes, "Paradoxically, the form of political organization which originated in America was developed into a much stronger and complex structure in western Europe ... " See Samuel P. Huntington, *Political Order in Changing Societies* (New Haven: Yale University Press, 1968), 132.

[48] Galen A. Irwin and J. J. M. van Holsteyn, "Decline of the Structured Model of Electoral Competition," in *Politics in the Netherlands: How Much Change?*, ed. Hans Daalder and Galen A. Irwin (London: F. Cass, 1989), 23.

[49] Vagn Dybdahl, *Partier og erhverv: Studier i partiorganisation og byerhvervenes politiske aktivitet ca. 1880–1913* (Aarhus: Universitetsforlaget i Aarhus, 1969), 12.

[50] See Maurice Duverger, *Political Parties: Their Organization and Activity in the Modern State* (London: Methuen, 1954); Panebianco, *Political Parties* (1988).

TABLE 2.3: *Two Conservative Party Strategic Responses to Pre-Democratic Electoral Competition, circa 1890s*

Formal Party Building	Informal Electoral Manipulation/ Corruption
• British Conservative Party (Great Britain)	• Deutsch–Konservative Partei (Germany)
• Højre (Denmark)	• Partido Regenerador (Portugal)
• Parti Catholique Belge (Belgium)	• Partido Conservador (Spain)
• Anti-Revolutionaire Partij (Netherlands)	• Italian Destra (Italy)
• Lantmanna Party or (after 1904) Allmänna valmansförbundet (Sweden)	• Orleanists, Bonapartists, and Legitimists Groupings (France)

wing socialist competitors, all in a context of restricted franchise, which would have a long-run impact on how politics developed in these countries.[51]

As Table 2.3 indicates, in a second group of countries, Spain, Germany, Italy, Portugal, and France, in which universal male suffrage came early but *without* mass party organization for conservatives, conservative parties initially opted for anti-competitive strategies of survival. Timing was all important: where conservative parties developed before the rise of universal male suffrage and the emergence of socialism, they adopted a strategy of formal party building, from which *strong* parties developed; where they followed the second route, however, strategies of informal electoral manipulation and collusion dominated, giving rise to much *weaker* conservative political parties.

WHAT ARE STRONG AND WEAK CONSERVATIVE PARTY ORGANIZATIONS?

It is important to clarify that the "strength" of a political party's organization is not simply read back from its electoral success. Rather, in historical context, as Table 2.4 depicts, the term has a very specific meaning and refers to four organizational features: the role of "professionals" in the leadership, the presence of local associations, the geographic spread of these associations,

---

[51] Below we will document precocious party building in the British Conservative Party. But the same insight has been elaborated regarding the first mass party in the Netherlands, the rightist Anti-Revolutionary Party; see Remco Boer, "The Anti-Revolutionary Vanguard: The Party Cadre of the Anti-Revolutionary Party in the Netherlands, 1869–1888" (Leiden University, 2008). For evidence of the early cross-class mass right Højre in Denmark, see Dybdahl, *Partier og erhverv: Studier i partiorganisation og byerhvervenes politiske aktivitet ca. 1880–1913* (1969); Luebbert, *Liberalism, Fascism, or Social Democracy* (1991), 329; Cathie Jo Martin and Duane Swank, *The Political Construction of Business Interests: Coordination, Growth, and Equality* (Cambridge: Cambridge University Press, 2012), 55–56.

TABLE 2.4: *Organizational Forms of Nineteenth-Century European Conservative Political Parties*

	Strong Hierarchical Mass Party	Weak "Contracting Out" Party
Structure of Leadership?	Parliamentary leaders *and* salaried professionals	Parliamentary leaders
Existence of Local Association of Parties?	Yes	Sporadic
Geographic Spread of Local Associations?	Wide	Sporadic
Role of Outside Interest Groups/ Radical Reactionary Groups?	Subordinated and contained	Competitive with parliamentary leaders and sometimes dominant

and the party leadership's relationship to its own local association and outside supporting interest groups.

Each feature taken together defines a political party as either a strong "hierarchical mass party" or what we can call a weak "contracting-out" party. While there are gradations across these dimensions of organizational strength or weakness and all dimensions do not necessarily cohere together, these two ideal types set a baseline of comparison that allows us to evaluate conservative political parties from Europe's pre-1914 transitional to the post-1918 phase of mass democracy. Parties that developed before the onset of mass suffrage and socialist competition closely approximate what I call a strong party, and those that attempted to develop afterwards, often unsuccessfully, possessed the attributes of what I identify as weak parties.

As Table 2.4 shows, the first critical dimension distinguishing the two types of conservative political parties is whether or not there was an early and sharp division of labor at the top between "professionals" and parliamentarians even though the leadership was still disproportionately comprised of aristocrats and traditional "notables." When Lord Salisbury, the Conservative holder of one of the oldest titles in Britain and one of its largest landowners, wrote to his party's highly competent chief agent, Aretas Akers-Douglas, at election-time in November 1885, "My dearest Douglas, Many thanks ... I should like to have a copy of your forecast for each constituency," his correspondence revealed a defining feature of one type of conservative party organization.[52]

---

[52] Salisbury to Akers-Douglas, November 27, 1885, Kent County Archive, Aretas Akers-Douglas Papers A 1226 U564 c 18/4.

Old-regime "patrician politicians" who had access to party organizations manned by professional "party agents" displayed more skill and therefore more confidence in their ability to compete as "office-seeking" electoral teams.

In the past, contemporaries often decried party agents as "wirepullers" – those who really exerted behind-the-scenes and pernicious influence in democracy.[53] But, making room at the top of the party hierarchy for professionals was a historic achievement, establishing an enduring division of labor that furnished old regime elite conservative politicians with specific political skills as well as an associated transactional orientation toward politics. Politics became a strategic enterprise, not a moral one. And professional politicians acquired a new ethos, summed up with a slogan familiar to professional athletes and surgeons alike: "Sometimes we win, sometimes we lose." In short, political parties came to be dominated by individuals who pragmatically looked to the future and treated politics above all as a "vocation."[54]

This "division of labor" mattered not only because it made compromise more likely, but also because politicians and their advisors, with access to the skills of modern politics that came with this division of labor within a political party, typically acquired an "investment" or "sunk cost" in democratic politics that rendered the system itself more likely to endure. Sociologist Arthur Stinchcombe impeccably spells out this logic:

When an action in the past has given rise to a permanently useful resource, we speak of this resource as a "sunk cost." ... Quite often such permanent resources are specialized, and they are only useful for the pattern of activity they were designed for. Such specialized sunk costs include especially skills developed in an activity, permanent or semi-permanent ... If these sunk costs make a traditional pattern of action cheaper, and if new patterns are not enough more profitable to justify throwing away the resource, the sunk costs tend to preserve a pattern of action from one year to the next.[55]

In this context, the "skills" in question are political and highly specific, including: (a) identifying the geographic location of voters; (b) estimating how voters are likely to line up on candidates and issues before election time; (c) grasping the nuances of electoral rules; (d) assessing the strengths and limits of a party's own organization; (e) possessing contacts able to facilitate electoral mobilization; and (f) knowing which issues effectively mobilize and demobilize

---

[53] As one contemporary, James Stephen, writing in the 1870s put it, "The strongest man in one form or another will always rule. If the government is a military one, the qualities which make a man a great soldier will make him a ruler. If the government is a monarchy, the qualities which kings value in counsellors, in administrators, in generals, will give power. In a pure democracy, the ruling men will be the wire-pullers and their friends." See James Stephen, *Liberty, Equality and Fraternity* (London: Smith, Elder and Co., 1874), 239.

[54] Max Weber, "Politics as a Vocation," in *From Max Weber: Essays in Sociology*, ed. H. H. Gerth and C. Wright Mills (New York: Oxford University Press, [1921] 1946), 77–128.

[55] Arthur Stinchcombe, *Constructing Social Theories* (New York: Harcourt Brace & World, 1968), 120–21.

voters. While these political skills may appear self-evident in a contemporary democracy, their historical emergence was linked to the professionalization of party leadership and the decline of the monopoly of the "notable politician."[56]

Conversely, then, the absence of party organization and division of labor gave way to what Richard Hofstadter once called "the paranoid style" – a dangerous fear and panic about the unfolding future order.[57] Lacking party professionals who could deliver office-seeking politicians a realistic confidence in victory, conservative politicians tended toward recalcitrance and what Max Weber termed "the politics of ultimate ends."[58] In this view, all political compromises are considered "rotten."[59] For example, when faced with a modest suffrage reform in Prussia in 1912, the leader of the Prussian Conservative Party, the east Prussian politician Ernst von Heydebrand, passionately explained his party's resistance in a way that precisely expresses this "paranoid" orientation. He argued against *any*, even modest, reform to his Prussian Assembly colleagues, insisting that "Rule by the undifferentiated masses ... is an attack against the basic laws of nature!"[60] In the midst of the First World War, General von Ludendorff went even further, illustrating the increasingly feverish view of German conservatism as he weighed the costs of ending the war against those of reforming the inegalitarian three-class voting system. He wrote to a friend, "With the equal franchise we cannot live ... I would rather an end with terror than a terror without end ... it would be worse than a lost war."[61] Germany's Conservative Party leaders and their allies found themselves in the spiraling grips of a cognitive style in which moral purposes substituted for strategic calculation, no matter the costs.

In addition to professionalization, there were several further dimensions that distinguished strong and weak conservative political party organization in this period. As outlined in the second and third rows of Table 2.4, these dimensions

---

[56] Indeed, as we will see in Chapter 3, in Britain a professional association of Conservative Party agents developed in the 1890s, which established a certification system for party agents, an examination system for potential party agents, and even a pension fund for association members: all the hallmarks of "professionalization." See the organization's own publication: Arthur William Potter Fawcett, *Conservative Agent: A Study of the National Society of Conservative and Unionist Agents and its Members* (Driffield (Yorks.): Published for the National Society of Conservative and Unionist Agents by East Yorkshire Printers, 1967).

[57] Richard Hofstadter, *The Paranoid Style in American Politics and Other Essays* (New York: Vintage Books, 1967).

[58] Weber, "Politics as a Vocation" [1921] (1946).

[59] For a broader elaboration of orientation, what has been called the "sectarian" view of compromise, see Avishai Margalit, *On Compromise and Rotten Compromises* (Princeton: Princeton University Press, 2010).

[60] For von Heydebrand's speech, see parliamentary debate in Preußen Haus der Abgeordneten. *Stenographische Berichte über die Verhandlungen des Preußischen Hauses der Abgeordneten.* Berlin: Verlag des Preussischen Hauses der Abgeordneten, 77. Sitzung, May 20, 1912, 6338ff.

[61] Cited by Hein Goemans, *War and Punishment: The Causes of War Termination and the First World War* (Princeton: Princeton University Press, 2000), 179.

describe whether or not political parties were built on the shoulders of well-organized local associations evenly spread throughout the country, which were active not only at election time but also between elections. Popular, local, permanent, and nationally encompassing organization helped with urgent tasks in elections: campaigning, canvassing, contributing membership dues, attending rallies, and distributing propaganda. It was this challenge that the Danish Right and the British Conservative Party overcame early. Joseph Chamberlain, Liberal MP from Birmingham and his "wirepuller" Mr. Francis Schnadhorst, pushed this model of "local associations" to new heights in the city of Birmingham; this was a paradigm of mass organization copied across the country in which all residents (including women), despite their voting rights, could join a party's local branch, which in turn would select a local ward committee that would appoint a city's general committee.[62] The "caucus" was an intricately organized machine and would operate at election time and between elections, organizing visits to each street and each home on a street, and assuring maximum turnout for party supporters.[63] The Conservative Party version of the organization, as we will see in Chapter 3, added a popular "entertainment" component to its work, as did the Danish Conservative Party in the 1880s, guaranteeing not only comprehensive coverage of the organization but continuous popular engagement as well.

In addition to a party's "vote-getting" or mobilizational capacity, a fourth dimension describes the *character* of the relationship of the party leadership to popular mass organization and outside mobilizing interest groups. Political parties are not simply unitary actors, and their positions on issues reflect not only the leadership's effort to court the electorate but also the party leadership's relationship to its own activists and supporting interest groups.[64] Organizationally weak parties with historically sporadic and lagging local associations find themselves – once strategies of manipulation and electoral fraud decline – more dependent than strong parties on *outside* interest groups and extra party resources. This in turn limits the leadership and autonomy of political office seekers. These parties followed what has been called a "contracting-out" model of party building, ceding autonomy in exchange for mobilizational support.[65] With diminishing opportunities for manipulation, and in desperate need of local party organization, these parties granted local associations greater influence in national party decisions. This balance of power is typically formalized in party statutes (i.e., party constitutions) that give local associations greater "grassroots" influence in selecting party leaders. For

---

[62] See Ostrogorski, *Democracy and the Organization of Political Parties* (1902), 165–66.
[63] Ibid.
[64] See, e.g., Karol, *Party Position Change in American Politics: Coalition Management* (2009).
[65] Marcus Kreuzer, *Institutions and Innovation: Voters, Interest Groups and Parties in the Consolidation of Democracy – France and Germany, 1870–1939* (Ann Arbor: University of Michigan Press, 2001), 119.

example, as we will see in Chapter 9, in Weimar-era Germany, the party statute of the loosely structured successor party that encompassed the heterogeneous strands of German conservatism (German National People's Party) granted local or grass-roots regional associations, and *not* national party leaders or national members of parliament, a majority of votes within the party congress to select the national party chairman. As a result, in 1928, an insurgent media magnate and industrialist, Alfred Hugenberg, could leverage his immense financial resources and access to outside pressure groups to capture the majority of local party associations to catapult himself into the position of party chairman, paving the way for the radicalization of Germany's right.

By contrast, if party leaders are able to *control* local associations and ancillary groups, a political party leadership oriented to pragmatic politics can remain ascendant.[66] As we will see in Chapter 3, Winston Churchill's father, the mercurial and ambitious Randolph Churchill, attempted to challenge the sitting party leadership of the British Conservative Party by first taking over the Central Union of Conservative Associations, a body of the Party's local associations. In that case, however, the party's center, already deeply institutionalized, crushed these efforts, leading to Henry Raikes' characterization of the British Conservative Party's local associations and supporting groups as the parliamentary group's "handmaid."[67] If a conservative party is well institutionalized at the top, then party leaders can have access to supporting organizations but are also able to *dominate* them.

It is a well-accepted notion that, whether a political party is on the left or the right, party activists are more likely to be deeply committed to a party's ideology, less willing to compromise for short run electoral gain, and hence ideologically more extreme than office-seeking party leaders who, for the sake of maintaining their wealth and status, tend to moderate their positions.[68]

---

[66] For example, the British Conservative Party faced internal factions and efforts by mobilized interest groups to radicalize the party, but its strong organizational core withstood these pressures (see Frans Coetzee, *For Party or Country: Nationalism and Dilemmas of Popular Conservatism in Edwardian England* (Oxford: Oxford University Press, 1990). The German Conservative Party was a weak organization, eventually a mere political arm of its robustly organized ancillary organizations that emerged before party leaders had the ability to develop their own party organization.

[67] This phrase "handmaid" has been used by other authors as well, including Robert Trelford McKenzie, *British Political Parties: The Distribution of Power within the Conservative and Labour Parties* (New York: St. Martin's Press, 1955), 146ff.

[68] See John Aldrich, "A Downsian Spatial Model with Party Activism," *American Political Science Review* 77, no. 4 (1983): 974–90; Geoffrey Layman, Thomas Carsey, John Green, Richard Herrera, and Rosalyn Cooperman, "Activists and Conflict Extension in American Politics," *American Political Science Review* 104, no. 2 (2010): 324–46; Herbert Kitschelt, "The Internal Politics of Parties: The Law of Curvilinear Disparity Revisited," *Political Studies* 37, no. 3 (1989): 400–21; Herbert McClosky, Paul J. Hoffmann, and Rosemary O'Hara, "Issue Conflict and Consensus Among Party Leaders and Followers," *The American Political Science Review* 54, no. 2 (1960): 406–27; Ryan D. Enos and Eitan D. Hersh, "Party Activists as

Strong parties by definition, however, build firewalls between office-seeking party leaders and these true-believing activists, bolstering party leaders' autonomy.[69] In turn, a strong party means that pragmatic office-seeking party leaders remain ascendant because of their dominance vis-à-vis "purer" and, in the case of conservative parties, often *antidemocratic* radical right elements of old regime interests.[70]

Taken together, strong leadership parties represent a delicate balancing act of fused authority and differentiated organizational function: professionalism at the top, local mobilizing structures at the bottom, and control by the center. One illustration of the difference between strong and weak political parties is how they appealed to voters. In all cases, a key group in the founding coalition of early conservative political parties was upper-class and old-regime elites. As a result, by the very nature of democratic competition, an expanded suffrage left such politicians as potential political losers in a democratic age, compelling them to innovate.[71] One way to survive this challenge was to introduce a cross-cutting cleavage (in this case, a cross-class "patriotism" cleavage), allowing the party the prospect of attracting a new majority.[72] Political scientist William Riker has formulated this dynamic more generally:

For a person who expects to lose on some decision, [a] fundamental ... device is to divide the majority with a new alternative, one that he prefers to the alternative previously expected to win. If successful, this maneuver produces a new majority coalition composed of the old minority and the portion of the old majority that likes the new alternative better.[73]

For conservatives on the losing side of the emerging class cleavage that accompanied nineteenth-century industrialization, a precondition for participating as "normal" actors in democratic politics, then, was the ability to successfully introduce and *manage* the introduction of new lines of conflict into battles over political power. However, these tasks were not automatically achievable and strong party organization was decisive for two reasons. First,

Campaign Advertisers: The Ground Campaign as a Principal-Agent Problem," 109, no. 2 (2015): 252–78.

[69] This dimension of the conceptualization is similar to the useful idea of "distancing-capacity," proposed by Bermeo, *Ordinary people* (2003), 238.

[70] This argument builds, in part, on Huntington's insights on parties and institutionalization. See Huntington, *Political Order in Changing Societies* (1968), 20. For a similar analysis of the conflict between moderate leaders and extremist activists in contemporary Social Democratic parties in Europe, see Herbert Kitschelt, *The Transformation of European Social Democracy* (Cambridge: Cambridge University Press, 1994).

[71] Kenneth A. Shepsle, "Losers in Politics (and How They Sometimes Become Winners): William Riker's Heresthetic," *Perspectives on Politics* 1, no. 2 (2003): 307–15.

[72] E. E. Schattschneider, *The Semi-Sovereign People: A Realist's View of Democracy in America* (New York: Holt, Rinehart, and Winston, 1960); William H. Riker, *The Art of Political Manipulation* (New Haven: Yale University Press, 1986); Shepsle, "Losers in Politics" (2003).

[73] Riker, *Art of Political Manipulation* (1986), 1.

old-regime party elites, often notables with a distaste for modern campaigns, needed "professionals" to help them identify which issues would activate voters, where to use these issues, and when to use them. Second, a significant challenge for the leaders of European conservative parties, even after identifying relevant issues, was to deploy cross-cutting cleavages *without losing control of the issues and, in turn, their party.* For example, parties of the electoral right often relied on religion, empire, and nationalism to mobilize activists but, as we will see in Chapters 5 and 7, they also ran the risk of letting these issues pull them away from constitutional politics. Only political party leaders sitting atop institutionalized mass party organizations with internal firewalls could effectively insulate themselves from this threat, and party organization allowed office seekers to exploit such issues while not being swallowed by them.

For example, the British Conservative Party's reliance on the slogan of "Queen, God and Empire," not unlike the Dutch Anti-Revolutionary Party's appeal to the trinity of "God, the Netherlands, and the House of Orange," was an effective conservative refrain, which could reach beyond a core upper-class constituency. But the galvanizing call of nationalism could also cause "blowback," as the British Conservative Party discovered when its now hyper-mobilized northern Irish "Ulster" Unionist activists took the Conservative and Unionist Party rhetoric and promises of support seriously in 1914, nearly leading, as we will discuss in Chapter 5, to armed rebellion and civil war. Similarly, in Sweden, the "battle for the Right" in the 1890s between a "very aggressive nationalist conservatism . . . modeled on German conservatism" and a "moderate conservatism" that accepted universal male suffrage was only resolved as party leaders deployed their robust party organization to defeat their internal opponents.[74] Well-institutionalized parties do not need to concede autonomy vis-à-vis their supporting activist and interest groups, which allows party leaders to take stances on issues independent of, and more *autonomous* from, the inevitable pressures of attempted right-wing insurgencies.

THE ORIGINS OF STRONG AND WEAK PARTIES

We are left, then, asking: under what conditions do these two types of political parties emerge? Part of the answer, as already suggested, hinges on timing: conservative parties that developed before universal male suffrage tended

[74] Niklas Stenlas, "Kampen om Högern – uppbyggnaden av Allmänna valmansförbundet 1904–1922," in *Anfall eller försvar?: Högern i svensk politik under 1900-talet,* ed. Torbjörn Nilsson (Stockholm: Santeus, 2002); Jan Hylén, *Fosterlandet Främst? Konservatism Och Liberalism Inom Högerpartiet 1904–1985* (Stockholm: Norstedts juridikförlag, 1991), 30. A similar battle erupted in the Swedish right between party leaders and the youth association (*Ungdomsförbund*) in the 1920s, a battle the party leaders won by ejecting the far right from the party. See Chapter 10 and Stefan Olsson, *Den svenska högerns anpassning till demokratin* (2000), 229ff; Hylén, *Fosterlandet Främst?* (1991), 32.

earlier to develop hierarchical mass organization that party elites themselves controlled; conservative parties that remained parties of "elite notables" despite universal male suffrage, which then tried to create mass organization only after universal male suffrage, ran into the pitfalls of "contracting out" and later were more easily captured by right-wing radicals. In the former set of cases, parties began to develop the tools of hierarchical mass organization under the stimulus of pre-democratic electoral competition. In the latter set of cases, under the stimulus of pre-democratic electoral competition, parties opted for collusive anti-competitive strategies of survival that delayed efforts at robust party-building.

It is self-evident that neither the presence of elections nor an expanded suffrage uniformly incentivizes party-building. In Britain, for example, elections and a *modest* suffrage reform in 1867 are often said to have "required" party organization. In France or Germany, however, even more expansive suffrage reforms in 1852 and 1871 at first did not. The galvanizing stimulus of electoral competition on party organization is mediated by another factor: the resources party leaders possess. In particular, resources from the state may reduce the imperative to organize formal parties in the first instance, even given an expanded franchise, and resources provided by society confer mobilizing structures, allowing the goal of party formation to be achieved.

The first set of resources, found in the structure of *state institutions*, shaped whether conservative parties had easy early access to various informal mechanisms of manipulation, including state and local rigging of elections and party pacts in national parliaments, as right-wing parties had in Spain, Italy, France, Germany, and Portugal. For these types of national cases, where absolutist traditions were historically strong, the state was a "substitute" for party, often operating through each country's Ministry of the Interior, which usually oversaw elections. The informal corruption of elections blocked party-building by providing a buffer that reduced the threat of electoral competition. In Portugal, for example, the *Partido Regenerador* dominated electoral politics during the constitutional monarchical period, where it reached up to 89 percent of the vote in 1881 and kept a steady 65 percent of the seats until regime change in 1910–11.[75] The governing majority dominated, however, chiefly through the elaborate rigging of election machinery, the system of *rotativismo*, rapid and frequent electoral reform during the 1880s, and localized electoral manipulation.[76] Similar local networks of power kept notables of the right in power despite possessing only organizationally weak

---

[75] Pedro Tavares de Almeida, "Materials for the History of Elections and Parliament in Portugal, 1820–1926" (Lisbon: Biblioteca Nacional de Portugal, 2006).

[76] Tavares de Almeida, *Eleições e caciquismo* (1991); Pedro Tavares de Almeida, "Portugal," in *Elections in Europe: A Data Handbook*, ed. Dieter Nohlen (Oxford: Oxford University Press, 2010).

parties in Italy after 1857. Here, Count Cavour who had had a vision of creating a "genuine conservative party," or, in his own words, a party of "Tories," soon found that his own collusive strategies of *connubio* and *trasformismo* blocked it.[77] In France until 1876, nobles controlled local prefectures, and thus political parties of the right lagged organizationally. As later chapters will show, this was also true in Spain after the 1880s, and in Germany until the 1890s, especially in Prussia.[78]

Conversely, in cases such as Britain, Sweden, the Netherlands, and Belgium, opportunities for such explicit strategies of election manipulation were limited earlier: pre-democratic election administration was either *not* in the hands of national executives (i.e., the Ministry of the Interior), often leaving local *parties* – and not government officials – with the task of overseeing elections; or, as in Sweden, state administration became insulated from elites. In England in the 1830s, for example, individuals were responsible for registration, and political parties, not the state, managed voter registration. In Sweden, between the eighteenth and nineteenth centuries, the professionalization of the bureaucracy insulated the administration of elections from private actor influence.[79] Without access to the state or without any informal state "substitutes" to turn to, formal political parties developed precociously. Thus, initially the institutional resource of an accessible state had undoubtedly appeared to be ex ante a "blessing," allowing conservatives in many countries to maintain power. However, this boon would come to haunt conservatives as they delayed developing the tools of organizational mobilization while their electoral competitors and internal rivals did.[80]

Successful party-building requires not only the absence of state resources but access to societal resources – mobilizing structures to provide the "raw materials" of organization-building. Deprived of the protections of a state and without a natural mass constituency, conservatives searched for pre-existing social groups and their related associations to provide themselves with the organizational resources for electoral mobilization. Given their initial status as defenders of elite old-regime interests, Europe's nineteenth-century conservatives everywhere found particularly powerful potential cross-class

---

[77] Cardoza, *Aristocrats in Bourgeois Italy: The Piedmontese Nobility, 1861–1930* (1997), 59.

[78] On France, see René Rémond, *The Right Wing in France from 1815 to De Gaulle* (Philadelphia: University of Pennsylvania Press, 1969). On Spain, see Varela Ortega, ed., *El poder de la influencia* (2001).

[79] Jan Teorell, "Cleaning Up the Vote: The Case of Electoral Fraud in Sweden, 1719–1909," *The Juan March Institute* (Madrid: 2011).

[80] Another related crucial resource in this second cluster of countries was the tendency for conservative parties in these cases to be founded inside national parliaments, therefore giving these parties institutions (e.g., party whip) that could easily be redeployed in the "countryside" to carry out elections. A founding in the "center" (i.e., the parliament) offered an easier route to institutionalization, as argued also by Panebianco, *Political Parties* (1988), 51.

mobilizing structures in religious cleavages.[81] In countries either fully or substantially Catholic, liberal secularizing states triggered movements of religious self-defense, and conservative parties tapped into these movements indirectly by drawing on lay organizations and social networks to construct popular local party organizations by casting themselves as defenders of the Roman Catholic faith.[82] Similarly, in Protestant countries, analogous conflicts erupted between an alliance of liberal reformers, who were opposed to the entrenched power of national churches, and nonconformist or "free churches" struggled against established state-affiliated churches such as the Anglican Church in England and the Lutheran Church in Sweden.[83] Here, like in Roman Catholic countries, established state Protestantism was under siege as other Protestant sects attacked the privileges held by the national churches, such as their control of education.[84] Thus, everywhere, conservatives discovered the electoral power of religion and turned themselves into defenders of traditional religious institutions.

However, party-building for conservatives was not always easy. The particular configuration of social cleavage made some societies more amenable than others to broad cross-class conservative coalitions built on pre-existing confessional social networks.[85] For example, in cases such as Britain and Sweden, where the upper-class economic elite tended to be predominately affiliated with the national church, it was easier to draw upon official Anglican and Lutheran lay organizations and cross-class social networks. But, if landed elites were split between Catholicism and Protestantism (e.g., Germany), shared

---

[81] Gould, *Origins of Liberal Dominance* (1999); Stathis N. Kalyvas, *The Rise of Christian Democracy in Europe* (Ithaca, NY: Cornell University Press, 1996); Thomas Ertman, "Western European Party Systems and the Religious Cleavage," in *Religion, Class Coalitions, and Welfare States*, ed. Kees van Kersbergen and Philip Manow (Cambridge: Cambridge University Press, 2009), 39–55; Kees van Kersberger and Philip Manow, eds., *Religion, Class Coalitions, and Welfare States* (Cambridge: Cambridge University Press, 2009).

[82] Kalyvas, *Rise of Christian Democracy* (1996); Thomas Ertman, "The Great Reform Act of 1832 and British Democratization," *Comparative Political Studies* 43, no. 8–9 (2010): 1000–22.

[83] David W. Bebbington, *The Nonconformist Conscience: Chapel and Politics, 1870–1914* (London: G. Allen & Unwin, 1982); Jonathan Parry, *The Rise and Fall of Liberal Government in Victorian Britain* (New Haven: Yale University Press, 1993); Ertman, "Western European Party Systems" (2009). In Britain, for example, leading conservatives such as future Prime Minister Lord Salisbury himself saw these precise analogies, linking the British Liberal party with other anticlerical parties of continental Europe. See Lord Salisbury to H. Lowthian, November 14, 1884, Salisbury Papers, as cited by Peter T. Marsh, *The Discipline of Popular Government: Lord Salisbury's Domestic Statecraft, 1881–1902* (Hassocks, Sussex: Harvester Press, 1978), 165.

[84] Kenneth D. Wald, *Crosses on the Ballot: Patterns of British Voter Alignment since 1885* (Princeton, NJ: Princeton University Press, 1983); Jonathan Parry, *Democracy and Religion: Gladstone and the Liberal Party, 1867–1875* (Cambridge: Cambridge University Press, 1986); Ertman, "Great Reform Act of 1832" (2010).

[85] On the role of religious networks, in particular, on fomenting partisan loyalties, see Jason Wittenberg, *Crucibles of Political Loyalty: Church Institutions and Electoral Continuity in Hungary*, Cambridge Studies in Comparative Politics (New York: Cambridge University Press, 2006).

economic interests did not automatically generate shared *party organization*; religious interests divided a potentially united right. This was so even in those rare moments of political opening, as, for example, in the 1848 Revolution in Germany, where party formation might have been possible. Similarly, in homogeneously Catholic countries, if the divisive secular–religious schism split the electoral right, as in Spain, France, and Italy into the twentieth century, party-building faced an analogous challenge.[86] Thus, successful cases of party-building were those aided not only by the absence of state resources for incumbent conservative but also by the absence of a divide on confessional and religious questions, or those rare cases where the electoral right had the ability to *overcome* such confessional divides.[87]

Thus, conservative party-building hinged on when it occurred. If conservatives benefited from state intervention in elections and other protections, party-building was delayed, leaving parties of the right playing a precarious game of "catch-up" at a later point when they now had to compete not with elitist liberal parties but instead against new and polarizing mass socialist parties. The resulting task was to confront their opposition's mobilizing efforts while simultaneously containing the growing radicalism of their own mass base. The subsequent treacherous path of political development was on full display in the persistent weakness of organized party conservatism in cases as diverse as Germany, Spain, Portugal, Italy, and France. By contrast, in those rare cases when parties of the right did not have access to these sorts of state resources, but *did* have access to social resources for party-building, strong conservative parties emerged before mass democratization, as seen in Britain, Belgium, the Netherlands, and Sweden.

THE TRAJECTORIES OF DEMOCRATIC TRANSITION AND CONSOLIDATION: 1914 AND BEYOND

Strong conservative political parties led to a stable long-run path of democratization because of five features of strong parties, which gave party

---

[86] Cardoza writes of the Italian right, "The possibilities of a conservative party guided by aristocrats" were constrained. He writes, "the crisis in church–state relations put Piedmontese aristocratic conservatives in an untenable position." Cardoza, *Aristocrats in Bourgeois Italy: The Piedmontese Nobility, 1861–1930* (1997), 59–60.

[87] The Calvinist Anti-Revolutionary Party of the Netherlands was founded in 1879 as the Netherlands' first mass party and went on to form governing coalitions with Catholics, overcoming a significant confessional divide, providing an anchoring stability for Dutch democratization into the twentieth century. See James Bratt, *Abraham Kuyper: Modern Calvinist, Christian Democrat* (Grand Rapids, MI and Cambridge, UK: Eerdmans Publishing, 2013). See also Thomas Ertman, "Liberalization, Democratization, and the Origins of a "Pillarized" Civil Society in Nineteenth Century Belgium and the Netherlands," in *Civil Society Before Democracy: Lessons from Nineteenth Century Europe*, ed. Nancy Bermeo and Philip Nord (Oxford: Rowman and Littlefield Publishers, 2000), 169. See Boer, "The Anti-Revolutionary Vanguard" (2008), 58.

leaders a realistic basis for assuming electoral success, the resources that allowed them to sideline their *own* radicals, as well as the organizational capacity to habituate themselves to the democratic game *after* democratic thresholds had already been passed.[88] Robust mass hierarchical party organization gives conservatives:

1) the capacity for a nationwide mobilization of supporters;
2) the capacity to stimulate but subordinate outside groups;
3) the availability of party professionals who deploy campaign resources effectively;
4) the capacity to self-consciously find and exploit issues that cross-cut and diminish the impact of social class as an electoral cleavage, supplanting it with issues such as nationalism, religion, and patriotism;
5) the establishment of organizational boundaries or "firewalls" to contain extremist groups that are stimulated by the new cross-cutting issues from penetrating the party's decision-making structure or forming alliances with internal party insurgents.

Taken together, these five factors, rooted in robust conservative party organization, lowered the stakes of losing, provided parties with resources to contain their own radicals, and made democracy safer for elites. Foreshadowing this argument in part, Argentinian sociologist Torcuato DiTella wrote in 1971,

Constitutional safeguards are not enough to convince powerful economic groups of the convenience of operating within the democratic system: what is needed is a party of the right that is capable, if not of winning elections, of at least making a good showing and of maintaining the hope of winning in the future, or of influencing a center party so that, in practice, it defends its interests.[89]

The presence or absence of strong conservative political party organization is a historical organizational legacy that *precedes* mass democratization. In turn, a strong or hierarchical mass conservative party transforms conservative politicians from recalcitrant opponents of democracy into reluctant democrats at two distinctive stages of democratization. Facing a democratic transition, if elites have access to a hierarchical mass party, they will be more willing to concede democracy. Party organization, unlike traditional informal personality-centered deference networks, is a resource that gives old elites reasonable expectation they can win, convincing them they can "*concede democracy without conceding defeat.*"[90] Further, armed with party

---

[88] The concept of "habituation" draws on Dankwart A. Rustow, "Transitions to Democracy: Toward a Dynamic Model," *Comparative Politics* 2, no. 3 (1970): 337–63.

[89] Torcuato S. Di Tella, "La búsqueda de la fórmula política argentina," *Desarrollo Económico* 11, no. 42/44 (1971/1972): 317–25.

[90] This phrase summarizes one of the key insights of Slater and Wong, "Strength to Concede" (2013), 731.

organization, party leaders can sideline their own "hardline" allies who typically occupy the grassroots.

Strong conservative party organization also helps a country avoid a second pitfall that leads to unsettled democratization: the problem that old-regime elites, or other new anti-democratic groups on the right that emerge along the way, might attempt to subvert a process of democratic consolidation even after a "democratic transition" has already been achieved. Indeed, longer-run democratic stabilization is also aided by the same structures of strong party organization for two reasons. First, strong party organization itself gives rise to a leadership coalition dominated by paid operatives and skilled politicians who then become increasingly invested in democratic politics. Party organization follows the logic of "sunk costs" and becomes self-perpetuating.[91] In particular, access to tightly coupled party organization makes a party's dominant leadership coalition, with specific investment in the skills and relationships of political party organization, less likely to seek out other non-institutionalized or non-electoral methods of contesting power (e.g., coups, cancelling elections, repression), since investments in these skills and relationships make abandoning democracy costly.

Second, this organizational resource also gives them the organizational leverage and power to sideline those "hard-line" groups that do advocate for such extra-institutional methods of acquiring and retaining power. Put simply, in moments of democratic transition and over longer periods where democracy is stabilized, party organization makes democracy safe for elites.

A NOTE ON THE UPCOMING CASES

The focus throughout this book is broadly comparative, and I return to briefer discussion of three cases (Spain, France, and Sweden) and several others in Chapter 10. But two countries, Britain and Germany from the late nineteenth century into the twentieth century, primarily occupy our attention (Chapters 3–9). While often held up as paradigmatically "successful" and "failed" cases of democratization, they are worth revisiting with the aid of a new theoretical lens for several reasons.[92] Recent work by political and economic historians has called into question the simple dichotomy of the comparison and made clear that, along key relevant dimensions, the two shared not only intense interconnections but some striking similarities in context that made them *both* promising cases for democratization. Nonetheless, Britain began to democratize before 1914 and endured as a democracy through the interwar

---

[91] Stinchcombe, *Constructing Social Theories* (1968), 123; Acemoglu and Robinson, *Economic Origins of Dictatorship and Democracy* (2006), 179; Pierson, *Politics in Time* (2004), 35.

[92] They are presented as paradigmatic illustrations in classic works in the field, including Luebbert, *Liberalism, Fascism, or Social Democracy* (1991).; Rueschemeyer, Stephens, and Stephens, *Capitalist Development and Democracy* (1992).

years, whereas Germany's path, while witnessing some significant institutional democratic reforms before 1914, was much more unhinged throughout, especially after 1918.[93]

What are the similarities that make the cases so useful to analyze? First, for scholars who emphasize that socioeconomic modernization is a driver of democratization, unlike southern or eastern edges of Europe, by 1890, Germany and Britain were both at the forefront of the industrial revolution in terms of total GDP, GDP per capita, as well as the size of the manufacturing sector and industrial output.[94] Germany, like Britain was a "capital abundant" economy in which democratizing lib–lab coalitions ought to have been robust.[95] Indeed, societal movements pushing for democratic reform were strong. Likewise for analysts ranging from Barrington Moore to more recent work by Ben Ansell and David Samuels that emphasize the importance of a rising middle class, revisionist accounts have made clear that the German middle class was much *stronger* economically and politically than traditional accounts have assumed.[96] Yet, democratic reform was not forthcoming.

As noted in the last chapter, others have highlighted the importance not of the "bourgeoisie" but of the working class as democracy's real driving force.[97] Again, the German case, when compared to Britain, appears anomalous: in the first decades of the 1900s, Germany's Social Democratic Party (SPD) was the most successful and powerful in the world as was its labor movement. Germany's SPD, itself a consistent advocate of democratic reforms, received a greater share of votes in Germany's national parliament than any other political party in Germany and than any other social democratic party in Europe. Its dense underlying social networks and organizations, furthermore, made it a formidable force for democracy.[98] Likewise, in the decisive first decade of the twentieth century, Germany on an annual basis experienced a greater number of strikes per capita than any other European country.[99] Some might suspect that the very intensity of labor unrest only frightened Germany's conservatives to block democratization. Not only does such an

[93] For an account that draws attention to Germany's nascent democratization before 1914, see Anderson, *Practicing Democracy* (2000).
[94] See data in B. R. Mitchell, *International Historical Statistics, Europe, 1750–2000*, 5th ed. (New York: Palgrave Macmillan, 2003).
[95] Rogowski, *Commerce and Coalitions* (1989). See, also J. Daniel Garst, "From Factor Endowments to Class Struggle: Pre World War I Germany and Rogowski's Theory of Trade and Political Cleavages," *Comparative Political Studies* 31, no. 1 (1998): 22–44.
[96] David Blackbourn and Geoff Eley, *The Peculiarities of German History: Bourgeois Society and Politics in Nineteenth-Century Germany* (New York: Oxford University Press, 1984).
[97] Geoff Eley, *Forging Democracy: The History of the Left in Europe, 1850–2000* (Oxford: Oxford University Press, 2002); Rueschemeyer, Stephens, and Stephens, *Capitalist Development and Democracy* (1992).
[98] Eley, *Forging Democracy* (2002), 89.
[99] See strike data in Mitchell, *International Historical Statistics, Europe, 1750–2000* (2003), 172–185.

argument run counter to the expectations of many theories, but also, it is worth noting that in the only other country that experienced similar (in fact higher) levels of strike activity in the same period, Sweden in 1907–1909, elites and, in particular, Arvid Lindman's Conservative Party responded not by blocking but rather by *adopting* and implementing universal male suffrage during these years.[100] In Britain, the labor movement was historically tamer; yet, its mobilization in pre-1914 led to significant democratic reforms. In Germany, however, economic modernization and intense demands for democratization went unanswered.[101]

Similarly, in the post-1918 years, when democracy swept across all of western Europe, in Germany, unlike Britain, this came bolstered by a remarkable and robust cross-class liberal–social democratic-Catholic party alliance (Center Party, Social Democrats and Left Liberals), the so-called "Weimar" coalition, which came into power in the first elections and was hegemonic into the early 1920s. For those who think that the first democratic election sets the terms, in path dependent fashion, of a post-transition polity, the fact that a thoroughly democratic governing coalition founded the Weimar regime ought to have set it on a democratic course.

What went wrong? Why, unlike in Britain, was democratic change so difficult to build before 1914; and why was it so vulnerable after 1918? Some argue that Germany's stalled democratization before 1914 and its fragility after 1918 was rooted in the economic power of the pre-modern landed elites.[102] Such a perspective is useful in directing our attention to not only those "demanding" democracy but also to occupants and societal allies of the old regime who might alternatively allow or impede democratic change. However, the idea that concentrated landed wealth was itself the chief barrier to democracy confronts a puzzle: the average size of agricultural holdings, as agricultural census data show, was far greater in Britain than in Germany in the nineteenth century; and tenant farming, rather than owner-occupied farms was more common in Britain than in Germany.[103] Further, historian David Cannadine elucidates the enduring social and political power of landed elites in Britain into the twentieth century.[104] This, then, is the puzzle: the *political party* that began its existence chiefly representing landed elites in Britain made its peace with democracy, while in Germany the equivalent political party, despite

---

[100] Lewin, *Ideology and Strategy: A Century of Swedish Politics* (1988), 70–71.
[101] Indeed, one of the claims I develop in Chapter 7 is that German labor's ideological and organizational intensity vis-à-vis other countries was itself an outgrowth of the reactionary strategies of conservative forces before 1914.
[102] Rueschemeyer, Stephens, and Stephens, *Capitalist Development and Democracy* (1992); Alexander Gerschenkron, *Bread and Democracy in Germany* (Berkeley: University of California Press, 1948); Daniel Ziblatt, "Does Landholding Inequality Block Democratization?" *World Politics* 60, no. 4 (2008): 610–41.
[103] Craigie, "The Size and Distribution of Agricultural Holdings in England and Abroad" (1887), 91; 139.
[104] Cannadine, *Decline and Fall of the British Aristocracy* (1999).

sitting in a very similar economy, remained resistant to democracy and could not contain a backlash of the far right after 1918.

The paired comparison of Germany and Britain commands our attention here because it offers such unambiguously different outcomes of long-run democratic development despite such striking similarities. The value of this type of comparison is that the most obvious explanations seem to fall short when the two countries are juxtaposed. However, in strict terms, the argument of the book is not empirically tested with this cross-country comparison alone, but at a more disaggregated level of analysis: with diverse sorts of micro-level evidence, including at the level of counties, provinces, individual politicians, and bond markets *within* each country.[105] This analysis is sometimes done qualitatively and other times quantitatively. Such an approach has two major benefits. We can use higher quality and richer data, drawn, for example, from archives, census reports, and the historical financial press, than is typically available in cross-national studies. And, by approaching the subject in this way, even though the focus is on several countries, we can increase the number of theoretically relevant observations by disaggregating our focus to examine unfolding political processes at the micro level within each national context. More direct evidence is then available for us to assess the plausibility of broad macro claims.

For example, for a case such as Britain, if conservative party strength actually gave rise to greater electoral self-confidence and willingness to comply with democratic practice, we should find disaggregated traces of evidence *within* Great Britain that Conservative Party politicians, given access to strong party organization, performed better electorally than those of organizationally weaker parties. Conversely, for a "negative" case such as Germany, if electoral weakness of the right made democracy more susceptible to collapse, as the argument and macro differences imply, then the core propositions become more plausible if we find micro-level evidence that German politicians of the right, with less electoral security and more frequent moments of organizational weakness, were more likely to opt for nondemocratic political strategies.

In short, while history rarely gives us "natural experiments" in a way that allows us to test the kinds of propositions we explore here, we can analyze political history with diverse sources of evidence and multiple analytical strategies to try to reconstruct the causes and consequences of why conservatives achieved party organization early in Britain but not in Germany. To that end, we first turn to the case of Britain to explore how these long-run divergent trajectories began.

---

[105] All the original data, the code for analysis, and output of statistical analysis for each table and figure in the book are available online: www.danielziblatt.com.

3

From 1688 to Mass Politics: British Democratization

One of the wealthiest and most powerful men in late-nineteenth-century Britain was Lord Robert Cecil (1830–1903), inheritor in 1868 of a prestigious and ancient title, Marquess of Salisbury, a Conservative peer, and later longtime Conservative Party Prime Minister of Great Britain. His family estate, Hatfield House, a grand home owned by the Cecil family since 1611, was surrounded by fifty acres of garden and sat twenty-five miles north of London. In 1860, Cecil, sitting atop the pinnacle of wealth in the wealthiest and most powerful country in the world, saw democratic changes on the horizon and was fearful. In a conservative periodical, the *Quarterly Review*, he wrote,

The mists of mere political theory are clearing away... The struggle between the English constitution on the one hand and the democratic forces that are laboring to subvert it on the other, is in reality, when reduced to its simplest elements and stated in its most prosaic form, a struggle between those who have, to keep what they have got, and those who have not, to get it.[1]

Were there reasons for a powerful landed elite in Britain to be so fearful of democracy? Was this merely inflammatory rhetoric of a reactionary oddity intended to strike fear into the hearts of his allies?[2] After all, the most enduring vision of British political history holds that the sinews of the British political system were so firmly entrenched that such a fear of disorder was exaggerated; in Britain, there was nothing to be afraid of. Property rights, in this view, had long been secure, and political elites had also long ago "mastered

[1] Lord Robert Cecil, "The Budget and the Reform Bill," *Quarterly Review* 107, April (1860): 523.
[2] This is the interpretation of nineteenth-century expressions of "conservative fear" offered in general by Ansell and Samuels, *Inequality and Democratization: An Elite-Competition Approach* (2014), 9.

the arts of competitive politics."[3] Put simply, this view holds that the road to settled democratization was guaranteed before the journey even began. First, beginning with the Glorious Revolution of 1688, it is often asserted, a "rough balance between the crown and nobility" constrained the expropriating tendencies of the English state, serving as a "decisive precondition for modern democracy."[4] Second, the formal institutional settlement after 1688, in turn, is thought to have provided time for political elites to learn "the norms and practice of competitive politics" in an insulated setting long before suffrage was expanded.[5]

How are we to assess this narrative? The British parliament was indeed developed long before the national legislature of many countries. And Britain's democratization over the long run was more settled than many of its European neighbors'. However, this chapter will argue that a "deep history" with parliamentarism was not a sufficient condition to assure a settled process of democratization. Something else intervened long *after* the 1688 Revolution. Indeed, in 1860, as I will show, the future Lord Salisbury may have had very good reason to be fearful of the rising democratic tide.

BRITISH DEMOCRATIZATION: THRESHOLDS OF DEVELOPMENT

The history of British democratization is normally told as an account of four major moments of suffrage reform: the 1832 Reform Act, the 1867 Reform Act, the 1884 Reform Act, and the Reform Act of 1918, along with a series of less high-profile reforms that altered Britain's political system.[6] The puzzle of why

---

[3] Douglas C. North and Barry Weingast, "Constitutions and Commitment: The Evolution of Institutions Governing Public Choice in Seventeenth-Century England," *Journal of Economic History* XLIX (1989): 803–32; Dahl, *Polyarchy* (1971), 38.

[4] Moore, *Social Origins of Dictatorship and Democracy* (1966), 417. Other important works agree on the importance of balance between crown and nobility. See Steven Pincus and James Robinson, "What Really Happened in the Glorious Revolution?" (National Bureau of Economic Research, 2011), 7. See also Francis Fukuyama, *The Origins of Political Order: From Prehuman Times to the French Revolution* (Farrar, Straus and Giroux, 2011), 325.

[5] Dahl, *Polyarchy* (1971), 36.

[6] See Michael Brock, *The Great Reform Act* (London: Hutchinson University Library, 1973); Maurice Cowling, *1867: Disraeli, Gladstone and Revolution: The Passing of the Second Reform Bill* (London: Cambridge University Press, 1967); Francis Barrymore Smith, *The Making of the Second Reform Bill* (Cambridge: Cambridge University Press, 1966); Robert Saunders, *Democracy and the Vote in British politics, 1848–1867: The Making of the Second Reform Act* (Farnham: Ashgate, 2011); Andrew Jones, *The Politics of Reform 1884* (Cambridge: Cambridge University Press, 1972); Martin Pugh, *Electoral Reform in War and Peace, 1906–18* (London: Routledge & Kegan Paul, 1978). One event that only recently has begun to receive the scholarly attention it deserves is the 1928 full female enfranchisement. In addition to suffrage reform, the literature also focuses on the introduction of reforms in how election corruption accusations were adjudicated (1868), the introduction of the secret ballot (1872), the introduction of limits on vote-buying (1883), and reform of the House of Lords (1911).

elites would willingly dilute their power by incorporating unfamiliar and poorer voters has been recounted many times, with scholars typically falling into two camps. Some argue that the impetus for reform came from a serious challenge or "threat of revolution" from below, while others emphasize that political elites only selectively altered the pool of voters in order to outmaneuver their political rivals in exclusively inter-elite political fights.[7]

In any case, two points are certainly true. First, the process of democratization in Britain, comparatively speaking, largely moved in one direction, with ever-expanding gradual democratization and without major moments of backsliding.[8] Second, though the process may have been more settled than many other national experiences, Britain's path was not predetermined by its "deep" parliamentary history. Rather, Britain's settled democratization was a modern construction, and it paradoxically became *more* settled over time as the suffrage was extended to ever-poorer voters. Why?

This chapter and the two that follow it make two arguments. First, the causes of democratization in Great Britain changed over time. For example, as we will see, in 1832 there was a genuinely revolutionary threat, but by 1867 this was no longer the case. And in 1884, the impetus for reform was paradoxically almost a non-event to property owners because both of the major political parties – not only Gladstone's pro–suffrage reform Liberal Party but also decisively the Conservative Party, originally the primary defender of landed wealth in Britain – had the organizational resources to survive and thrive in the face of an expanded electorate. Thus, in a critical development for British democratization, the organizational evolution of the Conservative Party between 1832 and 1884 endowed conservatives with a set of resources that itself began to alter the process of democratization. Second, the development of these organizational resources meant that in the major constitutional crises that might have sent Britain off its path, the Conservative Party, democracy's main *potential* saboteur in Britain, actually was pivotal in keeping democracy intact. The organizational development of the British Conservative Party made democracy safe for landed elites into the twentieth century.

---

[7] See, e.g., Daron Acemoglu and James A. Robinson, "Why Did the West Extend the Franchise? Democracy, Inequality, and Growth in Historical Perspective," *The Quarterly Journal of Economics* 115, no. 4 (2000): 1167–99; Adam Przeworski, "Conquered or Granted? A History of Suffrage Extension," *British Journal of Political Science* 39, no. 2 (2008): 291–321; Alessandro Lizzeri and Nicola Persico, "Why Did the Elites Extend the Suffrage? Democracy and the Scope of Government, with an Application to Britain's Age of Reform," *The Quarterly Journal of Economics* 119, no. 2 (2004): 707–65; Collier, *Paths Towards Democracy* (1999).

[8] I make this point fully aware of James Vernon's intervention that nineteenth-century British democratization, like nineteenth-century democratization more generally, also created new forms of exclusion (e.g., disenfranchisement of female property-owners) and demobilization via what is sometimes called the "privatization" of politics. See James Vernon, *Politics and the People: A Study in English Political Culture, 1815–1867* (New York: Cambridge University Press, 1993).

THE RISING TIDE OF DEMOCRACY AND CONSERVATIVE FEAR

Before examining how the British Conservative Party acquired party organization, let us return to Lord Robert Cecil and his fear of democracy. Of course political leaders – especially shrewd ones like Cecil – are often strategic in their rhetoric. It is always difficult to reconstruct politicians and pivotal actors' actual preferences based on their statements alone. Some, for example, interpret famous statements, such as Whig MP Thomas Babington Macaulay's 1831 exhortation to his colleagues to pass the Reform Bill – "Reform that you may preserve!" – as a sign that revolution was perceived as imminent. Others suggest that historians and historical protagonists exaggerated the threat of revolution. Gertrude Himmelfarb, for example, argues that the much-vaunted Hyde Park riots that preceded the 1867 Reform Act amounted to little more than "broken railings and trampled flower beds" in contrast to the revolutionary rhetoric of the moment.[9]

The problem of identifying concealed preferences has serious substantive and theoretical ramifications. If we assume elite fear of democracy is a major factor leading to unsettled pathways of democratization, then a first step in identifying the causes of *settled* democratization is to know exactly when elites overcame their fear of democracy. By being able to pinpoint *when* elites did so, we can isolate *what* might have tamed their fears.

If Lord Cecil's fears were exaggerated and propertied elites in general actually were no longer fearful of the prospect of expanding democracy by 1832, then the conventional view that 1688 made all the difference has greater plausibility – the causes of settled democratization may have been rooted in the distant past, long before mass democratization even began. If, by contrast, Cecil's fears were genuine and representative of broader fears of important property owners, then the causes of Britain's unusually settled path of democratization were likely rooted in some societal change that occurred *after* 1832. But, how do we assess how fearful elites actually were? There is certainly no reason to assume that Cecil must have spoken for property owners in general in 1860; in fact, there is good reason to think the future Lord Salisbury was an unusual and canny historical character.[10] Given this skepticism, is there in fact a way out of this bind; a method to determine how fearful property actually was of expropriation?

One surprisingly underutilized source suggests itself. The market for British sovereign bonds (the British 3 percent consol) provides a remarkably powerful opportunity to analyze a reliable contemporaneous indicator of perceived political risks. During the 1832 Reform crisis, contemporaries called the bond market a "barometer of the agitation which is working the public mind."[11] Were

[9] Himmelfarb, "The Politics of Democracy" (1966): 106.
[10] Bentley, *Lord Salisbury's World: Conservative Environments in Late-Victorian Britain* (2001).
[11] *The Times of London*, May 12, 1832.

investors fearful in the lead-up to democratization?[12] By recounting events through the lens of the sovereign bond market, we can focus on how investors responded to the chaotic "Days of May" of 1832, the Hyde Park riots of 1867, and the anti-House of Lords protests of 1884, as well as the parliamentary debates associated with the passage of each instance of suffrage reform. Because high frequency yield data on the British 3 percent consol – the most widely traded security in nineteenth-century Europe – incorporates default and currency risk associated with possible regime instability, fluctuations in bond yields are highly instructive of the actual perceptions of investors.[13] The actions of buyers and sellers of sovereign debt, unlike the statements of politicians, in this way represent revealed preferences and true perceptions of risk. Furthermore, the analysis of bond yields over time has two further benefits: it enables comparison of perceived political risk within Britain over the course of the entire nineteenth century, which contextualizes the significance of events in British political history; and it allows comparison of British reform episodes with analogous events in other countries.

What do the data show?[14] First, annual average yields on the whole period in the British 3 percent consol are displayed in Figure 3.1, with vertical lines representing plus or minus the standard deviation of monthly averages of

---

[12] The following analysis summarizes research I originally reported in Aditya Dasgupta and Daniel Ziblatt, "How Did Britain Democratize? A View from the Sovereign Bond Market," *Journal of Economic History* 57, no. 1 (2015): 1–29.

[13] This proposition follows how other analysts have used market data to quantify perceptions of political events. See Kristen Willard, Timothy Guinnane, and Harvey Rosen, "Turning Points in the Civil War: Views from the Greeback Market," *American Economic Review* 86, no. 4 (1996): 1001–18; Niall Ferguson, "Political Risk and the International Bond Market Between the 1848 Revolution and the Outbreak of the First World War," *Economic History Review* 59, no. 1 (2006): 70–112; Raymond Fisman, "Estimating the Value of Political Connections," *American Economic Review* 91, no. 4 (2001): 1095–102. A focus on British sovereign bonds follows the work of Larry Neal, *The Rise of Financial Capitalism: International Capital Markets in the Age of Reason* (Cambridge: Cambridge University Press, 1993), 14. He argues that the attractiveness of a sovereign bond "to the investing public depended on the relative ease by which it could be acquired and disposed of, the clear terms of the interest payments and the readily available information about its current price, and the military and political events likely to affect its price."

[14] Our two sources of 3 percent consol yield data are the Global Financial Database (www .globalfinancialdata.com/Databases/UKDatabase.html) and Robert Brown and Stephen Easton, "Weak-form Efficiency in the Nineteenth Century: A Study of Daily Prices in the London Market for 3 Per Cent Consols, 1821–1860," *Economica* 56, no. 221 (1989): 61–70. The Global Financial Database compiles data from various studies and historical publications, including the data-collection efforts of Neal (*The Rise of Financial Capitalism*, 1993), to produce an uninterrupted historical series of yields for the 3 percent consol, measured in terms of frequency at a minimum on a monthly basis. Brown and Easton ("Weak-form Efficiency," 1989) compile daily 3 percent consol price data for the period 1821–1860. The 3 percent consols in circulation during this time originated in legislation consolidating a variety of government securities into this form of bond in 1751, as well as periodical new issues of debt, especially for the purposes of war financing. The 3 percent consol made half-yearly interest payments, with no repayment of principal, for the time period under Brown and Easton, "Weak-form Efficiency"

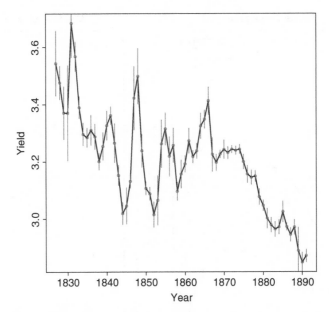

FIGURE 3.1: Plot of Mean and Volatility of Yields on 3 Percent Consol by Year
Note: Points represent annual averages of consol yields. Vertical bars represent annual average plus and minus one standard deviation of average monthly yields in the year. Data Source: Global Financial Database

yields in that year. Mean yields trend down over the course of the century, and there are clear spikes in the data corresponding to times of democratic tumult – 1832, 1848, and 1867. The general trend is ever-decreasing perceived risk, interrupted by momentary spikes at points in time that major democratic changes and attempted democratic changes occurred.

But how seriously should we take these trends, and what do they tell us about democratization? A more focused analysis of how bond markets responded in the lead-up to and after each of the major Reform Acts, in 1832, 1867, and 1884, as well as the failed moments of democratization in 1842 and 1848 that accompanied the Chartist uprisings, provides revealing information. In particular, the findings challenge the view that Britain's constitutional settlement was so firmly in place before 1832 that suffrage reform was simply a low-stakes political battle free from any substantial revolutionary turmoil. Figure 3.2 below summarizes Generalized Additive Model (GAM) estimates in the form of a partial regression plot (including residuals) of the estimated effect

(1989); Jan T. Klovland, "Pitfalls in the Estimation of the Yield on British Consols, 1850–1914," *The Journal of Economic History* 54, no. 1 (1994): 164–87.

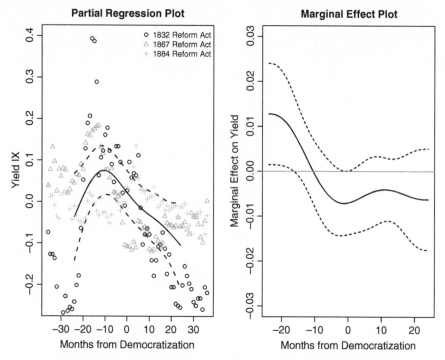

FIGURE 3.2: Semiparametric Estimate of Change in Yield around Passage of Reform
Note: Points in the partial regression plot represent the monthly average of consol yield, de-meaned by "episode fixed effect." Month zero coded for each Reform Act as the month in which the reform bill was passed in the House of Commons. Dashed lines represent 95 percent confidence interval.
Data Source: Global Financial Database

of *time to democratization* on *bond yields* along with a plot of the marginal effect of time to democratization on bond yields.[15]

---

[15] To semiparametrically estimate patterns in 3 percent consol yields in the periods of time around the passage of democratic reform, we estimate a generalized additive model (GAM) of the form:

$$Y_{it} = \tau_i + f(TIME_{it}) + \varepsilon_{it}$$
$$\varepsilon_{it} = \rho\varepsilon_{i,t-1} + v_{it}$$
$$v_{it} \sim N(0, \sigma^2)$$

where $TIME_{it}$ represents time in months (from –24 to 24) from the passage of Reform i (which occurs in month zero) and at time t. Bond yields are represented by Y_{it} for episode i at time t. Month zero is coded as the month in which reform took place in the House of Commons (June 1832; July 1867; December 1884). In this specification, the empirical sample includes only the 49-month windows around each Reform episode. The "episode fixed effect" τ_i is a vector of dummy variables, one for each episode to control for time-invariant omitted

Figure 3.2 can be interpreted as reporting the estimated rate of change in bond yields at different points of time relative to the passage of reform. The right panel "pools" the marginal effects of all three episodes, and the left panel shows that there was considerable heterogeneity across Reform Acts, with a large spike in bond yield in the months leading up to the 1832 Reform Act, on the order of a 65 basis point difference between minimum and maximum; a more moderate spike prior to the 1867 Reform Act, on the order of a 31 basis point difference; and a 21 basis point difference for the passage of the 1884 Reform Act. In other words, franchise extension was preceded by a sharp increase in perceived political risk in 1832 and 1867, but not for the 1884 Reform Act, with yields returning to pre-crisis levels upon passage of each Act. There is thus some evidence that the bond market volatility associated with reform episodes declined over the course of the nineteenth century, though instability was high in 1832.

But, even if apparently large in 1832 and moderately so in 1867, did these spikes indicate substantial concerns on the part of investors? And if so, what drove the concerns? To answer the first question, we can compare the reforms to other moments in British political history in the period. To do this, we randomly draw 1,000 49-month windows from the full monthly consol yield data series from 1825 to 1890 and calculate volatility statistics for each randomly drawn window: the percentage increase from minimum to maximum and the standard deviation and percentile in which each episode of reform falls. Table 3.1 reports the findings as compared to other major events in British history.

TABLE 3.1: *Comparison of Consol Yield Volatility within Britain*

Episode	Percent Increase Percentile	Standard Deviation Percentile
1832 Reform Act	88	85
1848 Chartist Agitation	84	88
Catholic Emancipation	82	85
1842 Chartist Agitation	70	71
1867 Reform Act	57	71
1884 Reform Act	25	10
Irish Land War	10	17

Note: Columns indicate different volatility statistics: percentage increase from minimum to maximum yield and standard deviation yields. Values represent the percentile in which each reform episode falls for a given volatility statistic, relative to 1,000 randomly drawn 49-month windows of British consol yield data between 1925 and 1980.
Data Source: Global Financial Database

variables in each 49-month period. The estimates are not particularly sensitive to the choice of time span outside of the 49-month span (from −24 to 24) used in the analysis.

Table 3.1 shows that consol yields were more volatile around the passage of the 1832 and 1867 Reform Acts as well as the failed 1842 and 1848 Chartist agitations than at other significant historical moments, including the Irish Land War and Catholic emancipation. Using a simple bond-price model of the default risk embodied in the changes, we can calculate that at the peak of the pre-1832 crisis, investors discounted the value of consols by 16.6 percent from the pre-crisis baseline, while at the height of the 1867 reform crisis investors discounted the value of consols by 8.7 percent.[16]

Two questions remain: how significant were these spikes compared to other revolutionary events in other countries during the same time period? And what about the suffrage reform episodes was driving the spike in yields? To answer the first question, we can compile a list of major nineteenth-century episodes of democratic reform and revolutionary events for a sample of western European countries – Austria, Belgium, Germany, France, and the Netherlands – based on compilations of major reform episodes constructed by other analysts.[17] For each episode, we can again compute the same two volatility statistics, ranking all episodes by the magnitude of volatility. Placing reform episodes in Britain within their cross-country context is revealing. The results reported in Table 3.2 suggest that the bond market volatility associated with reform in Britain is comparable to the volatility associated with similar episodes in other western European countries.

---

[16] Calculations are based on a simple bond-pricing model of the default risk embodied in these changes in yields. In an efficient market, the equilibrium price, P*, of a consol is equal to the net present value of coupon payments from the next period onward, discounted according to the per-period market interest rate, R, as well as political risk of default, θ, which we parameterize here in the form of a short-run risk of default on all future coupon payments:

$$P^* = \lim_{n \to \infty} \sum_{i=1}^{n} \frac{C}{(1+R)^2} \times (1 - \theta) = \frac{C}{R} \times (1 - \theta)$$

This implies that the yield, Y, computed by dividing the coupon by the market price, embodies the market interest rate and the short-run political risk of default:

$$Y = \frac{C}{P^*} = \frac{R}{1 - \theta}$$

In the case of the 1832 Reform Act, if we assume that the pre-crisis baseline yield of 3.25 represents the risk-free interest rate, R, and the increase to 3.9 is driven entirely by political-risk-induced changes in θ, we compute that at the height of the reform crisis the default risk was perceived to be 16.6 percent. Similar calculations can be performed using the monthly average maximum (3.46) and minimum (3.16) around the 1867 Reform Act, suggesting that the height of the reform crisis default risk was perceived to be 8.7 percent. These are large implied probabilities, based on the conservative simplifying assumption of a short-run political risk of total sovereign default.

[17] Toke Aidt and Peter Jensen, "Workers of the World, Unite! Franchise Extensions and the Threat of Revolution in Europe, 1820–1938," *European Economic Review* 72 (2014): 52–75; and Danièle Caramani, *Elections in Western Europe Since 1815: Electoral Results by Constituencies*, The Societies of Europe (London: Macmillan Reference, 2000).

TABLE 3.2: *Comparison of Bond Yield Volatility across Country Episodes*

Rank	Country	Year	Percent Increase	Standard Deviation
1	France	1848	113.18	1.14
2	Netherlands	1848	77.50	0.62
3	France	1830	64.60	0.54
4	France	1824	30.03	0.60
5	France	1870	46.13	0.66
6	Germany	1848	45.61	0.47
7	Belgium	1848	4.24	0.51
8	Netherlands	1887	27.29	0.20
9	Netherlands	1894	22.07	0.20
10	Britain	1832	20.45	0.17
11	Belgium	1893	20.24	0.11
12	Britain	1848	19.52	0.17
13	Britain	1842	5.67	0.13
14	Germany	1871	11.61	0.14
15	Austria	1896	10.52	0.09
16	Britain	1867	9.59	0.09
17	Belgium	1830	6.99	0.15
18	Britain	1884	6.42	0.03
19	Austria	1873	5.34	0.09

Note: Columns represent different volatility statistics: percentage increase of maximum from minimum yield and standard deviation of yields. Values represent the value of each reform episode for a given statistic, based on monthly long-term sovereign bond yields in the five years window of time around the recorded year of occurrence. Episodes are ranked by percentage increase of maximum from minimum yield. List of major reform episodes compiled from and Caramani 2000, Aidt and Jensen 2014, 59.
Data Source: Global Financial Database

To be sure, Britain's democratic episodes were associated with less bond market volatility than were some events in France, the Netherlands, and Germany. But the comparability of the 1832 and 1867 Reform Acts and the 1842 and 1848 Chartist agitations to major reform events in other European countries challenges the very widely held notion that the British constitutional settlement before 1832 was somehow "unique" and had already locked in a settled path of democratization. Further, a close reading of the financial press of the time, as well as an analysis of the major turning points in bond yields, reveal that massive social unrest and institutional dysfunction at the parliamentary level were driving these spikes.[18] For example, if we use structural break analysis of daily 3 percent consol yield data in the five-year window around the 1832 Reform Act, it becomes clear that there were six

[18] For a description, see Dasgupta and Ziblatt, "How Did Britain Democratize?" (2015).

major turning points.[19] Three of these prompted rises in bond yields: July 27, 1830; October 16, 1830; and February 14, 1831. The first, July 27, 1830, corresponds to the outbreak of the July Revolution in Paris, France, at which time yields rose sharply, corroborating, as others have argued, that this sparked fear within Britain.[20] The second corresponds to the height of the so-called "Swing Riots" of landless agricultural workers, in which attacks on landowners' property and arson occurred as well as calls for suffrage reform. And the third structural break point, February 14, 1831, comes six days before a party meeting of the conservative opposition that agreed to allow the introduction of the first reform bill in Parliament. This last moment may have reflected anxiety over advance news of the introduction of the bill and the anticipation that a divided elite implied conflict over its passage.

The broad lesson of these findings is this: while we cannot read the minds of political actors in the mid-nineteenth century, bond markets do represent a way of assessing how fearful investors and property holders were in the past of democratization. Recounting the major events of the era through the lens of the bond market reveals two points. First, the process of democratization was fraught, especially early in the century; as important as the settlement of 1688 was for England and beyond, it did not automatically secure a settled process of democratization for Britain, as evidenced by the fact that constitutional stability was not guaranteed as late as 1832.[21] Second, however, by 1884, something had changed. What, exactly?

WHAT SAVED DEMOCRATIZATION AND KEPT IT ON A SETTLED PATH, 1832–1884

Across Europe, landed elites were democracy's major opponents, and the British Conservative Party entered the nineteenth century representing precisely these kinds of elites.[22] Given that political parties with a similar core

---

[19] Dasgupta and Ziblatt, "How Did Britain Democratize?" (2015).

[20] Aidt and Jensen, "Workers of the World, Unite!" (2014), 60.

[21] On the importance of 1688, see most recently Steven Pincus, *1688: The First Modern Revolution* (New Haven: Yale University Press, 2009).

[22] Both the Whig and Tory Parties represented socioeconomic elites and landed wealth in Britain's pre-democratic oligarchic political system. Nonetheless, the most systematic estimates indicate that from the 1830s until at least the 1880s, the Conservative Party (even when combined with its Unionist allies after the 1880s) was more closely associated with landed wealth (rather than industrial and commercial wealth) than the Whig Party (and its Liberal successor) as indicated, by the professional and demographic background of MPs from the 1830s until the 1880s. See data in John Alun Thomas, *The House of Commons, 1832–1901: An Analysis of Its Economic and Social Character* (Cardiff: University of Wales Press, 1939), 4–5. See also Michael Rush, *The Role of the Member of Parliament Since 1868: From Gentlemen to Players* (New York: Oxford University Press, 2001), 95. More recent estimates using different data sources are found in Laura Bronner, "Property and Power: MPs' Assets and Support for Democratization in the 1867 Reform Act," *Legislative Studies Quarterly* 39, no. 4 (2014): 439–66.

constituency in other countries such as Germany did not respond to democratization by embracing party building, how did the British Conservative Party develop a tightly coupled mass party with well-organized mass structures across the entire country? Like a select cluster of other national elite conservative parties in Europe that successfully developed mass organization before mass democratization (e.g., Sweden before 1918, Belgium and Denmark in the 1880s), British conservatism stands out as a case that responded to early electoral competition by formal party building. Because of its contemporary durability, it can be easily forgotten that the British Conservative Party, originally the most loyal defenders of Britain's landed and Anglican *ancien régime*, spent much of the middle third of the nineteenth century as a weak minority party, limping from election to election, wracked by internal divisions and on the verge of collapse.[23] How could a party that began the century as the reactionary political defender of one of Europe's most powerful landed elite transform itself to survive and thrive in conditions of expanded suffrage?[24] If its base, especially after the schisms surrounding the Corn Law repeals in 1846, was a narrowly landed and aristocratic one, how could it perform so well electorally in an increasingly inclusive political system?

The following analysis lays out *two* phases of party formation, explaining how an elitist party developed, albeit in often disjointed and nonlinear fashion, into an electorally competitive party.[25] In the *first* period, described below, before 1874, the party was not entirely dissimilar from other conservative parties in Europe. An impressively strong parliamentary creature, it lacked a strong rank-and-file organizational base, leaving it poorly equipped to engage in free-ranging electoral competition. Despite important institutional innovations in the period, even the arrival of expanded suffrage in 1867 did not automatically trigger a "big bang" of organizational change. Instead the

---

[23] Between Britain's Great Reform Act of 1832 and 1874, the British Conservative Party held a majority of parliamentary seats only a single time (between 1842 and 1846). And after that brief spell in government, the party split over the controversial introduction of free trade that accompanied the repeal of the Corn Laws, as its leadership, under Peel, jettisoned the party entirely, taking with it the party's small central election fund, party whips, and election managers. The result was a protectionist aristocratic "rump party" that looked just as reactionary as any conservative party in Europe. A tentative recovery began in the 1850s with two brief minority spells in government; see Robert Blake, *The Conservative Party from Peel to Churchill* (London: Eyre & Spottiswoode, 1970). Beginning in 1874, however, and especially after 1884, the Conservative Party had begun a more complete comeback. It was in power for twenty of the twenty-six years between 1874 and 1900, becoming a powerful and electorally competitive party machine that occupied the right end of a robust two-party system into the twentieth century (Ertman, "Great Reform Act of 1832" (2010).).

[24] Cannadine, *Decline and Fall of the British Aristocracy* (1999).

[25] Stephen Skowronek and Karen Orren, *The Search for American Political Development* (Cambridge: Cambridge University Press, 2004); Kathleen Thelen, *How Institutions Evolve: The Political Economy of Skills in Germany, Britain, the United States, and Japan*, Cambridge Studies in Comparative Politics (Cambridge: Cambridge University Press, 2004).

organizational benefits of these reforms were only reaped in a *second* stage of development, after 1880, when the British Conservative Party discovered and took full advantage of the power of cross-cutting social cleavages.

In this second period, after 1880, the Conservative Party successfully accessed dense and robust cross-class social networks centered around a variety of actors including Anglican priests and a set of related cultural or symbolic issues in the late 1870s and early 1880s, deftly using them to create a mass organizational structure. The party gained a strong central organization that could quickly absorb and deploy pre-existing social networks, metamorphosing into a new political species altogether: a cross-class conservative party that looked uncannily like the cross-class Catholic conservative parties of continental Europe and the cross-class party of the right (*Allmänna valmansförbundet*) in Sweden.[26] Thus, the process of conservative party formation in Britain suggests that *party building*, as a strategy of conservative countermovement, was indeed triggered by electoral competition. But the impact of competition after 1832 was itself reinforced and moderated by political parties' gradual accumulation of political skills and resources, which allowed the Conservative Party's organizational innovative heresthetic strategies to be viable in the first place.

This view contends the most significant pivot of British political history occurred *after* 1832. How do we know that the adaptation of the British Conservative Party was itself not a function of a legacy of the 1688 settlement? Isn't it still possible that the legacy of this historical rupture compelled Tory MPs early on to learn "the norms and practice of competitive politics"?[27] There are two reasons to question this conventional wisdom. First, despite intense contestation and significant political change, for long periods of time between 1688 and 1832, the majority of British MPs who occupied parliamentary seats *never* faced an opponent at election time, relying instead on endorsements by local notables.[28] Uncontested parliamentary seats, or what analysts have called "silent elections" only permanently went into decline after 1832, long after the threshold of 1688.[29] It is hard to imagine politicians "learning the arts of contestation" when there was in fact so little contestation.[30] Second, the hardest evidence social scientists typically cite to support the idea that the Glorious Revolution propelled a modernizing

---

[26] For conservative parties of continental Europe, see Kalyvas, *Rise of Christian Democracy* (1996). For party information in Sweden, see Edvard Thermaenius, *Sveriges Politiska Partier* (Stockholm: Hugo Gebers Forla, 1933); Stenlas, "Kampen om Högern" (2002).

[27] Dahl, *Polyarchy* (1971), 36.

[28] For detailed data, see John Cannon, *Parliamentary Reform, 1640–1832* (Cambridge: Cambridge University Press, 1973), Appendix 3, 276–89.

[29] Daniele Caramani, "The End of Silent Elections: The Birth of Electoral Competition, 1832–1915," *Party Politics* 9, no. 4 (2003): 411–43.

[30] For a more detailed account of the emergence of various strands of pre-1832 conservatism in Britain, see James J. Sack, *From Jacobite to Conservative: Reaction and Orthodoxy in Britain, 1760–1832* (New York: Cambridge University Press, 1993).

transformation in political elite behavior is the low interest rates the British government paid to borrow money after 1688: an indicator of its low risk of default.[31] However, on top of the unrest we have uncovered immediately preceding 1832, recent scholarship has added a caveat even about the period after 1688 itself: in the eighteenth century, lower interest rates held when the Whig Party was in power, while investors in Britain's sovereign bonds actually *punished* British sovereign debt when the Tory Party was in government.[32] If low-yield rates on public debt are an indicator of the triumph of the "rule of law," it appears that in order for the historical break of 1688 to become *enduringly* stable, a series of additional developments were necessary, including a transformation in the Conservative Party itself. This process began only after 1832, and thus requires a different explanation altogether.

A STRONG PARLIAMENTARY PARTY WITH "FEET OF CLAY"? THE EARLY YEARS, 1832–1874

To fully grasp how well-organized conservative parties emerged in nineteenth-century Europe, three questions are useful: how did parties come to shape the parliamentary behavior of members of parliament? How and when did voters in the electorate come consistently to consider themselves as partisans, closely identifying with a particular political party? And, finally, when and why did parties develop the important organizational infrastructure "out in the country" that allowed them to cajole, campaign, and canvass voters between and during elections? In the case of nineteenth-century Britain, research on the first two questions is quite well developed. The latter question, however, has proven more difficult to answer. But there were four strategic organizational innovations that made significant headway in the formation of extraparliamentary party organization in this period: the creation of the office of party agent, the formation of local associations, the establishment of national umbrella organizations for these associations, and the inclusion of greater roles for salaried "professionals" in the party leadership.

---

[31] North and Weingast, "Constitutions and Commitment" (1989).

[32] For systematic evidence on this point, see David Stasavage, "Credible Commitment in Early Modern Europe: North and Weingast Revisited," *Journal of Law, Economics, and Organization* 18, no. 1 (2002): 155–86; and David Stasavage, "Partisan Politics and Public Debt: The Importance of the Whig Supremacy for Britain's Financial Revolution," *European Review of Economic History* 11 (2007): 123–53. In addition to different preferences about debt between landowning Tory Party and "monied interests" of the Whig party, a second possible explanation of this finding is that the Tory party remained more reliant on monarchical influence at election time than the Whigs for patronage, reducing the Tory Party as a credible check on monarchical power. For some supporting evidence of this hypothesis, see Bruce Morrison, "Channeling the restless spirit of innovation: Elite Concessions and Institutional Change in the British Reform Act of 1832," *World Politics* 63, no. 4: 691–92.

To place the challenges of building extraparliamentary party organization into proper perspective, we must begin our discussion with the role of parties *inside* parliament, since it is from here that parties developed. The scholarship of early political scientist Lawrence Lowell, and more recently of Gary Cox, Andrew Eggers, and Arthur Spirling, uses the tool of roll-call analysis to trace the evolution of parties' discipline on voting behavior of MPs.[33] Close historical analysis has also put institutional flesh on these findings by reconstructing the mechanisms by which the chief whip and the parliamentary party organization around him, including a small group of advisors, current MPs, and future or past ministers, met on a regular basis for "eve-of-session" meetings to establish the "party line."[34] Alternatively, meetings were held in the Prime Minister's home or at the Carlton Club to establish the preferences and strategy of the party.[35] But despite the importance of this informal parliamentary management structure, it is now clear that a decisive role was played by the chief parliamentary whip, whose job it was to translate these agreements at the top of the party into actual votes in parliamentary divisions.[36] If the prime minister was the public face of the party, the party's "chief whip" was the behind-the-scenes figure responsible for internal parliamentary work and the political "stagecraft" of "keeping a house."[37] His functions, as early political scientist Moshei Ostrogorski describes it, involved keeping the lobbies or smoking rooms of the parliament full in case a vote was called; maintaining a reserve of "fluent" speakers available to "run the clock" until the chambers were filled

[33] According to Lowell's data, as early as 1836, the British Conservative Party voted unanimously 56 percent of the time, compared to the Whigs' 40 percent, dipping in the 1850s and 1860s to 30–40 percent unanimity (after the rupture of the Corn Law debates in the 1840s), but achieving its earlier peaks of "party discipline" of 71 percent unanimity in the 1870s. See Lawrence A. Lowell, *The Government of England* (New York: Macmillan, 1912), 81. See, more recently, Gary Cox, *The Efficient Secret: The Cabinet and the Development of Political Parties in Victorian England*, Political Economy of Institutions and Decisions (Cambridge: Cambridge University Press, 1987); Andrew Reeves, "To Power through Reform: The Development of Party through Electoral Reform in the Victorian House of Commons" (Harvard University, 2008); Andrew Eggers and Arthur Spirling, "Party Cohesion in Westminster Systems: Inducements, Replacement and Discipline in the House of Commons, 1836–1910," *British Journal of Political Science* (2014): 1–23.

[34] Norman Gash, "The Organization of the Conservative Party, 1832–1846: Part I: The Parliamentary Organization," *Parliamentary History* 1 (1982): 140–41. More generally, see Ostrogorski, *Democracy and the Organization of Political Parties* (1902), 137–140; Tim Renton, *Chief Whip: People, Power and Patronage in Westminster* (London: Politico's, 2004).

[35] Disraeli and Gladstone both individually report that in the 1830s they sought to be included, from time to time, in this exclusive "club" of most trusted advisors; see Gash, "Organization of the Conservative Party" (1982): 141.

[36] The chief whip's name is borrowed from fox hunting to describe the huntsman's assistant who keeps the hunting dogs in line; see Ostrogorski, *Democracy and the Organization of Political Parties* (1902), 137–40; Gash, "Organization of the Conservative Party" (1982), 144.

[37] Ostrogorski, *Democracy and the Organization of Political Parties* (1902), 138.

for a vote; and distributing cash to MPs, who would line up after loyal party parliamentary votes for their payment at a window in the House of Commons itself.[38] Typically, the chief whip also was parliamentary secretary to the treasury, or patronage secretary and had access to "Secret Service" funds used to bolster his own personal powers of persuasion.[39] Thus, through a mixture of persuasion, monetary exchange, party loyalty, and "old corruption," the parties became entrenched and important actors in the British parliament beginning in the 1830s.[40]

Though creating cohesion inside the parliament, in terms of parties' relationship to individual voters, early research seemed to bolster the Liberal Party's agent Joseph Parkes's old proposition that "the pollbook is almost a topography of the estates."[41] From this view, the business of appealing to individual voters was not about partisan identification but was simply an outgrowth of "deference" to local patrons;[42] old corruption and coercion;[43] and making campaigns about local personalities, symbols and loyalties.[44] But more nuanced views have also altered these sweeping accounts, pointing out that in some contexts, as political scientist Gary Cox has substantiated through his analysis of "split-ticket voting," partisan loyalty, though low after 1832, increased as split voting declined throughout the course of the nineteenth century.[45] Similarly, other analysts trace thousands of individual voters *over time*, estimating hazard rates, or probabilities of whether voters will change partisan propensity after voting in one election.[46] This analysis, for a sample of

---

[38] Ibid.

[39] Tim Renton provides a summary of the types of funds to which chief whips had access. Renton, *Chief Whip* (2004), 139–41; Gash, "Organization of the Conservative Party" (1982): 144.

[40] Schattschneider, *Party Government* (1942); Aldrich, *Why Parties?* (1995). These two works provide the most convincing theoretical explanations of how a combination of collective-action problems and competition impel party "organization" and "counterorganization" inside legislatures, leading to parties-in-parliament. As Schattschneider puts it, party organization in legislatures flows from "the discovery that a few members agreeing in advance to concentrate their voting strength can control a large body in which the other members do not consult for this purpose." And counterorganization (generating a two-party system) happens "when organized efforts to concentrate voting strength on one side are opposed by equally well-organized efforts to concentrate support on the other side... and... [the result is] a kind of party system has been established," Schattschneider, *Party Government* (1942), 44.

[41] Cited by Norman Gash, *Politics in the Age of Peel: A Study in the Technique of Parliamentary Representation, 1830–1850* (Hassocks, UK: Harvester Press, [1953] 1977), 178.

[42] Moore, *The Politics of Deference* (1976).

[43] Norman Gash, "The Organization of the Conservative Party, 1832–1846: Part II: The Electoral Organization," *Parliamentary History* 2 (1983): 131–52.

[44] Vernon, *Politics and the People: A Study in English Political Culture, 1815–1867* (1993).

[45] Cox, *The Efficient Secret* (1987), 103–04.

[46] John A. Phillips, *The Great Reform Bill in the Boroughs: English Electoral Behaviour, 1818–1841* (Oxford: Clarendon Press, 1992); and John A. Phillips and Charles Wetherell, "The Great Reform Act of 1832 and the Political Modernization of England," *The American Historical Review* 100, no. 2 (1995): 411–36.

constituencies, demonstrates that the 1832 Great Reform Act – and, likely, the heated and high-profile debates surrounding it – was a watershed, establishing consistent party voting among many voters.[47]

What, finally, of party-as-organization outside of parliament? Since the core contention here is that conservative parties equipped with strong party organization in the electorate shape long-run democratic trajectories, this is our area of chief theoretical concern. How did parties, and the British Conservative Party in particular, gain formal structures for organizing and mobilizing the electorate *outside* of parliament? There were four main organizational innovations in this domain before 1874, but until the party was able to effectively mobilize religious cleavages in the 1880s, it remained an "elite" party without well-developed organization. Yet, these earlier innovations did have a long-run cumulative effect on the party that allowed it quickly to absorb the rapid creation of a mass social organization in the 1880s.[48]

The four innovations in this earlier period included the creation of the position of "party agent" in the 1830s; the proliferation of local associations beginning in the 1830s into the 1870s; the creation of a national umbrella organization, the National Union of Conservative and Constitutional Associations (NU), for these organizations in the late 1860s; and the increasing reliance on professional "organization men" to help run the party. The first innovation – the creation of the party agent position – occurred in the 1830s, a period, as historian Gash notes, in which governments had been made and lost not in elections but in defections inside the parliament.[49] Thus, until the 1830s, the task of electoral organization in the constituencies remained limited. "Outdoor" management, as Conservative leader in the House of Commons Sir Stafford Northcote dubbed it, received less attention from the party

---

[47] The authors conclude, quite stunningly, that the "central tendency in English electoral behavior after 1832" was that "voters became consistent partisans"; see Phillips, *The Great Reform Bill in the Boroughs: English Electoral Behaviour, 1818–1841* (1992), 435. According to Phillips's numbers, one interesting empirical finding is that Tory voters possessed higher partisan loyalty (i.e., lower hazard rates) than Whig voters (p. 431) in the crucial period between 1832 and 1861. One critic (Frank O'Gorman, "The Electorate Before and After 1832," *Parliamentary History* 12, no. 2 (1993): 171–83) has pointed out the selection-bias problems with this analysis, since Phillips's data usually come from urban and not rural constituencies, suggesting a line for future research. John A. Phillips, *The Great Reform Bill in the Boroughs: English Electoral Behaviour, 1818–1841* (1992); and Phillips and Wetherell, "The Great Reform Act of 1832 and the Political Modernization of England" (1995).

[48] As I will elaborate below, this reflects a particular nonlinear or discontinuous dynamic of institutional change (due to threshold effects) described by a range of theorists including Thomas Schelling, "Dynamic Models of Segregation," *Journal of Mathematical Sociology* 1 (1971): 143–86; Mark Granovetter, "Threshold Models of Collective Behavior," *American Journal of Sociology* 83 (1978): 1420–43; and Pierson, *Politics in Time* (2004).

[49] Gash, "Organization of the Conservative Party" (1983), 131.

management altogether.[50] The task was left to the chief parliamentary whip, who mainly focused on "indoor" work of party dynamics within the parliament.[51] However, after 1832, future Prime Minister Sir Robert Peel departed significantly from past practice by creating a new position in the party, the *party agent*, whose chief job it was to oversee and manage elections. This initial differentiation of function within the parliamentary party caused two main predictable tensions: first, with the chief whip, whose responsibility in the parliament initially had extended to "outdoor" work, and therefore with whom he stood in direct competition; second, with the informal and elitist amateurism of the Carlton Club, where the chief whip had usually conducted his "outdoor" activity.[52]

Though firmly entrenched in the central party organization and based in London, the party agent's chief task was different from the chief whip's: his purpose was to provide the link between the party leadership on the one hand and the emerging though limited local organizations and associations outside the parliament on the other. This new "professional" party agent's authority came not from his pre-existing status as a notable, but from his specialized and increasingly technical knowledge of the intricacies of voter registration rules and the number of electors. The first party agent, Francis Bonham, was a former MP who had worked closely in the *ad hoc* committee of the party leader and chief whip that had managed previous elections.[53] In the wake of the collapse of Peel's first government in 1835, Bonham wrote a letter to Peel indicating that what was needed was a "very small and quiet and active committee" to collect data and oversee elections. Bonham continued, "I am ready to devote my whole time out of the House of Commons to this work and with a very small committee hardly more than 7."[54]

The result was a committee that not only managed elections indirectly, but was in possession of a central election fund as early as 1835, which was used in the infrequent instances when candidates did not have enough money for

---

[50] Archie Hunter, *A Life of Sir John Eldon Gorst: Disraeli's Awkward Disciple* (London: Frank Cass, 2001), 120.

[51] Gash, "Organization of the Conservative Party" (1983), 131.

[52] For example, the chief whip had usually used the Carlton Club as a site to run his ad hoc "election committees," where he would meet aspiring candidates as well as local notables who would come to London in search of a candidate for "his" constituency, if an opening occurred. See Philip Salmon, *Electoral Reform at Work: Local Politics and National Parties, 1832–1841* (London: Royal Historical Society, 2002), 44–45; 50; Ostrogorski, *Democracy and the Organization of Political Parties* (1902), 148–149.

[53] The notion of a "professional" used here draws on Max Weber's "Politics as Vocation" as was the broader sociological literature on "professions." See Andrew Delano Abbott, *The System of Professions: An Essay on the Division of Expert Labor* (Chicago: University of Chicago Press, 1988); Harold L. Wilensky, "The Professionalization of Everyone?" *American Journal of Sociology* 70, no. 2 (1964): 137–58.

[54] Robert Stewart, *The Foundation of the Conservative Party, 1830–1867* (London: Longman, 1978), 136.

campaigning and the more frequent cases when candidates did not have sufficient money to undergo the complex and costly post-election dispute procedure.[55] Despite the presence of a central election fund, a central election committee, and a central election manager, the shift toward professionalism should not be overstated: the party agent's committee remained dominated not by experts but by cabinet ministers and officials in the government (e.g., Earl of Rosslyn and Granville Somerset). Moreover, the party agent position failed to become institutionalized, disappearing after 1841 with Bonham's departure. Though the position of "chief party agent" was resurrected at different points, his successors were not full-time party officials *per se*, but typically solicitors who worked part time for the party.

For example, Philip Rose, a lawyer in the firm of Baxter, Rose, Norton and Co. and Disraeli's personal lawyer, also served as party agent from 1853 until 1859.[56] Furthermore, Rose's successor after 1859 was another lawyer from the same firm, Markham Spofforth, who was aided by his clerks.[57] And, finally, in 1870, an even deeper transformation occurred when chief party agent John Gorst elevated the position to a permanent one, though still unpaid.[58] Several points about Gorst's well-studied tenure are worth mentioning. First, in 1867, the old divided regime was still intact (the solicitor, Spofforth, continued on as chief party agent as well in the 1868 election, and the whips oversaw the election).[59] It was only in 1870 that John Gorst, a former MP from Cambridge, was hired at Disraeli's intervention to help remake the party's central body: he created the Central Office at 53

---

[55] Gash, "Organization of the Conservative Party" (1983), 137.

[56] His nearly 600-page unpublished election notebook, dated in his last year of service in 1859, is filled with detailed accounts of nearly every constituency in Britain, each constituency's local agent, characteristics of MPs, and detailed reports on status of the constituency for the next elections, all making clear a distinctly empirical orientation toward party organization that contradicts any notion the party was being run by premodern amateurs. See Philip Rose, "Election Notebook" (Special Collections, Bodleian Library, Oxford, 1859).

[57] That this task would fall to a law firm may at first appear puzzling. However, as the discussion below makes clear, the key organizational issues facing parties in this period were election disputes and fights over voter-registration qualifications, which were primarily negotiated by lawyers until the 1850s. Being the party agent for a party was lucrative work for a law firm that specialized in election disputes. E. J. Feuchtwanger, "J. E. Gorst and the Central Organization of the Conservative Party, 1870–1882," *Bulletin of the Institute of Historical Research* 32, no. 85 (1959a):192.

[58] Hunter, *Life of Sir John Eldon Gorst* (2001), 83–84

[59] Spofforth's departure was not a self-conscious move of the party for more "professional" organization, stimulated by the 1867 Reform Act. Rather, it was the result of a more obscure legislative change that shifted the locale of election disputes from a London court to special provincial courts, making party work for the law firm Baxter, Rose, Norton and Co. less attractive and ending the relationship between the firm and the Conservative Party. See Feuchtwanger, "J. E. Gorst " (1959a): 194; E. J. Feuchtwanger, "The Conservative Party Under the Impact of the Second Reform Act," *Victorian Studies* 2, no. 4 (1959b): 298.

Parliament Street; settled the newly created federated body for local associations, the National Union, at the same address; and undertook a much more active agenda of creating electoral inroads in urban areas. Gorst, of a middle-class background, had advanced vague visions that would later constitute what Randolph Churchill dubbed "Tory Democracy" – including appeals to urban and middle-class voters and the commitment to forge a more professional party leadership.[60] As he wrote to Disraeli in 1874, "I do not dissent from your view the mass of the people is, or may be made, Tory. But masses cannot move without leaders."[61] What was needed, in short, was organization. Thus, Gorst sought to turn the Central Office, in the words of his biographer, into,

a repository of political information and data vital to the party's proper functioning. Apart from the list of candidates, this included in the course of time lists of all Conservative associations, records on registration of voters, and the results of revisions made in registration courts, draft model rules for local associations, publications and leaflets for distribution, statistics about parliamentary elections, and relevant information about forthcoming parliamentary bills.[62]

The turn to professionalism, a second major innovation in this period, put Gorst into conflict with an older style of political leadership represented by leading conservative aristocrats such as Lord Abergavenny, taking its toll on the transformation of the party. Indeed, though Gorst's remaking of the central leadership of the party is sometimes regarded as the source of the first electoral majority in thirty years in 1874, the closest analysis of Gorst concludes, "The period between the second [1867] and the third Reform Bills [1884] was a transitional stage in the development of party organization."[63] This is demonstrated by the fact that the position of party agent was hardly institutionalized: immediately following the election, Gorst set his eyes on an MP seat for himself, suggesting the limited appeals of the "party agent" position. The return to a massive Liberal majority in 1880 revealed that the status quo had indeed been re-established, and though Disraeli had called for a new special committee to revisit the question of party organization, the party remained stuck halfway between its aristocratic origins and a modern conservative organization.

Along with the party agent and the trend of professionalism, the third major area of organizational innovation was the systematic effort to create local constituency associations. After the Great Reform Act of 1832, and beginning as early as 1834–35, a web of local associations, some called "Conservative Operative Societies" or "Loyal and Constitutional Associations" and others

[60] Feuchtwanger, "J. E. Gorst " (1959a): 197.
[61] Disraeli Papers, Box A, Dyke, as cited by Feuchtwanger, "J. E. Gorst " (1959a): 200.
[62] Hunter, *Life of Sir John Eldon Gorst* (2001), 84.
[63] Feuchtwanger, "J. E. Gorst " (1959a): 197.

"Registration Societies," gradually emerged.[64] Again, this occurred before the British Liberal Party undertook similar efforts.[65] An infrequently noticed feature of the Reform Act of 1832, which installed a new system of voter registration, triggered the creation of these organizations.[66] While pre-1832 Britain had no system of voter registration, after 1832 each constituency was required to have a voter registry, updated annually by the voters themselves in county constituencies and less frequently in borough constituencies. The intent of this legislation, which constituted two-thirds of the Great Reform Act, was to control what many had expected to be an onslaught of new voters after the 1832 reform, prompted by the remaining provisions of the act.

However, the procedures for getting voters onto the local registries were so cumbersome and vague in the 1832 Act that a great deal was left to "private initiative." For example, voters themselves had to renew their registration annually.[67] Also, if another voter challenged the validity of a voter's qualifications, he was easily removed from the rolls.[68] To the surprise of many contemporaries, the result of this burdensome local procedure was less of an upsurge in voting after 1832 than had been expected.[69] Thus, after 1832, the profound electoral implications of voter registration thus became clear quite quickly. Sir Robert Peel, despite some ambivalence about extra-parliamentary organizations that might pressure the parliamentary party, announced in 1835 that a chief priority for the Conservative Party and its new associations should be to "Register, register, register!"[70]

The impetus for creating associations not only emerged from the party leadership but also came from local notables. First, by 1832, the old fiscal-military state of the late eighteenth century that had been sustained by "old corruption" to protect establishment interests had now been dismantled.[71] This left political parties as a newly important collective vehicle of elite self-

---

[64] Rather than having either an automatic process of voter registration or dedicated public officials to oversee the process of voter registration, it followed a different and highly "privatized" pattern of organization. Given the nature of the registration system in which "The State had trusted to private initiative" (Ostrogorski, *Democracy and the Organization of Political Parties* (1902), 142) all the activities of voter registration, it also makes sense that party organizations were formed to begin organizing challenges to voters who might vote against them and support for those who would vote for them. Blake, *The Conservative Party from Peel to Churchill* (1970), 39.

[65] Salmon, *Electoral Reform at Work* (2002), 58.

[66] Charles Seymour, *Electoral Reform in England and Wales: The Development and Operation of the Parliamentary Franchise, 1832–1885* (Newton Abbot: David & Charles, 1915; reprint, 1970), 107.

[67] Ostrogorski, *Democracy and the Organization of Political Parties* (1902), 141.

[68] Seymour, *Electoral Reform in England and Wales* (1915), 107.

[69] See data in Salmon, *Electoral Reform at Work* (2002), 22–23;

[70] Ostrogorski, *Democracy and the Organization of Political Parties* (1902), 150.

[71] See, e.g., Philip Harling, *The Waning of "Old Corruption": The Politics of Economical Reform in Britain, 1779–1846* (Oxford: Clarendon Press, 1996).

protection. But gaining access to voters was now critical for this to be viable. The conservative periodical *Blackwood's Edinburgh Magazine*, for example, spoke on behalf of local notables when it asserted that Conservative Party associations could solve the "collective action" problem of registering voters.[72] "Conservative associations might operate most efficaciously in aiding the cause of truth," the editors wrote.[73] They continued, making a plea for organization:

It is utterly unreasonable... that... the expenses incurred in securing the registration of Conservative voters should be incurred by [candidates]. In a few cases, indeed, where a great family has an interest in securing a county or borough from Radical invasion, this may be done; but generally speaking it is out of the question. The Conservative interest... must do it for themselves, or it will not be done at all.[74]

Thus, local agents, local notables, and prospective candidates formed new registration organizations. And when a particular constituency was well organized, it became a model for neighboring constituencies.[75] As Ostrogorski summarizes the dynamic, registration laws "became... a gap through which the parties, hitherto confined to Parliament, made their way into the constituencies and gradually covered the whole country with the network of their organization."[76]

According to one account, Conservative Party registration societies appeared, at one point or another, in virtually every constituency by the late 1830s, though, revealingly perhaps, no centralized or systematic record of them remains.[77] Some associations disappeared between elections, while others persisted. Their institutionalization was uneven, though their appearance did, according to several secondary accounts, outpace Liberal efforts. Moreover, once in place, registration societies were critical in the electoral proceedings that followed disputes in registration courts – explaining the lucrative attraction of the party agent position to attorneys – and they came to play an increasingly important role in electioneering, selecting candidates, and election-day canvassing.[78] While candidates' selection remained formally in the hands of the chief party whip in London, agents representing local associations often found themselves increasingly at an informational advantage to the central

---

[72] "Conservative Associations" *Blackwood's Edinburgh Magazine* (July 1835), 237 (38) 1–15.

[73] Ibid., 8.   [74] Ibid.,10.   [75] Salmon, *Electoral Reform at Work* (2002), 60.

[76] Ostrogorski, *Democracy and the Organization of Political Parties* (1902), 142.

[77] In the 1850s, the Conservative party manager Philip Rose also leaves us the earliest systematic record of the numbers of Conservative party associations in the constituencies in his unpublished "Election Notebook" that lists contacts, agents, and constituency association information in over 100 constituencies; reported in Edwin Jaggard, "Managers and Agents: Conservative Party Organisation in the 1850s," *Parliamentary History* 27, no. 1 (2008): 7–18. Matthew Cragoe, "The Great Reform Act and the Modernization of British Politics: The Impact of Conservative Associations, 1835–1841," *Journal of British Studies* 47 (2008): 581–603.

[78] Ostrogorski, *Democracy and the Organization of Political Parties* (1902), 151–53.

party.[79] Nonetheless, despite organizational innovation, these groups remained often still dominated by local notables, often disappearing between elections.

The fourth organizational innovation in this period came after the watershed of 1867 with the creation of a new national umbrella organization for pre-existing local associations, the National Union (NU), which aimed to give the party a nationally integrated organizational infrastructure. Founded by a group of young MPs, including John Gorst and Henry Cecil Raikes, with the approval of the party agent and chief whip, the NU served to provide a "propagandist organization" for the party, helping to distribute pamphlets, hold annual conventions, and provide a common platform for the disparate local associations unevenly spread across Britain.[80] The first gathering, in November 1867, was held at the Freemason's Tavern in London, chaired by the young Cambridge MP John Gorst who stepped in to replace a more notable MP who had canceled at the last minute. According to the meeting minutes, fifty-five cities sent delegates to this first annual gathering. Gorst began the session with a clear statement of his "professional" orientation to politics – in which strategy overrides principle – by declaring to the assembled, "This is not a meeting to discuss Conservative principles but to consider by which particular organization we may make those Conservative principles effective among the masses."[81] The goal, as several speakers at this first annual meeting proclaimed, was to support existing local associations and inspire the formation of new ones throughout Britain, giving the British Conservative Party a new organizational profile across the country.[82]

This auspicious start, however, quickly foundered. Table 3.3 reports the location of the meetings and number of delegates in attendance at annual conventions after 1867, showing that even seven years after the 1867 Reform Act, only 40 of the approximately 382 constituencies including Scotland and Wales (i.e., 20 percent) were represented at the annual meetings. It was only around 1874, and especially in 1875, when conservatives ironically were back in the majority, that local associations were organized enough to send more delegates to the annual meeting, though the number was still small.

Thus, we see that 1867 was hardly a "big bang" that sparked immediate organizational diffusion of the British Conservative Party. The lag after 1867 is in part explained by the nature of the internal debate within the party, between those who saw the "country element" as sufficient for the party's future and younger MPs, such as John Gorst, who argued that organizational transformation was necessary. Thus, when Disraeli appointed Gorst in 1870

---

[79] Gash, "Organization of the Conservative Party" (1983),133; Cragoe, "Great Reform Act" (2008).

[80] H. J. Hanham, *Elections and Party Management: Politics in the Time of Disraeli and Gladstone* (London: Longmans, 1959), 365–66.

[81] Minutes of Proceedings of First Conference of the National Union of Conservative Constitutional Associations, November 12, 1867, NUA 2/1/1, Conservative Party Archive, Bodleian Library, Oxford.

[82] Ibid.

TABLE 3.3: *Location of National Union Convention and Number of Delegates, 1867–1875*

Year	Location	Association Delegates
1867	London	55
1868	Birmingham	7
1869	Liverpool	36
1870	York	15
1871	Bristol	10
1874	London	40
1875	Brighton	93

Data Source: "Minutes of the Proceedings of Annual National Union of Conservative Constitutional Associations Convention," 1867–1876, NUA 2/1/1, Conservative Party Archive, Bodleian Library, Oxford

as the new party agent, an important shift occurred – one that prompted great resentment and resistance from what Gorst had derisively termed the party's "old identity."[83] The chief source of opposition came from the traditional leadership of the House of Lords and the House of Commons. Yet, John Gorst took several bold steps, including moving the NU to his new Central Office headquarters and having himself named honorary chair of the organization, more tightly linking the new entity to the party's Central Office.

The immediate result was greater activity, organization, and effort to reach out to urban districts. Gorst advocated the necessity of expanding the party beyond its "country" profile.[84] He astutely recognized, following the 1868 electoral loss, that the party's fortunes were now tied to the expanded electorates in cities – urban borough constituencies – where old patterns of "influence" were in decline and thus where party organization was most necessary. Further, Gorst's efforts to link the constituencies to the central party via the associations and the National Union were also a response to his sympathies for the "new men" of industrializing Britain who had sought to help the Conservative Party in organizing in exchange for the "spoils" and recognition of their party work. Gorst wrote candidly in an 1874 correspondence, "I cannot but perceive that all our patronage has been divided between the personal friends of the ministers and our political opponents; and that... nothing whatever has been done to reward those who have shared with us the labours and troubles of opposition."[85]

[83] James Cornford, "The Transformation of Conservatism in the Late Nineteenth Century," *Victorian Studies* 7, no. 1 (1963): 49.
[84] Ibid., 45.
[85] Disraeli papers, as cited by Cornford, "Transformation of Conservatism" (1963): 44.

Prompted by these pressures, the NU, under Gorst's leadership, campaigned to expand the breadth and density of local associations, and 447 associations existed by 1874 according to the party's own records.[86] At each annual meeting, the NU leaders announced how many newly affiliated local associations had been founded; and each year "progress" was announced. In 1875, the NU chairman declared at the meeting in Brighton that there were now 472 affiliated associations.[87]

However, at odds with this blooming landscape of local associations were two revealing developments. First, as noted above, immediately after the 1874 election, Gorst resigned, seeking a new seat for himself in the House of Commons, showing the limits of the institutionalization of the new reforms and the possibility that the status quo *ex ante* was quickly being re-established with party whips and the "old identity." Second, Gorst himself was increasingly critical of developments after 1874, appealing directly to Disraeli in 1877 and declaring in his correspondence that he feared "the misfortune to witness the whole system, to establish which so much trouble was taken, gradually to fall into decay"[88] Most in the party leadership had never been particularly sympathetic to Gorst's organizational initiatives, suspecting he might someday threaten to come back to capture the leadership of the parliamentary party. However, as long as the NU remained "handmaid" to the party, as H. C. Raikes put it in 1873, it was an organization that could be quietly tolerated. Yet, when Gorst, the chief proponent behind the organization, left office, the NU quickly went into decline until the 1880s.

Thus, we are left with two contradictory pictures, both built on a common periodization scheme of British political development that revolves around the frequently cited "turning point" of 1867. Did suffrage reform mean that the powerful party leadership finally had access to an effective "election machinery" that now could instantaneously mobilize voters? Or, alternatively, did this remain, as Gorst himself seemed to fear, a weak party organization essentially left without the kind of mobilizational capacity necessary for a true transformation in the party?

These are difficult questions to resolve systematically. However, we can weigh existing evidence to assess which argument finds greater support. In particular, one valuable data source on party organization provides us with important clues. In 1874, an election year, the Central Office produced a report entitled *Conservative Agents and Associations of the Counties and Boroughs of*

---

[86] This figure was reported in Minutes of Proceedings of National Union of Conservative and Constitutional Associations held at Westminster Palace Hotel, July 1, 1874 (8th annual meeting)," Conservative Party Archive, Oxford University, NUA 2/1/1

[87] This figure is reported in "Minutes of Proceedings of National Union of Conservative and Constitutional Associations held at Brighton, June 19, 1875," Conservative Party Archive, Oxford University, NUA 2/1/1.

[88] Gorst to Disraeli, March 3, 1877, Disraeli Papers, as cited by Cornford, "Transformation of Conservatism" (1963): 46.

England and Wales for private circulation only within the party leadership. This impressive handbook lists each constituency in England and Wales, the names of local party agents, the number of voters in each constituency, and the presence or absence of local association in any given constituency that year.[89] The document also lists the names of a wide range of disparate groups, including, for example, the West Gloucestershire Conservative Registration Association and the Salisbury Conservative and Working Man's Association. Using the party's document as a source, we can identify which of the 319 English and Welsh constituencies had associations (60 percent) and which did not.

But what effect did these organizations have on rallying voters? We can follow political scientist John Aldrich's lead to use election turnout data as a measure of party mobilization to give us a clue of whether local party organizations indeed led to greater electoral mobilization, as was intended.[90] If Conservative Party local associations were truly effective organizations, more than simply "parchment institutions," they ought to have led to substantial upturns in election turnout. Just as the pool of potential voters expanded, after 1867, so did the average percentage of eligible voters who actually turned out to vote. Table 3.4 shows, dividing the data into "borough" and "county"

TABLE 3.4: *Difference in Turnout Rates in Conservative Party Organized and Unorganized Counties and Borough, 1867–1880*

	Turnout Differentials, 1867–1880	Number of Constituencies
Counties		
Organized	1.8%	35
Not Organized	5%	5
Average	2.5%	41
Boroughs		
Organized	4.6%	112
Not Organized	4.7%	47
Average	4.6%	155
Total Average	4.2%	196

Data Source: Constituency party-organization data comes from the Conservative Party's own document *Conservative Agents and Associations of the Counties and Boroughs of England and Wales* (1874)

---

[89] I discovered this document in the British Library, London, England (April 2009). Hanham (*Elections and Party Management* (1959) and Cox (*The Efficient Secret* (1987) also both cite the document, though they use it for different purposes than I do here.

[90] Aldrich, *Why Parties?* (1995), 119.

constituencies, the increase in turnout as a percentage of registered voters between 1867 and 1880 in constituencies where the Conservative Party had local organization and where it did not.

In the new universe of elections after 1867 (e.g., 1867, 1874, and 1880), we see that overall turnout everywhere increased between 1867 and 1880, and more so in boroughs than in county constituencies. However, a first look at the data suggests, against the expectations of those who insist that these post-1867 party organizations were immediately effective, that the existence of conservative associations actually corresponds to *lower* levels of turnout increase. How do we explain this puzzling finding? Election results from 1868 show that it is precisely in the constituencies where the Conservative Party faired poorly that local associations were erected, suggesting that Gorst's Central Office was following a rational strategy.[91] In response to the Reform Act of 1867, efforts perhaps were made to build up party organizations precisely where they were weak, but such efforts may have remained unsuccessful.

To flesh out this argument and to incorporate the dynamics of electoral competition into a more complete explanation of voter turnout, we can use multivariate OLS analysis with robust standard errors to assess the impact of organizations while controlling for the competitiveness of elections. The dependent variable is the level of turnout for the period as a whole (1867–1880) in a time series cross-sectional analysis as well as in three cross-sectional analyses in the three election years (1867, 1874, and 1880).[92] The party organization variable is coded for each constituency dichotomously based on the presence or absence of party organization as reported in the Conservative Party handbook cited above. Also included are several controls for other variables that potentially mask the effect of party organization, including how competitive an election was in a particular constituency in a given year, since close elections can increase turnout,[93] and whether a constituency was a borough or a county constituency, since it is often argued that turnout tended to be lower in rural county districts turnout. Table 3.5 reports the results.

In Model 1, which is based on pooled data for all three elections in the period, as well as in the Models 2, 3, and 4, which report cross-sectional findings for each election year separately, we see several consistent findings. First, close elections (characterized by a high level of competitiveness) were associated

[91] Supporting evidence of this is that Conservative Party electoral outcomes (percentage of the vote for conservatives) in 1867, 1874, and 1880 are *negatively* correlated with the existence of Conservative Party associations.

[92] Ideally, it would have been useful to focus more narrowly on turnout for voters who cast their vote for conservative candidates. However, such data (distinguishing how those who turned out voted) do not exist.

[93] The measure of "competitiveness" used here assesses how close each election was (the percentage difference between the two top-scoring parties, using data from Caramani, *Elections in Western Europe* (2000).

TABLE 3.5: *Effect of Electoral Mobilization on Election Turnout, 1867–1880*

	(1)	(2)	(3)	(4)
Conservative Party	-5.994^{***}	-3.975^{**}	-7.837^{***}	-5.722^{***}
Organization	(1.074)	(1.992)	(2.053)	(1.570)
Competitiveness	16.352^{***}	11.028^{***}	14.227^{***}	27.418^{***}
	(2.087)	(3.174)	(3.966)	(3.919)
Borough	10.669^{***}	10.715^{***}	8.787^{***}	12.104^{***}
	(1.115)	(1.965)	(2.260)	(1.622)
Years	1867–1880	1867	1874	1880
Observations	680	219	213	248
R^2	0.200	0.166	0.149	0.318

Notes: * $p<0.1$, ** $p<0.05$, *** $p<0.01$; robust standard errors in parentheses. Hypotheses are direction specific; however, levels of significance reported throughout this chapter are for two-tailed tests.

with higher turnout. Also, confirming the conventional wisdom, turnout was higher in urban or borough constituencies, where it was easier to mobilize voters. But above and beyond these factors, we see that conservative-party organization not only did not have a positive relationship with turnout, it in fact had a statistically significant *negative* relationship with turnout, even controlling for a range of other factors. This finding is unexpected but suggests that either something about effective organization *per se* was driving down election turnout, or, alternatively, that the presence of party organization was itself correlated with some other third factor that led to lower turnout. One possible explanation for both John Gorst's own strategy as well as the negative correlation between the presence of party organization and electoral performance is this: party leaders self-consciously placed party organizations in districts where the party was weak.[94]

But, whatever the explanation, it is clear that the British Conservative Party, despite repeated efforts at extra-parliamentary organization building, remained a stunted organization even after the 1867 Reform Act. Its efforts to organize electoral mobilization did not have an immediate payoff. The expansion of suffrage had certainly incentivized enterprising political leaders to build extra-parliamentary organization in new locations, usually even before Liberal competitors. The push for local "popular" organization from the "new men" of middle-class urban Britain also had provided

---

[94] Further qualitative and quantitative analysis is certainly necessary to disentangle the question of why party organization was placed in some districts and not others. One might gain headway on this question by further consulting party archives and combining this with the type of analysis conducted here.

impetus. But despite the repeated efforts at reform, the party appeared, at least in the first fifteen years after 1867, to remain fundamentally fractured between the party leadership's old rural and still largely aristocratic identity and the urban and often middle-class propertied elements John Gorst had hoped to attract.

Thus, we see that the common periodization schemes structuring our politics analysis (e.g., pre- and post-suffrage reform) can distract us from the actual dynamics of organizational change, since a great deal of social and institutional change occurs at unexpected moments and in discontinuous fashion. However, we ought not dismiss the impact of these early party-building efforts altogether. A range of theorists, including Thomas Schelling, Mark Granovetter, and Paul Pierson, have argued that small or even invisible subterranean changes over time can accumulate, reaching critical "thresholds" in which earlier reforms provide a platform for rapid changes much later on.[95] In the case of the British Conservative Party, key organizational groundwork – the creation of the National Union, the Central Office, the precedent of local associations – was completed over a long time frame and would only prove useful down the road in the 1880s. While the basic contours of a strong extra-parliamentary party organization were created before the age of mass participation, the evidence suggests that in the short run, in the first ten years after the Second Reform Act, the party still lacked an effective popular organizational base. This left the urban middle-class strata still deeply lodged in the Liberal Party and keeping the old Tory party on the losing end of an increasingly dominant and therefore ominous-looking class cleavage.

DISCOVERING THE POWER OF GOD AND EMPIRE: THE RISE OF A MASS ORGANIZATION AFTER 1880

In the years after 1880, and especially after 1886, however, things changed: the old aristocratic and elitist British Conservative Party of 1846, after fits and starts of reform (e.g., 1867 and 1874), found itself in a position of near-permanent electoral dominance for the next twenty years, winning in head-to-head competition with Liberal opponents, appealing to middle-class and working-class voters in borough and county districts, and, with the aid of its new Liberal Unionist allies, securing parliamentary majorities in nearly every election until 1906.[96] Unlike Peel's efforts in the 1830s or Disraeli's in the 1870s, conservative party-building now succeeded.

---

[95] Schelling, "Dynamic Models of Segregation" (1971); Granovetter, "Threshold Models of Collective Behavior" (1978); and Pierson, *Politics in Time* (2004).

[96] Wald, *Crosses on the Ballot* (1983); Henry Pelling, *Social Geography of British Elections, 1885–1910* (London: Macmillan, 1967). See Chapter 4 below.

This newfound electoral competitiveness may come as a surprise given the expanded suffrage. But, historians and political scientists have correctly tried to explain the success as a result of the great "Victorian Realignment" in British politics in 1886 – a breach between the two halves of the emerging Liberal Party, composed of radical reformers on the one hand and traditional elite Whigs on the other. This split came to a head, analysts accurately note, with Prime Minister Gladstone's ill-fated effort to grant Ireland Home Rule in 1886.[97] However, the Conservative Party was neither a mere spectator to these disruptions nor was socioeconomic change the main driver of the split, as traditional views assume. In fact, the Conservative Party played an active role in fomenting rifts in the Liberal–Whig governing coalition; and the sources of the realignment were a set of symbolically connected *non-class* cleavages of religion (Anglican vs. Nonconformist), territory (center vs. periphery), and foreign policy (Empire vs. Radical Little Englander) that sealed together Liberal Unionism and British Conservatism in a new robust conservative alliance. The party structures that had emerged before 1880 had placed party leaders in a position that allowed them at a later point in time now to absorb and use these new developments.

First, Gladstone's embrace of Home Rule sparked the "flight of the Liberal Unionists" from the Liberal Party, who opposed Home Rule legislation and, on average, distinguished themselves from their Gladstonian counterparts primarily by being more likely to oppose Church disestablishment.[98] Furthermore, the separation of Liberal Unionists benefited the Conservative Party as it peeled away predominately conservative-minded Anglican Whigs and a smaller faction of Chamberlainite Liberals from the Liberals who opposed Home Rule to Catholic Ireland.[99]

In addition, the Home Rule issue highlighted a potent nexus of issues connecting religion, empire, and center-periphery relations (especially Home Rule), which cut right across class, and would ultimately win the Conservative Party itself a dedicated corps of activists. It is important to emphasize that these divisions within Liberalism that ultimately benefited the Conservative Party and its Unionist allies were only in part self-generating. Active machinations on the part of the Conservative Party itself contributed to these conflicts within Liberalism leading to the rise of the Home Rule issue in the first place as well as its endurance.[100] A young Winston Churchill's description of his father (Randolph Churchill, MP for

---

[97] See, e.g., Iain McLean, *Rational Choice and British Politics: An Analysis of Rhetoric and Manipulation from Peel to Blair* (Oxford: Oxford University Press, 2001), 84–86.

[98] W. C. Lubenow, "Irish Home Rule and the Great Separation of the Liberal Party in 1886: The Dimensions of Parliamentary Liberalism," *Victorian Studies* 26, no. 2 (1983): 161–80.

[99] The most recent work on the amalgam of groupings at the heart of Liberalism Unionism is Ian Cawood, *The Liberal Unionist Party: A History* (London: I. B. Tauris, 2012).

[100] Even Gladstone's initial embrace of Home Rule in 1885 itself was in part a product of Lord Salisbury's ruthless machinations: in the Fall of 1885, Salisbury surreptitiously backtracked on his previous support of Conservative Minister Lord Carnarvon's deal with Irish Nationalist leader Charles Parnell (support for Conservatives in exchange for some concessions to Ireland),

Woodstock) and his strategy vis-à-vis the Liberal government in the early 1880s gives us some sense of how this logic operated:

He [Randolph Churchill] was forever seeking for a chance to drive a wedge into the Ministerial array. To split the [Liberal] government majority by raising some issue on which conscientious radicals would be forced to vote against their leaders, or, failing that, by some question on which the Minister concerned would be likely to utter illiberal sentiments... No one understood better than [Randolph Churchill] the difficulties with which Mr. Gladstone had to contend, or the stresses which paralyzed the Cabinet and wracked the Liberal party.[101]

Thus, with an orientation that could not fit Riker's conception of "heresthetics" more perfectly, the mix of the three distinct issues of Irish Home Rule, Empire, and religion provided particularly explosive material in the hands of the Conservative opposition to both blow apart the Liberal government and to create a strong conservative party. Additional evidence that the 1886 Home Rule Crisis manifested itself as the culmination of ongoing efforts to split the Liberal majority along cultural issues, especially religion, is seen in the important debates of 1880 and 1881 surrounding Charles Bradlaugh. Upon the opening of the House in May 1880, the atheist radical MP Bradlaugh, newly elected from Northampton, refused to take his oath of office on a bible and instead sought to "affirm." In these opening days of Conservative opposition immediately following the elections, three Conservative Party MPs, Sir Henry Wolff, John Gorst, and Randolph Churchill, who would eventually form the "Fourth Party" (a particularly aggressive subset of the Conservative opposition), protested vigorously, extending the discussion over several days, bringing heated newspaper attention to the issue, and uncomfortably accusing the government (including Gladstone) of harboring "atheism, disloyalty, and immorality."[102]

The debate invigorated the ultimately ephemeral but notorious "Fourth Party" members of the Conservative Party opposition and more importantly accentuated tensions within the Cabinet. The long Whig and Liberal history of dismantling the entrenched interests and elevated status of the Church of England vis-à-vis Nonconformist churches (e.g., the Test and Corporations Act of 1828, the Irish Church Act of 1869, Forster's Education Act of 1870, political battles over the elimination of obligatory Church rates, and rumors of plans to disestablish the Church of England in Wales and in England) meant that frictions within the Liberal party between nonconformists and Anglicans were intense.[103] It was precisely this dynamic that fortified the many efforts including Churchill's to divide

leaving Gladstone's position exposed, now alone supporting a controversial policy of Home Rule. See McLean, *Rational Choice and British Politics* (2001), 84–86.
[101] Winston Churchill, *Lord Randolph Churchill* (New York: The Macmillan company, 1906), 230–31.
[102] For accounts of this event, see Harold Edward Gorst, *The Fourth Party* (London: Smith Elder, 1906), 51–62.
[103] See Parry, *Democracy and Religion* (1986), 6–8.

the Liberal government, using arguments about the importance of "traditional" values and the claim that Anglicans were threatened by "godless" Liberalism.[104]

But more than placing a cultural wedge within the Liberal majority, the British Conservative Party's fate also hinged on its ability to create a new mass electoral organization that could be used to access and solidify a new conservative cross-class majority of voters, in part built on the "defense" of Anglican and traditional interests. The project, thus, was not only "negative"; it required positive action to hold the potential alliance together.[105] While scholars have fixated on the debate over whether the post-1885 Conservative revival was built on urban working-class support or middle-class support, this debate has distracted us from a broader point: a new type of extra-parliamentary mass organization was necessary to reach and secure the loyalty of both groups of voters, whether middle class or working class.[106]

And, indeed, in the mid-1880s the Conservative Party, in contrast to its earlier efforts in the 1830s or 1870s, quickly found itself with access to precisely this kind of novel organizational infrastructure, which outpaced the relatively underdeveloped Liberal Party equivalents in the English countryside. In addition to the important official Conservative and Unionist associations, the most noteworthy in England was the Primrose League (PL). The PL was founded in 1883 as a secret society of Conservative loyalists, but quickly transformed into a mass membership social organization: in the words of Ostrogorski, a "Tory militia of moral order" with broad cross-class appeal.[107] Though its founders initially had visions for an exclusive, fraternal order like the Freemasons that was formally independent of the Conservative Party, by 1884 it had quickly morphed into a mass *social* organization, opening its membership to not only men, but also middle-class and working-class women, and even children. It was common for whole families, both working class and middle class, to join together.[108]

[104] This, again, was all further exacerbated by what Martin Pugh describes as the "fortuitous" timing in November 1885 of the excitement generated by the Chamberlain's call for the disestablishment of the Church of England. Martin Pugh, *The Tories and the People, 1880–1935* (Oxford: B. Blackwell, 1985), 26.

[105] Alex Windscheffel, *Popular Conservatism in Imperial London, 1868–1906*, Royal Historical Society Studies in History (Woodbridge, UK: Royal Historical Society, 2007), 17.

[106] On working-class support, see Robert McKenzie and Allan Silver, *Angels in Marble: Working Class Conservatism in Urban England* (London: Heinemann, 1968); Eric Nordlinger, *The Working Class Tories: Authority, Deference, and Stable Democracy* (London: MacGibbon and Kee, 1967). For middle-class support, see R. E. Quinalt, "Lord Randolph Churchill and Tory Democracy, 1880–1885," *Historical Journal* 22, no. 1 (1979): 141–65; cf. Jon Lawrence, "Class and Gender in the Making of Urban Toryism, 1880–1914," *English Historical Review* 108 (1993): 629–52.

[107] Ostrogorski, *Democracy and the Organization of Political Parties* (1902), xxxii; 535.

[108] Children above the age of six joined as "Primrose Buds" in "Juvenile Branches." Women, as I discuss below, joined as "Dames." See discussion in Janet Henderson Robb, *The Primrose*

The structure of the Primrose League, organized into local associations, quaintly called "habitations," and spread across the country, was an "odd combination of old bric-a-brac with well-contrived modern machinery."[109] Membership dues, anachronistically called "tributes," were mandatory for male members ("Knights"), female members ("Dames"), and working-class members ("Associates"). Oaths of membership were required in exchange for membership certificates granted by the Primrose League Grand Council. It all had a self-consciously "medieval" flair that corresponds to E. J. Hobsbawm's notion of "invented traditions," a form of social practice common in the late Victorian era.[110]

To the thousands of members who joined after 1884, the League and its local "habitations" appeared chiefly as a network of local social clubs that organized teas, music hall events, harvest suppers, dances, and concerts.[111] And, while these social activities appeared to be paramount, ultimately more significant were the political *uses* of these organizations. Local habitations boasted their own apolitical choirs and cycling clubs, the latter of which formed the Primrose League Cycling Corps.[112] But, when grand habitations were held once a year, the political tinge of the group became clearer, as local habitation members gathered with leading Conservative Party officials, notables of the day, and their wives.[113]

Whether at small-scale local events or at the Grand Habitations, the social gatherings were often held in halls decorated with ferns, flowers, and banners bearing Primrose League slogans or in the gardens and grand houses of local notables, allowing cross-class intermingling that held special appeal for its middle-class and working-class members.[114] PL members appeared at these events wearing pins, brooches, badges, and medals that identified their affiliation, rank, and position within the organization. Social events were marked by a mixed bag of entertainers, including flying trapeze artists, clowns, minstrel shows, trick bicycle riders, jugglers, ventriloquists, marionettes, and brass bands. These events usually began at around 5:00 p.m. as teas, followed by musical performances at 7:00 p.m., and then ending late in the evening with dances.[115] Conservatives had, in effect, discovered the

---

League, *1883–1906*, vol. 402, Columbia Studies in the Social Sciences (New York: Columbia University Press, 1942); Pugh, *Tories and the People* (1985).
[109] Ostrogorski, *Democracy and the Organization of Political Parties* (1902), 538.
[110] Eric J. Hobsbawn and Terrence Ranger, eds., *The Invention of Tradition* (Cambridge: Cambridge University Press, 1992).
[111] Pugh, *Tories and the People* (1985), 29.   [112] Pugh, *Tories and the People* (1985), 28–31.
[113] Diane Sheets, "British Conservatism and the Primrose League: The Changing Character of Popular Politics" (PhD, Columbia University, 1986), 83–125.
[114] Pugh, *Tories and the People* (1985), 31.
[115] This account draws on vividly descriptive "habitation notes" submitted by local associations to the league's own newspaper, the *Primrose League Gazette*, as well as a lively collection of flyers advertising Primrose entertainment events, reprinted in Pugh, *The Tories and the People* (1985), 33–34 and Ostrogorski, *Democracy and the Organization of Political Parties* (1902), 543.

mobilizing power of mixing social entertainment and politics at the dawn of what cultural historians have called the age of "public amusements."[116]

This emphasis on "entertainment" rather than "political education" was, at first, ridiculed by more austere Liberal Party organizers.[117] From the perspective of conservative notables, some of the mass social entertainment also left something to be desired. But, unlike the PL's Liberal critics, conservative notables within the PL recognized the political benefits of mass entertainment. As Lady Salisbury described the circus-like atmosphere of PL events, "Of course it's vulgar; but that's why we are so successful."[118] Indeed, though the program of social entertainment was the chief appeal for many Primrose League members, politics was never far from the surface, and it is precisely this potent organizational innovation that the Liberal Party first criticized but by 1900 tried unsuccessfully to imitate.[119]

The first modern historian of the Primrose League, Janice Robb, notes that the political propaganda of the League was "disguised with a coating of popular entertainment, or was so surreptitiously introduced into the evening's gaiety as to be almost unnoticed."[120] Indeed, the political functions and themes of the Primrose League – alluded to between events, in after-dinner talks, and in small and intimate teas – were no accident, but rather the outgrowth of a conscious effort to bring the organization's mass appeal under the control and direction of the Conservative Party leadership. The message was one of broad "conservative" principles: defending the Church of England against the onslaught of atheism and defending the monarch, Empire, Union with Ireland, and the House of Lords from radical reformers.[121] These principles were broad but cut across class, attracting those possessing anti-Nonconformist and anti-Irish sentiments.[122] Most important, they were articulated within the

---

[116] See, e.g., David Nasaw, *Going Out: The Rise and Fall of Public Amusements* (New York: Basic Books, 1993).

[117] Patricia Lynch, *The Liberal Party in Rural England, 1885–1910: Radicalism and Community*, Oxford Historical Monographs (Oxford: Oxford University Press, 2003), 58. Lynch reports that the local party organizers of the Liberal Party in places like Essex mistakenly diagnosed and dismissed PL tactics as a "mere smoke screen" to distract voters from their lack of organization. Within several years, however, Lynch (*The Liberal Party in Rural England* (2003), 85) also notes that Liberal Party recognized the power of the PL methods and began imitating them themselves.

[118] Robb, *The Primrose League* (1942), 204.

[119] Lynch, *The Liberal Party in Rural England* (2003), 85.

[120] Robb, *The Primrose League* (1942), 88–89.

[121] New members had to take an oath of allegiance that articulated the Conservative principles clearly: "I declare on my honour and faith that I will devote my best ability to the maintenance of Religion, of the Estates of the Realm, and of the Imperial Ascendency of Great Britain... and that consistently with my allegiance to the Sovereign of these Realms, I will obey all orders coming from the constituted authority of the League for advancement of these objects." Cited by Sheets, "British Conservatism" (1986), 18–19.

[122] See also E. H. H. Green, *The Crisis of Conservatism: The Politics, Economics, and Ideology of the British Conservative Party, 1880–1914* (London: Routledge, 1995), 68; 128.

context of an increasingly tightly coupled party, directed more and more by the very top of the Conservative Party national leadership.

First, beginning in 1885, a year or so after the PL's founding, Salisbury and Northcote, the Conservative Party's respective leaders in the House of Lords and House of Commons, began to take hold of the mass social organization by placing Conservative Party leadership in top positions of the growing "grassroots" organization. For example, Salisbury's new, personally selected party agent, Richard Middleton, volunteered his services as *ex officio* member of the Primrose League's leading body, the Grand Council, along with that of the party's chief parliamentary whip, Akers-Douglas. Next, Northcote and Salisbury had themselves named as co-presidents, or "Grand Masters," of the PL's Grand Council. And leading Conservative Party figures, such as Salisbury and Northcote, had their wives and daughters named to leading positions in the Ladies' Grand Council.[123] Scholar Diane Sheets notes that of the fifty-one members of the National Union's leading executive body, twenty-two had become members of the PL's Grand Council by 1889, suggesting overlapping leadership that quite self-consciously tilted toward the Conservative Party's increased control over the PL.[124]

Along with the party's capture of personnel came its leadership's absorption of key functions: Richard Middleton, also head of the NU in the late 1880s, established regular contact with the PL's Grand Council and provided advice on how to register voters who lived outside the constituencies in which they voted.[125] Middleton, in one meeting before the 1885 elections, authorized the Conservative Party's payment of funds to lecturers to attend PL events. In a decision in June 1885, the PL's Grand Council agreed to keep the Conservative Party's party agent informed of political activities; in exchange, the party's political secretary was empowered to provide a staff of lecturers to the Primrose League free of charge.[126] The Primrose League lecture circuit also provided the launching pad for the political careers of a variety of figures, including, most notably, a young Winston Churchill who in 1898 gave his first public speech, in what he called his "maiden effort" at a small-scale Primrose League event, alongside carnival games and races.[127]

By 1888, an even more elaborate structure of party-directed collaboration was put in place: Primrose League "Wardens" were assigned to subdistricts to help register voters, requested to post registration lists on church doors, and

---

[123] Sheets, "British Conservatism" (1986), 88.
[124] Sheets, "British Conservatism" (1986), 115.
[125] Minutes of Grand Council March 25, 1885; April 15, 1885, as cited by Sheets, "British Conservatism" (1986), 89.
[126] Minutes of Grand Council, June 17, 1885, as cited by Sheets, "British Conservatism" (1986), 93.
[127] Winston Churchill, *My Early Life* (New York: Charles Scribner's Sons, 1958), 203–5. See also Keith Owen, "The Fourth Party and Conservative Evolution, 1880–1885" (Texas Tech University, 2000).

instructed, as the Grand Council's minutes report, to go "street by street, village by village, and hamlet by hamlet" to assure conservative public opinion was organized.[128] The Ladies' Grand Council also became increasingly involved in elections as effective canvassers and planners, for example, providing carriages to transport candidates in rural districts. This was an organizational innovation – the active participation of female non-voters – in canvassing and political organization that far outpaced Liberal party efforts. The result was, as Sheets puts it, that the Primrose League had become "instrumental in registering voters... conveying individuals to the polls, distributing pamphlets, and directly assisting campaign efforts by the local candidates."[129]

Naturally, some tensions between NU local associations and local habitations of the Primrose League did arise through these overlapping functions. One disappointed Conservative Party agent critic sent a letter published in the National Society of Conservative Agents' publication, *The Tory*, "I fear it [the Primrose League] is only in those constituencies where the same management controls both Associations and League that the resources of the Primrose League are usefully deployed." The critic goes on to write that the main problem in his view was,

...the League [has been insisting] that it is not a Conservative organization. The idea is no doubt to get the enemy to join; but I am certain the persistent repudiation of Conservatives does more harm than good. It damps the enthusiasm of your Conservative working men, who think you are ashamed of your party; and further, it doesn't deceive a single Radical![130]

But, this subtle appeal was at the heart of its strategy and over time the PL was absorbed into the pre-existing official party structure.[131] Salisbury himself began this process in his 1887 annual speech to the PL's Grand Habitation on the anniversary of Disraeli's birthday, revealing the fused self-identity and organization of the Conservative Party and the PL. He proudly proclaimed,

[Gladstone] had forgotten that we were an unorganized body but are an organized body now (cheers)... [We] have an organization with which no party in any country would be able to offer any comparison.[132]

Salisbury's tendency to refer to "we," as Sheets notes, is particularly revealing.[133] The absorption of the PL by Conservative Party leaders meant that the PL was "acclaimed by the end of the century as the most permanently

---

[128] Primrose League Special Minutes Book, June 18, 1888, Sheets, "British Conservatism" (1986), 97.

[129] Sheets, "British Conservatism" (1986), 95.

[130] "Is the Primrose League of Use?" *The Tory* (1892), 126–27.

[131] Robb, *The Primrose League* (1942), 78; Windscheffel, *Popular Conservatism in Imperial London* (2007), 99–100.

[132] *The Times*, April 21, 1887, 8, as cited by Sheets, "British Conservatism" (1986), 112.

[133] Sheets, "British Conservatism" (1986), 112.

successful of all the political organizations that ever existed in Britain."[134] Furthermore, it became a model of conservative "counterorganization," leading, according to one account, Royalists in France to imitate it.[135] In some respects the successful absorption of the PL into party structures was not surprising, given the long history of developed party organization.

By the 1880s, the previous era's efforts to build robust party organization had begun to pay off. Even Lord Salisbury, who like other traditional conservatives at first possessed strong prejudices against "wirepullers," turned to the importance of party organization with the full conviction of a convert. His party agent, Captain Middleton (his title of "Captain" came from his service in the British navy, though he was in fact a Navigation Lieutenant), quickly built on the pre-existing structures that had roots back to the 1830s, but rendered them permanent and professional.[136] In fact, improving on Gorst's handiwork from the 1870s, a full-time professional network of party agents ran the National Union by 1886. A new professional association was founded for Conservative Party agents (the "National Society of Conservative Agents"), establishing its own journal, *The Tory*, and a new set of professional requirements for officials – including apprenticeships, rigorous exams on voter registration laws, membership dues, and even the possibility of expulsion for professional misconduct.[137] The professional association's journal, published monthly, indicated a highly professionalized party structure: it included regular reports on recent judicial rulings governing voter registration, ongoing advice for Conservative Party agents on how to "canvass out-voters," sample forms for Conservative Party agents to use to defend against the Liberal Party's objections of a voter's registration status, sample exam questions for qualifying to be a Conservative Party agent, and monthly reports on the association's pension fund.[138] In short, given its long history of party organization, growing professionalism, and a committed party leadership, the Conservative Party could quickly and effectively co-opt and absorb the new mass organization that appeared ripe for partisan mobilization.

Yet, it is not self-evident how a mass conservative-minded cross-class *social organization*, independent of party, arose in the first place. We can highlight

---

[134] Marsh, *The Discipline of Popular Government* (1978), 203.   [135] Ibid.

[136] "Captain" Richard Middleton, like Aretas Akers-Douglas, earned his early political experience as a party agent in Kent County, a region of the country that appeared to provide kind of training ground for national Conservative Party agents. See, for example, *Nottingham Guardian* February 28, 1905 in Middleton Papers, Oxford University Special Collections, MS Eng Hist c. 1129.

[137] For a short history of the professional agent organization, see the organization's own publication, Fawcett, *Conservative Agent: A Study of the National Society of Conservative and Unionist Agents and its Members* (1967).

[138] "Digest of Scottish Registration Cases, 1891–1893," *The Tory* 1894; "Out-Voters and How to Canvass Them," *The Tory* 1894. "To Defend a Radical Objection Occupation," *The Tory* 1894. For details on party agent exam, see Appendix A.

four factors that help explain the rapid birth and success of the PL: political ambition, recently changed parliamentary rules on election spending, the organizational countermodel found in the Liberal Party's Birmingham Caucus, and *the availability of religious cleavages and networks* which provided the "raw materials" necessary for a cross-class conservative party organization. The first factor, "political ambition," which according to Joseph Schlesinger often drives party organization, was a crucial ingredient.[139] An important catalyst in the case of the British Conservative Party and the PL was Lord Randolph Churchill, a highly ambitious thirty-one-year-old Conservative MP elected for the first time in 1874, who viewed himself as an outsider to party hierarchy but had high-flying hopes of placing himself in a position of leadership.[140] His career was meteoric. He landed at center stage of British politics in the early 1880s, and though his career quickly fizzled – he died at the age of forty-six in 1895 – his impact on the Conservative Party was notable though controversial.[141] In the early 1880s, he viewed extra-parliamentary party organization, namely the National Union structure, as a powerful potential platform to be used to gain party leadership "from the outside." In the wake of major defeat in 1880 and Disraeli's death in 1881, the party was in disarray, run by a "dual leadership" structure in which Lord Salisbury led the Conservatives in the House of Lords and Sir Stafford Northcote in the House of Commons. This structure was ripe for an "insurgent" such as Churchill because it had led to "chaos," "uncertainty," "rivalry, indecision, and infirmity of purpose," as Churchill and his increasingly reliable but less glamorous partner, John Gorst, wrote in a highly critical anonymous article (signed by "Two Conservatives") entitled, "The State of the Opposition," published in the leading conservative magazine, *The Fortnightly Review* in 1882.[142]

The ambitions for party leadership first led Churchill (aided by Gorst) to attempt a takeover of the Conservative Party – or at least its national party

---

[139] Joseph Schlesinger, *Ambition and Politics: Political Careers in the United States* (New York: Rand McNally, 1966); Joseph A. Schlesinger, *Political Parties and the Winning of Office* (Ann Arbor: University of Michigan Press, 1991).

[140] R. Churchill's "Tory" pedigree was unassailable; his father, the Duke of Marlborough, was Lord Lieutenant in Ireland, and, of course, his son would become Conservative Prime Minister in the twentieth century. For biographies, see Churchill, *Lord Randolph Churchill* (1906); Gorst, *The Fourth Party* (1906); Robert Foster, *Lord Randolph Churchill: A Political Life* (Oxford: Oxford University Press, 1981).

[141] Francis H. Herrick, "Lord Randolph Churchill and the Popular Organization of the Conservative Party," *The Pacific Historical Review* 15, no. 2 (1946): 178–91. For a more skeptical view of Churchill's impact, see Foster, *Lord Randolph Churchill: A Political Life* (1981).

[142] Two Conservatives, "The State of the Opposition," *Fortnightly Review* 32, no. 191 (1882), 675. Though anonymous, the article caused such a stir that in November 1882, Gorst resigned from the position he had taken up again in the organization of the party in 1880 at precisely the same moment the article appeared.

organization – by gaining chairmanship of the National Union at the Fall 1883 annual meeting (with 450 local association delegates in attendance), where Churchill and Gorst pushed for the passage of a resolution that called for a "legitimate share" of influence for the NU in the Conservative Party structure.[143] The purpose was to give the "representative body" more say and control over the management of the parliamentary party and was modeled on an understanding of how the Birmingham Caucus operated, intending to grant local associations and the NU financial and some decision-making control over the party's center. After a heated set of political maneuvers, Churchill was successful in his bid for NU chairmanship, but by 1884 Lord Salisbury had outflanked the insurgents. Salisbury made a private deal with Churchill that disappointed Churchill's associates like Gorst and left the *status quo ex ante* intact: the party's central committee continued to dominate the local associations, not the other way around.

However, Churchill's apparent defeat at the hands of Lord Salisbury only prompted new machinations. Having been prevailed over by the official organization of constituency associations, Churchill and his two allies, John Gorst and Henry Drummond Wolff, met in a card room at the Carlton Club in November 1883 to create their *own* ancillary organization, which they first named the Tory Primrose League to commemorate Disraeli's death and putatively his favorite flower. The history of this very first meeting has not yielded many further details on the origins of the organization.[144] However, careful scholarship has concluded that, though the organization was at first secretive, it was, like Churchill's tactics in the official party organization, primarily conceived as a vehicle for his ambitions.[145] But, when the Primrose League's founding was discovered in December 1883 by Salisbury and Northcote, Wolff wrote a conciliatory note to Northcote, elaborating a possible function of the organization beyond simply serving Churchill:

[The Primrose League] is intended to obtain the help of volunteers to replace the paid canvassers abolished by the Corrupt Practices Act [of 1883]. The League is obtaining such strength that I think you will take an interest in its progress as being likely to stimulate Conservative efforts in constituencies where it is often sufficiently active.[146]

On the one hand, party leaders Salisbury and Northcote privately ridiculed the plan, as seen in Northcote's Christmas Day message sent to Salisbury two days later, in which he wrote of the proposed organization, "It seems to be something

---

[143] Marsh, *The Discipline of Popular Government* (1978), 48.

[144] For an account of founding, see Pugh, *Tories and the People* (1985), 13. According to Robert Blake, *Disraeli* (London: Eyre & Spottiswoode, 1966), 752, Queen Victoria sent two wreaths of primroses to Disraeli's funeral, in part triggering the oft-repeated account that it was Disraeli's "favorite flower." See, for example, Dorothy Nevill and Ralph Nevill, *The Reminiscences of Lady Dorothy Nevill* (London: E. Arnold, 1906), 210–11.

[145] Sheets, "British Conservatism" (1986), 27.

[146] Wolff to Northcote, December 22, 1883, cited by Sheets, "British Conservatism" (1986), 26.

between the Ribbon Association and the 'Ancient Order of Buffaloes' though I did not submit this comparison to its author."[147] On the other hand, party leaders did quickly and publicly embrace the plan. That the message appealed to the Conservative Party leadership at all suggests a second major factor stimulating the search for new forms of party organization beyond political ambition alone: electoral reforms restricting campaign expenditures and the available "material" selective incentives to help parties organize.[148] It was the Corrupt and Illegal Practices Act of 1883 that limited the opportunity to use the informal and often explicitly manipulative patterns of adaptation that we will see endured in countries such as Germany, Spain, and Italy in this same period. This led the Conservative Party's chief agent, George T. C. Bartley, to report at the 1883 annual convention of the National Union,

I believe the day is quite gone by when any success can be hoped for without the great mass of the electors being organized and encouraged themselves to take an active part in the work of the party. Their active services will be required at the election as voluntary canvassers and assistance such as this cannot be expected unless they have been taught to understand that they are part and parcel ... of the organization of the party.[149]

In a related fashion, conservatives received further stimulus from the apparent success of Joseph Chamberlain's model of Liberal party organization and from the 1877 founding of the National Liberal Federation, which built on the impressive and innovative party organization based out of the city of Birmingham during Chamberlain's tenure as mayor.[150] The label "Birmingham Caucus," at first a term of derision invented by Disraeli to discredit Chamberlain's project by associating it with the "American style" caucus, was quickly embraced by its founders, Joseph Chamberlain and Francis Schnadhorst, and became, when incorporated by breakaway Liberal Unionists after 1886, part of Liberal Unionist success.[151] The Birmingham

---

[147] Northcote to Salisbury, December 25, 1883, Salisbury Papers, Hatfield House.

[148] Mancur Olson, *The Logic of Collective Action: Public Goods and the Theory of Groups* (Cambridge: Harvard University Press, 1965).

[149] George T. C. Bartley, "The Condition of the Conservative Party in the Midland Counties" Conservative Party Archive, National Union of Conservative and Constitutional Associations Convention (1883), Conservative Party Archive, NUA2/1/2; "Seventeenth Annual Conference of National Union, Bodleian Library, Conservative Party Archive, Oxford University

[150] See Ostrogorski, *Democracy and the Organization of Political Parties* (1902), 204–49.

[151] See statements by F. Schnadhorst, "The Caucus and Its Critics" Federation Pamphlets (1880); Joseph Chamberlain, "The Caucus and a New Political Organization" Federation Pamphlets (1883). The organizational innovations of the Birmingham Caucus, described closely but critically by Ostrogorski (*Democracy and the Organization of Political Parties*, 1902) included the use of local wardens to "encourage" (and sometimes coerce) voters to cast their multiple votes in multimember urban districts, a feature of the electoral system created in a minority clause of the 1867 Reform Act, to help assure Liberal majorities. Second, this was supported by the creation of an elaborate system of ward committees ("block captains") that expanded upwards into more general municipal-wide committees (committee of "hundreds"), which assured the bottom-up selection of candidates, thereby removing power from the traditional

political organization became a model, emulated across British cities and the basis of the Liberal party's elaborate national-level extra-parliamentary party organization structure, allowing the Liberal party a short-run "competitive advantage" after having lagged for so long behind the Conservative organization.[152] The 1880 elections in which Liberals trounced Conservative opponents were explained by Chamberlain himself in the April 13, 1880 *Times* as a product of the success of the new caucus organization. He wrote, "This remarkable success is a proof that the new Organization has succeeded in uniting all sections of the party." Chamberlain continued, "Know ye the power of the Caucus and bow before it!"[153]

If the Liberal caucus was, in Bryce's terms, the equivalent of a "Spartan" military invention, then what was needed for Conservatives was, as noted above, in Ostrogorski's terms, a "Tory Militia" for counterorganization for the defense of "moral order."[154] Gorst and Churchill led the charge in this direction in their anonymous critique of the party structures, arguing, "If the Tory party is to continue to exist as a power in the state, it must become a popular party."[155] In short, personal ambition plus the dynamics of party competition stimulated opposing groups of party leaders to search for more robust and effective mass structures for their formerly elite party.

But as an explanation for how parties develop mass organizational base, these factors alone are insufficient in explaining the development of the party's mass organizational base. We still must ask: how did a narrow vehicle for Churchill's political ambitions rapidly metastasize in just five years into a mass organization of "social integration" and mass membership?[156] And, given the problems of the NU before 1880, what was different about conditions now? The chief barrier to organization remained, as it had been in the 1870s, the deep fracture between the new urban middle class, its new potential corps of activists and voters, and the party's old "aristocratic" and rural supporters based in the counties. Churchill's calls for "Tory Democracy" and his efforts to empower the NU vis-à-vis the party's Central Committee had been intended to appeal precisely to the new urban middle classes. But his efforts had been thwarted by the old identity, represented by Lord Salisbury, who still

Liberal parliamentary party but also, according to its critics, exerting coercive control on the parliamentary behavior. See also Trygve Tholfsen, "The Origins of the Birmingham Caucus," *Historical Journal* 2, no. 2 (1959): 161–84.

[152] Parry, *The Rise and Fall of Liberal Government in Victorian Britain* (1993).
[153] Ostrogorski, *Democracy and the Organization of Political Parties* (1902), 204.
[154] Ostrogorski, *Democracy and the Organization of Political Parties* (1902), 535.
[155] Conservatives, "The State of the Opposition" (1882): 668. A broader debate was sparked in conservative circles as seen in, e.g., "A Conservative Caucus" *The Saturday Review* (May 17, 1884): 628–629; "Conservative Reorganization," *Blackwood's Edinburgh Magazine* (June 1880): 804–811.
[156] Sigmund Neumann, *Modern Political Parties: Approaches to Comparative Politics* (Chicago: University of Chicago Press, 1956).

controlled the party, and revealed the barriers to building up a new party organization.

One way of assessing the sources of the PL's organizational appeal is to use the forty-four counties of England and Wales as our units of observation and the detailed individual membership data that exists after 1884 (published by the PL in its annual *Roll of Habitations*), to try identify where and why some counties were densely organized by the PL and others were not. Table 3.6 below shows that membership totals grew consistently from 1884 to 1901. As noted above, the PL divided its members into three categories: Knights, who paid the highest membership fees, Dames, which included all women, and Associates, working-class members who paid lower membership dues, or no fees at all.[157]

Before proceeding to identify where and why the organizational density of the PL varied within Britain, we should note that using membership totals as an indicator of organizational strength, though a powerful potential empirical tool, requires proceeding with caution.[158] As Table 3.6 demonstrates, the growth in the number of members was so explosive – for example, between 1886 and 1888 – that critics and analysts might at first glance be skeptical of the data's validity. Indeed, this impressive organizational growth led critics at the

TABLE 3.6: *Primrose League: Official Membership Totals, 1884–1901*

Year	Total Members	Knights	Associates	Dames
1884	857	747	57	153
1885	11,366	8,071	1,914	1,381
1886	200,837	39,206	149,266	21,365
1887	550,508	47,234	442,214	36,800
1888	672,616	54,580	575,235	42,791
1889	810,228	58,180	705,832	46,216
1890	910,852	60,795	801,261	48,796
1891	1,001,292	63,251	887,068	50,973
1901	1,556,639	75,260	1,416,473	64,906

Data Source: These data originally come from the *Primrose League Gazette* but have been reprinted in Robb 1942, 228; Pugh 1985, 27; Sheets 1986, 123–124

[157] One important note, evidenced in Table 3.6, is the growth of not only female members but the *cross-class* nature of the PL as seen in rapid expansion of working-class elements in the party ("Associate" category), reaching a clear majority of members in the 1880s.

[158] For a discussion of methodological issues involved with this measure, see Theda Skocpol, *Diminished Democracy: From Membership to Management in American Civic Life* (Norman: University of Oklahama Press, 2003); Robert Putnam, *Bowling Alone: The Collapse and Revival of American Community* (New York: Simon and Schuster, 2000); Marc Howard, *The Weakness of Civil Society in Postcommunist Europe* (Cambridge: Cambridge University Press, 2003).

time, including several Liberal periodicals, to challenge the PL figures. The *Pall Mall Gazette* charged in 1886 that the PL membership rolls included the "dead, the dying, the decayed, and the seceded," and the Liberal publication the *Truth* carried out its own investigation in 1890 and estimated membership figures far beneath the official figures, itself using scattered, though it turns out, incorrect data on membership dues.[159]

Careful contemporary scholarship has investigated these concerns, often coming to the conclusion that these critiques by the PL's competitors were largely exaggerated.[160] However, there is nonetheless a serious methodological problem, as Robb, Pugh, and Sheets all admit: whereas new and current members were quite meticulously added to the membership rolls annually, members who had *de facto* relinquished their membership, by either not contributing member fees (in the Knight and Dame category) or not attending events and meetings (in the Associate category), were rarely removed from the official rolls.[161] Thus, the accuracy of these membership data as precise measures of organizational strength can certainly be questioned, especially beginning in the early 1890s, when there appears to have been a drop-off in membership dues but continued gains in the total accumulation of members as the official membership figures report.[162] However, Pugh's own research leads him to conclude, "despite an undeniable element of inflation, the figures brandished during the 1880s and 1890s are unlikely to have been grossly misleading; they paint a picture of the largest and most widely spread political organization of the time."[163]

Beyond this reassurance, is there further systematic evidence that can bolster our confidence in the validity of PL membership data? One potentially powerful approach would be to track how annual fluctuations in membership relate over time to other plausible indicators of PL organization.[164] For example, one could try to infer the *actual* number of PL members in any given year from the total PL membership dues collected by the PL Grand Council. As promising as this method may at first sound, its usefulness is limited: the only data available on total PL annual membership dues are for the two categories of "Knights" and "Dames," and no data exist for the much more numerous working-class

---

[159] "The Secrets of the Primrose League by an ex-Leaguer" *Pall Mall Gazette*, March 23, 1886, cited by Robb, *The Primrose League* (1942), 58. The *Truth* report is discussed and dismissed by Sheets, "British Conservatism" (1986), 156–58.

[160] Pugh, *Tories and the People* (1985), 28; Sheets, "British Conservatism" (1986), 156.

[161] Ibid.

[162] This, however, it should be added, is less of a concern in the early years (i.e., the mid and late 1880s) when the organization was in its infancy and membership rates were growing, by all accounts, extremely rapidly. Sheets, "British Conservatism" (1986), 157.

[163] Pugh, *Tories and the People* (1985), 28.

[164] On the concept of measurement validity, see Robert Adcock and David Collier, "Measurement Validity: A Shared Standard for Qualitative and Quantitative Research," *American Political Science Review* 95, no. 3 (2001): 529–46.

"Associates" category that constituted 86 percent of members by 1888.[165] Nonetheless, as a first-cut test of the accuracy of the figures in Table 3.6, this method is revealing. In 1888, for example, the total contributions of Knights and Dames reported to the Grand Council were £5,663.[166] Given that membership dues after 1887 were two shillings, this suggests there were 56,630 Knights and Dames in the PL in 1888, 60 percent of the "official" number of Knights and Dames, as reported in Table 3.6.[167]

An additional, perhaps more comprehensive, "check" on the idea that membership data as a valid measure of PL organizational density is a measure of the activity of the important Ladies' Grand Council (LGC), headed by Lady Salisbury, which included both working-class and upper-class women. This was a subgroup within the PL that had its own membership rolls, income, and sponsored lectures on public events.[168] In periods of rapid PL membership growth, these indicators drawn from LGC activity should also have shown positive growth. To check the validity of our main measure, we track the changes over time as depicted in the left panel of Figure 3.3 in the total membership in PL membership figures, according to the official *Roll of*

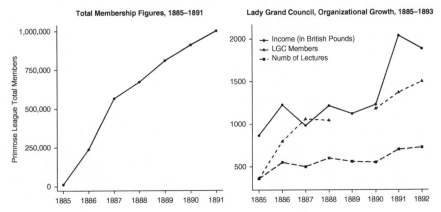

FIGURE 3.3: Primrose League Organizational Growth vs. Lady Grand Council (LGC) Organizational Growth, 1885–1893
Data Sources: Lady Grand Council data from Sheets 1986, 142; Primrose League membership data from Pugh 1985

---

[165] The year 1888 is selected here and in the analysis that follows because this marks a point at which data at the county level are available and also is prior to the period in the early 1890s that analysts have expressed greater concern over the accuracy of the membership data. See Sheets, "British Conservatism" (1986), 157.
[166] Robb, *The Primrose League* (1942), 59.   [167] Sheets, "British Conservatism" (1986), 156.
[168] Robb, *The Primrose League* (1942), 106–37.

Habitations, against the Ladies' Grand Council's own data as displayed in the right panel of Figure 3.3, on (a) the number of LGC members each year, (b) the total income flowing into the organization, and (c) the number of lectures sponsored annually.

We see, as Pugh asserts, that while the total "official" membership figures (in Table 3.6 and the left panel of Figure 3.3) generally capture the organizational trends of the age, they are indeed likely inflated and do not track perfectly other measures of party organization, as seen in the right panel of Figure 3.3.[169] Yet, the LGC data does confirm the general current of the period: upward growth in the number of members in the late 1880s.[170] In this sense, the official membership figures do seem to reflect the broader organizational dynamic of the period. Thus, while by no means perfect, in the absence of other data, these membership figures do give us the most systematic picture of organizational density available.

In light of these caveats, what qualitative evidence would convince us that strong conservative political party organizations are more likely when they are able to tap into pre-existing cross-class religious networks to become political "defenders" of established religion? There are three main reasons why this logic might hold. First, as Philip Salmon has demonstrated, beginning as early as the 1830s Anglican priests began to serve as the "unseen backbone... of many Conservative associations," taking on roles as leading local activists for the Conservative Party's organization-building efforts.[171] Socially respectable and politically unambitious, the clergy possessed a "kaleidoscope" of multifaceted social resources that could be redeployed for political ends.[172] Since their function was not a narrow religious one as we might imagine today – but rather had historically involved the supervision of a diverse range of public local activities such as poor relief, medical services, education, social club organization, and entertainment – the result was that Anglican clergy, even into the 1880s, had refined "the art of being indispensable."[173] It was not uncommon, for example, that four of the six school committee members of the small Norfolk village of Burston included the Anglican vicar, the vicar's

---

[169] Pugh, *Tories and the People* (1985), 28
[170] The slower rate of growth in the number of lectures is explained in Sheets, "British Conservatism" (1986). She notes that in the late 1880s, a division of labor sprung up in which the National Union tended to organize lectures while the PL was left organizing other events and forms of outreach.
[171] Salmon, *Electoral Reform at Work* (2002), 70.
[172] See Robert Lee, *Rural Society and the Anglican Clergy, 1815–1914: Encountering and Managing the Poor* (Woodbridge, UK: Boydell & Brewer Press, 2006), 182.
[173] Christopher K. Ansell and M. Steven Fish, "The Art of Being Indispensible: Noncharismatic Personalism and Contemporary Political Parties," *Comparative Political Studies* 32, no. 3 (1999): 283–312; Jeffrey Cox, *The English Churches in a Secular Society: Lambeth, 1870–1930* (New York: Oxford University Press, 1982), 64–89.

wife, and the vicar and churchwarden of the neighboring village of Shimpling.[174] Likewise, it was not unusual that in the rural constituency of North Dorset there were fourteen local habitations of the Primrose League, seven of which were chaired by local Anglican clergy.[175]

Second, the chief programmatic agenda of the Primrose League was the defense of Crown, Empire, and the Church of England. Its goal was the "defense of Christianity," and building on the sharpening confessional cleavage of the 1870s that had been exacerbated by the Home Rule conflict, the Primrose League was, along with the Church Defence Society, self-consciously the defender of Anglican influence in decline.[176] The source of the cleavage was not theological; rather, it was symbolic of a broader political conflict between the establishment Church and its rivals. As Martin Pugh puts it, "religion, the crown and property represented but different aspects of one indivisible good."[177] In Lady Maidstone's words, "Take away Religion and their chief cornerstone is gone... for if the Crown and the rights of property do not derive their authority from God they have no right to exist at all."[178] Thus, while confessional fights chiefly mattered as elite disputes, according to the most systematic and comprehensive ecological analyses of voting behavior in late-nineteenth-century Britain, religion – whether or not a voter was Anglican or Nonconformist – remained even into the late nineteenth century a stronger predictor of partisan leaning than any other factor.[179]

Third, political actors themselves viewed the Conservative–Anglican vs. Nonconformist–Liberal couplet as the core cleavage shaping British politics.[180] Lord Salisbury saw the parallel between British Liberals and anti-Catholic Liberals in continental Europe, and cast himself and his Conservative Party as the defender of the established Anglican interests.[181] Likewise, Liberal critics frequently attacked the "conservative complexion" of the Anglican Church. A leading Liberal publication, *Westminster Review* (founded by James Mill, owned at one point by John Stuart Mill, and an outlet for authors such as T. H. Huxley) published one piece, for example, in the 1890s accusing Anglican clergy of being "political mercenaries" in the "clutches" of Conservatism.[182] Thus, theory and qualitative evidence instruct us that

---

[174] Lee, *Rural Society and the Anglican Clergy* (2006), 158.

[175] Pugh, *Tories and the People* (1985), 101.

[176] "The New Electioneering," *The Speaker* February 16, 1895: 182.

[177] Pugh, *Tories and the People* (1985), 81.   [178] Ibid.

[179] Wald, *Crosses on the Ballot* (1983). See also David W. Bebbington, "Nonconformity and Electoral Sociology, 1867–1918," *Historical Journal* 27, no. 3 (1984): 633–56.

[180] Among others see Bebbington, *The Nonconformist Conscience: Chapel and Politics, 1870–1914* (1982).

[181] Marsh, *The Discipline of Popular Government* (1978), 165.

[182] T. M. Hopkins, "The Conservative Complexion of the English Church," *Westminster Review* 147 (1897): 334.

organizations are often built and can endure via cross-cutting social networks such as religious institutions.[183]

But beyond this scattered information, what systematic evidence is there of the proposition that the British Conservative Party deployed cross-cutting Anglican social networks to coalesce its organization? The 1888 Primrose League publication *The 1888 Roll of Habitations* provides information that allows us to locate in which of Britain's forty-four counties each of the PL's 672,606 members resided. How do the data look? Figure 3.4 reveals that – measured by individual membership total as a portion of total county population – in 1888, there was wide-ranging variation across Britain in organizational density, ranging from slightly above 8 percent in Rutlandshire and 6 percent in Lincolnshire in the east and Dorsetshire in the south, to less than 2 percent in Bedfordshire and Surrey.

What explains this disparity in organizational density? Was it a product of socioeconomic differences, a reflection of where the Conservative Party was already electorally strong or weak? Or, above and beyond these factors, does it reflect the types of social networks described above? First, we can present some *prima facie* evidence to begin to test the proposition that counties with denser Anglican religious social networks gave rise to higher concentration of PL membership.

In this analysis, the dependent variable is concentration of Primrose League membership and the chief independent variable is the density of Anglican religious networks. To measure this main independent variable, rather than using the more distant religious census data of 1851, a more *direct* measure is available in the occupational data from the 1881 British census that reports, for each county, the number of males and females in hundreds of occupational categories, including Anglican priests, nonconformist ministers, and Catholic priests.[184]

---

[183] It should be added that a similar conflict erupted in mid-nineteenth-century Scotland, where a schism opened between an evangelical Free Church movement and the establishment Church of Scotland. See A. Allan MacLaren, *Religion and Social Class: The Disruption Years in Aberdeen* (London: Routledge & K. Paul, 1974). The Free Church movement increasingly identified itself with calls for church disestablishment in Scotland, a policy stance in turn adopted by the Scottish Liberal Party, which received disproportional electoral support from Free Church and Presbyterian clergy and was resisted by the establishment Church clergy who disproportionately were represented by the Conservative Party, giving confessional conflict a partisan tinge. The post-1885 rise of the Scottish Unionist Party and the resurrection of the Scottish Conservative Party had its roots in this conflict. Beginning in 1886, like in England, however, the Home Rule issue became the definitive issue shaping support for Scottish Unionism. See Pelling, *Social Geography of British Elections, 1885–1910* (1967), 374; Catriona Burness, *"Strange Associations": The Irish Question and the Making of Scottish Unionism, 1886–1918* (East Linton: Tuckwell Press, 2003).

[184] I do not rely on Britain's religious census of the population to assess density of Anglicans for two reasons: first, the last nineteenth-century religious census was conducted in 1851 and was possibly outdated by the 1880s. See Wald, *Crosses on the Ballot* (1983). Second, my interest is in the direct impact of Anglican priests as key actors in social networks, rather than degree of Anglican religious affiliation. Many have argued – and Wald (*Crosses on the Ballot*, 1983),

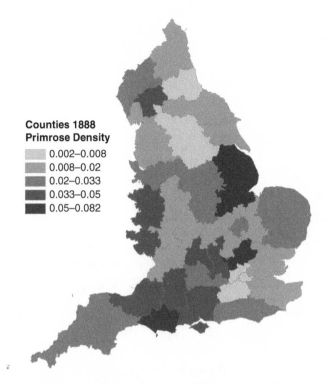

Counties 1888
Primrose Density
  0.002–0.008
  0.008–0.02
  0.02–0.033
  0.033–0.05
  0.05–0.082

FIGURE 3.4: Primrose Membership Rates in British Counties, 1888
Data Source: "The Roll of County and Borough Habitations" The Primrose League
Gazette, multiple issues, 1886–1888

These rich data provide an opportunity to test directly the proposition that there
is a statistically significant and *positive* relationship between the density of Anglican
clergy and the development of Primrose League membership.[185] Graphical
evidence in Figure 3.5 supports an apparent link between Anglican priests and
Primrose League strength. We see that where there are more Anglican priests as
a percentage of the population, the Primrose League was stronger.

Figure 3.5 suggests that a basic correlation between these variables holds.
However, secondary accounts also suggest there is a range of possibly
confounding factors that might affect the organizational concentration of the
Primrose League, including urbanization, population level, agricultural

---

using these data, convincingly demonstrates – that Anglicanism is correlated with support for
the Conservative Party.

[185] The measure of the density of Anglican religious networks is Anglican priests per capita in each
county. The data source is Census of England and Wales, *Ages, Conditions as to Marriage,
Occupations, and Birth-Places of the People*, vol. III (Presented to both Houses of Parliament by
Command of Her Majesty) (London, 1881).

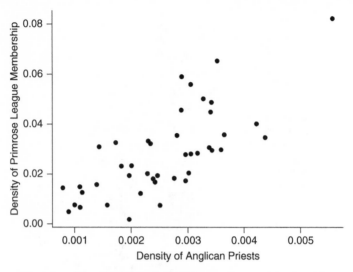

FIGURE 3.5: Density of Anglican Priests and Primrose League Membership, 1886–1888
Data Sources: County-level Anglican priest data from *Census of England and Wales,* 1881; "The Roll of County and Borough Habitations," *Primrose League Gazette* (1886–1888)

structure, *and* the electoral strength of the parties in districts.[186] Pugh, for example, has argued that the Primrose League found greater support in rural areas where landed estates were more predominant. We can use a multivariate OLS model with robust standard errors to try to disentangle these issues.[187]

In the analysis, the dependent variable (the percentage of a county's population with membership in the Primrose League) is measured again using the Primrose League *Roll of Habitations* from 1888. The key independent variable, as outlined above, is the density of Anglican priests per capita.[188] We also control for a set of additional variables for each county: population, level of industrialization, the electoral strength of the opposition Liberal Party, and inequality of the distribution of farms. The data source for the first two

---

[186] The bivariate relationship between Anglican density and PL density is strong (r = 0.73). But, one of the benefits of the graphical representation is that, as Figure 3.5 makes clear, there is an "extreme" case (PL membership = 0.08) in the far upper-right corner of the figure. Even dropping this case, gives us a strong correlation coefficient of r = 0.65.

[187] Pugh, *Tories and the People* (1985), 99–100.

[188] A key assumption in the analysis that follows is that the number of Anglican priests in each county was, in effect, assigned by history "randomly," or at least had causes that are so distant in the past that it is "exogenous" in the analysis that follows. A vast historiography on the organizational structure of the Anglican Church lends some initial support to the idea that regional variations in Anglicanism have deep historical roots. See the classic work of Owen Chadwick, *The Victorian Church* (New York: Oxford University Press, 1966).

controls, "population" and "level of industrialization," is the occupational census of 1881.[189] The pre-existing electoral strength of the Liberal Party might suggest a weaker potential basis for organization building, and is measured as the average portion of seats in a county won by the Liberal Party in national parliament in the two previous elections.[190] Finally, since it has been argued that it was in the counties still dominated by large estates where the Primrose League found its greatest support, we can use data from the 1885 agricultural census on the average size of farms as a proxy for rural social structure.[191] According to the agricultural census, the average size of farms varied between 37 acres in Lancashire to 119 acres in Northumberland.[192] Also, for each county, the data given by Major P. G. Craigie in the *Journal of the Royal Statistical Society* report the number of farms in every size category, allowing us to estimate the Gini coefficient that captures the underlying inequality in landholding sizes.[193] Table 3.7 reports the results for two multivariate OLS regressions.

In Model 1, we see that the density of Anglican clergy is significantly correlated with concentrations of PL membership in a simple bivariate relationship. In Model 2, the pre-existing electoral strength of the Liberal party is also included as a control variable along with a few other relevant control variables, and the density of Anglican clergy remains highly statistically significant. In other words, political organization appears to have been developed out of religious networks, above and beyond all other characteristics of counties. However, we should be cautious about drawing any conclusions of the *non-significance* for any of the other controls, including level of socioeconomic modernization. Indeed, the concentration of PL membership and percentage of agricultural workers are highly correlated ($r = 0.67$).[194] It is therefore difficult to rule out the possibility in this analysis that the level of industrialization (or socioeconomic modernization) in a district

---

[189] Census of England and Wales, *Ages, Conditions as to Marriage, Occupations, and Birth-Places of the People*, vol. III (Presented to both Houses of Parliament by Command of Her Majesty) (London, 1881). In addition to reporting population, we can use this source measure the level of "industrialization" in a county, using the proxy of agricultural employment as a share of total employment. For purposes of checking the robustness of this measure, I substitute several alternative measures of this variable, none of which change the findings in any significant way: (a) all agricultural employment *without* fishing; (b) all agricultural employment *with* fishing, (c) all agricultural employment, including land proprietors.

[190] Data source is Fred W. S. Craig, *Electoral Facts, 1885–1975* (London: Macmillan Press, 1976).

[191] Source: Major P. G. Craigie, "The Size and Distribution of Agricultural Holdings in England and Abroad," *Journal of the Royal Statistical Society* 50, no. 1 (1887): 86–149.

[192] Craigie, "Size and Distribution of Agricultural Holdings" (1887), 131.

[193] The Gini coefficient in landholding for each county is estimating with (a) the number of farms and (b) the size of farms. For a similar analysis in the German context, see Ziblatt, "Shaping Democratic Practice" (2009). See also Chapter 6.

[194] None of the other control variables are correlated with the chief independent variable of interest above $r = 0.30$.

TABLE 3.7: *OLS Analysis of Primrose Membership Density, 1888*

	Dependent Variable: *Primrose Membership Density in 1888*	
	(1)	(2)
Anglican Priest Density	12.335***	9.935***
	(1.800)	(3.492)
Economic Modernization (% of Population in Agriculture Sector)		6.539
		(40.570)
Population		−0.004
		(0.003)
Liberal Electoral Strength		−3.632
		(6.818)
Landholding Inequality		−23.735
		(40.780)
R^2	0.534	0.543
Adjusted R^2	0.523	0.476
Observations	43	40

exerts some indirect effect on Primrose League membership concentration. However, to reiterate, whatever the nature of this more complex causal relationship, the concentration of Primrose League membership appears to be consistently associated with Anglican priest density.[195]

More broadly, we see confirming evidence of a critical insight: the "most important political organization" in British politics in the nineteenth century was built in large part on the shoulders not of class actors but of religious institutions and networks that cut across class.[196] It is precisely the availability of Anglican networks that gave British Conservatism and Lord Salisbury – the pessimist who thought he might be the "last conservative" – the organizational resources and the ability to survive and *thrive* in the age of mass politics.

CONCLUSION AND COMPARATIVE REFLECTIONS

The building of conservative political parties in the nineteenth century differed from the building of other types of political parties. Unlike liberal parties or

---

[195] In another analysis not reported here, I include the interaction of Anglican density and economic modernization, which is statistically significant (p = 0.05), showing that the impact of Anglican density is not the same across all levels of socioeconomic modernization as the above models assume. Instead, the marginal impact of Anglican priest density on PL membership concentrate *increases* as districts become more rural. A closer analysis of the political activities of rural Anglican priests versus what were often called the "slum" priests of districts such as East End London and other major cities would be particularly revealing.

[196] Marsh, *The Discipline of Popular Government* (1978), 203.

especially socialist parties, whose forward-looking ideologies provided mobilizing impetus to party-building, conservatives were primarily reliant on their access to pre-democratic states. Thus, they conceived of themselves as the greatest potential "political losers" in the age of mass democracy, facing the "rearguard" dilemma of striving to preserve their power, prestige, and wealth without undermining their "way of life." In order to untangle the distinctive dynamics of conservative party building, our empirical focus has been on the British Conservative Party, tracing the barriers to effective party organization which that particular party faced and seeking to understand its ability to overcome them, all before full-blown democratization came to Europe. In large part because the British Conservative Party's adaptation was so impressive, there is a great temptation to view this story as an exceptional one, an evolution rooted in Britain's distinctive trajectory to modernity.[197]

One of my contentions has been that British Conservatism, while certainly unusual vis-à-vis many other conservatives, is by no means unique. The landed interests that the British Conservative Party represented at the beginning of the period – especially after 1846 – were narrow, protectionist, and resistant in principle to suffrage extension.[198] Conservative parties and interests everywhere in Europe, from Belgium and Sweden to Germany and Spain, faced a similar challenge at the outset of the modern age: how to survive and defend their interests and way of life, while inhabiting the shrinking end of what appeared to be an increasingly dominant class cleavage. The responses to this challenge varied even among the specific group of countries in which successful party building occurred, including not only Britain but Belgium, the Netherlands, Denmark, Sweden, and, after the 1880s, France. Yet, in these countries (some marked by high landholding inequality and others not; some marked by early national parliaments and others not), conservatives were propelled by similar dynamics, gradually successfully adapting to the challenge of mass politics by building formal party organization. By contrast, in Italy, Portugal, Germany, and Spain, conservative parties, representing an equally diverse mixture of landed and urban interests, did not build party organization but instead developed new informal mechanisms of manipulation and collusion (e.g., *Trasformismo, el Turno Pacífico, Wahlbeeinflussung*) that allowed the right to survive without competing. This disjuncture cast a long shadow on European

---

[197] This is analogous to the problem of British democratization more generally. See, for example, Rueschemeyer, Stephens, and Stephens, *Capitalist Development and Democracy* (1992), 5. They in fact argue, "The British case is so singular in so many ways, both in terms of the antecedents to democracy and the process of democratization, that is impossible to decide which factor was the most important on the basis of comparative analysis."

[198] It is worth repeating here because it is all too often forgotten that in the mid to late nineteenth century, territorial wealth was consolidated in fewer hands in Britain than nearly anywhere in Europe, including in eastern Prussia. See data in Cannadine, *Decline and Fall of the British Aristocracy* (1999); and Ziblatt, "Shaping Democratic Practice" (2009), and Craigie (1887), 91; 139.

history and represented a decisive pivot which, as I will argue in subsequent chapters, contributed to broader patterns of century-long regime trajectories.

How precisely did the British Conservative Party successfully create strong party organization that left it electorally competitive? And what are the implications of this case for how we think about the ability of conservative parties more generally to adapt to the challenges of political competition? The chief accomplishment of British Conservatism came around 1880–1886, and was two-fold. First, the party created new mass organization for the defense of key elite social groups; second, the party leadership came to control this mass organization. This "balancing act" of possessing *fused* authority but *differentiation* of organization was achieved in two main steps.[199] First, the party's fused authority (i.e., the party leadership's tight control over the party) developed out of a long-run process of organizational development. Beginning in the 1830s, the party leadership established the decisive elements of centralized authority in the form of strong parliamentary parties, the pivotal position of party agent, a robust though still underdeveloped system of local associations, and a national umbrella organization to direct and oversee these structures. Though the party was still relatively weak "in the electorate" until 1880, the effort to build these institutions was great, and these costly investments in very "institution specific" organizations such as constituency associations and party agents rendered the organizations themselves self-reinforcing.[200] The result was that institutions "at the top of the party" persisted and shaped subsequent developments, including the party's rapid absorption in the 1880s of a mass-mobilized social organization.

And, indeed, it is here where the second and decisive innovation transpired: the creation of mass organization, which allowed for the kind of symbolic appeals and political argument that were critical to election success. The shift from an "elite" party to a mass party was undoubtedly a delicate one for a conservative party, but its various official organizations along with the Primrose League, first introduced in the 1880s, filled this role to great effect. Due to the endurance of a cohesive Anglican confessionalism in elite circles that was connected to patriotism, Empire, the Home Rule issue, and embrace of monarchy, British Conservatives had a natural constituency from which to build a party. As Kalyvas has noted more generally about conservatives in this era, "Because they were unwilling [or unable] to create mass organizations, conservative politicians had only one way to survive as significant political players. They sought organizational resources elsewhere."[201]

All of this runs counter to a common but misleading orthodoxy that the Conservative Party's survival was due to Britain's two-party system.

---

[199] These categories borrow from Huntington, *Political Order in Changing Societies* (1968), 110.
[200] Stinchcombe, *Constructing Social Theories* (1968); Acemoglu and Robinson, *Economic Origins of Dictatorship and Democracy* (2006), 179; Pierson, *Politics in Time* (2004), 147.
[201] Kalyvas, *Rise of Christian Democracy* (1996), 53.

As nineteenth-century economic modernization gave rise to a new middle class that voted both Liberal and Conservative, Britain's electoral system is sometimes thought to have assured that the Conservative Party could reap the rewards that single-member plural electoral systems promise for center-right parties.[202] In this mistaken view, since single-member district electoral institutions favor two-party systems, the British Conservative Party could easily shift from being the party of landed elites to the "party of property," compelled by the external stimulus of late-nineteenth-century economic life, and that Britain's electoral system guaranteed its adaptation and survival.[203]

But this falls short as an explanation of the origins of parties. The idea that Britain's mid-nineteenth-century electoral system determined the internal structure of British political parties overlooks the fact that *all* European political systems had similar and weakly institutionalized electoral systems in the mid-nineteenth century, including Britain, where still three-quarters of the seats were multimember until 1867.[204] Thus, a strong conservative political party began to develop in Britain *despite* the existence of high numbers of multimember districts, which are normally thought to thwart development of a strong two-party system.[205] Furthermore, even to argue that pre-1867 Britain was a "two-party" system ignores the fragmented nature of the ephemeral and constantly shifting factions – Peelites, old Tories, Whigs, Irish, and radicals – that constituted British parliamentary politics at the time. Indeed, the consolidation of a two-party majoritarian electoral system was arguably *an outgrowth* of the Conservative Party's strength, since single-member districts were an institutional innovation initiated and implemented in 1867 and 1885 at the hands of an increasingly well-organized and professionalized party leadership that had the

---

[202] See, e.g., Torben Iversen and David Soskice, "Electoral Institutions and the Politics of Coalitions: Why Some Democracies Redistribute More Than Others," *American Political Science Review* 100, no. 2 (2006): 165–81. They provide a model and evidence demonstrating institutionalized majoritarian systems disproportionately benefit Center-Right parties.

[203] For an example of this view, see Peter G. J. Pulzer, *Political Representation and Elections in Britain*, Studies in Political Science (London: Allen and Unwin, 1972), 102. Pulzer puts it this way, "Especially since the Second Reform Act [in] 1867, the further one went down the social scale, the more likely one was to find support for the party of the left (Liberal until 1914, Labour thereafter)." And, conversely, the Conservative Party, according to this view, became the defender of property rights, appealing to middle-class voters who felt threatened by the radical elements in the Liberal party. See Cornford, "Transformation of Conservatism" (1963).

[204] Josep Maria Colomer, "On the Origins of Electoral Systems and Political Parties: The role of elections in multi-member districts," *Electoral Studies* 26, no. 2 (2007): 262–73.

[205] Conversely, it is worth also noting that Germany's single-member districts for national parliamentary elections after 1871 did little to assure a strongly organized conservative party in that context, though some have argued that Germany's majoritarian requirement (assuring frequent run-offs) contributed to a fragmented party system. This is discussed more fully in Chapter 6.

organizational skills and know-how to view such an electoral rearrangement in a positive light.[206]

In short, it is only by making the mistake of "reading history backwards" that we can identify Britain's stable constitutional order and twentieth-century two-party system as the causes of the Conservative Party's transformation. Even if evolving parliamentary institutions and socioeconomic changes drove party organizational change, the question remains: What was the "social glue" that sealed a mass electoral base to the elitist British Conservative party in post-1832 Britain? Rather than regard the old British Tory Party as the "passive recipient" of external stimuli of changing class configurations within a fixed set of institutions, we must recognize that the British Conservative Party after 1832 actively reshaped not only electoral institutions but also the electorate. The Conservatives elevated the themes of religion, empire, and nation in British politics, transforming it from a one-dimensional "class-centered" politics – an increasingly losing prospect – into a two-dimensional electoral space that generated their enduring electoral competitiveness. How precisely this helped generate Britain's settled path of democratization after 1884 is the subject we turn to next.

---

[206] The idea that electoral systems reflect party and other interests is demonstrated in Carles Boix, "Setting the Rules of the Game: The Choice of Electoral Systems in Advanced Democracies," *The American Political Science Review* 93, no. 3 (1999): 609–24; Thomas Cusack, Torben Iversen, and David Soskice, "Economic Interests and the Origins of Electoral System," *American Political Science Review* 101, no. 3 (2007): 373–91; and Kenneth Benoit, "Electoral Laws as Political Consequences: Explaining the Origins and Change of Electoral Institutions," *Annual Review of Political Science* 10 (2007): 363–90.

4

A Virtuous Cycle? Conservative Strength and Britain's Settled Path, 1884–1906

Bond markets talk. And what they tell us about British democratization, as we saw in the last chapter, is that in the lead-up to the 1884 Third Reform Act, the most democratizing of Britain's three major nineteenth-century suffrage reforms, investors hardly took notice. Even more striking, as this chapter will show, is that following the act's passage, the unexpected happened: almost nothing changed. Or more precisely, what occurred ran counter to leading theories of redistribution and democracy: Britain's Conservative Party, originally based (in the 1840s) on power, privilege, and landed wealth, not only survived, but electorally flourished.

How do we explain this curious turn of events? How did Britain appear to end up at least by 1884 on a path of settled democratization? And how secure was this path, really? Any analysis must begin by noting an underappreciated ambiguity at the heart of Britain's experience from 1884 into the twentieth century. On the one hand, the suffrage expansion and its immediate aftermath appears to confirm an "exceptionalist" narrative about Britain – that it had long been, and firmly remained, on a settled path of political development. Even if not fully democratic, the median voter was, after all, now much poorer and more likely to be propertyless than ever before in modern British political history.[1] Sixty percent of adult males could now vote. And, yet, after suffrage reform there was neither an ascendency of Radicals and Liberals nor an attempt by displaced and disgruntled old elites to dismantle democratic change. Instead, Radicalism and left Liberalism nearly disappeared from the stage of political

---

[1] See Seymour, *Electoral Reform in England and Wales* (1915). The 1884 Reform Act increased the voter rolls by over a million (1,762,087). This is in contrast to the much more modest 1832 Reform Act pushed by the Whig Party, which expanded the electorate from 435,391 to 652,777 voters (217,286 voter increase), or the 1867 Reform Act that had been pushed by Tory Prime Minister Disraeli against traditional forces in his own party, to "dish the Whigs," which expanded the electorate by less than a million (938, 427 voters). These numbers are from Seymour, *Electoral Reform in England and Wales* (1915), 533.

power, and it was the *Conservative Party*, originally a party associated with traditional landed wealth, and its Unionist allies that emerged as the dominant competitive forces at the very moment of democratic expansion. To the surprise of many contemporaries, the so-called "Unionist alliance" that had the Conservative Party at its core, governed for the next twenty years, from 1886 to 1906, interrupted only by a thirty-four-month interregnum between 1892 and 1895. It won governing majorities in three of four general elections – something it had managed to do only once since 1846 – and the party made inroads into new urban and suburban constituencies, acquiring a diverse cross-class voter base. The old Conservative party of landed wealth – the most unequal landed wealth in Europe – had organizationally insulated itself and thrived in tandem with democratic reform, appearing to follow a trajectory of "democracy through strength."[2]

As settled as democratization may have looked over this twenty-year period, a long-run view is still imperative because this pattern suddenly looked much less steady after 1906. In the biggest swing to the left in British history, the General Election of 1906, the Unionist alliance collapsed and lost its parliamentary majority, shrinking from 400 to 157 seats and being replaced by a new and much more progressive Liberal majority. Democracy was put to a sharp test as Conservatives feared becoming a permanent minority: and the result was a period of severe constitutional crisis as they sought extreme methods to protect their interests. The unelected House of Lords inserted itself into politics in ways previously unimaginable; the rhetoric of the Conservative Party radicalized, even calling for violence; and the leadership of the Party deployed new methods of reacquiring power that violated long-standing constitutional norms. One author sums it up as the age when Britain's "unwritten constitution" was "destroyed."[3] As long the Conservatives won, democracy was settled; as soon as they lost, a constitutional crisis appeared to shake the state. Thus, we ask: Had organized conservatism *really* helped secure a path of settled democratization in Britain, after all?

In this chapter and the next I untangle these issues and trace the development of British democratization from 1884 to the interwar years. First, I demonstrate that the Third Reform Act of 1884, a moment of partial democratic transition, partly transpired so seamlessly because conservatives had access to the unusual inheritance of party organization that the British Conservative Party had incrementally acquired over the past fifty years. Party organization made

[2] The useful phrase "democracy through strength" is from Slater and Wong, "Strength to Concede" (2013): 718. They use the concept to explain cases in contemporary East Asia, where incumbent authoritarian parties concede democratic reforms because of their own organizational strength.
[3] Iain McLean, "The 1909 Budget and the Destruction of the Unwritten Constitution" *History and Policy (Policy Papers)* November 3, 2009 (www.historyandpolicy.org/policy-papers/papers/the-1909-budget-and-the-destruction-of-the-unwritten-constitution).

democracy safe for conservatives. But, this is not the end of the story. The destabilizing moments of crisis between 1906 and 1914, which appeared to challenge Britain's democratic development, give us reason to pause.

Though historians know well the nature of the fundamental constitutional crises of 1906–1914, most political scientists discount them because they contradict the traditional "deep" Whig historical interpretation of British history. According to that view, implicitly accepted by many analysts, early parliamentary sovereignty was achieved in 1688 and its aftermath inoculated Britain from serious revolutionary and counterrevolutionary crises. But, the events of 1906–1914 challenge this view, and we see the importance of the British Conservative Party, which was implicated in two ways: first by triggering the crises, then by helping resolve them. It was the party's persistent internal factionalism that led to disorder in the first place. However, by 1922, it was the party's inheritance of robust organization that had averted full democratic disaster.

THE FIRST STEPS OF MASS DEMOCRATIZATION IN BRITAIN: THE 1884 REFORM ACT

Britain's mass democratization did not begin in 1832 or even 1867, which left the political system a largely oligarchic order that would hardly meet any contemporary definition of democracy.[4] Instead, the story really begins in 1884 in the parliamentary battles over Britain's Third Reform Act, which extended the suffrage to 67 percent of the male population. Though Liberals and Conservatives in Britain predictably disagreed on the desirability of expanding the electorate, many leaders of both groups could agree on one point: an enlarged electorate that left propertyless voters as the new majority was a potential threat to the Conservative Party and would unleash dramatic changes on the structure of government and public policies. In mid-1884, as Gladstone's Third Reform Bill wound its way through the House of Commons, Lord Salisbury, now the Conservative Party leader, expressed this precise concern. Salisbury feared, as we noted in the last chapter, the risk that suffrage expansion might lead to massive expropriation.[5] But facing the prospect of competing against Liberals for the votes of the explosive population of landless labor, he also privately expressed strategic fear over the narrower *electoral* fate of his party, justifying to a friend his initial unyielding opposition to Gladstone's bill: "[The] alternative which Mr. Gladstone

---

[4] See Chapter 3 above.

[5] One of his more provocative assertions of this concern was, "[Suffrage expansion] means that the whole community shall by governed by an ignorant multitude, the creature of a vast and powerful organization, of which a few half-taught and cunning agitators are the head... it means, in short, that the rich shall pay all the taxes, and the poor shall make all the laws." See Cecil, "The Budget and the Reform Bill" (1860): 286.

presented to us was the absolute effacement of the Conservative Party. It would not have reappeared as a political force for 30 years."[6]

But, as we will see, Salisbury's nervousness provoked a realistic plan and vision for how the Conservative Party might compete and survive. If anyone was unrealistic, it was the left wing of the Liberal Party, the Radicals, who had successfully pressed the democratizing suffrage reform agenda onto the legislative agenda of their ambivalent Whig–Liberal allies.[7] For example, even after the passage of the reform, a pamphlet circulated one Warwickshire constituency calling 1885 an *"annus mirabilis,"* playfully providing a mock epitaph with the statement "In memory of Lord Tory, who died in great agony on December 1, 1885, notwithstanding all the medical and clerical attention, and female nursing given to him in his last moments!"[8]

At first glance, Radicals had good reason to hope for the future, since by 1884 the three major historical preconditions of pre-democratic Conservative Party electoral success had now dissolved. The first was a set of informal repressive social controls wielded by dominant county magnates – bolstered by a culture of "deference" and an immobile rural labor force – that allowed landed elites to dominate and shape voting practices in the countryside.[9] Second was an oligarchic electoral system with a narrow suffrage, especially in the countryside, that represented the interests of property owners alone.[10] And third, a rural social structure marked by a rural labor movement of propertyless workers that was unusually quiescent and disorganized when viewed in cross-national perspective.[11] By 1884, these historical underpinnings of old-regime Conservative political success were crumbling; nevertheless, as we will see, the Conservative Party thrived *after* the most significant democratizing reform of the century.

We begin by presenting the three challenges to traditional Tory power. First of all, in the thirty years before 1884, profound socioeconomic changes had gradually eliminated the traditional repressive and informal social controls wielded by landed elites over labor. Until the mid-nineteenth century, these controls had been embedded in the social structure of England as well as parts of Scotland, Ireland, and Wales in which rural employment remained primarily agricultural and labor markets had been highly immobile, giving landlords and employers the ability to engage in pre-election intimidation and post-election

---

[6] Cited by William Hayes, *The Background and Passage of the Third Reform Act* (New York: Garland Publishing, 1982), 171.

[7] See description in Hayes, *The Background and Passage of the Third Reform Act* (1982).

[8] William Tuckwell, *Reminiscences of a Radical Parson* (London, Paris, New York and Melbourne: Cassell and Company, 1905), 51.

[9] Hanham, *Elections and Party Management* (1959); Moore, *The Politics of Deference* (1976).

[10] Seymour, *Electoral Reform in England and Wales* (1915).

[11] David Spring, "An Outsider's View: Alexis de Tocqueville on Aristocratic Society and Politics in 19th century England," *Albion* 12, no. 2 (1980): 122–31.

reprisals through the threat and use of layoffs.[12] Further, political life in rural England, including the management of elections, had been firmly in the hands of England's powerful landed elites via magistrate appointments, quarter sessions, and the local offices of Lord Lieutenant and Justice of the Peace.[13] And, it has been argued, in a critical twist on Bagehot's notion of Britain as a distinctive "community of deference," that this entire premodern regime was undergirded by a rural cultural *milieu*. Even if being undermined in many places, "deference" appeared to assure cohesive group voting dominated by powerful landlords or factory owners, especially in the pre-1872 period of the open ballot.[14] As T. J. Nossiter describes county elections in the 1860s, "the polls leave no doubt that the disposition of the great estates constituted the political geography of rural England."[15]

If traditional patrons were the masters of local life and also the key point of access to national politics, then a set of socioeconomic changes beginning in the early years of the nineteenth century weakened these traditional controls.[16] These changes included increased labor mobility, as migration to cities and manufacturing undermined the landlord monopoly on agricultural employment;[17] increased global competition in agricultural markets from the great plains of North America, Argentina, and continental Europe, leading to significant drops in agricultural prices and a sharp decline, especially between the 1870s and 1890s, in rents that British landlords could charge; and finally, a drop in the price of land prices and values that led landed elites to become increasingly indebted.[18] As their control over labor markets weakened and their

---

[12] See description in Thomas Johnson Nossiter, *Influence, Opinion and Political Idioms in Reformed England: Case Studies from the North East 1832–1874* (New York: Barnes & Noble Books, 1974); Hanham, *Elections and Party Management* (1959).

[13] According to modern estimates, until the 1880s, landed elites occupied approximately three-quarters of all county magistrates; Tories dominated the office of JP into the twentieth century; and though landed Liberals had made up an important portion of England's Lord Lieutenants, in the 1880s, Conservatives systematically appointed young patrician Lord Lieutenants to secure control over this office (Cannadine, *Decline and Fall of the British Aristocracy*, 1999, 154–55).

[14] See Moore, *The Politics of Deference* (1976). For a critique of the limits of the notion of deference in nineteenth-century Britain, see David Eastwood, "Contesting the Politics of Deference: The Rural Electorate, 1820–1860," in *Party, State, and Society: Electoral Behavior in Britain Since 1820*, ed. Jon Lawrence and Miles Taylor (Aldershot, England: Scolar Press, 1997), 27–49.

[15] Nossiter, *Influence, Opinion and Political Idioms* (1974), 47.

[16] Remarkably, as late as 1883, among the largest landowners in Britain, *less* than 10 percent was "new wealth," achieved after 1780, suggesting traditional, pre-nineteenth-century elites predominated until the 1880s. See data in W. D. Rubinstein, "New Men of Wealth and the Purchase of Land in Nineteenth-Century Britain," *Past & Present*, no. 92 (1981): 137

[17] E. P. Thompson, *The Making of the English Working Class* (New York: Vintage Books, 1963), 213–33.

[18] Cannadine reports an average drop in agricultural rents between the 1870s and 1890s of 26 percent, and notes the scale of the drop was even greater in certain regions. Cannadine, *Decline and Fall of the British Aristocracy* (1999), 92.

material and coercive resources dissipated, old elites' leverage over tenants also dissolved. In short, there was good reason to think the social bases of the Conservative Party's survival were being undermined.

Just as landed elite's informal and local hold over elections was declining, a second shock came in the form of national electoral reforms, which transformed the oligarchic and exclusive political institutions that had long benefited landowners and their primarily Conservative Party political representatives. The 1884 Reform Act altered the playing field of political competition, making it dramatically less biased in favor of property. The reform reached further down the income distribution in sheer numbers than the two previous (1832 and 1867) acts combined, expanding the electorate by 67 percent (from 2,618,453 to 4,380,540), the largest absolute increase of the electorate in the nineteenth century.[19] The result was that landless laborers, miners, and working-class voters now comprised, for the first time, the majority of the electorate. Furthermore, unlike previous reforms, the Third Reform Act was simultaneously passed in Ireland, Scotland, and England, ensuring it had an instantaneous impact across the entire United Kingdom.

The view that Britain was fully "democratic" after its Third Reform Act of 1884 is thus understandable, though mistaken.[20] Despite the Act's clear limits (e.g., a full 30 percent of adult males still could not vote and undemocratic plural voting remained in place), the reforms appeared more threatening to Conservative party success, especially in county districts, than the more-often-studied 1867 Reform and the extremely modest 1832 Reform. The first reason is that the 1884 reforms were preceded by series of smaller but significant electoral reforms, including the introduction of the secret ballot in 1872 and the Corrupt and Illegal Practices Prevention Act of 1883, which further debilitated "informal" election control in the countryside. In addition, the 1884 franchise reform left the median British voter poorer and much less likely to own property than ever before in county districts, the heart of traditional Tory power.[21] Historian David Cannadine – referring to Trollope's fictional but iconic

---

[19] The total increase in the size of the electorate in 1884 was 1,762,087, while the increase in the electorate in 1832 and 1867 was 217,386 and 938,087, respectively. See Seymour, *Electoral Reform in England and Wales* (1915), Appendix 1, 533.

[20] Britain after 1884 was certainly not democratic for several reasons. For a concise overview of the argument, see Ross McKibbin, *Ideologies of Class: Social Relations in Britain, 1880–1950* (Oxford: Oxford University Press, 1990).

[21] For example, Duncan Tanner, *Political Change and the Labour Party, 1900–1918* (Cambridge: Cambridge University Press, 1990), 119. Tanner estimates that three-quarters of voters in the Edwardian period were working class. More precisely, in 1867, the "occupier" category was expanded in the boroughs alone but not the counties, leaving the older "ownership" voters in a position of dominance. In 1883, *before* the Third Reform Act, in the counties ownership voters (freeholders, leaseholders, etc.) constituted 54 percent of the electorate, outnumbering "occupiers" (tenants and owners of lower value properties) by almost one-and-a-half (Seymour, *Electoral Reform in England and Wales* (1915), 286). Meanwhile in 1886, after the reform, ownership voters now constituted only 20 percent of the electorate, and the remaining 80 percent

county of Barset – wrote that the 1884 reforms, "were far more significant, and far more threatening, than the earlier measures of 1832 and 1867: for they emphatically spelt the end of the politics of Barset."[22] Indeed, a cross-national examination during this period of other Conservative Party defenders of landed interests – say, Germany, France, or Spain – suggested that conservative parties were not made to survive mass suffrage.[23]

Certainly, accompanying the reform was a series of measures that arguably mitigated, in the view of the Conservative Party, some of the "worst" or most democratic elements of the suffrage reform. These included, in 1885, a voter registration bill that, while addressing some of the most egregious features of a decentralized system of voter registration, nonetheless allowed local overseers to remove voters from the voting lists with little constraint, leading to the potential disenfranchisement of significant numbers of voters.[24] Also, the Redistribution of Seats in 1885, as many scholars have argued, created safe seats for Conservatives.[25] Yet, even the latter reform had unintentionally disruptive and democratic elements. For example, the reform not only redistributed 174 seats and created thirteen new constituencies from scratch, but it also redrew boundaries on an entirely new basis: single-member districts became the dominant form of electoral constituency, in effect demolishing the previous multimember district model.[26] Additionally, the worst forms of malapportionment were dramatically reduced, which certainly made the political system more geographically equitable than it ever had been.[27]

---

constituted the new "occupier" combined with the "lodger" category, which included, among other groups, miners, landless labor. For data and discussion, see Seymour, *Electoral Reform in England and Wales* (1915), 487.

[22] Cannadine is not alone in thinking the 1884 the most important Reform Act. Agreeing with him is Mary Chadwick, "The Role of Redistribution in the Making of the Third Reform Act," *Historical Journal* 19, no. 3 (1976): 665; Eric Evans, *Parliamentary Reform in Britain, c. 1770–1918* (Abingdon: Routledge, 2000), 134; G. R. Searle, *A New England? Peace and War, 1886–1918* (Oxford Clarendon Press, 2004), 133–34; Cannadine, *Decline and Fall of the British Aristocracy* (1999), 142.

[23] See data in Caramani, *Elections in Western Europe* (2000).

[24] Neal Blewett, "The Franchise in the United Kingdom, 1885–1918," *Past and Present* 32 (1965): 27–56.

[25] Cornford, "Transformation of Conservatism" (1963); Chadwick, "The Role of Redistribution in the Making of the Third Reform Act" (1976); Hayes, *The Background and Passage of the Third Reform Act* (1982); Amel Ahmed, "Reading History Forward: The Origins of Electoral Systems in European Democracies," *Comparative Political Studies* 43, no. 3/4 (2010): 931–68.

[26] Amel Ahmed, *Democracy and the Politics of Electoral System Choice: Engineering Electoral Dominance* (Cambridge: Cambridge University Press, 2013), 117–38.

[27] The drop in malapportionment between 1880 and 1886 was momentous. One measure notes this drop: 0.33 in 1880 to 0.11 in 1885. This is calculated so that $MAL = (1/2)\Sigma|si - vi|$ where sigma stands for the summation over all districts i, si is the percentage of all seats allocated to district i, and vi is the percentage of the overall population (or registered voters) residing in district i.

Further careful empirical work has disputed the importance of single-member districts to Conservative Party success, leaving the true impact of redistribution an open question.[28]

In any case, even with the Redistribution Act and the persistence of some undemocratic features in British elections, the shifting socioeconomic conditions and the enlarged electorate appeared to jointly pose an unprecedented threat to the Conservative Party's survival; without the resources to control voters and facing a new, much poorer median voter, Britain's Conservative Party had good reason to believe – as some of its opponents and defenders did – that it had passed the apex of its power. But, it was a *third* and final challenge that made the fate of the British Conservative Party appear especially vulnerable: the rural landless, beginning in the 1870s, became intensely and explosively mobilized in what social historians call the "revolt of the field" under the auspices of the Conservatives' chief opponents, agricultural labor unions and Liberal–Radical leaders powerfully armed with a coherent doctrine of anti-landlordism.[29]

The heated debate over land reform in Britain in the 1870s and early 1880s took on a sharp edge with the emergence of this well-organized anti-landlord movement, inspired in part by the American reformer Henry George's visit to the United Kingdom.[30] Fractures developed between tenants and landlords on the one hand and tenants and landless laborers on the other. Calls for land reform, lower rents for tenants, higher wages for laborers, new land taxes, and even outright land redistribution – prompted by Radicals such as John Bright in England and the Land League in Ireland – were a reaction to the "Himalayan" levels of land inequality, but were also triggered by the global economic crisis of the late 1870s.[31]

---

[28] J. P. D. Dunbabin, "Some Implications of the 1885 British Shift towards Single-Member Constituencies: A Note," *English Historical Review* 109, no. 430 (1994): 89–100.

[29] J. P. D. Dunbabin, "The 'Revolt of the Field': The Agricultural Labourers' Movement in the 1870s," *Past and Present* 26, November (1963): 68–97.

[30] Rural union memberships (often under the auspices of organization Farmer Defense Association) reached levels of 150,000 in the 1870s, mostly in southeast England, including east Devon, Herefordshire, Warwickshire, and Lincolnshire (Dunbabin, "Revolt of the Field," 1963: 68). Local studies have identified all the variations in social demands and organization, including the especially radical and threatening three-year "Land War" in Ireland (See, for example, Rollo Arnold, "The 'Revolt of the Field' in Kent, 1872–1879," *Past and Present* 64, August (1974): 71–95); Samuel Clark, *Social Origins of the Irish Land War* (Princeton: Princeton University Press, 1979). Yet, even across England, the traditional way of life was on the precipice; and, new politically potent organization emerged, in the eyes of rural conservatives, coming from outside and therefore perceived as profoundly threatening. See Dunbabin, "Revolt of the Field" (1963).

[31] The term "Himalayan" to describe the scope of land inequality in Britain in this period is from David Cannadine, "The Landowner as Millionaire: The Finances of the Dukes of Devonshire, c. 1800–c.1926," *The Agricultural History Review* 25, no. 2 (1977): 78.

Further, this socioeconomic conflict had political dynamics as well, heightening the sense of a coming showdown. Conservative-minded landlords viewed this "revolt of the field" through a distinctly political lens, regarding it as a pretext for a Liberal project of party building in the countryside. In his memoirs, one conservative landlord observes precisely this link when recalling "the demagogues who came out of Birmingham at election time, black-coated, gamp-umbrellaed, cotton-gloved *a la* Stiggins... interfered with farmhands. This they call 'farmyard canvassing.'"[32]

Not surprisingly, soon voting rights and the suffrage reform for the counties also became part of the political battle, and were regarded as a way "to liberate a lost people," the unrepresented householders of British counties.[33] In the early 1880s, the agricultural union leader Joseph Arch, an advocate of suffrage reform, put it this way:

I hold that the farm labourers of this country would not have been in the degraded condition they are if the *rights of citizenship* allowed their betters had been granted them... we are now rising up to a sense of our manhood and we are determined that we will have our rights as citizens.[34]

Thus, socioeconomic conflict coupled with calls for suffrage reform led to a third major challenge to conservative power: an increasingly mobilized rural poor. Restricted suffrage in the countryside not only protected the socioeconomic interests of landlords, but now after the Conservative Party's national victory in 1874, it was clear that it also protected the Conservative Party's *electoral* interest. The Liberal Party had outperformed the Conservatives in borough districts under the new suffrage rules, but in the predominately rural county districts, under the old suffrage rules, Liberals were overwhelmed by Conservatives. Thus, Liberal politicians saw in the rural movement a means of possibly altering the electoral balance of power in national politics.[35]

In sum, though not technically facing a socialist party, Conservative Party leaders, such as Lord Salisbury, were vehemently critical of democracy as the socioeconomic, electoral, and organizational bases of their electoral success came under siege. The British Conservative Party faced diminished resources to control voters, a transformed electoral system that left the median vote in the hands of a daunting propertyless class of laborers, and, above all, a new electorate that had *already* been mobilized and courted for the previous ten years by the most radical wing of the Liberal Party. When confronted with

[32] John Bridges, *Reminiscences of a Country Politician* (London: T. W. Laurie, 1906), 127–29.
[33] Parry, *The Rise and Fall of Liberal Government in Victorian Britain* (1993), 274.
[34] Cited by Hayes, *The Background and Passage of the Third Reform Act* (1982), 23–24.
[35] And, furthermore, the radical or "forward" wing of the Liberal Party also viewed rural suffrage reform as both a way of dislodging Conservative hegemony in the counties and also as part of an *internal* battle within the Liberal Party, as "a lever in their struggle to move the Liberal Party to the left" (Hayes, *The Background and Passage of the Third Reform Act* (1982), 41), by eclipsing the traditional Whig landlords who still dominated the Liberal Party.

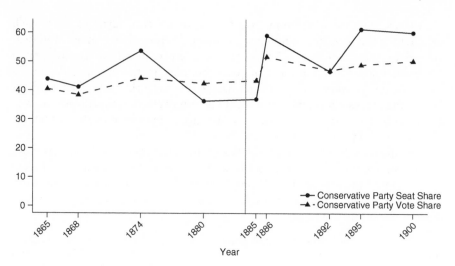

FIGURE 4.1: Conservative Party Vote Share and Seat Share, 1865–1900
Data Sources: Craig 1976, Caramani 2000

suffrage reform in 1867, Lord Salisbury feared that he may be the "last Conservative." But there were good reasons to think the 1884 Reform represented an even *more* significant challenge.

Yet, here we turn to the heart of the paradox of 1884. Despite the crumbling traditional bulwarks of conservative power – and the rise of a liberalized rural social structure, an expanded franchise, and a mobilized rural labor force – conservatism not only survived in Britain, it thrived. The British Unionist alliance dominated elections between 1885 and 1906, especially in England. It won an electoral majority in three of this period's four elections (1886, 1895, and 1900) and only lost its majority briefly in 1892. In the twenty years between 1886 and 1906, the Conservative Party and its Liberal Unionist allies held a majority of seats in the parliament every year but three (see Figure 4.1). On average, the party won a remarkable 58 percent of votes in the twenty-year period after suffrage reform, even including the years it lost its majority (1885 and 1892), which surpassed its 37 percent in the twenty-year period before the reform.

And, the party, unlike many other European conservative parties of the era, received support across a wide range of electoral constituencies.[36] It had nationalized its electoral machinery to compete in rural, urban, and suburban districts. And, though, as Ross McKibbin has written, around the turn of the century "the standing of the Conservative Party seemed hardly more firm than that of the Liberals," within twenty years it was that *other* great party of the late

---

[36] One standard measure of this is a Gini coefficient of share of votes spread out over geography, which measures how concentrated a party's electoral support is. For cross-national historical evidence on party vote share concentration, see Chapter 6.

Victorian age that had gone extinct. In George Dangerfield's old but still evocative phrase, the Liberal Party experienced a sudden and "strange death."[37] So, the question remains: How did Britain's Conservative Party manage this feat?

TO THE RESCUE: CONSERVATIVE PARTY ORGANIZATION
AND SUFFRAGE REFORM

While the "strange death" of Liberal England has attracted much attention, the equally "strange survival" and revival of the Conservative Party in England until 1906 also deserves careful scrutiny.[38] Two kinds of arguments are present in the historical literature on the question. An early generation of scholarship emphasized, broadly speaking, structural or demographic determinants of party success. In one variant of this view, the British Conservative Party was a passive beneficiary of the shift away from older status identities to the modern class identities that accompanied socioeconomic modernization, seamlessly becoming the political defender of the increasing number of middle-class voters in homogenously redrawn electoral districts in 1885.[39] Compatible with classical sociological accounts of partisan affiliation, this view regards the revival of British conservatism as tied to an expanding middle class and the rise of a class cleavage in British politics, noting conservative success in wealthy suburban districts outside major cities, in which Lord Salisbury himself sought the reliable Conservative "villa vote."[40] However, it remains puzzling why Britain's Conservative Party benefited from this phenomenon while parties of the right in other countries did not.

A second variant of the demographic argument, which challenges the class-centered analyses of the older tradition, makes the important observation that the effect of religion, in particular Anglicanism, did not in fact pass away with modernity.[41] Wald's landmark work *Crosses on the Ballot* makes clear that religion mattered: in districts where Anglicanism was more prevalent, the Conservative Party did better, electorally.[42]

---

[37] Ross McKibbin, *Parties and People, England, 1914–1951* (Oxford: Oxford University Press, 2010), 12; George Dangerfield, *The Strange Death of Liberal England* (Stanford: Stanford University Press, [1935] 1997).

[38] Dangerfield, *Strange Death of Liberal England* (1997); Ross McKibbin, *The Ideologies of Class: Social Relations in Britain, 1880–1950* (Oxford: Clarendon Press, 1990); McKibbin, *Parties and People* (2010).

[39] Cornford, "Transformation of Conservatism" (1963).

[40] For citation and discussion, see Richard Shannon, *The Age of Salisbury* (London and New York Longman, 1996), 60–69; Seymour Martin Lipset and Stein Rokkan, *Party Systems and Voter Alignments: Cross-National Perspectives*, International Yearbook of Political Behavior Research (New York: Free Press, 1967).

[41] See Wald, *Crosses on the Ballot* (1983).

[42] Wald's *Crosses on the Ballot* (1983) made a major empirical contribution by systematically incorporating nineteenth-century census data (on class and religion) in an analysis of election

In the last ten years, Wald's focus on the demographic drivers, like Cornford's, has given way to a second generation of scholarship.[43] This line of thought emphasizes the strategic and positive action of the Conservative Party in activating issues, political arguments, and appeals to voters; in deploying party expertise to carve out safe seats and reaching voters; in seeking out working-class voters; and in using non-class appeals of "sociability" and identity to establish a solid electoral foundation for itself. Rejecting the largely passive role that scholars previously assigned the Conservative Party, the new generation, to paraphrase E. P. Thompson, argues that it "did not rise like the sun at an appointed time. It was present at its own making."[44] From this view, the British Conservative Party shaped its own fate. Homogeneously middle-class districts did not arise on their own; rather, they were created by party professionals equipped with maps, census data, and close knowledge of local dynamics. Similarly, the party's effective deployment of "issues" – Irish Home Rule, Empire, and defense of the established church – simultaneously prompted "the flight" of Liberal Unionists from Liberals in the House of Commons in 1885 and 1886 and attracted new voters in 1895 and 1900.[45] A *precondition* for the survival of the Conservative Party was its robust party organization, which allowed it to take advantage of structural conditions.

THE POWER OF PARTY ORGANIZATION

The two broad arguments outlined above – the first centered on demographic factors and the second on strategic action of the Conservative Party itself – are

results, something that been hitherto impossible because matching census units and electoral units is a logistically difficult task. Wald solves the problem by creating a novel database of 115 "surrogate" units.

[43] Wald, *Crosses on the Ballot* (1983); Cornford, "Transformation of Conservatism" (1963); Matthew Roberts, "'Villa Toryism' and Popular Conservatism in Leeds, 1885–1902," *Historical Journal* 49, no. 1 (2006): 217–46; Windscheffel, *Popular Conservatism in Imperial London* (2007); Barry Doyle, "A Crisis of Urban Conservatism? Politics and Organisation in Edwardian Norwich," *Parliamentary History* 31, no. 396–418 (2012).

[44] Thompson, *The Making of the English Working Class* (1963), 9.

[45] A first school of thought has argued that the British Conservative Party was not unlike many former authoritarian incumbents in seeking to *repress the vote* (i.e., depress turnout) after suffrage expansion and it was only with a smaller electorate that the Party could thrive (Blewett, "The Franchise in the United Kingdom, 1885–1918," 1965). A second school of thought, less critical of the party's democratic credentials, argues that the party only survived not by repressing the vote but by *reshaping the vote* via electoral gerrymandering in the 1885 Redistribution Act, creating safe electoral districts for middle-class and upper-middle-class voters, and making positive appeals to voters (Cornford, "Transformation of Conservatism," 1963). See John D. Fair, "From Liberal to Conservative: The Flight of the Liberal Unionists after 1886," *Victorian Studies* 29, no. 2 (1986): 291–314; Paul Readman, "The 1895 General Election and Political Change in Late Victorian Britain," *Historical Journal* 42, no. 2 (1999): 467–93; Paul Readman, "The Conservative Party, Patriotism, and British Politics: The Case of the General Election of 1900," *Journal of British Studies* 40, no. 1 (2001): 107–45.

sometimes treated as mutually exclusive alternatives. Identifying which precise structural or cultural contexts provided favorable conditions, which positive strategies mattered, and the relative weight of each certainly provides a rich set of debates amenable to empirical testing. But one key and underappreciated factor that links these two explanatory frames is the concept of party organization itself.

"Party organization" has certainly been highlighted in other accounts, but its impact on democratization has never been systematically theorized or tested empirically at the level of electoral constituencies.[46] Furthermore, scholars of British conservatism have tended to perceive party organization as "merely" a source of organizational efficiency.[47] But this narrow view fails to recognize that party organization both elevates "party professionals" and allows parties to articulate political arguments and mobilize through mass appeals. Indeed, political scientists who analyze the effects of campaigns on election outcomes have long agreed on the difficulty of verifying the impact of party organization empirically.[48] However, more recent work has demonstrated a discernable impact of campaigns and organization on elections. Experimental work clarifies that campaign contact via canvassing affects turnout;[49] appealing to voters via social networks does as well; and "organizing" affects election outcomes.[50]

Building on this extensive literature, we can expect that effective party organization is a crucial component of Conservative Party dominance via two main channels. First, as argued in Chapter 2, well-developed party organization means that experts with scientific and professional orientations are in positions of decision making, allowing them, for example, to draw electoral districts that maximize vote share efficiently and to identify and effectively use issues to appeal to voters. Second, party organization also results in mass or popular organizations that can more efficiently and effectively access and persuade voters to vote through social networks, organizations, and group affiliations.[51]

---

[46] See, e.g., Cornford, "Transformation of Conservatism" (1963); Matthew Roberts, "Popular Conservatism in Britain, 1832–1914," *Parliamentary History* 26, no. 3 (2007): 399–400.

[47] Cf. Doyle, "A Crisis of Urban Conservatism? Politics and Organisation in Edwardian Norwich" (2012), 409.

[48] See Bernard R. Berelson, Paul Lazarsfeld, and William McPhee, *Voting: A Study of Opinion Formation in a Presidential Campaign* (Chicago: University of Chicago Press, 1954).

[49] Alan Gerber and Donald Green, *Get out the Vote: How to Increase Voter Turnout* (Washington, DC: Brookings Institution Press, 2008).

[50] Steven J. Rosenstone and John Mark Hansen, *Mobilization, Participation, and Democracy in America*, New Topics in Politics (New York: Macmillan, 1993); Sidney Verba, Henry Brady, and Kay Schlozman, *Voice and Equality: Civic Voluntarism in American politics* (Cambridge: Harvard University Press, 1995); Seth E. Masket, *No Middle Ground: How Informal Party Organizations Control Nominations and Polarize Legislatures* (Ann Arbor: University of Michigan Press, 2009); Kathleen Bawn, Martin Cohen, David Karol, Seth Masket, Hans Noel, and John Zaller, "A Theory of Political Parties: Groups, Policy Demands and Nominations in American Politics," *Perspectives on Politics* 10, no. 3 (2012): 571–97.

[51] Rosenstone and Hansen, *Mobilization, Participation, and Democracy* (1993).

122   *A Virtuous Cycle?*

Given a certain demographic profile, voters may have a predictable though loose set of predispositions. But without the party apparatus to identify, register, and canvass those voters they are unlikely to vote in predictable ways.[52] Similarly, "issues" and "appeals" may be a major source of electoral success, as scholars of British conservatism and political scientists alike agree.[53] Yet, again, party organization itself is what provides politicians the skills to decide which political arguments to make, which "issues" to prioritize, and what stances to take in order to incorporate new constituencies and maintain coalitions within a party.[54] In short, while a certain demographic profile is certainly likely to be highly correlated with Conservative Party vote share, we can hypothesize that two features of party organization – party expertise and political pundits today call the popular organizational "ground-game" – should have an impact on election performance.

As traditional forms of influence declined in the nineteenth century, the Conservative Party's organization, as we saw in the last chapter, took two new main forms. First, it acquired official local party associations and full-time professional party agents, who possessed their own professional organization and systematic knowledge of districts.[55] In addition, in the 1880s it developed the first popular or truly mass grassroots political organization in Britain, the Primrose League. With its mass membership, garden parties, elaborate picnics, excursions, and firework extravaganzas – coupled with its subtle campaigning and political mobilization – the Primrose League became a powerful tool for accessing and canvassing voters as well as strategically employing "issues" (e.g., anti-Home Rule, religion, crown, Empire) to generate a loyal cross-class conservative base.[56]

Likewise, by appealing to working-class and middle-class voters at events often held at the grand homes of Britain's glittering landed elites, the Primrose League tapped into the status and gender identities of the citizenry, providing a powerful vehicle of grassroots organization.[57] But, how important was "party organization" conceived in these two ways – as "party expertise" and "mass organization" – to the British Conservative Party vis-à-vis the normal demographic variables, let alone its other more manipulative strategies such as suppressing the vote?

---

[52] On the role of political party agents registering voters in this period, see Blewett, "The Franchise in the United Kingdom, 1885–1918" (1965): 38–40. See also Kathryn Rix, "The Party Agent and English Electoral Culture, 1880–1906" (Cambridge University, 2001).

[53] Windscheffel, *Popular Conservatism in Imperial London* (2007), 26.

[54] Karol, *Party Position Change in American Politics: Coalition Management* (2009).

[55] Rix, "The Party Agent and English Electoral Culture, 1880–1906" (2001).

[56] The Primrose League is described in greater detail in Chapter 3. See, also Robb, *The Primrose League* (1942); Sheets, "British Conservatism" (1986); Pugh, *Tories and the People* (1985).

[57] As noted in the last chapter, women members were a central part of the organization; and much of the appeal of the organization was the "mixing" of middle-class and working-class voters, hosted at the homes and gardens of the local notables and the prominent. See Pugh, *Tories and the People* (1985), 43–44.

HOW DO WE KNOW PARTY ORGANIZATION MATTERED?

Two kinds of evidence can be deployed to assess these arguments. In what follows I report the results of a multivariate OLS analysis in which the dependent variable is Conservative Party (and Unionist Party) vote share in each electoral constituency in England for each of the general election years: 1885, 1886, 1892, 1895, and 1900.[58] Since the goal of the analysis is to link "party organization" to electoral performance, I adopt a two-pronged approach. As noted above, "party organization" comes in two guises: (1) the popular organizational "ground game" and (2) the party expertise of party agents and professionals.

Our first hypothesis is that after 1884 in constituencies where the Primrose League was more organized (i.e., had more members per capita), even holding all other demographic variables constant, the Conservative Party performed better. The causal logic of the argument is that the "treatment" of a robust popular organizational "ground game" should increase vote share for the reasons outlined above: the party can more effectively canvass and use cross-class issues to mobilize voters. While certainly other features of party organization matter – e.g., the skill and "organizational intelligence" of party officials as they redrew electoral boundaries, not to mention the professionalism of party agents and local associations at election time – to assess the first hypothesis, I focus on the impact of the Primrose League alone.

However, a narrow focus on the Primrose League, by ignoring other facets of "party organization," would arguably understate the significance of the broader variable. Thus, a second hypothesis I test, albeit in this case indirectly, is that a reliance on "party experts" in the 1880s helped the Conservative Party. The most frequently cited handiwork of nineteenth-century Conservative Party "party expertise" was the careful redrawing of electoral boundaries in 1885. I focus here on the observable implication that close consideration of a district's class profile is purported to have decisively boosted Conservative Party vote share, leaving Conservative candidates safe in

---

[58] The analysis focuses on all of England, while Wales, Scotland, and Ireland are dropped from the empirical analysis for several reasons. First, the census for Ireland and Scotland were separate from the Welsh and English census, posing substantial difficulties of matching census and electoral units outside of England. Second, in this period, the heartland of British Conservatism and Unionism was in England due in part to its sheer size. In 1886, for example, 343 of the UK's 397 Conservative and Unionist MPs were from England, the remaining from Wales, Scotland, and Northern Ireland (Craig, *Electoral Facts* (1976).) Certainly Scottish Liberal Unionism and Conservatism, which formally fused in 1912, broke Liberal Party hegemony in Scotland in this period, providing critically important MPs for the Conservative and Unionist dominance in Westminster. However, secondary literature directly asserts that arguments developed here about England – that well-developed party organization was critical to Unionist electoral success – apply in Scotland too; see Cawood, *The Liberal Unionist Party: A History* (2012), 138. For details of organizational activity in West of Scotland where Unionism thrived in contrast to North and East Scotland, see Catriona Burness, "The Making of Scottish Unionism, 1886–1914," in *Mass Conservatism: The Conservatives and the Public Sphere Since the 1880s*, ed. Stuart Ball and Ian Holliday (London: Routledge, 2013), 16–35.

their own districts.[59] While the "mobilizational effect" of the Primrose League can be tested directly by looking at the impact of Primrose League membership density on election performance at the local level, the "party-expert effect" can only be tested indirectly with this hypothesis: holding constant all other variables, the carving out of more homogeneously upper-middle-class districts in 1885 ought to have continued to have a positive relationship with election performance for the next twenty years, despite the intervening demographic changes.

To test both hypotheses, I use an empirically novel research design. Because Britain's nineteenth-century decennial population census only collected data at a level of analysis that did not correspond to election constituencies, the rich literature on late Victorian and Edwardian elections has faced severe gaps, and to date no one has systematically combined census data for all electoral constituencies in England in the post-1885 period.[60] The analysis that follows combines systematic census data with electoral constituencies, taking advantage of recent GIS technology that allows us to assign, for the very first time, each of the over 8,000 English parishes in 1881 (the level of analysis for which census data are reported) to all 438 English constituencies, based on which constituency-polygon the parish's centroid fell within, and assigning all census data for the parish to that constituency.[61] Without the benefit of GIS technology and the recent work of geographers at the University of Portsmouth, the task of matching up constituencies and census units would have been simply impossible.[62]

---

[59] Cornford, "Transformation of Conservatism" (1963): 583.

[60] Because of the mismatch, to date, scholars have resorted to one of two techniques: (1) focusing on highly aggregated but usually artificial units of analysis at the "regional" level (Pelling, *Social Geography of British Elections, 1885–1910*, 1967), or at the level of artificially created "surrogate" units (Wald, *Crosses on the Ballot*, 1983) to allow for census data and electoral data to be matched; or (2) a focus on a smaller subset of districts, either contained within a single region, such as London (Windscheffel, *Popular Conservatism in Imperial London*, 2007), or within a type of constituency, e.g., Borough constituencies (Jon Lawrence and Jane Elliott, "Parliamentary Election Results Reconsidered: An Analysis of Borough Elections, 1885–1910," *Parliamentary History* 16, no. 1, 1997: 18–28), preventing the ability to identify average effects across all of England. Recent progress has been made, though to date is unpublished by Karen Long Jusko, "Who Speaks for the Poor? Electoral Geography and the Political Representation of Low-Income and Working Class Citizens" (Stanford University, 2013).

[61] As noted above, the analysis focuses on England only and reports on a "work in progress" since the process of matching census units to constituency units has been done so for about two-thirds of districts, leaving about one-third of districts still unmatched, mostly in big cities, where parishes covered much larger areas than constituencies. Nonetheless, for the first time, we can assess the average effect of demographic variables on election performance for a great majority of English constituencies in a way that simply was impossible for an earlier generation of scholars (Pelling, *Social Geography of British Elections, 1885–1910*, 1967; Cornford, "Transformation of Conservatism," 1963).

[62] Great Britain Historical GIS Project (2012) "Great Britain Historical GIS." University of Portsmouth. I am grateful to Humphrey Southall for aid on this collaborative project.

Explanatory Variables: The goal is to assess whether and by how much party organization helped secure greater electoral success for the Conservative Party, all else held equal. "Party organization," however, as mentioned earlier, is notoriously difficult to measure, especially in a historical context. In the context of this analysis, as mentioned above, party organization has two facets, one that can be directly measured and the other second indirectly. For the first "direct" measure, I draw upon a hitherto unused source, the Primrose League's own publication, the *Primrose League Gazette* which in 1887 published a detailed listing of the total numbers of Primrose League members for nearly every electoral constituency (n = 314) in England between 1885 and 1886.[63] For purposes of analysis, I measure "party organization strength" as "Primrose League organizational density" (number of members per voter for each electoral constituency in England in the period between 1885 and 1887). The Primrose League itself was a mass organization with thousands of members spread unevenly across England, ranging from a maximum of 6,486 members in the district of Wilton in Wiltshire County to no members in a district in London, and an average constituency level membership total of 1,470 across England.[64]

Because I am also interested in whether the "party expertise" associated with robust party organization also mattered in electoral success, I use an indirect proxy for this variable by looking at whether homogeneously upper-middle-class electoral districts, the purported handiwork of party elites armed with census data and maps, had an enduring relationship with electoral success over the five subsequent elections by creating safe districts. Lord Salisbury, in the early 1880s, famously regarded the "villa vote" of the new leafy and wealthy suburbs of major cities such as London as "requiring organization." The degree to which middle-class districts constructed in 1885 were in fact correlated with higher Conservative Party vote share tells us about the actual capacity of party elites to identify demographic predictors. Thus, this second "party expertise" hypothesis is tested by analyzing whether the portion of an electoral constituency constituted by the 1881 census category of Class I employment (professionals) is positively correlated with Conservative Party vote share, holding other variables constant.[65]

Dependent Variable: The dependent variable in this analysis is Conservative and Unionist Party vote share in each constituency averaged over the five elections in the period of conservative hegemony: 1885, 1886, 1892, 1895, and

---

[63] This publication is held in special collections at Bodleian Library at Oxford University, "Roll of County and Borough Habitations" *The Primrose League Gazette, October 8, 1887–1889.*

[64] For purposes of analysis, total constituency member totals are coded as "PL membership totals per number of voters in a district," ranging from 0 to a full 79 percent (Wiltshire) with a mean value of 15 percent.

[65] The precise measure used is Class I employment category as a percentage of total employment in each district, according to the 1881 census. For purposes of robustness, I also substitute a measure that others have used from the 1881 census for similar purposes, "domestic servants/total employment." The findings are not significantly affected.

1900.[66] Though we have data for each election in each constituency, the dependent variable is most usefully measured as "average vote share" over the entire period for two reasons. First, most of the independent variables in the analysis below are available at the constituency level as cross sections at a single moment in time at the beginning of the period (e.g., the 1881 census or the 1887 *Primrose League Gazette* report), thus making a time-series cross-section a problematic method of analysis. Second, the purpose of the analysis is not to explain every minor fluctuation in vote share, but instead to identify broad patterns determining Conservative Party performed better electorally. Thus, by averaging the vote share over the entire period, I am able to focus on these patterns in a more accurate fashion.[67]

Control Variables: In addition to the variables listed above, I also include a set of controls for several demographic variables that we might expect to influence Conservative Party vote share: portion of the population that is Anglican, which has been argued to increase support for the Conservative Party, and portion of workers in a district employed in the agricultural sector.[68] I rely on employment data from the 1881 census to measure Anglican priests as portion of total employment and agricultural workers as a portion of total employment. Additionally, because other scholars have argued that the Conservative Party only thrived by suppressing the vote, I include a control for average turnout over the entire period (valid votes as a percentage of the total electorate) in each constituency.[69] Finally, I also include a dummy variable for whether or not a district was a borough constituency or a county constituency, a distinction with deep historical roots that possibly affects election outcomes.

ANALYSIS AND RESULTS

The theoretical expectations can now be examined against the data. I conduct an OLS multivariate analysis model that allows us to assess the impact of "party organization" relative to more traditional demographic and turnout variables. Table 4.1 presents the results with several different specifications.

Table 4.1 reports the findings for an OLS analysis that covers the entire time period and every electoral constituency in England for which data are available.

---

[66] Average vote share is calculated using data available from Ken Kollman, Allen Hicken, Daniele Caramani, David Backer, and David Lublin (2014), *Constituency-Level Elections Archive* (Ann Arbor, MI: Center for Political Studies, University of Michigan [producer and distributor]). www.electiondataarchive.org/, accessed September 15, 2013.

[67] I also do the analysis as a pooled time-series cross section but do not report the findings below. The findings show generally consistent results: the two measures of "Party Organization" remain statistically significant in most specifications.

[68] Wald, *Crosses on the Ballot* (1983).

[69] See Cornford, "Transformation of Conservatism" (1963). But more recently, Luke Blaxill and Taym Saleh, "The Electoral Dynamics of Conservatism, 1885–1910: "Negative Unionism" Reconsidered," *Historical Journal* 59, no. 2 (2016): 417–45.

TABLE 4.1: *OLS Analysis Results, Average Conservative Party Vote Share, 1885–1906*

	(1)	(2)	(3)	(4)	(5)
Party Organization (Measure #1: PL Density, 1885)	0.211*** (0.071)	0.252*** (0.066)	0.163*** (0.057)	0.173*** (0.058)	0.163*** (0.057)
Party Organization (Measure #2: class-1 employment share, 1881)		6.276*** (0.730)	4.814*** (0.596)	4.300*** (0.676)	5.116*** (0.761)
Anglican Density (Anglican Priests)			15.474*** (6.389)	18.787*** (6.705)	0.399 (10.450)
Voter Turnout			−0.353*** (0.029)	−0.366*** (0.030)	−0.360*** (0.030)
% Employment, Agricultural Sector					0.234** (0.102)
Borough				0.033 (0.021)	0.046** (0.021)
Observations	314	314	286	286	286
R²	0.028	0.233	0.517	0.522	0.530

Notes: *p<0.1, **p<0.05, ***p<0.01; robust standard error in parentheses.

In Model 1 of Table 4.1, I include a measure of Primrose League density, showing the positive correlation between this first measure of "party organization" in 1885 and the subsequent average electoral performance between 1885 and 1906. In Model 2, I add the second measure of party organization, Class I employment share. In Models 3, 4, and 5, I include additional control variables in different combinations. We see in all three of these models, as other authors have argued, that average voter turnout over the period is negatively related to average Conservative and Unionist Party vote share, providing confirmation that the party did perform better when the electorate was restricted.[70] In Models 3 and 4 we see evidence that, as Wald has argued, the measure of Anglican religiosity is positively correlated with Conservative Party vote share.[71] This finding is revealing because, as we saw in the Chapter 3, the Primrose League itself was built upon social networks revolving around the Anglican Church. But, even holding this variable constant, additional Primrose League density had a positive impact on election performance.[72]

---

[70] This provides confirming evidence of Blaxill and Saleh, "The Electoral Dynamics of Conservatism, 1885–1910: 'Negative Unionism' Reconsidered" (2016).

[71] Wald, *Crosses on the Ballot* (1983).

[72] This certainly poses some difficulties for interpretation – the value of the coefficients may be misleading because of the correlation of these variables.

In Model 5, however, I include a control variable for how important agriculture was to a region. Here we see that the Anglican variable drops out in its substantive and statistical significance.[73] In Models 4 and 5, we see, finally, that when controlling for the type of election district (borough vs. county), the basic findings remain intact. Most crucially for our purposes, in each specification the statistical and substantive impact of the two primary variables of interest remain significant.

In sum, even accounting for demographic variables, we find that, on average, Primrose League density in a constituency is positively related to average Conservative Party vote share. Also, there is evidence that the Redistribution Act of 1885, by creating homogeneous upper-middle-class districts, had the expected relationship with party success, suggesting that party expertise may have played an important role. We will return to this last point in the discussion of causal mechanisms below.

To illustrate the precise impact of party organization on vote share, as reported in Table 4.1, we can simulate the impact of party organization on vote share by using Model 5 and setting Primrose League density for each constituency at "0" while leaving all other values at their actual values. This allows us to assess the counterfactual: what would have election results been *had there been no Primrose League?* The Primrose League in some cases altered the outcome of elections, though demographic variables on their own played a major role. For example, if we take a district like Stalybridge, where the average observed Conservative vote share was just over 50 percent over five elections, we see a small but decisive impact: without any Primrose League membership, the district would have dropped below 50 percent to 44 percent, altering, on average, the outcome of the elections. To take another example, in the City of London the actual average vote share over five elections was 96 percent, making it an extremely "safe seat." By contrast, a counterfactual simulation shows that without any Primrose League membership, that same district would have become much more competitive, dropping over 30 percentage points to a 64 percent average vote share during the same period. Despite a diverse range of experiences, and with the Primrose League and all other variables included, the average Conservative Party vote share across all districts was 60 percent.

At first glance, when simulating the average effect had there been no Primrose League, the impact looks relatively small. In the counterfactual simulation with Primrose League density set at "0," Conservative Party average total vote share for all districts drops to only 57 percent, showing that demographic variables on their own gave the Conservatives a substantial head start in building electoral majorities in this period. However, this conceals the variation in impact of Primrose League membership across different types of districts, since it

---

[73] This is perhaps explained by the fact that correlation coefficient between these two variables – agricultural employment and Anglican density – equals 0.76.

includes districts where the Conservative Party never earned a majority, and even some uncontested districts with no votes at all. For example, if we subset the data to examine those districts where the Conservative Party had a near hegemonic position over five elections – in the districts where it achieved over 80 percent of the vote (n = 56) – the counterfactual simulation reveals that without Primrose League membership, the average drop in average vote share would have been a very substantial 13 percent, making some safe seats much more competitive. The average Conservative vote share when it earned more than 50 percent of the vote was 69 percent, a supremely safe share of the vote; without the Primrose League, the vote share would have been 62 percent.

For purposes of illustrating the differences, Figure 4.2 presents the observed Conservative Party vote share for a sample of constituencies (triangles) and the predicted vote share if the Primrose League density were "o" (circles) for those same districts.

In sum, we can see, for the first time, precisely how much of an impact the Primrose League had on electoral performance. The impact was real and statistically significant. However, the benefit of our analysis here is that we can, very precisely, identify where "party organization" was most substantial: for districts where the Conservative Party already had a majority due to demographic and other factors. Second, it is also likely that our findings understate the importance of "party organization" as a variable in helping explain Conservative Party success by focusing mostly on the role of the Primrose League. We see in the broader analysis that "party expertise" also mattered a great deal, as elaborated below. Yet, even with this narrow focus, by making what might have been competitive seats into extremely "safe seats," the party's grassroots organization played a crucial and hitherto not fully appreciated role in making democracy safe for Conservatives.

THE TRIUMPH OF THE POLITICAL WIREPULLERS

Before discussing the later consequences of party organization for Britain into the twentieth century, it is worth dwelling on two narrower questions about the causal mechanisms underpinning these findings. First, how and why exactly did the Primrose League have such an impact, independent of demographic and other factors, on securing safe seats for the British Conservative Party? And, second, if homogeneously drawn upper-middle-class districts help explain a major portion of Conservative Party share, what evidence is there that we can attribute this to the far-sighted expertise of party elites, the so-called "political wirepullers," rather than to impersonal forces of socioeconomic modernization?

The answer to the first question has been explored in the growing secondary literature on the British Conservative Party. The positive grassroots status and identity appeals of organizations such as the Primrose League have been emphasized by scholars who have studied the Edwardian Conservative Party

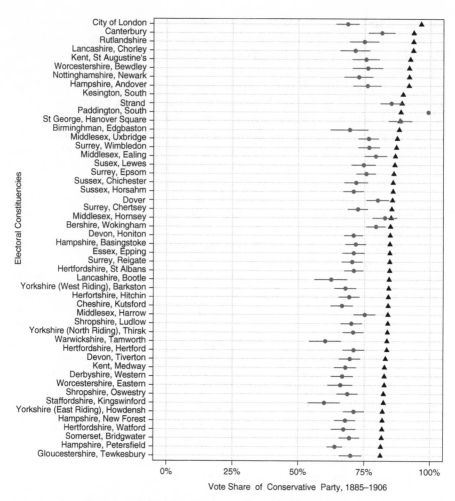

FIGURE 4.2: Actual Conservative Vote Share and Predicted Vote Share (with and without Primrose League Membership, 1885–1906)

Note: Triangles indicate *actual* average vote share of the Conservative Party in the districts listed and dots indicate simulated estimates of what the Conservative Party vote share would have been had the Primrose League not existed, all other variables being held at their actual values.

Data sources for analysis are discussed in the text.

in its Unionist alliance in socioeconomically diverse settings, including Leeds and London.[74] This literature notes that the Conservative Party did well electorally even among working- and middle-class voters in these districts.

[74] Roberts, "Popular Conservatism in Britain, 1832–1914" (2007); Windscheffel, *Popular Conservatism in Imperial London* (2007).

How precisely? And how does the Primrose League help us understand this puzzle? As our discussion in Chapter 2 made clear, William Riker's notion of "heresthetics," which characterizes how politicians remake or, in Riker's terms, "manipulate" an issue space when on the losing end of a cleavage provides a powerful framework to make sense of this puzzle.[75]

Given the size and makeup of the electorate, election appeals on socioeconomic issues were a losing proposition for the Conservative Party. The Primrose League, however, a cross-class organization built around sociability and entertainment, provided a powerful vehicle to appeal to voters through non-class issues, political arguments, and political values including prominently anti-Home Rule sentiment, as well as empire, religion, and monarchy. Is there any evidence this was the basis of Conservative Party election success? Though more suggestive than conclusive, evidence drawn from election addresses of Conservative Party MP candidates suggests that a Rikerian heresthetic logic was at work. In the *British Political Party General Election Addresses* for the elections of 1892, 1895, and 1900 we can assess directly the kinds of appeals British Conservative and Unionist candidates made in elections.[76] Did British Conservative politicians utilize these cross-class "cultural" appeals (e.g., "Queen, Empire, and Church") in their campaigns, which a Rikerian heresthetic perspective might presume?

For the two elections for which systematic data exist (1895 and 1900), the answer appears to be a definitive "yes." In a careful reconstruction of the 1895 and 1900 elections, historian Paul Readman codes and reports different themes raised in candidate speeches for the 1895 and 1900 elections in London as well as counties and boroughs across the United Kingdom.[77] Drawing on his data, we can report findings below that are largely consistent with the "heresthetic" model of conservative electoral self-defense elaborated in Chapter 2. We can separate his twenty-one themes into two groups, "social policy appeals" (e.g., old-age pensions, workers' compensation, poor law reform, hours of labor) and cross-class "cultural appeals" (e.g., Irish Home Rule, religion, Empire, South Africa).[78] Figure 4.3 reports the percentage of total Conservative and Unionist speeches that cluster into each category. Because politicians often referred to more than one theme in a single speech, the total percentage for each year exceeds 100 percent.

Though it is difficult to tease out the causal impact of election campaigns on outcomes, it is certainly true that in the two highly successful election campaigns of 1895 and 1900 the Conservative Party disproportionately relied

---

[75] Riker, *Art of Political Manipulation* (1986).

[76] *"British Political Party General Election Addresses, [1892–ca. 1970] from the National Liberal Club collection, Bristol University,"* ed. Library University of Bristol (1986).

[77] Readman, "The 1895 General Election" (1999); Readman, "The Conservative Party, Patriotism, and British Politics" (2001).

[78] See Readman, "The 1895 General Election" (1999): Appendix, Table 12.

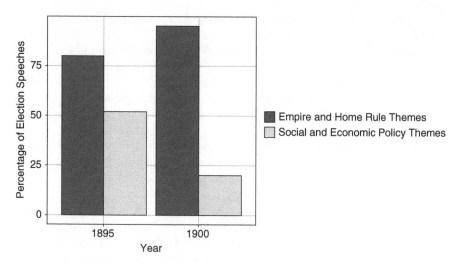

FIGURE 4.3: Percentage of Conservative Party Candidate Election Speeches in 1895 and 1900 That Refer to Two Clusters of Themes
Data Source: Readman 1999 and 2001

on the kinds of cross-cutting issues that helped seal robust majorities. Furthermore, this finding conforms quite closely with the immense secondary literature on the benefits of the "Home Rule" issue for Conservatives in this period, as well as the role of Empire, patriotism, and the Boer War for the Conservative Party in 1900's so-called "Khaki election." The Primrose League became central as the organized vehicle that delivered these messages. A classic instance of this is found in a report about social and campaign events held in the Bredbury Habitation of Cheshire, published in the Primrose League's own publication, the Primrose League Gazette on October 13, 1888, in which the account reads that "a most able address was delivered by the Rev. David Avans, Vicar of Abergel," who spoke to his audience powerfully about the threats of disestablishing the Church of England,

Confiscation is contagious ... if it began by attacking the tall spires and towers, it would not stop short of leveling the castle turrets and factory chimneys.[79]

And, what about the second question, the degree to which we can attribute the positive relationship of homogeneous districts and party success to "party expertise" – i.e., the role of "political wirepullers" – or to the impersonal forces of economic modernization? Certainly, the latter dynamic played a role. However, close analysis of party elites in the negotiation of the 1884 Reform Act and the 1885 Redistribution Act confirms that party experts and

[79] *The Primrose League Gazette*, October 13, 1888, 11

party agents were clear players in this process, aware of the problems of not conceding suffrage reform without redistribution, and were active participants in a process that elevated party experts to help draw the boundaries of electoral constituencies during the course of 1885.

For example, evidence from three sources – the private papers of Lord Salisbury; those of his chief party whip, Aretas Akers-Douglas; and the Conservative Party Archive – expose the party's decision-making process in the heated moments of uncertainty as it negotiated the details of the suffrage reform bill in 1884 and 1885. The Conservative Party, by now a modern, hierarchical, centralized, and specialized organization, had developed several key traits: "organizational intelligence," the containment of factionalism and rivalry among competing groups, the adoption of a relatively flat hierarchy, and the presence of informal channels of communication.

First, at a very basic level, the British Conservative Party could effectively gather and transmit information about the electorate and threats to its popularity. Before the Liberal government began its February 1884 push to expand suffrage, in September 1883 the Conservative Party's chief agent, George T. Bartley, a full-time Central Office employee with the responsibility of overseeing party agents and local associations, composed a detailed, statistical assessment. He submitted the report, "The Condition of the Conservative Party in the Midland Counties," to party leaders and presented it at the Annual Conference of the National Union of Conservative Associations in Birmingham.[80] The report included statistical tables based on a careful analysis of vote share, electorate size, and number of representatives in each of the five Midland counties (Derbyshire, Leicestershire, Staffordshire, Warwickshire, and Worcestershire) and thought to be revealing of broader trends. Bartley offered many important recommendations to party leaders, who reflected on the consequences of democratizing suffrage reform and considered the importance of redrawing electoral constituencies (called "redistribution" in the parlance of the day). He wrote,

The first point is that the figures given by the polling show that Conservative party has not the representation in Parliament which the number of the electors would justify. Thus, in the counties, although the number of Liberal and Conservative members is equal, the Conservatives polled 38,000 against the Liberals' 31,000.... In the boroughs this is even more the case... These figures which are as nearly accurate as possible point to several considerations as the working of the new redistribution scheme, and although it is not my object on this occasion to dwell upon this subject, I merely refer to it as important.[81]

[80] George T. Bartley "The Condition of the Conservative Party in the Midland Counties" National Union of Conservative and Constitutional Associations Convention, (1883) Conservative Party Archive, Bodleian Library, Oxford University, NUA2/1/2.

[81] George T. Bartley "The Condition of the Conservative Party in the Midland Counties" (1883) Conservative Party Archive, Bodleian Library, Oxford University. NUA2/1/2.

The party apparatus was beginning to provide the kind of detailed and reliable "intelligence" about the future needed for redistribution (i.e., redistricting). Support for democratizing suffrage reform could be made safer if the party could construct a favorable redistricting plan. Thus, on October 25, 1884, at the pivotal moment when protests in Hyde Park and elsewhere had reached their peak, Salisbury had the option of asserting a House of Lords veto to block suffrage reform outright when he received a detailed report, again from George Bartley, which delivered a warning:

I think it right to lay before the leaders of the Conservative Party, my view as to the present aspect of affairs and the result which has attended the recent demonstrations, together with the influence that they have on the action of the party in the future... I feel... that if the agitation is to go on, particularly as indications have been recently seen of riot on the part of the Radicals, serious damage will be done to our case unless the steps we take now are to such to ensure the sympathy and support of that great mass of the sober-minded public, who lie between the Radicals and the Conservatives, and whose oscillation from one side to the other is amply sufficient to control the result of the election.[82]

Bartley concluded his memo by "emphatically" urging that "We should without delay ... announce our programme concerning redistribution." The party experts were imploring the party leaders to accept suffrage reform, if accompanied by a redistricting to make the democratic reform sufficiently palatable for Conservatives.

Aside from formal channels, Salisbury and Northcote also quite effectively sought out informal channels of information on how districts should be redrawn by Boundary Commissions. Northcote and Salisbury received notes from local associations across Britain, including one typical example from the Edinburgh branch of the Scottish Conservative Club on November 19, 1884, with the following advice:

I have consulted with some of our friends here best conversant with the state of political feelings in various parts of Scotland and I think it is desirable to inform you at the earliest moment... that household franchise in counties without a bold application of the grouping principle will annihilate the Conservative Party in Scotland.[83]

[82] Bartley Report to Salisbury/Northcote, October 25, 1884, Conservative Central Office, "Memorandum to the Marquess of Salisbury and Sir Stafford Northcote," Salisbury Papers, Hatfield House.
[83] Scottish Conservative Club, Edinburgh, Mackintosh to Northcote, November 18, 1884, Hatfield House, Salisbury Papers. Other similar memos from other MPs and local officials include one on November 19, 1884 from the Carlton Club making special pleading for a mid-Cheshire constituency. See Talbot to Northcote, November 18, 1884, Hatfield House, Salisbury Papers. See also a note from Howler to Northcote from November 20, 1884, in which he writes, "My dear Stafford... I enclose a note from Roland Winn (chief whip). His views as the superiority of the single seated constituencies... are I think well worth consideration. The immense physical labour involved in "stumping" a large double seated constituency, added to the expense of supporting every village cricket, football, and bicycle club all over a large electoral area must

Thus, there was certainly evidence that party agents, local associations, and above all, the chief agent, who knew the lay of the electoral land, also counseled party leaders that (a) sustaining the status quo by blocking suffrage reform was self-undermining, and (b) redistricting was necessary.

But was this "intelligence" in turn effectively conveyed to party elites, altering decision making? Two forms of evidence are quite suggestive. The first is the basis and justification of Salisbury's own insistence that redistribution was a necessary and useful feature of reform for Conservative Party survival. As he put it in his October 1884 article "The Value of Redistribution," published at the moment of decision in *The National Review*, "it is dictated by the strongest instincts of self preservation."[84] In fact, this assessment was based on careful and arduous analyses, apparently conducted by Salisbury himself, using data supplied to him not only through formal channels by Bartley but also via informal ones from statistician Henry Bernhard.[85] Second, even more conclusive, is what followed in the wake of Bartley's October 24, 1884 memo insisting that the Party make its position on redistribution explicit to the government. Two days later when, as Hayes describes it, the Tories finally made their "leap," Sir Michael Hicks Beach, Conservative Chancellor of the Exchequer, secretly met with Lord Hartington.[86] Many observers describe this meeting as the moment when the stalemate ended and a "breakthrough" to calmer negotiations began.[87] Beach presented Hartington the first concrete set of proposals to come from a Conservative. The proposal, stipulating single-member districts and political equality of districts went so far beyond anything the government had considered that, according to Powell, it "shocked" Hartington.[88] What prompted the leap? Hayes reports the conventional view that Hicks Beach unofficially operated on his own.[89]

The record suggests a different account, underscoring the importance of intelligence and advice from the "organization" man, George Bartley. Only two days after Bartley, the chief whip, urged Northcote and Salisbury make their proposal explicit, Northcote wrote Salisbury, "... I am inclined to think that Beach had better see Hartington. I am writing to ask him to come up

not be lightly considered..." James Howler to Northcote, November 20, 1884, Hatfield House, Salisbury Papers.

[84] Lord Salisbury, "The Value of Redistribution: A Note on Electoral Statistics," *The National Review*, October 20, 1884, 145.

[85] Salisbury cites Bernard's "very useful pamphlet on Redistribution" as the basis of his analysis. Salisbury, "The Value of Redistribution: A Note on Electoral Statistics," 150.

[86] Hayes, *The Background and Passage of the Third Reform Act* (1982), 223.

[87] Hayes, *The Background and Passage of the Third Reform Act* (1982), 223; Leigh Michael Powell, "Sir Michael Hicks Beach and Conservative Politics," *Parliamentary History* 19, no. 3 (2000): 377–404. See also Lady Victoria Hicks-Beach, *Life of Sir Michael Hicks Beach* (London: Macmillan and Co, 1932), 217.

[88] Powell, "Sir Michael Hicks Beach and Conservative Politics" (2000): 381.

[89] Hayes, *The Background and Passage of the Third Reform Act* (1982), 223.

tomorrow."[90] Beach approached Hartington and presented the party's "unofficial" plan, opening a channel of negotiations between Conservative and Liberal party leaders (including Dilke, Northcote, Salisbury, Hartington, and Gladstone) three weeks later that persisted until a settlement was reached in the so-called Arlington Street Compact of November 28, 1884. Though the content of Beach's recommendation differed from the final outcome, it was precisely that which broke the stalemate between Liberal and Conservatives and made a resolution possible. Bartley, as chief whip, often felt his views were not taken as seriously as he hoped.[91] However, his work then had a major impact that has hitherto not been fully appreciated.[92]

That the Conservative Party would rely on its chief agent to gather and transmit intelligence, identify and communicate the threats of inaction, and strategically propose suffrage reform plans reveals a broader point: a party in which non-aristocratic experts – possessing analytical and interpretive skills and access to election results and census data – were allowed to play a major role in decision-making was also a party that could craft constituencies to preserve itself. This was even more the case as the putatively "neutral" Boundary Commission, constituted by appointees of each party, did the work of dividing up constituencies. Already in November 1884, Ellis Ashmead-Bartlett wrote the future Conservative Prime Minister, Balfour, about how districts should be redrawn: "Sheffield, Bradford, Bristol, Hull ought certainly to be divided into single member wards. If so we shall win [each]."[93]

This practice of estimating electoral futures based on "organizational intelligence" continued even after the Reform. Beginning in 1885, Akers-Douglas, a Kent County landowner and "organization man" from the "Kentish gang" (a group of Conservative party men who focused on party organization, including the long-time chief agent, Richard Middleton) worked in a remarkably informal and friendly way with Lord Salisbury and provided

---

[90] Northcote to Salisbury, October 26, 1884, Hatfield House, Salisbury Papers.

[91] At one point he even threatened resignation over this issue but agreed, later, to stay on in his position. See Northcote to Salisbury, December 12, 1884, Hatfield House, Salisbury Papers.

[92] There has been a debate about the relative importance of Queen Victoria in helping bring the main parties to an agreement. Weston has argued that the monarch's interventions were crucial precisely because of divisions among Conservatives. See Corinne Weston, "The Royal Mediation in 1884," *English Historical Review* 82, no. 323 (1967): 296–322; Corinne Weston, "Disunity on the Opposition Front Bench, 1884," *English Historical Review* 106, no. 418 (1991): 80–96. In two responses to this research, Fair has quite convincingly argued that while the Queen played a role, Salisbury's control of his own party was very high (confirmed, incidentally by a look at roll call votes in the period) and it is important not to exaggerate monarch's interventions, since the main action was taking place at the level of political party leadership, with some genuflection to the Queen's wishes. See, in particular, John D. Fair, "Royal Mediation in 1884: A Reassessment," *English Historical Review* 88, no. 346 (1973): 100–13; John D. Fair, "The Carnarvon Diaries and Royal Mediation in 1884," *English Historical Review* 106, no. 418 (1991): 115.

[93] From Salisbury Papers, cited by Cornford, "Transformation of Conservatism" (1963): 58.

him critical election information and intelligence at decisive moments.[94] For example, before the 1885 elections, Salisbury, as I noted in Chapter 2, depended on Akers-Douglas' precise election predictions for all constituencies while weighing different strategies."[95] And, more than just simply supplying figures, party agents and party leaders together puzzled through the new subtleties of democratic politics. Party leader Stafford Northcote, who after July 1885 became Lord Iddesleigh, traveled across several constituencies, and thereafter sent a "private" note from 10 Downing Street to his party's chief party agent Captain Middleton in August 1885:

My dear sir, since coming down here I have heard great complaint of W. Lyons' work in this neighborhood. As long as he is addressing a friendly audience he does very well, but when it is a mixed one he is unnecessarily irritating, picks up bits of personal gossip and makes them matter for attack and when interrupted loses his temper so that there have been some disagreeable scenes in which it has sometimes been necessary to protect from assaults. This is what I am told by friend . . . They think he should be employed elsewhere as here he is only doing harm. This has been a very radical district which is now conservatizing and needs delicate handling.[96]

CONCLUSION

Beyond a remarkably nationally encompassing mass organization, the British Conservative Party thus possessed the "organizational intelligence" to detect and impart crucial information to party leaders. Suffrage reform in 1884 remained a risky proposition. But, it was not entirely a "leap in the dark"; it was a move made with a keen sense of how events might unfold. That safe seats drawn up in 1885 would endure, helping the Conservative Party survive, in part reflects the expanded size of the middle class. But, party organization operated through the two distinct channels, "popular organization" and "party expertise," to help minimize the uncertainty and risk of suffrage reform for British Conservatives in the late nineteenth century; the aim was to reduce the

[94] In addition to having elaborate systems in place to collect and exchange useful electoral information, important for overcoming the pitfalls of centralized organization was the relatively flat hierarchy of party leaders and their "organization men." While Bartley, as chief party agent, at times felt slighted, Salisbury was on particularly friendly basis with his friend Akers-Douglas (e.g., "My dear Douglas") and Middleton, even inviting him, for example, from time to time, to stay at his country home for evenings (at Hatfield House) for social occasions such as hunting (Salisbury to Middleton, January 27, Middleton Papers, MS Eng C 4838, Oxford University Special Collections). For a nineteenth-century organization that needed the "specialization" of "organization men," status distinctions were surprisingly kept to a minimum.

[95] Salisbury to Akers Douglas, November 27, 1885, Kent County Archive, Aretas Akers Douglas Papers A1226 U564 c 18/4. Akers Douglas provided the forecasts, for which Salisbury thanks him.

[96] Northcote to Middleton, August 17, 1885, MS Eng C 4838, Middleton Papers, Special Collections, Oxford University.

potential downsides of suffrage reform. A mass organization in the form of the Primrose League built through Rikerian strategies of cross-class appeals gave party leaders some hope that they could win elections. And, the elevating of party experts and "organization men" who both urged moderation and possessed the skills to create districts from which the party could benefit electorally, helped make democracy safer for Conservatives than it would have otherwise been.

In this sense, contemporary critics of parties and democracy, such as Henry Maine, were correct that the new era of the 1880s in Britain was one in which "wirepullers" operated behind the scenes, exerting the kind of influence advisors to kings and generals had in the past.[97] However, though correct in their assessment of the wirepullers' power, critics like Maine wrongly diagnosed the consequences of this development for democracy.[98] Rather than being a pernicious influence, wirepullers played a positive role, as did the increasingly institutionalized political party organizations in which they were embedded. They tamed the fears of Britain's most powerful opponents of democracy, helping the Conservative Party accommodate itself to democracy and turning potentially destabilizing democratic breakthroughs into near non-events.

[97] Henry Maine, *Popular Government* (London: John Murray, 1886), 29–30.
[98] Maine, *Popular Government* (1886), 29–30.

5

Averting a Democratic Disaster in Britain, 1906–1922

A single democratic breakthrough is no assurance of further breakthroughs, let alone long-run democratic survival. Indeed, a long-run view makes clear that *staying settled* – or in the more traditional language of political science, "consolidating" democracy – is a major challenge for newly democratizing regimes. What shapes the prospects of democratic consolidation?

To answer this question, we have at least two options: first, investigate a case of democracy transition gone wrong and identify the factors that play a role in blocking consolidation; second, examine a democratic "near miss" – a moment when a newly democratized state just barely sidesteps disaster – to understand what allowed it to survive. Later chapters tracing the development of German democracy employ the former strategy, but in this chapter, we shall adopt the latter, to explore a little-known case of a *democratic disaster averted* in Britain in the years leading up to and immediately after the outbreak of the First World War. In the process we will recognize the pivotal role played by British Conservatism.

CONTAINING RADICALISM: THE ANATOMY OF A CRISIS AVERTED

At the turn of the twentieth century, Britain at first glance appeared to have securely landed on a pathway of settled democratization. In 1902, after decades at the head of the Conservative Party, Lord Salisbury resigned as Prime Minister, and his nephew Arthur Balfour, in an orderly and predictable succession, took over leadership of the party and premiership of Great Britain. Even if the suffrage had not legally been expanded since the 1884 Reform Act, more people had the right to vote than ever before, and Britain's old-regime elites appeared to be graciously accommodating themselves to the modern age.[1]

---

[1] Serious restrictions persisted. See Blewett, "The Franchise in the United Kingdom, 1885–1918" (1965). Yet, despite the fact that formal suffrage rules did not significantly change in period,

Looks, however, were deceiving. England's long Indian Summer, the age of "Edwardian equipoise," was only stable on the surface.[2] There was an analogue in the realm of international politics. Norman Angell's *The Great Illusion*, written in the warm glow at the tail end of the long "first globalization," argued that European national economies were then so interlinked by trade that war had become self-destructive and futile.[3] A similar faith in the appearance of prewar *domestic* equilibrium, reinforced in this case by the "infallibility" of Britain's long-standing unwritten constitution, misled contemporary observers about the sources of stability in British domestic political life.

After 1906 the British order was tested as key Conservative Party elites began to believe they faced "existential" threats that justified extreme extraconstitutional means of self-defense. Crisis was brewing. Conservative diehards found themselves in the grips of what Lord Salisbury in 1903 had called a "catastrophical theory of politics," in which everything was perceived to be getting worse.[4] The British Conservative Party – or the Unionist Alliance or Party, as it was increasingly called even before its formal merger with the Liberal Unionists in 1912 – both triggered and helped resolve the political instability in these years. As we will see, it remained the main pivot of British democratization into the twentieth century.

The period from 1906 to 1922 highlights three themes. First, all conservative political parties that rely on cross-class appeals of religion and patriotism, even strong ones like the British Conservative Party, are vulnerable to populist backlash if they lose control of these issues; in such moments, they are pulled toward the most explosive rhetoric of hardline and even "disloyal" right-wing extremism. Second, even if conservative politicians believe they are merely "play-acting" or posturing at such moments, all democratizing states, even those with long histories of constitutionalism, run the risk of constitutional crisis. And, third, the particular legacy of organized conservatism in a country determines if such posturing leads, as it did in Germany, to democratic collapse. In Britain it did not. Though British conservatism may have experienced an unprecedented upsurge in right-wing rhetoric and activity before 1914, the main lesson is that by 1922, even facing the challenge of a growing Labour Party, a legacy of robust party organization helped check major deviations from Britain's settled path of democratization.

---

growing wealth alone with fixed income/property thresholds meant the size of the electorate increased by 35 percent, from 5,708,030 in 1885 to 7,694,741 in 1910. Data source: Craig, *Electoral Facts* (1976).

[2] See Ross McKibbin, "Edwardian Equipoise and the First World War," in McKibbin, *Parties and People* (2010).

[3] Norman Angell, *The Great Illusion* (1909).

[4] See Cannadine, *Decline and Fall of the British Aristocracy* (1999), 517.

TABLE 5.1: *Members of Parliament, Elected in British General Elections, 1900 and 1906*

	1900 General Election	1906 General Election
Progressive Alliance	262	508
Liberal Party	183	399
Irish Party	77	82
Labour Party	2	29
Conservative and Liberal Unionist Parties	402	156

Data Source: Craig 1976, 32

THE 1906 POLITICAL EARTHQUAKE: A THREAT TO STABILITY

What triggered the political crisis of the Edwardian era in the first place? The event was a political earthquake in the form of the British general election of 1906. After decades of Conservative and Unionist dominance, the "Liberal landslide," as Table 5.1 shows, gave rise to the largest leftward swing in British parliamentary history. The Conservative Party and its Unionist allies lost their majority, dropping from 402 to 156 seats. Meanwhile, Liberals won 399 seats and were supported in their majority by the Irish nationalists (with 82 seats) and the Labour Party (with 29 seats).[5]

Beyond the sheer size of the parliamentary shift, the election reverberated more ominously for conservatives because it exposed their own vulnerabilities as well as their opponents' strengths.[6] The old patrician order appeared to face its final assault, and the electoral shift was not merely temporary. In the next two elections, both held in 1910, the progressive alliance of Irish, Labour, and Liberalism – a frightening, perhaps even "unconstitutional" configuration of forces in the eyes of traditional Tories – retained its majority in parliamentary seats, leaving the Unionist alliance increasingly desperate. In addition, the election stirred up a strategic dilemma that soon wracked party elites with internal schism and self-doubt.[7]

At the heart of this dilemma was the disintegration of the party's foundational cross-class appeal, which revolved around confession, Empire, and anti–Home Rule mobilization. In the 1880s and 1890s, the Conservative

---

[5] The precise balance depends on how one counts some new MPs who ran under joint Lib–Lab tickets and other ambiguities. My summary relies on the authoritative numbers in Craig, *Electoral Facts* (1976), 32.

[6] As we will see in the discussion below, the shift in votes was by no means as substantial as the shift in seats would suggest, bringing attention to the extreme disproportionality of the British electoral system.

[7] See discussion in Stuart Ball, *The Conservative Party and British Politics, 1902–1951* (London: Routledge, 2013), 44–46.

Party mobilized voters to great effect, galvanizing them on patriotic issues and in response to Liberal plans to grant Catholic Ireland greater political autonomy via Home Rule. In 1893, the second Liberal attempt at devolution for Ireland under Gladstone's final premiership only bolstered this appeal. However, after the failure of the bill in the House of Lords, the issue disappeared as Liberal leaders finally convinced themselves that Gladstone's "obsession" had been electorally counterproductive.[8] In the 1900 General Election (the "Khaki Election"), the Boer War in South Africa left the public, in James Bryce's words, "intoxicated with militarism," giving the Conservatives a useful substitute issue to campaign on.[9] The 1906 election, however, found the Unionist alliance suddenly at the precipice – facing an increasingly mobilized labor movement and strife over female enfranchisement, but with no obvious campaign themes with which to win an election. After the mixed record of the Boer War removed Empire as an easily beneficial "patriotic" issue, the Liberal Unionist Joseph Chamberlain pushed the Unionist alliance to instead make a vocal case for the Imperial tariff system – a kind of Imperial protectionist *Zollverein*. In 1903, protection's advocates founded the Tariff Reform League (TRL), which provided them an organizational vehicle to pressure Unionist MP backbenchers to shift their allegiances, to seek out and support loyal Unionist MP candidates, and even to help run fratricidal candidates against free trade Unionists.[10] The tariff agenda was thought to solve many problems simultaneously. As E. H. H. Green writes,

The tariff campaign offered Conservatives a chance to reestablish their credentials as the party of Empire. But it also provided a means of renewing the Conservative attack on the Liberal Party as the anti-imperial party.[11]

But, as the results of 1906 proved, the issue was electorally a dismal failure. The "last best hope," for Unionists, or, as Chamberlain himself described it, "the great question of the future," failed to appeal to voters and only caused destructive rifts within Unionist ranks between free-traders and protectionists.[12] Antagonized by these developments, the young backbencher Winston Churchill, for example, bolted from the party altogether and became a Liberal. The sudden strategic vulnerability left economic and party elites nervous and plagued with the nagging sense of being once again on the losing end of the most important political fights of the day.[13]

---

[8] Roy Jenkins, *Asquith: Portrait of a Man and an Era* (New York: E. P. Dutton, 1966), 46.
[9] James Bryce to Goldwin Smith, January 23, 1900, as cited by Green, *Crisis of Conservatism* (1995), 74.
[10] See, e.g., Larry L. Witherell, *Rebel on the Right: Henry Page Croft and the Crisis of British Conservatism, 1903–1914* (Newark: University of Delaware Press, 1997).
[11] Green, *Crisis of Conservatism* (1995), 203.
[12] Chamberlain's description comes from Ball, *The Conservative Party and British Politics* (2013), 42.
[13] The best accounts of this include Green, *Crisis of Conservatism* (1995) 268; and Cannadine, *Decline and Fall of the British Aristocracy* (1999).

Unionists also worried over the ideological coherence and self-confident organizational prowess of the new governing Liberal Party. Led by Prime Minister H. H. Asquith and David Lloyd George as Chancellor of the Exchequer, this was no longer the old patrician Whig party of landed notables, described by one account during Gladstone's time as a "people's crusade at the bottom and like a gentlemen's club at the top."[14] Instead, the party, while still appealing to its traditional nonconformist base, transformed "liberal ideals away from pure self-help and distrust of state intervention toward 'new' or 'progressive' liberal conceptions."[15]

From 1906 to 1914, the Liberal-led government oversaw Britain's transformation into a pioneer welfare state.[16] In 1906, the Liberal cabinet quickly enacted an all-encompassing web of policies, including industrial accident insurance; the 1906 Trade Disputes Act, which limited union liability during labor strikes; the 1909 Trades Board Act, which set up boards of government officials to supervise work conditions in heavy industry; the 1909 Old-Age Pensions Act; and the 1911 National Insurance Act, which provided health and unemployment insurance for the first time.[17]

The new, innovative welfare system was coupled with an aggressive tax system to finance it. This culminated in the Budget Bill of 1909, the famous "People's Budget," which Lloyd George declared was a "war budget" in a battle against "poverty and squalidness." It included proposals for a "super tax" on high incomes, a land tax aimed at wealthy landowners, a graduated income tax, and an inheritance tax primarily shouldered by the rich. The Liberal government's recasting of the role of the state had multiple, overlapping aims: to win working-class voters, to assure the support of the still-nascent Labour Representative Committee, to co-opt public reform campaigns, and to resolve genuine governance problems. Whatever the motivation, standard political science theories of two-party systems would predict that, given the leftward shift of Asquith's "new" Liberalism, the center-right conservative party would move to the center. But, it did not; it moved to the right. Why did this happen? To understand the crisis of 1906–1914, we must understand the conservative response to this new challenge.

Rather than pursuing conciliation, Conservative Party leaders adopted a combative, hard-edged and distinctly right-wing profile because the party fell into the grips of its activist base. Not just a revolt of the "radical right," as Alan Sykes calls it, the nature of the shift was even more

---

[14] Peter Clarke, *A Question of Leadership: Gladstone to Thatcher* (London: Penguin, 1992), 67.
[15] Ann Orloff and Theda Skocpol, "Why Not Equal Protection? Explaining the Politics of Public Social Spending in Britain, 1900–1911 and the United States, 1880s–1920," *American Sociological Review* 49, no. 6 (1984): 735.
[16] Peter Flora and Arnold Heidenheimer, eds., *The Development of Welfare States in Europe and America* (New Brunswick: Transaction Publishers, 1984).
[17] See Orloff and Skocpol, "Why Not Equal Protection?" (1984).

subversive.[18] Beginning slowly after 1906, "His Majesty's Loyal Opposition" – the Unionist Party – took on behavioral and rhetorical traits that arguably matched what Juan Linz identifies as precursors to democratic breakdown: opposition "semiloyalty" and "disloyalty" to basic democratic or constitutional procedures.[19] Unionist leadership appeared increasingly willing to tolerate, and even actively participate in, outright defiance of accepted constitutional rules. This characterization is perhaps surprising, but consider Linz's "litmus test" for determining whether political actors react "disloyally" to democratic "rules of the game":

- Ambiguities in public statements about the need to use force to gain power;
- Expressions of interest and willingness to seek out armed forces support (i.e., "knocking on the barracks door");
- Public statements that deny the legitimacy of political party leaders to rule, despite election success;
- Descriptions of opposition as "instruments" of secret, foreign, and conspiratorial forces;
- Willingness to encourage, tolerate, excuse, or justify the actions of political participants that go beyond limits of peaceful patterns of politics in a democracy;
- Readiness to curtail civil liberties of leaders and supporters of the opposition.[20]

After 1906, but especially from 1911 to 1914, the Conservative Party remarkably adopted all but the last of these tactics while seeking to force an election. In one historian's account of the period, the British Conservative Party appeared "prepared to defy the laws and legislature of the land to resort to extra-parliamentary and non-constitutional means, to preach violence and to practice it if needs be, and even to support rebellion and risk civil war, in an attempt to recover their position."[21]

How did it come to this? Reconstructing the process by which the Unionist leadership radicalized reveals clues about the triggers of the crisis, the depth of its severity, and how it was overcome. We recognize immediately the proximate causes – an old elite confronted by the onslaught of democratic mobilization without apparent capacity to compete electorally, thus conspiratorially plotting and seeking undemocratic shelter.[22] But is the case as clear as it first appears? And was British democracy truly threatened?

---

[18] Alan Sykes, "The Radical Right and the Crisis of Conservatism before the First World War," *Historical Journal* 26, no. 3 (1983): 661–76.

[19] Linz and Stepan, *Breakdown of Democratic Regimes* (1978), 27.

[20] Linz and Stepan, *Breakdown of Democratic Regimes* (1978), 27–34.

[21] Cannadine, *Decline and Fall of the British Aristocracy* (1999), 517.

[22] On this logic in general, see Loxton, "Authoritarian Inheritance and Conservative Party-Builiding in Latin America" (2014), 9–10.

There were two distinct stages to the evolution of Britain Unionism in this period. In the first (1906–1910), constitutional rules remained intact, but were made more pliable as the outlines of the crisis emerged. Three main issues were at stake: the ambitious social policy programs of the Liberal government, the Budget Bill of 1909, and the proposed Parliament Act, which would eventually remove the House of Lords' unrestricted ability to veto elected government's legislation. The Parliament Act was especially threatening because the House of Lords, dominated by Unionist peers, was the last safeguard of influence.[23] The Unionist Party was also still weakened by the Tariff Reform League's insurgent and acrimonious campaign to "capture" it.[24] Between 1903 and 1907, the party continued to deteriorate as free-traders abandoned its ranks and press reports probed what *The Economist* then called the "causes of party weakness."[25]

In this first stage, a "Tory rebellion" was brewing.[26] Party infighting and the disastrous 1906 election caused power to shift momentarily to the conservative-minded Unionist Peers in the House of Lords who collaborated with Unionist leaders in the House of Commons. The Lords' leader, Lord Lansdowne, assured the House of Lords played the role, in Lloyd George's memorable phrase, of "Balfour's poodle" by killing Liberal bills as they appeared before the body. The most diehard landed elites who themselves were unelected could afford to baldly protect their sectoral interests without considering the electoral consequences. To be sure, many Liberal bills and core features of the government's program proceeded through the House of Lords untouched. But, normal constitutional protocol was subverted as Unionist loyalists in the Lords sought new protections: an unprecedented number of items – the Education Bill and the Plural Voting Bill in 1906, the Licensing Bill in 1908, and so on – were blocked, and others such as Irish Home Rule were not even proposed since they faced inevitable veto from the outset.[27] Roy Jenkins notes that the period was marked by the "slaughter of Liberal bills on a scale from which their more robust predecessors, the Duke of Wellington or Sir Robert Peel, would have recoiled in horror."[28] For the reeling Unionists, party

---

[23] The usual estimate for the number of self-identified Liberal peers in the House of Lords in 1906 are 88 out of 602 members (i.e., 15 percent). The origin of the imbalance in Tory favor goes back to at least William Pitt the Younger (1759–1806) whose use of patronage expanded the House of Lords by 40 percent. While the gap diminished over the nineteenth century, it expanded again in the 1880s when 100 Liberal Unionists joined Conservative ranks. See, Norton, "Resisting the Inevitable? The Parliament Act of 1911" (2012).

[24] Ball, *The Conservative Party and British Politics* (2013), 43.

[25] "Causes of Party Weakness" *The Economist* November 26, 1904: 1887.

[26] Dangerfield, *Strange Death of Liberal England* (1997), 72.

[27] To be sure, the Liberal majority passed some ambitious reforms including the 1906 Trade Disputes Law (which gave unions exemption from lawsuits) as well as the Workmen's Compensation Act and the Eight Hours Act. For an analysis of the strategic restraint of Unionists on these issues, see Jenkins, *Asquith* (1966), 170–71.

[28] Jenkins, *Asquith* (1966), 169.

weakness meant that class interests was ascendant in the unelected House of Lords without the moderating influence of electoral accountability, easily trumping conciliatory party politics.

The 1909 Budget Bill represents a revealing test case.[29] By convention, the House of Lords held no ability to block the House of Commons' budget bills. The House of Commons' supremacy over finance had gone unchallenged since the English Civil War of 1640–1649, which was fought over precisely this issue.[30] But the bill's inclusion of a land tax as well as a "super tax" on the wealthy – even if modest by today's standards – was seen as a genuine threat by landed elites. The Lords, remarkably, were willing to defy constitutional custom to vote 350 to 75 against the bill. To explain this deviation from normal practice, it is insufficient to highlight the importance of landed wealth in the House of Lords; this constituency had always dominated that institution. Instead, one must factor in the momentary *organizational weakness* of the Conservative Party leadership and the self-perceived "crisis of conservatism" that allowed the Lords' extreme preferences to take on added weight. With the Unionists unable to re-obtain power in the House of Commons anytime soon, the *unelected* House of Lords rose in importance. While Karl Marx famously once argued that the repeal of the Corn Laws in 1846 decisively eclipsed the power of landed wealth in Britain, this group puzzlingly appeared momentarily to gain a new lease on life in the first decades of the twentieth century.[31]

The critical point is this: facing a perceived redistributionist onslaught, challenges to traditional conceptions of Empire, and the unexpected *weakness* of their party, the unelected House of Lords became a bulwark of renewed importance in the political system for groups that had appeared to have waning influence. After Labour's birth, the old rules seemed no longer to apply, and a core feature of Britain's constitutional system – the conventional House of Commons monopoly on the budget – fell to the side.[32] Most strikingly, electoral weakness of the Unionist alliance made the extraordinary veto appear necessary, which ultimately threatened the stability of Britain's democratic evolution.

---

[29] That the Budget Bill became the "real" showdown was not entirely an accident; as McLean rightly notes, Lloyd George intentionally chose this issue, as a particularly mobilizing one, to push a constitutional reform onto the House of Lords. McLean, *Rational Choice and British Politics* 156–57.

[30] McLean, *What's Wrong with the British Constitution?* (2012), 97.

[31] On the idea that landed classes had been eclipsed, see Karl Marx, "The elections in England–Tories and Whigs (New York Daily Tribune)," in *Karl Marx and Friedrich Engels on Britain* (Moscow: Foreign Languages Publishing House, [1852] 1962), 351–57. For a more recent version of the argument, see Moore, *Social Origins of Dictatorship and Democracy* (1966).

[32] Indeed, there was no precedent for the House of Lords blocking budget bills, though Unionist-minded jurists tried to make the argument that the House of Lords was simply protecting the constitution given the nature of the coalition government, the nature of the bill (that included a land valuation procedure), and the Liberal Party's slim majority.

THE REVENGE OF THE BASE: PARTY ACTIVISTS AND THE UNIONIST
ALLIANCE, 1911–1914

If the Conservative Party's implosion had removed one protective buffer for old-regime interests, then the passage of the 1911 Parliament Act – abolishing the future use of the House of Lords veto – eliminated a second safeguard, making the situation even more dire. Control of the political system appeared to be slipping away, and the next few years witnessed even more vitriol, as the far right publicly sought to remake long-standing constitutional rules. For example, the party leadership, now under Andrew Bonar Law, expressed willingness to abandon two touchstones of English constitutional doctrine: civilian control of the military and the merely ornamental character of the British crown. Also, Unionist party leaders employed a provocative rhetoric of violence that justified the use of force in domestic politics and even tacitly supported military insubordination.

What caused this shift? While the period was marked by the progressive and relatively modest redistributionist goals of the Liberal-Irish government, the second period pivoted around the "nationalist" themes of Ireland and Home Rule. As a strategy of electoral mobilization, the rhetoric of defending Great Britain's territorial integrity empowered extreme party activists at the grassroots, especially in Ulster, to strike back at the Unionist leadership. This political approach, dubbed a "doctrine of disorder" by *The Economist*, was prompted by pressure to grant Ireland greater autonomy. *The Economist*, a normally sober-minded publication, critiqued the Unionist party leadership in 1912 with this scathing observation:

[We] cannot escape from the one outstanding and extraordinary fact—that the leader of the Conservative party has definitely and repeatedly encouraged the outbreak of civil war.[33]

Broadly speaking, the drive to extra-constitutional and even anti-constitutional posturing was instigated by two factors: (1) Conservative Party electoral insecurity and (2) pressure from outside groups. The House of Lords veto of the Budget Bill in November 1909 had prompted a general election in 1910 in which Conservatives recovered but not enough to dislodge the Liberal government.[34] The Parliament Act, which transformed the constitution by restricting future efforts to block House of Commons legislation, passed the Commons for the first time in the summer of 1910. It then passed the House of Lords after King George V reluctantly promised to swamp the Lords with new peers once the general election of December 1910 had endorsed the Liberal

---

[33] "Doctrine of Disorder," *The Economist*, August 17, 1912: 310.
[34] The January 1910 elections returned 274 Liberals to parliament, 272 Unionists, and 71 MPs from the Irish Party. See Craig, *Electoral Facts* (1976), 32

Party.[35] While Liberals regarded the Parliament Act as a major democratic achievement, the self-described "no-surrender" faction of intransigent "diehards" in the House of Lords saw it differently.[36] They believed it was a revolutionary emasculation of what Walter Bagehot called the "dignified parts" of the constitution.[37] Not only was the Liberal "revolution" illegitimate, the Conservative Party's leadership's willingness to concede revealed them to be heading a "Judas" party or "Court Party" of treasonous "Mandarins."[38] With this last constitutional weapon in their arsenal removed, and following Balfour's forcible ejection from the leadership, conservative self-defense took more extreme measures.

The subsequent three years left the Liberal Party leadership and the Unionist Party extremists playing a dangerous game of "chicken." On the one hand, the Liberal Party's own electoral triumph of 1906 sagged in the two 1910 elections, leaving it equally strong as the Unionists but politically dependent on its Irish Party coalition partner. The price to be paid for Irish Party support was the promise to pass home rule for *all* of Ireland, a deal that hardened the Liberal position and that Unionists saw as a "corrupt bargain."

On the other hand, Balfour's successor, Andrew Bonar Law, despite intense sympathy for predominately Protestant northern counties of Ireland (his father was born in Ulster), found himself crushed between conflicting imperatives. Law agreed with the ruthless advice of Lord Milner who wrote, "To my mind there is only one road to salvation for Unionists now, and it is to shout 'Ulster, Ulster' all the time... no running after Lloyd George, no mention of Tariff reform."[39] After all, in the 1880s and 1890s, anti–Home Rule mobilization had in Rikerian fashion destroyed Liberalism, and as McLean argues, realigned electoral competition to make economic and cross-class issues (i.e., Empire and religion) structuring features of British party politics.[40] After Asquith's apparent stumble into the morass again after 1910, the Unionist leadership spotted an opportunity. Reflecting on the possibility of compromise, Law admitted to one colleague, "From a party point of view, there is the disadvantage that [with] Home Rule moved out of the way, our chance of winning an election is very probably diminished."[41] As in the past, the ferocity of Unionist resistance – now under Edward Carson's leadership – to

---

[35] In the December 1910 General Elections, Asquith's Liberals won 272 seats and the Unionists 271. The Liberals governed with the aid of the Irish Party's 74 seats. Labour won 42 seats. See Craig, *Electoral Facts* (1976), 32

[36] Gregory Phillips, "Lord Willoughby de Broke and the Politics of Radical Toryism, 1909–1914," *Journal of British Studies* 20, no. 1 (1980): 205–24. 215.

[37] Walter Bagehot, *The English Constitution* (London: Chapman and Hall, 1867), 118.

[38] Phillips, "Lord Willoughby de Broke" (1980): 212.

[39] R. J. Q. Adams, *Bonar Law* (Stanford: Stanford University Press, 1999), 116–17.

[40] McLean, *Rational Choice and British Politics* (2001), 96–97.

[41] Cited in Jeremy Smith, "Bluff, Bluster and Brinkmanship: Andrew Bonar Law and the third Home Rule Bill," *Historical Journal* 36, no. 1 (1993):163.

Home Rule provided useful mobilizing material for Conservatism. One account asserts "the Conservative Party backed Carson with giddy relish."[42]

But, this time around things were different. Unlike in the 1880s or even the 1890s, Protestant Ulster resistance – distrustful of Conservative Party leadership commitment – had begun to self-organize. In 1905, William Moore, MP, founded the Ulster Union Council (UUC), a permanent umbrella organization for the constituency associations of the Ulster Unionist Party and local MPs. With Carson at the head, its purpose was to aggressively influence debate in Westminster. English and Ulster Unionists mobilized mass participation in the form of the solemn and symbolic "Ulster Day" on September 28, 1912, when a covenant was presented to and signed by hundreds of thousands of normal citizens. With financial encouragement from some well-known right-wing Tories, Ulster Unionists began to organize themselves in paramilitary groups, which fused together in 1913 into the Ulster Volunteer Force (UVF). In short, under the leadership of Carson, recalcitrance to Home Rule provided Unionists with a promising mobilizing issue that put dangerous pressure on Law. The *Irish Times* reported a story of a "prominent Tory [election] agent" who, upon attending a meeting of the UUC, found that if he did not advocate armed rebellion, he would be regarded as a "traitor."[43]

Thus, Law walked a tightrope: On the one hand, a "small but formidable" group of Unionist backbenchers and peers – supported by mobilized Ulster party activists – restrained his ability to give away any of Ireland.[44] On the other hand, in order to win the general election with a broader electorate, he had to tame his supporters' intensity and give the *appearance* of being willing to negotiate with Asquith.[45] "The marriage of convenience" between British Conservatives and their Ulster Unionist allies had been beneficial electorally, but Carson's increased willingness to threaten violence pushed Law to extremes that made compromise difficult.[46]

How did Law land himself in this difficult dilemma? A leading historian of the Home Rule Crisis writes that the Unionist leadership was "in the talons of

---

[42] Jack Beatty, *The Lost History of 1914: Reconsidering the Year the Great War Began* (New York: Bloomsbury Publishing, 2012), 97.

[43] Thomas Kennedy, "Troubled Tories: Dissent and Confusion concerning the Party's Ulster Policy, 1910–1914," *Journal of British Studies* 46, no. 3 (2007b): 580.

[44] To be sure, there were tensions between opponents of Home Rule for all of Ireland (e.g., southern Protestants such as Lord Lansdowne) and narrower advocates of Ulster exclusion. It was hard to argue, Carson even admitted, for ongoing resistance to Home Rule writ large if the Liberals granted an exclusion to Ulster. "It is hard to see" Carson said, "if separate treatment was given to Ulster, how I could be justified in asking men to go on preparing for resistance when their only object could be to obtain what they had been offered to them." Cited in Alvin Jackson, *Home Rule: An Irish History, 1800–2000* (Oxford: Oxford University Press, 2003a), 125.

[45] On the latter point and for evidence that Law thought in these terms, see Jackson, *Home Rule: An Irish History, 1800–2000* (2003a), 112.

[46] The term "marriage of convenience" is from Kennedy, "Troubled Tories" (2007b): 572.

the hawks" and had become "prisoners of their own logic, penned in by their own indecision over violence and their own supporters' desire for a more assertive command."[47] In 1912, *The Economist* agreed with this diagnosis:

Mr. Law is more orator than statesman, and... his speeches control his policy instead of his policy controlling his speeches.... [He] is constantly tempted by the prospect of "loud Opposition cheers" to go beyond his purpose and play to the most violent, *because they are the most noisy members of his party.*[48]

The repeated inability of the Unionist Party to gain power via the ballot box left the Conservative Party leadership lacking in the short-run "victory confidence" and desperate to use any institutional lever to regain power. In 1912, Law provocatively announced his willingness to embrace "whatever means seem to us most effective" to block the elected majority.[49] But, the advent of unruly right-wing pressure groups in Ulster and across England in his own camp left him feeling deeply insecure about this leadership *within* the party. After all, his own allies now had the power to oust non–tariff supporting MPs and to challenge party candidates, including his predecessor, former party leader Arthur Balfour.

This organized pressure became more consequential for the party's stance vis-à-vis constitutional issues as the UVF began recruiting tens of thousands of men in Ulster in January 1913.[50] Law was happy to join Carson on stage at "monster demonstrations" in Belfast after 1912, for example. But by clasping Carson's hand and trying to match his rhetoric, Law aligned himself with uncomfortably extreme positions. The result was, in political scientist Ian Lustick's assessment, a "regime-threatening alliance" of British Tories and Ulster Rebels that represented a "vehement challenge to parliamentary authority."[51]

This was visible in the rise of two major right-wing groups, the Union Defense League (UDL) and its competitor, the British League for the Support of Ulster and the Union, which pushed the crisis to an ominous apex.[52] These two groups spread propaganda, raised funds for Ulster militias, and applied pressure on more moderate British Unionist MPs. The former was launched in 1907 by Walter Long, a Unionist politician from an old Wiltshire gentry family and Law's chief competitor for the party chairmanship in 1911. The latter was founded by Lord Willoughby de Broke, a notoriously incendiary right-wing Tory peer of one of the most ancient baronies in England. De Broke, frustrated

---

[47] Alvin Jackson, "The Larne Gun Running of 1914," *History of Ireland* 1, no. 1 (1993). 37.

[48] *The Economist*, August 17, 1912: 310.

[49] Quoted by Robert Blake, *Unrepentant Tory: The Life and Times of Andrew Bonar Law, 1858–1923* (New York: St. Martins Press, 1956), 130.

[50] Kennedy, "Troubled Tories" (2007b): 582.

[51] Ian Lustick, *Unsettled States, Disputed Lands: Britain and Ireland, France and Algeria, Israel and the West Bank-Gaza* (Ithaca: Cornell University Press, 1993), 200.

[52] Also important were two other groups that exerted leverage on party leaders, the socially imperialist Reveille Group founded in 1910 and the diehard Halsbury Club founded in 1911.

by his own party's conciliatory stances to Liberals over the Parliament Act in 1911 and Home Rule after that, forged a group that secured the support of 100 Unionist peers and 124 members of the House of Commons.[53] With the hypermobilized "grassroots" of the party pushing for ever-greater resistance, Law sought to compel the Liberal Party to subject itself to another election. But, the compromise necessary to avoid constitutional crisis appeared to be drifting out of reach.

Whatever Law's intention, he was deeply constrained in his capacity to reshape his party's profile vis-à-vis the median voter in the British electorate. In particular, the balance of organized power within the party clearly weighed heavily on his mind as he scrambled to maintain his own position as party leader. First, he knew that the "revolt of the right" helped orchestrate the ejection of the conciliatory Arthur Balfour from his position as party leader in 1911. Supported by de Broke, the right wing conducted a successful press assault dubbed the "B. M. G." ("Balfour Must Go") campaign, and Law was keenly mindful of the implied threat this posed to his own leadership. Second, the activist groups pushed an eclectic and sometimes incoherent set of issues, including demands for more military spending, a preference for tariff revenue rather than direct taxation, criticisms of parliamentary rule in principle, and greater intransigence on Home Rule. And, finally, the pressure reduced Law's maneuverability on the Irish question. Such groups wielded influence to a degree unrivaled in British history and entirely out of proportion when considering the British electorate as a whole.

SPIRALING TOWARD CRISIS? THE CRISIS OF CONSERVATISM
AND THE THREAT OF DEMOCRATIC BREAKDOWN

In the view of most historians, the threat of regime-upending violence increased after 1913, primarily because of constraints put on Law by his own party's radical allies. As his biographer writes, "If Bonar Law meant to put compromise on the table, he would have to convince these men [de Broke, Curzon, Long] first."[54] Likewise, historian Richard Murphy writes that Law "knew that he could accept no compromise without taking on the formidable section of the party on whose support [Walter] Long could rely – a particularly unattractive prospect in view of the fact that Long had been a principal contender for the party leadership in November 1911."[55] In short, even the well-institutionalized British Conservative Party, when squeezed between an internal crisis on the one hand and Liberal challenges on the other, was vulnerable to the threat of organizational breakup from an activated and insurgent right wing.

---

[53] Phillips, "Lord Willoughby de Broke" (1980): 219.   [54] Adams, *Bonar Law* (1999), 128.
[55] Richard Murphy, "Faction in the Conservative Party and the Home Rule Crisis, 1912–1914," *History* 71 (1986): 225.

The resulting push against "normal" constitutional politics can be seen at three levels. First, in terms of rhetoric, Law, along with members of the House of Lords, increasingly used violent language and expressed a tolerance for the idea of using violence to gain power. In 1913, de Broke, who had spent the past year helping arm the UVF should Home Rule come to pass, justified his actions by writing, "If [a] settlement is denied to us, then we must fall back on the only other means at our disposal." De Broke also announced that he had "instituted a league," with a street address that was "curiously enough next door to a gunmaker's shop."[56] The warning could not have been clearer.

Similarly, the week the Home Rule Bill was introduced in the House of Commons in April 1912, Law traveled to Ulster where in front of 100,000 Ulstermen and on a stage adorned by a massive Union Jack flag, he told his audience "You are a besieged city... The Government by their Parliament Act have erected a boom against you, a boom to cut you off from the help of the British people. You will burst that boom."[57] His rhetoric intensified later that summer at Blenheim Palace where he infamously declared,

In our opposition to [the Liberal Party and Home Rule] we shall not be guided by considerations, we shall not be restrained by the bonds which would influence us in ordinary political struggle. We shall use *any means* to deprive them of the power which they have usurped and compel them to face the people they have deceived.[58]

And then, in the most frequently quoted statement of his political career, Law said,

I repeat now with a full sense of the responsibility which attaches to my position, that, in my opinion, if such an attempt [to include Ulster within the scope of Home Rule] is made, *I can imagine no length of resistance to which Ulster can go in which I should not be prepared to support them*, and in which, in my belief, they would not be supported by the overwhelming majority of the British people.[59]

Law's extreme statements have understandably preoccupied historians, as British constitutional politics genuinely seemed at risk. But, how seriously should we take this rhetoric? We might ask, in the words of one historian, was this not merely "the legitimate bombast of a disgruntled opposition"?[60] Others have dismissed the importance of his threats, noting that "grand set-piece speeches such as those at Blenheim Palace... [merely] gave Bonar Law an opportunity to speak tough and raise party morale."[61] In short, Law was perhaps just play-acting. While still criticizing Law, in August 1912, *The Economist* confidently downplayed the significance of his rhetoric:

Few English Unionists, if any, believe that Ulster really will revolt, that Sir Edward Carson is the destined president of a new republic, or that Lord Willoughby de Broke has

---

[56] Phillips, "Lord Willoughby de Broke" (1980): 219.   [57] Adams, *Bonar Law* (1999), 103.
[58] Adams, *Bonar Law* (1999), 109.   [59] Ibid.
[60] Dangerfield, *Strange Death of Liberal England* (1997), 96.
[61] Smith, "Bluff, Bluster and Brinkmanship" (1993): 176.

at last found a ditch in which to die with glory and distinction. Whatever may happen next month or next year, we in England certainly do not believe that there is going to be a civil war, and at present the discussion of a possible outbreak is carried on mainly by party men anxious to score a point through the folly of the other side.[62]

In short, what was the actual risk of civil war and regime breakdown? We may examine that "barometer of public agitation," the sovereign bond market, to see how yield rates on British sovereign bonds responded to the potential unsettling events. While the task is complicated in this instance by the near-simultaneous arrival of continental war in 1914, we can nonetheless map how bond market responded to the most significant Ulster-related events between 1910 and 1914. These include (1) the first mass Ulster Rally of September 11, 1911; (2) Law's Blenheim speech on July 27, 1912; (3) the Ulster Covenant Rally on September 28, 1912; (4) the Curragh Mutiny of March 19–24, 1914, when fifty-seven British officers based in Ireland resigned rather than enforce Home Rule; (5) the Larne Gun-Running Incident of April 24–25, 1914, in which Irish nationalists received weapons from abroad; and (6) the final passage of the Home Rule Bill in the House of Commons on May 29, 1914.

Weekly fluctuations in the price of British consols in this period likely reflected macroeconomic factors as well as political events.[63] But many of the most significant Ulster events were in fact correlated with significant yield decreases (i.e., price increases), suggesting that the risk of disorder was taken seriously.[64] For example, the first Ulster Rally, Law's well-known Blenheim speech, and the Ulster Covenant Rally (events 1, 2, and 3) all are correlated with significant yield shocks. But, revealingly, until 1914, the financial press itself did not discuss any of the Ulster events when assessing the factors driving bond yields, instead emphasizing traditional factors such as the money supply and the size of the British public debt. Thus, while the statistical evidence supports the

---

[62] *The Economist*, August 17, 1912: 310.

[63] This point is made clear by a careful reading of the financial press at the time, which attributed shifts in British consols to macroeconomic factors – money supply and the size of British public debt – as well as political events, including the events connected to Ulster. My analysis is based on a reading of "The Stock Markets" column in *The Economist*, 1910–1914; as well as the financial pages of *The Times* (1910–1914).

[64] This conclusion is supported by an OLS regression of yields on dummy variables that 'switch on' following the event. This allows for an assessment of how the mean of the yield series is changing after each event. A brief summary of results of the first three events in Figure 5.1 is given below. We discuss the next three events noted in Figure 5.1 in the paragraphs that follow:

	Coefficient	Std. Error	t value	Pr(>|t|)
(Intercept)	3.119714	0.008237	378.741	< 2e-16 ***
event1	0.098525	0.010930	9.014	2.99e-16 ***
event2	0.123316	0.017762	6.943	6.83e-11 ***
event3	0.035146	0.017167	2.047	0.042089 *

idea that worried investors had real concerns about Law's rhetoric and the state of affairs in Ulster, it is difficult to disentangle the effect of political events from broader macroeconomic factors in the years 1911–1913.

However, by 1914 it is much clearer that the rhetoric carried political and economic weight. Large price changes in consols that correlated with Ulster events were now also accompanied by articles in the financial press, which reported that investors' decisions were affected by political uncertainty. On February 14, 1914, *The Economist*'s "Stock Markets" column reported that

[the] factor most talked of this week as being a cause of dullness in the Consol market was the Ulster question. The bears profess to see in the Volunteer movement a real menace to the security of peace.[65]

The next month, the same column still had "Ulster" on its mind but was nonetheless more optimistic, reporting that "the stock exchange sent prices up with a swing on the strength of the Prime Minister's offer regarding Ulster."[66] But only seven days later, on March 21, the column was again anxious and conceded that "the promising strength evident in last Saturday's markets was not maintained when it became apparent that the Ulster question is by no means settled. Consols went back…"[67] Similarly, on March 20, *The Times* financial page reported, "The stock markets were very depressed yesterday morning, the Ulster question, the development of which was regarded as having reached a dangerous stage, occupying the principal attention of members."[68]

Events in Ulster now appeared to be driving weekly shifts in yields. This persisted into July 1914, when Nathan Rothschild, senior partner of the bank N M Rothschild and often described as the elder statesman of the "City," wrote to his cousin on the mood of the British markets: "The chief anxiety here is always Ulster."[69] Continental war appeared far from his mind. This Ulster anxiety came to a head over the weekend of March 18–21, 1914, in the infamous "Curragh Incident" or "Curragh Mutiny," as it is sometimes called.[70] Rumors circulated that the Ulster militias were planning raids on British weapons depots with the aim of acquiring weapons and blocking any efforts to enforce Irish Home Rule "by force."[71] Facing this prospect, the War Office ordered its Ireland-based

---

[65] "The Stock Exchange Position," *The Economist*, February 14, 1914: 340.
[66] "The Position in Stock Exchange Markets," *The Economist*, March 14, 1914: 651.
[67] "The Stock Markets," *The Economist*, March 21, 1914: 728.
[68] "Markets and Ulster," *The Times*, March 20, 1914: 21.
[69] Correspondence cited by Richard Roberts, *Saving the City: The Great Financial Crisis of 1914* (Oxford: Oxford University Press, 2014), 7.
[70] A vast literature exists. See for a representative sample, A. T. Q. Stewart, *The Ulster Crisis* (London: Faber and Faber, 1967); Adams, *Bonar Law* (1999), 153–60; McLean, *What's Wrong with the British Constitution?* (2012), 100–27; Paul O'Brien, *A Question of Duty: The Curragh Incident 1914* (Dublin: New Island, 2014).
[71] Winston Churchill's famously bombastic rhetoric and plans – including troop movements – have attracted attention; see Dangerfield, *Strange Death of Liberal England* (1997), 341.

troops – many of whom were based at the Curragh Camp, fifty kilometers southwest of Dublin – to safeguard the weapons. However, relations between the military hierarchy – especially Major General Henry Wilson, Director of Military Operations at the War Office – and the Unionist Party were especially close, a problem that would undermine the Liberal government's position.[72] Thus, at the urging of Unionist sympathizers inside the London War Office, many of whom had close relationships with Law and other opposition politicians, fifty-seven out of seventy mid-ranking British officers in Ireland resigned rather than implement the Liberal government's decision. This triggered a constitutional crisis of the first order; rather than implementing a decision of the elected government, the military hierarchy effectively *subverted an elected government's decision*, aiming to force a change in the policy itself.

As the news of the mass resignations spread, the Prime Minister Henry Asquith and his Secretary of War, J. E. B. Seely, quickly scrambled, abandoning their initial plan and called the Irish commander to London to "clarify" the situation. In the minds of its critics, the military had set policy in an outright act of insubordination. *The Daily Chronicle* reported, for example,

For the first time in modern English history a military cabal seeks to dictate to government the bills it should carry or not carry into law... We are confronted with a desperate rally of reactionaries to defeat the democratic movement and repeal the Parliament Act. This move by a few aristocratic officers is the last throw in the game.[73]

Lloyd George asserted, "We are confronted with the greatest issue raised in this country since the days of the Stuarts... We are not fighting about Ulster. We are not fighting about Home Rule. We are fighting for all that is essential to civil liberty in this land."[74] And Churchill put forth his camp's perspective most clearly: "The Army have done what the Opposition failed to do."[75]

Yet, the bond markets reacted curiously. While events of the pre-1914 period *raised* the risk of default in the minds of investors, the Curragh Mutiny, as Figure 5.1 shows, had the opposite effect: It was preceded by a rise in yields, followed the next week and thereafter by a significant drop in yields.[76] In short, *the "mutiny" lowered*

---

[72] Adams, *Bonar Law* (1999), 157.   [73] Quoted in Beatty, *Lost History of 1914* (2012), 120.

[74] Lloyd George, as cited in *Illustrated London News*, vol. 54, March 28, 1914: 511.

[75] Quoted in Beatty, *Lost History of 1914* (2012), 120.

[76] This is evident in another OLS regression of the last three events in Figure 5.1. The negative sign of the coefficient for event 4 (the Curragh Incident) indicates that not only was it the only statistically significant event but it was the only one to lead to a drop in yields. Results summarized below:

	Coefficients	Std Error	t value	Pr(>|t|)
(Intercept)	3.119714	0.008237	378.741	< 2e-16 ***
event4	−0.087301	0.022490	−3.882	0.000146 ***
event5	0.038350	0.032690	1.173	0.242296
event6	0.007550	0.028830	0.262	0.793713

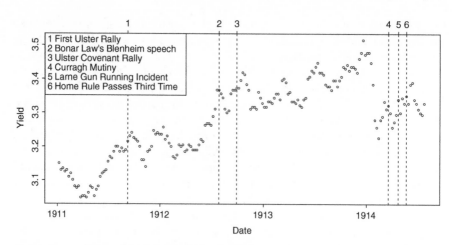

FIGURE 5.1: 3 Percent Consol Yield Rates and Ulster Political Crisis Events, 1911–1914
Data Source: The yield rates report weekly closing rates. The data are available from the
Global Financial Database (www.globalfinancialdata.com/Databases/UKDatabase.html),
which is a product of collection efforts of Neal 1993

the perceived risk of conflict and default. How do we explain this? Again, the
financial press is revealing. On March 23 – the Monday following the weekend of
the crisis – *The Times* "Stock Exchange" column reported the following:

When stock markets opened on Saturday, there appeared to be a consensus of opinion
that the morning's news regarding the home political situation indicated a slight
improvement... [T]he reports as to the attitudes of the Army officers were taken as an
additional reason why the Government would be bound to modify its policy in the
direction of a settlement on terms acceptable to Ulster.[77]

Likewise, *The Economist* "stock markets" column made a similar point a few
days later:

The stock exchange has been fully occupied in discussing Ulster... The week has been
a fairly good one with a sharp rise in the early half... As happened last week, the
Saturday market was cheerful after several days of depression and rumors of
insubordination in the Army were regarded as a bull point on the grounds that the
Government would have to give way to Ulster.[78]

A constitutional crisis appeared to be approaching but the markets supported
the defeat of the government's plans. Law's maneuvers to bring the Unionist
Party back from the electoral precipice were more than "mere" words affecting
financial markets. Even if the Unionist leaders *thought* they were engaged in
high-stakes "playacting," hoping to trigger a crisis to get back in power, this

[77] "Stock Exchange: Improved Tone," *The Times*, March 23, 1914: 19
[78] "The Stock Markets," *The Economist*, March 28, 1914: 787.

electoral strategy opened up constitutional crises that even bond markets recognized.

Diary entries from Liberal cabinet members also make clear that while the cabinet collectively ignored early provocations, by the end of 1912, they recognized the serious possibility that the imposition of Home Rule would face stiff military resistance.[79] But this was not the end of the crisis. In addition to the military veto, Law took specific and unusual steps to escalate the crisis often hidden beyond the view of bond markets that clearly constituted extra-constitutional strategies of conservative self-defense. In July 1913, he shocked King George by advising him to consider using the prerogative of the veto for the first time in centuries. Austen Chamberlain, who was present at the meeting, recalled Law's words to the monarch:

They may say that your assent is a purely formal act and the prerogative of the veto is dead. That was true as long as there was a buffer between you and the House of Commons, but they have destroyed that buffer and it is true no longer.[80]

In addition to prodding the king, Law pushed hard, finding some resistance within his own party, to alter a cornerstone of the British constitution unquestioned since the Glorious Revolution: namely, civil authority's supremacy to military authority. Since 1688, the Army Annual Act had been automatically passed each April to legalize the existence of the armed forces for the next year. Law informed at least two Unionist peers, Lord Selborne and Lord Milner, that he intended to propose an amendment to the Annual Army Act that would sabotage Liberal efforts to impose Home Rule using troops.[81] Law did not proceed once the Curragh incident occurred, abandoning his plans once it became clear that the Curragh officers had sparked a crisis.

THE RECOVERY OF CONSERVATISM AND THE ROAD TO DEMOCRATIC RESTABILIZATION, 1914–1922

By June 1914, the situation remained unresolved. *The Economist* summed up the mood of the period: "Ulster still weighs on the market, and though there seems to be a general belief that *some way out* will be found, the continued uncertainty is bad for business."[82] But, what was the way out? And what does it teach us about Britain's sources of stability as its political system was democratizing?

---

[79] Lustick, *Unsettled States, Disputed Lands: Britain and Ireland, France and Algeria, Israel and the West Bank-Gaza* (1993), 211.

[80] Adams, *Bonar Law* (1999), 107.

[81] This plan was abandoned with the onset of the Curragh incident. See Adams, *Bonar Law* (1999), 151.

[82] "The Stock Markets," *The Economist*, June 27, 1914: 1575.

Despite flirting with constitutional violations from 1910 to 1914, ultimately crisis was averted and constitutional stability would be restored. Some historical accounts have offered a historically particular, partially correct, but incomplete answer: The exogenous shock of the First World War arrived like a "bolt from the blue," quickly turning attention away from Ireland toward the continent.

At one level, this view is certainly correct. After repeated efforts in July 1914 to seal a deal for Ulster, Asquith and Law suspended their domestic battle once news from the continent grew dire. The two parliamentary combatants agreed on a compromised Home Rule – leaving out counties in Ulster – with a mollifying delay in implementation.[83] But two important questions remain: why did threat of war prompt compromise among former combatants? After all, political self-interest "rightly-understood" does not always triumph with the onset of war. Second, what happened to the armed opponents of Home Rule who had appeared on the verge of derailing Britain's constitutional order? In democratic politics, as we have frequently seen, losers rarely disappear for good; defeated parties usually regroup and plan a later comeback. While the war certainly put the conflict on hold, we must thus account for why the external shock of the First World War (a) altered the political game in a conciliatory direction, and (b) why this apparent toleration endured through the 1920s.

On the first question, it is critical to note that the initiative for the successful Home Rule truce ultimately came from Bonar Law. Asquith recollects the invitation from Bonar Law on July 30, 1914,

I was sitting in the Cabinet room with a map of Ulster, and a lot of statistics about populations & religions, and some choice extracts from Hansard (with occasional glances at this morning's letter from Penrhôs), endeavouring to get into something like shape my speech on the Amending Bill, when a telephone message came from (of all people in the world) Bonar Law, to ask me to come & see him & Carson at his Kensington abode – Pembroke Lodge. He had sent his motor, which I boarded, and in due time arrived at my destination: a rather suburban looking detached villa in a Bayswater street.[84]

Asquith continues,

I found the two gentlemen there, & B. Law proceeded to propose, in the interest of the international situation, that we should postpone for the time being the 2nd reading of the Amending Bill. He said that to advertise our domestic dissensions at this moment wd. weaken our influence in the world for peace.[85]

To explain this shift we must recognize that there was confidence *on both sides* that political compromise ultimately could be reached. The international situation did undo the deadlock but only because of a pre-existing stock of

---

[83] For a more nuanced view, see Jackson, *Home Rule: An Irish History, 1800–2000* (2003a), 143.
[84] As cited in Jenkins, *Asquith* (1966), 221.   [85] Ibid.

organizational capital and confidence. Asquith recounts Bonar Law warning him in 1912, on the eve of the "Irish imbroglio's" dominance of the political agenda, of the forthcoming gamesmanship that would accompany this issue:

> I remember the first time that [Bonar Law] and I walked side by side in the annual procession of the Commons to hear the King's speech in the House of Lords . . . he said to me on the way back: "I am afraid I shall have to show myself very vicious, Mr. Asquith this session. I hope you will understand." I had no hesitation in reassuring him on that point.[86]

Not only did Bonar Law regard the Irish question as a political game, but also, critically, Asquith himself *knew* he did. The distant constitutional settlement of 1688 was thus less immediately relevant as an explanation for the sidestepping of the 1914 crisis. Instead, much more important was that the political actors, especially Bonar Law, were in possession of political party structures not only invested in the political system but also that elevated political gamesmanship over the virtues of the "true-believer." Bonar Law sitting atop a political party with an accumulated stock of organizational capital viewed politics in a transactional manner that allowed for compromise, but, especially so when it became politically expedient.

Two key pieces of evidence expose the shifting political expediency of the Home Rule issue from 1910 to 1914: by-election results and the content of by-election campaigns themselves. While analysts often primarily focus on British general election results, historians have demonstrated that parliamentary by-elections are valuable "political barometers." In an age without opinion polls, by-elections – held on a rolling basis when politicians died, unexpectedly retired, or moved on to the House of Lords – revealed otherwise invisible shifts in public sentiments. Then known as a form of "political meteorology," observers closely watched by-elections in an attempt to predict political trends,[87] and dairies of leading Tory figures are filled with reflections on the significance of each result.[88] Party leaders adjusted their political strategies accordingly, even in the domain

[86] Herbert Henry Asquith, *Memories and Reflections: 1852–1927, Volume 1*, ed. Alexander Mackintosh (Boston: Little, Brown, and Company, 1928), 271.

[87] For example, see Matthew Roberts, "A Terrific Outburst of Political Metereology: By-elections and the Unionist Ascendancy in Late-Victorian England," in *By-Elections in British Politics, 1832–1914*, ed. Thomas G. Otte and Paul Readman (Woodbridge: Boydell Press, 2013), 177–200; Ian Packer, "Contested Ground: Trends in British By-elections, 1911–1914," *Contemporary British History* 25, no. 1 (2011): 157–73.

[88] See, especially Robert Sanders, *Real Old Tory Politics: The Political Diaries of Sir Robert Sanders, Lord Bayford, 1910–35*, ed. John Ramsden (London: The Historians' Press, 1984), 50; 72. Other notable diaries of leading Conservatives in this period include Philip Williamson, ed., *The Modernisation of Conservative Politics: The Diaries and Letters of William Bridgeman 1904–1935* (London: Historians Press, 1988); John Russell Vincent, ed., *The Crawford Papers: The Journals of David Lindsay, Twenty-Seventh Earl of Crawford and Tenth Earl of Balcarres (1871–1940), During the Years 1892 to 1940* (Manchester: Manchester University Press, 1984).

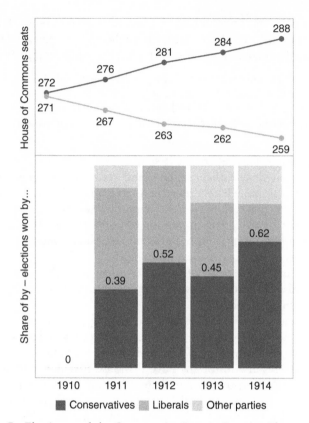

FIGURE 5.2: By-Elections and the Conservative Party's Growing Electoral Advantage, 1910–1914
Data Source: Craig 1987, 32; 47–48

of foreign policy,[89] while even an emerging political betting market of MPs and British investors adjusted its spread in response to them.[90]

Figure 5.2 tracks two indicators of a shifting parliamentary balance of power due to the unusually high number of by-elections (eighty-five) held between the general election of December 1910 and the outbreak of the First World War in August 1914. First, as Figure 5.2 makes clear, the Conservative Party held a growing share of total parliamentary seats due to the by-elections. Second, we see the increasing share of by-elections won by Conservatives annually between

[89] Thomas G. Otte, "The Swing of the Pendulum at Home: By-elections and Foreign Policy, 1865–1914," in *By-elections in British Politics, 1832–1914*, ed. Thomas G. Otte and Paul Readman (Woodbridge: Boydell Press, 2013), 121–50.

[90] Sanders, *Real Old Tory Politics: The Political Diaries of Sir Robert Sanders, Lord Bayford, 1910–35* (1984), 72–73.

1910 and August 1914. By the peak of 1914, not only did the Conservatives hold more seats than the Liberal Party in the House of Commons (though the Liberal Party was still in power, aided by the Irish Party), the Conservative Party was winning a growing share of by-elections each year, and could expect to win a majority in the next general election.

In a diary entry made on February 11, 1914, Sir Robert Sanders, Conservative MP from Somerset, reports on a dinner at which Bonar Law was "apprehensive that any announcement of concessions would put us in a bad position in the country."[91] Law also confided to Walter Long that a compromise "from a party point of view" would mean that "our best card will have been lost."[92] Thus, the political expediency of escalating the Home Rule issue is not to be underestimated and was self-evident to the Conservative party leadership even as far back as 1911. On July 18, 1911, Sanders reports in his diary on a conversation with Lord Hugh Cecil, the son of the former Prime Minister,

I had a talk with Hugh Cecil this morning. He loves the idea of a Constitutional row. He always did, even at Oxford... He is very anxious to get up a violent agitation in Ulster in the autumn and have a session of the northern counties worked out in every detail.[93]

In short, although Britain may have appeared on the verge of a genuine constitutional crisis, the Unionist leadership had largely manufactured the crisis for political gain within the existing political system. On the one hand, a moment of weakness in the Conservative Party (1906–1910) unleashed a chain of events that appeared to bring the country to the precipice of civil war. But a rapid recovery, and growing conservative electoral self-confidence *after* 1910, helped prevent a complete democratic breakdown; operating within the confines of the parliamentary system would bring them back to power.

Similarly revealing is that if we read the by-election campaign manifestos of the Conservative candidates in this period, critiques of the Liberal Home Rule agenda played a central role in many of them, demonstrating that Unionist MP candidates thought that Home Rule was a winning issue.[94] In Figure 5.3, we see examples of conservative campaign material that was very typical for this period. In this case, the Conservative Party candidate in a February 1911 by-election, Archibald Weigall, made Home Rule central to his campaign and distributed campaign flyers focused on the issue in the long-standing Tory Lincolnshire constituency of Horncastle.

Thus, electoral performance and the content of by-election campaigns suggest that electoral *self-confidence*, not simply "crisis," was the driver of

---

[91] Ibid.   [92] Adams, *Bonar Law* (1999), 139.
[93] Sanders, *Real Old Tory Politics: The Political Diaries of Sir Robert Sanders, Lord Bayford, 1910–35* (1984), 30.
[94] "British Political Party General Election Addresses, [1892–ca. 1970] from the National Liberal Club collection, Bristol University."

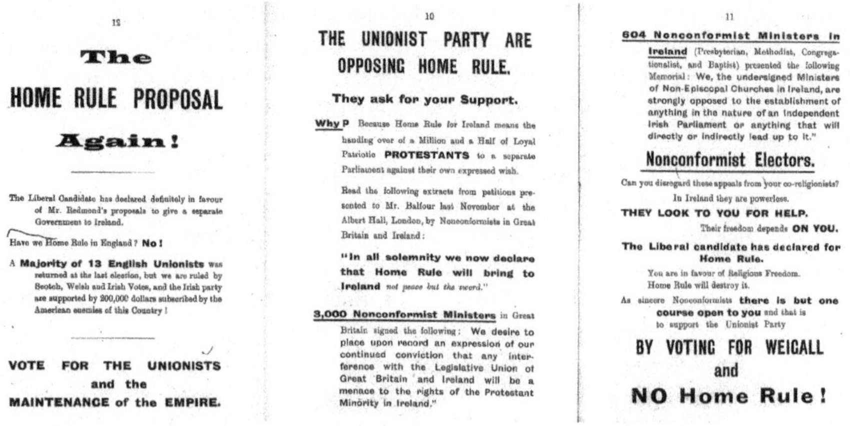
12

The

HOME RULE PROPOSAL

Again!

The Liberal Candidate has declared definitely in favour of Mr. Redmond's proposals to give a separate Government to Ireland.

Have we Home Rule in England? **No!**

A **Majority of 13 English Unionists** was returned at the last election, but we are ruled by Scotch, Welsh and Irish Votes, and the Irish party are supported by 200,000 dollars subscribed by the American enemies of this Country!

VOTE FOR THE UNIONISTS and the MAINTENANCE of the EMPIRE.

10

THE UNIONIST PARTY ARE OPPOSING HOME RULE.

They ask for your Support.

Why? Because Home Rule for Ireland means the handing over of a Million and a Half of Loyal Patriotic **PROTESTANTS** to a separate Parliament against their own expressed wish.

Read the following extracts from petitions presented to Mr. Balfour last November at the Albert Hall, London, by Nonconformists in Great Britain and Ireland:

"In all solemnity we now declare that Home Rule will bring to Ireland *not peace but the sword.*"

3,000 Nonconformist Ministers in Great Britain signed the following: **We desire to place upon record an expression of our continued conviction that any interference with the Legislative Union of Great Britain and Ireland will be a menace to the rights of the Protestant Minority in Ireland."**

11

604 Nonconformist Ministers in Ireland (Presbyterian, Methodist, Congregationalist, and Baptist) presented the following Memorial: **We, the undersigned Ministers of Non-Episcopal Churches in Ireland, are strongly opposed to the establishment of anything in the nature of an Independent Irish Parliament or anything that will directly or indirectly lead up to it."**

Nonconformist Electors.

Can you disregard these appeals from your co-religionists?

In Ireland they are powerless.

THEY LOOK TO YOU FOR HELP.

Their freedom depends **ON YOU.**

The Liberal candidate has declared for Home Rule.

You are in favour of Religious Freedom.
Home Rule will destroy it.

As sincere Nonconformists **there is but one course open to you** and that is to support the Unionist Party

BY VOTING FOR WEIGALL and NO Home Rule!

FIGURE 5.3: Conservative Party Campaign Flyer, Horncastle, February 1911
Source: "British Political Party General Election Addresses, [1892–Ca. 1970] from the National Liberal Club Collection, Bristol University" 1986

events.[95] Of course, to the so-called "diehard" opponents of Home Rule – such as Willoughby de Broke, provocatively described by George Dangerfield as "not more than two hundred years behind his time" – the combination of poor election performance in 1910 and the elimination of the House of Lords veto had triggered a chain reaction that could only end with a constitutional crisis.[96] Nonetheless, while historians have found moments of self-doubt in the correspondence of party leaders, the bulk of the evidence after 1910 suggests Conservative party leaders were in control and their party was on the rebound.[97]

A LEGACY OF ORGANIZATION AND DEMOCRATIC CONSOLIDATION INTO THE POSTWAR ERA

The revitalization of the Conservative Party before 1914 was not just due to the usual shifting of political winds. Rather, the losses of 1910 had triggered far-reaching internal reforms that built upon a longer legacy of organizational prowess and adaptation reaching back into the previous century. The success

[95] For a very different interpretation of these same by-election results, see Green, *Crisis of Conservatism* (1995), 269.

[96] Dangerfield, *Strange Death of Liberal England* (1997), 48.

[97] For contrasting accounts, and some evidence of self-doubt, see Green, *Crisis of Conservatism* (1995), 269. See also David Dutton, "Conservatism in Crisis, 1910–1915," in *Recovering Power: The Conservatives in Opposition since 1867*, ed. Stuart Ball and Anthony Seldon (London: Palgrave, 2005), 129.

of these efforts provided a solid basis for self-confidence that lasted through the postwar period.

In 1911, faced with growing pressure from the conservative press, Balfour, like his predecessors conceded to organizational reform: namely, the formation of the Unionist Organization Committee, a committee of nine leading party figures, chaired by former party whip Aretas Akers-Douglas.[98] The Committee carried out in-depth investigations, interviewing 103 witnesses and receiving written testimony from 289 others.[99] The modernizing reforms sponsored by the group – including the creation of the positions of Party Chairman to oversee the Central Office and Party Treasurer to raise money, along with the merging of the National Union office with the Central Office – created a pattern of party organization that would stay in place until the Maxwell Fyfe reforms of 1948.[100] By all accounts, the reorganization was successful, facilitating the recovery of the party even before 1914. More than this, the Unionist Party also benefited from a pre-1914 revitalization of its rank-and-file organization, especially among women's organizations such as the Women's Unionist and Tariff Reform Association, which surpassed even the Primrose League in its organization for women.[101] All of this prepared the revamped Conservative Party for full male and especially partial female enfranchisement in 1918.[102] If desperate old-regime parties provoke constitutional crises, by 1914 the old Conservative Party had become increasingly nimble and self-confident, which suggests democratic disaster could be averted.

Indeed, as strong as Liberals looked in 1906–1910, the following two decades were not years of conservative collapse but rather of conservative ascendancy – and this all despite the rise of universal male (and partial female) suffrage reform and the Labour Party, increasing labor unrest, economic insecurity, and disruptive media and technological change.[103] Like elsewhere in Europe (see Chapter 8),

---

[98] For details, see John Ramsden, *The Age of Balfour and Baldwin, 1902–1940* (London: Longman, 1978), 44–62.

[99] David Thackeray, *Conservatism for the Democratic Age: Conservative Cultures and the Challenge of Mass Politics in Early Twentieth Century England* (Manchester: Manchester University Press, 2013), 23.

[100] Ramsden, *The Age of Balfour and Baldwin, 1902–1940* (1978), 44–62.

[101] Thackeray, *Conservatism for the Democratic Age: Conservative Cultures and the Challenge of Mass Politics in Early Twentieth Century England* (2013). In Thackeray's account (see Chapter 1, in particular), a major source of regeneration was thus not only formal organizations but the "grassroots" tariff movement as well as rank-and-file female-led Women's Unionist and Tariff Reform Association (WUTRA), which served in his account as a kind of twentieth-century substitute for the declining Primrose League.

[102] See, e.g., Neal R. McCrillis, *The British Conservative Party in the Age of Universal Suffrage: Popular Conservatism, 1918–1929* (Columbus: Ohio State University Press, 1998), 46–82; David Jarvis, "Mrs Maggs and Betty: The Conservative Appeal to Women Voters in the 1920s," *Twentieth Century British History* 5 (1994): 129–52.

[103] For one statement of these challenges, see Maurice Cowling, *The Impact of Labour 1920–1924: The Beginning of Modern British Politics* (Cambridge: Cambridge University Press, 1971), 15–44.

wartime radically altered British politics. The end of the war brought transformative electoral reform suffrage (universal for men and limited for women) *without* proportional representation. Like in 1884, the status quo before 1914 was preferable to any suffrage reform. But, again, rich organizational continuities were again a buffer for Britain's Conservatives. Also, just as Labour's success after the First World War had its roots in the prewar period, so too did a similar logic apply to Unionism.[104] As historian Philip Williamson states, we should neither exaggerate the prewar crises of conservatism nor the postwar ascendance of the British Conservative Party.[105] Across both periods, and unlike many of their European countries, conservatives in Great Britain were particularly adept at navigating political and social change.[106]

This was vividly on display in the October 1922 destruction of the national (Lloyd George Liberal–Conservative) coalition wartime government – an event with important consequences for democratic consolidation in Britain. After the passage of universal male suffrage (and partial female enfranchisement) in 1918 in Britain, two major thresholds of democratization – universal male enfranchisement and parliamentary dominance – had been passed.[107] Full female enfranchisement still was to come in 1928, but before that one critical threshold remained: would political parties previously systematically excluded (e.g., the Labour Party) finally be allowed access to executive power?[108]

This question pivoted on whether or not the Unionist Party decided to extend its collusive wartime governing coalition with Lloyd George's (coalition) Liberal faction into a permanent governing coalition, which would prevent Labour from gaining executive office despite growing electoral strength.[109] It can be contended that this decision shaped the future of democratic consolidation in Britain in two ways: (1) The *de facto* exclusion of a growing working-class party through an anti-competitive collusion of two establishment

[104] For this argument applied to the Labour Party, see Ross McKibbin, *The Evolution of the Labour Party, 1910–1924* (London: Oxford University Press, 1974).

[105] Philip Williamson, "The Conservative Party, 1900–1939: From Crisis to Ascendancy," in *A Companion to Early Twentieth-Century Britain*, ed. Chris Wrigley (London: Blackwell Publishing, 2003), 3–22.

[106] Recent analyses make clear that the Conservative Party was particularly adept at surviving and in fact benefiting from partial female enfranchisement in 1918 as well as full female enfranchisement in 1928. Of the many works on female enfranchisement in Britain, the most compellingly analytical is Dawn Teele, "Ordinary Democratization: The Electoral Strategy That Won British Women the Vote," *Politics & Society* 42, no. 4 (2014): 537–61.

[107] On the 1918 electoral reform, see Pugh, *Electoral Reform in War and Peace, 1906–18* (1978).

[108] For an elaboration of the importance of this "third threshold" of democratization, see Stein Rokkan, *State Formation, Nation-building, and Mass Politics in Europe: The Theory of Stein Rokkan Based on his Collected Works*, ed. Peter Flora, et al. (New York: Oxford University Press, 1999).

[109] Dan Slater and Erica Simmons, "Coping by Colluding: Political Uncertainty and Promiscuous Powersharing in Indonesia and Bolivia," *Comparative Political Studies* 46, no. 11 (2013): 1366–93.

parties was itself inherently undemocratic and might have led to a political monopoly that would have diminished the quality of British democracy; (2) Such a move also might have radicalized British Labour (as some contemporaries claimed to fear) and potentially might have destabilized the new political order.[110] For example, future Conservative prime minister, Stanley Baldwin, though highly critical of the Labour Party, feared that permanently excluding it from power and pushing it away from constitutional politics would backfire and have grievous consequences. As his close ally and future party chairman, J. C. C. Davidson, put it in correspondence in 1922, "To deprive Labour of their constitutional right – is the first step down the road to revolution."[111]

How did events unfold? In the run-up to the expected general election of 1923, the Conservative backbench increasingly had pressured their leaders to end the party's eight-year-old alliance with Lloyd George's Liberal faction, while most Liberals in the coalition nonetheless sought to preserve it.[112] On the morning of October 19, 1922, in a secret meeting of all sitting Conservative Party MPs on at London's Carlton Club, 187 voted against continuing the wartime coalition with Lloyd George Liberals, while a total of 87 wanted it to continue.[113]

This showdown was a turning point in interwar British politics. So-called "coalitionists" such as Winston Churchill pursued the formation of a single "fusion" party, a constantly governing Liberal–Unionist bloc that would permanently exclude Labour from power.[114] By breaking the coalition, the Conservative Party allowed the possibility that Labour would gain executive office. And, indeed, within fifteen months, the election ultimately resulted in a Labour government for the first time, led by Ramsay MacDonald.

What led Conservative MPs to embrace this strategy? Ironically, it was the *legacy of conservative party's organization strength* that contributed to the toleration of Labour and, unintentionally, postwar democratic stability. Sitting MPs from districts where the Conservative Party had been historically dominant before 1914 were most likely to support a break with

[110] Across the political spectrum the question of how to think about and respond to the "upheaval" of Labour's rise was a key issue shaping strategy. At issue was not whether Labour should take office but rather what was the best means to prevent Labour from winning elections. For a sense of the debate see Cowling, *The Impact of Labour 1920–1924: The Beginning of Modern British Politics* (1971).

[111] John Colin Campbell Davidson, *Memoirs of a Conservative: J. C. C. Davidson's memoirs and papers, 1910–37* (London: Weidenfeld and Nicolson, 1969), 189.

[112] See Michael Kinnear, *The Fall of Lloyd George: The Political Crisis of 1922* (London: Macmillan, 1973).

[113] For a first-hand account of this event Davidson, *Memoirs of a Conservative: J. C. C. Davidson's memoirs and papers, 1910–37* (1969), 100–33.

[114] Andrew J. Taylor, "Stanley Baldwin, Heresthetics and the Realignment of British Politics," *British Journal of Political Science* 35, no. 3 (2005): 434.

the Liberal coalition while organizationally weak districts voted for the coalition. In short, despite its own opposition to the Labour Party, Conservative Party strength (and self-confidence) actually *facilitated* democratization.

Evidence for this proposition comes from an unusual historical source. Though the vote at the Carlton Club was secret at the time, Austin Chamberlain's papers and party chairman J. C. C. Davidson's memoirs provide a complete list of how all sitting MPs voted on the crucial day. Using these data and F. S. W. Craig's historical election data, we can assess the proposition that a robust prewar legacy of conservative organizational prowess was associated with postwar support for Conservative Party independence by calculating the share of seats the Conservative Party won in each sitting MP's district in the last three prewar elections (1906, 1910a, and 1910b).[115] Did supporters of party independence (i.e., non-coalition) in fact come from historically dominant conservative districts?

I estimate a simple logit model where a sitting Conservative Party MP vote in the 1922 Carlton Club is the dependent variable, coded as either "yes" (for coalition) or "no" (against coalition). The main independent variable is average share of votes for the Conservative Party in the MP's district in last three prewar general elections (1906, 1910a, and 1910b), which ranges from 0 to 1. To illustrate the findings, Figure 5.4 graphs the predicted probability of voting for independence at the meeting based on the historical dominance of the Conservative Party in a district.[116] We see that the greater the historical dominance, the greater the probability a MP would vote against coalition, which in effect allowed for the rise of the first Labour government in British history in 1924.

Rather than being anchored in a broad-minded concern about accountability or potential abuses of power, the rejection of collusion in this case was primarily

---

[115] Craig, *Electoral Facts* (1976), 32.

[116] Data in Figure 5.4 draws on a bivariate logit equation with the following results:

internal_vote	Coef.	Std. Err.	z	P>|z|	[95% Conf. Interval]	
conserv_dom	.6050742	.329414	1.84	0.066	−.0405654	1.250714
_cons	.4767675	.199274	2.39	0.017	.0861976	.8673375

For purposes of robustness in some specifications, I included one control variable using census data estimating the percent of a constituency population that is Anglican since in other work I show this is correlated with Conservative Party success. The findings are not significantly altered. Data on religious profile of districts in 1922 draws on Michael Kinnear, *The British Voter: An Atlas and Survey Since 1885* (London: Batsford, 1968).

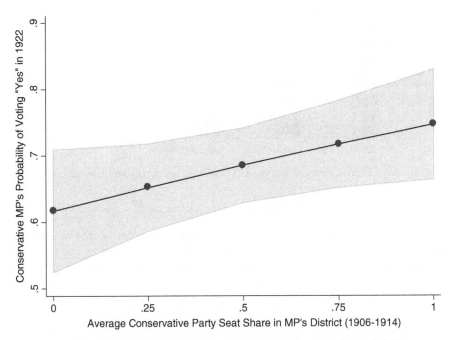

FIGURE 5.4: Legacy of Conservative Party Strength and 1922 Carlton Club Vote
Data Sources: MP's 1922 Carlton Club vote listed in Kinnear 1973; and Davidson 1969,
127; Seat share (1906–1914) from Craig 1976, 32

self-interested.[117] The efforts were driven by a web of MPs from safe seats and
conservative operatives – including party agents and constituency association
members – who resented accommodating Liberals in their constituencies. They
confidently believed the most effective response to the rise of Labour was an
independent and united Conservative Party capable of winning elections.[118]
Again, party strength unintentionally democratized British politics. Moreover,
the day before the Carlton Club vote, a Conservative candidate won a high-
profile and much discussed three-way (Labour, Liberal, Conservative) by-
election at Newport. This reinforced the view of Central Office's chief
organizer, Leigh Maclachlan, who informed party leaders in October 1922
that "if the Conservatives stood against all comers, they would get a clear
majority."[119]

---

[117] On this case, see Cowling, *The Impact of Labour 1920–1924: The Beginning of Modern British
Politics* (1971). For a broader comparative treatment of collusion as a strategy for dealing with
electoral uncertainty, see Slater and Simmons, "Coping by Colluding: Political Uncertainty and
Promiscuous Powersharing in Indonesia and Bolivia" (2013).

[118] McKibbin, *Parties and People* (2010), 40.

[119] Sanders to Wilson, correspondence, October 8, 1922, in Sanders, *Real Old Tory Politics:
The Political Diaries of Sir Robert Sanders, Lord Bayford, 1910–35* (1984), 190.

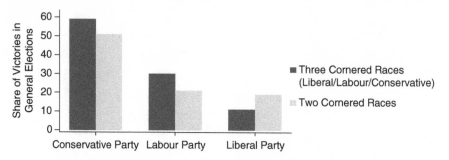

FIGURE 5.5: Three-Cornered Races vs. Two-Cornered Races and Conservative Party
Election Victories, 1918–1930
Data Source: Craig, 1976, 123–136

While Labour gained office twice over the next ten years (1924 and 1929),
the Conservatives were organizationally prepared to thrive in the resulting
unstable three-party system. Once the Conservatives abandoned coalition
with Lloyd George Liberals, the Labour Party became "the fulcrum of
British politics," and in the historian Ross McKibbin's words, "the position
of the Conservative Party became almost impregnable."[120] But, in the
meantime, the monopolistic collusion of the two old regime parties broke,
putting Britain on a steady path of democratic consolidation.

The heightened electoral competition also elevated the electoral game of the
Labour Party, which responded to Conservative propaganda with its own
effective political campaigns.[121] But Conservatives ultimately benefited from
the rise of the Labour Party at the Liberals' expense. This is seen in Figure 5.5
above, which shows that while the Conservatives were more likely to win
elections in general, they won even *more* seats in three-cornered elections where
Labour was also present along with the Liberal Party than in head-to-head two-
cornered Liberal–Conservative races. By contrast, Liberals, while less likely to
win seats in general, were relatively *worse* off in three-cornered races than in two-
cornered races. These data support the proposition that the rise of Labour split
the left-leaning vote to the benefit of the Conservative Party.

But the dominance of the Conservative–Labour cleavage was not
preordained. In 1923, in the wake of the Carlton Club split that ousted sitting
party leader Austen Chamberlain, the party's future remained uncertain.
Further, new leader Stanley Baldwin's campaign emphasis on trade
protectionism united competing factions within his party but failed to appeal
to the general electorate sufficiently to retain a majority in the House of
Commons. In the quickly called general election of 1924, Baldwin adopted

---

[120] McKibbin, *The Ideologies of Class: Social Relations in Britain, 1880–1950* (1990), 281.
[121] Laura Beers, "Counter-Toryism: Labour's response to anti-socialist propaganda, 1918–1939,"
in *The Foundations of the Labour Party: Identities, Cultures and Perspectives*, ed.
Matthew Worley (London: Ashgate, 2009), 231–68.

a new campaign strategy that elevated the perils of the Labour Party to the center of their election campaigns.[122] Some argue that the Conservative Party (increasingly renamed this after 1922) found success then by moving to the "middle ground," which is descriptively accurate but presumes the dimensions of electoral competition were already fixed. Indeed, as several analysts demonstrate, the party's mastery of new media technologies – not to mention its formidable party organization – allowed it to reshape and define the ideological "middle ground" in the first place.[123] Before 1914, British Conservatism had sought above all to highlight its core "political values" including Empire and eliminate "class" as an issue (see evidence in Chapter 4). But after 1923, as William Riker would certainly have appreciated, their campaign speeches did the opposite, presenting the party's commitment to deflationary economic policies as a protective "common sense" reaction against a potentially destabilizing Labour Party.[124]

At the heart of this strategy was an alarmist red-baiting campaign. Beginning in 1923, the Conservative Party worked hand-in-hand with the conservative press to portray the Labour Party as a "foreign" Russian- and German-inspired menace to property, political order, and family. The *Daily Mail's* release of the "Zinoviev Letter" four days before the 1924 general election, for example, which sought to emphasize Labour's relations with Soviet Union central to the campaign was only the most notorious. Historian Laura Beers documents the iconography of campaign posters that portrayed the Labour Party as a "foreign threat" to women and traditional family, and accused Labour leaders of being "our Kerenskys," mere fronts for Bolshevik extremists.[125] The shift from the 1923 campaign, which essentially ignored the "threat of Labour" to the 1924 campaign, which made it the centerpiece of its electoral appeal, makes clear how Conservatives sought to recast themselves as "common sense" conservatives and defenders of "English values" against class and foreign threats.

Whatever the contemporary analyst might think of this political maneuvering, the renewal of British Conservatism after 1910 and its postwar endurance helped keep Britain on a settled path of democratization in several very specific ways. First, before 1914, as a semi-loyal alliance of diehards and Ulster Unionists threatened to form an outright anti-regime alliance, Conservative Party electoral success kept these groups interested in playing the democratic game. Jettisoning the political rules was unnecessary since not only was "bourgeois

[122] "British Political Party General Election Addresses, [1892–ca. 1970] from the National Liberal Club collection, Bristol University."

[123] See in particular Philip Williamson, *Stanley Baldwin: Conservative Leadership and National Values* (Cambridge: Cambridge University Press, 1999). See also Taylor, "Stanley Baldwin, Heresthetics and the Realignment of British Politics" (2005).

[124] For an elaboration of this interpretation, see McKibbin, *The Ideologies of Class: Social Relations in Britain, 1880–1950* (1990), 259–93.

[125] Laura Beers, *Your Britain: Media and the Making of the Labour Party* (Cambridge: Harvard University Press, 2010), 58–67.

propriety and dignity" intact, but, as Ross McKibbin puts it, "The Conservative Party was the best defence against a politicized working class."[126]

Second, after 1918, party organization helped to contain certain "semi-loyal" elements within interwar British conservatism. For example, in the late 1920s, two right-wing media moguls, Lord Beaverbrook and Viscount Rothermere, owners of the three largest daily newspapers in Britain at the time (Beaverbrook's the *Daily Express*, Rothermere's the *Daily Mail* and *Daily Mirror*), challenged the party leadership. Both Beaverbrook and Rothermere, the latter of whom was both sympathetic to Nazi Germany in the 1930s and would later briefly but openly endorse Oswald Mosley's fascism, disapproved of Baldwin's apparent moderation vis-à-vis Labour in the mid-1920s. Together, they organized the Empire Crusade, an insurgent campaign that ran candidates against the Conservative Party in 1929 and 1930. The efforts of these diehards were remarkably similar to those of Germany's own notorious right-wing media magnate, Alfred Hugenberg, whom we will discuss in detail in Chapter 8, who *successfully* took over Germany's Conservative Party in the late 1920s. In the case of Britain, the Conservative Party's own organization and candidates defeated the insurgency, and Stanley Baldwin publicly ridiculed the media magnates with his famous words that the two aimed at "power without responsibility... the prerogative of the harlot throughout the ages."[127] Professional party agents, a revived Central Office loyal to the party leader, and robust local associations played a major part in containing these efforts.

Finally, Conservative Party hegemony in the interwar years also assisted in blocking another challenge: the emergence of anti-system radical right, which then thrived across Europe in the interwar years.[128] The reasons for the relative absence of British fascism are undoubtedly complex. As Martin Pugh convincingly argues, fascism in Britain was not a "foreign" threat but homegrown, making itself most significantly felt in Oswald Mosley's British Union of Fascists.[129] However, the enduring electoral appeal of Britain's well-organized conservatism simply meant there was no *electoral space* for a party of the far right. Confirming a point we will elaborate in our discussion of Germany, John Stevenson argues,

> Unlike in interwar Germany, where there was no single, strong party of the right until the Nazis rose to power, Britain's strong Conservative Party virtually monopolized the ground on which any fascist movement might hope to base itself.[130]

[126] McKibbin, *The Ideologies of Class: Social Relations in Britain, 1880–1950* (1990), 281.
[127] Beers, *Your Britain: Media and the Making of the Labour Party* (2010), 21.
[128] Ertman, "Great Reform Act of 1832" (2010).
[129] Martin Pugh, *Hurrah for the Blackshirts! Fascists and Fascism in Britain Between the Wars* (London: Pimlico, 2006).
[130] John Stevenson, "Conservatism and the Failure of Fascism in Britain," in *Fascists and Conservatives: The Radical Right and the Establishment in Twentieth Century Europe*, ed. Martin Blinkhorn (Abingdon: Routledge, 1990), 276.

This was evident in the elections of 1931 and 1935, when economic conditions were ripe for the disintegration of the center-right, as occurred in other European countries. But in Britain, under Stanley Baldwin, Conservatives retained a mass appeal intact in a way that proved impossible to replicate elsewhere with the exceptions of Belgium, Switzerland, and Scandinavia. As participants in MacDonald's Labour-led National Government from 1931 to 1935 and the National Government's leading party after 1935, the Conservative Party remained a major player in interwar politics. As Philip Williamson argues, the result was that the British Conservative Party was the "most effective obstacle to all extremist groups in interwar Britain."[131] There is certainly a great deal to criticize about Conservative-influenced economic policies in Britain in these years.[132] Yet, we must nonetheless concede this fundamental proposition: at the pivot points of British political history – 1884, 1914, and after 1922 – a legacy of well-organized Conservatism, when compared to conservatives in other countries, helped assure a transition to, and consolidation of, British democracy, clearing the way for democratic stability in a period of remarkable global instability.

CONCLUSIONS AND LOOKING AHEAD

Social scientists may no longer believe that the path to British democracy was settled by 1688 or even 1715. The Whig interpretation of Britain's political development has largely been discredited; however, a more modest form of predetermination still resonates. In that view, the creation of a "rough balance of power" within British society after 1688 was both necessary and sufficient to eventually produce a "political culture" that made settled democracy inevitable.

However, as I have shown over the past several chapters, path-dependence is not predetermination. The early period may be necessary to explain the settled path that Britain took – but no way was it sufficient. The reorganization of a British Conservative Party equipped to play electoral politics was also a precondition of democratic transition and consolidation. This conclusion becomes clearer when comparing the case of Britain with that of Germany – a case in which a relatively precocious political system went off the rails. In the next four chapters, we investigate the German case to explore a different phenomenon: the emergence of weak conservative parties marked by particular syndromes of disorganization that, as we shall see, exert a negative impact on the stability of democratization.

---

[131] Williamson, "The Conservative Party, 1900–1939: From Crisis to Ascendancy" (2003).

[132] For an overview of economic policies of the Conservative Party in this period, see Philip Williamson, *National Crisis and National Government: British Politics, the Economy and Empire, 1926–1932* (Cambridge: Cambridge University Press, 1992).

6

Weak Party Conservatism and the Case of Germany

In his 1925 *Memoirs of a Junker* (*Erinnerungen eines Junkers*), east Prussian notable Hellmut von Gerlach recounts election day in rural Silesia shortly after Germany's early adoption of universal male suffrage for national parliamentary elections in 1871. He writes,

No village innkeeper dared to grant the use of his dancing-hall for any other than a Conservative meeting; otherwise the neighboring landlord, who was also the local magistrate, could make it exceedingly disagreeable for him. On election day laborers were marshaled in a column during the noon interval and marched off to the polls, with the bailiff in front and the forester behind. At the door of the polling-place the bailiff gave each laborer a Conservative ballot, which the landlord immediately collected from him in his capacity as judge of elections. The machine worked perfectly.[1]

Von Gerlach's view vividly suggests a second route to conservative party survival: the use of local power and the state to undercut fair and competitive elections, in order to cushion old elites from the threats posed by universal male suffrage. This mode of conservative survival contrasts with the one described in the last chapter in which the British Conservatives and their leader, self-professed opponent of democracy, Lord Salisbury, early on embraced "wirepullers" and other features of modern party organization in order to use *competition* to defend themselves against electoral challenges and the profound redistributive threats associated with the gradual rise of democracy. Comparing the experience of Germany's Conservative Party (*Deutschkonservative Partei,* or DKP) before 1918 to that of the British Conservative Party highlights a paradox that, once resolved, further bolsters our account. The landed elite of both countries came to be represented by two very different types of political parties. In Britain, an institutionalized, tightly coupled Conservative Party with a well-organized base increasingly competed in elections throughout the

[1] Gerlach, *Erinnerungen eines Junkers [Memoir of a Junker]* (1925), 29.

country, including urban and suburban areas, and hence became a formidable opponent; whereas Germany's landed elite, despite efforts to build party organization during the Imperial period, remained represented by an organizationally weak political party of notables.[2] Increasingly trapped in its East Elbian rural strongholds, the DKP was unable to forge a territorially integrated, nationally encompassing center-right defense of the old regime, and as a result was profoundly frightened of democracy.[3]

In both instances, the political party representing this crucial and powerful social class was no minor historical detail: the way in which old elites are incorporated into the modern world shapes the long-run development of democracy. When viewed comparatively, two distinctive symptoms make the organizational weakness of Germany's Conservative Party particularly clear. First, the party relied on a combination of state-assisted electoral fraud and anti-socialist election-time coalitions with other parties of the right until 1918, in place of party organization, surviving primarily in rural strongholds alone. Second, in a somewhat surprising turn, by the 1890s this "party of notables" had been gradually overrun by extremist party activists and outside insurgent interest groups. The party leadership, without its own election machinery or mass base, traded decision-making independence for mobilizational support and as a result was unable to maintain autonomy from these supporting groups. A dynamic of cooptation from below prevailed, in which party ideologues, interest groups, and insurgent civil society organizations overwhelmed party leaders and set the agenda for the party.[4]

---

[2] Below I study the German Conservative Party (DKP) and the German Empire Party (*Reichspartei*) as conservatives because they both represented economic elites and were tightly associated with the predemocratic political establishment in Prussia and Germany. In the context of Prussia and national politics, I do not consider the Center Party, the German Catholic party, a "conservative party" for our purposes despite conservative ideologically leanings because it was an "outsider" party, opposed to the Protestant Prussian-centered regime and thus while representing Catholic landed elites was not institutionally a part of the Prussian old regime. For an account of its outsider status, see Margaret Lavinia Anderson, *Windhorst: A Political Biography* (Oxford: Clarendon Press, 1981); Dirk Stegmann, *Die Erben Bismarcks: Parteien und Verbände in der Spätphase des Wilhelminische Deutschlands* (Köln: Kipenheuer & Witsch, 1970); Retallack, *The German Right* (2006).

[3] Compared to other countries' conservative parties, the German Conservative Party's electoral base was highly geographically concentrated. See data in Chapter 7.

[4] The idea that interest groups overrun "weak" parties is not an entirely original one. See, for example, Morris Fiorina, "The Decline of Collective Responsibility in American Politics," *Daedalus* 109 (1980): 25–45. He writes, "[As parties] decline they lose control over nominations and campaigns, they lose the loyalty of the voters, and they lose control of the agenda. Party officeholders cease to be held collectively accountable for party performance, but they become individually exposed to the political pressure of myriad interest groups. The decline of party permits interest groups to wield greater influence, their success encourages the formation of still more interest groups, politics becomes increasingly fragmented, and collective responsibility becomes still more elusive" (Fiorina, "Decline of Collective Responsibility" (1980): 41–42).

This chapter will examine the two critical symptoms of party weakness: the party's reliance on electoral fraud and anti-socialist cross-party elite coalitions as substitutes for party organization on the one hand; and its organizational cooptation by ideologues and outside interest groups, on the other. Second, we provide a brief account of the general phenomenon of "party development gone wrong" exemplified in the historical development of the DKP, highlighting how a constitutional legacy that left conservatives with a heavy reliance on the state and geographically concentrated religious divides posed serious barriers to party building.

THE SYMPTOMS OF PARTY WEAKNESS

Unlike Europe's nineteenth-century socialists, whose only two strategic options were revolution or electoral competition, Europe's conservatives, as noted in Chapter 2, because of their incumbent status, had *four* alternative strategies when facing elections: repression, electoral competition via the building of party organization, institutional engineering (e.g., proportional representation and plural voting), and electoral manipulation and collusion.[5] Each strategy had its own short-run costs and benefits; each had its own unintended consequences in the long run. In a range of cases, including Spain, Portugal, Italy, France before 1879, and Germany, the secondary literature makes clear that old elites with only poorly developed party organization survived primarily by relying on the fourth strategy alone: the refinement and deployment of localized and often informal "social power" in which access to local state institutions led to electoral manipulation.[6]

Absent "tightly coupled" party organization, however, there was a downside to this route of electoral self-defense: as the scope of competition widened and the political temperature of mass politics heightened during the 1880s and 1890s, outside interest groups and civil society organizations, which acted as surrogates for party organization, quickly and easily overran and captured weak and institutionally porous parties.[7] If armed with their party's *own* financial and organizational resources, party leaders could build "solid boundaries" between themselves and interest groups and activists. Only by insulating itself from such pressures could an organization become the

---

[5] Przeworski and Sprague, *Paper Stones* (1986).

[6] Tavares de Almeida, *Eleições e caciquismo* (1991); Moreno-Luzon, "Political Clientelism, Elites, and Caciquismo in Restoration Spain, 1875–1923" (2007); Varela Ortega, ed., *El poder de la influencia* (2001); José Varela Ortega, *Los amigos políticos: Partidos, elecciones y caciquismo en la Restauración, 1875–1900* (Madrid: Alianza, 1977); Arsenschek, *Die Kampf um die Wahlfreiheit im Kaiserreich* (2003); Theodore Zeldin, *The Political System of Napoleon III* (New York: St. Martin's Press, 1958).

[7] See Coetzee, *For Party or Country* (1990); Geoff Eley, *Reshaping the German Right: Radical Nationalism and Political Change after Bismarck* (New Haven: Yale University Press, 1980).

focused, electoral-minded entity that behaves according to the classic Downsian "unitary" model of rational politicians.[8] But without strong party organization, loosely coupled incumbent parties confronted a dual problem of "porous boundaries." First, weak parties, by definition, depend on organized interests to act as "surrogates" and hence are vulnerable to the demands of interest groups.[9] Second, ideologically extreme party activists are given immediate access to the main levers of party power, in turn constraining the autonomy of party leaders.[10]

For Europe's nineteenth-century conservatives, well-developed self-contained party organization was more than a tool to defeat socialist opponents. Just as crucially, *party organization was a firewall against radicalism from within*. Lacking their own autonomous organizational infrastructure, party leaders were unable to respond to electoral signals or reshape the electorate in moderate directions when such moves clashed with the countervailing pull of well-organized interests, such as military pressure groups (e.g., the Naval League), protectionist societies (e.g., the Agrarian League), or populist Anti-Semitic movements that emerged throughout western Europe in this period.[11] The result was that these groups could wield enormous influence on issues – including democratic constitutional reform – completely *out of proportion* to their real significance in the economy as a whole or even in the distribution of actual voters.[12] In brief, for the leaders of weak conservative parties, the aim was not to appeal to a moderate "median voter" but rather to appease well-organized activists.

These two syndromes – electoral malpractice and cross-party elite collusion on the one hand, and organizational co-optation on the other – are two sides of the same coin: symptoms of conservative party organizational weakness. In the following, we shall see how both dynamics played out in the context of German conservatism in the nineteenth century.

---

[8] Kitschelt, "Internal Politics of Parties" (1989). This assumption of the "unitary actor" model is illustrated in Anthony Downs, *An Economic Theory of Democracy* (New York: Harper, 1957).

[9] On the distinction of "solid" and "porous" boundaries, see John Leslie, "Parties and other Social Functions" (University of California, Berkeley, 2002); Fiorina, "Decline of Collective Responsibility" (1980).

[10] For a more elaborated discussion, see Chapter 2. Kitschelt, "Internal Politics of Parties" (1989).

[11] Similar protectionist, Imperialist, and nationalist strands were present in Britain in the same period as well; the crucial issue is how parties coped with these new popular forces after 1890. On these dynamics in Britain, see Coetzee, *For Party or Country* (1990).

[12] A variant of this argument is also made in the classic and influential work, Stegmann, *Die Erben Bismarcks* (1970). More recently, Axel Grießmer, *Massenverbände und Massenparteien im wilhelminischen Reich: zum Wandel der Wahlkultur 1903–1912* (Düsseldorf: Droste, 2000).

THE PROBLEMS OF ELECTORAL MALPRACTICE AND CROSS-PARTY ELITE COORDINATION IN GERMANY, 1871–1914

Universal male suffrage, adopted in 1871 in Germany, did not instantaneously bring autonomous, self-financing, and institutionalized party organization to Germany's Conservative Party. The Social Democratic Party (*Sozialdemokratische Partei Deutschlands*, or SPD) and the Catholic Center Party (*Deutsche Zentrumspartei*) responded, over time, with a robust type of partisan "counterorganization" that theorists such as Schattschneider and Duverger would expect to find with universal male suffrage.[13] Hellmut von Gerlach's description of elections in Silesia after 1871 at the beginning of this chapter suggests a different story for Germany's conservatives: elections became a ritualistic exercise in "dependent voting," particularly in rural areas where Germany's so-called "Bread Lords" predominated.[14]

It is not entirely surprising that in the first years after 1871 traditional landed notables, who lacking formal party organization, at first deployed the potent mix of deference and coercion that their long-standing wealth, power, and status assured them.[15] After all, such practices were also common in Britain before the rise of mass party organization, providing electoral boosts to both the oligarchic Liberals and Conservatives, and rural bases delivered "deferential" – or perhaps more accurately *intimidated* voters.[16] What is striking, then, is that the German Conservative Party (DKP) as well as the small and more narrowly urban *Reichspartei*, despite representing some of Germany's most powerful social classes, failed to develop the type of tightly coupled formal party organization we saw in Britain after 1867.

It is true, however, that party leaders – as well as insurgent organizers – attempted to build a strong party of the right during key intervals in German political history. We will return to this theme later on. But it is worth emphasizing that German conservatism was by no means, as it has been commonly portrayed, a backwater of unchanging organizational stasis. Instead, at pivotal moments when the old regime was challenged – 1848, 1871, 1890, 1909–1914, and 1918 – the Conservative Party was ironically constrained both by its own ongoing access to the state and the *history* of its

---

[13] Schattschneider, *Party Government* (1942), 44; and Duverger, *Political Parties* (1954).

[14] This is true despite the fact that scholars have usefully points to the rising competitiveness and contentiousness of German elections. See Anderson, *Practicing Democracy* (2000); Stanley Suval, *Electoral Politics in Wilhelmine Germany* (Chapel Hill: University of North Carolina Press, 1985). Though certainly correct when Social Democrats and the Center Party were involved, Germany's Conservatives did not develop the institutions of modern party organization that contemporaries such as James Bryce and Max Weber identified as transforming the politics of the era. See Bryce, *The American Commonwealth* (1908); and Weber, "Politics as a Vocation" [1921] (1946).

[15] See discussion and examples in Suval, *Electoral Politics in Wilhelmine Germany* (1985), 102–03; Anderson, *Practicing Democracy* (2000), 152–98.

[16] Moore, *The Politics of Deference* (1976).

access to the state. While outsiders such as Catholics and socialists formed robust parties, the German Conservative Party and the *Reichspartei* initially had less of an impetus to do because they were aided by the Interior Ministry at election time, and became reliant on that aid. Further, as we will see, even as such assistance diminished over time, Conservatives were encumbered by a second weakness: confessional divides that split the German right and raised the barriers to party building even higher.

Over time, Germany's conservatives, especially the DKP, with an ever-narrowing electoral base, continued to refine and redeploy new techniques of electoral manipulation well into the twentieth century, drawing on notables' auxiliary social resources as a "substitute" for the absence of institutionalized formal party organization.[17] But if electoral fraud is one symptom of party weakness, then that begs an empirical question: how do we know that Germany's old elites continued to rely on it throughout the nineteenth and into the twentieth century? What historical evidence can we draw upon to bolster this claim?

We start by turning to eastern Prussia, to those seven rural regions east of the Elbe River dominated by the old Junker class, where, if our core proposition – that old-regime landed elites used electoral fraud to achieve their conservative electoral goals – holds, it ought to be immediately evident.[18] We can begin by more closely examining one election district, a "most likely" case, from this region, Prenzlau-Angermunde (the fourth district of Brandenburg). With a population of 120,000 in the 1890s, Prenzlau-Angermunde was located 100 kilometers northeast of Berlin, just west of the Oder River and squeezed up against the eastern edge of the state of Mecklenburg-Strelitz. Of Germany's 397 single-member parliamentary districts, the fourth district of Brandenburg was a place where the power of Prussia's aristocratic Junkers ought to have been intact.[19] Despite the general weakening of landlord power after 1872, the district had among the highest levels of landholding inequality in Germany.[20] So, too, according to available evidence, it was among German regions

---

[17] In this sense, Germany's Conservatives shared less with Britain's Conservatives and more with incumbents in Spain, Portugal, France, and Italy, who also used a variety of inventive manipulative techniques. On the parallels of Germany's conservatives and parties in these other countries, see Christopher Clark, *Iron Kingdom: The Rise and Downfall of Prussia, 1600–1947* (Cambridge: Harvard University Press, 2006), 502–03.

[18] This follows the logic of a "most likely" or "crucial" case selection, which generates insights that are more suggestive than conclusive. Selecting cases with extreme values on independent (high land inequality) and dependent variable (high election manipulation) are more likely initially to expose the causal mechanisms at work. As we will see below, I follow up this discussion with a more systematic analysis below. See John Gerring, *Case Study Research: Principles and Practices* (Cambridge: Cambridge University Press, 2007).

[19] See, William Hagen, *Ordinary Prussians: Brandenburg Junkers and Villagers, 1500–1840* (Cambridge: Cambridge University Press, 2002); Wagner, *Bauern, Junker und Beamte* (2005).

[20] Based on Kaiserliches Statistisches Amt. 1898. *Statistik des Deutschen Reichs*. Bd. 112. Berlin: Verlag des Königlich Preussichen Statistischen Bureaus, pp. 351–413 [Table 9]. Data available as

exhibiting with the highest levels of electoral manipulation.[21] Not far from the Junker-dominated landscapes conjured up in Theodor Fontane's 1899 novel *The Stechlin*, the two rural counties of Prenzlau and Angermunde boasted open green fields, lakes, and a heavy reliance on agriculture.[22]

Memoirs, parliamentary reports of election misconduct, and election results from this district allow us more precisely to understand how "the machine" that *substituted* for modern party organization endured until the end of the century. In fact, as late as 1890, we see electoral manipulation and extra-party maneuvering was still very much alive. First, in Prenzlau-Angermunde's six parliamentary elections between 1890 and 1912 in, the DKP won every election. Second, according to the detailed reports, which were reviewed by the parliamentary Reichstag committee charged with investigating election misconduct, the DKP's electoral success relied less on landlords directly dominating their tenants and more on capitalizing on the blurred boundaries between local landlord power and state power, and on local officials' (in particular the office of the prefect or *Landrat*) willing intervention in the electoral process. For example, in the 1893 election, the first election after 1890 for which we have evidence, the longstanding local prefect, Karl Ulrich von Winterfeldt, was also one of the most prominent landowners in the district and had occupied his position as Landrat since 1863.[23] In 1893, he sought to add to these achievements: he ran for the first time as his district's German Conservative Party parliamentary candidate. His simultaneous status as one of the region's largest landowners, the central government's most important local administrator, *and* Conservative Party candidate for the national parliament was not an entirely uncommon political phenomenon. This overlapping of positions gives us a sense of how local landed elites maintained their electoral success. Rather than relying on *direct* old-style social power over tenants ("marching them to the polls"), they shaped elections *indirectly* by accessing and deploying local state power quietly to capture the election process itself. Above all, local notables as local government officials shaped two essential

Daniel Ziblatt, 2011, "Replication data for: Shaping Democratic Practice (APSR)," http://hdl .handle.net/1902.1/16066, Harvard Dataverse, V2

[21] Based on *Stenographische Berichte, Deutscher Reichstag,*1871–1914 as constructed and available in Daniel Ziblatt and Robert Arsenschek, 2010, "Complete Reichstag Election Dispute Dataset, 1871–1914," http://hdl.handle.net/1902.1/15015, Harvard Dataverse, V3

[22] Fontane, *The Stechlin* (1995).

[23] Despite a change in the rules in 1872 that removed the selection procedure from the hands of local notables and placed it under the control of the central government, the persistence of old elites in the *Landrat* position, it turns out, was not uncommon. Indeed, into the 1890s, an estimated 56 percent of *Landräte* in Prussia as a whole were nobility (always landowners in the district where they worked) and an even greater 81 percent in the province of Brandenburg, where Prenzlau was located (Christiane Eifert, *Paternalismus und Politik: Preussiche Landräte im 19. Jahrhundert* (Münster: Westfälisches Dampfboot, 2003), 98–99). The consequence was that a narrow stratum of powerful local landed elites was often in control of the local state electoral apparatus.

functions normally performed by parties: the candidate nomination process and the mobilization of voters.[24]

Underpinning this system was a "grand bargain," not unlike contemporary arrangements in post-1874 Spain (*el Turno* and *caciquismo*) or in late-nineteenth-century Portugal (*rotativismo*), between the central government and the local elites who nominally represented the central government and oversaw election administration. Especially in Eastern Prussia, the Landrat was not only a major landowner but usually a member of the small group of local landed notables that constituted the "local branch" of the Conservative Party. He attended DKP election rallies and often traveled around the district to local villages, pressuring mayors, whom he appointed and who needed his approval to stay in office, in order to generate Conservative victories. In addition to visiting local officials during campaigns, it was not unusual for the *Landrat* to call on local tavern owners, pressuring them to not let their facilities be used for opposition gatherings of the Social Democratic and Left Liberal parties.[25] In exchange for generating conservative votes, the *Landrat* used his personal network to convey to local rural mayors and poll station chairs that conservative victories would be rewarded with infrastructure programs. Conversely, conservative defeats might prompt unfavorable tax assessments.[26] In Prussia, a series of clientelist tactics, familiar to students of nineteenth-century Spain, Portugal, and Italy, were used as top-down resources to help sustain the DKP's electoral success in its strongholds.[27]

The resulting "machine" was effective indeed. In 1893, Karl Ulrich von Winterfeldt was elected from Prenzlau-Angermunde with a decisive 64 percent of the vote, undoubtedly aided by his own threefold role as local notable, election administrator, and candidate for office, against the outsider Social Democratic Party candidate who only received 20 percent.[28] Immediately after the votes were counted, a group of voters submitted a complaint to the Reichstag election disputes committee that voters' secret ballots were systematically violated by polling station officials appointed by von Winterfeldt.[29]

Likewise, in 1898, the Conservative Party's candidate was again Karl Ulrich von Winterfeldt, who won again by a forty-point margin over the same opponent.[30] Further illustrating how the "machine" managed the problem of

---

[24] On the role of local government officials in the process of selecting candidates, see Arsenschek, *Die Kampf um die Wahlfreiheit im Kaiserreich* (2003), 173ff.

[25] Wagner, *Bauern, Junker und Beamte* (2005), 422.

[26] Wagner, *Bauern, Junker und Beamte* (2005), 422–23.

[27] As unconventional as it may sound to view nineteenth-century Prussia through the lens of Portugal, Spain, and Italy, the outlines of a potentially revisionist historiography has begun to emerge that does precisely this. See Wagner, *Bauern, Junker und Beamte* (2005); Clark, *Iron Kingdom* (2006), 502–03.

[28] Carl Wilhelm Reibel, ed., *Handbuch der Reichstagwahlen, 1890–1918: Bündnisse, Ergebnisse, Kandidaten* (Droste Verlag, 2007), 40.

[29] *Stenographische Berichte*, January 17, 1884: 686.

[30] Reibel, ed., *Handbuch der Reichstagwahlen, 1890–1918: Bündnisse, Ergebnisse, Kandidaten* (2007), 40.

succession, this time the election was administered by a new Landrat: Joachim von Winterfeldt, the elder von Winterfeldt's thirty-two-year-old son, who had trained at his father's side the year before.[31] Thus, in 1898, the complex logistical task of running the election fell to Joachim, who recounts his experiences in his memoirs.[32] In that same year, he helped assure his father's victory, which drew even more vigorous outcry from the Social Democratic opposition. Petitions were filed to the Reichstag claiming that the younger von Winterfeldt had removed massive numbers of seasonal workers from the voting rolls; that local election officials had purposely and thoroughly abused the secret ballot; and that qualified voters were denied the right to vote for invalid reasons, which had all resulted in his father's victory.[33]

Again in 1907 and 1912, the Conservative Party still prevailed over the Social Democratic Party, which once more won around 20 percent of the vote in both elections. Then in the latter election, following the illness and death of the elder von Winterfeldt in 1908, it was the younger the Joachim von Winterfeldt who successfully ran for office on the Conservative ticket. In both 1907 and 1912, petitions were again filed challenging the validity of the election, but this time by the election committee of the Left Liberal Party, who had split the opposition vote with the Social Democrats in 1907 and 1912. The petitions objected that the new *Landrat* had once again systematically excluded large numbers of seasonal workers from voting rolls, expelled voters from the voting stations, violated the secret ballot, thrown away ballots for the opposition parties, and thwarted opposition efforts to mobilize and organize rural workers.[34]

In short, this account of Prenzlau-Angermunde offers us a snapshot of weak incumbent party organization at work: landowning elites, closely tied to the local state and often *manning* it, worked entirely on behalf of the DKP to assure electoral victories. Where unchecked rural landholding patterns gave rise to a narrow stratum of landowning elites, the "machine" of electoral manipulation operated quite smoothly. Without party organization, landed elites used state-assisted electoral fraud to provide the DKP with a powerful extra-party mechanism of electoral self-defense.

This single case of DKP election fraud in Prenzlau-Angermunde does not bar the possibility that other parties used such tactics; nor that the concentration of industrial power also had similar effects.[35] But, the question remains whether election misconduct was more likely to occur in constituencies dominated by landowning notables than without. Since voters and parties could dispute the results of elections in their electoral constituency without paying a fee, the

---

[31] Joachim von Winterfeldt, *Jahreszeiten des Lebens* (Berlin: Propylän-Verlag, 1942), 88.
[32] von Winterfeldt, *Jahreszeiten des Lebens* (1942), 80–111.
[33] *Stenographische Berichte*, March 9, 1899: 1431.
[34] *Stenographische Berichte*, July 13, 1909: 9462; March, 9, 1914: 7939.
[35] This latter point is an insight developed in Isabela Mares, *From Open Secrets to Secret Voting: Democratic Electoral Reforms and Voter Autonomy* (Cambridge: Cambridge University Press, 2015).

Reichstag minutes between 1871 and 1914 present massive paper trail of which of the Imperial Germany's 397 single-member electoral constituencies in which years were most marred by electoral irregularities. Historians have studied this historical record, with varying degrees of comprehensive coverage.[36] In collaboration with German historian Robert Arsenschek, in 2008 I digitized the records of the parliamentary papers of the German Reichstag between 1871 and 1914 to code each district by whether or not it was subject to election disputes.[37] The results have been reported elsewhere.[38] Other scholars have also analyzed the data.[39] If we code each of the over 5,000 elections (thirteen elections in Germany multiplied by the 397 single-member electoral districts) by whether it was subject to an official election dispute, we can reconstruct a more complete picture of electoral corruption "on the ground" in nineteenth-century Germany. In Figure 6.1, we see the cumulative number of total disputed elections for each of the thirteen elections in the period in all 397 districts, giving us an idea of where elections were most problematic.

Though I analyze these findings more systematically below, even a casual look at the map in Figure 6.1 reveals that the incidence of challenged elections was greatest in those eastern parts of Prussia where the old landed elite were most dominant, landed estates were large, and where traditional social power endured the longest, even if it was increasingly challenged in the nineteenth century.[40] Moreover, it is worth noting that Germany's two conservative parties (the *Reichspartei*, an urban-based right-wing party and the Conservative Party), which fared better in areas where landholding inequality was highest, were also disproportionately accused of election manipulation.[41] Between 1871 and 1914, their election victories were subject to 35 percent of

---

[36] Anderson, *Practicing Democracy* (2000); Arsenschek, *Die Kampf um die Wahlfreiheit im Kaiserreich* (2003).

[37] Do election petitions really give us an accurate picture of where electoral fraud was most prevalent? I examined the content of each of the detailed individual petitions emerging from the 1890 and 1912 elections that generated 155 disputed seats. Of the combined total of 617 petitions from those two years, the content of these individual petitions reflected precisely the types of election practices (e.g., vote-buying, intimidation, influence) that today count as electoral fraud. Second, there are several reasons we can have relative confidence in the source used here. The process overseeing the investigation of elections in Germany was notably robust and fair. See, for example, Arsenschek, *Die Kampf um die Wahlfreiheit im Kaiserreich* (2003); Anderson, *Practicing Democracy* (2000). Also, while there might be reasonable concerns that data do not only measure fraud but actually also measure willingness to complain, degree of social mobilization, or other phenomena (e.g., partisan interests), statistical controls for each of these potential sources of error can be introduced into the analysis below for each possible threat to validity. For a fuller discussion, see Ziblatt, "Shaping Democratic Practice" (2009).

[38] Ziblatt, "Shaping Democratic Practice" (2009).

[39] Mares, *From Open Secrets to Secret Voting: Democratic Electoral Reforms and Voter Autonomy* (2015); Johannes C. Buggle, "Law and Social capital: Evidence from the Code Napoleon in Germany," *European Economic Review* 87 (2016): 148–75.

[40] Gerschenkron, *Bread and Democracy* (1948); Hagen, *Ordinary Prussians* (2002).

[41] Suval, *Electoral Politics in Wilhelmine Germany* (1985) 100–01.

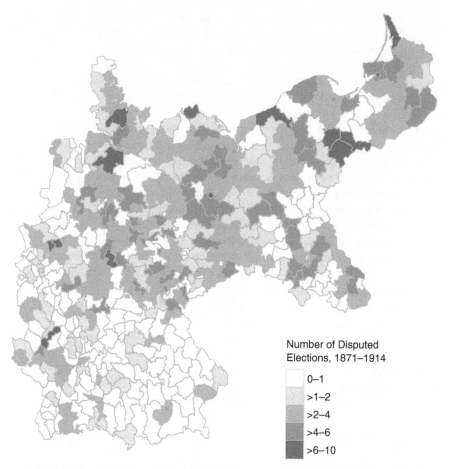

FIGURE 6.1: Total Number of Disputed Elections in Germany, 1871–1914
Data Sources: (a) Disputed election data: Daniel Ziblatt and Robert Arsenschek, 2010, "Complete Reichstag Election Dispute Dataset, 1871–1914." [Online] http://hdl.handle .net/1902.1/15015, Harvard Dataverse, V3
(b) Geographic shapefiles: Daniel Ziblatt and Jeffrey Blossom (2011) "Electoral District Boundaries, Germany, 1890–1912" Harvard University Geospatial Library

the disputes, though they won only 20 percent of the seats in this period, giving us further confidence in the measure.

Also, to help us grasp where elections confronted disputes over time, we see in Figure 6.2 the incidence of disputed elections in each year during the entire time period. As Figure 6.2 depicts, it was particularly in the period after 1890 that elections came become more problematic.

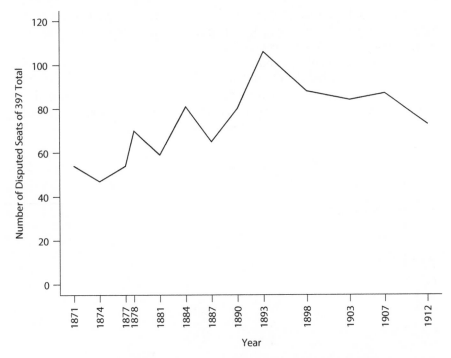

FIGURE 6.2: Number of Disputed Elections in Imperial Germany, per Year, 1871–1912
Data Source: Daniel Ziblatt and Robert Arsenschek (2010) "Complete Reichstag Election Dispute Dataset, 1871–1914." [Online] http://hdl.handle.net/1902.1/15015, Harvard Dataverse, V3

But the question remains: was landholding inequality – as a rough measure of traditional social power in this period – systematically correlated with the incidence of electoral fraud?[42] In Appendix B, I provide detailed regression results of a multivariate cross-sectional time-series logit analysis of all thirteen national parliamentary elections between 1871 and 1914 and in all German constituencies, for which we include the most important relevant controls, including variables that measure the competitiveness of elections in each

[42] To measure "landholding inequality," I draw upon an agricultural census of 1898 that surveyed over 5,000,000 agricultural units in all of Germany to give us a picture of the size and number of farms in each electoral constituency. From this, for each electoral constituency, we can calculate land Gini coefficients, the average size of farms, and the percentage of farms over 1,000 hectares (as alternative measures of landholding inequality) to estimate levels of landholding inequality in each electoral constituency. The analyses that follow are based on a land Gini score as a measure of landholding inequality for each of Germany's 397 electoral constituencies. See Ziblatt, "Shaping Democratic Practice" (2009); Daniel Ziblatt, "Landholding Inequality in Germany, at the Reichstag Constituency Level, and Prussian Chamber of Deputies Constituency Level, 1895" (Harvard Dataverse, 2010). http://dvn.iq.harvard.edu/dvn/dv/dziblatt

district, turnout for elections, share of vote for SPD, and other attributes of each district such as employment structure, population, and religious makeup. Here I simply describe the substantive results.[43]

First, over the whole period (1871–1914), we can ask: if an electoral constituency was marked by landholding inequality, did the probability of election fraud increase? In Figure 6.3, I present the relationship graphically (using Model 1 from the regression table in Appendix B). [44] Figure 6.3 shows

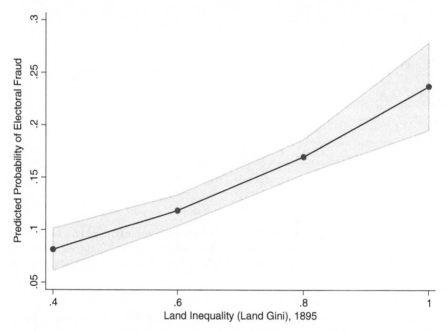

FIGURE 6.3 Predicted Probabilities of Incidence of Electoral Fraud (Based on Model 1) Data Sources: For land inequality data, Daniel Ziblatt, 2010, "Landholding Inequality in Germany, at the Reichstag Constituency Level, and Prussian Chamber of Deputies Constituency Level, 1895," http://hdl.handle.net/1902.1/15023, Harvard Dataverse, V1; For election petition data, Daniel Ziblatt and Robert Arsenschek, 2010, "Complete Reichstag Election Dispute Dataset, 1871–1914." [Online] http://hdl .handle.net/1902.1/15015, Harvard Dataverse

[43] For a listing of control variables, see Appendix B. For a fuller description of sources and measures, see Ziblatt, "Shaping Democratic Practice" (2009). For how other variables affect the analysis, see Mares, *From Open Secrets to Secret Voting: Democratic Electoral Reforms and Voter Autonomy* (2015), Chapter 5.

[44] Probabilities are calculated by adjusting inequality and holding all other variables at their mean values. Probabilities and probability changes presented in this paper can be calculated in stata 11 using the prchange and prvalue commands available as part of the sPost package created for stata 11 by Jeremy Freese and J. Scott Long. The simulations all use Model 1 as reported in Appendix B.

that over the whole time period, if we hold all the other control variables at their mean values, as the levels of landholding increase in electoral constituencies, the probability that a district would be subject to election fraud investigation increases quite dramatically. For example, holding all other variables at their mean, moving from minimum level of landholding inequality (0.49) to the maximum level of landholding inequality (0.92) increases the chances that a district would be subject to electoral fraud by 15 percent.

We can further refine the analysis by conducting cross-sectional analyses of each individual election year from 1871 until 1912 to interrogate how the relative importance of landholding inequality as a determinant of electoral fraud changed over time. This is a crucial way of assessing how the rise *of mass politics*, associated in particular with the "turning point" of 1890, might have affected old-regime strategies.[45] Though this analysis is limited by the fact that the earliest landholding inequality data are only available in 1895, it generates some revealing inter-temporal variations.[46] I have examined cross-sectional data for each of the thirteen elections between 1871 and 1914, and I report the logit regression results in Table 6.1 in B for each election year between 1871 and 1912.

First, as reported in Appendix B, a few of the control variables are statistically significant, but the chief independent variable of interest, landholding inequality, has an uneven relationship with electoral fraud across time. However, there does appear to be a pattern that closely maps onto a sharp divide that fits the general argument of this chapter. A shift occurs in 1890, a year that leading scholars of Germany have argued represented a "turning point," a "refounding of the Reich," and a moment in which "one pattern of politics began to be replaced by another."[47]

In 1890, the government-friendly *Kartell* Reichstag majority of National Liberals (*Nationalliberale Partei*), German Reich Party *(Deutsche Reichspartei)*, and Conservatives were decimated at the polls, Bismarck resigned from power, the ban on the Social Democratic Party expired, and the Conservative Party faced the

---

[45] Eley, *Reshaping the German Right* (1980), 19.

[46] Though no constituency-level data are available before 1895, provincial-level data do confirm in Germany what economic historians note about landholding inequality in other world regions – that it changed very little. In Germany, while county-level agricultural census data on the number and size of agricultural units do not exist for years before 1895 (thus preventing inclusion in the empirical analysis here), highly aggregated data that break Germany into 80 large provinces do exist for the census from the 1880s. If we aggregate the 1895 data into the same 80 provincial units that were reported for the 1882 census, we can estimate a Gini coefficient for the same 80 provinces in 1882 *and* 1895. The correlation between each province's Gini scores in 1882 and 1895 are nearly identical ($r = 0.987$), suggesting very limited change in landholding inequality between the 1880s and 1890s.

[47] A "turning point" in Richard Evans, *Rethinking German History: Nineteenth Century Germany and the Origins of the Third Reich* (London: Allen and Unwin, 1987b), 87; "Refounding the Reich" in David Blackbourn, *Religion, and Local Politics in Wilhelmine Germany: The Centre Party in Württemberg before 1914* (New Haven: Yale University Press, 1980), 14; Eley, *Reshaping the German Right* (1980), 19.

onset of increasingly well-organized mass party politics and rural and urban mobilization.[48] In the period before 1890 (columns 1–7 in B), landholding inequality is only inconsistently related to electoral fraud, a finding possibly explained by the relatively security of the Conservative Party during these years, unchallenged by the still-banned SPD and more safely entrenched in the political environment of *Honoratiorenpolitik* ("politics of notables"). By contrast, in all six elections between 1890 and 1912 (summarized in columns 8–13 in Appendix B), landholding inequality had a strong and statistically significant positive relationship with electoral fraud, with the exception of the last election of the Reich in 1912.[49]

The Conservative Party's apparently growing dependence on electoral manipulation in areas of high rural inequality after 1890 is likely a component of the party's "counteroffensive" campaign against more robustly organized parties, single-issue groups, and a revived Social Democratic Party.[50] Indeed, after the SPD's ban was lifted, its leadership announced a new slogan and a new strategy: "Out into the Countryside!"[51] Thus, with traditional forms of power under siege, the increase in rural electoral fraud is not altogether unexpected. In a related development, the results of the 1890 Reichstag election and the perceived frailty of the governing National Liberal-Conservative coalition (the so-called *Kartell* of 1887) gave to rise to serious rumors of a coup d'état (*Staatsstreich*) orchestrated by Bismarck and the military against the Reichstag.[52] Absent party organization, alternative strategies, ranging from electoral fraud to rumors of coups, became plausible.[53]

Recent work by other scholars supplements these findings. Isabela Mares' analysis of the same election irregularities data uncovers two main additional factors relevant here. First, as part of a broader analysis of German politics in the period, she identifies a logic explaining the incidence of election irregularities in Germany's industrial heartland. She discovers that in those

[48] Eley, *Reshaping the German Right* (1980), 24–30.

[49] In 1912, German electoral politics was turned upside down, with the Social Democratic Party (SPD) "breaking through" and becoming, for the first time, the largest party in the Reichstag. A fuller discussion of this follows below.

[50] James N. Retallack, *Notables of the Right: The Conservative Party and Political Mobilization in Germany, 1876–1918* (Boston: Unwin Hyman, 1988), 156–58.

[51] Eley, *Reshaping the German Right* (1980), 24.

[52] Historians have made vividly clear, drawing on correspondence between Bismarck and the Emperor, as well as instructions sent to the War Ministry shortly following the elections of 1890, that force might be necessary in a coming showdown. Further, rumors of a coup d'état persisted, off and, on throughout the 1890s. See John C. G. Röhl, "Staatsstreichplan oder Staatsstreichbereitschaft? Bismarcks Politik in der Entlassungskrise," *Historische Zeitschrift* 203, no. 3 (1966): 610–24.

[53] Also, it should be noted, simultaneous to this, in the period of flux after 1890, there were serious discussions and efforts to "refound" a new party of the right. See discussion in Dirk Stegmann, "Between Economic Interests and Radical Nationalism," in *Between Reform, Reaction, and Resistance: Studies in the History of German Conservatism from 1789 to 1845*, ed. Larry Eugene Jones and James Retallack (Providence, RI: Berg, 1993), 157–85.

regions of Germany where employment and economic output were in fewer firms' hands, election intimidation and election manipulation were more rampant.[54] In these "autarkic," largely industrial regions, electoral fraud was a mode of protecting entrenched industrial interests. Second, she finds that, on average, where the electoral right was more fragmented (i.e., where all three right-wing parties, National Liberals, Conservatives, and Free Conservatives, campaigned for the same single-member MP spot in an individual district), the probability of electoral manipulation increased. There may be different ways to interpret this latter finding, but it does appear consistent with the idea that in Germany electoral manipulation was a rightist alternative mechanism of defense when such parties found themselves organizationally weak and incapable of winning elections.[55]

However, the weakness of formal party organization for the electoral right also found a second and related substitute that also has resonance with southern European political systems in this period: informal cross-party elite coalitions among political parties of the right *against* regime outsiders. A distinctive feature of Imperial German Reichstag elections, like many other early democratizers, was that they were single-member "run-off" or two-round systems, requiring each candidate earn a majority in his election district to win a parliamentary seat. For the decentralized conservative political parties of Imperial Germany, this electoral system exacerbated party weakness by incentivizing local party branches to form rotating cross-party election-time coalitions – rather than a nationally encompassing party organizations – in order for candidates to earn a full majority of a district's votes. In historian Carl Wilhelm Reibel's analysis of the structure of these coalitions in every district in Germany in every election between 1890 and 1918, he identifies eight separate types of coalitions.[56] Further, he identifies a consequential asymmetry: Social Democrats and the Center Party, regime outsiders, were least likely, and parties of the right, *most likely* to form cross-party coalitions with partners at the local level. The conservative *Reichspartei* owed 94 percent of its mandates to such coalitions, the National Liberals 83 percent, and the German Conservative Party 80 percent whereas Socialists and Catholic Party were less likely to rely on coalitions.[57] Thus, especially for parties of the right, loose, shifting, and informal cross-party coalitions substituted for weak national party

[54] Mares, *From Open Secrets to Secret Voting: Democratic Electoral Reforms and Voter Autonomy* (2015), 117.

[55] Indeed Mares (p. 112) finds that when a second-round of elections occur, where forging anti-socialist coalitions of the right were typically easier, the fragmentation of the right does not have a positive relationship (indeed, a slightly negative relationship) with electoral irregularities. See Mares, *From Open Secrets to Secret Voting: Democratic Electoral Reforms and Voter Autonomy* (2015), 115.

[56] Reibel, ed., *Handbuch der Reichstagwahlen, 1890–1918: Bündnisse, Ergebnisse, Kandidaten* (2007), 33.

[57] Ibid.

organization to keep "outsider" parties (Center Party and the Social Democrats) away from power.

One might imagine the counter-argument that these types of election-time coalitions represented an auspicious precursor for Germany's democratic cross-party coalition-building in the second half of twentieth century.[58] While the long-run consequences of the practice of forging election-time coalitions are open for debate, in the context of nineteenth-century Germany, this strategy's immediate consequence was to block party development on the right, disproportionately benefiting electorally right-oriented political parties dominated by structurally-advantaged groups (employers, landowners, etc.) to keep outsider parties (i.e., socialists and Catholics) out of power.

To illustrate, consider the case of the Merseburg district of Bitterfeld-Delitzsch in 1903. In the first round of the Reichstag election that year, the Social Democratic candidate beat four rivals, earning 41 percent of the vote, outpacing two close competitors, a conservative *Reichspartei* candidate, a locally prominent owner of a coal mine and early chemical industry founder, Louis Bauermeister who received 37 percent of the vote and a Liberal candidate who earned 22 percent of the vote. With no candidate receiving a full majority in the first round, a second round election took place in which the right parties coordinated to support the conservative Reichspartei candidate, who narrowly triumphed over the Social Democratic candidate in a two-man second-round race by just over a thousand votes (52.2 percent to 47.8 percent).[59] In short, political parties of the right used coordination, if not collusion, *among* parties of the right as a substitute for strong parties of the right.

In sum, using various types of evidence, we have drawn a portrait of some key symptoms of Conservative Party weakness in nineteenth-century Germany: state-assisted electoral manipulation and patterns of coalition formation among right-leaning political parties that substituted for traditional party organization. In terms of the former, the DKP's core constituency of landed elites had enormous local power to manipulate elections late into the nineteenth century, by controlling both the practice of candidate nomination and the process of voter mobilization on election day. In terms of the latter, while possibly providing a pattern for future coalitional bargaining, in the hands of structurally advantaged socioeconomic and political insiders, this was an anti-competitive strategy to keep regime outsiders out of power. It is correct that historians have often argued that, in order to assure its survival *without* party organization, the style of notable politics employed by organized conservatism in Imperial Germany required a potent combination of collusion, deference, coercion,

---

[58] For a general elaboration of this argument in the context of Prussian elections, see Kühne, *Dreiklassenwahlrecht und Wahlkultur* (1994), 209–215; 242–256.

[59] Reibel, ed., *Handbuch der Reichstagwahlen, 1890–1918: Bündnisse, Ergebnisse, Kandidaten* (2007), 131.

and state access.[60] We now see, even more clearly, how this elaborate arrangement worked in practice.

THE PROBLEM OF INTEREST GROUPS, PARTY ACTIVISTS, AND "CAPTURED" POLITICAL PARTIES

The second broad type of symptom of conservative party weakness, or "loosely coupled" organization, in nineteenth-century Germany was the problem of insurgent cooptation "from below" by interest groups and radical party activists. It is instructive to begin by contrasting Britain's Conservative Party and its relationship with the Primrose League on the one hand to the German Conservative Party's relationship with its party activists and key interest groups on the other. As I demonstrated in the last several chapters, a key ingredient in the British Conservative Party's ability to survive an expanded suffrage was the remarkable capacity of its leaders to deploy Rikerian heresthetic tactics to create and shape cross-class cultural cleavages to divide the opposition.[61] But simultaneously activating voters *indirectly* via their groups and social networks while remaining autonomous is no simple task.[62] In the case of the British Conservative Party, supporting organizations such as the Primrose League were available for mobilization, but the party leadership had already developed high levels of autonomy to insulate itself from the demands that often come with interest groups and civil society organizations.[63]

But, these two characteristics – group availability and party leadership autonomy – do not hold in all times and places.[64] Indeed, as Table 6.1 shows, we can in fact identify four scenarios that describe four different types of relationships between parties and their interest groups.

As Table 6.1 illustrates, the longstanding "top down" tendency to treat parties as unitary actors with little consideration for their interaction with supporting interest groups describes only one type of party and completely misses the variation among political parties.[65] Political parties not only build parliamentary majorities; they also have two further functions: to nominate candidates and, given their limited resources, *to mobilize groups* to access voters indirectly, rather than mobilize voters themselves.[66] The nature of

---

[60] Retallack, *Notables of the Right* (1988); Retallack, *The German Right* (2006); Suval, *Electoral Politics in Wilhelmine Germany* (1985); Thomas Nipperdey, *Die Organisation der Deutschen Parteien vor 1918* (Düsseldorf: Droste Verlag, 1961).

[61] Riker, *Art of Political Manipulation* (1986); McLean, *Rational Choice and British Politics* (2001).

[62] Rosenstone and Hansen, *Mobilization, Participation, and Democracy* (1993), 27–30.

[63] See, e.g., McKenzie, *British Political Parties* (1955); Samuel Beer, "Pressure Groups and Parties in Britain," *American Political Science Review* 50, no. 1 (1956): 1–23.

[64] Bawn, Cohen, Karol, Masket, Noel, and Zaller, "A Theory of Political Parties: Groups, Policy Demands and Nominations in American Politics" (2012).

[65] Downs, *An Economic Theory of Democracy* (1957).

[66] Aldrich, *Why Parties?* (1995); Rosenstone and Hansen, *Mobilization, Participation, and Democracy* (1993), 27.

TABLE 6.1: *A Typology of Party-Interest Group Relations, with Illustrations*

	Autonomous and Institutionalized Party Leadership	Poorly Institutionalized Party Leadership
Mobilized Groups	**Leadership Party with Mass Base** (e.g., British Conservatives c. 1867)	**Captured Party** (e.g., German Conservatives after 1893)
No Mobilized Groups Activated	**Tightly Coupled Elitist Leadership Party** (e.g., British Conservatives c. 1832)	**Loosely Coupled Party of Notables** (e.g., German Conservatives in 1849)

a party's relationship to its interest groups therefore is a defining feature of all political parties.

As parties begin to rely on outside interest groups, a "balancing act" between pursuing voters and managing the groups used to mobilize voters is delicate and can easily spiral into a difficult dynamic, especially if a party is *poorly institutionalized*. In this circumstance, because an interest group may have access to critical outsourced or "surrogate" organization, personnel, and resources, it can gain powerful leverage over a party in its most defining functions: selecting candidates, delivering programmatic statements to appeal to voters, and taking stances on issues in legislative bodies. Indeed, it is precisely when a party becomes overrun or swamped by its organized interests that it may be described as a "captured party."[67] So too can insurgent party activists become a threat. If a party leadership is "loosely coupled," whether because of porous or decentralized organization, party activists can easily and quickly gain access to levers of power, exposing party leaders to pressures that may hamper strictly electorally minded decision-making.[68] This, then, is the crux of

[67] This definition borrows from the concept of "regulatory capture" developed by George Stigler, "The Theory of Economic Regulation," *Bell Journal of Economics and Management Science 2*, no. 1 (1971): 3–21. In the context of German political parties, the idea that "interest groups" and "parties" developed in tension and in competition with each other was prominently proposed by Stegmann, *Die Erben Bismarcks* (1970) and more recently developed in Grießmer, *Massenverbände und Massenparteien* (2000).

[68] Kitschelt, "Internal Politics of Parties" (1989).

the difference between a "strong" and "weak" party: the degree to which party leaders are able to dominate their interest groups and activists, in the manner, for example, of the British Conservative Party and its Primrose League (i.e., a strong party); or, conversely, the extent to which interests and activists overrun parties (i.e., a weak party) – for example, the DKP.

Further examples from our two cases illustrate this point. In Britain, where the hierarchical British Conservative Party emerged early – after 1832 – as an increasingly institutionalized collective actor, organized interests were, in Raikes' famous phrase, mere "handmaids" of the party.[69] For the DKP, the situation was the opposite: without their own organization, *parties became, over time, handmaids of their interests.* But, this was not simply, as one might imagine, a function of contrasting degrees of extra-party interest-group mobilization. Conservatives in Britain and Germany both faced highly mobilized societies, especially after 1890, including radical right demands from each country's respective naval leagues, agrarian protectionist societies, and other similar groupings.[70]

Rather, a vital difference in timing separates the two cases. In Britain, the party's organizational infrastructure – including party whips, the central office, and a network of professional party agents – was developed before appealing to civil society and interest groups. In Germany, partly owing to its heavy and early reliance on state-assisted electoral manipulation and cross-party coalitions, the DKP's development was stalled, and the party did not successfully evolve into an autonomous organizational infrastructure until long after interest groups and associational life had outpaced party development.

INTEREST GROUPS AND THE TRANSFORMATION OF GERMAN CONSERVATISM

To demonstrate empirically the phenomenon of organizational cooptation, or "capture," we can focus on the German Conservative Party and one prominent organized group, the Agrarian League or the *Bund der Landwirte* (BdL) that supported it beginning in 1893. While the alliance of the BdL and the German Conservative Party at many points was not a monolithic bloc and the two groups were sometimes in conflict, a pattern of *organizational capture* of the DKP by the BdL was predominant. Thus, we can ask: how were the conditions ripe for activists and interest groups, such as the BdL to capture the DKP?

[69] McKenzie, *British Political Parties* (1955), 146.
[70] On Britain and right-wing challenges (in the form of tariff societies and naval leagues) to conservatism around 1900, see Coetzee, *For Party or Country* (1990); and Green, *Crisis of Conservatism* (1995). On the same theme in Germany, see Hans-Jürgen Puhle, *Agrarische Interessenpolitik und preussischer Konservatismus im wilhelminischen Reich, 1893–1914: Ein Beitrag zur Analyse des Nationalismus in Deutschland am Beispiel des Bundes der Landwirte und der Deutsch-Konservativen Partei.* (Hannover: Verlag für Literatur u. Zeitgeschehen [1966] 1967); Eley, *Reshaping the German Right* (1980).

There are several reasons for thinking that the DKP in the 1890s was extremely vulnerable to organizational takeover. To begin with, by all accounts, it remained a loose party of notables who had little contact with each other late into the nineteenth century.[71] Indeed, even in the 1890s, the DKP had limited centralized organization in the three defining areas of party organization: nomination of candidates, mobilization of voters, and parliamentary discipline. The nomination of candidates was still largely handled by "collegial" local, self-selecting committees of notables.[72] Further, despite repeated efforts (e.g., by *Verein für König und Vaterland* in 1849 and *Preussenverein* in the 1860s) throughout the DKP's history, no integrated mass mobilization within the party hierarchy had developed across the national territory.[73] And, even in the domain of the parliament, the early 1890s found the party increasingly torn asunder by diverging stances on free trade and tariffs.[74] In roll call votes in the Reichstag on the all-important Italian and Austrian tariff treaties of 1891, for example, the DKP members of parliament were deeply divided: on the Italian treaty, fourteen of sixty-eight Conservative MPs voted for the legislation and the remaining voted against, were absent, or abstained.[75] On the Austrian treaty, eighteen of sixty-eight Conservative MPs opted for trade liberalization with the government, and the remaining MPs either abstained or voted against the reform.[76] The party was weak, due to the localized notable control of party nominations, and, fracturing even further in 1890, it was on the lookout for the auxiliary resources to provide nationally integrated extra-party organization.

In addition to the party's poor formal organization, after 1890 German Conservatives found themselves suddenly marginalized vis-à-vis the Imperial government itself. The motivations for DKP counter-organization then were clear. First, Bismarck's removal from power in March 1890 meant the elimination of a crucial ally and advocate of the hegemonic Conservative-Liberal *Kartellpolitik*. Second, the antisocialist laws expired in 1890, despite conservative efforts for their renewal, sparking a new socialist challenge to old regime power. And, third, Chancellor Leo von Caprivi's moderate "new course" aided by the non-Junker complexion of the new government suggested a fundamentally transformed political climate that suddenly appeared aggressively opposed to traditional conservative interests. Immediately after

---

[71] Nipperdey, *Die Organisation der Deutschen Parteien vor 1918* (1961); Puhle, *Agrarische Interessenpolitik und preussischer Konservatismus* (1967); Retallack, *Notables of the Right* (1988); Retallack, *The German Right* (2006).

[72] Puhle, *Agrarische Interessenpolitik und preussischer Konservatismus* (1967) 213–14.

[73] Retallack, *The German Right* (2006).

[74] Sarah Tirrell, *German Agrarian Politics After Bismarck's Fall. The Formation of the Farmer's League* (New York: Columbia University, 1951).

[75] Tirrell, *German Agrarian Politics (1951)*, 132–35.

[76] *Stenographische Berichte*, Reichstag, December 18, 1891, 3567–69. For an account of this, see Tirrell, *German Agrarian Politics* (1951), 135.

1890, for example, legislation was passed, granting East Prussian municipal authorities more autonomy, and in turn undermining local control of landed elites.[77] Even more crucially, over the course of 1891 and 1892, a series of liberalizing trade agreements with Austria–Hungary, Italy, Switzerland, Belgium, Serbia, and Romania were *perceived* to have caused dramatic collapse in agricultural prices, leaving landed elites in a fearful panic about their futures.[78] The political consequences for Conservatives were dramatic, as they now, in effect, were in the opposition. This serious threat to agrarian interests represented one of the great shifts of late-nineteenth-century German history, which altered, for a brief period, the dynamics of politics. As Paul Massing vividly puts it,

The Conservatives no longer dared remain a government party by definition... the Caprivi administration was an enemy to be fought and destroyed before its policy led to the destruction of the conservative society and all it stood for. But with the Kaiser and Chancellor in collusion with the forces of liberalism and revolution, even Conservative diehards could not think of having recourse to "direct action," that is having the executive branch scrap the constitution and rule with bayonets. The battle had to take place in the arena of parliamentary politics. More than ever before the Conservative Party needed the vote of the little man. A mass movement from the Right and led by the Right was what the hour demanded.[79]

Unlike in Britain in the same period, the DKP now found itself, politically speaking, consistently far to the right of the monarchy itself, an ultra-royalist movement dissenting from the monarchy's own government.[80] The motive for counter-organization therefore was clear. But without pre-existing and

---

[77] The focus here on eastern Prussia is not to deny the importance of agrarian radicalism and the BdL itself west of the Elbe, as is highlighted by Geoff Eley, "Anti-Semitism, Agrarian Mobilization, and the Conservative Party: Radicalism and Containment in the Founding of the Agrarian League, 1890–189," in *Between Reform, Reaction, and Resistance: Studies in the History of German Conservatism from 1789 to 1945*, ed. Larry Eugene Jones and James Retallack (Oxford: Berg Publishers, 1993), 187–228; Georg Vascik, "Agrarian Politics in Wilhelmine Germany: Diederich Hahn and the Agrarian League," in *Between Reform, Reaction, and Resistance. Studies in the History of German Conservatism*, ed. Larry Eugene Jones and James Retallack (Berg, 1993), 229–60.

[78] See Puhle, *Agrarische Interessenpolitik und preussischer Konservatismus* (1967), 28–36.

[79] Paul Massing, *Rehearsal for Destruction: A Study of Political Anti-Semitism in Imperial Germany* (New York: Harper, 1949), 63.

[80] This development was only the latest stage of development in a constantly shifting relationship of German conservatism and the state. A long strand of scholarship has attempted to reconstruct the chronological evolution of German conservative *ideas* vis-à-vis government through a series of stages. These works typically emphasize that before the French Revolution, Prussian conservatism, associated with Justus Möser, was anti-absolutist and associated with the defense of estates rights; after the French revolution, it took the form of the defense of absolutism against constitutionalism; in the 1850s, now associated with Julius Stahl, it became a defender of Prussian constitutionalism against revolution democracy; in the 1870s, Prussian conservatism was critical of nationalism, but by the 1880s and 1890s, a defender of the Reich. See, for example, Sigmund Neumann, *Die Stufen des Preussischen Konservatismus* (Berlin: E. Ebering,

nationally integrated party organization, conservative parliamentarians had to scramble and look elsewhere to other organizations for resources to bolster party building.[81] In particular, two groupings were relevant: the loose but highly mobilized and increasingly well-organized anti-Semitic Christian socialist groups, who viewed themselves, in part, as a potential mass organization for conservatism; and second, the Agrarian League (*Bund der Landwirte*).[82] The Anti-Semitic movements, particularly those of Protestant minister Adolf Stoecker, promised access to new, urban, and often *Mittelstand* (i.e., lower middle class) voters that could be used to rescue the old Conservative Party.[83] Stoecker himself argued, "Under the prevailing universal suffrage [it cannot] be doubted that the Conservative Party will gain its strength only in the social question."[84] Likewise, for the old *Mittelstand*, it was commonly claimed, first by the anti-Semitic journalist Otto Glagau, that "the Social Question is the Jewish Question."[85] Anti-Semitism would give conservatism a mass base and a "bridge" to conservatism for urban and nonagrarian voters.[86] This move to provide a popular base for conservatism did not occur, however, without resistance. Immediately, intense internal battles emerged within the party between, on the one hand, agrarian notables such as the party founder and chairman Otto von Helldorff-Bedra, and, on the other hand, the populist insurgency led by Stoecker and other provincial anti-Semitic agitators. A splinter group also developed centered on the long-standing and influential traditional elite conservative newspaper founded after 1848, the *Kreuzzeitung*, including its chief editor Wilhelm von Hammerstein.[87]

1930); Klaus Epstein, *The Genesis of German Conservatism* (Princeton: Princeton University Press, 1966). For a recent overview, see Retallack, *The German Right* (2006), Chapter 1.

[81] On the concept of "resources" in social movement theory, see John McCarthy and Mayer Zald, "Resource Mobilization and Social Movements: A Partial Theory," *American Journal of Sociology* 82, no. 6 (1977): 1212–41.

[82] See Peter G. J. Pulzer, *The Rise of Political Antisemitism in Germany and Austria* (Cambridge: Harvard University Press, [1964] 1988); Richard S. Levy, *The Downfall of the Anti-Semitic Political Parties in Imperial Germany* (New Haven: Yale University Press, 1975); Retallack, *The German Right* (2006).

[83] The main outlines of Adolf Stoecker's biography are worth briefly noting: he was the son of a blacksmith who later became a prison warden. Stoecker studied theology and began his career as a pastor in the Lutheran church, also serving as a tutor for a noble family in Courland; in the Franco-Prussian war, he served an army chaplain, and because of his reputation as a dramatic and charismatic figure in these years, he was called to Berlin where he served as "court preacher" in Berlin's largest Lutheran church. It was his activities in Berlin, including his efforts to build a "Christian socialist" alternative for Berlin's working class, that drew him to politics. See Pulzer, *Rise of Political Antisemitism* (1988), 85.

[84] Cited by Pulzer, *Rise of Political Antisemitism* (1988), 112.

[85] Levy, *The Downfall of the Anti-Semitic Political Parties in Imperial Germany* (1975), 276.

[86] Ibid.

[87] Indeed, the DKP's founding chairman, Helldorff-Bedra, resisted efforts to include the successful anti-Semitic Christian Social faction led by Stoecker in the parliamentary group and was forced to resign on April 6, 1892, though he was replaced by another "governmental" or traditional

The first fateful moment exposing the vulnerability of the poorly institutionalized DKP transpired at the Tivoli Congress of 1892. Stoecker and others had called for a conference to provide a forum to consider changes to the DKP's party program. Pressure had grown from provincial groups across Germany, provoked in large part by the efforts of Stoecker and Hammerstein to create a leadership crisis within the party itself, until the new party chairman, Otto von Manteuffel, very reluctantly called a party convention.[88] The rowdy event that unfolded at the Tivoli Brewery on the outskirts of Berlin on December 8, 1892, was described vividly by Stoecker in these terms: "It was not a party congress in dress coat and white gloves, but in street clothes. It was the Conservative Party in the era of the universal equal suffrage."[89]

Owing to the new nature of this conservative gathering, the Tivoli Congress represented an event of paramount historical significance for two reasons. First, for the first time in German history, a major political party assumed an explicitly anti-Semitic plank in its platform, introducing into the DKP program the ominous phrase, "We combat the widely obtruding and decomposing Jewish influence on our popular life. We demand a Christian authority for the Christian people and Christian teachers for Christian pupils."[90] But, second, most reflective of the lack of organizational autonomy of Conservative Party leaders, this stance was remarkably adopted against their explicit wishes and plans. Von Helldorff-Bedra had long been critical of the populism of anti-Semitism[91] as had his sober and traditionalist successor, Otto von Manteuffel, who chaired the Tivoli Congress.[92] Manteuffel, newly installed as party chair as of 1892, began the Congress with a draft program in hand, prepared by moderate allies and circulated ahead of time, that included the phrase, "We condemn the excesses of Anti-Semitism."[93] However, before the

---

conservative, von Manteuffel, who, however, was more willing to tolerate the new right-wing populism. See Levy, *The Downfall of the Anti-Semitic Political Parties in Imperial Germany* (1975), 79.

[88] Prussian parliamentary conservatives, under the leadership of classic "notable" party chairman Helldorff-Bedra had resisted calls for a popular party congress, preferring for affairs to be conducted "en petit comité" (Massing, *Rehearsal for Destruction* (1949), 64) because, as Helldorff-Bedra argued, "the lack of discipline" among party activists would give rise to "chaos" and would not allow for the benefits of "expert opinions" (cited by Retallack, *The German Right* (2006), 336). But, Stoecker had mobilized anti-Semitic groupings in his own constituency to produce an ultimatum, insisting to (and thereby embarrassing) the leadership into calling a convention.

[89] Quoted by Massing, *Rehearsal for Destruction* (1949), 64.

[90] Cited by Pulzer, *Rise of Political Antisemitism* (1988), 112.

[91] Retallack, *The German Right* (2006), 336.

[92] Revealingly, Helldorff-Bedra and Manteuffel were two of the eighteen Conservative Party Reichstag MPs who voted against the wishes of the agrarian interests and for government's free-trade treaty with Austria in 1891 (Tirrell, *German Agrarian Politics* (1951), 148).

[93] Retallack, *The German Right* (2006), 337. The most thorough account of this is found in Retallack, *Notables of the Right* (1988), 91ff.

leadership could assert itself, the dynamics of co-optation, or capture "from below," stormed the scene. As recorded in the minutes and a range of careful secondary accounts, the Tivoli Congress went rapidly and wildly off course as activists effectively seized the party, shoving the party to a new extreme outer limit.[94] How did this happen?

In the first place, party leaders had no method of checking credentials at the door, meaning that of the 1,200 attendees, most were not "party associates," but instead were Berlin-based anti-Semitic activists associated with Stoecker and local journalists. Second, because the purpose of the convention was to hold a highly symbolic debate over the party program and not to select candidates, a group of twenty-one relatively moderate "notable" Reichstag caucus members refused to attend the convention in protest, leaving Manteuffel alone to read aloud their statement that they wished to "stand by" the old 1876 party program. This proposal was shouted down, as was the condemnation of anti-Semitism. The arguments for anti-Semitism triumphed, as loud and unruly "reformers," such as a haberdasher from Saxony, Eduard Ulrich-Chemnitz, who introduced himself as a "man of the people," voiced entreaties like the following:

The Conservative Party wishes to be a *Volkspartei* (popular party); it therefore does not want to see itself all the more insulted with the talk of "demagoguery." It is common practice today among the leading circles of the Conservative Party, that everything... which moves the people is very easily dismissed with the stock phrase "demagogic." I must ask our honorable deputies themselves to become a little more "demagogic."[95]

Thus, in this chaotic party convention, we apparently find evidence for what John May originally described as the "law of curvilinear disparity": party activists, whether of the left or right, are always more extreme ideologically than election-minded party leaders.[96] Upon closer examination, however, we see that the Tivoli Congress is consistent with an amended and more nuanced version of that claim: it is in *loosely coupled or porous* party organizations that party leaders become victim to the demands of their activists as they are given unguarded access to decision-making bodies.[97] Thus, in such circumstances, party activists, commonly a party's "true believers," will more likely gain the upper hand over more moderate party leadership. Hence, party structure helps

[94] Retallack, *The German Right* (2006). See *Neue Preußische Zeitung*, Number 603, December 24, 1892, Levy, *The Downfall of the Anti-Semitic Political Parties in Imperial Germany* (1975), 276; Pulzer, *Rise of Political Antisemitism* (1988); Retallack, *Notables of the Right* (1988); Retallack, *The German Right* (2006).
[95] Retallack, *Notables of the Right* (1988), 92.
[96] John D. May, "Opinion Structure of Political Parties: The Special Law of Curvilinear Disparity," *Political Studies* 21, no. 2 (1973): 135–51.
[97] Kitschelt, "Internal Politics of Parties" (1989).

explain the turn to anti-Semitism in Germany's leading right-wing party in the late nineteenth century.[98]

But, just as quickly as it materialized, the moment of organized anti-Semitism seemed to fade. Historian and political scientist Peter Pulzer argues that organizational conflict among various anti-Semitic factions emerged and the severity of the agricultural crisis coupled with declining corn prices demanded a different political reaction.[99] In the effort to build a mass base, Conservatives discovered, as Levy describes it, that anti-Semites proved unreliable partners who might disappear as quickly as they arrived on the scene.[100] The cross-class anti-Semitic *Mittelstand* rhetoric and ideology persisted, but was now attached to a more effective organization: the remarkably efficient interest group and chief defender of agricultural interests into the twentieth century, the Agrarian League, or *Bund der Landwirte* (BdL).[101]

A NEW STAGE: CAPTURE BY THE AGRARIAN LEAGUE

Within two months of the Tivoli Congress, conservatives had discovered a new, more valuable ally in the BdL a joint project of landlords, activists from the Peasant's Union (*Bauerverein*), and one Reichstag MP.[102] But a misleadingly bifurcated debate exists over the degree to which agrarian mobilization developed "from above" by manipulative agrarian elites or "from below" out of small farmer or peasant grievances.[103] Certainly real grievances, as Eley has noted, such as growing indebtedness, the foot-and-mouth epidemic of 1891–92,

---

[98] It should be added that the Tivoli Congress has been interpreted as having longer-run consequences for German political life. As Hellmut von Gerlach recalled many years later, this moment was crucial in German history because it was here that anti-Semitism "made the greatest gain in prestige it could hope for" when it became part of the Conservative Party's program. Previously it had been represented only in various small splinter parties; now it became the legitimate property of one of the biggest parties, of the party nearest to the throne and holding the most important positions in the state. Anti-Semitism had come close to being accepted at the highest levels of social respectability (von Gerlach, cited by Massing, *Rehearsal for Destruction*, 1949, 66–67).

[99] Pulzer, *Rise of Political Antisemitism* (1988), 113.

[100] Levy, *The Downfall of the Anti-Semitic Political Parties in Imperial Germany* (1975).

[101] In addition, analysts argue that the Social Democratic Party's electoral success of 1903 was another important threshold prompting the formation of the *Reichsverband gegen die Sozialdemokratie* as a crucial tool of mobilization. See *Massenverbände und Massenparteien* (2000), 74. Grießmer also makes the case one could also point to the formation of the Pan-German League, formed in 1891 as a decisive "extraparliamentary" interest group (see Roger Chickering, *We Men Who Feel Most German: A Cultural Study of the Pan-German League, 1886–1914* (Boston: George Allen and Unwin, 1984)). For purposes of space, I limit myself to the BdL, which in many ways was a forerunner in organizational innovation.

[102] See account of founding in Puhle, *Agrarische Interessenpolitik und preussischer Konservatismus* (1967), 32–36.

[103] Compare, e.g., Puhle, *Agrarische Interessenpolitik und preussischer Konservatismus* (1967); Eley, *Reshaping the German Right* (1980), 21.

and the threat of increasing taxes, played a role in activating a populist mobilization in both western and eastern Germany.[104] But, in any case, the key point is that organization developed from both above and from below, providing a resource that could be redeployed for electoral purposes.

An elaborate and rapidly growing behemoth rivaled only by the Social Democratic Party, the BdL had attracted 160,000 members by October 1893, fusing together and absorbing membership and finances of existing farmer alliances and associations (the Congress of German Farmers, the Peasants' League, etc.).[105] The organization was both hierarchically centralized and territorially diffuse: local and regional associations were built from the ground up and clustered together to form *Wahlabteilungen* (i.e., one local organization per electoral district); this pattern of mass assemblage demonstrated the BdL's main objective – to influence electoral politics for the narrow economic interests of its members. In 1893, 271 of Germany's 397 parliamentary districts had a local BdL association;[106] the remaining districts were either urban or had no chance of electing a BdL sympathizer. The league had solidified its base.

In addition to its massive membership, the BdL was marked by a sprawling organization: in the early years after 1900, it had over 700 employees, including staff, agricultural-scientific experts, journalists, and political professionals, while its national headquarters in Berlin spread out across two building complexes near the Prussian Chamber of Deputies building.[107] The BdL also included several scientific divisions that distributed technical advice on best agricultural practice to farmers; a publishing house that oversaw at least three newspapers, book production, and other propaganda efforts; a press archive; fertilizer manufacturing facilities dispersed across Germany; and a social services and insurance office that oversaw old age and accident insurance for members. Most crucially, the BdL had formed a "political" division – run in the late 1890s by Dr. Diederich Hahn – that included a staff of full-time professionals single-mindedly running election campaigns, staging events, selecting sympathetic candidates, and offering strategic advice on agricultural interests for affiliated MPs and candidates.[108]

The BdL was, as historian and political scientist Hans-Jürgen Puhle has convincingly argued, not a political party. Indeed, it supported all parties, except the Social Democrats and Left Liberals.[109] It conceived of politics as a battle of organized interests rather than political party organizations; and it

---

[104] Eley, *Reshaping the German Right* (1980), 21.

[105] The history of this organization's founding, in response to the passage of tariff reform in 1891, is recounted in Tirrell, *German Agrarian Politics* (1951), 144–67.

[106] Puhle, *Agrarische Interessenpolitik und preussischer Konservatismus* (1967), 43 (footnote 22).

[107] Puhle, *Agrarische Interessenpolitik und preussischer Konservatismus* (1967), 45.

[108] See Puhle, *Agrarische Interessenpolitik und preussischer Konservatismus* (1967) 165–67; Tirrell, *German Agrarian Politics* (1951).

[109] Puhle, *Agrarische Interessenpolitik und preussischer Konservatismus* (1967) 184–209.

sought, over the long run, to create an autonomous arena for consultation among economic actors' decision making that eventually might exclude political parties altogether. It was, in short, self-consciously conceived of as a new type of interest group, far surpassing in its "machine-like" qualities all existing notable organizations of the right, such as the *Centralverband Deutscher Industrieller*, founded by Reichspartei politician Wilhelm von Kardoff or the *Vereinigung für Wirtschaft and Steuerreform* (Association of Economic and Tax Reformers). The BdL's purpose was to vigorously protect agriculture, its ideology manifesting a malignantly aggressive and populist edge to much of the group's ideology.[110] At one level, it was a perfect match for the German Conservative Party, which had long conceived of itself as the defender of agricultural interests; and since the DKP still lacked its own nationally integrated party organization on the scale necessary for political competition, the BdL became the surrogate to provide counter-organization for conservatism in an age of mass politics.

Still, what evidence is there that the organizational boundaries between the BdL and the DKP were blurred? And, given our claims of capture and co-optation, how do we know who set the terms of this alliance? Relations between political parties and interest groups are typically regulated by internal rules that establish either solid boundaries between their respective hierarchies or porous ones in which organizational blurring occurs.[111] If there is interpenetration, it usually involves interlocking personnel, as well as sharing of resources and organization, and formal and informal decision-making.[112] On each of these dimensions, the BdL and the DKP overlapped to a remarkable extent after 1893. Moreover, and most importantly, close analysis reveals that, over time, the balance of power tilted in the direction of the BdL, leading to the DKP's gradual capture by its surrogate.

First, by 1903, the DKP's leading executive body, the so-called "committee of eleven," consisted of MPs from throughout Germany and two members of the BdL.[113] Between 1898 and 1912, not only was every single Reichstag Conservative Party MP endorsed by and programmatically committed to the BdL, but also one-third of Conservative Party MPs were simultaneously high-level BdL functionaries.[114] Yet, it is very important to emphasize the following point: the BdL was self-consciously and formally "nonpartisan," and neither its leaders nor its members conceived of it as a political party. Nor did the

---

[110] In addition to not allowing non-Christian members, the BdL's mix of anti-Semitism, national-ism, and protectionism has been described in great detail by Puhle (*Agrarische Interessenpolitik und preussischer Konservatismus*, 1967) as a form of proto-fascism.

[111] Leslie, "Parties and other Social Functions" (2002), 16.   [112] Ibid.

[113] Also worth noting is that the troika who ran the BdL after 1898 (Dr. Gustav Roesicke, Conrad Wangenheim, and Diederich Hahn), the first was a Conservative Reichstag MP, while the latter two were not officially committed to the German Conservative Party. Puhle, *Agrarische Interessenpolitik und preussischer Konservatismus* (1967), 220.

[114] Puhle, *Agrarische Interessenpolitik und preussischer Konservatismus* (1967), 168–69.

organization directly nominate candidates for office, though evidence below
suggests this was not always the case. Indeed, the organization's chief political
function was to provide campaign materials and logistical support for
candidates from any political party (except the SPD and the Left Liberals) that
would endorse its program. Since the BdL's chief aim was the protection of
a narrow agrarian interest, it was thus willing to work with any political party
that carried out this agrarian agenda. Nonetheless, the amount of overlap
between BdL personnel and the DKP is particularly striking: while
100 percent of Conservative Party MPs were "committed" (*verpflichtet*) to
the BdL between 1893 and 1912, only 18 percent of the remaining Reichstag
MPs had any affiliation with the BdL during this whole period.[115] In other
words, the interest organization had a key function of providing organizational
resources, especially personnel, to the DKP.

A further telling instance of interpenetration is also evident in the case of the
DKP's General Secretary, Dr. Josef Kaufhold.[116] Appointed in 1905, Kaufhold
was in fact an employee of the BdL: his salary was paid by the BdL, he worked
out of his BdL office on Dessauerstrasse in Berlin, and he had the status of being
officially "on loan" from the BdL while leading the DKP. This unusual
arrangement stands in marked contrast to that of Britain, where the
relationship of parties and pressure groups was precisely the opposite: indeed,
the British Conservative Party leadership often "lent out" its own staff,
including Richard Middleton of the Central Office, to its supporting interest
group, the Primrose League (see, e.g., Chapter 3).

The result of this blurring of personnel was that, despite occasional
disagreements and conflicts, organizational resources and decision-making
were extensively shared between the two. The most relevant tools provided by
the BdL to the DKP were its elaborate publishing operations, which included by
1912 five newspapers and twenty-five periodicals, thus granting Conservatives
access to a well-developed production and national distribution network that
could reach Germany's largest and most remote communities.[117] Materials
included campaign pamphlets, "friendly" news accounts, and interpretations
of events in the lead-up to elections with enthusiastic slogans and headlines such
as *"Auf zu den Wahlen!"* ("Off to the Elections!"). The BdL also organized
innovative petition drives and signature-gathering campaigns, which became
vital tools for mobilizing voters and building organization.[118] If a candidate
from any party received the BdL endorsement, this machinery was instantly and

---

[115] Puhle, *Agrarische Interessenpolitik und preussischer Konservatismus* (1967), 168–70; 214–15.
[116] Puhle, *Agrarische Interessenpolitik und preussischer Konservatismus* (1967), 220.
[117] Puhle, *Agrarische Interessenpolitik und preussischer Konservatismus* (1967), 55.
[118] One example was the 1899 petition drive on a Reichstag law regulating meat production, which
Puhle (*Agrarische Interessenpolitik und preussischer Konservatismus*, 1967) reports might have
generated over 3 million signatures. On the more general theme of the relationship of petitions
and organization building, see Dan Carpenter, "The Petition as Tool of Recruitment" (Harvard
University, 2003).

energetically put to work on his behalf, usually starting six months before election day, with increasing frequency and vigor (e.g., anti-Social Democratic and anti-Semitic rhetoric) up until the day's arrival.

Aside from its media resources, the BdL independently organized and sponsored public events in non-election years and rallies during election years. In 1899, not even an election year, for example, the BdL held 5,000 separate events. It relied on a pool of "mobile" professional party speakers (*Wanderredner*), trained by the BdL in annual courses as well as through "public speaking" manuals. In 1896, Puhle reports a staff of eighteen BdL *Wandnerredner*, and by the 1903 elections, there were seventy-four of them working on behalf of predominately DKP candidates, supplying precisely the type of "agitational" resources the traditional party had lacked.[119]

Finally, the BdL furnished the DKP and other parties with crucial resources for parliamentary work. After 1893, the "parliamentary group" of the BdL, based in Berlin, was instrumental in effecting what had previously been elusive: closer coordination between the Prussian Chamber of Deputies Conservative parliamentary group and the Reichstag Conservative parliamentary group.[120] Until that point, the lack of a party "center" had meant that the DKP comprised several competing parliamentary groups that often clashed with each other. Further, by maintaining close relations with the DKP parliamentary leadership, the BdL's parliamentary group regularly consulted with DKP *Fraktion* leaders, offered policy expertise, allowed the DKP access to its archive resources, and, in fact, helped the DKP draft legislation and write speeches that were delivered by MPs on the Reichstag floor.[121] Finally, given the close collaboration and overlapping between the two entities in Berlin, it was common for formal and informal meetings to be held at BdL headquarters or the homes of BdL officials, as the BdL and the DKP forged joint stances on a wide range of topics, from trade issues to foreign policy and domestic politics.

Thus, despite occasional conflicts between the groups that we elaborate below, we see an extreme case of organizational blurring between the German Conservative Party and its chief interest group. Yet, the question remains: which way did power and influence run? One way to address this is to examine the dynamics surrounding the DKP's candidate selection process for the Reichstag elections. It is, after all, this key linchpin of power that reveals the ultimate organizational authority within a party. As E. E. Schattschneider has argued, "The nature of the nominating procedure determines the nature of the party; he who can make the nominations is the owner of the party."[122]

Given Schattschneider's insight, it is surprising how little we actually know systematically about the selection procedure of party candidates in Imperial

[119] Puhle, *Agrarische Interessenpolitik und preussischer Konservatismus* (1967), 61–62.
[120] Puhle, *Agrarische Interessenpolitik und preussischer Konservatismus* (1967), 221.
[121] Puhle, *Agrarische Interessenpolitik und preussischer Konservatismus* (1967), 220–21.
[122] Schattschneider, *Party Government* (1942), 64.

Germany.[123] Yet, some key facts about the relationship between the BdL and DKP expose the influence of interest groups over party leaders. First, as I have noted, for the German Conservative Party until the 1890s, it was local notables, usually among the largest landowners in a district and loosely belong to local and always shifting electoral committees, who were officially charged with selecting a constituency's candidates.[124] But, by the early 1890s, the actual dynamics at play in constituencies across Germany began to diverge from this model because, like many interest groups, the BdL offered official endorsement of candidates and, more importantly, provided key logistical help in mobilization and campaign organization.[125]

For example, in the unpublished papers of Baron Conrad von Wangenheim, member of the BdL's executive board, we see that the BdL at times actively intervened in the selection of candidates. In November 1906, for example, Wangenheim's fellow board member, Dr. Roesicke, reported to the former on his "behind the scenes" machinations to find an appropriate MP candidate in the district of Stargard.

Herr von Liebermann has told me in the strictest of confidence that [candidate] Kasell is impossible in Pyritz. Liebermann told me, however, that it would be an appropriate electoral constituency for Dr. Oertel. We would need to get into touch with the director of the creamery, Mr. Neumann, in Stargard.[126]

More important than the direct selection of candidates, however, was the issue of BdL's endorsements. Because of the organizational vacuum at the center of the DKP on the one hand and the BdL's vast organizational resources on the other, the endorsement system resulted in a new anticipatory dynamic of candidate selection described by Puhle in these terms: "Because the Conservative Party had no 'agitation machinery' of its own at its disposal, it could only nominate candidates that the BdL would support."[127] Thus, after 1893, according to Puhle, 100 percent of the DKP's MPs received BdL endorsement.[128] But this is only a very rough indicator of this dynamic. Additional evidence further supports

---

[123] Cf. Nipperdey, *Die Organisation der Deutschen Parteien vor 1918* (1961).

[124] Nipperdey, *Die Organisation der Deutschen Parteien vor 1918* (1961), 241ff.

[125] The conditions attached to endorsement were substantial: DKP candidates, like all Reichstag MP candidates, did not merely offer a pre-election "verbal" agreement to protect agricultural interests in exchange for BdL's campaign and logistical support. Instead, candidates subjected themselves to a written agreement with the local BdL branch whose support they sought.

[126] "Briefwechsel Conrad Freiherr von Wangenheim/Dr Roesicke im Jahre 1906" November 27, 1906, Nachlass Wangenheim, Bundesarchiv Berlin-Lichterfelde, N 2323 Nr. 2 (1906). More evidence of this type of intervention of an interest group to select candidates is seen in correspondence between the same two BdL executive board members in 1908. See, e.g., "Briefwechsel Conrad Freiherr von Wangenheim/Dr Roesicke im Jahre 1908" July 31, 1908, Nachlass Wangenheim, Bundesarchiv Berlin-Lichterfelde, N 2323 Nr. 3 (1908). In this instance the discussion was with regards to the difficult relationship of the BdL to the Catholic Center Party.

[127] Puhle, *Agrarische Interessenpolitik und preussischer Konservatismus* (1967), 214.

[128] Puhle, *Agrarische Interessenpolitik und preussischer Konservatismus* (1967), 168–70.

the idea that interest groups, led by the BdL, exerted control over the DKP's candidate selections and, more broadly, the behavior of its MPs.

To unpack these issues, I have constructed an original dataset on Prussian candidates for Reichstag office in Prussia's 236 Reichstag electoral constituencies during the course of the six national elections between 1890 and 1912.[129] The data, which includes information on thousands of candidates, reports each constituency's partisan makeup for each election year.[130] Of all the electoral competitions after 1890 for which we have data, we can focus our attention on a smaller universe of cases, the total number of districts in which at least one of the two major conservative parties (DKP and *Reichspartei*) fielded at least one candidate, which ranged from 164 districts in 1890 to a low of 131 districts in 1907. In Figure 6.4, we see that of those races, the two main conservative political parties often failed "to bind" their own right-wing interest allies to the candidates, facing candidates from the BdL and other right-wing interest groups.[131] In particular, Figure 6.4 shows that in 1890 this occurred 11 percent of the time; in 1893 and 1898, 38 percent of conservative candidacies confronted right-wing interest group opponents; in 1903, 19 percent of conservatives faced opposition from within their own camp; and in 1912, 20 percent ran against other competitors from the right.

If, as Schattschneider has argued, the true "test" of a party's power is whether its nomination authoritatively "binds," we see that the DKP often failed this test, facing an internal right-wing insurgency in a number of constituencies every year after 1890.[132] While these challenges usually did not end in electoral victory for the party outsiders, the mere presence of a right-wing rebellion was a serious challenge because, as Schattschneider also writes, "Unless [a] party makes authoritative and effective nominations, it cannot stay in business."[133] A close analysis of these insurgencies, furthermore, reveals that they were chiefly interest groups efforts to exert disciplinary leverage over DKP MPs who had strayed from the interest group's stance on issues.

To take one example, we can reconstruct political dynamics in the predominately rural East Prussian district of Deutsch Krone, today in northwestern Poland, that was represented throughout the 1890s by a Reichspartei MP, Karl Friedrich Oskar

---

[129] The total number of electoral constituencies for the Reichstag in Germany as a whole was 397. The data analysis here focuses on Prussian electoral constituencies since this was the heartland of Conservative Party power.

[130] The data for this are compiled from the two-volume data handbook by Reibel, ed., *Handbuch der Reichstagwahlen, 1890–1918: Bündnisse, Ergebnisse, Kandidaten* (2007).

[131] The groups coded as "right-wing interest groups" include *Mittelstandsvereinigung, Wirtschaftliche Vereinigung, Bund der Landwirte,* and the collection of anti-Semitic groupings that tried, at points, to organize as independent political parties: *Christlich-Sozial, Antisemiten, Antisemitische Volkspartei, Deutsche Reformpartei, Deutsche Sozialpartei,* and *Deutsch Soziale Reformpartei.* A key to these groups is provided in Reibel, ed., *Handbuch der Reichstagwahlen, 1890–1918: Bündnisse, Ergebnisse, Kandidaten* (2007), 52–53.

[132] Schattschneider, *Party Government* (1942), 64.   [133] Ibid.

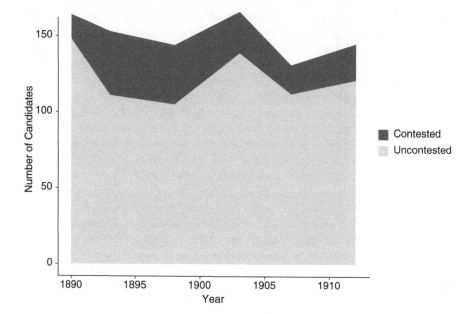

FIGURE 6.4: Conservative Party Candidates, Contested and Uncontested by Right-Wing Interest Groups, 1890–1912
Data Source: Reibel 2007

Freiherr von Gamp-Massaunen. In 1890 and 1893, Gamp-Massaunen received the endorsement of the DKP and the National Liberals, not only winning these races, but also receiving the all-important campaign support that came with the BdL's 1898 endorsement. However, by 1903, all that changed with one reverberating political rupture. In the tariff reform debates and legislation leading up to the race, Gamp-Massaunen had supported free-trade tariff reform that ran directly counter to the BdL's position. This vote also violated Gamp-Massaunen's formal agreement with the BdL, which had been the price of the organization's endorsement. Consequently, shortly before the election, the local BdL chairman, undoubtedly in coordination with the Berlin office, abruptly announced that Gamp-Massaunen no longer enjoyed the "trust" of the BdL. Gamp-Massaunen scrambled, promising a return to his previous protectionist stance if the opportunity arose, but the BdL formally withdrew its support from the Reichspartei MP and ran its own candidate.[134] While in this particular case the incumbent won a closely fought race, garnering 57 percent of the vote in the second round even without BdL support, an unmistakable message had been sent.[135]

---

[134] Reibel, ed., *Handbuch der Reichstagwahlen, 1890–1918: Bündnisse, Ergebnisse, Kandidaten* (2007), 29–30.
[135] Gamp-Massaunen appeased the BdL's criticism, earning their endorsement in the next election. Puhle, *Agrarische Interessenpolitik und preussischer Konservatismus* (1967). Puhle recounts in great detail how the ideology and the party program of the DKP was gradually altered over the

In short, while the interest groups were rarely electorally victorious, the mere threat of rebellion had the potential to transform conservative political parties and conservative politics more generally. Puhle asserts that the BdL "deformed" German conservatism by supplying an institutional anchor for anti-Semitism, radical agrarianism, militarism, and protectionism.[136] The repercussion was that German conservatism was thrust to the right of the monarchy and the old regime it sought to defend. More broadly, a new form of influence on parties emerged in Germany that was ironically analogous to, albeit quite different, from what Ostrogorski had feared might come to pass in Britain between "party organization" and members of the British Parliament.[137] Ostrogorski famously argued that the rise of the "party caucus" was a pernicious trend that damaged the tradition of MP independence and measured discretion. Because conservative party organization was weak in nineteenth-century Germany, the "venerable" tradition of MP independence was replaced not by an institutionalized party organization but instead by a much more pernicious force: a professionalized but narrow *interest group* radicalism – a dynamic that, as we will see in later chapters, would have devastating consequences for the long-run development of democracy.

EPILOGUE: WHAT WENT WRONG WITH GERMAN CONSERVATISM?

Before turning to the consequences of weakly institutionalized party structure on the democratization, we must ask two questions. First, while I have laid out the symptoms of party weaknesses, such as those of the DKP and the *Reichspartei*, why was the German right so fractured to *begin* with? And, second, why were repeated attempts at German party organization in the form of the DKP, for example, thwarted before 1914? There were in fact efforts, in 1848 and 1871, and before 1914, at building mass organization, but they all collapsed. Further, other parties, including the Center Party and the SPD, two outsider parties to the old regime, built up their party organization while existing in the same institutional context, which presumably was not conducive to party building. With universal male suffrage national parliamentary elections already in existence beginning in 1871, the DKP thus represents a puzzle.

The answer, consistent with the account of British conservatism elaborated in Chapter 3, entails a two-step path-dependent logic. First, there was a critical "window of opportunity" for the German Conservative Party to emerge as an effective nationally encompassing mass party with a professional leadership and division of labor at the top. As the case of Britain illustrates, during this "age of

---

1890s; indeed, he notes, the DKP economic program eventually itself was lifted entirely from the BdL's own economic program.
[136] Puhle, *Agrarische Interessenpolitik und preussischer Konservatismus* (1967), 274.
[137] Ostrogorski, *Democracy and the Organization of Political Parties* (1902).

pressure groups," the party of the right had to emerge *before* mass interest groups in order to fill the mobilizing space that appeared after 1890. While Britain's Conservative Party filled this sociological space by the 1880s, becoming the key organizer of its own domain, in Germany, efforts to organize on the right from the late 1840s through the 1880s had faltered. By the 1890s, the aftermath was a realm of well-organized interest groups *outside* of, and substituting for, parties on the electoral right, and the DKP grew increasingly reliant on "surrogate" groups.

If timing was critical, then we ask: why did the traditional German electoral right miss the window of opportunity to build itself before the "age of the pressure group" triumphed? In other words, why, by the beginning of the 1890s, was the German right still so poorly organized and ceding political mobilization to non-partisan groups like the BdL? The answer is partly rooted in the German Conservative Party's unusually close access to the state, its reliance on electoral fraud, and the long constitutional legacy of weak parliaments and unconstrained executives that limited not only liberals' organization efforts but also conservatives.' We know this to be true; but this account is incomplete for three reasons. First, if elites were so firmly protected by Germany's dualistic constitutional structures, this explanation assumes that there ought to have been no serious *efforts* at party building on the electoral right in the first place, which as we shall see is incorrect. Universal male suffrage beginning in 1871, as well as flirtations with it as far back as 1848, after all prompted serious experiments with popular conservative party-building that simply failed to bear fruit. Second, other national cases marked by a dualistic constitutional structure, such as Sweden and Denmark, show that a weak parliamentary history does not always preclude the advent of a well-organized electoral right.[138] And, finally as the last chapter also made clear, the purported nexus between a strong parliament, as England had after 1688, and "strong parties" may not be as automatic as we think. Thus, we must also consider other factors.

First of all, prior to and during Germany's Imperial period tensions intensified between the Conservative Party and the monarchy hastening the conservative need to formally organize. It is not fully appreciated that in the 1848 revolution, self-described Prussian Conservatives "discovered" party organization and invented a normative *theory* of party, which, on its face, paved the way for the creation of effective party organization.[139] The Prussian king's unexpected adoption of a new constitution in March 1848 not only provoked association-building on the left, but also on the right, as old-regime allies increasingly found

---

[138] See Discussion in Chapter 2.
[139] See Dieter Langewiesche, "Die Anfänge der deutschen Parteien. Partei, Fraktion und Verein in der Revolution von 1848/49," *Geschichte und Gesellschaft* 4, no. 3 (1978): 324–61; Wolfgang Schwentker, *Konservative Vereine und Revolution in Preussen, 1848/49: Die Konstituierung des Konservatismus als Partei* (Düsseldorf Droste, 1988).

the new regime's unpredictable moves reason for self-organization. As described in the careful work of historians Schwentker and Schult, in Prussia, landowners, military officials, and high government officials feared for their lives, retreating to family estates in the spring of 1848.[140] One set of groups, revolving around the von Gerlach brothers, however, actively sought to build a "Conservative Party" to respond to the new reality. The result was a proliferation of articles in the *Kreuzzeitung*, a newly founded and rapidly growing newspaper, with titles such as "The Formation of a Conservative Party" (*"die Bildung einer conservative Partei"*), calls for a new "constitutional-monarchical" response to unrest, as well as the formation of associations and "political clubs" throughout the country. Presaging James Bryce's insight about the Spartan-like power of "party organization" cited in Chapter 3, one conservative author presented his case to his readers on the importance of party organization.[141] He wrote,

One can think of political clubs what one wants to, however this much is certain: one must fight the opponent on his own terrain if one does not want to go extinct. There is a wonderful power in the regularized and planned activities of a corporate organization. As soon as twenty or thirty comrades of the same persuasion meet together on a regular basis, the corporate organization gains in power and influence more than if there were ten-times more individuals involved... it is by organizing as a political "Club" that a small minority can dominate an opposition of fully opposite convictions.[142]

Reflecting on the same contested and possibly conflicted relationship of "party" and "democracy" that would occupy Anglo-American and European contemporaries such as M. Ostrogorski and James Bryce, German conservatives had discovered the promise and perils of "party organization."[143] In a letter to Otto von Bismarck, influential editor Hermann Wagener argued that "in terms of building organization we can learn from our opponent."[144] And the paper's founder, Ernst Ludwig von Gerlach, in a pair of important articles published in August and September 1848, entitled "The Formation of a Conservative Party" (*"Die Bildung einer conservativen Partei"*), elaborated his "appreciation" of political parties.[145] Four points were crucial in von Gerlach's articles. First, he asserted that with the recent "events," "nothing else remains" for the opponents of

---

[140] Schwentker, *Konservative Vereine und Revolution* (1988); and Richard Schult, "Partei wider Willen: Kalküle und Potentiale konservativer Parteigründer in Preußen zwischen Erstem Vereinigten Landtag und Nationalversammlung, 1847/1848," in *Deutscher Konservatismus im 19. und 20. Jahrhundert* ed. Dirk Stegmann, et al. (Bonn: Verlag Neue Gesellschaft, 1983), 33–68.

[141] Bryce, *The American Commonwealth* (1908).

[142] Neue Preußische Zeitung, nr. 55 September 7, 1848, cited by Schwentker, *Konservative Vereine und Revolution* (1988), 87.

[143] See Nancy Rosenblum, *On the Side of the Angels: An Appreciation of Parties and Partisanship* (Princeton: Princeton University Press, 2008); Bryce, *The American Commonwealth* (1908); and Ostrogorski, *Democracy and the Organization of Political Parties* (1902).

[144] Cited by Schwentker, *Konservative Vereine und Revolution* (1988), 90.

[145] On the "appreciation" of parties, see Rosenblum, *On the Side of the Angels* (2008).

revolution than a "monarchical-constitutional party."[146] The defense of property rights was a central preoccupation behind this movement, and it was only a political party that could now help secure this.[147] Second, as conservative associations developed across Prussia during the summer of 1848, he maintained that it was a centralized body (i.e., a central committee) that was most necessary – one that could serve as a point of connection for "the local *Vereine*, that are otherwise often isolated from each other... to thereby provide a strong, internal organization for the conservative party."[148]

Third, von Gerlach sharply criticized the prominent conservative-minded extraparliamentary "interest group" that had developed among eastern Prussia's agrarian elite, the *Verein zur Wahrung der Rechte des Grundbesitzes und zur Aufrechtererhaltung des Wohlstands aller Volksklassen* (the Association for the Protection of Landowners and All Classes). Here, he argued against what he viewed as the group's excessively "narrow" program and instead insisted that conservative interests must be pursued within the context of a *political party*. To illustrate his point, von Gerlach drew upon the example of the 1830s Anti-Corn Law League in Britain, contending that group's free trade agenda was precisely "aided by its close connection to political parties."[149] Finally, fourth, in a follow-up article on the same topic on September 7, 1848, von Gerlach elaborated a further crucial task for conservative party organizers: an innovative "school for voters and candidates" that would over the long run train conservatives to fight against republicanism and anarchy.[150]

In short, this evidence suggests that Prussian conservative interests were *not* always simply so securely protected in a bureaucratic and military apparatus and thus uniquely predisposed against parties. The idea that Prussian conservatives simply never needed party organization finds itself on shaky ground, because in Prussia in 1848, what can be called a normative "breakthrough" occurred from an "old conservatism" to a fundamentally new form of conservatism.[151] Political parties were now seen as viable and legitimate vehicles for political "self-defense" against liberalism and radicalism.

Grass roots organizing exploded in Prussia between May and December 1848, when three new self-identified conservative *Vereine*, some even with cross-class ambitions, sprang up outside the parliament as civil society organizations in cities and in the countryside across Prussia: the *Patriotenverein*, the *Preussenverein*, and the *Verein für König und Vaterland*.

[146] *Neue Preußische Zeitung*, Nr 53, August 31, 1848, Zweite Beilage, 333.
[147] Schwentker, *Konservative Vereine und Revolution* (1988), 111
[148] *Neue Preußische Zeitung*, Nr 53, August 31, 1848, Zweite Beilage, 333.
[149] Ibid., as cited in Schwentker, *Konservative Vereine und Revolution* (1988), 113.
[150] "Die Bildung einer conservativen Partei und der Verein für König und Vaterland, II *Neue Preußische Zeitung*, Nr. 59, September 7, 1848, as cited by Schwentker, *Konservative Vereine und Revolution* (1988), 114.
[151] See Clark, *Iron Kingdom* (2006), 503.

Their ideological profiles, social membership, and political purposes differed, but shared some core commonalities, including the geographical basis of support and broader rejection of the results of the 1848 Revolution.[152] Indeed, precisely because of this incredibly successful "bottom up" proliferation of extraparliamentary groups, each with its own distinctive constituency, von Gerlach and his closest *Kreuzzeitung* associates nervously recognized the possible problems posed by the absence of a coherent party center to coordinate these rapidly growing organizations.

In late June 1848, a group of prominent conservatives, including von Gerlach, Carl Wilhelm Lancizolle, Adolf von Thadden-Trieglaff, Ernst von Senfft, Victor Aimé Huber, Robert Heinrch von der Goltz, and a young Otto von Bismarck convened in Berlin to formulate a strategy to unite conservative movements. In a jointly issued statement, they called on conservatives to overlook their own differences; to overcome confessional, class, and occupational divisions; and to develop a system of coordinating, funding, and overseeing the activities of existing associations in the "political education" of voters. As von Gerlach urged, laying his scheme in detail in his two-part essay in the *Kreuzzeitung*, the formation of a conservative central party was needed.

What, then, prevented this from happening? First, one pitfall was the nature of the founding via a process of "diffusion" rather than "penetration."[153] In sociologist Angelo Panebianco's terms, a party founded via "penetration,"

---

[152] The *first*, the Patriot's Association (*Patriotenverein*), was largely an organization of landlords, former government officials, and other notables and emerged in different locations in early summer 1848 partly in reaction to the failure to mobilize for the first parliamentary elections but also in response to fissures within the Liberal "constitutional associations" that had encapsulated both Liberals and Conservatives in the post-March 1848 period. Micro-level organizational evidence (Schwentker, *Konservative Vereine und Revolution*, 1988) from Ministry of Interior sources as well as organization membership lists, pamphlets, and brochures of found in various German archives, adds up to an aggregate picture of surprising activity (Schwentker, *Konservative Vereine und Revolution*, 1988, 75–76). Similarly, the *second* group, the *Preussenverein*, also began to appear across Prussia in the summer months of 1848. This group was, perhaps, the first cross-class conservative organization in modern German history. It built its appeal on calls to "protect" Prussia against outside threats (including in the rest of Germany), and proclaimed that its goal was to fight against "republican and absolutist tendencies." This group spread rapidly, as a cross-class organization, including urban and rural members. A founding meeting was held in Berlin at the end of May 1848; an association was set up in Halle, with 300 members in July 1848; in Königsberg, a founding assembly occurred in August 1848; and associations were set up across eastern Prussia. Membership was not limited to landlords, officers, bureaucrats, and soldiers. Schwentker (*Konservative Vereine und Revolution*, 1988, 83–85) reports that Preussenverein recruiters for the organization went into poor neighborhoods and distributed brandy to celebrate the King's birthday with a mass appeal to patriotism and the monarch. Finally, a third group, the *Verein fur König und Vaterland*, also emerged in this founding period. For an account of right "constitutional" groups in Bavaria as they organized in spring 1849, see Klaus Seidl, '*Gesetzliche Revolution' im Schatten der Gewalt: die politische Kultur der Reichsverfassungskampagne in Bayern 1849* (Paderborn: Verlag Ferdinand Schöningh, 2014).

[153] Panebianco, *Political Parties* (1988), 64–65.

one in which the central organization forms local organizations, leads to centralized parties. A party formed via "diffusion" is one in which local organizations exist first and join together to create a national organization, which leads to a less centralized party.[154] The formation of the Prussian Conservative Party was a clear instance of the latter. After the meeting of the several leading figures mentioned above, a "convention" meeting was held in Magdeburg on July 14, 1848, with 500 representatives of existing *Vereine* in attendance, as well as a second follow-up convention in Halle on July 24, 1848. The founding of the conservative party was a "mass" event, with a remarkably high dose of popular involvement. At the first general party congress for the *Verein für König und Vaterland* on July 14, 1848, in Magdeburg, for example, 500 activists, mostly landowning aristocrats from local *Patriotische Vereine, Preussenvereine*, and other groups such as farmers' associations attended. The minutes report that the chairman began the meeting by proposing a central committee, which was immediately and publicly denounced by a local *Preussenverein* member who skeptically expressed that all the local "associations were already established and were not interested in submitting themselves to an obscure central committee in Berlin."[155]

A second, highly charged and largely symbolic issue then was discussed: whether the Liberal ministry should be praised or criticized for having taken a middle road in parliamentary proposals to recognize and officially honor the revolutionaries killed in the March 1848 uprisings. The ministry did not reject parliamentary proposals outright but removed some of the more radical proposals in order to maintain support from the monarchy.[156] This compromise split the conservative gathering, with some calling for complete resignation of the Liberal ministry for having made any concessions at all to the "radicals," and others lauding the ministry for having rejected the most "radical" calls for a full embrace of the "republican" efforts to memorialize the fallen revolutionaries.

But, in addition to the obstacles posed by this surprisingly "grassroots" founding, which made party building difficult (as Panebianco would predict), confessional divides loomed large in a way they did not in Britain, further complicating the rift.[157] In brief, in Prussia, while Protestant areas could be organized along popular lines for partisan Conservative Party purposes, Catholic areas could not.[158] Europe's nineteenth-century conservative political parties required, as I argued in the last several chapters, cross-class

---

[154] Panebianco, *Political Parties* (1988), 49–68.
[155] Schwentker, *Konservative Vereine und Revolution* (1988), 92.
[156] On the debate, Schwentker, *Konservative Vereine und Revolution* (1988), 93.
[157] Panebianco, *Political Parties* (1988).
[158] As we will see below, the opposite was the case in Bavaria: it was in Catholic regions, not Protestant regions, that the right or conservative forces organized in Bavaria. See discussion in Seidl, *'Gesetzliche Revolution' im Schatten der Gewalt: die politische Kultur der Reichsverfassungskampagne in Bayern 1849* (2014).

appeals and mobilization techniques usually centered on confessional networks to bolster nationally integrated organization (see Chapter 3). For this reason the structure of religious cleavages in Prussia, and even more so in Germany generally, presented a major dilemma. On the one hand, orthodox Lutherans provided the initial "political talent" of German conservatism, as Marjorie Lamberti has argued, and Lutheran landed elites comprised its core constituency.[159] It is no accident, for example, that almost one-quarter (twelve of fifty) of the chairs of the local branches of the *Treubund für König und Vaterland* in 1849 were Protestant ministers.[160] Furthermore, as Schult has argued, orthodox Protestantism offered, in terms of mobilization and propaganda, a common "starting point that could speak to *all social classes* of Protestants."[161]

On the other hand, the population of eleven of Prussia's twenty-seven *Regierungsbezirke* in 1848 had Catholic majorities, each with its own parallel universe of Catholic landed elites, priests, peasants, workers, and *Vereine*, leaving these regions entirely inaccessible to Prussian conservatism's strictly Lutheran cross-class confessional appeals and mobilizational strategy. Thus, the strategy to build a conservative mass party organization across the whole territory of Prussia – let alone Germany – contained a fatal flaw. Unlike in Britain, Belgium, and Sweden, where religious affiliation provided a point of convergence and at least commonality, the presence of parallel Protestant and Catholic "strongholds" in Prussia and Germany effectively divided the core constituency of landed elites, rendering any single religiously based mobilizational strategy severely diminished.

This dynamic was also visible in Catholic Bavaria, where similar but parallel popular conservative Catholic movements sprung up in the spring of 1849, mobilizing mass protest events and hundreds of petition campaigns to pressure the Bavarian government to take anti-revolutionary stands vis-à-vis the ongoing negotiations at the Frankfurt National Assembly.[162] Again, it was not only the pro-revolutionary left that was organizing. Two key Catholic conservative groups, the *Piusverein* and the *Verein für konstitutionelle Monarchie und religiöse Freiheit (Association for Constitutional Monarchy and Religious Freedom)* were Catholic-based groups that recent archival work makes clear

---

[159] Defense of king, fatherland, and god was the founding principle. See Dagmar Bussiek, *"Mit Gott für König und Vaterland!" die Neue Preussische Zeitung, 1848–1892* (Lit Verlag: Muenster, 2002); Marjorie Lamberti, "Lutheran Orthodoxy and the Beginning of Conservative Party Organization in Prussia," *Church History* 37, no. 4 (1968): 439–53.

[160] Schwentker, *Konservative Vereine und Revolution* (1988), 286.

[161] For an elaboration of the theological issues at stake, see Schult, "Partei wider Willen" (1983): 65–66, 83.

[162] James Harris, "Rethinking the Categories of the German Revolution of 1848: The Emergence of Popular Conservatism in Bavaria," *Central European History* 25, no. 2 (1992): 123–48; Seidl, *'Gesetzliche Revolution' im Schatten der Gewalt: die politische Kultur der Reichsverfassungskampagne in Bayern 1849* (2014).

both possessed a mass *cross-class* membership.[163] Further these groups' anti-revolutionary organizing was centered around Catholic religious holidays (e.g., *Pfingstsonntag*) and church services. But these groups' activity, careful spatial historical research has also made clear, were as a result entirely isolated to only homogenously Catholic regions of *Niederbayern* and *Oberbayern*. In confessionally mixed regions of Bavaria such as Franken and Schwaben, only limited popular conservative organizing took place.[164]

The constraining effect of Germany's deep confessional divides on conservative party organizing was thus visible in Catholic Bavaria and predominately Protestant Prussia. Using the Prussian example, one more systematic clue of this is seen in the way self-identified "conservative party" associational life in the high point of 1848–49 was geographically concentrated in Protestant parts of Prussia and – in sharp contrast to Bavaria – almost entirely absent in Catholic regions of Prussia.[165] It has of course long been argued that in terms of voters, Prussian conservatism was essentially a Protestant phenomenon, anchored in Lutheran circles of northern Germany.[166] However, less fully recognized until recently is that efforts to build conservative party organization were similarly constrained by confessional divides.[167] Catholic landlords, a natural socioeconomic ally of Protestant landlords, for example, operated in different social circles and thus lent their support to the emerging Catholic political grouping that would eventually constitute Germany's *Zentrumspartei*. Mass organization of course developed in Catholic regions, but as it developed into Germany's first mass party, the *Zentrumspartei*, it ran at conflicting purposes with Protestant conservatism despite overlapping potential interests. In short, cross-class confessional networks, a crucial social resource for European conservative parties more generally, were deeply fractured by schism in Prussia and consequently less useful for purposes of building a nationally integrated popular conservative party.

To demonstrate this point systematically, we can draw upon a meticulous reconstruction of the number of all conservative associations of the type described above in each Prussian *Regierungsbezirk* collected by the Prussian Ministry of the Interior at the end of 1848.[168] While no comprehensive data on

---

[163] See detailed individual-level data on membership in local branches of the *Piusverein* and the *Association for Constitutional Monarchy and Religious Freedom* in Seidl, '*Gesetzliche Revolution' im Schatten der Gewalt: die politische Kultur der Reichsverfassungskampagne in Bayern 1849* (2014), 253–55.

[164] For geo-coded protest-event and petition data demonstrating this point, see Seidl, '*Gesetzliche Revolution' im Schatten der Gewalt: die politische Kultur der Reichsverfassungskampagne in Bayern 1849* (2014), 205; 21.

[165] Schwentker, *Konservative Vereine und Revolution* (1988), 159–60.

[166] Suval, *Electoral Politics in Wilhelmine Germany* (1985), 99.

[167] See also Retallack, *The German Right* (2006).

[168] These data were originally reported by Schwentker, *Konservative Vereine und Revolution* (1988), 158.

individual conservative association membership exists as for the British Conservative Party's Primrose League, the Prussian Ministry of Interior data does give us one rough measure for "organizational density" by identifying and listing the number of conservative party associations (e.g., *Preussenverein, Patriotenverein*) in each province at the end of 1848.

Is there any systematic relationship between the density of local conservative party organizations and the portion of Protestants in particular regions? Schwentker suggests a positive relationship but does not account for possibly confounding variables, such as urbanization, employment structure, or population.[169] There are several reasons to include controls for these variables. Conservative party leaders such as von Gerlach repeatedly noted that it was the *"platten Land"* (i.e., rural or agricultural hinterlands) that were most promising terrain for conservative *Verein* activity. Scholarly analysts have long argued, by contrast, that it was primarily artisans or preindustrial craftsmen (*Handwerker*) who provided a bulwark of conservative or reactionary sentiment against the revolution.[170] Finally, social movement theory more generally suggests that greater urbanization and population density helps organization and mobilization.

We can address the question of whether Conservative Party associations were significantly shaped by religious cleavages by using multivariate OLS analysis (with robust standard errors), in which the dependent variable is the number of conservative associations adjusted for population (i.e., per 10,000 citizens) in each of Prussia's twenty-six *Regierungsbezirke* (or provinces) as reported in the Prussian Ministry of Interior's 1848 report. The chief independent variable of interest is "Protestants as a portion of population" in 1848. The hypothesis is that Conservative Party associational density is greater in Protestant areas. Table 6.2 reports the findings.

In Models 1–3, we include all the main controls and see that conservative party association organizational density is significantly correlated with percentage of Protestants. In other words, the Conservative Party found its strongest organization-building potential in Protestant regions. As in the analysis of British counties in the last chapter, the very small number of units in this universe of study, however, should caution us about reading too much into the non-significance of the control variables. But since our main purpose is to assess the hypothesis that a confessional variable, in particular Protestantism, positively affected party building, the statistically significant findings for this variable, despite the small number of cases, provide surprisingly firm support. The findings confirm the idea that Prussian Conservative Party was able to find denser organization where the portion of Protestants (vis-à-vis Catholics) was higher. What mattered was not the absence of sufficient incentive to build

[169] Schwentker, *Konservative Vereine und Revolution* (1988), 160.
[170] Schwentker, *Konservative Vereine und Revolution* (1988), 170.

TABLE 6.2: *OLS Analysis of Conservative Association Organization Density, 1848*

	Dependent Variable: Conservative Association Organizational Density (per 10,000 Residents)			
	(1)	(2)	(3)	(4)
Protestant as	0.108***	0.113***	0.095***	0.088***
Proportion of Population	(0.033)	(0.036)	(0.037)	(0.038)
Proportion of Population in Agricultural Sector		0.071 (0.146)		−0.182 (0.212)
Proportion of Population Employed as Craftsmen			−0.166 (0.116)	−0.279 (0.176)
Urbanization		−0.003 (0.135)	0.010 (0.082)	−0.088 (0.141)
Population (per 10,000)		0.0001 (0.001)	0.0002 (0.001)	0.0002 (0.001)
R^2	0.315	0.349	0.403	0.425
Adjusted R^2	0.285	0.219	0.284	0.274
Observations	25	25	25	25

Notes: *$p<0.1$; **$p<0.05$; ***$p<0.01$; robust standard errors in parentheses.
Data Source: Conservative Association data draws on Schwentker 1988,158

a party; it was the absence of "raw materials" of social organization for party building.

In sum, due to many causes, the German Conservative Party entered the twentieth century as a weak, fractured, and loosely coupled organization reliant on outside interest groups for electoral mobilization. Despite the presence of mass franchise in Germany after 1871, a variety of systematic and idiosyncratic factors exogenous to democratization itself conspired to block party building in Germany. By 1911, conservative reformers within the conservative milieu, such as Dr. Adolf Grabowsky, feared it was "too late" – that history had "deformed" German Conservatism in fundamental ways.[171] As we will see in later chapters, Grabowski's assessment was largely correct, with dire consequences for democracy.

[171] Adolf Grabowsky, "Der Kulturkonservatismus und die Reichstagswahlen" *Der Tag* 19, 22 (January 1911)

7

Stalled Democratization in Germany Before 1914

On the spring evening of May 20, 1912, a fleet of black automobiles drove up the graveled side driveway of Berlin's Prussian House of Representatives, unloading a group of men clad in dark suits. Earlier in the evening, these Reichstag Conservative Party members had hurriedly left that body's chambers, located just down the street, in the middle of debate. They lined into the chambers of the Prussian House of Representatives because that evening their vote was required on a piece of legislation before the Prussian provincial parliament.[1] This exclusive group, composed mostly of landed notables representing rural east Prussian constituencies, all with dual mandates in both the Prussian state and Reichstag chambers, had been called away by their leaders in the Prussian state assembly to exercise their vote. The bill they faced would have altered the so-called "three-class" suffrage rules for elections to the state House of Representatives in Prussia, then Germany's largest state. They cast their vote to "rescue" the three-class voting system and then quickly returned to their idling cars. In that decisive vote, summarized in Table 7.1, the seemingly overwhelming coherence and power of late Imperial German conservatism appeared to be at work. The Conservative and *Reichspartei* votes, along with critical abstentions from the Center Party and National Liberal Party, killed the bill with a vote of 188 to 158, as in the sixteen previous reform efforts since 1869.

Given the Prussian Conservative Party's apparent near veto-like power in Prussia that evening, we might ask: does it really make sense to blame this outcome on *weakly organized* political parties representing old-regime interests, as described in the last chapter? After all, at least at first glance, landed elites appeared immensely powerful, not weak. This chapter will make a very different argument: Germany's old regime landed elites were represented by a weak political party, loosely coupled without national integrated structures to integrate diverse

---

[1] *Berliner Tageblatt*, May 21, 1912, 1.

TABLE 7.1: *Parliamentary Vote on Prussia's May 1912 Legislation on Reforming the Suffrage*

Party	Total Representatives	Yes	No	Abstain
Conservative (K)	152	0	139	13 (0)
National Lib (N)	65	45	0	20 (13)
Center (Z)	102	58	0	44 (33)
Reichspartei (R)	59	0	49	10 (0)
Left Liberals (F)	36	33	0	3 (0)
Polish Party (P)	15	14	0	1 (1)
Social Dem (S)	6	6	0	0 (0)
Danes (D)	2	2	0	0 (0)
All	437	158	188	91 (47)

Note: In the "abstain" column, the figures in parentheses refer to the number of delegates who "abstained without excuse." A discussion of this follows in the text.
Data Source: *Verhandlungen des Hauses der Abgeordneten 77*. Sitzung, 21. Legislative Period, May 20, 1912, 6428–32.

broad constituencies. As a result, these elites and their party *acutely* feared democracy more severely. Further, it was paradoxically the very weakness and fragmentation of party organization representing these groups that allowed a single, narrow socioeconomic interest – landed elites – to gain such exclusive control over the parties, thereby keeping the old regime in place. In Germany, the result was profound: between 1890 and 1914, despite promising conditions, a democratic transition in Prussia's key voting system did not take place. And, as we will see in the next two chapters, the long-run effect of weak party organization on the electoral right subverted a potential consolidation of German democracy after 1918.

THE PRUSSIA FACTOR

Long before the First World War, at the founding of Germany's Empire in 1871, a question was already present: was Imperial Germany's political system doomed to authoritarian institutional stasis, or was democratic reform possible?[2] A British journalist reportedly confronted Count Otto von Bismarck with precisely this question in the years after unification, when he asked, "How far do you regard the present constitutional system of the Empire as final?" Bismarck apocryphally is said to have answered, with his characteristic mix of foresight and equivocation,

---

[2] For a discussion of the complications of this framing of the problem, see James Retallack, "Meanings of Stasis," in *The German Right* (2006), 108–36.

Final it is not. Doubtless we shall pass through the stages which you in England have passed through. But it will be a slow, gradual process and we cannot foresee the direction which development will take.[3]

Whether or not Britain is a useful frame of reference, on the eve of the First World War, Germany's imperial constitutional order, forged during the 1871 national unification, indeed came under unprecedented agitation for change. Democratic reforms were put on the political agenda of the "commanding heights" of the German political state. The unusual hybrid political regime that Bismarck is chiefly credited with designing – comprising a powerful monarch and his appointed chancellor; a weak national parliament; universal male suffrage; a federated executive in the form of a second chamber (the *Bundesrat*); and powerful states with their own suffrage systems, public finance, and bureaucracies – was not static, but it did face serious pressure for change.[4] Yet, in those last five years before the First World War, the grand ambition of democratic reformers met a disappointing fate.

On the one hand, the early-twentieth-century collision of three forces had generated very real impulses toward democratization in Germany, as they had in much of Europe at the time. These included (1) the transnational revolutionary turmoil emanating from Russia's 1905 Revolution; (2) an increasingly cohesive and self-confident center-left pro-democratic social coalition of German Left Liberals and Social Democrats, the latter of which was by 1903 the most electorally successful socialist party in Europe; and (3) state-led conservative efforts at "political modernization" to catch up with the global "leader" Great Britain and to head off more radical reform.[5] But,

---

[3] Cited by Walter Shepard, "Tendencies to Ministerial Responsibility in Germany," *American Political Science Review* 5, February (1911): 57.

[4] Each of these institutions has spawned wide-ranging literatures unto themselves. On the question of universal male suffrage for the Reichstag, see Anderson, *Practicing Democracy* (2000). On the power of the Reichstag, see Manfred Rauh, *Die Parlamentarisierung des Deutschen Reiches* (Düsseldorf: Droste Verlag, 1977); Dieter Grosser, *Vom monarchischen Konstitutionalismus zur parlamentarischen Demokratie* (Hague: Martinus Nijhoff, 1970); Christoph Schoenberger, "Die Überholte Parlamentarisierung. Einflussgewinn Und Fehlende Herrschaftsfähigkeit Des Reichstags Im Sich Demokratisierenden Kaiserreich," *Historische Zeitschrift* 272 (2001): 623–66; Kreuzer, *Institutions and Innovation* (2001). On variations in state suffrage systems, see Simone Lässig, "Wahlrechtsreformen in den deutschen Einzelstaaten: Indikatoren für Modernisierungstendenzen und Reformfähigkeit im Kaiserreich?" in *Modernisierung und Region im wilhelmischen Deutschland*, ed. Simone Lässig (Bielefeld: Verlag für Regionalgeschichte, 1998), 127–70; Retallack, *The German Right* (2006). On state bureaucracies and systems of public finance, see Peter-Christian Witt, *Die Finanzpolitik des Deutschen Reiches von 1903 bis 1913: Eine Studie zur Innenpolitik des Wilhelminischen Deutschland* (Lübeck: Matthiesen, 1970); and D. E. Schremmer, "Taxation and Public Finance: Britain, France and Germany," in *The Cambridge Economic History of Europe. Volume VIII. The Industrial Economies: The Development of Economic and Social Policies* ed. Peter Mathias and Sidney Pollard (Cambridge: Cambridge University Press, 1989), 315–494.

[5] There are a number of older but still important works on these three subjects. On the impact of the Russian Revolution of 1905 on the German left, see Carl E. Schorske, *German Social Democracy*

unlike the successful passage of analogous democratic reforms such as Britain's Parliament Act of 1911, or those of relative socioeconomic and geopolitical "laggards" such as Sweden (1907) and Denmark (1901), Germany's political experiences in this period of global tumult ended in timid "non-events." In these moments, to borrow A. J. P. Taylor's memorable phrase, history "failed to turn," not just once, but many times and with increasing frequency as Europe's statesmen tragically "sleepwalked" into the First World War.[6]

To make sense of the "German catastrophe" of the first third of the twentieth century, some have employed a misleading retrospective image of Imperial Germany as a static society, without significant democratizing forces at play.[7] This account severely misconstrues the central puzzle of the political regime: in Germany, democratic reforms were vigorously, articulately, and passionately pursued by socialists like Karl Kautsky, Left Liberals such as Friedrich Naumann, and more tentatively before 1914 by Catholics such as Matthias Erzberger. German cities such as Berlin, Dresden, and Hamburg were scenes of hotly contentious and well-organized social unrest, strikes, "suffrage storms," and mass protest.[8] Parliamentary showdowns over proposed democratic reforms of the ballot and parliamentary sovereignty in the halls of the Reichstag and the Prussian House of Deputies captivated public minds and reverberated in newspaper accounts.[9] And even in what we normally think of as the reactionary Prussian State Ministry, moderate proposals at political reform were broached in the atmosphere of increasing panic after 1906.[10] In all of these instances, despite political noise from the street and from a newly self-confident proto-coalition of Social Democracy and Left Liberals, bolstered by discussion buzzing in the pages of the popular press, the political system appeared to be stuck in what contemporary political scientists would call a "reform trap," in

1905–1917: The Development of the Great Schism (Cambridge: Harvard University Press, 1955). On the potential of a "Lib–Lab" coalition of Liberals and social democrats, see Beverly Heckart, *From Basserman to Bebel: The Grand Bloc's Quest for Reform in the Kaiserreich* (New Haven: Yale University Press, 1974).

[6] Christopher Clark, *The Sleepwalkers: How Europe Went to War in 1914* (Penguin Press, 2013).

[7] Cf. Anderson, *Practicing Democracy* (2000); James Retallack, "'Get out the Vote!' Elections without Democracy in Imperial Germany," *Bulletin of the German Historical Institute* 51 (2012): 23–38.

[8] See, e.g., Evans, "Red Wednesday' in Hamburg: Social Democrats, Police and Lumpenproletariat in the Suffrage Disturbances of 17 January 1906" (1979); Retallack, "Citadels against Democracy," in *The German Right* (2006).

[9] See *Berliner Tageblatt* in particular. For an overview of heated academic debates about the constitution in this period, see Mark Hewitson, "The Kaiserreich in Question: Constitutional Crisis in Germany before the First World War," *The Journal of Modern History* 73, no. 4 (2001): 725–80.

[10] A ten-volume record of German *Staatsministerium* minutes have recently been digitized and published by the Berlin-Brandenburg Akademie der Wisseschaften, ed., *Die Protokolle des Preussischen Staatsministeriums, 1817–1934/38*, 10 vols. (Hildesheim: Olms Weidmann, 1999).

which major reform appears extraordinarily ripe in its societal preconditions, but blocked in its political reality.[11]

To be sure, it is a mistake to say that Germany experienced only political institutional stasis before the First World War: some significant and particular democratic reforms did occur.[12] Political reformers altered the electoral systems – via redistricting and changing the tax requirements for voting – for elections to the state parliaments of several of Germany's smaller southern states between 1899 and 1914;[13] the secret ballot was given more institutional reality with a national reform of Reichstag voting procedures in 1903;[14] and the profile and power of MPs in the Reichstag was altered when reform in 1906 gave them regular salaries for the first time.[15] Yet, the two defining political institutions of the pre-1914 regime, those that had attracted the most passionate criticism from democratic activists of the day, stubbornly persisted, untouched by reform.

First, despite proposals in the Reichstag, the political system remained, in deeply undemocratic fashion, a dualistic constitutional structure in which *the executive remained formally unaccountable to the parliament or popular control.*[16] Modeled after the 1814 French *Charte Constitutionnelle* and pre-1848 German constitutions, the king appointed the chancellor without requiring approval of a parliamentary majority, and the government formally

---

[11] Fritz Scharpf, "The Joint-decision Trap: Lessons from German Federalism and European Integration," *Public Administration* 66, no. 3 (1988): 239–78.

[12] Anderson, *Practicing Democracy* (2000); Retallack, "Get out the Vote!" (2012).

[13] Lässig, "Wahlrechtsreformen in den deutschen Einzelstaaten" (1998).

[14] Anderson, *Practicing Democracy* (2000) 250; Mares, *From Open Secrets to Secret Voting: Democratic Electoral Reforms and Voter Autonomy* (2015), 137.

[15] Lässig, "Wahlrechtsreformen in den deutschen Einzelstaaten" (1998); Anderson, *Practicing Democracy* (2000), 356.

[16] For students of German political development, my label of an "unaccountable executive" or an absence of parliamentarization as "undemocratic" likely prompts some confusion requiring immediate clarification. Early twentieth-century German observers (e.g., Max Weber) and contemporary constitutional historians (e.g., Scherer and Kühne) very usefully distinguish between "parliamentarization" and "democratization," noting that an expanded suffrage and growing power of parliamentarization did *not* accompany each other but actually may have run at cross purposes. See Thomas Kühne, "Demokratisierung und Parlamentarisierung: Neue Forschungen zur politischen Entwicklungsfähigkeit Deutschlands vor dem Ersten Weltkrieg," *Geschichte und Gesellschaft* 31, no. 2 (2005): 293–316. I also make this point in Daniel Ziblatt, "How Did Europe Democratize?" *World Politics* 58, no. 2 (2006): 311–38. Nonetheless for purposes of the discussion here, I follow common contemporary usage. See, for example, Charles Tilly, *Contention and Democracy in Europe, 1650–2000* (Cambridge: Cambridge University Press, 2004); Larry Diamond, *Developing Democracy: Toward Consolidation* (Baltimore: Johns Hopkins University Press, 1999). These works regard three institutional reforms under the broader normative umbrella category of "democratization": (1) increased constraints on executives, (2) expanded scope and equality of electoral participation, and (3) protections of civil liberties. Calling these reforms all democratic is not intended to suggest that there are not tensions between these institutions or that they always travel together empirically.

did not reflect the results of elections. This was not unlike the Swedish, Danish, and Norwegian systems before the early twentieth century; but, unlike in Sweden and Denmark, reform did not then come to Germany.[17] In federal Germany, the chancellor's "cabinet," which was in reality a group of "state secretaries" and not cabinet ministers, was chosen not from the majority party of the Reichstag – as one typically finds in "fused" parliamentary systems such as those of the UK or France after the birth of the Third Republic – but instead by the chancellor and king. These secretaries often were career bureaucrats with no party affiliation; the parliament, in this sense, chiefly only had the power to approve and propose legislation.[18] While by the early twentieth century the Reichstag had gained enough leverage, in at least one high-profile instance, to eject the Emperor's handpicked chancellor from office when Chancellor Bernhard von Bülow's 1909 Finance Bill failed, the Reichstag never possessed, before 1914, the ability to *form* governments and pick ministers.[19] It is for this reason that while the German national parliament's power increased in the last years before 1914, the possibility of a "type-shift" from a dualistic constitution to a parliamentary system was limited by the very institutional tensions between the government and the Reichstag that have mistakenly been called a "silent" parliamentarization."[20]

In addition to its unconstrained executive, the second major fortification of the nondemocratic Imperial German political system was the institution that I mentioned at the start of this chapter, one that had emerged before the founding the Reich: the three-class voting system for the Prussian state legislature, designed by Prussia Interior Ministry officials in the wake of the 1848 revolution.[21] Although universal male suffrage had been formally adopted, members of the Berlin-based state assembly were elected indirectly via electors, no guarantees for a secret ballot existed, and the relative weight of the vote in each constituency was dramatically skewed by total tax contribution: wealthier citizens'

[17] Denmark's parliamentarization is normally dated as 1901, while Sweden's formally came after 1915; elections in 1905 put Liberal party leaders at the head of government, in effect parliamentarizing the system. For a comparative overview, see Collier, *Paths Towards Democracy* (1999), 82–83.

[18] A crucial constraint was Article 9 of the constitution, which forbade members of the Bundesrat to also be a MP in the Reichstag, thereby, in principle, blocking parliamentarization of a ministry.

[19] See Rauh, *Die Parlamentarisierung des Deutschen Reiches* (1977).

[20] See Schoenberger, "Überholte Parlamentarisierung" (2001). For a useful intervention in this debate that distinguishes among three key dimensions of parliamentarization: (1) the ability to dismiss governments, (2) the ability to form governments, and (3) the ability to affect legislation, see Marcus Kreuzer, "Parliamentarization and the Question of German Exceptionalism: 1867–1918," *Central European History* 36, no. 3 (2003): 327–57. While on the first and third dimensions, the Reichstag was growing in strength, on the second dimension, it did not and looked more like the Swedish parliament.

[21] Günther Grünthal, "Das preußische Dreiklassenwahlrecht. Ein Beitrag zur Genesis und Funktion des Wahlrechtsoktrois vom Mai 1849," *Historische Zeitschrift* 226, no. 1 (1978): 17–66.

TABLE 7.2: *German States: Suffrage Regimes, 1913*

	Criteria #1 Universal Male?	Criteria #2 Equal?	Criteria #3 Secret?	Criteria #4 Direct?	Criteria #5 Lower Chamber All Elected?
Prussia	*Yes*	*No*	*No*	*No*	*Yes*
Saxony	Yes	No	Yes	Yes	Yes
Hamburg	Yes	No	Yes	Yes	Yes
Bavaria	Yes	Yes	Yes	Yes	Yes
Baden	Yes	Yes	Yes	Yes	Yes
Württemberg	Yes	Yes	Yes	Yes	Yes
Lübeck	Yes	No	Yes	Yes	Yes
Hesse	Yes	No	Yes	Yes	Yes

Note: Saxony, Bavaria, Württemberg, Lübeck, and Hessen all also relied on census or direct tax requirements, which qualified universal male suffrage

Data Sources: for Prussia, Huber 1994, 351–82; for Saxony, Huber 1994, 401–410; for Hamburg, Eckardt 2001, 46; 51ff; for Bavaria, Huber 1994, 385–400; for all other states, Vogel, et al. 1971, 70ff; Schröder 1995, 825–59, Hallerberg 1996, 324–57

votes counted for more than poorer citizens' in each district. By the first decade of the twentieth century, this system became the main target of reformers who recognized its severe violations of basic democratic norms. They drew attention to the fact that, by 1903, the wealthiest 3 percent of the voters (who fell into the "first class") had the same electoral weight as the poorest 85 percent of voters (the "third class").[22] If we compare Prussia to the other major German states in terms of the basic elements of democratic franchise, as Table 7.2 summarizes, we see Prussia was an outlier in the regressiveness of its rules. In only two other cases was the Prussian system imitated: in Hamburg and Saxony beginning in 1896 and 1906.

The significance of these rules and the differences between southern Germany and Prussia are evident, as they were to their contemporary critics and defenders. When liberalizing reforms were passed in Württemberg in 1906, for example, the Prussian Conservative newspaper *Kreuzzeitung* fearfully reported to its readers that "the reform mania is an epidemic illness of the southern states," but then reassuringly asserted, "It will not, however reach up north of the River Main [into Prussia]."[23] The Prussian system was not only uniquely regressive within Germany; in a cross-national perspective, as Stein Rokkan and Dieter Nohlen report in separate analyses, the Prussian case was an

[22] Kühne, *Dreiklassenwahlrecht und Wahlkultur* (1994), 423.
[23] *Neue Preußische Kreuzzeitung*, Nr. 321, July 12, 1906 (Abendausgabe), 1

outlier in pre-1914 Europe, the only state within the twenty-two future OECD membership states still *without* a secret ballot and *with* indirect parliamentary elections.[24]

But most important of all, the centrality of Prussia's particular electoral system within Germany's national political structure makes it worth closer attention. On the one hand, there has been a careless and frequent conflation of Prussia with Germany, leading some to erroneously think that the German Reichstag had a three-class voting system or to incomprehensibly assume that Prussia (approximately two-thirds of German territory) *was* in fact all of Germany before 1914. This has understandably produced ire among careful political historians, who in recent decades have explored and emphasized the importance of developments *outside* of Prussia as a way to counter the notion that Prussia is "identical" with Germany and as a strategy to stress the internal diversity of Germany's political and social developments.[25] As valuable as this corrective has been, it is equally crucial not to make the opposite mistake of diminishing the unusually important institutional linkages between the Prussian political system and the federal political system, chief among these the critical three-class voting system. Thus, it is crucial to carefully reconstruct the intricate and subtle institutional interconnections between Prussia's three-class voting system and national politics, which were decisive in shaping the political regime as a whole.[26]

First, we note that these two institutions – parliamentarization (rules governing constraint over executive power at the national level) and the three-class voting system (rules governing the suffrage) – were not entirely discrete, as they are sometimes treated. Instead, they were tightly interlinked, a self-reinforcing bundle of authoritarian institutions that were tricky to unwind unless done so simultaneously, thereby defining the contours of the broader political regime. This nexus elevated Prussia's consequences for Germany and protected its broader "way of life" within the country.[27] When the First World

[24] Both are authors are cited by Kühne, *Dreiklassenwahlrecht und Wahlkultur* (1994), 26. For the original sources see Rokkan, *Citizens, Elections, Parties* (1970); and Dieter Nohlen, *Wahlrecht und Parteiensystem* (Leverkusen: Leske & Budrich, 1986).

[25] See, e.g., Blackbourn, *Religion, and Local Politics in Wilhelmine Germany: The Centre Party in Württemberg before 1914* (1980); Lässig, *Wahlrechtskampf und Wahlreform in Sachsen, 1895–1909* (1996); Lässig, "Wahlrechtsreformen in den deutschen Einzelstaaten" (1998); Reinhold Weber, *Bürgerpartei und Bauernbund in Württemberg: konservative Parteien im Kaiserreich und in Weimar (1895–1933)* (Düsseldorf Droste, 2004).

[26] Kühne also makes this argument in a review essay. Kühne, "Demokratisierung und Parlamentarisierung" (2005).

[27] One clue of this elevated power is recounted by Reinhold von Sydow (Reich State Secretary of the Treasury), who is reported to have "recalled in his memoirs that one question was repeatedly asked... when a crucial question of domestic policy was discussed: 'What does Heydebrand [Conservative Party chair in the Prussian chamber of deputies] say about this?'" This quote is from Retallack (*The German Right* (2006), 387.

War neared its end, Max Weber provided a clue to how these institutional links operated in an important essay on the future of German constitutionalism.[28] He argued that even had constitutional reforms passed before 1914, leaving Germany's chancellor and his state secretaries' appointment reliant on a national Reichstag vote, the persistence of an unreformed three-class voting system in Prussia's state legislature would have resulted in majorities there for the Conservative Party, indirectly blocking national parliamentarization because of the distinctive structure of Germany's second chamber, the Bundesrat.[29]

Without a reform of the three-class voting system, Prussia's seventeen delegates to the fifty-eight member Bundesrat would still have continued to reflect the deeply undemocratic Prussian electoral system that obstructed Social Democrats from representation in that body. The result would have been that conservative-minded Prussian ministers, as Prussian delegates in the Bundesrat, had maintained their virtual absolute veto over all Reichstag legislation, since only fourteen votes in the Bundesrat could stop any Reichstag legislation.[30] In this way, as Max Weber put it, the three-class voting system "poisoned the political system as a whole." Parliamentarization could only come to national politics in Germany through a democratization of Prussia, not merely through more parliamentary control at the national level over the chancellor.[31]

To better comprehend Prussia's institutional and national interconnections, it is useful to compare it to the U.S. South before the second half of the twentieth century, where a similar "subnational" authoritarian political system affected the character, extent, and outer limits of *national democratization* in important ways. There, like in Germany and in other federal systems such as those of Argentina and Mexico, a variety of elaborate institutional mechanisms exist by which powerful authoritarian subnational units, also governed by a restricted-suffrage regime generating near single-party rule, could exert disproportionate influence on national politics.[32] For example,

[28] Max Weber, "Das Preussische Wahlrecht," in *Zur Politik im Weltkrieg*, ed. Wolfgang Mommsen and Gangolf Huebinger (Tuebingen: JCB Mohr, [1917] 1984).

[29] The Bundesrat consisted of fifty-eight seats, occupied by delegates of the member-states of the federation. The body had legislative and administrative functions and was occupied chiefly by ministers of the member states. The Prussian Minister President (typically also the Imperial Chancellor) was chair of the body.

[30] Important for understanding this is that Prussian Ministers, while formally not required by the constitution to be reflective of election results had themselves undergone a "parliamentarization," but in this instance a conservative parliamentarization that benefited the German Conservative Party. See Werner Frauendienst, "Demokratisierung des Deutschen Konstitutionalismus in der Zeit Wilhelms II," *Zeitschrift für die gesamte Staatswissenchaft* 113, no. 4 (1957): 721–46.

[31] The quote about the Prussian electoral system is from Weber, "Das Preussische Wahlrecht" [1917] (1984): 233.

[32] See Edward L. Gibson, *Boundary Control: Subnational Authoritarianism in Federal Democracies* (Cambridge: Cambridge University Press, 2012); Ira Katznelson, *Fear Itself: The New Deal and the Origins of our Time* (New York: W. W. Norton, 2013).

in the United States, Senate rules granted committee chairmanships, including those of the judiciary committee, which approved Supreme Court appointees, to the longest-serving members of the Senate. Low competitiveness in southern states had the effect of typically guaranteeing many of the powerful committee chairmanships to Senators from those states.[33] Also, in the United States, the "solidly" Democratic, effectively single-party South exerted disproportionate influence via the presidential candidate selection process, which required a three-fifths majority, thereby giving the South a de facto veto – not unlike the Prussian veto in the Bundesrat – on the selection of U.S. presidential candidates.[34] In short, democratizing the United States as a whole required democratizing its own "authoritarian enclaves."[35]

Similarly, Prussia was the pivot of the broader German national political regime. As political scientist Walter J. Shepard vividly put it in 1911, the three-class voting system was the "citadel of the powers" of autocracy and bureaucracy in Germany. Shepard continued, "Its abandonment would give the enemy possession of the entire fortress."[36] It is sometimes argued that Germany's early universal male suffrage for the Reichstag and its failure to parliamenterize perniciously shaped its democratic trajectory. But even had there been national parliamentarization but no Prussian suffrage reform, a nondemocratic national political regime would have remained in place until war and revolution demolished *both* sets of institutions.[37] In sum, the three-class voting system was arguably the thread that held the whole political regime together, and, if tugged, would bring the whole regime down with it. Thus, we see why democratic activists ran under the slogan "Abolish the three-class voting system!" – a political catchphrase of the age – and why, at a DKP Party Congress in December 1907, Manteuffel ominously warned that any Prussian minister who would dare propose the Reichstag franchise for the Prussian House of Representatives *should be charged with treason!*[38]

THE PUZZLE OF DURABLE AUTHORITARIANISM IN PRE-1914 GERMANY

The stakes of reform thus were especially high in Prussia. So, then, why did its system persist for so long? Some argue that authoritarian regimes survive because their rulers are lucky enough, or perhaps skilled enough, to rule over

---

[33] V. O. Key, *Southern Politics in State and Nation* (New York: A. A. Knopf, 1949); Gibson, *Boundary Control* (2012), 64.

[34] For a classic discussion, see Key, *Southern Politics* (1949), 317.

[35] Mickey, *Paths Out of Dixie: The Democratization of Authoritarian Enclaves in America's Deep South, 1944–1972* (2015).

[36] Shepard, "Tendencies to Ministerial Responsibility in Germany" (1911): 66.

[37] Schoenberger, "Überholte Parlamentarisierung" (2001).

[38] Cited by Retallack, *Notables of the Right* (1988), 163.

quiescent societies with fragmented, timid, and disorganized oppositions, thereby buying political stability for themselves. But the endurance, then, of authoritarianism in Prussia, and hence Germany, is puzzling.[39] German society, and especially Prussian society after 1905, was anything but quiescent; rather, the Germany state was under siege, facing what looked to be unstoppable societal challenges that took increasingly disruptive, organized, and visible forms. Further, even if "economic backwardness" had once been a barrier to democratization, by 1900 both Germany as a whole and the state of Prussia, with its transformative industrialization, had joined the ranks of the world's most capital-abundant advanced economies of the world.

Strictly in terms of socioeconomic development, it is of course correct that "economic backwardness" is normally a barrier to democratization.[40] In the German context, the antidemocratic dominance of the infamous industrialist-landlord "iron-rye" protectionist coalition has frequently been used to link relatively late industrialization to stalled political development.[41] Landed elites and industrialists in this account share preferences for protectionism and antipathies to democracy. In his analysis of the impact of expanding global trade on political coalitions, Ronald Rogowski incisively links socioeconomic development to pro-democratic political coalitions.[42] Building on core axioms of trade theory (e.g., the Stolper–Samuelson theorem) that identify which sectors benefit from trade protectionism in different types of economies, Rogowski argues that in developing "backward" or, more precisely, capital-poor societies, a labor-abundant but land scarce society's growing exposure to trade tends to generate a reactionary coalition of protectionist industrialists and rural landlords, a configuration that certainly matches traditional accounts of German political life until at least the 1890s.[43] This contrasts to the impact of growing trade in a "capital advanced" economy, in which both labor and capital are plentiful and only land is limited. In this latter scenario, a progressive pro–free trade alliance between labor and capital is

---

[39] Accounts that emphasize the role of well-organized "working class" or "threat of unrest" as cause of democratization run from classic sociological accounts such as Rueschemeyer, Stephens, and Stephens, *Capitalist Development and Democracy* (1992), to contemporary political economists (e.g., Acemoglu and Robinson, *Economic Origins of Dictatorship and Democracy*, 2006; Acemoglu and Robinson, "Why Did the West Extend the Franchise?" 2000). It should be added, "threat of unrest" is of course not always treated entirely as "exogenous" – it can be suppressed, bought off, redirected, and otherwise suffocated.

[40] Lipset, "Some Social Requisites of Democracy" (1959); Boix, *Democracy and Redistribution* (2003).

[41] Gerschenkron, *Bread and Democracy* (1948).

[42] Rogowski, *Commerce and Coalitions* (1989), 9–10.

[43] Rogowski, *Commerce and Coalitions* (1989); Gerschenkron, *Bread and Democracy* (1948); Arthur Rosenberg, *Imperial Germany: The Birth of the German Republic 1871–1918* (Boston: Beacon Press, 1964).

expected to form against the reactionary and protectionist interests of landed elites. Rogowski's account has eminent plausibility for the British context.[44]

While these accounts may be correct about the mid to late nineteenth century, by 1890, Prussia was growing rapidly socioeconomically, even joining the ranks of the "capital abundant" advanced economies, and yet, the expected Lib–Lab coalition that followed to challenge the old Junker-and-industrialist-dominated political system did not bring democratic change to Germany, let alone to Prussia itself.[45] By 1913, Germany, with Prussia at its core, was among the leaders of Europe's industrializing economies, behind only the United Kingdom, Belgium, Switzerland, and the Netherlands – the only five countries on the entire continent with less than 35 percent of their working populations still employed in the agricultural sector. Meanwhile the remaining thirteen countries of eastern, southern, and northern peripheries of Europe lagged behind with over 40 percent and up to 80 percent of their working populations in the agricultural sector.[46] Further, Germany became a net exporter of capital after 1890, and the nature of its exports shifted away from low-capital-intensive products – such as textiles, leather, and silk – to the capital-intensive electrical, engineering, and chemical sectors.[47] By all accounts, Germany actually surpassed Britain in total industrial output before the First World War, and Prussia, with a shrinking proportion of agricultural workers, was at the forefront of these developments.[48] Yet, reform did not come to the most significant *national* barrier to democracy, the three-class voting system *within* Prussia.

If it is difficult to blame insufficient socioeconomic development, it is even more implausible to place the burden of Germany's stalled democratic transition on an *absence* of social contention, unrest, and working-class mobilization. Before 1914, Germany was not a quiescent authoritarian state; it was under

---

[44] See Frank Trentmann, *Free Trade Nation: Commerce, Consumption, and Civil Society in Modern Britain* (Oxford: Oxford University Press, 2008); Rogowski, *Commerce and Coalitions* (1989).

[45] Gary Herrigel, *Industrial Constructions: The Sources of German Industrial Power* (Cambridge: Cambridge University Press, 1996).

[46] Stephen Broadberry, Giovanni Federico, and Alexander Klein, "Sectoral Developments, 1870–1914," in *The Cambridge Economic History of Modern Europe: 1870 to the Present*, ed. Stephen Broadberry and Kevin H. O'Rourke (Cambridge: Cambridge University Press, 2010), 59–83. Drawing on data from B. R. Mitchell, the authors (p. 61, Table 3.1) rank economies based on employment data, which demonstrate Germany was more industrialized in 1913 on average than cases of more stable democratization, including Sweden, France, and Denmark.

[47] Garst, "From Factor Endowments to Class Struggle" (1998); Herbert Feis, *Europe, the World's Banker, 1870–1914: An Account of European Foreign Investment and the Connection of World Finance with Dplomacy before World War I* (New York: W. W. Norton, 1965).

[48] Rüdiger Hohls and Hartmut Kaelble, eds., *Die Regionale Erwerbsstruktur im Deutschen Reich und in der Bundesrepublik 1895–1970* (St. Katharinen: cripta Mercaturae Verlag, 1989).

assault on two related fronts: first, extra-parliamentary contention in the form of labor unrest, strikes, and protests; second, an irrepressibly rising Social Democratic Party that represented a major electoral challenge within the realm of formal parliamentary politics. A wide-ranging literature – from Dahl; Rueschemeyer, Stephens, and Stephens; and Tilly to Acemoğlu and Robinson – asserts that social conflict or the social "threats" of a disruptive and well-organized and mobilized opposition are essential to regime change.[49] This contention is typically thought to provoke acute fear among incumbent nondemocratic elites, who, in a classic democratic "transition game" may quickly become convinced they are stuck between a "rock" (i.e., growing unrest and contestation) and a "hard place" (i.e., democracy), leaving democratization increasingly preferable to an unsustainable *status quo*.[50] Real political change, it is thus often asserted, requires serious contestation and a robust opposition.

While this logic certainly captures a main ingredient of the process of dislodging powerful old-elite networks of power, it leaves one unexplained puzzle: protests, strikes, and opposition to the old regime were *more* well-organized, disruptive, and visible in Germany than in other European countries such as Sweden and Britain, yet the contention achieved far *fewer* substantive democratic concessions. In the years before 1914, chiefly in the peak years of 1899, 1905, and 1912, the dockyards of the major shipping ports such as Hamburg along the northern coast, the coal mines of the Ruhr Valley in Prussia's west, and the streets of nearly all German cities became the sites of an unprecedented social mobilization that stood out even in the famously protest-filled days of *fin de siècle* Europe. With his eye on the reverberating effect of the Russian Revolution, Carl Schorske has called the year 1905 a "turning point in European history," but notes its particularly ferocious edge in Germany:

> Repercussions of the Russian Revolution were felt throughout the European labor movement, but above all in Germany, where indigenous sources of class antagonism were strengthened by the Russian example. Labor conflict of unprecedented scope dominated the economic scene in 1905–06. In politics there began a mass movement to democratize the discriminatory suffrage systems in the federal states...[51]

To put Germany's political environment in comparative context, Figure 7.1 reports national census data on the total number of industrial strike participants

---

[49] Dahl, *Polyarchy* (1971); Rueschemeyer, Stephens, and Stephens, *Capitalist Development and Democracy* (1992); and Tilly, *Democracy* (2007); Acemoglu and Robinson, "Why Did the West Extend the Franchise?" (2000). See Eley, *Forging Democracy* (2002).

[50] Social contention and protest alter the calculations of incumbents as they weigh the "costs of toleration" vs. the "costs of suppression" in Dahl's classic formulation (*Polyarchy*, 1971). When the latter outweigh the former, democratic reform becomes a possibility. See also Guillermo A. O'Donnell, Philippe C. Schmitter, and Laurence Whitehead, eds., *Transitions from Authoritarian Rule: Comparative Perspectives* (Baltimore: Johns Hopkins University Press, 1986).

[51] Schorske, *German Social Democracy* (1955), 28.

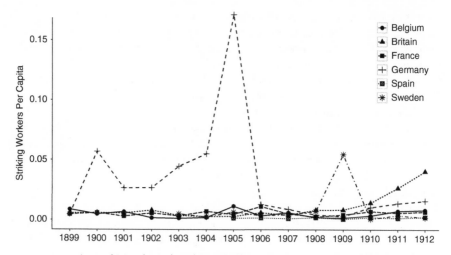

FIGURE 7.1: Annual Number of Striking Workers Per Capita, 1899–1912
Data Source: Mitchell 2003, 3–8, 172–85

annually (per capita) over the period before 1914 for the major European countries for which data are available. We see that over nearly the entire period, Germany did not lag behind but actually far outpaced the rest of Europe, only matched in the years 1910–1914 by Sweden and Britain.

Still, while suffrage was reformed in some German states, in its largest state, Prussia, where most of the strikes occurred, reform was nonexistent.[52] To make sense of this oddity, we must identify the causes of the social unrest presented in Figure 7.1. First, we know the 1890 lapse of the Anti-Socialist Law catapulted rapid growth of "free" Social Democratic unions, which comprised 27 percent of all laborers by 1913, a level matched only by other advanced economies of the day.[53] Other increasingly well-organized unions played a similarly crucial though often underestimated role as well, including the Polish coal miners' union, *Zjednoczenie Zawodowe Poslkie*, which represented the vast number of Polish-speaking miners in the Ruhr (in Prussia) and helped spearhead mass mobilization in the area in 1899 and 1905.[54] Responding to real injustices and pursuing real ambitions, the German working class, broadly understood,

[52] It is worth noting that in my analysis of data that I discuss more fully below, between 1899 and 1906, half of all industrial strikes took place in Prussia. See "Kaiserliches Statistisches Amt, Streiks und Aussperrung im Jahre 1909," in *Statistik des Deutschen Reichs* (Berlin: Verlag von Puttkammer & Mühlbrecht, 1910).

[53] Stefano Bartolini, *The Political Mobilization of the European Left, 1860–1980: The Class Cleavage*, Cambridge Studies in Comparative Politics (Cambridge: Cambridge University Press, 2000), 531; Garst, "From Factor Endowments to Class Struggle" (1998): 33.

[54] See John J. Kulczycki, *The Foreign Worker and the German Labor Movement: Xenophobia and Solidarity in the Coal Fields of the Ruhr, 1871–1914* (Providence: Berg, 1994).

became, in historian Mary Nolan's assessment, "the best organized workers' movement in the late nineteenth century."[55]

A second factor contributing to unrest was that unions altered their main strategy of agitation, abandoning the older plant-by-plant, "one-off" strike (*Einzelabschlachtung*) to adopt, quite controversially, the coordinated strike and later the general strike, motivated largely by the example of the Belgian suffrage strike of 1902.[56] Even the moderate revisionist Eduard Bernstein embraced the new and remarkably effective "radical" strategy of mass mobilization with an explicitly political goal of securing universal and equal suffrage.[57] Finally, crucial for the broadening impact of the German labor movement was how union leaders linked political and institutional goals (e.g., suffrage reform) to everyday uncoordinated economic fights over pay, working conditions, and control of the shop floor – the more immediate concerns that had brought Ruhr Valley coal miners and Hamburg dockworkers onto the streets. The issue of how "private problems" become "public concerns" is of course a critical one, and no small part was played by the recalcitrant Prussian House of Representatives, which in reaction to the January 1905 coal miners' strike rejected a proposal to introduce state monitoring of Prussian mines. This move sparked renewed outrage against the three-class voting system, which blocked workplace reforms.

A third noteworthy development was the spectacular rise of the Social Democratic Party (SPD) in Germany. Indeed, this was a major front of the challenge to Germany's old regime. Though the SPD was restricted in its activities by Bismarck's anti-socialist laws until 1890, its organizational prowess allowed it to compete in nearly all electoral districts long before its competitors, contesting nearly all constituencies by 1898. Its official coordination with the German Free Trade Unions that began at the 1906 Mannheim Congress gave it an organizational apparatus that helped create a mass base (with associated "proletariat" civic associations), and provided it with a wide-ranging membership. These trends were most visible in Prussia. As the introduction of free and fair elections in Prussia after 1918 demonstrates, without restrictions on voting equality and because of the advanced level and nature of heavy industrialization, socialists would come to dominate the state's political life.[58]

---

[55] Mary Nolan, "Economic Crisis, State Policy and Working Class Formation in Germany, 1870–1900," in *Working Class Formation: Nineteenth Century Patterns in Western Europe and the United States*, ed. Ira Katznelson and Aristide Zolberg (Princeton: Princeton University Press, 1986), 352.

[56] Schorske, *German Social Democracy* (1955), 33.

[57] See Eduard Bernstein, *Der politische Massenstreik und die politische Lage der Sozialdemokratie in Deutschland: Vortrag gehalten im Sozialdemokratischen Verein* (Breslau: Verlag der Volkswacht, 1906). For a discussion of Bernstein's place in the evolution of German social democracy, see Sheri Berman, *The Primacy of Politics: Social Democracy and the Making of Europe's Twentieth Century* (Cambridge: Cambridge University Press, 2006), 42–44.

[58] See Dietrich Orlow, *Weimar Prussia, 1918–1925: The Unlikely Rock of Democracy* (Pittsburgh: University of Pittsburgh Press, 1986).

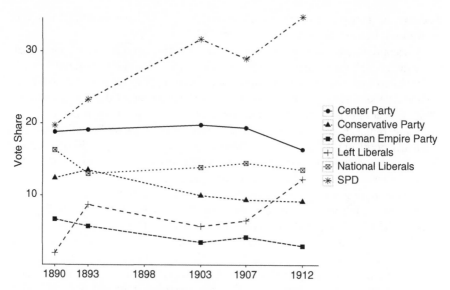

FIGURE 7.2: National Reichstag Vote Share of SPD and Other Parties, 1890–1912
Data Source: Vogel, et al. (1971), 290–92. Reichstag results under universal, equal, direct, and secret ballot. The SPD's performance in state elections varied enormously because of the variation in suffrage systems

But over the prewar period, the rise of the SPD at the national level was just as impressive. Figure 7.2 provides evidence of the SPD's soaring electoral dominance and outright plurality of Reichstag seats after 1890, outperforming socialist parties *anywhere* in Europe at the time.[59]

The growing intensity of strikes in the international reverberations of the Russian Revolution, coupled with the threatening electoral rise of Social Democracy, caused panic, hasty action, and innovative efforts at founding new reactionary pressure groups, parties, and organizations as self-defense.[60] But, as creative as these responses were, democratic reform of the state was still not forthcoming.

Given the arguments of Rueschemeyer, Stephens, and Stephens; Eley; and Acemoğlu and Robinson, we must ask: why didn't Germany undergo more far-reaching democratization?[61] One intuitive but ultimately unsatisfactory argument is that the very strength of the strikers and the SPD backfired,

[59] See also Bartolini, *Political Mobilization of the European Left* (2000).
[60] On older work on the response of the right to the rise of socialism is Stegmann, *Die Erben Bismarcks* (1970). More recently, see Heinz Hagenlücke, *Deutsche Vaterlandspartei: die nationale Rechte am Ende des Kaiserreiches* (Düsseldorf: Droste, 1997).
[61] Rueschemeyer, Stephens, and Stephens, *Capitalist Development and Democracy* (1992); Eley, *Forging Democracy* (2002); Acemoglu and Robinson, "Why Did the West Extend the Franchise?" (2000).

rendering the goals of reform coalitions actually *more* difficult to achieve than in countries with a "tamed" reformist left, as the old regime in Germany stubbornly resisted democratization more than it might otherwise have.[62] This claim is certainly appealing at first glance. However, it is deeply misleading in the German context for three main reasons, and hence suggests a general gap in the account of how contention, unrest, and democratization are connected. First, as the strike data from Figure 7.1 depict, the only other national cases in which industrial strike movements were as strong as Germany's (e.g., Sweden and Britain) are normally considered "settled" cases of democratization. In these countries, unrest did not bring de-democratization; in Sweden, for example, a massive general strike in 1909 occurred without derailing the Swedish Conservative Party's transformative bill, led by Arvid Lindman, for universal male suffrage that passed through the political system between 1907 and 1909, just in time for the 1911 parliamentary elections.[63] By contrast, Spain, a case of low strike participation in this period, experienced no equivalent democratization before 1914, suggesting it is a mistake to assume a direct link between strikes and de-democratization.

Second, faulting the ideological radicalism of the Prussian left reverses the actual historical sequence; it is the long-standing and repeated intransigence of the regime, particularly the terms of the Prussian government's three-class voting reform proposal released on February 4, 1910, which triggered the "final break" of Prussian Socialists, planting the seeds for the "Swing to the Left" or what Carl Schorske famously called "the Great Schism" between socialists and communists during the First World War.[64] The details are crucial: at their September 1909 national Leipzig Congress, the SPD agreed to a positive parliamentary agenda to collaborate with Liberals to push for a "joint offensive" for constitutional reform in Prussia, and even warned its rank and file "against excessive street demonstrations or demonstration strikes which might weaken the united front."[65]

But the potential Lib–Lab coalition, already extremely fragile from diverging electoral interests between Left Liberals and Socialists and years of living under the three-class voting system, finally collapsed when the government released its reform proposal in February 1910. The socialist daily paper *Vorwärts* immediately criticized the bill proposal as a "brutal and contemptuous declaration of war."[66] Two days later, mass street protests erupted. Schorske describes the dynamic this way: "The proposed reforms were so inadequate that

---

[62] This argument is implicit in Luebbert's analysis of what he calls "abortive Lib-Labism." Luebbert, *Liberalism, Fascism, or Social Democracy* (1991), 115. I discuss the cases of Saxony and Hamburg below.

[63] Lewin, *Ideology and Strategy: A Century of Swedish Politics* (1988), 53–86.

[64] Schorske, *German Social Democracy* (1955), 171.

[65] Schorske, *German Social Democracy* (1955), 173.

[66] Schorske, *German Social Democracy* (1955), 177.

far from satisfying democratic opinion they only aroused it further."[67] He also writes,

That the Prussian wing would have reversed the trend toward a reform coalition... was not unnatural. The Prussian comrades lived under the three-class suffrage system; they had had the spirit of compromise beaten out of them by years of petty persecution at the hands of the Prussian administration and courts. The ire of the rank and file... could not easily be converted into friendship for the Liberals.[68]

In more general terms, in the most definitive cross-national study of the determinants of radicalism and reformism before the First World War, Gary Marks and his collaborators analyze the ideologies of socialist parties in eighteen countries before 1914 on a twelve-point scale, demonstrating that a prehistory of restricted or unequal suffrage, on average, radicalizes socialist parties.[69] Another recent cross-national study illustrates that repression of the organized working class more accurately predicts the radicalization than a range of other socioeconomic variables.[70] The point is this: to attribute stalled democratization in Germany to the radicalism or the strength of the German left is to reverse the causal arrow that underpins the relationship. Intransigent and repressive conservatives in power and blocking reform radicalized the left, leaving open the core question of why some pre-democratic regimes responded to threats with repression and others with democratic concessions.

A final, more general problem with the view that leftist strength triggered conservative repression and thus stalled democratization is theoretical: it requires an intricate, if not convoluted, causal logic, given the insights of Dahl and Rueschemeyer, Stephens, and Stephens.[71] If both claims are correct – that democratization requires social unrest *and* that it can also lead to de-democratization – then one must argue that some contention is necessary for democratization but that too much stymies it. Indeed, this argument has been ingeniously proposed and elaborated in theoretical terms by recent formal work.[72] But, *empirically* identifying the charmed middle ground without relying on *post hoc* "just-so stories" becomes, at best, a tricky business.

Such theoretical contortions, however, become unnecessary if we shift our analytical focus to a different agent: the political representative (party or group)

---

[67] Schorske, *German Social Democracy* (1955), 177.

[68] Schorske, *German Social Democracy* (1955), 175.

[69] Gary Marks, Heather Mbaye, and Hyung-min Kim, "Radicalism or Reformism: Socialist Parties before World War I," *American Sociological Review* 74 (2009): 615–35.

[70] Konstantin Vössing, "Social Democratic Party Formation and National Variation in Labor Politics," *Comparative Politics* 43, no. 2 (2011): 167–86.

[71] Dahl, *Polyarchy* (1971); Rueschemeyer, Stephens, and Stephens, *Capitalist Development and Democracy* (1992).

[72] This is the innovative argument about a "U-shaped" relationship between inequality and democratization elaborated by Acemoglu and Robinson, *Economic Origins of Dictatorship and Democracy* (2006).

of the main social elite in a nondemocratic system. We can concede that socioeconomic changes may alter coalitional dynamics, giving rise to a push for democratization. Also, mass unrest as well as election success of opposition groups may place democratic reform on the political agenda. But, in responding to such unrest, three options exist for old-regime incumbents and their allies: (1) democracy may simply be blocked, (2) an intensification of repression may follow, or (3) democratic reforms may be adopted. What, then, determines whether the third option, and not the first two, follows from social unrest and changed socioeconomic conditions?

As elaborated more fully in Chapter 2, democratization is usefully conceived as a "two-step" process, each step being analytically distinct. Demands for democratization may emerge from changing socioeconomic conditions, but how the political representatives of elites respond – through obstruction, repression, or democratization – hinges on the organizational resources of the incumbent elite at the moment they are challenged. First, *with* party organization, old-regime elites can concede with greater self-assurance that they can survive electorally, whereas *without* party organization, the dilemma of finding themselves stuck between a "rock" (i.e., unrest) and a "hard place" (i.e., democracy) is exacerbated, and democracy becomes much less appealing since the prospects of survival in free and fair democratic competition only worsen. Then, party weakness intervenes at a second step in the causal chain: even if party elites within an old regime perceive "democracy" as preferable, without tightly coupled party organization, they have a more difficult, potentially impossible, time containing the backlash of hardliners or reactionaries. This will thwart the strategies of more moderate conservative office seekers, blocking the faintest tendencies toward reform. In short, even facing propitious conditions, *without party organization, incumbents may be simply too weak to acquiesce.*[73]

WEAK CONSERVATIVES AND THE DEFEAT OF SUFFRAGE REFORM IN PRUSSIA, 1910 AND 1912

The consequences of party organization becomes visible as we explore the details of two major moments of potential but *failed* democratic reform in

[73] The analysis that follows focuses on the decisive three-class voting system. A similar analysis could be made of the absence of "parliamentarization" in Germany in the same period. Indeed, it has been argued that a major hindrance to parliamentarization in Germany was that, aside from the Social Democrats who were in favor of parliamentarization, no party had sufficient electoral prowess to win an outright majority, thereby diminishing their enthusiasm for cabinet responsibility to a parliamentary majority (Grosser, *Vom monarchischen Konstitutionalismus*, 1970). Thus, in addition to the barrier of the three-class voting system, it was also precisely the fragmentation of parties due to the kinds of religious and confessional divides I have identified above that made parliamentarization difficult in Germany (cf. Rauh, *Die Parlamentarisierung des Deutschen Reiches*, 1977).

Prussia: 1910 and 1912. It is one task to show how party organization aided the navigation of successful democratic reform, as in our analysis of British Conservatives and the 1884 Reform Act in Chapter 4. But the challenge we take up here is the inverse: to analyze a case of a "dog that did not bark." – that is, to show how, even though Left-Liberal Party and Socialist Party agitation put suffrage reform on the Prussian political agenda after 1908, it was the organizational weakness of regime-defending conservative parties that stalled democratization. The inaction witnessed in Prussia can be explained through two dynamics: *electoral concerns* and *dynamics of organizational capture.*

TOO WEAK TO ACQUIESCE: THE ELECTORAL CONCERNS
OF A WEAK CONSERVATIVE PARTY

In order to understand the electoral concerns of Prussian Conservative Party MPs, we must first ask: How was suffrage placed on the government agenda in the early 1900s, and was there ever a real possibility of reform?[74] The most serious efforts came before the First World War, but the 1910 Reform, the most likely to have succeeded in Prussia in that period, was originally introduced by Theobald Bethmann-Hollweg, the government's new and ambitious chancellor. Bethmann-Hollweg did not merely expect reform, but thought substantial suffrage reform was inevitable. Before taking up his chancellorship, he had previously broached the subject in 1906:

Our Prussian franchise is impossible to preserve in the long run... Its Conservative majority is so banal in spirit and so complacent in its feeling of inviolable power that it must be humiliating to any progressively minded man; we *must* find a new basis.[75]

The perception that reform, even if modest and at the edges, was not only desirable but *necessary* reflected the very real structural dynamics of socioeconomic change and social unrest; it would be the political price paid to contain socialist electoral success. Further, Bethmann-Hollweg, like his predecessor Bernhard von Bülow, viewed suffrage reform as part of a broader package of "modernizing" institutional reforms, such as public finance reform and internal improvements (e.g., canal-building), that would allow Germany to compete on the international stage with Great Britain and other great powers.[76] But, the issue of suffrage reform initially forced itself onto the political agenda – in

---

[74] There were repeated efforts at reform from 1848 until the twentieth century, some from the government to bolster the three-class voting system, others as symbolic proposals to eliminate it altogether. Kühne (*Dreiklassenwahlrecht und Wahlkultur*, 1994, 377–574) provides the most thorough overview of all sixteen reform proposals to be discussed and voted on in the Prussian Chamber of Deputies.

[75] Emphasis in original. Cited by Retallack, *Notables of the Right* (1988), 163.

[76] There is an extensive literature on the connections of international politics to domestic but most recently, see Sebastian Conrad and Jürgen Osterhammel, eds., *Das Kaiserreich transnational. Deutschland in der Welt 1871–1914* (Goettingen: Vandenhoeck & Ruprecht, 2004).

fact compelling the Prussian king himself to announce a commitment to suffrage reform at the opening session of the Prussian Chamber of Representatives in an October 1908 "Crown Speech" (*Thronrede*). State elites found suffrage reform essential to pursuing their project of political and institutional "modernization," while sustaining an anti-socialist governing coalition in the Reichstag. The Chancellor, as well as the government, thus regarded suffrage reform not just as possible, but also as a political imperative.

From the late nineteenth century onwards, the national government's need for parliamentary majorities was filled by cobbling together ever-shifting ad hoc coalitions – dubbed *Sammlungspolitik* – in the Reichstag to pass its legislative agenda through *without* the aid of the SPD. After Bismarck's fall and the Anti-Socialist Law's expiration in 1890, however, there arose a governing coalition of an increasing number of political parties, including National Liberals, Conservatives, Free Conservatives, and the Catholic Center Party, thereby only excluding Left Liberals, Social Democrats, and other smaller minority parties. Until 1906, the *Sammlung* governing grouping, as Kühne reports, maintained reasonable consensus on economic policy (e.g., protectionism) and on Prussian constitutional questions (e.g., antireform), but often disagreed on foreign policy (e.g., colonialism) and cultural questions (e.g., education) especially the pivot of the coalition, the Catholic Center Party.[77] By 1906, the coalition began to destabilize as the Crown and his chancellor unintentionally elevated suffrage reform as a key political issue in the process in their attempts to garner liberal support for a more expansive foreign and colonial policy.

With the Reichstag facing the prospect of an irrepressibly growing SPD plurality, multiple fissures began to develop with the national government's coalition. First, in 1905–06, the Catholic Center Party grew more critical of Germany's brutal response to uprisings in east Africa, making the government nervous about relying on these allies in the future. Second, socioeconomic development heightened tensions between National Liberals on the one hand and Conservatives on the other. These two groups increasingly clashed over trade policy, which disproportionately benefited agrarian interests at the cost of new industrial groups, and provided the nearly tax-exempt status to landed wealth in the countryside.[78] Thus, National Liberals started to collaborate with

---

[77] Kühne, *Dreiklassenwahlrecht und Wahlkultur* (1994), 494–95.
[78] Imperial Germany's system of fiscal federalism and public finance had long been notoriously defective since the national parliament (governed by universal male suffrage) only had access to tariffs and limited indirect taxes on consumption, while the states (with restricted suffrage rules) had access to potentially very substantial income taxes and land taxes. The result was a growing fiscal crisis that increased the risk premium on government bonds and resulted in insufficient resources to fund Germany's own ambitious military goals. See Schremmer, "Taxation and Public Finance: Britain, France and Germany" (1989); and Niall Ferguson, "Public Finance and National Security: The Domestic Origins of the First World War Revisited," *Past and Present* 142, no. 1 (1994): 141–68.

Left Liberals, both in campaigns and in parliamentary debates, through their shared critique of Germany's decentralized finances as well as the three-class Prussian voting system, the core institutional bulwark that prevented tax reform.[79] Further, the rise of socialists in urban districts and demands for suffrage reform in "suffrage strikes" pressured Liberals of all stripes, even in the Prussian State Assembly, for a non-socialist reform agenda.[80] Even the National Liberals, who were historically ambivalent if not outright reactionary vis-à-vis suffrage issues, also announced their support for the secret ballot at their October 1907 Wiesbaden Congress.[81] With fractures separating its party allies in the parliament, the government sought a new coalitional foundation and a solid fiscal basis so that it could develop its much sought-after expansionist foreign policy (*Weltpolitik*).

The result was the 1907 Reichstag election, which marked a turning point in the evolution of Prussian suffrage.[82] In this national election, the government's strategically crafted campaign invoked nationalism and patriotism that sought to remake, in a move of Rikerian heresthetics, the coalitional landscape by *excluding* Catholics and for the first time *including* Left Liberals, who had displayed growing support for colonies and the navy.[83] The new nationalist majority consisting of the *Reichspartei*, Conservatives, National Liberals, and now Left Liberals, together gained 216 of the Reichstag's nearly 400 seats. The coalition seemed prepared to support the government's agenda.[84]

But, the majority came at a political price: like the Irish Party's role in the UK Parliament Act debate after 1910, the Left Liberals, the new swing-member of the coalition, elevated Prussian suffrage reform as a condition of cooperation.[85] Though criticism of "Empire" and cultural questions over education had

---

[79] This subtle shift of Left Liberals and even National Liberals, who represented urban and industrial interests along with Left Liberals, was decisive; they had historically supported the oligarchic three-class suffrage system for electoral reasons and had begun to shift on this issue because of their view that the growing SPD success that would result from suffrage reform was a reasonable price to pay for decreasing the wealth that the three-class voting system protected. Kühne, *Dreiklassenwahlrecht und Wahlkultur* (1994), 495.

[80] A further factor pushing for a convergence of Left Liberals, Liberals, and even Social Democrats was their increasingly reliance on each other in election campaigns in Prussia. For systematic data on the frequency of alliances over time, see Kühne, *Dreiklassenwahlrecht und Wahlkultur* (1994), 264–65.

[81] Kühne, *Dreiklassenwahlrecht und Wahlkultur* (1994), 515.

[82] On the 1907 election, see George Crothers, *The German Elections of 1907* (New York: Columbia University Press, 1941).

[83] On the Left Liberal support for expanded colonies and navy, see Alastair Thompson, *Left Liberals, the State, and Popular Politics in Wilhelmine Germany* (Oxford University Press, 2000), 161; Riker, *Art of Political Manipulation* (1986).

[84] Thompson, *Left Liberals, the State, and Popular Politics* (2000), 158.

[85] According to Kühne (*Dreiklassenwahlrecht und Wahlkultur*, 1994, p. 513), a key point came with the publication of Left Liberal MP Friedrich Naumann's agenda-setting article in *Berliner Tageblatt* on July 31, 1907, which asserted the critical importance of suffrage reform to the new governing bloc.

previously been the central cleavages dividing the Catholic Party and its conservative and National Liberal allies, after 1907, these issues were successfully submerged. Prussian suffrage reform now took center stage as the prerequisite for reforming public finances to support the government's colonial ambitions. In his memoirs, the future head of the German Conservative Party in the Reichstag, Count Kuno Westarp, reports that the precise wording of the King's throne-speech was fine-tuned by the chancellor to win-over Left Liberals for tax reform.[86]

Yet, between 1908 and 1914, no reform was achieved, despite the combination of economic development, social unrest, SPD electoral success, and the new coalitional dynamics. In order for us to grasp how the Conservative Party's weakness was at the root of stalled reform, we must pose two separate questions: First, why did the sweeping alterations of the three-class voting system envisioned by Left Liberals and Social Democrats, which would have included *equal, direct, secret,* and *universal male suffrage,* repeatedly fail?[87] And, second, perhaps more realistically, why were even the government's own modest reforms, which included myriad institutional safeguards, political nonstarters? We know that nondemocratic monarchs under massive social pressure – for example in Britain in 1884 or Sweden in 1907 – could "buy off" initially reluctant Conservatives when such safeguards were included as part of a reform "package." In Germany, however, under no conditions did Conservatives let down their resistance.

To answer the first question we can first demonstrate how the Conservative Party's weak organization shaped their electoral motivations in such a way that it increased Conservatives' *unwillingness* to support reform proposed by Left Liberals and Social Democrats. For example, the parliamentary record in the Prussian parliament includes two notable votes that occurred on bills that would have introduced sweeping reforms. The first was an amendment offered by Left Liberals to the government's own more modest bill, voted upon on March 11, 1910.[88] The second was a stand-alone bill offered by Left Liberals in May 20, 1912. By analyzing these two bills side by side – and setting aside the predicament that passing both through the *Herrenhaus* (upper

---

[86] Westarp quotes Bülow's explanation that the King's words were necessary so that "mood of the Liberals would not be damaged for the [upcoming] public finance reform." Graf Westarp, *Konservative Politik im letzen Jahrezent des Kaiserreichs,* vol. 1 (Berlin: Deutsche Verlagsgesellschaft, 1935), 99–100.

[87] Left Liberals and Social Democrats were committed to a wholesale reform; National Liberals were advocates of secret and direct elections; Free Conservatives conceded to allow the elimination of indirect elections; and only the German Conservative Party remained stalwart against all reforms. See Joachim Bohlmann, "Die Deutschkonservative Partei am Ende des Kaiserreichs: Stillstand und Wandel einer untergehenden Organisation" (Ernst-Moritz-Arndt-Universität Greifswald, 2011), 87.

[88] Below we will discuss the fate of the modest yet nonetheless failed government bill, which initially passed the Chamber of Deputies on March 16, 1910.

chamber) would have been presented another barrier – we can cast light on the *sources* of opposition to major democratic reforms, ranging from more conservative structural attributes of particular districts to electoral challenges facing individual MPs. Both bills would have added the secret ballot and direct elections to the Prussian suffrage system, and this thereby provides a revealing window on barriers to far-reaching suffrage reform.[89]

Following my argument in Chapter 2 and the general insights of Schattschneider and Llavador and Oxoby, I can test the hypothesis that electoral or "office-seeking" motivations, shaped by the strength of electoral organization at the disposal of old-regime political parties, determine willingness to embrace suffrage reform *above and beyond* the structural variables that the literature typically identifies.[90] With access to "stronger party organization," we would expect more willingness to accept suffrage reform; with "weaker party organization," we would expect less willingness to accept suffrage reform.

But how do we test whether "party organization" and its associated electoral benefits increased willingness to accept suffrage reform? While detailed constituency-level party organization data for this period is not available, the Imperial multilevel electoral system fortunately offers an unusual and revealing source of information that allows us to indirectly test this hypothesis. Since the candidates for the Prussian state assembly and the German Reichstag were elected from nearly matching (i.e., similar) geographical electoral districts, we can estimate how each sitting member of the Prussian Parliament, elected under Prussia's restrictive suffrage system would have fared under the universal, direct, equal, and secret ballot already in place in national Reichstag elections by comparing his vote actual vote share in Prussian elections to Reichstag candidates' vote share of his same party (in the corresponding election district) in the more democratic national Reichstag elections. In short, we can assess whether politicians of all parties who would have had *poorer* electoral prospects under these conditions (i.e., in Reichstag elections) were in fact *more* resistant to democratic reform; and whether those with *better* electoral prospects, were *more* supportive of reform.

---

[89] Part of this analysis (the analysis of the May 20, 1912 bill) draws on Ziblatt, "Does Landholding Inequality Block Democratization?" (2008). Mares has also reanalyzed these data but extended the analysis by examining the 1910 and 1912 bill with a different theoretical interest on the impact of "labor mobility" in a district on the willingness of MPs to vote for reform. See Mares, *From Open Secrets to Secret Voting: Democratic Electoral Reforms and Voter Autonomy* (2015), Chapter 7.

[90] We will control for these types of "structural variables" at the level of the electoral constituency: agrarian employment, landholding inequality, population, population density, and religious profile of district. See below for more details. Humberto Llavador and Robert Oxoby, "Partisan Competition, Growth and the Franchise," *The Quarterly Journal of Economics* 120, no. 3 (2005): 1155–89; and Schattschneider, *Party Government* (1942).

For the 1910 roll call vote, I match up electoral results from the most recent Prussian state elections (1908) with those of the candidate's same political party in the corresponding national district for most recent Reichstag elections (1907) to construct an "electoral incentive" variable for nearly every member of the Prussian state parliament. I also do the same for the 1912 vote, constructing an "electoral incentive" variable that contrasts the MPs' results from the 1908 Prussian elections with those of his co-partisan in the corresponding district in the 1912 Reichstag elections. This variable is built, in effect, by asking the following question: how much better or worse off would an individual legislator be, given the last national elections, if the national electoral system were adopted for state elections?

I also include three main control variables that measure different structural features of an MP's home constituency that might shape prospects of supporting reform. First, following a long-standing view that Junker landed wealth counteracted the democratizing impact of strong democratic oppositions, creating an unmovable political system, I include a measure of landholding inequality from the 1895 agricultural census for each district (discussed in Chapter 6), with the expectation that higher land inequality would make an MP less likely to support democratic reform.[91] Second, following the basic assumption that socioeconomic modernization promotes democratization, I include a variable that measures the percentage of the population employed in the agricultural sector for each constituency, with the expectation that the higher the proportion of agricultural workers, the more likely an MP is to resist democratization. Third, I include a variable that measures the religious makeup of a constituency, measured by the percentage of the total population in each constituency that was Catholic in the same year, with the expectation that greater religious heterogeneity makes support for democratization less likely.[92]

For the 1910 and 1912 votes, I code the dependent variable (support for democratic reform) in several ways for purposes of robustness. First, I code "yes" votes as 1 and all other votes (noes and abstentions) as 0. Second, I focus on "yes" and "no" votes only and exclude abstentions from the analysis. Finally, I also include an ordinal ranking where I code "yes" votes as 2, abstentions as 1 (since abstentions were used strategically), and "no" votes as 0.[93] The coding of dependent variables makes little difference. Table 7.3 summarizes the findings.

We see that across all specifications, even holding all other variables constant, that the more an MP is to lose out *electorally* with the new suffrage

---

[91] See, e.g., Rueschemeyer, Stephens, and Stephens, *Capitalist Development and Democracy* (1992).

[92] For more details on these control variables, measurement issues, and sources, see Ziblatt, "Does Landholding Inequality Block Democratization?" (2008): 629–30.

[93] See Ziblatt, "Does Landholding Inequality Block Democratization?" (2008): 623–24.

TABLE 7.3: *Probit and Ordered Probit Analyses of Roll Call Vote on Prussian Suffrage Reform (March 1910 and May 1912)*

	1910			1912		
	Yes vs. All Other Votes	Excluding Abstentions	Ordinal Ranking	Yes vs. All Other Votes	Excluding Abstentions	Ordinal Ranking
Electoral Incentive	0.01***	0.01***	0.01***	0.02***	0.02***	0.01***
	(0.00)	(0.00)	(0.00)	(0.00)	(0.00)	(0.00)
Land Inequality (Gini)	0.06	0.16	0.08	-0.77	-3.11**	-1.20
	(1.17)	(0.89)	(1.05)	(1.08)	(0.02)	(0.20)
Agricultural Employment	-0.03***	-0.01***	-0.03***	-0.04***	-0.08***	-0.04***
	(0.01)	(0.00)	(0.00)	(0.01)	(0.00)	(0.00)
% Catholics	-0.01*	-0.01**	-0.01*	0.01**	0.03***	0.01***
	(0.00)	(0.00)	(0.00)	(0.00)	(0.00)	(0.00)
N	264	240	264	264	214	264

Notes: * p<0.1, ** p<0.05, *** p<0.01; robust standard error in parentheses.
Data Source: For a description of data sources, see Ziblatt (2008)

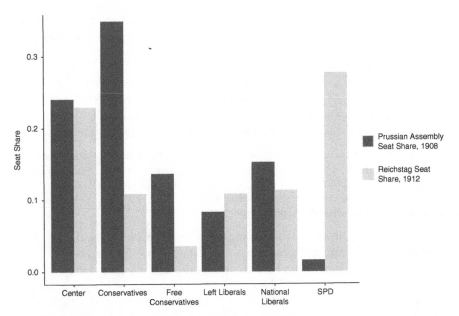

FIGURE 7.3: Seat Share by Each Party in Prussian State Elections and Federal Reichstag Elections, 1908/1912
Data Sources: Data on Federal election results from ICPSR (Inter-university Consortium for Political and Social Research). 1984. "German Reichstag Election Data, 1871–1912." Data on Prussian state elections from Kühne (1994b)

rule, the likelier he is to oppose suffrage reform.[94] We also see, unsurprisingly, that many of the other control variables are also statistically significant: MPs from more rural regions are consistently more likely to oppose reform in all specifications, and landholding inequality makes MPs from such districts less likely to support reform in some specifications.[95] A similar logic, although not linear, holds for the traditional structural variable: increasing rural employment decreases likelihood of supporting reform.

Conservatives (both Free Conservatives and German Conservatives) had the most to lose electorally under Reichstag suffrage rules, as Figure 7.3 illustrates. And the Social Democrats, with their expansive and robust nationally integrated party organization, had the most to gain. We see, therefore, why, in addition to any

[94] The positive sign on the coefficient for the variable "electoral incentive" reflects how this variable was measured (an MP's party's vote share in Reichstag elections *minus* the same party's vote share in Prussian state elections). If a member of Prussian assembly's own political party would do better under rules more closely approximating the Reichstag rules, the MP was more likely to vote for reform. The worse the MP would do, the less likely he was to vote against the reform. For more elaborate discussion, see Ziblatt, "Does Landholding Inequality Block Democratization?" (2008).

[95] In several models not reported here, this variable is more important (e.g., when a broader sample of districts is included). But the electoral incentive variable remains important in *all* specifications.

ideological motivations, instrumental electoral calculations were certainly not far
from the minds of MPs: with their feeble party organization, as I described in the
last chapter, Conservatives realized that they were simply *too weak to acquiesce* to
transformative suffrage reform.

These last-ditch efforts to block reform are found again and again
throughout this era's political landscape. The Conservative Party leader in the
Prussian State Assembly, Ernst von Heydebrand, decried suffrage reform in
parliamentary debate in 1912 in strident ideological terms, asserting:

Rule by the undifferentiated masses – which is the core ideal of universal equal suffrage –
is an attack against the basic laws of nature, according to which the capable, the best and
the worthiest [should] contribute to a country's fate; and this contribution of the ablest
and the best has been the foundation of every civilization. In fact, it is impossible to
conceive of a civilization that makes no such distinctions.[96]

Certainly not far from consideration behind such rhetoric was the short-run
instrumental calculation that stifling suffrage reform would keep the Reichstag
system of suffrage away from Prussia, an idea the DKP itself used in a campaign
brochure published in time for the June 2, 1908, election: "Hold tight on to what
the [Prussian] suffrage rule still protects! An elimination of the [three-class]
suffrage and its substitution with the general Reichstag suffrage rule represents
the final domination by the masses!"[97]

THE SECOND FACE OF WEAKNESS: THE DYNAMICS OF
ORGANIZATIONAL CAPTURE

If comprehensive suffrage reform faced staunch opposition from conservatives,
then what explains the failure of more modest government-sponsored proposals?
Suffrage reform in Britain (1884) and Sweden (1907 and 1909) included
safeguards that secured the interests of existing political parties. Was not the
same possible in Prussia? Though unlikely to transform the political regime as
a whole, the Prussian reform proposed in February 1910 by Bethmann-Hollweg
himself and endorsed by the Crown, had a better chance of success. But, while the
proposed reform disappointed Left Liberals and Social Democrats, this "top-
down" route of gradual democratization was not so unusual when we consider
British crown's interventions in the reform debate of House of Lords in
1910–1911 or the Swedish crown's parliamentary interventions in 1907 and
1909. Bethmann-Hollweg's proposal, like most democratic reforms by "elite
negotiation," had ulterior and not strictly democratic motives.[98] Nonetheless, it

---

[96] Stenographische Berichte, Haus der Abgeordneten 77 Sitzung, 21 Legislative Period, May 20, 1912
[97] *Kreuzzeitung* 256, June 2, 1908 cited by Bohlmann, "Deutschkonservative Partei am Ende des
Kaiserreichs" (2011), 88.
[98] On idea of 'elite negotiations in democratization', see Collier, *Paths Towards Democracy*
(1999), 33ff.

would have (1) substituted direct elections for indirect elections (eliminating electors); (2) enlarged the size of electoral districts to reduce the worst forms of income malapportionment; and (3) granted educated and other groups that did not qualify under income qualifications access to "first-class" voting status.[99]

The proposal was, however, admittedly modest insofar as it did *not* introduce the secret ballot; nor did it eliminate the three-tiered voting system itself. Though the reform was largely a move to bolster the status quo while appeasing Left Liberal democratic reformers, its goal was not unlike those of other democratic reforms in history: to empower a more moderate center-right collaboration of National Liberals and Conservatives and to reduce social unrest (*"Beruhigung im Land"*).[100]

The ultimate cause of the bill's failure, though in part owed to some small government missteps, was twofold: first, party leaders were unable to impose electoral losses on their own party's incumbents (what Benjamin Disraeli in 1867 had called his own party's "dying swans"), a necessary ingredient in any democratization reform, as British reforms in 1867 and 1884 demonstrate.[101] Second, as Kühne has also argued, the intense urban-rural rivalry that had developed between the two partners expected to carry the bill, National Liberals and the German Conservative Party, made forging an alliance between the two more complicated than the crown had imagined.[102] The potential center-right reform coalition was not forthcoming despite Bethmann-Hollweg's hope that the bill would "help the Conservatives make good the errors they had committed" and to "help them regain touch with the mood of the people."[103]

Instead, the Conservative Party leadership in Prussia, under von Heydebrand, chose to resist the monarchy's own plans and so proposed its own, alternative initiative without National Liberals in March 1910.[104] But, while National Liberals supported the original bill, the gap between the two parties widened too far as the Conservative leadership employed a new, ultra-conservative strategy, criticized as "demagogic" by Bethmann-Hollweg. In particular, this strategy, best summed up in Retallack's words, as being *"plus royaliste que le roi"* ("more royalist than the king"), left German

---

[99] The results for reducing the worst income malapportionment of the existing system were modest, increasing the portion of voters in the first class from 3.8% of the electorate to 7%; voters in the second class from 13.8% to 17%; and reducing the portion of third class voters from 82.4% to 76%. The more significant reform would have been the introduction of direct elections. See Bohlmann, "Deutschkonservative Partei am Ende des Kaiserreichs" (2011), 89.

[100] "Sitzung des Staatsministeriums am 26 Februar 1910," in *Die Protokolle des Preussischen Staatsministeriums, 1817–1934/38* (1999), vol. 10, 54.

[101] Kühne, *Dreiklassenwahlrecht und Wahlkultur* (1994), 568.

[102] Kühne, *Dreiklassenwahlrecht und Wahlkultur* (1994), 567.

[103] Retallack, *Notables of the Right* (1988), 164.

[104] For an account of the bill's passage through the upper chamber, see Spenkuch, *Das Preussische Herrenhaus: Adel und Bürgertum in der ersten Kammer des Landtags 1854–1918* (1998), 542–48.

Conservatives increasingly antagonistic toward the king and isolated in the German political system, unable to forge alliances with any group except the Catholic Center Party.[105]

The formerly "state loyal" Conservative Party now also contested the government's internal modernization and canal-building projects (1899, 1901, 1904) as well as the 1909 public finance bill that would have removed tax privileges of landed wealth, bills that both Left Liberals and National Liberals supported. More fundamentally, the irresolvable tensions between National Liberals and Conservatives were rooted in an important consequence of weak party organization: the *geographic isolation* of the party. Lacking nationally encompassing party organization, the German Conservative Party was increasingly concentrated in a smaller number of districts (as Figure 7.4 depicts) chiefly in eastern Prussia, which by any estimate had starkly different median preferences about suffrage than those of the liberal parties.

I follow Jones and Mainwaring in proposing a Party Nationalization Score (PNS) based on a Gini coefficient of electoral support, which assesses the degree to which a party wins equal vote shares across all subnational units (in this case electoral constituencies). Figure 7.4 reports electoral geography Gini coefficients for the traditional right or conservative party in parliamentary elections in four countries for which systematic over-time data are available.[106] In this case, the higher the value, the higher the geographical concentration of the votes. As Figure 7.4 shows, the German Conservative Party was unique among similar traditional right parties in Europe in gaining most of its Reichstag election votes in a concentrated set of districts.[107]

If a political party's electoral support is spatially concentrated, the median voter of its median district is likely to be very ideologically distant from the median voter of the country as a whole.[108] Further, this suggests that MP incumbents had resisted efforts from party leadership to more efficiently distribute their electoral victories, further indicating party weakness. Figure 7.5 which plots agricultural employment as a share of total employment on the

[105] See Retallack, *The German Right* (2006), 347. In addition to the instability of parliamentary coalitions, Kühne's (*Dreiklassenwahlrecht und Wahlkultur*, 1994, 264) data on which parties formed electoral coalitions with other parties makes clear that Conservatives' electoral cooperation with Left and National Liberal Parties was in decline after 1890, but increasing only with the Catholic Center Party.

[106] For an elaboration of the method, see Mark Jones and Scott Mainwaring, "The Nationalization of Parties and Party Systems: An Empirical Measure and Application to the Americas," *Party Politics* 9, no. 2 (2003): 139–66. Data source is Caramani, *Elections in Western Europe* (2000).

[107] Equally intensive concentration was found also with the Prussian Assembly delegation where 126 MPs were from east of the Elbe River (the heartland of "eastern Prussia") and only seventeen were from west of the Elbe. Retallack, *Notables of the Right* (1988), 167.

[108] See Jonathan Rodden, "The Geographic Distribution of Political Preferences," *Annual Review of Political Science* 13 (2010): 321–40.

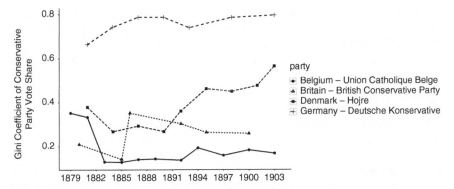

FIGURE 7.4: Geographic Concentration (Gini-Coefficient) of Conservative Party Vote Share, National Parliamentary Elections, 1881–1903
Note: The figure reports Gini coefficients in vote share across electoral districts for all national parliamentary elections between 1880 and 1903.
Data Source: Caramani 2000

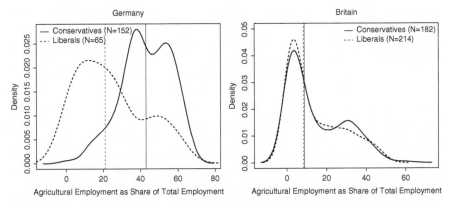

FIGURE 7.5: Median and Distribution of Conservative and Liberal Party Seats Across Varying Levels of Agricultural Districts in Germany and Britain in Years of Suffrage Reform (1910 and 1885)
Data Sources: Election data from Caramani (2000); Employment data for Britain's constituencies from Great Britain Historical GIS Project (2012) "Great Britain Historical GIS." University of Portsmouth; Employment data for German constituencies, see Ziblatt (2009), 9

x-axis (as a proxy of the type of district) against the density of seats won by Conservative and Liberal Parties, indicates that this was the case in Germany

We see greater overlap in Britain, suggesting that Conservatives and Liberals won very similar types of districts (strictly in terms of where agricultural employment predominated). By contrast, in Germany, Conservatives won in much more rural districts, overlapping less with Liberals. Thus, unlike in Britain, where British Conservatives and Liberals competed over similar suburban districts, in Germany, the profile of Conservative districts was starkly different demographically – more rural and marked by low population density, a higher portion of Protestants, and high landholding inequality. This ensured that their constituencies' preferences were likely far from those of other parties.[109] The result was simple: lacking the necessary party organization to reach beyond safe seats *without losing their base*, the German Conservative Party's stances on highly ideological questions were constrained by the simple fact that its median voter was very distant from the center of the political space as well from other parties, which were necessary partners to negotiate suffrage reform.

The concept of "party weakness" also implies an *organizational logic* that unfolds in several ways: unlike Swedish Conservatives in 1907–09 or British Conservatives in 1884, German Conservative leadership, because of its weak party organization and resulting geographic isolation, was more dependent upon, more vulnerable to, and thus more easily "captured" by the narrowly focused and effectively organized Agrarian League (BdL) as described in Chapter 6.[110] As I have noted earlier, between 1898 and 1912, all Conservative Party MPs in the Reichstag were endorsed by and took pledges to support the BdL; and the interpenetration of the interest groups' leadership and party leadership was extensive.[111] Further, Conservative MPs were disproportionately reliant on campaign financing and logistical support from the BdL. Because of the ever-present threat that the BdL might run its own candidates against disloyal DKP members, the interest group, which defined itself as exclusively defending agrarian interests, exerted enormous leverage over a Conservative Party consigned to rural districts. This was seen in stages: first, as the BdL incited internal factionalism in the party over infrastructure bills, tariff bills, and tax bills in the early years after 1900; and second, as it definitively shaped the party's stances on voting rights and suffrage in 1909 and 1910, entirely out of proportion to the importance of agriculture in the broader German economy.

With the BdL's influence giving the rural cast to their party, some conservatives began to try to gain back control of the party. In the years after

[109] See Jonathan Sperber, *The Kaiser's Voters: Electors and Elections in Imperial Germany* (Cambridge: Cambridge University Press, 1997). For parallel evidence on Prussia, see Ziblatt, "Does Landholding Inequality Block Democratization?" (2008).

[110] The idea that interest groups can more effectively capture political parties when parties are spatially concentrated in their support is not one, as far as I know, that exists in the literature. However, there is good theoretical reason, building on basic theories of collective action as well as theories of regulatory capture to think spatially concentrated actors are more vulnerable to capture. See Olson, *Logic of Collective Action* (1965); Stigler, "The Theory of Economic Regulation" (1971).

[111] Also exerting influence in the Prussian Chamber of Deputies, 122 of 152 Conservative MPs in the Prussian Chamber of Deputies in 1908 declared themselves in favor of the BdL program and received campaign assistance in exchange. See Retallack, *Notables of the Right* (1988), 166.

1903, and especially after the rejection of the government's public finance bill in 1909, a movement within the Conservative Party developed to "step across the Elbe" and "ride to the west" by building local party associations (*Vereine*) and running campaigns outside of the East Elbian heartlands in a new "urban conservatism" modeled in part on British Toryism.[112] For example, the conservative mayor of Dresden, Dr. Gustav Otto Beutler, argued that Conservatives' anti-industrial views were limiting its prospects in Saxony. Dr. Beutler, at the Conservative Party Congress of December 1909, criticized his fellow delegates, asserting that "there is a widespread understanding that the party has become a complete dependent of the BdL."[113] Also, in reaction to the failure of the government's public finance bill at the hands of the BdL-dominated DKP Reichstag caucus, disaffection emerged among a group of conservative *Vereine* from the leafy suburban districts outside of Berlin including Lichterfelde, Moabit, and Pankow, similar to the districts outside London that Conservatives thrived in beginning in the 1880s. In addition to policies that would benefit cities (i.e., tariff reform, public finance reform), local party activists from the suburban Vereine actually advocated more sweeping suffrage reform and a political program based around this revealing slogan:

> More contact with the people!
> Independence from the Agrarian League!
> Equity between city and country!
> Away from the Center Party!
> Back to the Bloc concept [alliance with National Liberals]
> against Social Democracy!
> Then the Conservative Party will become a *Volkspartei*![114]

However, these groups had little hope of influencing the party leadership, already comprised of agrarian BdL insiders – in the Reichstag, the Prussian Assembly, and *Herrenhaus* parliamentary groups – which, along with a single Saxon MP, constituted its central decision-making body, the so-called "Committee of Twelve."[115] Facing a party leadership already dominated by well-organized agrarian interests, these new provincial groups could garner

---

[112] A prominent figure in this movement was led by Dr. Adolf Grabowsky, a prominent publicist and later political scientist whose 1911 article "Cultural Conservatism" explicitly compared British and German Conservatism, arguing the latter had been "deformed" and required fundamental organizational and ideological reform.

[113] Deutsche Konservative Partei, ed., *Der Allgemeine Delegiertentag der Deutsch-Konservativen Partei. Stenographischer Bericht, 11 December 1909* (Berlin: Hauptverein der Deutsch-Konservativen, 1909), 27.

[114] On this group's stance on suffrage reform, see Bohlmann, "Deutschkonservative Partei am Ende des Kaiserreichs" (2011), 92. On the group's program, Retallack, *Notables of the Right* (1988), 182–83.

[115] Retallack, *Notables of the Right* (1988), 229. By 1912, the highest body in the party, the so-called "committee of twelve" consisted of Wedel, Heydebrand, Beutler, Buch, Erffa, Klassing, Kroecher, Limburg, Mehnert, Mirbach, Normann, Pappenheim, and Westarp.

little immediate influence, instead leaving a simmering grassroots factionalism in the provincial *Vereine* to reemerge after 1918.[116] Thus, a powerful legacy of the past and internal party politics blocked a rational strategy to maximize votes.

How did this dynamic of "organizational capture" shape the party's stance on democratization? And, why would an agricultural interest group have such a strong position on electoral reform? Though Ernst von Heydebrand, nicknamed the "uncrowned King of Prussia," was said to have run the Conservative Party with an "iron fist" and was widely regarded as a brilliant politician, by 1910, the impact of the BdL's influence was far-reaching. Indeed, part of von Heydebrand's unusual political talent was precisely his ability to act on behalf of a narrow interest while simultaneously playing the role as commanding leader fully in charge of the party.[117] However, illustrating one of the classic paradoxes of political power, the full scope of influence between the two organizations is difficult to identify empirically unless the analyst carefully traces *over time* how what at first might have been open conflicts was gradually muted and replaced with a subtle, quiet domination, with one group entirely limiting another group's room for maneuver.[118] In the earliest ultraconservative stances *contra* the chancellor over the canal bill (1899, 1902, and 1905), tariff bills (1902), and the public finance bill (1909), we see the BdL issuing overt threats and rewards to Conservative Party MPs, and we witness open power struggles between the two groups. But over time, these overt inner-party struggles were submerged, BdL members occupied a greater portion of leadership positions in the DKP, and the political positions and actions of the two groups became increasingly fused and difficult to disentangle.

The first great clash came in 1899 when the king's government pushed for a "modernizing" canal to link western Prussia and eastern Prussia. The bill's introduction into the Prussian Chamber of Deputies sparked a sharp split in Conservative Party. The BdL released propaganda materials decrying the destructive "incursion" into eastern Prussia that a canal would cause, and also warned that the massive infrastructure project would strengthen labor movements to the west (driving up the price of labor in the east) and decrease the price of grain by depressing the costs of foreign imports. Not unlike the Tariff League campaign launched in Britain in 1903 (described in Chapters 4 and 5), in Germany conservative-leaning pressure groups coerced sitting MPs. In a well-organized campaign in the summer of 1899, the BdL threatened to withdraw its endorsement from Conservative MPs who expressed support for

---

[116] Retallack, *The German Right* (2006), 378–83.
[117] A range of opponents, from National Liberal Eugen Schiffer to Left Liberal newspaper editor Theodor Wolff, express admiration. See Retallack, *The German Right* (2006), 387.
[118] Paul Pierson, "Power and Path Dependence," in *Advances in Comparative Historical Analysis*, ed. James Mahoney and Kathleen Thelen (Cambridge: Cambridge University Press, 2015); Peter Bachrach and Morton Baratz, "Two Faces of Power," *American Political Science Review* 56, no. 4 (1962): 947–52.

the bill; following the wholesale adoption of the BdL's rhetoric by Conservative Party MPs, the bill was defeated.[119] But the BdL's influence was by no means complete; in an ensuing backlash, the so-called "canal rebels" came under a major counterattack as the king's government announced no BdL members would be welcomed to the court, and, more importantly, all current and future officials in the government instantly had to drop their BdL membership.

Yet, the government's actions, while important, only heightened the stakes of the BdL–DKP battle. Three years later, conflicts again erupted over efforts to increase Caprivi's old low tariffs on grain. In 1902, though tariffs were ultimately raised, BdL chairman Wangenheim threatened to form his own party to run against the thirty-four Conservative MPs who had voted for the bill because the tariff rate increase was insufficiently *large*. While "governmentalist" Conservative MPs critiqued the power of the BdL, Wangenheim intervened in public debate, asserting that parties that supported the bill needed to be "destroyed."[120] The conflict exploded into the open: while some leaders such as Manteuffel called for the expulsion of Wangenheim from the party, Wangenheim himself and the BdL leadership ran fifty-five candidates of their own in the next Prussian elections of 1903. It is true that only five of the BdL candidates won seats. But, a message clearly had been sent, and by 1905, the balance of power had begun subtley to tilt in favor of the BdL. Oskar von Normann, the Reichstag caucus leader, favored Wangenheim during the 1903 conflict, and when a new party chairman of the Prussian Chamber, Ernst von Heydebrand, was elected, BdL chairman Wangenheim enthusiastically wrote that of all the candidates, Heydebrand was "the only one who would lead the cause energetically and along agrarian lines."[121]

Indeed, by 1908, when von Bülow's government introduced its major public finance bill that would have removed the tax privileges of landed wealth, the BdL and the party leadership now worked closely together to defeat it. On June 24, 1909, only six deputies from the entire DKP Reichstag caucus voted for the bill, which in turn led to the eventual fall of Chancellor von Bülow and the passage, with Center Party support, of an alternative bill written jointly by the BdL leadership and that taxed "mobile" wealth and not landed wealth. The future party leader, Count Kuno von Westarp recalled in his memoirs a revealing private moment in the heated public debate:

On April 20, 1909 as I was preparing to speak to a Conservative gathering in Charlottenburg... I received two letters from the two chairman of the Bund der Landwirte [including von Wentzel] in my home constituency... they had heard that I would make the case for the inheritance tax and they had to tell me that the Agrarian League had raised protest at constituency meetings and would not support my future

[119] Bohlmann, "Deutschkonservative Partei am Ende des Kaiserreichs" (2011), 57.
[120] Ibid., 60. [121] Cited by Retallack, *The German Right* (2006), 361.

candidacy and insisted I lay down my mandate. I telegraphed von Wentzel "Assumption of letter is false. Am astounded that that threat was even necessary."[122]

Indeed, by the fall of 1908, when the king made his "throne speech" calling for reform of the three-class voting system, the alignment of the BdL and the DKP's main leadership on key issues was apparent. It was no longer necessary to threaten party leaders to implement the BdL agenda, though it is certainly true that subterranean resistance and criticism did persist, especially from western Vereine and disgruntled associations. In the case of the three-class voting system, the DKP and BdL shared a common interest. Not unlike the House of Lords in Britain until 1911, the Prussian suffrage system was a buffer that protected the immediate electoral interests of DKP MPs, while also blocking the passage of potentially damaging tax initiatives – since major direct taxes existed *only* at the state level – on rural property and land.

At their annual general gathering in 1909, BdL delegates raucously criticized suffrage reform plans. One Prussian BdL member and Reichstag Conservative MP, Herr von Oldenburg-Januschau, made clear the importance of the three-class voting system in Prussia, noting that three linked topics dominate the agenda: tax reform, suffrage reform, and the rising power of the parliament.[123] Addressing the liberalizing suffrage reform in southern German states, to the applause of his colleagues, he proclaimed, "We will defend the Prussian dam for you all to maintain the influence of the countryside and the strength of the monarchy!"[124] In a meandering speech, another BdL member, F. von Bodelschwingh-Schwarzenhasel, defended the three-class voting system in even more pernicious terms and with a warning to MPs who might defect:

Gentleman, I know that in some places people are shy to criticize Judaism or to name oneself as an opponent of Judaism. It is a weakness of our times to not want to call things by their proper name... With all emphasis, I would like to speak out against a changing of the suffrage/constituency boundaries which will reduce the influence of the countryside. And, I would like to add: from my view, any of the MPs from one of the parties that is close to us that have come out unconditionally for the redrawing of electoral districts, *should find no support and no contact from us.*[125]

But, the BdL leaders, Roesicke and von Wangenheim, though just as firmly opposed to any suffrage reform, argued against taking an explicit stand. After all, von Heydebrand proved a reliable ally. Though von Heydebrand had initially proposed a secret ballot in 1910, proving his "loyalty" to the crown

---

[122] Westarp, *Konservative Politik im letzten Jahrezent des Kaiserreichs* (1935), 64–65.

[123] "Stenographische Bericht über die 16 General-Versammlung des Bundes der Landwirte," *Korrespondenz des Bundes der Landwirte*, Nr. 15 February 23, 1909: 66.

[124] Ibid.

[125] "Stenographische Bericht über die 16 General-Versammlung des Bundes der Landwirte," *Korrespondenz des Bundes der Landwirte*, Nr. 15 February 23, 1909: 70.

to the annoyance of many in his party, it is uncertain whether he was simply playing both sides of the issue. After all, the bill had little chance of surviving the *Herrenhaus*, and in 1910 he led a vote *against* the final version of the government bill, revealing his ultimate position.[126] In short, the BdL toned down. In his correspondence to von Wangenheim on November 2, 1908, Roesicke argues precisely against an overly "aggressive" and "open" stance and proposed an alternative strategy of resistance:

If we take up an *open* struggle against the suffrage plans of the King, this will lead to renewed tensions. These tensions will deeply annoy a large number of the members of the Conservative faction. Nonetheless, we can prevent a change in the suffrage rules that would run counter to our position while avoiding tensions and this break by furthering the enlightenment of the public that we began in the last campaign, a shaping of the public mood that von Bülow will take into consideration.[127]

One can argue that open conflict was no longer necessary; and yet, following this subtle strategy, the right-wing "diehards" achieved their aim: the three-class voting system remained untouched until war and revolution destroyed the entire political regime in 1918. The king's own effort at suffrage reform was defeated despite the presence of mass unrest and widespread support from across the political spectrum, from Social Democrats all the way to National Liberals.

In short, given the importance of the three-class voting system to Germany's dualistic constitutional structure, we see that the repeated failure of suffrage reform before 1914 reveals a paradox: an organizationally weak old-regime party, arguably in decline, was vulnerable to takeover by a *radicalizing* narrow interest that constrained the party leadership's room for maneuver. The similarities to Britain's Unionist Party – constrained by its own die-hards – before 1914 are certainly striking. However, while similar battles between British Conservative Party right-wingers and moderating "party men" were common at pivotal points in the evolution of Britain's Conservative Party – as in fights over the 1867 and 1884 Reform Acts, for example – the "party men" were then on the winning side. In Germany, by contrast, the victories ran the other way. It was the German Conservative Party's diehards who triumphed; and the party was incrementally swallowed by them. In sum, Conservative Party weakness ironically blocked the reform of what ultimately remained an unwieldy and nondemocratic political regime. The failures to innovate organizationally in 1848 haunted Germany until at least 1914 and beyond.

---

[126] Kühne, *Dreiklassenwahlrecht und Wahlkultur* (1994), 565–69.
[127] G. Roesicke to C von Wangenheim on November 2, 1908, "Briefwechsel Freiherr von Wangenheim/Dr. Roesicke im Jahre 1908" Nachlass Wangenheim, Bundesarchiv Berlin-Lichterfelde N 2323 Nr. 3 (1908).

EPILOGUE: WHY WE CAN'T JUST BLAME GERMANY'S AGRARIAN
ELITES

We return now to our central claim: that it was the nature of the political parties representing Germany's socioeconomic elite that made any possibility of democratic transition in Prussia, and hence in Germany, so difficult before 1914. But, to lay the heavy burden of Germany's political development on highly depersonalized factors such as "political organizations," "political parties," and "interest groups" is to offer, one might contend, an acontextual view of political history – one that does not take seriously the deeply embedded character of the social structure, groups, and individuals being represented. After all, a long line of literature – from Gerschenkron, Rosenberg, and Wehler to Rueschemeyer, Stephens, and Stephens – notes that it was above all *agrarian elites* in Prussia, sitting atop highly concentrated landed wealth, who possessed deeply antidemocratic cultural orientations. They, thus, were the true culprits, doing all they could to thwart democratization whether or not they had effective political party organization.[128] Recent historiography has certainly not given us a more flattering picture of the political orientations of Germany's and Prussia's landed elites.[129] Also, there are good *theoretical reasons* to believe that the holders of immobile assets like land, such as east Prussian Junkers, no matter how they are organized politically, will be particularly formidable defenders of nondemocratic political regimes even in the face of great social unrest.[130]

The Prussian case study I have presented above uses wide-ranging sources of quantitative and archival evidence to illustrate the importance of party organization. However, this account does not fully absolve agrarian elites of their direct responsibility for one simple reason: weakly organized political parties may have represented socioeconomic elites, but those socioeconomic elites were also chiefly *agrarian* elites. Indeed, the coexistence of *both* weak party structures on the one hand and an antidemocratic agrarian elite on the other, aggravates the challenge of disentangling the relative importance of each. Both factors were present, so to speak, at the scene of the crime. Indeed, the evidence we saw above of Prussian roll call votes on suffrage reform in 1910 and 1912 not only points to the importance of "electoral incentives" flowing from weak party organization, but also partially confirms the conventional account: MPs from more rural districts – typically those with higher land inequality and disproportionately located in eastern Prussia, the heartland of traditional

---

[128] Gerschenkron, *Bread and Democracy* (1948); Rosenberg, *Imperial Germany* (1964); Hans-Ulrich Wehler, *Moderne deutsche Sozialgeschichte*. (Köln: Kiepenheur u. Witsch 1966); and Rueschemeyer, Stephens, and Stephens, *Capitalist Development and Democracy* (1992).

[129] Sebastian Malinowski, *Vom König zum Führer. Sozialer Niedergang und politische Radikalisierung im deutschen Adel zwischen Kaiserreich und NS-Staat* (Berlin: 2003).

[130] Boix, *Democracy and Redistribution* (2003); Acemoglu and Robinson, *Economic Origins of Dictatorship and Democracy* (2006).

agrarian power – were more likely to oppose democratic reform whether or not they had effective party organization.

To give us more *prima facie* confidence in the claim about the *independent* impact of party organization on democratization, it would be helpful to find a case with the following attributes: (a) intense social unrest and working-class mobilization demanding democratic reform; and (b) homogenously non-agrarian or *urban* "bourgeois" socioeconomic elites that are at the center of a nondemocratic regime; and which in turn (c) do *not* possess party organization. The case of nineteenth-century and prewar Britain (Chapters 3 and 4) is useful comparatively because landed elites were powerful into the twentieth century, but, because they were armed with political party organization, they *could* accommodate themselves to democracy.[131] However, we still must ask: without the presence of an agrarian elite in Germany, would weak political parties have still blocked democratization before 1914? If so, we certainly would have greater confidence that weak party organization itself matters and is not simply an outgrowth of a particular type of rural social structure; and we could more self-assuredly assert the importance of party organizations representing the elites in a nondemocratic political regime, no matter its socioeconomic or sociocultural complexion.

THE LESSONS OF A "CRUCIAL" CASE

A case within pre-1914 Germany allows us to analyze precisely this scenario: Hamburg in 1906.[132] A longtime self-governing republic and an economically vibrant commercial hub on Germany's North Sea, Hamburg, like Lübeck, the city portrayed in Thomas Mann's novel *Buddenbrooks*, had roots in its distant past as a medieval trading port. But, unlike Lübeck, which went into relative decline, nineteenth-century Hamburg became Germany's second-largest city and also one of its wealthiest states. Initially dominated by a group of distinguished merchant family firms built on an expansive global trade across the Atlantic, Asia, and Africa, the city also became the site of a massive shipping and ship-building industry as well as growing financial and service sectors. Crucially for our purposes, this was a city-state that featured not only

---

[131] For evidence on the persistence of landed elites in positions of dominance into the twentieth century, see Chapter 2 and Cannadine, *Decline and Fall of the British Aristocracy* (1999), 280ff.

[132] The following brief case study builds on an extensive literature, but major works it relies on are Richard Evans, *Death in Hamburg: Society and Politics in the Cholera Years, 1830–1910* (Oxford: Clarendon Press, 1987a); Madeleine Hurd, *Public Spheres, Public Mores, and Democracy: Hamburg and Stockholm, 1870–1914* (Ann Arbor: University of Michigan Press, 2000); Jennifer Jenkins, *Provincial Modernity: Local Culture and Liberal Politics in Fin-de-Siecle Hamburg* (Ithaca: Cornell University Press, 2003); and Meike Schallert, "Why the Poor Organized and Lost Their Vote: Suffrage Robbery in Hamburg" (Harvard University, 2008).

a strong bourgeois elite but a vibrant working class as well. Further, like all states in Germany's fiscally loose federation, Hamburg had jurisdiction not only over its own constitutional and suffrage rules but its own tax and fiscal systems as well, making its two representative groups – the Citizens' Assembly and the *Senat* – consequential elected bodies.

Beyond this, three factors are particularly telling. First, it was a state *without* an agrarian elite, and, thus, arguably the urban merchant-class bourgeoisie dominated to a degree unmatched by any European state at the time. If there is anything to Barrington Moore's famous insight "no bourgeoisie, no democracy," Hamburg, a city with a long republican tradition and a self-confident urban elite, certainly qualified as a promising case for democratization.[133] An almost entirely urban state in the German federation, by 1914 Hamburg had a greater share of world trade than any port in continental Europe and was moreover a national financial center, with a stock exchange equaled in activity only by Frankfurt.[134] The economic elite of the city, as Niall Ferguson notes in his case study of the city in the late Imperial and Weimar period, included "merchant houses like Shuback & Söhne; the shipping lines R. M. Sloman, Hapag, and the Woermanns; [and] the shipyards Blohm & Voß, Vulkan and Reiherstieg ... "[135] This ruling economic class was a close-knit group of bourgeois families with wealth primarily drawn from international trade, shipbuilding, and the trading houses. With no royal bureaucracy or agrarian elite, the Hamburg merchant classes were both politically and culturally hegemonic, sponsoring a rich urban culture of theaters, natural history museums, art museums, libraries, and public spaces.[136] The case appeared a promising one for theories that maintain the indispensability of a rising bourgeois class for democracy.

But more than this, Hamburg was then also arguably the "capital of the labor movement" in Germany, the home of a particularly strong working class aligned with the Social Democratic Party and increasingly organized trade unions. Thus, for theories that emphasize not the bourgeoisie but the role of the organized working class as "torchbearers of democracy," Hamburg is also clearly a case where conditions were ripe for democracy.[137] Hamburg was,

---

[133] Moore, *Social Origins of Dictatorship and Democracy* (1966).

[134] R. Gömmel, "Entstehung und Entwicklung der Effektenbörsen im 19. Jahrhundert bis 1914," in *Deutsche Börsengeschichte*, ed. H. Pohl (Frankfurt a. M.: Fritz Knapp Verlag, 1992), 133–207.

[135] Niall Ferguson, *Paper and Iron: Hamburg Business and German Politics in the Era of Inflation, 1897–1927* (Oxford: Oxford University Press, 2002), 47.

[136] Schallert, "Why the Poor Organized and Lost Their Vote" (2008), 6; Jenkins, *Provincial Modernity: Local Culture and Liberal Politics in Fin-de-Siecle Hamburg* (2003); Sven Beckert, "Die Kultur des Kapitals: Bürgerliche Kultur in New York und Hamburg im 19. Jahrhundert," in *Vorträge aus dem Warburg-Haus 4*, ed. Warburg Haus (Berlin: Akademie Verlag, 2000), 143–75.

[137] Eley, *Forging Democracy* (2002).

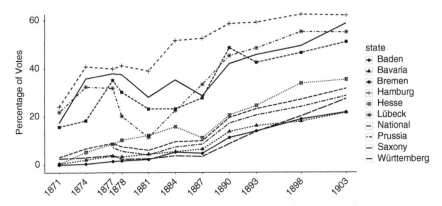

FIGURE 7.6: Electoral Support for SPD, by German State in Reichstag Elections
Data Source: Kaiserliches Statistisches Amt. ed., *Streiks und Aussperrungen im Jahre 1909*, Statistik des Deutschen Reichs, Vol. 239 (Berlin: Verlag von Puttkammer & Mühlbrecht, 1910), 49–58

electorally speaking, a socialist stronghold, even during the time of the anti-socialist laws.[138] After 1890, all three of Hamburg's Reichstag seats were in the hands of Social Democrats, thanks to the universal male suffrage system in place for national elections. As displayed in Figure 7.6, the SPD held a higher percentage of votes in Hamburg than in all other German states, including Bremen, Lübeck, and Saxony, similarly urban, industrialized states with sizeable labor movements. In 1871, Hamburg's SPD received four times as high a vote share as it did nationwide; and in 1903, its support was twice as high.

In addition to electoral politics, the working class increasingly exerted pressure through extra-parliamentary means. Hamburg, as historian Richard Evans explains, became the central site of massive labor strikes (e.g., in the dockyards) in the years before 1910, attracting attention across Europe. In response to a cholera outbreak in 1892 and the city's failed response to this crisis, social pressure grew to improve working and living conditions – and to alter the suffrage.[139] As summarized in Figure 7.7, we can draw upon German census industrial strike data, reported by state, to show that despite Hamburg's small size, the incidence of strikes there was matched only by the much larger states of Saxony and Bavaria.

---

[138] Helga Kutz-Bauer, "Arbeiterschaft und Sozialdemokratie in Hamburg vom Gründerkrach bis zum Ende des Sozialistengesetzes," in *Arbeiter in Hamburg. Unterschichten, Arbeiter und Arbeiterbewegung seit dem ausgehenden 18. Jahrhundert*, ed. Arno Herzig, et al. (Hamburg: Verlag Erziehung und Wissenschaft, 1983), 179–92.

[139] Evans, *Death in Hamburg: Society and Politics in the Cholera Years, 1830–1910* (1987a). Evans, "Red Wednesday' in Hamburg: Social Democrats, Police and Lumpenproletariat in the Suffrage Disturbances of 17 January 1906" (1979).

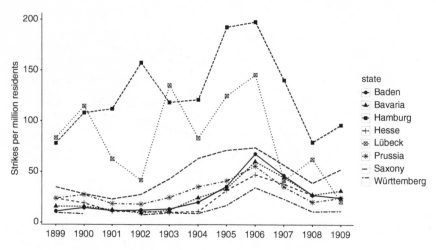

FIGURE 7.7: Incidence of Annual Strikes in German States, 1899–1909 (per Million Residents)
Data Source: Schröder, *Sozialdemokratische Parlamentarier in den Deutschen Reichs- und Landtagen, 1867–1933*, 825–889

Hamburg was a center of German bourgeois *and* working-class power. In short, few cases seemed as over-determined for democratic success. So, then, what was the outcome of a robust bourgeoisie coming face-to-face with a vocal working class demanding political representation? The result, ironically, was what historians and activists at the time called a *"Wahlraub"* ("suffrage robbery"). In 1906, facing massive social unrest, the political elite of Hamburg, already protected by a comparatively restrictive franchise, introduced a remarkable further *retraction* of political rights by reducing political equality through restrictions on voting rights.[140]

Confronting similar unrest after 1900, many southern German states, including Baden (1904), Bavaria (1906), and Württemberg (1906), democratized their voting systems in important ways – institutionalizing the secret ballot, expanding who could vote, and weighing lower income voters more. Hamburg, however, followed Saxony (1896) and Lübeck (1902, 1905) by imposing new restrictions and, most importantly, decreasing the equality of the vote, modeling itself after Prussia. The Hamburg government, employing an elaborate system of income malapportionment divided up the general electorate into two income-based classes and gave them highly unequal voting

[140] See Wolfgang Schneider, "Die Begrenzungen des Wahlrechts in Deutschland, Preußen und Hamburg (im 19. und 20. Jahrhundert)" (Hamburg, 1955). According to Schneider's data (p. 220–21), only 4 percent of Hamburg's residents could vote in state elections: a remarkably low figure, lower than that found in Bavaria, Hesse, Baden, Württemberg, and Prussia.

rights.[141] Between 1879 and 1906, the general curia (which included both high-income and lower-income citizens) had elected 80 of the 160 representatives, while the second curia of high-income notables elected 40, and the third curia of high-income property owners elected 40, totaling 160 seats. After the 1906 reform, however, a new distinction was added to the general curia: the top third by income had the right to elect a disproportionate 48 representatives, while the bottom two-thirds elected only 24 representatives. The citizens of outlying districts elected the remaining 8 representatives, while notables and property owners preserved their respective shares of 40 representatives each.[142] In short, facing socialist mobilization, power was expropriated from the poorest of citizens.[143] The political redistribution rendered Hamburg's electoral system among the most unequal in Germany.

How was this possible? Given existing theory, why, with a well-organized bourgeoisie and working class, and no agrarian elite, was de-democratization the result of social contention? Why was there *not* the opposite, some movement toward democratization? A focus on the balance of social forces is clearly insufficient, and the puzzle persists unless we focus on the more complicated question of how the economic elite during this time of mass unrest *organized themselves politically*. Though an urban merchant class with mobile assets, Hamburg's economic elite was ineffective at organizing political parties.[144] In a revealing analysis, Meike Schallert argues that the groups that occupied Hamburg's governing institutions indeed were "party-precursors" and not political parties.[145] Though organized in Hamburg's Assembly as three groups, Right, Center, and Left, they were *not* political parties for three reasons. First, unlike their well-organized socialist opposition, the bourgeois "notable" politicians formed factions *after* elections, not before, and thus lacked party programs. Second, as a result, the "parties" failed to exert any party discipline in decision-making, a key hallmark of party organization, even regarding such measures as "distastefully" coercive.[146] Third, the groupings did not collect membership dues nor did they raise funds, hire staff, or print publications, leaving them extremely skeletal organizations.[147] In sum, with

---

[141] Hans Wilhelm Eckardt, *Privilegien und Parlament: Die Auseinandersetzungen um das allgemeine und gleiche Wahlrecht in Hamburg* (Hamburg: Landeszentrale für politische Bildung, 1980), 40–49. This account draws on Schallert, "Why the Poor Organized and Lost Their Vote" (2008).

[142] In Hamburg, the result was a highly inequitable voting system: even within the third, general curia of the 1907 elections, one-third of Hamburg's citizens now elected twice as many representatives as the remaining two-thirds, a fact compounded by the continued privileges of notables and property owners, leaving lower income citizens electing 24 of 160 representatives.

[143] Analogous pressures for urban disenfranchisement, it should be added, were found in far-flung locations, including New York City, though these proposals foundered. See Beckert, "Democracy and Its Discontents" (2002).

[144] Boix, *Democracy and Redistribution* (2003).

[145] Schallert, "Why the Poor Organized and Lost Their Vote" (2008).   [146] Ibid.   [147] Ibid.

none of the core attributes of party organization, Hamburg's bourgeois elite was left wanting for the electoral machinery necessary to compete with its socialist rival, which thrived in national elections.

It thus comes as no surprise that leading figures in Hamburg politics such as Senator O'Swald, of a prominent merchant family, summarized the opposition he now faced with nervousness, calling out several of the opposition's attributes that the Hamburg's elites could learn from,

> [Social Democratic] power is based on tight organization... such excellent organization as I would wish for other political parties... [The Social Democrats] are used to tight discipline, a type of discipline that one can hardly find in the military... the Social Democrat who as a worker cannot take care of political affairs betakes himself into the hands of the leaders of the SPD, and as such he must follow the leader's orders; he has no independent will. The Social Democratic leaders do not accept opposition, and if a Social Democrat fails to obey rules, he will simply be expelled or admonished... This is why Social Democracy won twelve seats in the last half-time renewal of the Assembly.[148]

Confronting this political reality with a mix of acute fear and loathing, it is not surprising that Hamburg's bourgeois elite, like Prussia's agrarian elite – just as *any* economic elite without party organization likely would respond – repressed and *de-democratized*. It is possible that Hamburg's urban elite, like the prominent merchant family in Thomas Mann's novel *Buddenbrooks*, was merely the victim of the diffusion of the Prussia's landed elites' pernicious political ethos, one that expressed admiration for aristocratic life and extreme distaste for competitive politics. However, even if correct, a more immediate and concrete factor in Hamburg was that economic elites, as in Prussia, were simply unwilling and unable to harness the "new" power of political party organization – a fact that might actually *explain* the origins of that political ethos. This organizational absence hindered these groups' ability strategically to defend their interests in a lasting way. And, the long-run result was, tragically, unhinged democratization for more than a century.

---

[148] William H. O'Swald, Stenographische Berichte der Hamburger Bürgerschaft, eighteenth session, May 24, 1905: 454, cited by Schallert, "Why the Poor Organized and Lost Their Vote" (2008).

8

The Unsettled Path: Conservative Weakness in Weimar Germany, 1918–1928

A well-worn historiographical interpretation argues that Weimar Germany, emerging out of the destruction of the First World War, suffered a flawed origin and was doomed from the start. Illegitimate because of the terms of Versailles Treaty that ended the war, and born from an incomplete and compromised revolution, this account runs, the Weimar system left footholds in place for reactionaries to creep back into power. Like many orthodoxies, this set of claims has a grain of truth. The new postwar political regime did have substantial vulnerabilities rooted in Germany's peculiar path of political development. However, the vulnerabilities were not the ones that most analysts have assumed. The most important constraint on the viability of democratic consolidation in Germany after 1918 was not the enduring dominance of old regime forces in the new era as an older strand of work has it.[1] Rather, the opposite is the case – decisive was the enduring *fragmentation* of former old regime forces and *how* these forces organized themselves as political parties. In short, the key vulnerability was an inheritance from the pre-1914 period: a legacy of organizational weakness as Germany's conservative parties entered the age of mass democracy.

REASSESSING WEIMAR GERMANY'S VULNERABILITIES:
PROBLEMS OF DEMOCRATIC CONSOLIDATION

If the last two chapters focused on the incremental steps of democratic "transition" in Germany before 1914, this chapter and the next move into the twentieth century, past the trauma, violence, and death of what Winston Churchill called the "world crisis" of the First World War. We turn to the theme of how the main political parties that inherited the highly diverse and

---

[1] Fritz Fischer, *Bündnis der Eliten: zur Kontinuität der Machtstrukturen in Deutschland 1871–1945* (Düsseldorf: Droste, 1979).

fragmented strands of Germany's pre-1918 conservatism, including chiefly the new *Deutschnationale Volkspartei* or the DNVP, fared in the resulting "brave new world" of mass democracy that was imposed in the aftermath of the First World War.[2] We shift, then, from the challenges of democratic transition to the problem of democratic consolidation or, in this case, the challenge of *avoiding* democratic breakdown.

Until 1918 in Germany, as we have seen, the roadblocks to democratic reform had appeared immovable making it a case where movements toward democratic transition were consistently thwarted. But with the war's end, exogenous triggers for democratic transition were now overwhelming, leaving the chief issue not whether a democratic transition could be achieved but whether the new fully democratic political system would endure. The causes for the apparent democratic breakthrough were multiple and complex. The First World War's destruction and the associated mobilization of resources and labor altered the balance of power within European societies, including, in Germany, empowering the forces for democracy. Reinforcing this, the "Wilsonian moment" of 1918 witnessed the simultaneous collapse of four autocratic multinational empires, the Ottoman, the Austrian, the Russian, as well as the Hohenzollern German empires, destroying the international context of old regime Europe.[3] Further, at war's end, given the massive destruction of prewar wealth and income, organized labor now had increased leverage to demand its inclusion in national politics. This in turn was reinforced by the Russian Revolution in 1917 and unrest across Europe from 1918 to 1920 in work councils on the factory floors of Turin, Hamburg, and Cologne, and the Red Clydeside movement in Glasgow.[4] Finally, for defeated countries such as

---

[2] As we will see, Germany's highly diverse pre-1918 conservatism, split between, for example, Protestant landed elites in Prussia, Catholic landed elites in Westphalia and Silesia, Catholic conservatives in Bavaria, and certain industrial elites throughout Germany, recast themselves into many different party formations after 1918: many Catholic conservatives of Westphalia and Silesia defected from the Center Party to join the DNVP (see Larry Eugene Jones, "Catholic Conservatives in the Weimar Republic: The Politics of the Rhenish-Westphalian Aristocracy, 1918–1933," *German History* 18, no. 1, 2000: 60–85). Some former *Reichspartei* leaders lent their support to the new DVP but other leading figures played a major role in founding the DNVP; and most former DKP supporters ended up in the DNVP camp. One outlier was the Catholic conservative milieu of Bavaria, which aligned primarily with the Bavarian People's Party (BVP).

[3] See Erez Manela, *The Wilsonian moment: self-determination and the international origins of anticolonial nationalism* (Oxford: Oxford University Press, 2007). See also Jörg Fisch, *Das Selbstbestimmungsrecht der Völker: die Domestizierung einer Illusion* (München: Verlag C. H. Beck, 2010).

[4] Thomas Piketty, *Capital in the Twenty-First Century* (Cambridge, MA: The Belknap Press of Harvard University Press, 2014). For a comparative view on labor mobilization in this period, see James E. Cronin, "Labor Insurgency and Class Formation: Comparative Perspectives on the Crisis of 1917–1920 in Europe," *Social Science History* 4, no. 1 (1980): 125–52. On the role of labor in Germany, see the authoritative works by Richard Bessel, *Germany After the First World War* (Oxford: Oxford University Press, 1993); Gerald D. Feldman, *Army, Industry, and Labor in Germany, 1914–1918* (Princeton: Princeton University Press, 1966); Bessel, *Germany After the*

Austria and Germany, President Wilson's insistence that constitutional reform was a precondition for a negotiated or "just peace" rather than a "violent peace" pressured elites to adopt new identities: autocrats such as Quartermaster Erich Ludendorff became, even if superficially, at least self-proclaimed "democrats."[5]

But, if new national democracies, of different shapes and sizes, emerged after 1918, we know all too well that only a very few survived the subsequent turmoil that wracked Europe and the broader Atlantic world in the 1920s and 1930s. Weimar Germany was not one of them. Historical research has identified many plausible factors as to why some countries survived as democracies and others did not in this era, including the extent of economic crises of inflation and later recession, poorly designed constitutions, the strength of liberal political parties, the coherence and ideological self-confidence of anti-systemic extremists, the presence of overly dogmatic socialist politicians, and poor decisions of national political leaders.[6]

The more focused scholarship on Weimar Germany has highlighted many of these factors as well, but two genetic errors of the Weimar political system have attracted most attention: (1) the terms of the international settlement after 1918 and (2) the compromised nature of the revolution of 1918. First, the terms of the international settlement after Germany rejoined the gold standard in 1924, coupled with reparations, it is often said, imposed major constraints on the German economy, which were exacerbated by the economic crisis of

First World War (1993). Also critical was the failure of Kerensky's liberal revolution in Russia in 1917, sharpening the options facing Europe after 1918. See Adam B. Ulam, *Russia's Failed Revolutions: From the Decembrists to the Dissidents* (New York: Basic Books, 1981).

[5] One example of the linking of the armistice question and domestic reform is seen in Woodrow Wilson's third note to the German government of October 23, 1918, in which the issue was made explicit: "It is evident that the German people have no means of commanding the acquiescence of the military authorities of the Empire in the popular will; that the power of the King of Prussia to control the policy of the Empire is unimpaired; that the determining initiative still remains with those who have hitherto been the masters of Germany... If [the government of the United States] must deal with the military masters and the monarchical autocrats of Germany now... it must demand not peace negotiations, but surrender," in James Brown Scott, *Official Statements of War Aims and Peace Proposals, December 1916 to November 1918* (Washington, DC: Carnegie Endowment for International Peace, 1921), 436.

[6] See, respectively, Jørgen Møller, Alexander Schmotz, and Svend-Erik Skaaning, "Economic Crisis and Democratic Breakdown in the Interwar Years: A Reassessment," *Historical Social Research* 40, no. 2 (2015): 301–18; Ferdinand A. Hermens, "Proportional Representation and the Breakdown of German Democracy," *Social Research* 3, no. 4 (1936): 411–33; Michael H. Bernhard, *Institutions and the Fate of Democracy: Germany and Poland in the Twentieth Century*, Pitt Series in Russian and East European Studies (Pittsburgh: University of Pittsburgh Press, 2005); Luebbert, *Liberalism, Fascism, or Social Democracy* (1991); Hanson, *Post-Imperial Democracies: Ideology and Party Formation in Third Republic France, Weimar Germany, and Post-Soviet Russia* (2010); Sheri Berman, *The Social Democratic Moment: Ideas and Politics in the Making of Interwar Europe* (Cambridge: Harvard University Press, 1998); Capoccia, *Defending Democracy* (2005).

the late 1920s.[7] But more than the economic consequences, particularly pernicious for German democratization, many scholars have asserted, was a psychological component of the international settlement: the "war guilt" clause of the Versailles Treaty. This clause was used by nationalists, entirely out of proportion to its actual significance, to magnify right-wing anti-regime sentiment. Feelings of this sort are what Hans Mommsen has called the "inner rejection of the peace."[8] Because of how the Weimar regime was founded, this account concludes, the Weimar constitution was neither legitimate nor sustainable.[9]

In addition to the terms of the international settlement after 1918, critics often also note a second genetic error that is said to have made Weimar a precarious case from the start: political decisions and compromises by the Social Democratic leaders that suffocated a genuine revolutionary break from the imperial past.[10] As German analyst Sebastian Haffner writes, "To this day, Germany is crippled by the betrayal of 1918."[11] What exactly was the betrayal Haffner refers to? First, the establishment of a parliamentary monarchy in October 1918 via a "revolution from above" arguably jeopardized the democratic tenor of the regime change.[12] Also, consequential was the state's official reaction when the Hohenzollern monarch was dethroned on November 9, 1918, and the ongoing uncontained diffusion of revolutionary tumult that spread across the country, beginning in the naval yards of Kiel as sailors rebelled against orders, extending to the work councils of industrial cities, and culminating in the activities of the Marxist Spartacus League of Rosa Luxemburg and Karl Liebknecht in Berlin. These movements had

[7] See, e.g., Manfred F. Boemeke, Gerald D. Feldman, and Elisabeth Gläser, *The Treaty of Versailles: A Reassessment After 75 years* (Washington, DC: German Historical Institute, 1998).; Barry J. Eichengreen, *Globalizing Capital: A History of the International Monetary System*, 2nd ed. (Princeton: Princeton University Press, 2008). Because of the international monetary system's reliance on the gold standard, economic historians have argued, Germany's current accounts deficit, exacerbated by reparations, convinced political leaders that the only way out was the adoption of extreme deflationary measures that made the political regime vulnerable to political extremism on the left and right.

[8] Mommsen, *Rise and Fall of Weimar Democracy* (1996), 89.

[9] In perhaps the clearest single statement of this view, Fritz Stern writes, "Born in defeat, humiliated by Versailles, mocked and violated by its irreconcilable enemies at home, the Weimar Republic never gained the popular acceptance which alone could have given its parliamentary system permanence, even in crisis." Fritz Stern, *The Failure of Illiberalism: Essays on the Political Culture of Modern Germany* (New York: Columbia University Press, 1992), 162.

[10] For a recent summary and critique of the traditional view of the 1918 Revolution, see Conan Fischer, "A Very German Revolution? The 1918–1920 Settlement Reconsidered," *German Historical Institute London Bulletin* 28, no. 2 (2006): 6–32.

[11] Haffner, *Die verratene Revolution: Deutschland 1918/1919* (1969), 245.

[12] For a recent account that reconstructs Erich Ludendorff's critical role in the collapse of the Imperial order, see Manfred Nebelin, *Ludendorff: Diktator im Ersten Weltkrieg* (München: Siedler, 2010), 461–508.

various goals, but even if ultimately destructive, chief among them was the deep social transformation of Imperial Germany.

When long-time Social Democrat parliamentary leader Friedrich Ebert was thrust into office after November 9, 1918, he sought to contain the revolutionary tumult and reconcile his own democratic aspirations with the tamer goals of orderly military demobilization, economic stabilization, food security, and political "order" more generally. As a result, Ebert pragmatically forged alliances with the German High Command, kept the Imperial civil and military services intact, rejected calls to create a "people's militia," and relied on the voluntary *Freikorps* to squash *leftist* mobilization in Munich and Berlin, and the March 1920 Ruhr workers' rebellion.[13] Many historians have argued that the accommodations and implicit toleration of the right – i.e., "the betrayal" – stifled the necessary social revolution, leaving it "incomplete" and even "aborted."[14] Haffner notes:

On the Monday after Revolution Weekend, the same civil servants went back to the same public offices, and even the policemen (who on Saturday afternoon had been glad to get home unmolested) were back again a few days later; in the armies in the field in the East and West, the same generals and officers remained in command.[15]

Historians such as Gordon Craig have argued that this "compromise" with the old regime would have dire consequences. Craig provocatively concludes,

[Weimar] Republic's basic vulnerability was rooted in the circumstances of its creation, and it is no exaggeration to say that it failed in the end partly because German officers were allowed to put their epaulettes back on again so quickly and because the public buildings were not burned down, along with the bureaucrats in them.[16]

Some argue that concessions were unavoidable, asking, for example, whether it is realistic to expect Ebert, having only ascended to the presidency in November 1918, to have overseen the demobilization of 6 million soldiers in three short weeks *without* working closely with the General Staff.[17] Yet, historians often seem to agree that the combination of unhappy international circumstances and flawed decisions at its birth – especially concessions to the German military – jointly provided the motives and institutional niches for Imperial antidemocratic forces to regroup and conspire for their later comeback.

---

[13] In particular, the agreement, sealed by telephone, between Friedrich Ebert and the military's new Quartermaster Groener on November 10, 1918, to leave the military hierarchy untouched in exchange for support for the new regime has received the most significant criticism. See account in Gordon Craig, *Germany, 1866–1945* (New York: Oxford University Press, 1978), 404–05.

[14] Craig, *Germany, 1866–1945* (1978), 396.

[15] Haffner, *Die verratene Revolution: Deutschland 1918/1919* (1969), 122.

[16] Craig, *Germany, 1866–1945* (1978), 398.

[17] See, e.g., Gerald D. Feldman, *The Great Disorder: Politics, Economics, and Society in the German Inflation, 1914–1924* (New York: Oxford University Press, 1997), 103.

However, even if we accept that international conditions and an incomplete social revolution constrained Weimar's subsequent development, to draw a direct link between these two particular shortcomings and democracy's ultimate demise in 1933 is to overlook the actual sources of Weimar's vulnerabilities. Indeed, there were at least three specific reasons to question this conventional view. While it is important not to understate the challenges facing the regime, it is also critical to recognize that democrats felt a profound sense of hope and reactionaries, fear.[18]

First, the democratic opposition was electorally *triumphant* in the founding days of the regime. This view was not merely misguided optimism; there was good reason for it. A powerful insight of the comparative politics literature on regime change contends that the distribution of electoral power – between the old regime and the opposition – at the moment of transition shapes the stability and character of the subsequent democracy, since it is in these moments that the basic rules of the new political regime are created.[19] For example, McFaul summarizes his findings on post-communist democratic transitions,

A distribution of [societal] power clearly favoring democrats at the moment of transition has helped to produce liberal democracy ... a distribution of power favoring dictators of the *ancien régime* has yielded new forms of authoritarian rule...[20]

In general, the "moment of transition" is thought to matter so disproportionately because decisive political victories at critical moments, all else held equal, increase the likelihood of future victories via *three* interrelated mechanisms: (1) the transfer of resources away from the vanquished to the victor; (2) the signals sent to competitors about relative strength, thereby altering alliance preferences of "fence-sitters"; and (3) the inducing of political losers to adopt strategies that effectively reinforce the new status quo.[21] While a variant of this argument has been developed to explain the wide range of post-communist experiences, McFaul's argument about the relative strength of democratic proponents and old-regime

---

[18] In the decisive month of October 1918, even the traditional leader of the reactionary Prussian loyalist Conservative Party in the Reichstag, Kuno von Westarp, felt it would help him more than hurt him to proclaim, "The shift in political conditions resulting from the war impels the Conservative party to refresh its old and honored traditions with the new spirit of the time so that it will be in a position to meet the challenges of present-day life." See Kuno Graf von Westarp, *Die Regierung des Prinzen Max von Baden und die Konservative Partei 1918* (Berlin: Deutsche Verlagsgesellschaft für Politik und Geschichte, 1928), 128.

[19] See, e.g., Michael McFaul, "The Fourth Wave of Democracy and Dictatorship: Noncooperative Transitions in the Postcommunist World," *World Politics* 54, no. 2 (2002): 212–44; Michael Albertus and Victor Menaldo, "Gaming Democracy: Elite Dominance During Transition and Prospects for Redistribution" *British Journal of Political Science* 44, no. 3 (2014b): 575–603.

[20] McFaul, "Fourth Wave of Democracy and Dictatorship" (2002): 226.

[21] Pierson, "Power and Path Dependence" (2015), 134.

incumbents highlights an important dynamic in democratic transitions more generally.[22]

These considerations are all important because in the case of Weimar Germany, the early and overwhelming electoral *dominance* of the vigorously cohesive founding democratic coalition of Left Liberals, Catholics, and Social Democrats was not superficial; it suggested a genuine shift in political power formed during the last days of war. Until 1917, the cross-party wartime "truce" (*Burgfrieden*) between the left and right persisted, leaving the possibility of a democratic majority in the Reichstag sidelined. But, the Russian Revolution of March 1917 emboldened the far left side of Social Democracy in its push for "peace without annexations."[23] The entry of the United States into the war the very next month also altered the balance within Germany, increasing the resonance of the call for a peace without territorial demands among Left Liberals and the Center Party, leading to the crumbling of the Supreme Command's acquiescent parliament. Chancellor Bethmann-Hollweg's government desperately scrambled to appease domestic pressure arising from these developments and the related massive strike of 200,000 Berliners in the Spring of 1917, promising to reform the Prussian three-class voting system at war's end.[24] But as the war dragged on, such gestures could not quell the emerging democratic majority coalition in the Reichstag.

In a decisive turning point, the previously pro-annexation Catholic Center Party leader Matthias Erzberger dramatically switched sides and joined the leaders of the Social Democratic and Left Liberal Reichstag groups. Historian William Halperin dubbed this the "Weimar coalition in embryo," and they pushed for constitutional change, such as ministerial accountability and equal suffrage in Prussia, and peace without annexations.[25] In a well-crafted move of Rikerian "issue linkage," the emerging coalition of Social Democrats, Left Liberals, and Centre Party members demanded reform on both fronts, using "the peace issue, about which the public was so exercised, to wrest concessions in the constitutional domain."[26]

---

[22] How is "societal power" in the moment of transition typically measured? For a new political regime, one rough but useful indicator is the electoral performance of old regime parties vis-à-vis former opposition or democratic parties in the very first legislative elections *after* the transition (McFaul, "Fourth Wave of Democracy and Dictatorship," 2002: 226).

[23] Roger Chickering, *Imperial Germany and the Great War, 1914–1918* (Cambridge: Cambridge University Press, 2004), 158.

[24] Ludwig Bergsträsser, *Die Preussische Wahlrechtsfrage im Kriege und die Entstehung der Osterbotschaft* (Tübingen: Verlag von Mohr, 1929).

[25] Samuel William Halperin, *Germany Tried Democracy: A Political History of the Reich from 1918 to 1933* (New York: W. W. Norton, 1965), 28. On Matthias Erzberger and his critical contributions, see Klaus Epstein, *Matthias Erzberger and the Dilemma of German Democracy* (Princeton: Princeton University Press, 1959).

[26] Halperin, *Germany Tried Democracy: A Political History of the Reich from 1918 to 1933* (1965), 28. See also Chickering, *Imperial Germany and the Great War, 1914–1918* (2004), 158.

The resulting peace resolution passed in July 1917 was important for the subsequent development of the war and, even more critically for our purposes, for the formation of an unofficial interparty parliamentary committee of what had previously been only a *potential* kind of "Gladstonian coalition" of Left Liberals, Social Democrats, and Catholic Center Party.[27] The pro-democratic coalition, a variant of what political scientist Ruth Collier has dubbed a cross-class "joint project" now had powerful institutional "flesh" inside the Reichstag in the form of the Inter-Party Committee (*Interfraktionelle Ausschuss*, or IFA).[28] The IFA was a coordinating body of the three majority parties in the Reichstag, with some collaboration of National Liberals, which existed for fifteen decisive months (July 7, 1917, to September 30, 1918) to push for peace without annexation and major constitutional changes, forming a kind of "cabinet-in-exile" in the midst of war.[29] With the collapse of the Hohenzollern monarchy and the rapid implosion of the rightist parties, the working partnership of the three leaders in the IFA – Friedrich Ebert, Friedrich von Payer, and Matthias Erzberger – stood as the most cohesive grouping left standing on the political stage as the Imperial regime crumbled around it.[30]

Indeed, as Table 8.1 summarizes, the result was a new postwar balance of societal power, on full display in the first democratic elections in January 1919. The three groupings that had constituted the IFA – Left Liberals (now the German Democratic Party), the Center Party, and the Social Democrats – garnered a remarkable 76 percent of the vote of the national constituent assembly (the de facto parliament), which would approve the new constitution in August 1919. The electoral victory was nothing short of overwhelming. Meanwhile, the first post-constitutional elections, held in June 1920, are sometimes retrospectively described as "disastrous for the Republic" since the Weimar coalition fell below fifty percent.[31] However, it is important to remember the founding coalition still managed to win 43.6 percent of votes, and the SPD remained the single largest party in the Reichstag despite a swing toward the DNVP and the German People's Party (*Deutsche Volkspartei*, or DVP).

---

[27] The phrase "Gladstonian coalition" refers to the proto-Labor, Liberal, and Irish Catholic party coalition that was a prodemocratic force in Britain beginning in the 1880s. See Arthur Rosenberg, *The Birth of the German Republic, 1871–1918* (New York: Oxford University Press, 1931), 18.

[28] Collier, *Paths Towards Democracy* (1999), 168.

[29] See Klaus Epstein, "Der Interfraktionelle Ausschuß und das problem der Parlamentarisierung 1917–1918," *Historische Zeitschrift* 191, no. 3 (1960): 562–84; Erich Matthias and Rudolf Morsey, eds., *Der Interfraktionelle Ausschuß 1917/18* (Düsseldorf: Droste, 1959).

[30] On the collapse of the right, see Lewis Hertzman, *DNVP: Right-wing Opposition in the Weimar Republic, 1918–1924* (Lincoln: University of Nebraska Press, 1963); Maik Ohnezeit, *Zwischen "schärfster Opposition" und dem "Willen zur Macht": Die Deutschnationale Volkspartei (DNVP) in der Weimarer Republik 1918–1928* (Düsseldorf: Droste Verlag, 2011).

[31] Ruth Henig, *The Weimar Republic 1919–1933* (Hoboken: Taylor and Francis, 2002), 28.

TABLE 8.1 *Weimar Coalition Vote Share, 1919 and 1920 Federal Parliamentary Elections*

	January 19, 1919	June 6, 1920
Weimar Coalition	76.2%	43.6%
Social Democratic Party (SPD)	37.9%	21.7%
Democratic Party (DDP)	18.6%	8.3%
Center Party	19.7%	13.6%
All other parties	23%	56%

Data Source: *Elections in Europe: A Data Handbook* 2010

Even more notable than the national electoral performance of the founding coalition in these early critical moments was the deep transformation of state politics in Prussia, which then comprised three-fifths of Germany. Under the three-class voting system, reactionary forces had dominated the state, but in the Weimar period, it became the opposite: Prussia was, in one historian's phrase, Germany's "unlikely rock of democracy."[32] Aided by a new and equal democratic suffrage, the founding parties' wartime cooperation, and the collapse of the old-regime parties, the three Weimar coalition parties dominated the 1919 Prussian state elections, winning 76 percent of the votes. But, unlike in national politics, the group continued to dominate the state parliament until 1928, never holding less than 45 percent of seats, and Prussia was a model of cabinet stability even when national politics shifted.

The traditional narrative is quick to emphasize, correctly, that the three founding parties experienced a drop-off in national support beginning in 1920, making way for a "recovery of the right."[33] As an explanation of Weimar's instability, however, this view fails to consider a few critical points. A "recovery of the right" does not mean that democracy was necessarily doomed; after all, alternations in power – often between left and right – is the *sine qua non* of democratic consolidation. Even if Germany's electoral right was only at best marginally committed to the new regime at the outset, the key issue is why the right's return to political power then triggered its own *further* radicalization and disintegration, culminating in the decomposition of the entire party system; after all, a post-transition "return of the right" does not always lead to the disintegration of a new democracy. Additionally, while in retrospect we can easily identify patterns of electoral decline for the pro-democratic coalition, in 1918 and 1919, the playing field was still wide open. If anything, the ability of the Weimar coalition to dominate politics in the regime's euphoric founding months gave good reason for figures such as SPD politician and publicist Konrad Haenisch to believe in the self-reinforcing

[32] Orlow, *Weimar Prussia* (1986). [33] Henig, *The Weimar Republic 1919–1933* (2002), 22.

power that typically emerges out of founding moments. He confidently wrote, "we socialists, with the strength of our character and willpower, shall inscribe our handwriting on the blank pages of Germany's political future...."[34]

Indeed, this point constitutes the *second* reason to have been optimistic about Weimar's founding: because of their early electoral dominance, the constitution-writing process also disproportionately reflected the input of the democratic coalition. For example, most critically, in the national body charged with drawing up the Weimar constitution in January 1919, Social Democrats had the largest number of representatives, followed by the Center Party and the Left Liberal Party (DDP), together forming 79 percent of the delegates. At the January 1919 constitutional convention of one of the historically most reactionary German states, Prussia, Social Democrats, Left Liberals, and the Center Party shared 76 percent of the delegates; the SPD claimed the largest portion of that group with over 30 percent of the delegates.[35] This experience was repeated across Germany, giving rise to a political system that chiefly reflected the designs and visions of the core Weimar coalition; meanwhile the old right, though participating in important ways, did not take a leading role in these proceedings.[36]

But more than mere formal constitutional change, a *third* political bargain struck at the very heart of the postwar German economy, suggesting a sharp departure from the past. On November 15, 1918, Germany's leading representatives of industry and organized labor forged the outlines of what would become continental Europe's highly vaunted coordinated model of democratic corporatism in the Stinnes–Legien Agreement. This granted unions firm bargaining rights with employers, an eight-hour workday, and workplace labor committees in all plants with more than fifty employees, as well as, conversely, trade union recognition of property rights and the rights of private shareholders.[37] The agreement had immediate consequences for union membership in Germany and the long-run development of Germany's political economy, even after the Second World War.[38]

The initiation of formalized labor-employer relations also indicated an altered societal landscape underpinning German democracy. In his classic work on industry and army between 1914 and 1918, historian Gerald Feldman appropriately places this agreement in its broader context. He notes that, with big business' acceptance of the Stinnes–Legien Agreement, industrialists "were, in effect, abandoning their long-standing alliance with

[34] Konrad Haenisch, "In erstester Stunde," *Glocke* 4 (October 5, 1918): 843, as cited by Orlow, *Weimar Prussia* (1986), 51.

[35] Orlow, *Weimar Prussia* (1986), 18.

[36] Christian F. Trippe, *Konservative Verfassungspolitik 1918–1923: die DNVP als Opposition in Reich und Ländern* (Düsseldorf: Droste, 1995).

[37] Feldman, *The Great Disorder* (1997), 107.

[38] Thelen, *How Institutions Evolve: The Political Economy of Skills in Germany, Britain, the United States, and Japan* (2004), 68.

the Junkers and the authoritarian state for an alliance with organized labor."[39] However, it was "an ambiguous labor achievement."[40] Critics have noted that the foundational Stinnes–Legien Agreement did not represent an outright *ideological conversion* on the part of industry, but was rather an opportunistic co-opting of labor mobilization and an effort to inoculate industry against radicalism.[41] But, such flexible opportunism suggests that the societal balance of power in Germany had been transformed, at least temporarily. The point more broadly is this: the adaptive self-serving opportunism or "contingent consent" of old-regime elites in key founding moments can at times launch a political process that results in far-reaching institutional change.[42] In this case, however, it was tragically insufficient. Why?

While the concessions to the military that Gordon Craig identifies as so pernicious may be to blame, it is worth remembering that even these sorts of compromises to old regime elements can be interpreted in a different light. Many analysts of "democratic transitions" more generally have argued that targeted compromises or "pacts" with an old regime can generate "buy-in" or mutual protections for both sides that secure rather than undermine democratization.[43] From this perspective, Weimar Germany's electorally transformative founding combined with targeted compromises to old regime elements actually appears to follow the textbook model of a *successful* democratic transition. That these concessions failed to secure democracy means that interwar Germany of course had genuine vulnerabilities. But, that there were promising features of Weimar Germany's founding suggests that it is a misdiagnosis to focus exclusively on the nature of the political regime's founding to explain its ultimate demise.

THE REAL SOURCES OF WEIMAR'S VULNERABILITY: THE WEAKNESS OF AN ORGANIZED ELECTORAL RIGHT

On the particularly sunny morning of June 24, 1922, only three years into the young life of Weimar Germany, German Foreign Minister Walther Rathenau, one of the first foreign ministers in the new democratic regime, was chauffeured in a convertible from his villa in the leafy Grunewald suburb to his office on

---

[39] Feldman, *Army, Industry, and Labor* (1966), 523.

[40] Feldman, *The Great Disorder* (1997), 107.

[41] Volker Berghahn, *Modern Germany: Society, Economy, and Politics in the Twentieth Century*, 2nd ed. (Cambridge: Cambridge University Press, 1987), 68–69; Maier, *Recasting Bourgeois Europe* (1975), 60.

[42] See O'Donnell and Schmitter, *Transitions from Authoritarian Rule. Tentative Conclusions about Uncertain Democracies* (2013 [1986]), 68.

[43] See, especially, O'Donnell and Schmitter, *Transitions from Authoritarian Rule. Tentative Conclusions about Uncertain Democracies* (2013 [1986]).

Wilhelmstrasse.[44] A Mercedes Touring automobile pulled up alongside the car, and two occupants, armed with machine guns, opened fire and assassinated Rathenau in broad daylight.[45]

While a moment of great tragedy, public reaction to the murder also ironically underscores the idea that the founding years of the Weimar regime did not doom it. On the one hand, the murder by rabid right-wingers certainly crystallized in a moment the perilous social contention facing Europe as a whole after 1918. Germany's new democracy, like other European states', was in crisis, having already faced a recent coup attempt and galloping inflation.[46] The early 1920s had left a trail of turmoil in its wake not only in Germany but across Europe. Hungary's brief Bolshevik republic had been replaced by the authoritarian regime of Admiral Horthy in March 1920; Mussolini's *squadistri* were on the march and would take power in Italy in the fall of 1922; and, responding to growing unrest in 1922 and 1923, Primo de Rivera would lead a successful military coup in Spain. Echoing the tenor of these events, in the days immediately following Rathenau's death, ominous calls of treason and accusations of murder ricocheted between the far right and left on the floor of the German parliament.[47]

However, only three days later, on June 27, 1922, German politics experienced an unexpectedly hopeful quasi-truce, bolstered in part by the persistent electoral dominance of the Social Democratic Party: the first state funeral since the death of Otto von Bismarck in 1898 was held in the chambers of the Reichstag for Rathenau. Wreaths of red roses, tea roses, and blue hydrangeas adorned the chamber floor; the symbol of the eagle appeared overhead as the red, black, and gold flag of the Republic draped the plain oak coffin at the center of the assembly floor.[48] President Friedrich Ebert, a Social Democrat, rose before a chamber that was filled to capacity with dignitaries ranging from Albert Einstein to foreign diplomats and members of the German parliament. Reactionary conservatives and communists alike all were solemnly dressed in black.[49] Ebert delivered brief remarks honoring Rathenau's life and

---

[44] The tragic fate of Walther Rathenau has been recounted in several biographies. Rathenau was a cosmopolitan polymath – a liberal, a Jew, and cofounder of the German Democratic Party (*Deutsche Demokratische Partei*, DDP), a successor organization to the Left Liberals, who now advocated cooperation with Germany's Social Democrats. He was also an engineer, a scholar, an industrialist and chairman of the AEG electrical company, and fascinated with innovative modes of incorporating labor into corporate governance. Yet he was also an unapologetic German nationalist who had held senior posts in the Raw Materials Department of the War Ministry during the First World War. See Shulamit Volkov, *Walther Rathenau: The Life of Weimar's Fallen Statesman* (New Haven: Yale University Press, 2012).
[45] Volkov, *Walther Rathenau* (2012), 1.
[46] On this period, see Feldman, *The Great Disorder* (1997), chapter 4.
[47] "Storm Renewed in Reichstag: 'Cries of Revenge!' Interrupt Speeches on Rathenau Murder," *New York Times*, June 26, 1922.
[48] Cyril Brown, "Rathenau Is Buried as Martyr," *New York Times*, June 27, 1922.
[49] Brown, "Rathenau Is Buried as Martyr."

contributions to the "German people." In the grave hour of the state funeral, American journalist Cyril Brown astutely observed that "even the communists behaved decorously, as did the arch-reactionaries."[50] Rather than catapulting the new German Republic into collapse, this moment of potential breakdown was instead one of apparent solidarity, sidestepping the type of institutional crisis that proved lethal to so many of Europe's other new democracies.[51] Weimar, despite its later reputation, started the 1920s with a moment of impressive regime legitimacy, bolstered by the founding democratic Weimar coalition, one that other political regimes would be envious of.

Thus, in this we find a paradox for those accounts that assume the new regime was doomed from the start: the political system, after initial years of instability, appeared to begin to stabilize in its middle years, falling prey to fatal political radicalization, as we will see, beginning in large part in 1928. To explain Weimar Germany's collapse, we therefore must come to terms with this puzzle about the timing of democracy's disintegration. After difficult initial years (1918–1924), there was what historians often call a "golden age" (1924–1928) that made some believe the most difficult times had passed. But, evidently they had not. Given this variability *over time* of the self-perceived promise and stability of the political regime, determining "what went wrong" must mean more than identifying some fixed, and therefore implicitly *essential* or congenital feature of the political system. A moving target cannot be explained by an unmoving cause. Explaining the collapse of Weimar thus requires explaining this variation over time in the stability of the regime.

To do so, we will see that Weimar democracy was intimately tied to a battle within the largest party of the electoral right, the DNVP, between its "fundamentalists" and "pragmatists." This struggle unfolded over time, beginning in 1918 but ending with a radical takeover of the party in 1928 that was, in my view, a key turning point making the endurance of democracy dramatically less likely from that point forward.[52] More generally, how old-regime elites' conservative political parties had historically coped with the advent of elections in the nineteenth century cast a long shadow, determining how institutionalized these political parties were during the age of mass democracy after 1918. This factor, and the vulnerability of the traditional right to internal radical right-wing insurgencies, altered the course of a promising democratic transition and led to a tragic and calamitous breakdown.

---

[50] Brown, "Rathenau Is Buried as Martyr."

[51] Though responses on the right and left of course varied dramatically to Rathenau's murder, the rallying of public support, with an estimated 200,000 mourners lining the streets of Berlin, prompted the Reichstag to respond by passing the decree for the protection of the republic in July 1922. See Volkov, *Walther Rathenau* (2012).

[52] On the notions of "fundamentalists" and "pragmatists" in the DNVP, see Hermann Beck, *The Fateful Alliance: German Conservatives and Nazis in 1933. The Machtergreifung in a New Light* (Oxford and New York: Berghahn Press, 2008), 30ff.

Other analysts have observed that across Europe, the degree of the electoral right's organizational inheritance was correlated with democratic consolidation or failure after 1918.[53] Such a view is also consistent with the literature on Latin American democratization regarding the role of conservative political parties in helping avert democratic breakdowns there.[54] Yet, all such cross-national evidence remains only *suggestive*, at best, for two main reasons. First, as with any effort at causal inference, problems of endogeneity arise when the number of national cases is limited. Above all, a complex range of other factors – economic, institutional, or even cultural – are plausibly correlated with the organizational condition of parties of the traditional right in 1918, which may have shaped the subsequent survival of democracies. Such limitations inevitably complicate any effort to elevate one particular factor above all others.

Second, these cross-national correlations tell us little about the actual causal mechanisms that might plausibly link "conservative party organization" and democratic consolidation. The Latin American experience suggests one mechanism: when a cohesive old regime and reactionary elite is not equipped with equally cohesive party organization to defend its interests in a new democratic regime through established electoral channels, it seeks out extra-constitutional or conspiratorial "authoritarian" strategies such as military coups instead.[55] For a reactionary old-regime elite without party organization, military coups are an appealing strategy of extra-constitutional defense and, moreover, *a plausible mechanism linking party weakness to democratic breakdown.*

Was this the logic at work in Weimar Germany? This logic is powerful, but it assumes that old-regime elites are implausibly single-minded in their preferences, and not wracked by the normal divisions of ideological disagreement, problems of collective action, disagreement over economic questions, and organizational schism that made politics messier than our theories. Here, therefore, I propose an alternative link that explicitly highlights elite ideological and organizational schism. If we conceive of political parties not as inherently cohesive and unconstrained "unified teams of politicians," guided by vote-maximizing and office-seeking considerations alone, but instead recognize that they are made up of politicians enmeshed and constrained by their own *coalition of interest groups and activists,*[56] then we see the possibility of a different mechanism.

---

[53] Ertman, "Western European Party Systems" (2009); Ertman, "Great Reform Act of 1832" (2010); Philip Manow and Daniel Ziblatt, "The Layered State: Patterns and Pathways of Modern Nation State Building," in *The Oxford Handbook of Transformations of the State*, ed. Stephan Leibfried, et al. (Oxford: Oxford University Press, 2015).

[54] See, e.g., Di Tella, "La búsqueda de la fórmula política argentina" (1971/1972); Gibson, *Class and Conservative Parties* (1996); Kevin J. Middlebrook, ed., *Conservative Parties, the Right, and Democracy in Latin America* (Baltimore: Johns Hopkins University Press, 2000).

[55] See, e.g., O'Donnell, Schmitter, and Whitehead, eds., *Transitions from Authoritarian Rule: Comparative Perspectives* (1986), 73.

[56] Bawn, Cohen, Karol, Masket, Noel, and Zaller, "A Theory of Political Parties: Groups, Policy Demands and Nominations in American Politics" (2012).

From this perspective, the DNVP's party weakness did not merely provide an "authoritarian temptation" to old-regime elements.[57] Rather, party weakness mattered for reasons related to a distinctly internal organizational logic: DNVP leaders operated in a loosely coupled party organization, with less autonomy vis-à-vis their own activists and pressure groups than in highly institutionalized parties – such as Britain's Conservative Party in the same period – because of the *porousness* of organizational boundaries between party leaders and grassroots activists, and between party structures and outside pressure groups. Outside groups wielded increasingly disproportionate influence over mobilization and financing, and local associations elevated their leverage over party leaders, leaving positions in place for the well-organized radicals that finally took over the party entirely in 1928. History *did* repeat itself: similar to the dynamic found in DKP before 1914 (see Chapters 6 and 7), after 1918, office-seeking party leaders were unable to contain an internal radical backlash led by activists and external pressure groups. As a review of the three key stages of Weimar's political evolution – 1918–1924; 1924–1928; and after 1928 – reveals, these dynamics in the case of the Weimar's political right.

THE RISE AND FALL OF WEIMAR: THREE PERIODS BETWEEN 1918 AND 1933

This internal organizational evolution of the DNVP shaped the rise and fall of the Weimar regime itself. Though Weimar Germany is often regarded as a case of "interwar democratic collapse," its history is in fact more variegated than this account lets on, and it is usually divided by historians into three periods. The first (1918–1924) was an uncertain time of democratic transition marked by two major right-wing coup attempts, assassinations of major democratic leaders, and near civil war; the second (1924–1928), an era of apparent democratic consolidation, Weimar's so-called "golden age"; and finally, the third (1928–1933), a stage of democratic disintegration and breakdown that began even before the onset of the Great Depression in the fall of 1929.[58] That the political regime had phases of stability and hope alongside those of instability is striking as this variety occurred all within the same formal institutional structure of proportional representation and federalism, suggesting that factors other than a flawed constitution intervened to steer the fate of the political regime.

As Figure 8.1 depicts, the rise and fall of the DNVP appears to track the growth and decline of the regime as a whole, with the DNVP's electoral peak

---

[57] On this understandably contentious issue, see Henry Ashby Turner, *German Big Business and the Rise of Hitler* (New York: Oxford University Press, 1985); Gerald D. Feldman, "Big Business and the Kapp Putsch," *Central European History* 4, no. 2 (1971): 99–130; David Abraham, *The Collapse of the Weimar Republic: Political Economy and Crisis*, 2nd ed. (New York: Holmes & Meier, 1986).

[58] See, e.g., Detlev Peukert, *The Weimar Republic* (New York: Hill and Wang, 1993), 4–5.

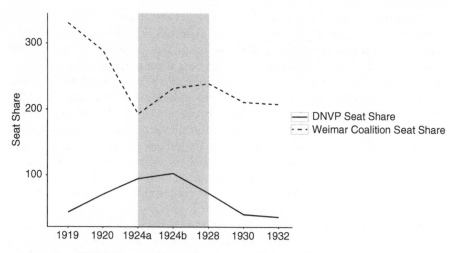

FIGURE 8.1: DNVP Seats and Vote Share across Weimar's Three Periods, 1919–1932
Data Source: *Elections in Europe: A Data Handbook* 2010

between 1924 and 1928 mapping onto the most stable period in Weimar's history. Figure 8.1 is instructive because it demonstrates that despite the DNVP's inherited organizational weakness, its performance in the middle years suggests at least the possibility of mass appeal. The DNVP's best electoral performance (20 percent of the vote), furthermore, was achieved in the two Reichstag elections of 1924, which also coincided with the inauguration of the "golden age" (1924–1928). It was also then that the DNVP began to behave in a way that more closely approximated an electorally minded "team of politicians," becoming not only the largest non-socialist party in the Reichstag, but one that participated in government under the moderate leadership of what Thomas Mergel has called "*Tory-Konservativen*," a group that reluctantly but effectively embraced "republicanization."[59] By contrast, in Weimar's unstable and violent early years (1918–1924), the DNVP never earned more than 12 percent of the vote. And, in the last period (1928–1933), the party's electoral collapse in 1928 (with 14 percent of vote) prompted a full-blown anti-regime orientation for the party and heightened political polarization, a full year *before* the 1929 Wall Street crash.

This inter-temporal pattern suggests that economic conditions, while always a key contextual favor, are not the only variable that explains the radicalization or moderation of the center-right. And further, it implies that the two paths of the DNVP and the regime as a whole might actually be interlinked in counterintuitive ways. Is it when the DNVP thrived electorally that the regime

---

[59] Thomas Mergel, "Das Scheitern des deutschen Tory-Konservatismus. Die Umformung der DNVP zu einer rechtsradikalen Partei 1928–1932," *Historische Zeitschrift* 276 (2003): 323–68.

was most stable? If so, why? Finally, while the same institutional context of proportional representation decisively shaped all electoral considerations in each period, a static contextual variable on its own cannot determine why the same political party was first ideologically recalcitrant, moderated its ideology in 1924, and then radicalized and disintegrated beginning in 1928. Put simply, other factors, which we explore below, *internal* to the life of the political party, intervened.[60]

To examine how the internal balance of power inside the DNVP and the decline of the regime as a whole were connected, we turn to the party's development in the age of mass democracy. We also see, in brief, three periods characterized by shifting power between two groups. The first group is what Hermann Beck has called "pragmatic" party leaders, who attempted to coax the DNVP to behave in the office-seeking manner typically expected by political scientists. The second group was made up of what Beck calls "fundamentalists" among the activists of local associations and nationalist pressure groups, who often derailed these organizational efforts.[61]

The balance of power between these two elements set the tenor of the party. The first period (1918–1924) was characterized by a *stalemate* between them. The second period (1924–1928) was marked by a *tenuous triumph* for the pragmatists as they steered the party into electoral success and into government two times, even gaining six federal ministries in these years.[62] In these "golden years," the triumph was, however, ultimately *tenuous* because the fundamentalists were only temporarily sidelined, the moderates' hold on power was insecure, and splinter groups emerged dissatisfied with the compromises the DNVP was making with the Weimar political system. The third period (1928–1933), was one of *radical takeover*, in which precisely this post-1924 splintering further weakened the DNVP, creating space for fundamentalists to reassert themselves and captured the party, with disastrous consequences for Germany.

A comparative view is revealing: beginning in the mid-1920s in Britain under Stanley Baldwin's Conservative Party and in France under Raymond Poincaré, the electoral right's electoral triumph assured a "conservative political stabilization" in the same period compatible with the new political regime.[63] All three countries returned to the gold standard in these years, and democracy began to stabilize under the electoral right's auspices.[64] But, was a similar dynamic underway in Germany beginning in 1924? The answer is a definitive no. The

---

[60] See Kitschelt *The Transformation of European Social Democracy* (1994) for a similar argument about the importance of "internal organization" vis-à-vis "environmental stimuli," in a different context.

[61] See, e.g., Beck, *Fateful Alliance* (2008), 33.

[62] Mergel, "Scheitern des deutschen Tory-Konservatismus" (2003).

[63] See, e.g., Maier, *Recasting Bourgeois Europe* (1975), 481.

[64] On the return to the gold standard in Germany (1924), Britain (1925), and France (1926), see Eichengreen, *Globalizing Capital: A History of the International Monetary System* (2008), chapter 3.

crucial difference between Britain and France on the one hand, and Germany on the other, was disruptive character of Germany's electoral right in national politics. While right-wing radicals were marginalized within the DNVP, the party's leaders and moderates had *not* achieved a durable organizational victory that would permanently subordinate the fundamentalists; their victory was constantly challenged and, at best, only short-lived. Thus, in Germany's third period, after 1928, and at the first sign of serious electoral faltering at the top, unlike in Britain or France, outside groups and party activists successfully staged an open revolt. As opposed to the remarkably analogous failed interventions in British Conservative Party politics by Lord Beaverbrook and Viscount Rothermere, the owners of the three largest daily newspapers in Britain in the 1920s, the German millionaire media magnate Alfred Hugenberg – one of the founders of the Pan-German League, a nationalist pressure group – was backed by influential local associations to whom he provided important financial support. Hence, he actually gained leadership of the DNVP in 1928. The loosely coupled party structure had in fact enabled his ascent to the top. In 1928, Hugenberg injected financial resources into regional associations, and maneuvered radical and antidemocratic candidates into upper-level positions on regional candidate lists, ultimately triggering a mass exodus of the DNVP's moderate party leaders. When the economic crisis hit in the fall of 1929, the key center-right "border party" had *already radicalized* with Hugenberg at the helm, endangering both party and regime.

THE FIRST PERIOD: FORGING A NEW PARTY ON FRAGILE FOUNDATIONS AND REGIME INSTABILITY, 1918–1924

The origin of Germany's democratic failure can be traced to organizational decisions made in the *first* period of relative stalemate between pragmatists and fundamentalists within the *Deutschnationale Volkspartei*.[65] In the pivotal months of October and November 1918 – as the German emperor fled, the monarchy broke down, and the emergence of a new regime appeared imminent – all politicians, but especially of the right, were given powerful incentives to forge new, more effective party organization.[66] The end of the Imperial political system had left old parties of the right scrambling without the

---

[65] My conception of internal party "stalemate" draws on Stanley Hoffmann's notion of the "stalemate society," a concept developed to explain fragile stability in a very different context: Third Republic France. See, for example, Stanley Hoffmann, *Decline or Renewal? France since the 1930s* (New York: Viking Press, 1974).

[66] Annelise Thimme, *Flucht in den Mythos: die Deutschnationale Volkspartei und die Niederlage von 1918* (Göttingen: Vandenhoeck and Ruprecht, 1969); Marcus Funck, "Shock und Chance: Der Preussische Militäradel in der Weimarer Republik zwischen Stand und Profession," in *Adel und Bürgertum in Deutschland*, ed. Heinz Reif (Berlin: Akademie, 2000), 127–71.

institutional protections that they had so long relied upon.[67] In the midst of war, the emperor announced the end of the three-class voting system; and at the war's end, suffrage for German national parliamentary elections was expanded to women, doubling the size of the electorate overnight and prompting new electoral strategies, particularly on the right, to appeal to women.[68] Additionally, given the cohesive new coalition dominating national politics and Social Democrats winning in Prussia, old elites, as in 1848, developed clear motives for party counter-organization.

But, there was one additional factor incentivizing more effective party organization: the adoption of proportional representation in the 1919 constitution.[69] Proportional representation, even while fragmenting political party *systems*, provided centralizing motives and authority for individual political party organizations themselves. Party leaders now had to undertake two new tasks: (1) the creation of national lists of candidates at the regional and national levels; and (2) the construction of a nationwide campaign for the "party vote."[70] Additionally, party leaders had a new tool with which to enforce discipline: favorable placement on party lists in exchange for good behavior within the parliament.[71] While the old single-member two-round majoritarian system (1867–1918) in relatively smaller districts had left candidate selection in the hands of local notables – as they could identify the most well-recognized, and hence most electable, of candidates – proportional representation, in which candidates were likely to be elected if they ranked higher on party lists, gave *national* party leaders more power. If there was anywhere where Duverger's logic of the "contagion of the left" should have

---

[67] On this early period in the DNVP, see Werner Liebe, *Die Deutschnationale Volkspartei, 1918–1924*, Zusammenarbeit mit dem Forschungsausschuss der Vereinigung für die Wissenschaft von der Politik (Düsseldorf: Droste-Verlag, 1956); Hertzman, *DNVP* (1963); Ohnezeit, *Zwischen 'schärfster Opposition'* (2011).

[68] See Kirsten Heinsohn, *Konservative Parteien in Deutschland 1912 bis 1933: Demokratisierung und Partizipation in geschlechterhistorischer Perspektive* (Düsseldorf: Droste, 2010); Raffael Scheck, *Mothers of the Nation: Right-Wing Women in Weimar Germany* (Oxford: Berg, 2004).

[69] The list system included both regional lists for parties in thirty-five large electoral districts as well as national party lists. For a recent account, see Philip Manow, Valentin Schroeder, and Carsten Nickel, "Germany's 1918 Electoral Reform and the Reichstag's Efficient Secret" (paper presented at the Historical Democratization and Redistribution in Advanced Industrialized Democracies, Juan March Institute, Madrid Spain, October 20–22, 2011).

[70] On these two general tasks of parties, see Gregory R. Stephens and John Leslie, "Parties, organizational capacities and external change: New Zealand's National and Labour parties, candidate selection and the advent of MMP," *Political Science* 63, no. 2 (2011): 205–18. See also John M. Carey and Matthew Soberg Shugart, "Incentives to Cultivate a Personal Vote: A Rank Ordering of Electoral Formulas," *Electoral Studies* 14, no. 4 (1995): 417–39.

[71] Also critical with the adoption of proportional representation was the thirty-three-fold enlargement in the average physical size of electoral districts from 36,000 to 1,200,000 registered voters from the Imperial to the Weimar period, requiring in one analyst's assessment an "organizational quantum leap" for political parties. See Kreuzer, *Institutions and Innovation* (2001), 97.

led to the creation of centralized mass parties by reluctant parties of the right, it indeed was in Weimar Germany after 1918 and 1919.

How did the electoral right respond to these challenges and opportunities? The implementation of proportional representation and the changed political reality after 1918 required new forms of party organization. Like authoritarian successor parties throughout history, in a remarkable turnaround – in this case, within two weeks of the November 9, 1918 Revolution – a new, more heterogeneous political party formally established itself as a new political actor of the electoral right.[72] As the leader of the DKP in the Reichstag, Kuno von Westarp, reluctantly put it in November 1919, "The shift in political conditions resulting from the war impels the Conservative party to refresh its old and honored traditions with the new spirit of the time so that it will be in a position to meet the challenges of present-day life."[73]

Motivated by such considerations and the historical disunity on the right, forty-nine prominent conservative politicians signed a statement published in the pages of the old DKP's newspaper, the *Kreuzzeitung*, on November 24, 1918, proclaiming the new nationally encompassing party of the right, the *Deutschnationale Volkspartei* (DNVP), and calling for a set of new guiding principles. Over the following several weeks, the DNVP became the third new major party on the political stage, following a model set by the other two "bourgeois" parties: the former National Liberal Party had become the *Deutsche Volkspartei*, and the more reliably democratic Left Liberals had reconstituted themselves as the *Deutsche Demokratische Partei* (DDP).[74]

The DNVP, as the third and most conservative of these, effectively became a successor to the heterogeneous conservative and right-wing political parties and pressure groups of the Imperial period. These included, most prominently, the urban-based monarchist Free Conservative Party; the Christian Socialists, which had its roots in Adolf Stoecker's movement from the 1890s; right-wing elements of the National Liberal Party; the multiple anti-Semitic *völkisch* nationalist party groupings, which ran in election campaigns before 1914; and leaders of pressure groups ranging from the Pan-German League and the Steel Helmets (*Stahlhelm*) veterans' association to the renamed Agrarian League. But, the core predecessor to the DNVP, from an organizational and financial perspective, was the old Prussian *Deutsche Konservative Partei* (DKP), equipped with the most robust institutional resources. However, the new

---

[72] Historical analogues can be seen in the reconstitution of former communist parties in Eastern Europe after 1989. See Anna M. Grzymala Busse, *Redeeming the Communist Past: The Regeneration of Communist Parties in East Central Europe* (Cambridge: Cambridge University Press, 2002). And in Latin America after democratization Loxton, "Authoritarian Inheritance and Conservative Party-Building in Latin America" (2014).

[73] See von Westarp, *Regierung des Prinzen Max von Baden* (1928), 128.

[74] See Larry Eugene Jones, ed., *The German Right in the Weimar Republic: Studies in the History of German Conservatism, Nationalism, and Antisemitism from 1918 to 1933* (New York: Berghahn Books, 2014).

DNVP was distinctly *not* a continuation of the East Elbian Junker-dominated party of the past. In fact, key elements in the DKP leadership initially resisted the creation of the DNVP, fearing that their core constituency would be diluted in this entity. In this, they were correct. In 1912, 38 percent of DKP parliamentary representatives were members of the aristocracy; but by 1924, only 9 percent of the new DNVP were aristocrats and half of the party's votes came from west of the Elbe River.[75]

Yet for all this pragmatism, a second important strand of reaction was also present in the DNVP, described aptly by historian Annelise Thimme as a "flight into mythology." Conspiratorial rightists built a series of revanchist myths to explain Germany's "humiliating" defeat in the First World War: the army had not truly been "defeated"; it had been merely "stabbed in the back" by the "November 1918 traitors" – typically some mix of scapegoats including Socialists, Jews, and Left Liberals.[76] In 1918, future foreign minister Gustav Stresemann incisively explained what the loss of the war meant to German nationalists: "We thought we were the Romans, but we turned out to be Carthaginians."[77]

This peculiar psychological coping mechanism inevitably led some to question the very legitimacy of the resulting political regime.[78] And this posture, widespread in Germany but most coherent in the so-called "conservative revolution" – an intellectual movement of "reactionary modernism" – found its most fertile environment in the heterogeneous DNVP.[79] But, as important as the anti-Semitic and Pan-German-laced rhetoric was, it was only one of many strands in the political life of the DNVP.[80]

So, how was the DNVP constructed amid these very real right-wing tensions? The strategic calculations and organizational machinations behind the merger of right-wing forces were demanding, and they unintentionally but predictably gave rise to a compromised, *weak* political organization for the new political party, not unlike its prewar precursor.[81] Pressure to break with the past came largely from Free Conservative and Christian Socialist leaders such as Oskar Hergt, Siegfried von Kardoff, and Franz Behrens, who wanted to shatter the dominance of the agrarian-minded East Elbian Prussian Conservative Party.

---

[75] Mergel, "Scheitern des deutschen Tory-Konservatismus" (2003): 327. One important group – the so-called "young conservatives" represented by figures such as Ulrich von Hassell – had already been sidelined by 1920, leaving the core of the DNVP in place.

[76] See Thimme, *Flucht in den Mythos* (1969).   [77] Thimme, *Flucht in den Mythos* (1969), 76.

[78] See Thimme, *Flucht in den Mythos* (1969).

[79] On the "conservative revolution," see Jeffrey Herf, *Reactionary Modernism: Technology, Culture, and Politics in Weimar and the Third Reich* (Cambridge: Cambridge University Press, 1984).

[80] Hermann Beck (*Fateful Alliance* (2008). Beck (2008) goes so far as to argue that "When the DNVP was founded in November 1918, anti-Semitism did not play a role in the party's self-image" (p. 37). See also discussion p. 176ff.

[81] This "merger" pattern of formation is theorized to lead to weakly institutionalized parties. See Panebianco, *Political Parties* (1988).

The greatest resistance against internal reform came from the leaders of most important group, the DKP, who were reluctant to hand over their organizational and financial resources to the group they feared would be a more politically moderate.

But a settlement was reached in intense discussions that began informally at the funeral of Karl Friedrich Freiherr von Gamp-Massaunen, a prominent Conservative Party Reichstag MP in mid-November 1918 and continued among a committee of right party leaders, including some sympathetic DKP leaders, over the next several weeks. By late November 1918, the founding committee had accepted the new name, adopted a new program, embraced a new collective self-conception emphasizing the defense of the "nation," and self-consciously articulated a new strategic orientation to appeal to middle-class and non-agrarian interests. Critically, while in principle calling for monarchy and resisting the new political order, an equivocal party declaration in 1918 also proclaimed its willingness to work "on the basis of the parliamentary form of government, which is the only one possible after recent events."[82]

The DNVP was formed of heterogeneous elements, but – we should remember – so are most political parties. In this case, ideological fissures would be exacerbated because the party was constructed from previous groups possessing their own long histories. These already quasi-institutionalized groups and pre-existing political parties were only incompletely fused, and their own varied constituencies, continued formally to exist, as in the case of the DKP. This led to a new overarching party organization exhibiting all the hallmarks of a "loosely coupled" political party (see Chapters 2 and 6).[83] In particular, local associations had inordinate power over the center; outside pressure groups, upon whom the party leaders depended excessively, played a principal role in decision making; and the parliamentary center had an unusually limited degree of control. This *organizational porousness* left in place particular organizational niches, which in the late 1920s would become sites of an intense right-wing insurgency based precisely in these outside groups.

Thus, though the party leaders of the old DKP agreed to join the DNVP, it was only a partial union. Not only did DKP party leaders insist – in a noteworthy memorandum distributed in November 1918 – that their party executive would continue to exist as an autonomous entity alongside the new national party, but the same memo also reassured the *Kreisvereine* (local constituency associations) of the DKP that they would not be disbanded, though members were encouraged also to join the DNVP.[84] The approximately forty-five local DKP *Kreisvereine* went by different names in different districts, and when they were reorganized roughly at the level of the thirty-five electoral constituencies, they remained mostly autonomous.

---

[82] Cite Craig, *Germany, 1866–1945* (1978), 507.   [83] Panebianco, *Political Parties* (1988).
[84] The memo is cited by Ohnezeit, *Zwischen 'schärfster Opposition'* (2011), 32.

In Ohnezeit's words, they stayed as a "legacy of the founding of the DNVP."[85] These *Kreisvereine*, unlike equivalent bodies in the British Conservative Party in the same period, gained a special de jure status in the *Parteivertretung* (the sovereign executive body of the party), which selected party chairmen, as well as greater *de facto* leverage in formulating Reichstag candidate lists than has typically been recognized.[86]

In short, the result was not an electorally minded "team of politicians," deploying activists and interest groups to achieve their own ends, as McKenzie characterized the British Conservative Party.[87] Rather, "the resulting political creation" of the DNVP, in historian Hertzmann's words, was a "complex coalition of interests, often so disparate in their tendencies as to threaten the effective existence of the new party."[88] This was certainly exacerbated by the autonomy of the party's regional constituency associations (*Landesverbände*), which Ohnezeit describes as "a legacy of the origins of the DNVP in different parties" that could in turn result in an "orientation of opposition of the *Landesverbände* to the Berlin central office."[89] Even a DNVP brochure published in 1928 concludes, "Germans are often said to be born organizers. Unfortunately in nationalist organizational life, they are in the minority."[90] In short, German conservatives, *contra* the dominant narrative, were organizationally ill-equipped to cope with the new Weimar era.

The resulting organizational disunity, therefore, was not just a reflection of the heterogeneous opinions of the party's founders. Rather, as William Riker reminds us in a broader perspective, "outcomes depend as much on the procedure of amalgamation as on the tastes of the participants."[91] In this case, given the pre-1914 history of fragmentation, the procedure of organizational combining these groups formed was what another analyst has called a loose "composite."[92] The recreation of fragmentation was the immediate effect of the divide between grassroots fundamentalists and the pragmatists within the first generation of Reichstag leaders.[93] In 1918–1919, a group of former Prussian civil servants appeared to dominate the new party leadership ranks. These were politicians and former statesmen whose overwhelming loyalty to the *idea* of the

---

[85] Ohnezeit, *Zwischen 'schärfster Opposition'* (2011), 47.

[86] See, by contrast, Manow, Schroeder, and Nickel, "Germany's 1918 Electoral Reform and the Reichstag's Efficient Secret."

[87] McKenzie, *British Political Parties* (1955).

[88] Lewis Hertzman, "The Founding of the German National People's Party (DNVP), November 1918–January 1919," *The Journal of Modern History* 30, no. 1 (1958): 25.

[89] Ohnezeit, *Zwischen 'schärfster Opposition'* (2011), 47–48.

[90] Deutschnationale Volkspartei, *Der nationale Wille: Werden und Wirken der Deutschnationalen Volkspartei 1918–28*, ed. Max Weiss (Essen: Deutsche Vertriebsstelle Rhein und Ruhr, 1928), 362.

[91] Riker, *Art of Political Manipulation* (1986), 11.

[92] Attila Chanady, "The Disintegration of the German National Peoples' Party 1924–1930," *The Journal of Modern History* 39, no. 1 (1967): 68.

[93] Beck, *Fateful Alliance* (2008), 30.

German state overcame their substantial antipathy to the new regime, prompting them to participate in it without undergoing any deep democratic conversion. This group of DNVP leaders included Oskar Hergt, former Prussian Finance Minister; Clemens von Delbrück, former Lord Mayor of Danzig and Undersecretary for the Interior; Arthur Graf von Posadowsky-Wehner, also a former undersecretary; and Karl Helfferich, Undersecretary of the Treasury and well-regarded finance expert.[94] They were, in O'Donnell and Schmitter's terms, "contingent consenters"; they saw the need for a new conservative organizational response to democratic elections, unintentionally helping the new regime incorporate its most vociferous critics.

But, from 1921 to 1923, a power struggle within the DNVP erupted which took the form of an anti-Semitic and radical counterreaction in the wake of foreign policy and economic crises, including the onset of inflation, the French occupation of the Ruhr, and well-publicized French military rulings against Germans. Had there been a "tightly coupled" party hierarchy, these groups would have more easily been sidelined, as equivalent grassroots groups were in Britain or Sweden, to the margins of the party organization. But, in Germany, these extremists had relatively easy access to the levers of party authority, even though often located closer to local *Kreisvereine* than the halls of the Reichstag. They exercised their power via three mechanisms. First, party statute gave local party associations de jure authority to cast key votes in the annual *Parteivertretung* for the selection of the party leader, which amounted to 188 of the total 286 votes in 1928.[95] This would carry weight in the fall of 1928, but it was already a source of leverage for party activists early in the 1920s. The second mechanism was the DNVP's *de facto* candidate selection process: as Ohnezeit puts it, "the formulation of candidate lists for the elections to the [first National Assembly to meet in mid-January 1919] were left in the hands of the provincial associations."[96] This localized model of candidate selection, despite proportional representation, presented a substantial challenge to party leadership. For example, in 1918, local associations dropped at least ten of the national leadership's preferred candidates.[97] Certainly, as Manow and his collaborators note, over time national party leaders attempted to assert control over their selection of candidates.[98] But the initial patterns were tough to undo, as fights over candidate lists between interest groups and party leaders demonstrate as late as 1928.[99]

---

[94] This list comes from Beck, *Fateful Alliance* (2008), 31.

[95] Ohnezeit, *Zwischen 'schärfster Opposition'* (2011), 51; Mergel, "Scheitern des deutschen Tory-Konservatismus" (2003): 327; Heidrun Holzbach, *Das "System Hugenberg": Die Organisation bürgerlicher Sammlungspolitik vor dem Aufstieg der NSDAP* (Stuttgart: Deutsche Verlags-Anstalt, 1981).

[96] Ohnezeit, *Zwischen 'schärfster Opposition'* (2011), 159.

[97] Ohnezeit, *Zwischen 'schärfster Opposition'* (2011), 160, footnote 8.

[98] Manow, Schroeder, and Nickel, "Germany's 1918 Electoral Reform and the Reichstag's Efficient Secret."

[99] See Ohnezeit, *Zwischen 'schärfster Opposition'* (2011), 81–83.

A third mechanism, related to candidate selection, was the position of extra-party pressure groups in the party structure, especially industrial groups associated with Pan-German League founder Alfred Hugenberg. One analyst writes, "Industry made donations for campaigns dependent on the selection of their preferred candidates."[100] More than just industrial groups, a total of ninety right-wing pressure groups and nationalist associations – from the Pan-German League to the German Officer's League to the Steel Helmets – represented a heterogeneous array of interests.[101] Theories of "conditional party government" predict that heterogeneity among "principals" tends to inhibit centralized and strong party leadership for the simple reason that disparate groups are unlikely to hand over power to a party leader who will advantage some groups over others.[102] This logic was clear here. The ninety groups were, it should be noted, joined together to form an umbrella organization, the United Fatherland Association of Germany (*Vereinigte Vaterländische Verbände Deutschlands*, or VVVD) in 1923 to provide mobilizational aid to the electoral right and push an agenda centered mostly on foreign policy questions. However, this was done in exchange for influence over the party and candidate selection.[103] As a result, the party leadership held very little sovereignty over its supporting coalitions of activists and pressure groups.

Though the interdependence of the DNVP and the VVVD has been noted, trying to assess precisely the extent of porousness, or *how much* influence outside groups had on party leaders' decisions, is more problematic.[104] Yet, by examining Reichstag MPs' voting patterns, we can systematically see evidence of two types of party fragmentation: (1) a weak ability to control DNVP MPs votes in the Reichstag ("voting cohesion"), and (2) the degree to which sitting DNVP MPs abandoned their party for another group in the middle of parliamentary sessions ("organizational cohesion"). In Figure 8.2, we see that, in general, the DNVP was on average weaker than most other parties on these two dimensions. But, consistent with our chronology of the linked fate of the DNVP and Weimar regime, the one exceptional period was between 1924 and 1928 when the DNVP had *higher* levels of party discipline than it did throughout the rest of the decade.

Thus, we must ask: is there a plausible link between the fragmented nature of the DNVP and the fragility of the regime in these early years of Weimar?

---

[100] Ohnezeit, *Zwischen 'schärfster Opposition'* (2011), 160.

[101] Barry A. Jackisch, *The Pan-German League and Radical Nationalist Politics in Interwar Germany, 1918–39* (Farnham: Ashgate Publishing Limited, 2012).

[102] John Aldrich and David W Rohde, "Measuring Conditional Party Government" (paper presented at the American Political Science Association Annual Convention, Chicago, 1998).

[103] For the party's own account of this, see Deutschnationale Volkspartei, *Der nationale Wille* (1928); James M. Diehl, "Von der "Vaterlandspartei" zur "Nationalen Revolution": die Vereinigten Vaterlaendischen Verbaende Deutschlands (VVVD) 1922–1932," *Vierteljahrshefte für Zeitgeschichte* (1985): 617–39.

[104] See, e.g., Ohnezeit, *Zwischen 'schärfster Opposition'* (2011), 116.

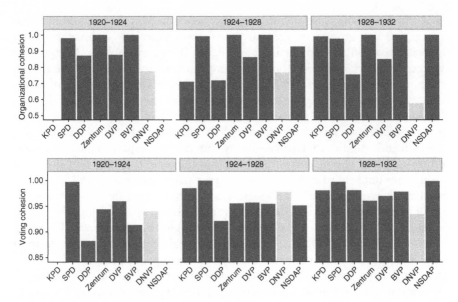

FIGURE 8.2: Organizational and Voting Cohesion of the DNVP and Other Political Parties in Weimar Germany, 1920–1932
Notes: This analysis estimates "organizational cohesion" and "voting cohesion" scores for each party over each period. "Organizational cohesion" is measured by subtracting the percentage of MPs in a party who switched party affiliation in a legislative session from 1. "Voting Cohesion" is based on a Rice Index, the standard measure of assessing "party discipline" in parliamentary settings.
Data Source: Data used for this analysis is the replication data for Hansen, Martin Ejnar/ Marc Debus. 2012. "The Behaviour of Political Parties and MPs in the Parliaments of the Weimar Republic." *Party Politics* 18, 5: 709–26

Between 1918 and 1924, moderate party leaders and radical outside pressure groups both seemed to have similar levels of influence. But did this matter for the Weimar political system? This impasse can indeed be linked to the two most significant institutional weaknesses in the period: first, cabinet instability, which subtly undermined the resilience of the new political regime itself; and second, attempted right-wing military coups that sought to violently dismantle the entire regime outright.

First, while a chronic syndrome for interwar Europe more generally, the Weimar government's cabinet instability became particularly acute and notorious.[105] In 1920, the Weimar coalition – SPD, DDP, and Center Party – dropped from its nearly 76 percent supermajority to 43 percent of the vote,

[105] For a comparative account on the rise and consequences of cabinet instability for economic policy in interwar Europe, see Beth A Simmons, *Who Adjusts?: Domestic Sources of Foreign Economic Policy during the Interwar Years* (Princeton: Princeton University Press, 1994), 123–24.

shifting the political center of gravity away from the founding left-wing coalition to a new "middle" constellation of the DDP, the Center Party, and the more right-wing liberal DVP.[106] Lacking an outright majority, this centrist coalition needed to decide whether to move left and include the SPD in a "grand coalition," or move right to include the DNVP in a non-socialist "bourgeois coalition."[107] Though the DNVP Reichstag leadership was willing to moderate itself and was "anxious to enter the government," grassroots radicalism presented a stumbling block to the formation of a bourgeois coalition.[108] Thus, the DNVP as a whole – deadlocked between fundamentalists and pragmatists – leaned too far right for the tastes of the DDP and Center Party.[109] Unwilling to forge alliances with the DNVP, the moderate middle parties instead sought minority governments without it, giving rise to four brief minority governments from November 1922 to May 1924.[110] Given the coalitional possibilities in the Reichstag after 1920, the ideological standoff inside what would soon be the largest non-socialist party in Germany left the national party system itself more fragile.

In addition, the inability of the DNVP's pragmatists to control factionalism sheds light on the most significant challenge to the political regime in this period: the failed Kapp Putsch of 1920, in which Wolfgang Kapp, General Lüttwitz, and a group of *Freikorps* (free-corps) troops occupied Berlin and set the national government briefly on the run.[111] The coup survived only several days and ultimately was defeated at the hands of a general strike and resistance by a "state loyal" civil service, but it nonetheless represented a perilous trial for the new regime. The leaders of the putsch were disgruntled military officers, some with ties to the DNVP such as party member Kapp, who resented the government's efforts to reduce the military and dissolve the Freikorps. The driver of the unsuccessful putsch was not, as Gerald Feldman has demonstrated, "big business" lacking a party to represent its interests; rather, it was dissatisfaction from the DNVP's own grassroots. Business leaders, though ambivalent about the new regime, were in fact critical of Kapp's

---

[106] This short-lived government of DDP, Center Party, and DVP was led by Chancellor Constantin Fehrenbach (Center Party).

[107] This framing of the electoral dynamics draws on Robert P. Grathwol, *Stresemann and the DNVP: Reconciliation or Revenge in German Foreign Policy 1924–1928* (Lawrence: University Press of Kansas, 1980), 14–15.

[108] Grathwol, *Stresemann and the DNVP* (1980), 22.

[109] See Michael Stürmer, *Koalition und Opposition in der Weimarer Republik 1924–1928* (Düsseldorf: Droste Verlag, 1967).

[110] The four governments were these: (1) the November 1922–August 1923 minority government was led by Chancellor Cuno without the SPD or the DNVP; (2) the August–October 1923 government led by Chancellor Stresemann was a "grand coalition" that included the SPD; (3) the October–November 1923 government also led by Stresemann reshuffled the same "grand coalition" cabinet including the SPD; and (4) the November 1923–May 1924 minority government led by Chancellor Marx of the Centre Party excluded the SPD and the DNVP.

[111] See Craig, *Germany, 1866–1945* (1978), 430.

strategy. A crucial catalyst instead was the failure of DNVP party leaders to control radical elements loosely affiliated with the party.[112] For example, party chairman Oskar Hergt, who was disparaging of the Kapp Putsch from the outset, and party manager Hans-Erdmann von Lindeiner-Wildau actually actively tried, but failed, to disrupt the unfolding coup – a failure that hurt them electorally. The inability of the party leadership to control its own allies was tied to the fragility of the new regime as a whole.

But, interestingly, if the causes of the coup attempt itself were rooted in the relative autonomy of the DNVP's grassroots radicals, then the failure of the coup, too, can be attributed not only to loyal civil servants and a robust labor strike, but also to the ambivalence of Germany's most powerful business leaders.[113] Important economic interests regarded the DNVP's office-seeking moderates as viable players in the new democratic game. In the words of Fritz Semer, the chief Berlin lobbyist for the powerful Thyssen interests, within two weeks of the attempted coup, "the act of Kapp and Lüttwitz was, in the manner in which these people undertook it, a crime." But even more critically for our purposes, Semer went on to argue, "The [electoral] drive to the right was powerfully underway, and we actually would have had good elections if this miserable Kapp had not come along with his putsch!"[114] Once again, we see that if conservative interests feel they have a way of winning the electoral game, they will be inclined to compete within the bounds of the democratic arena. While powerful business interests were certainly no enthusiasts for the new regime, the relative promise of the DNVP in the Reichstag left such players unsupportive of Kapp's "clumsy" interventions.

In short, the hallmark of the DNVP's internal stalemate was the simultaneous *absence* of decisive organizational control over its own radical elements and the *presence* of sufficient electoral self-confidence among the party's "pragmatists" to reject extra-constitutional channels of obtaining power. Thus, between 1918 and 1924, the DNVP's organizationally stalemated status – where pragmatists and fundamentalists both appeared ascendant – played a major role in triggering the coup *and* its ultimate failure in the precarious first years of the Weimar period.

SECOND PERIOD: THE PERIOD OF STABILIZATION, 1924–1928

The second part of the Weimar regime, spanning 1924 and 1928, was distinctive in two respects. First, DNVP party leaders, nearly always more moderate than their activist base, appeared to decisively obtain the upper

---

[112] Beck, *Fateful Alliance* (2008), 33–35; Ohnezeit, *Zwischen 'schärfster Opposition'* (2011), 198–207.

[113] Craig, *Germany, 1866–1945* (1978).

[114] Cited by Feldman, "Big Business and the Kapp Putsch" (1971): 102. He draws this correspondence from Semer's Thyssen papers, dated April 2, 1920.

hand in their own party. They not only increasingly controlled the selection of candidates, but they also achieved great electoral success. They won 21 percent of the vote early in May 1924 and just under 20 percent in December 1924, entered two short-lived non-socialist governments – the First Luther Cabinet (January 1925–January 1926) and the Fourth Marx Cabinet (January 1927– June 1928) – and held six government ministries. While the DNVP weathered severe criticism from their own grassroots base, one author captures the scholarly consensus about changes in the party during this period,

The DNVP's whole relationship to the politics of the Weimar Republic began to change. Its entry into the government had certainly been a tactical accommodation, hedged about with mental reservations... Now, however, they were brought face-to-face with a conflict between their world of nationalist ideals and the world of political reality... For the first time, but not for the last, the leaders of the DNVP suspended their myths and opted for reality.[115]

In this period, the pursuit of office overwhelmed ideological concerns, and party leaders were willing to make foreign policy concessions to maintain two coalition governments. Extensive and regularized policy collaboration between such ideologically opposed parliamentary figures as Social Democratic leader Rudolf Hilferding, Heinrich Brüning, and DNVP leader Reinhold Quaatz was now possible.[116] Further, the parliamentary elite of the DNVP, though often holding an intransigent line on foreign policy, participated in normal, everyday transactional politics of domestic policy making. This included supporting protectionist tariffs for their core economic constituencies; pushing for unemployment insurance reform; pushing for a revaluation of the currency in 1924 that would benefit small investors; and even, in 1927, abandoning their previous unyieldingness by supporting the government's renewal of the "Law for the Defense of the Republic" (*Republikschutzgesetz*), initially passed in the wake of Walther Rathenau's murder in 1922.[117] This latter move was particularly notable because it predictably antagonized the core worldviews of the party's own right wing by banning all groups in Germany that supported the restoration of monarchy, a remarkable about-face for what was still officially a monarchist party.

In sum, the DNVP clearly appeared to be "habituating" itself, albeit grudgingly, to the unwelcome grinding work of parliamentary politics.[118]

---

[115] Grathwol, *Stresemann and the DNVP* (1980), 75. See also Mergel, "Scheitern des deutschen Tory-Konservatismus" (2003); Stürmer, *Koalition und Opposition in der Weimarer Republik 1924–1928* (1967); Ohnezeit, *Zwischen 'schärfster Opposition'* (2011).

[116] Evidence of this is found in Brüning's memoirs. The notion that the DNVP opted for "power over purity" appears in Grathwol, *Stresemann and the DNVP* (1980), 115.

[117] It should be added that the DNVP Minister Walter von Keudell has also been criticized for having watered down the low and undercutting non-nationalist Interior Ministry personnel. See Mommsen, *Rise and Fall of Weimar Democracy* (1996), 246.

[118] This notion of "habituation" is the fourth phase of a democratic transition, in Dankwart Rustow's influential framework. See Rustow, "Transitions to Democracy: Toward a Dynamic Model" (1970). For an application of this framework to the pre-1914 Imperial

One prominent historian's label for this phase of the DNVP's political life was "Tory-Konservatismus" – a pragmatic conservatism that was willing to comply with the "rules of the game" of modern parliamentary politics, without necessarily having undergone a deep ideological conversion.[119] This appeared to be an opportunity for the regime to stabilize. Was it?

For the political regime as whole, the middle years, the "golden age" of Weimar, are often characterized as politically stable, during which parliamentary politics worked "with a semblance of normality."[120] Cabinets were more secure, the inflation crisis appeared at first glance to be coming under control, military coups were now beyond the pale, negotiated settlement with western powers was achieved, and democratic stabilization appeared imminent. So, how precisely were these two phenomena – the moderation and success of the DNVP on the one hand and the apparent stabilization of the fragile democracy on the other – related?

Undoubtedly, a crucial factor was the rapid process of economic stabilization that ended the hyperinflation crisis of 1923–24.[121] As with other European states in this period – France, Britain, and Belgium – Germany's return to the gold standard in these years (1924–1927) under the leadership of the electoral right suggested a new interwar stabilization with "bourgeois" backing.[122] However, a precondition of this reconciliation in Germany, including the acceptance of the Dawes Plan in 1924, was the changed balance of power within the increasingly important DNVP itself. As the DNVP after 1924 was the largest non-socialist party in the Reichstag, it also possessed the most potentially destabilizing forces for the regime, and its endurance was vital to the settling of the German economy and its democracy as a whole.

Further, the DNVP became not only the biggest "bourgeois" party, thanks to the Reichstag elections of May 4, 1924: when the vote totals of its ally, the *Reichslandbund*, are included, it was the largest party in the Reichstag as a whole, even outpacing the SPD's vote share by winning approximately 21 percent of seats. The president of the Reichstag was now the well-respected DNVP Catholic MP Max Wallraf, the former mayor of Cologne, who also happened to be the uncle of young Konrad Adenauer's first wife and

---

period that uses some of this same language, see Anderson, *Practicing Democracy* (2000). It could be added that, though sometimes regarded as naïve in retrospect, this was all suggestive evidence that there is something to the thesis that learning "the arts of political compromise" is an *effect*, not a cause, of democratization.

[119] Mergel, "Scheitern des deutschen Tory-Konservatismus" (2003).

[120] Heinrich August Winkler, *Der Schein der Normalität: Arbeiter und Arbeiterbewegung in der Weimarer Republik 1924 bis 1930* (Berlin: J. H. W. Dietz, 1985).

[121] Maier, *Recasting Bourgeois Europe* (1975), 481–515; Feldman, *The Great Disorder* (1997), 803–37.

[122] Simmons, *Who Adjusts? Domestic Sources of Foreign Economic Policy during the Interwar Years* (1994).

the future post-war Chancellor's political mentor.[123] Even while the SPD recovered in the December elections of that year, the DNVP remained the strongest party of the right and had the potential to become a new steadying pole in Germany's multiparty system. Gustav Stresemann, the DVP leader and Foreign Minister, though often a vocal critic of the DNVP, hoped that, for Germany's sake, "size" would "create responsibility."[124] Indeed, if a "conservative stabilization" under democratic auspices was possible in France and Britain, so too, it seemed for a brief interlude, might it be even in the tenuous context of Germany.[125] With moderation in the right, at least at the level of the party leadership, democratically elected center-right coalitions were now finally possible.

In addition, the 1924 election victory was the consequence of a power shift within Germany's right. As the DNVP achieved electoral success, the millions of voters who had supported a turn to the right began to pressure the DNVP's participation in government.[126] Further, the DNVP's electoral victories meant that "fundamentalists," who decried any and all participation in government, began to lose control of the candidate selection process. In the view of one party leader, Gottfried Treviranus, until 1928 the national party list was now firmly in the hands of the party leadership.[127] In addition, between 1920 and 1924, a series of three key developments had already sapped radicals of their influence.

First, Kapp's botched coup attempt had discredited nondemocratic putschist strategies in general, particularly in the DNVP. While certain major participants in the coup – Gottfried Traub, Wolfgang Kapp, and less directly Graf von Westarp – were connected with the DNVP, party chairman Oskar Hergt and party manager von Lindeiner-Wildau quickly had condemned the action (after its failure), and even Westarp did his best to distance himself from it. The dismal defeat of the Putsch – owing to civil servant resistance, a labor strike, and the displeasure of big business – left this mode of counterrevolutionary activity, by all accounts, fully discredited.[128] Soon afterward, Oskar Hergt himself announced in his party's publication, "There is no space in the DNVP for anyone who undertakes participation in anti-constitutional enterprises."[129] Business leaders also publicly denounced the unsuccessful coup.[130] Historian

---

[123] Hans-Peter Schwarz, *Konrad Adenauer: A German Politician and Statesman in a Period of War, Revolution, and Reconstruction* (Providence, RI: Berghahn Books, 1995), 89.

[124] Cited by Grathwol, *Stresemann and the DNVP* (1980), 22.

[125] See Maier, *Recasting Bourgeois Europe* (1975), 481–82.

[126] Chanady, "Disintegration of the German National Peoples' Party" (1967): 71.

[127] Gottfried Treviranus to Manfred Dörr, July 19, 1962, Family Collection, Bern, Switzerland. In this unpublished correspondence, Treviranus writes, "Before the fall of 1928, the national party list was set by the party executive" (*Parteivorstand*).

[128] Beck, *Fateful Alliance* (2008), 35.

[129] Korrespondenz der DNVP, Nr. 79, April 15, 1920, as quoted by Ohnezeit, *Zwischen 'schärfster Opposition'* (2011), 204.

[130] Feldman, "Big Business and the Kapp Putsch" (1971).

Thomas Mergel describes the situation within the DNVP this way: "From this point on, under the dominant influence of Oskar Hergt and Karl Helfferich, a violent change of the political system was no longer a [viable] theme in the DNVP."[131] Though perhaps prompted less by ideological commitment to the Republic than a pragmatic recognition that the world had changed, violent interventions were now off the agenda of the DNVP leadership.

A second event that allowed DNVP party leaders to momentarily sideline destructive die-hards within their own ranks was the internal party showdown in 1922 over the second major barrier to DNVP moderation: the anti-Semitic or *deutschvölkisch* groups that had sprung up with ever greater vociferousness across Germany in the early 1920s. Two years after the Kapp Putsch, these factions were nearly expelled from the DNVP. As Gordon Craig puts it, "at the [DNVP] Görlitz Party Conference of 1922... it appeared that the party was on the point of breaking definitively with primitive *Junkertum* and radical anti-Semitism."[132]

Since early in the life of the party, *völkisch* anti-Semitic tendencies ran rife among political leaders, including Oskar Hergt. However, though these politicians may have been deeply anti-Semitic and did not regard it as a taboo, they were nonetheless ambivalent about the strategic benefit of deploying the ideology as an electoral strategy.[133] Hergt and Helfferich were anxious about the anti-Semitic movement, because of the internal power struggles and concerns about the groups' growing autonomy inside the DNVP itself.[134] But until 1922, the broader stalemate in the party also left this issue effectively unaddressed.

Finally, an unexpected event intervened to alter the balance of opinion: a vitriolic anti-Semitic essay critical of Walther Rathenau written by one of the three anti-Semitic leaders in the party, Wilhelm Henning, was published in the *Konservative Monatsschrift* immediately preceding Rathenau's assassination. This coincidence in timing generated widespread public censure of the DNVP and growing concern from party leaders that radicals in their midst were making the party *koalitionsunfähig* (not respectable enough for coalition government).[135] For electorally minded politicians, increasingly

---

[131] Mergel, "Scheitern des deutschen Tory-Konservatismus" (2003): 333.

[132] Craig, *Germany, 1866–1945* (1978), 507.

[133] See quotes from Hergt, cited by Hertzman, *DNVP* (1963), 126.

[134] This group was led by the triumvirate of radical right DNVP Reichstag members, Albrecht von Graefe-Goldebee, Reinhold Wulle, and Wilhelm Henning, that was critical of what they perceived as the DNVP leadership's "opportunistic" pursuit of political office at all costs. For a description of these dynamics, see Ohnezeit, *Zwischen 'schärfster Opposition'* (2011), 147–52.

[135] For example, see discussions in Hertzman, *DNVP* (1963); Beck, *Fateful Alliance* (2008). Both recount a well-known and revealing episode surrounding Anne von Gierke, daughter of Otto von Gierke, the prominent legal scholar (whose wife was Jewish): Ms. Gierke, a prominent member of the National Assembly in 1919, was dropped for this reason from the DNVP party list by a local constituency association, once again, a hotbed of radicalism, in Potsdam, triggering no small level of embarrassment on the part of party leaders.

desperate for office, such politics were irresponsible and damaging to the party's goals. Further, the key DNVP anti-Semitic group's effort to form an independent group with its own local branches, modeled in part on the old DKP successor group within the DNVP, was perceived as a challenge to party authority, triggering a test of the leadership's ability to control the grassroots. Taken together, what was regarded as overly vitriolic and embarrassing anti-Semitism and a serious internal power struggle, Hertzman writes, now convinced Hergt "to dissociate the party... from the stigma of 'rowdy' or 'pogrom' anti-Semitism."[136]

The efforts at sidelining this group were at first tentative but, given the obstacles the party typically faced with such insurgent groups, at least partly successful. Party leaders orchestrated the Görlitz Party Congress of October 1922 to assure that the anti-Semitic insurgency was officially condemned by a majority of delegates.[137] It is true that the anti-Semitic leaders were not expelled immediately from the party; however, the official denouncement led to the triumvirate's rapid secession.[138] Two months later, the three leaders founded their own party, the German Racist Freedom Party (*Deutsch-völkische Freiheitspartei*), leaving the office-seeking party leadership greater room to accommodate the political center.

A third major hindrance to the party's accommodation with the Weimar political system was the terms of the international peace agreement, which had at first seemed utterly incompatible with the unreconstructed and reactionary nationalist self-identity of the DNVP.[139] Shifting foreign policy dynamics in Europe during 1924–25, however, unintentionally elevated the pragmatists in the DNVP, leaving office-seeking party leaders more room for maneuver. In particular, the most proximate element in this regard, as historian Charles Maier has put it most concisely, was that "American loans... transform[ed] the internal politics of Germany."[140] In response to the shock of the 1923 occupation by 60,000 French troops of the Ruhr Valley to coerce timely reparations "in kind" of coal, France, Britain, and the United States collaborated and also competed with each other to develop a more viable reparations plan for Germany.[141] The highly effective DVP Foreign Minister, Gustav Stresemann

[136] Hertzman, *DNVP* (1963), 128.
[137] Ohnezeit, *Zwischen 'schärfster Opposition'* (2011), 147–49.
[138] Ohnezeit, *Zwischen 'schärfster Opposition'* (2011), 152–54.
[139] Grathwol, *Stresemann and the DNVP* (1980); Thimme, *Flucht in den Mythos* (1969).
[140] Maier, *Recasting Bourgeois Europe* (1975), 481.
[141] The French occupation itself of the Ruhr was triggered in large part by French Prime Minister Raymond Poincaré's perception that the United States and Britain were being too passive toward Germany and the fear that this passivity was even intentional as a way of balancing France's new strength vis-à-vis Germany's weakness. The resulting Dawes Plan can be interpreted, as it was by Stresemann, as the U.S. response to this intensification of European rivalries. See, John F. V. Keiger, *Raymond Poincaré* (Cambridge: Cambridge University Press, 1997), 287.

played a pivotal role in the negotiation, as the Americans proposed the Dawes Plan to resolve international tensions.[142]

The details of the Dawes Plan were released in the month before the May 1924 elections, promising huge loans in exchange for a new payment schedule and supervision of Germany's railroad system and national bank, all premised on Germany's growing economy and its subsequent ability to pay off reparations. The potential benefits – 800 million marks in loans to facilitate economic recovery – to powerful agricultural and industrial pressure groups directly affiliated with the DNVP, such as the National Agricultural Federation (*Reichslandbund*) and the National Federation of German Industry (*Reichsverband der deutschen Industrie*), again altered the balance of power within the party. A constituency for compromise had thus instantly been created, giving DNVP Reichstag moderates an unusual ally within the party.[143] Previously, party leaders had faced an intractable impasse with radical groups who viewed the Dawes Plan as a treasonous acceptance of the Versailles Treaty. But, the offer of loans to influential economic interest groups concentrated minds on the material virtues of holding office, including the tantalizing prospect of vigorous protectionist tariffs for agriculture. All of this tilted the internal balance of power toward the Reichstag's *Tory-Konservativen*.[144] Material interests, in short, eclipsed revanchist nationalist ideology. As Maier observes, "Republicans neither by commitment, nor by reason, they consented briefly to become republicans [out of] interest."[145]

But the outcome of the showdown between the "pragmatic" and "fundamentalist" wings of the DNVP was no foregone conclusion. Things came to a dramatic head in August 1924, as negotiations over a center-right cabinet remained stalled and a parliamentary vote on the Dawes Plan appeared before the Reichstag. While the DVP, the Center Party, and the DDP all supported the plan, its terms stipulated constitutional changes that necessitated a supermajority in the Reichstag, and thus DNVP support. DNVP party chairman Hergt and his secretary von Lindeiner-Wildau both favored joining the government despite public criticism, even with the Dawes Plan attached, though they pushed the interim minority government for deep alterations to the initial plan. The other leading figure in the DNVP

---

[142] Jonathan Wright, *Gustav Stresemann: Weimar's Greatest Statesman* (Oxford: Oxford University Press, 2002); Grathwol, *Stresemann and the DNVP* (1980).

[143] Direct evidence of perceived pressure on DNVP on this issue from industrial groups, found especially in the west, is provided by Ohnezeit, *Zwischen 'schärfster Opposition'* (2011), 264; Maier, *Recasting Bourgeois Europe* (1975), 385. Interestingly, while Hugenberg himself opposed the Dawes Plan, his organization, the RDI, supported it, generating a split in industrial interests.

[144] Undoubtedly helping this, and also demonstrating the lack of autonomy of the DNVP leadership, half of the parliamentary group belonged to the Reichslandbund. See Maier, *Recasting Bourgeois Europe* (1975), 486.

[145] Maier, *Recasting Bourgeois Europe* (1975), 481.

parliamentary group, Westarp, was even more disparaging of the Dawes Plan, straddling the party's middle. He sought to placate the vocal opposition of DNVP local party activists, who viewed the proposed international supervision of German railroads as treasonous. Their intransigence was expressed in a last-minute meeting of forty-two of the forty-five constituency associations in August 1924, in which thirty-nine chairmen voted against support for the Dawes Plan, sending a clear message to the Reichstag MPs.[146] This impatient pressure, increasingly outspoken and unsympathetic, would only grow over time, and local associations charged party leaders with opportunism and even betrayal. The DNVP leadership, which depended on local associations to legitimize them as leaders and to select MP candidates on local party lists, felt the intensifying squeeze and expressed in its public statements and discussions severe criticism of the plan, advocating for a less burdensome reparations agreement until the bitter end.[147]

Yet, profound pressure to support the proposal asserted itself from the other side – in particular from the largest German industrial association, the National Industrial Association (*Reichsverband der deutschen Industrie*, or RDI) and the agricultural association, the *Reichslandbund*. Both groups saw the benefits of loans and having a presence in the government. Finally, on the eve of the vote, the DVP and Center Party Reichstag leadership sent an explicit promise – without Chancellor Marx's approval, to be sure – to the DNVP that support for the Dawes Plan would assure their inclusion in the new government.[148] For ambitious party leaders and Reichstag MPs attempting to balance voter preferences on the one hand with the conflicts among powerful pressure groups and party activists on the other, the result was a strategic minefield. But, the same day, the DNVP Reichstag caucus held its own vote in which a majority of MPs expressed their *support* for the Dawes Plan. In light of this, though still frightened of the formidable and organized grassroots opposition, Chairman Hergt, rather than altering the party's official stance, adopted a more passive strategy of "releasing" his Reichstag group from the obligation to vote for what was still the official party line of opposition. The all-important final result was a close split in favor of the Dawes Plan: on the constitution-altering article, forty-eight DNVP MPs voted for the bill and fifty-two against it (including Oskar Hergt himself), providing the necessary two-thirds majority for the bill's passage.[149]

The way was now also nearly cleared for DNVP participation in government: in the fall of 1924, right liberal DVP leader and longtime foreign minister Gustav Stresemann made multiple efforts to expand the existing government to incorporate the DNVP, but this foundered on left liberal DDP resistance.

[146] Ohnezeit, *Zwischen 'schärfster Opposition'* (2011), 265.
[147] See Grathwol, *Stresemann and the DNVP* (1980), 51.
[148] Wright, *Gustav Stresemann* (2002), 292; Grathwol, *Stresemann and the DNVP* (1980), 50.
[149] Beck, *Fateful Alliance* (2008), 41.

According to his biographers, Stresemann had many reasons for trying to include the DNVP: he sought to bring the largest parliamentary opponent to his foreign policy "on board," thinking that appealing to its moderates might someday split the party, peeling off support for the DVP. Finally, Stresemann himself argued – in a fashion entirely consistent with this chapter's argument – that doing so would in the short-run help stabilize Weimar democracy: he himself attributed Britain's political stability in part to the experience that *all* of its parties had in governing.[150]

The DVP resigned after it became clear it would not – absent a new election – be able to convince the more left-leaning DDP of Stresemann's vision of uniting all "constitutional bourgeois parties" in a single government. Yet, in the wake of new elections in December 1924, Stresemann's vision was still in reach: after the Dawes Plan acceptance, support had declined for the political extremes – the Communists (*Kommunistische Partei Deutschlands*, or KPD) and the Nazis (*Nationalsozialistische Deutsche Arbeiterpartei*, or NSDAP). And, while the SPD amassed new strength, the DNVP actually increased its vote totals, suggesting support for its path of accommodation.[151] This gave rise to plans for a new, officially nonpartisan government with the DNVP, led by Chancellor Hans Luther, filled out by ministers from the DVP, the Center Party, and the center-right Bavarian People's Party (*Bayerische Volkspartei*, or BVP). By January 1925, the DNVP was, at last, officially in the government.

In sum, Stresemann's strategy of inclusion and Hergt's move against his own activist base drove Germany to what appeared to be a major turning point.[152] After all, the economy stabilized in the wake of the Dawes Plan, passed with the reluctant and ambivalent aid of the DNVP. Further, the DNVP itself showed a potential for moderation in the three years that followed, including after its entry into government in 1925 and its re-entry in 1927. It was willing to participate in the everyday politics of coalition building and parliamentary politics; it pursued a more transactional, center-right democratic politics; it defended trade protectionism for key interest groups including agriculture; and it advocated tax reform. And, critically for its electoral success in 1924, it had also made promises to voters to support a generous revaluation, even placing figures from the growing revaluation pressure group movement on the

[150] Wright, *Gustav Stresemann* (2002), 296–97; Grathwol, *Stresemann and the DNVP* (1980), 29.
[151] A key part of the election success was the DNVP's successful adoption of the mantle of revaluation – putting itself at the head of a growing movement of revaluation groups – to restore the losses of middle-class investors, a move that put it in collaboration with a group of increasingly powerful pressure groups. See Larry Eugene Jones, "Inflation, Revaluation, and the Crisis of Middle-Class Politics: A Study in the Dissolution of the German Party System, 1923–28," *Central European History* 12, no. 2 (1979): 143–68.
[152] The passage of the Dawes Plan is called a "turning point," an opportunity "for consolidating the republic," or as the beginning of a "new era" Beck, *Fateful Alliance* (2008), 41; Wright, *Gustav Stresemann* (2002), 292; Maier, *Recasting Bourgeois Europe* (1975), 488.

party ticket.[153] Although certainly taking different forms than in other countries, the DNVP was beginning to show tendencies not unlike the center-right politics of Britain under Stanley Baldwin and France under the right-leaning postwar leader, Raymond Poincaré.[154] The balance of power within Germany's largest potential opponent of parliamentary democracy had now tilted, even if ever so barely, in favor of moderates; and the result was that democracy appeared, for the first time in Weimar's history, to be moving toward stabilization. But, as we shall see, the moderation of party leaders in Germany's main conservative party remained tenuous because of the party's weak organization and its inability to dominate and distance itself from its grassroots base. In 1925, the DNVP, as part of the coalition, made the types of compromises that inevitably come from being in government, including stepping-back from its promise of full and equitable revaluation for middle-class voters.[155] This perceived concession sparked a further proliferation of interest groups, which insisted the DNVP had sold out to big business at the expense of small investors. As one Saxon creditor is quoted as saying at the time, DNVP had left voters "in the lurch" and had "dug its own grave."[156] New pressure groups and splinter parties sprung up on the right in 1926 including the *Volkrechtspartei*, focused especially on this issue, as well as the German Reich Party for the Middle Class (*Reichspartei des deutschen Mittelstandes*), This splintering of the middle-class vote for the right would ultimately spell trouble for the DNVP by 1928, creating an opening for other groups. In the wake of the inflation crisis, an organizationally more robust center-right party might have been able hold the disparate economic groups at its core together, while simultaneously forging compromises and keeping disaffected groups inside the party. As we will see in the next chapter, this could not happen; the ordinary work of parliamentary politics was simply not sustainable for a weak center-right party.

CONCLUSION

The overwhelming triumph of the pro-democratic Weimar coalition in 1918–1919 at one level had suggested a democratic breakthrough and a transformed regime. However, since democratic elections inherently involve alternations in power, a main factor shaping Weimar's longer-term democratic

---

[153] Jones, "Inflation, Revaluation, and the Crisis of Middle-Class Politics: A Study in the Dissolution of the German Party System, 1923–28" (1979).

[154] On the economic policy profile of conservative parties in general in the interwar years, see Simmons, *Who Adjusts?: Domestic Sources of Foreign Economic Policy during the Interwar Years* (1994); and Maier, *Recasting Bourgeois Europe* (1975).

[155] Jones, "Inflation, Revaluation, and the Crisis of Middle-Class Politics: A Study in the Dissolution of the German Party System, 1923–28" (1979).

[156] Benjamin Lapp, *Revolution From the Right: Politics, Class, and the Rise of Nazism in Saxony, 1919–1933* (Atlantic Highlands, NJ: Humanities Press, 1997), 159.

stabilization was the organizational character of pro-old-regime political parties. Could a shift of power happen without undermining the political regime? Sometimes analysts assert that the new political regime was doomed from the outset because of "disloyal" elements, such as the DNVP, that rejected the regime's legitimacy. However, I have demonstrated that this perspective sidesteps the major issue facing the new regime. The position of old-regime "spoilers" vis-à-vis a new regime is rarely, if ever, set in stone. Rather, old-regime parties facing a new democratic regime often equivocally cycle between "disloyalty," "semi-loyalty," and "contingent consent" in ways that must be explained. Given the DNVP's weakness in the early years, disloyalty to the regime escalated and the political regime itself possessed undeniable frailties. However, beginning in 1924, a pragmatic "semi-loyal" DNVP faction emerged as dominant, and the political regime itself stabilized. But, was this the end of the story? As we will see in the next chapter, this apparent internal party equilibrium was not durable and tragically neither was the political regime as a whole.

9

A Deluge: Conservative Weakness and Democratic Breakdown in Germany

The auspicious "turning point" of 1924–28, Weimar's so-called "golden age," seemed to suggest a decisive shift in the balance of power from "fundamentalists" to "pragmatists" within the German Conservative Party's successor organization, the DNVP.[1] But this accommodation with the political regime was short-lived. The fall of 1928 inaugurated the third period of the DNVP's evolution, a new and destructive cycle of organizational schism, as the grassroots right wing of the DNVP orchestrated a remarkable recovery in the form of a radical takeover from below. Their open revolt successfully dislodged the traditional conservative electoral right that had grudgingly habituated itself to democratic politics.

This takeover *from within* decisively narrowed the possibilities for the political regime as a whole and marked the beginning of democracy's "endgame" in Germany.[2] The rebellion removed from power the relatively pragmatic founding establishment coalition of the DNVP originally associated with Oskar Hergt. By seizing local associations, radicals established a platform

---

[1] Beck, *Fateful Alliance* (2008), 38.

[2] There is a broad debate, which my argument does not aim to resolve, on the scope of maneuverability for political elites in this "endgame" of democracy of political elites after 1928–1930. Foremost have been the classical perspectives of Werner Conze, "Brünings Politik unter dem Druck der großen Krise," *Historische Zeitschrift* 199 (1964): 529–50; and Karl Dietrich Bracher, *Die Auflösung der Weimarer Republik* (Stuttgart: Ring-Verlag, 1955). See also William Patch, *Heinrich Brüning and the Dissolution of the Weimar Republic* (Cambridge: Cambridge University Press, 1998). This debate has primarily focused on whether Brüning's turn to a presidential cabinet "above parties" in March 1930 represented a justifiable effort to save democracy or, the view more consistent with my own, the first step toward democratic collapse. I seek here to show that the radicalization and associated weakness of the DNVP beginning in the fall of 1928 – before the Great Depression – made the Weimar system more politically vulnerable than it would have been otherwise. In this sense, I date the beginning of heightened vulnerability to democratic collapse not in March 1930 (Brüning's cabinet), or the fall of 1929 (the stock market crash) but rather to the fall of 1928, when the DNVP radicalized.

to wrestle control of party leadership from the traditional parliamentary leaders, swallowing and radicalizing the DNVP and splintering it into many pieces in the process. The result was defiantly celebrated by the insurgents as creating "not a large but a strong right," one that would create a more "reliable" core for the new party chairman.[3] The goal, in short, was less about offering a new alternative to maximize votes than securing an ideological "purification" of the party in an inner-party fight with only the vaguest of plans about what would happen next.[4]

But more than just a localized power struggle within a political party headed to history's dust heap, this radical turn had far-reaching consequences. Because DNVP was the largest non-socialist party within the Weimar system and played a key role in integrating potential "spoilers" of democracy, the radicalization and rapid erosion of it altered the fate of German politics in sweeping ways. The "capture of the party by radical nationalists," according to historian Larry Eugene Jones, "was one of the seminal turning points in the politics of the Weimar Republic, and... had a profound impact on the subsequent course of events right up to and including Hitler's appointment as chancellor in January 1933."[5] Indeed, the quick collapse of the traditional right, although a longtime opponent of democracy, did not help democracy's advocates further their case; rather, the DNVP's internal battle in 1928 triggered a destructive dynamic of political disintegration, and the resulting "disunity of the right... constituted a prerequisite for the Nazi seizure of power."[6]

This chapter will elaborate the step-by-step process by which the change in DNVP party leadership in the fall of 1928 further radicalized a "border party" only instrumentally committed to the political regime, and thereby softened a major barrier – or, to use Karl Dietrich Bracher's term, created a "power vacuum" – contributing to the National Socialists' rise to power.[7] But before

---

[3] Axel Freiherr von Freytagh-Loringhoven, "Nicht grosse sondern starke Rechte," in *Die Deutschnationale Volkspartei 1925 bis 1928*, ed. Manfred Dörr (Marburg: Philipps-University Marburg/Lahn, [Der Tag 177 (1928)] 1964; reprint, reprinted as Anlage Nr. 38), 579–580. For evidence that Pan-Germans viewed the narrowing of the appeal of the party as creating a more "reliable" party, see Class' memoirs, cited in Jackisch, *Pan-German League* (2012), 153.

[4] As we will see, the language of ideological "purification" (*"Reinigung"*) was repeated frequently in this period and was used to justify the power grab that followed the 1928 change in party leadership.

[5] Larry Eugene Jones, "German Conservatism at the Crossroads: Count Kuno von Westarp and the Struggle for Control of the DNVP, 1928–30," *Contemporary European History* 18, no. 2 (2009): 147–77.

[6] We will elaborate this below, but Beck (*Fateful Alliance*, 2008) gives the most detailed account of the "fateful alliance" of the DNVP and the rise of the National Socialist Party after 1928. For a recent more general set of essays on the topic, see Jones, ed., *The German Right in the Weimar Republic: Studies in the History of German Conservatism, Nationalism, and Antisemitism from 1918 to 1933* (2014).

[7] On the idea of a "border party," see Capoccia, *Defending Democracy* (2005). The inferential challenge of showing that an increasingly "small" and even eventually "absent" phenomenon (i.e., a robust moderate center party) has a "big" causal impact on outcomes is substantial.

investigating the consequences of the DNVP's collapse, we must address a key puzzle: given the incentives of the institutional environment as well as the power-reinforcing advantages of holding political office, why was the gradually entrenched and highly experienced Reichstag DNVP establishment utterly incapable of maintaining power and "taming," as they stated they hoped to, their own radical grassroots in 1928? Why, in short, did Stresemann's strategy of making the DNVP leadership "responsible" for government, apparently successful between 1924 and 1928, not lead to the reinforcement of those atop the party hierarchy, but instead to their demise?

THE PATH TO RADICAL TAKEOVERS IN MODERN CONSERVATIVE POLITICAL PARTIES

A long literature has traced the emergence of the historical schism between "radicalism" and "reformism" within "working class" or left-leaning parties as they began, even if at times reluctantly, to participate in democratic politics.[8] Another literature covers the broad ideological affinities, or lack thereof, between fascism and conservatism in Germany and cross-nationally.[9] But, less attention has been focused on the organizational balance of power *within* "mainstream" or "upper class" conservative political parties that seek to participate as normal democratic players as they coped with the shock of democracy.[10] This deficiency reveals a major gap because, as the German case instructs us unequivocally, the threat of a radical takeover inside moderate conservative party organizations is a significant vulnerability of modern democratic politics. The need to reconstruct the dynamics of radical takeovers – their preconditions and their consequences for democratic stabilization – is therefore paramount.

However, the case-centered, process-tracing method of this chapter is particularly well suited to the challenge by showing how, *over time*, outcomes change due to over-time changes in the independent variable.

[8] Schorske, *German Social Democracy* (1955); Seymour Martin Lipset, "Radicalism or Reformism: The Sources of Working-class Politics," *American Political Science Review* 77 (1983): 1–18; Przeworski and Sprague, *Paper Stones* (1986).

[9] Klemens von Klemperer, *Germany's New Conservatism, Its History and Dilemma in the 20th Century* (Princeton: Princeton University Press, 1957); Martin Blinkhorn, ed., *Fascists and Conservatives* (Abingdon: Routledge, 1990).

[10] Certainly a large and important literature exists on the radical right in advanced democracies; see Herbert Kitschelt, *The Radical Right in Western Europe: A Comparative Analysis* (Ann Arbor: University of Michigan Press, 1995); Pippa Norris, *Radical Right: Voters and Parties in the Electoral Market* (New York: Cambridge University Press, 2005); David Art, *Inside the Radical Right: The Development of Anti-Immigrant Parties in Western Europe* (New York: Cambridge University Press, 2011). However, this literature at times assumes that the "far right," while shaping and being shaped by the strategies of mainstream constitutional conservative political parties, is itself a discrete phenomenon apart from the mainstream right.

Before accounting for the consequences, we will first explore the causes of conservative party radicalization beginning in 1928. The remarkable history of the DNVP's capture by outside radical groups, which culminated in media magnate Alfred Hugenberg's insurgent campaign and dramatic election to party chairman in October 1928, has been recounted before by historians of Germany's right.[11] But the larger significance of this story for us is how it helps explain the difficult trajectory of German democracy after 1918. Notwithstanding the "auspicious" conditions identified in the last chapter, a critical reader might ask whether Weimar Germany was, in some sense, already headed toward democratic breakdown because of the factors other scholars have typically highlighted, thereby diminishing the importance of the factors emphasized here.[12] Yet, even if multiple forces conspired against German democracy, we can see, upon closer examination of Weimar Germany, the enormous impact of the *backlash and takeover from within by radicals of a moderate conservative party*. Indeed, the collapse of the DNVP is only an extreme illustration of a more general dynamic to which all conservative political parties were susceptible – even putatively more "moderate" and "tamed" parties such as the British Conservative and Unionist Party before 1914 or the Swedish Right in the 1920s. Since ideologically extreme party activists are always located in the grassroots of party organizations, the party organizational structure is crucial to determining the radicals' relative effect.[13] Organizationally strong political parties can sideline extremists, but weak party organizational structures reduce the barriers to their influence, leaving moderates less able to combat radicals in their midst.[14] The result is that loosely coupled political parties are more vulnerable to the "revenge of the base."

But, a second lesson is that these structural preconditions are on their own insufficient to explain democratic breakdown; also crucial is the base's deployment of successful strategies of "radical takeover." In the case of the DNVP, these strategies, developed and elaborated by Pan-German League leader Heinrich Class and media magnate Alfred Hugenberg, leveraged the advantages of a well-organized minority against the *status quo*. Their techniques of organizational "capture" were similar to those of Leninist

---

[11] See Beck, *Fateful Alliance* (2008); Ohnezeit, *Zwischen 'schärfster Opposition'* (2011); Mergel, "Scheitern des deutschen Tory-Konservatismus" (2003); Chanady, "Disintegration of the German National Peoples' Party" (1967).

[12] See Chapter 8 for a list of the factors that are said to have "predisposed" German democracy for breakdown.

[13] May, "Opinion Structure of Political Parties" (1973); Herbert P. Kitschelt and Staf Hellmans, *Beyond the European Left: Ideology and Political Action in the Belgian Ecology Parties* (Durham: Duke University Press, 1990).

[14] May, "Opinion Structure of Political Parties" (1973): 135–51; Kitschelt and Hellmans, *Beyond the European Left* (1990).

Parties in the same period.[15] The strategies they employed, such as colonizing easily accessible local branches and reshaping public opinion through local press infiltration, are also of broader relevance. After all, it was the potent *combination* of particular types of party structures and corresponding tactics of takeover that *explain the dissolution of the DNVP and the onset of German democracy's heightened vulnerability.*

FLAWED PARTY STRUCTURE AND VULNERABILITIES TO ORGANIZATIONAL CAPTURE

We can begin with an account of the party structures that made the DNVP particularly susceptible to organizational capture. Historians sometimes tell the story of its undoing with little systematic reference to party organization, instead focusing on the proximate triggers for the sharp shift in power that came in October 1928.[16] The first of these, in the usual narrative, was the shock of the DNVP's major electoral loss in the Reichstag parliamentary elections of May 20, 1928, the most devastating defeat in its history to that date. This created an opportunity for the usual recriminations from the far right that Reichstag party leaders had opportunistically compromised the party's identity ideology in order attain office; poor electoral performance, in this view, was the result of too *much* pragmatism and compromise.[17] After the DNVP served two terms in office, the sudden loss of a third of its voters (sinking from 20.5 percent and 4 million voters to 14.5 percent and 2 million voters), as well as nearly one-third of its seats (from 111 to 78), led to allegations of failure all around, prompting a fight for the party leadership.[18]

A related secondary trigger, also frequently noted in the literature, was the resulting public debate over the causes of the election outcome. Of particular importance was an article published in July 1928 by the leader of the DNVP's "pragmatic" Christian union wing, Walther Lambach, who blamed not party leaders but the far right for the election loss. Lambach's hotly debated article, entitled "Monarchism," argued that the defeat indicated the declining electoral appeal of monarchism itself, and that a fuller accommodation to the Republic

[15] Philip Selznick, *The Organizational Weapon: A Study of Bolshevik Strategy and Tactics* (Santa Monica: Rand Corporation, 1952).

[16] It is frequently noted that the DNVP had a relatively weak party organization and that its decentralized party structure made it vulnerable to Pan-German influence. But these two points are rarely linked, nor have the broader implications of this case ever been fully fleshed out. See below for further discussion.

[17] See Chanady, "Disintegration of the German National Peoples' Party" (1967): 81; Ohnezeit, *Zwischen 'schärfster Opposition'* (2011), 424.

[18] Undoubtedly a critical factor behind the DNVP collapse was the severe agricultural crisis of 1927, which sparked, according to one assessment, defections away from the DNVP's core constituency. See Kreuzer, *Institutions and Innovation* (2001), 117.

was now necessary to make the party appealing to a new generation of younger conservatives.[19] Though one could easily attribute the electoral decline of 1928 to the normal cycle of electoral politics, the dire reading of the 1928 election and the intense reaction of Pan-Germans and many local associations to Lambach's article caused a storm in the conservative press, leading to Lambach's ejection from his own Potsdam DNVP provincial association (*Landverein*), suggesting more was at stake. Importantly, Lambach's ejection transpired *against* the wishes of some high-ranking party leaders.[20] Also, not coincidentally, the surrounding controversy launched a power struggle within the party leadership that rapidly elevated one unusual figure – Alfred Hugenberg, a sharp critic of Lambach's – who had been waiting in the wings to forge a new, more extreme party of the right. The election defeat had triggered an authoritarian turn.

Yet, why did the electoral setback yield this reaction? Parties' electoral fortunes always rise and fall, driven by a myriad of factors. While major electoral losses do tend to open challenges against incumbent party leaders, they do not necessarily ignite the kind of all-encompassing firestorm from below that overwhelmed the DNVP after 1928. In this case, the uproar swallowed the party entirely, transforming not only the dominant leadership coalition but the very political orientation of the party. This is surprising because scholars of political power have observed that, "there is no reason to assume that those originally favored by [a distribution of power] will not be able to use their superior resources and political connections to their advantage."[21]

Indeed, in politics, usually the outcomes of earlier victories become self-reinforcing. "Power begets power" by signaling to others who is dominant within an organization, altering how politics are talked about, and inducing other social actors to reorient their "investments" in such a way that slowly entrenches those atop political organizations in ways that are hard to unwind even in the face of short-run defeats.[22] As a result, existing dominant coalitions can typically withstand shocks such as electoral setbacks, even if an individual political leader must be sacrificed to do so.[23]

---

[19] See Walter Lambach, "Monarchismus," in *Die Deutschnationale Volkspartei 1925 bis 1928*, ed. Manfred Dörr (Marburg: Philipps-University Marburg/Lahn, [Politische Wochenshrift IV/ 24 June 14, 1928] 1964), 554–56.

[20] Jackisch, *Pan-German League* (2012), 154.

[21] Frank Baumgartner and Bryan Jones, *Agendas and Instability in American Politics* (Chicago and London: University of Chicago Press, [1993] 2009), 8.

[22] See Pierson, "Power and Path Dependence" (2015), 134.

[23] The idea that former dominant political parties must "learn to lose" is a precondition of democratic consolidation is developed by Edward Friedman and Joseph Wong, eds., *Political Transitions in Dominant Party systems: Learning to Lose* (New York and London: Routledge, 2008). For an illustration of how a dominant coalition remains intact while sacrificing individual leaders, see Stuart Ball and Anthony Seldon, eds., *Recovering Power: The Conservatives in Opposition since 1867* (Houndmills, Basingstoke, Hampshire: Palgrave Macmillan, 2005).

Yet, in other instances, seemingly powerful coalitions turn out to be temporary and flimsy, suddenly appearing precariously vulnerable following relatively minor events such as electoral defeat. In such cases, the "outs" of an organization, rather than quietly fading away, use short-run crises to destabilize what had only *looked* to be a stable political equilibrium. Political comebacks happen then because the former "outs," waiting for the propitious moment to reappear, have *already* regrouped by, for example, inventing new discourses, seeking alternative venues to assert their interests, or leveraging different financial and organizational resources.[24]

In this case, we see that the latter organizational trajectory was at work. Though the moderate "pragmatic" wing of the DNVP appeared ascendant between 1924 and 1928, its power was precarious for two reasons: (1) its organizational scaffolding of power was shaky *and* (2) the radical party outsiders employed innovative strategies of comeback. First, the organizational compromises hatched to transform the party from a pre-1918 "party of notables" into a mass party had several consequences: local activists had leverage over the party leadership that was built into the party's basic formal and informal rules; outside interests had greater leverage over local party organizations because of their indispensability for providing funding and mobilization aid. Both of these dynamics left the party leadership exposed to the local radicalism of groups such as the Pan-German League.

Historians have noted this same dynamic, though not always systematically disentangling what were in fact two distinct dimensions of organizational vulnerability. For example, Hermann Beck observes,

The regional DNVP Land Associations, which enjoyed considerable influence on financial and organizational matters because of the party's decentralized structure, were particularly unrelenting in their opposition to parliamentary government and the Republic... Since the DNVP was dependent upon contributions from industry to maintain the apparatus and finance election campaigns (membership dues alone were insufficient), financial contributors exercised disproportionate leverage. Alfred Hugenberg capitalized on this dependency.[25]

Likewise, Grathwol writes, "District organizations were more susceptible to the pan German point of view than was the DNVP Reichstag delegation."[26] And Leopold agrees, making a similar point when he argues that one of two main culprits of the radical takeover

was the weakness of the German National party structure. The independence of regional party associations and the sociological structure of these associations left ample room for Pan-Germans to exert coordinated pressure.[27]

---

[24] See Shepsle, "Losers in Politics" (2003).   [25] Beck, *Fateful Alliance* (2008), 48.
[26] Grathwol, *Stresemann and the DNVP* (1980), 102.
[27] John A. Leopold, *Alfred Hugenberg: The Radical Nationalist Campaign against the Weimar Republic* (New Haven and London: Yale University Press, 1977), 35.

These dynamics were visible in October 1928 at the watershed moment when Alfred Hugenberg was elected the fourth party chairman. First, in the lead-up to that vote, the party's reliance on outside funds gave outside interests, such as a group of Ruhr industrialists called the *"westliche Gruppe"* that included representatives from the major steel firm, Krupp, leverage over the party's profile. Hugenberg's donations to the DNVP election fund (*Wahlfond*) in 1928 and his role throughout the 1920s as indispensible broker of industrial contributions had also elevated his importance.[28] In the DNVP, industrial contributions played an extensive role as funds from party members had always lagged, as had contributions from local associations.[29] Further, it is worth noting the degree to which this funding dynamic differs from the model of party efficiency – the SPD. In this classic case of a strong party, outside analysts and party officials have estimated that a full two-thirds of total expenditures were covered by individual member contributions.[30] But, for the DNVP, things were dramatically different: local associations throughout Germany were themselves reliant on industrial donations and in particular on Hugenberg, who by most assessment now played a central role in channeling money and resources from Ruhr industrialists to these organizations.[31]

The raised status of local and provincial party associations also rendered the party defenseless: the body charged with electing the party chairman, according to the statute, was not the politically dominant Reichstag delegation as one might have expected, but rather the 288-member *Parteivertretung*, in which the forty-five provincial party associations had a veto-proof majority of 186 members.[32] The *Parteivertretung* met annually and was constituted, also according to party statutes, by chairmen of the state parliamentary delegations, representatives of party committees, and, most importantly, chairmen of each of the "peripheral" state/provincial local associations, "grassroots" actors who dominated the body through their sheer numbers.[33] Further, as noted in the last chapter, local associations mattered more for candidate selection than has generally been recognized, as was seen in the frequent fights between party leaders and local associations over candidate placement on regional party lists.[34] The authority of local interests over the party center, combined with a party structure reliant on outside sources of

[28] Leopold, *Alfred Hugenberg* (1977), 44.

[29] Manfred Dörr, ed., *Die Deutschnationale Volkspartei 1925 bis 1928* (Marburg: Philipps-University Marburg/Lahn, 1964).

[30] Protokoll vom Parteitag der SPD, Heidelberg, 1925, p. 108, as cited by an early American political scientist James Pollock, drawing on SPD party yearbooks, who also provides further evidence that these data are accurate. See, James Pollock, *Money and Politics Abroad* (Freeport: Books for Libraries Press, 1932), 230–31, 46.

[31] See, e.g., Ohnezeit, *Zwischen 'schärfster Opposition'* (2011), 75.

[32] Holzbach, *System Hugenberg* (1981), 242.

[33] Ohnezeit, *Zwischen 'schärfster Opposition'* (2011), 51.

[34] See Jackisch, *Pan-German League* (2012), 152–53.

money and mobilization, resulted in the DNVP's extreme porousness to organizational influence by grassroots radicals, giving them easier access to power.

This vulnerability was already seen in 1924 and 1925 even during the DNVP's period of "successful" moderation, a period in which ominous indications of splintering emerged due precisely to this organizational weakness. Further, this prepared the ground for the party's eventual decomposition in 1928. In particular, as mentioned in the last chapter, the precariousness of the party's apparent coherence was illustrated by the near "capture" of the DNVP campaign agenda in fall 1924 by the rapidly expanding currency revaluation movement, led by various associations such as the "Mortgage and Savings-account Protection Association."[35] There were over 30 million German small investors with savings accounts who had been especially hard hit with the German inflation in the early 1920s.[36] This diverse and disgruntled social base prompted the formation of an increasingly well-organized movement claiming to speak for the German *Mittelstand*, which culminated in the national *Sparerbund für das Deutsche Reich* (Saver's Association for the German Reich). This group had the specific aim of ending repayment of loans and mortgages in devalued currency for all those who had lost money in the inflation. Facing the prospect of new single-issue political parties springing up to push this issue and lacking its own resources, the DNVP leveraged the resources of these vociferous groups and embraced their agenda in the December 1924 election – the DNVP promised unrealistic and full revaluation and even placed movement leaders on its party list. While aiding at election-tine, this alliance ended poorly. By July 1925, the DNVP was now in government and made concessions on its promises, fracturing the heterogeneous coalition and hemorrhaging the electoral support upon which it had relied at its peak.[37]

This indicated a basic organizational fragility in the DNVP and also provided an opening for other groups, in part explaining the DNVP's election performance in 1928.[38] In particular, with a party in which authority was still found at the local level, it was both harder for a party to hold together and easier for Pan-Germans to target it. As with all pressure groups and all political

---

[35] On this movement, see Jones, "Inflation, Revaluation, and the Crisis of Middle-Class Politics: A Study in the Dissolution of the German Party System, 1923–28" (1979).

[36] The figure 30 million small investors is reported in Jones, "Inflation, Revaluation, and the Crisis of Middle-Class Politics: A Study in the Dissolution of the German Party System, 1923–28" (1979): 148.

[37] In particular, rather than the one hundred percent revaluation, the July 1925 bill gave 15–25 percent revaluation on private debt and 0–12.5 percent revaluation on public debt. See discussion in Maier, *Recasting Bourgeois Europe* (1975), 489–94.

[38] The emergence of new splinter groups on the right sprang from this episode, as did a similar compromise the DNVP made over tariff policy in 1925, which sparked the emergence of competing farmers' leagues and organizational fragmentation.

parties, capturing *local* and provincial "peripheral organizations" manned by local party activists was more viable than it would have been to go after upper echelons of the elected national party leadership.[39] Moreover, in this particular case, there was a pre-existing ideological affinity between the grassroots in many areas of Germany and the Pan-German League. The local and provincial party bodies were always short of financial and staffing resources; and, because the DNVP, unlike the SPD, lacked an integrated media structure in local communities across Germany, access to Hugenberg's vast network could serve as a "substitute."

The DNVP was thus a highly attractive target for outside groups; as local party structures had significant influence over the center, their capture could enormously benefit them. After all, these accessible local units possessed direct *de jure* control over the selection of the party chairman and the party executive (*Vorstand*) as well as *de facto* control, in many instances, over candidate selection. This was no complicated, circuitous path of influence: loosely coupled organizational rules indeed paved a quick and clear path to power for local activists. Taken together, the low costs and large payoffs of capture made the DNVP a textbook case of a loosely coupled party, an easy target.[40]

RULES FOR CONSERVATIVE RADICALS: SUBTERRANEAN STRATEGIES OF RADICAL TAKEOVER

Neither structural vulnerability of the party organization nor the election losses made the radical takeover of the DNVP inevitable. Rather, an awareness of the radicals' conscious strategy is necessary to understand the rapid fall of conservative moderation. While the moderate Reichstag group appeared to entrench itself in power between 1924 and 1928, radical insurgents were inventing and gradually implementing a series of less visible but highly impactful long-run strategies of recovery.[41] This set of "rules for conservative radicals" weakened the foundations of moderate legitimacy from *within*, laying the groundwork for a far-right comeback, and the vote on October 20, 1928,

---

[39] This insight is consistent with a diverse set of literature, ranging from Selznick, *Organizational Weapon* (1952), 113–224.

[40] Systematic data on Pan-German League membership of Verein chairman is not available. However, one analyst notes that a majority of the provincial association chairman who were the strongest supporters of Hugenberg's chairmanship (seventeen provincial associations) were also leading figures on the Pan-German league, evidence of the interpenetration of the two groups. See Holzbach, *System Hugenberg* (1981), 241.

[41] This strategy of pursuing subterranean or slow-moving institutional change resonates with broader theories of institutional change developed by Pierson, *Politics in Time* (2004); Thelen, *How Institutions Evolve: The Political Economy of Skills in Germany, Britain, the United States, and Japan* (2004); and Wolfgang Streeck and Kathleen Thelen, "Introduction: Institutional Change in Advanced Political Economies," in *Beyond Continuity*, ed. Kathleen Thelen and Wolfgang Streeck (Oxford: Oxford University Press, 2005), 1–39.

was only the last step of a deliberate and highly sophisticated strategy of radical takeover. The plan was tentatively launched in 1925, when the DNVP appeared to be firmly in the hands of relative moderates, and fully activated in 1927, a full year before Hugenberg became party chairman.

The specifics of the internal takeover plans are reconstructed in the work of Barry Jackisch, who identifies new historical source material in the executive committee meeting minutes of the Pan-German League as well as in the private papers and correspondence of many of the actors involved.[42] The plans to takeover were outlined in part in several critical memos from Heinrich Class,[43] and they include different tactics of "organizational combat" and working "from below," which uncannily shared qualities with the Leninist strategy of organizational colonization, representing the effort of a minority or "political loser" to alter the balance of power in its political party.[44] Drawing on memos cited by Jackisch and general actions of the party, we can reconstruct four key elements:

- Shaping public opinion via a centralized network of local and regional press outlets to bolster allies and undercut legitimacy of "moderate" rivals within the DNVP
- Channeling financial resources and industrial resources to allies
- Colonizing local and provincial party positions with insurgent allies
- Shaping provincial candidate lists for Reichstag elections

The architects of this strategy were Heinrich Class and Alfred Hugenberg. Class was the leader of the Pan-German League (*Alldeutscher Verband*, or ADV), an extra-party pressure group founded in 1891 that reached a peak of 38,000 members in 1921 and had long allied itself with the DNVP.[45] Hugenberg was a former civil servant who was also cofounder of the Pan-German League in 1891, member of the board of directors at Krupp, and cofounder of the National Industrial Association (RDI) as well as a series of other overlapping steel and mining companies and association boards based in

---

[42] Jackisch, *Pan-German League* (2012), 151.

[43] Among the several memos, the most important is dated November 26/27, 1927, and outlined by Barry Jackisch (*The Pan-German League*, 2012, 151) as a "set of guidelines" or a "blueprint" to help League members "set to work with the greatest zeal" to aid Hugenberg's "takeover of the party and the Reichstag delegation" [Class' phrase]. The guidelines included five key tactics: (1) Pan-German members are encouraged to take on a more active role in DNVP regional associations to shape candidate selection; (2) the Pan-German League will not approve of DNVP candidates who had taken stances counter to its expectations; (3) the Pan-German League will not support DNVP candidates who had taken stances counter to its expectations; (4) the Pan-German League will insist MPs maintain close contact to local associations, and if necessary, against Reichstag leadership; and (5) the Pan-German League insists on an ideological requirement that all candidates must be "ready to fight the parliamentary system."

[44] On this strategy in a Leninist context, see Selznick, *Organizational Weapon* (1952).

[45] See Johannes Leicht, *Heinrich Class, 1868–1953: Die politische Biografie eines Alldeutschen* (Paderborn: Ferdinand Schoeningh Verlag, 2012).

the Ruhr region.[46] Together they formed a formidable duo. Both Class and Hugenberg were "organization men" and insurgent political entrepreneurs, characterized by an absence of charisma, and instead for organizational effectiveness and their "indispensability" to a complex right-wing network of organizations, firms, media outlets, and groups.[47]

Endowed with vast organizational resources, Class's Pan-German League had long pushed for German colonial expansion and played a critical role in making racism socially acceptable to Weimar's political elite. However, by the late 1920s, the mass movement organization had begun to give way to even more virulent groups.[48] By contrast, Hugenberg's clout had been increasing since before the end of the First World War, but picked up pace beginning in the 1920s. In addition to his industry connections, he had made a shrewd and profoundly modern discovery, unprecedented in the history of German conservatism: "that sporadic attempts to influence the electorate only during election years... had been inefficient and ineffective";[49] and *that greater coordination in systematically shaping political opinion through the media* could be the best defense against socialism.

Thus, Hugenberg, cooperating in part with Class and others, used his sway with Ruhr industrialists such as Krupp to secure investors and construct a right-leaning media empire. Hugenberg's operation would eventually be based on three pillars: a major advertising firm (*Allgemeine Anzeigen GmBH*); the largest private news agency in Germany, to which 50 percent of German newspapers, mostly local and regional, had subscriptions (*Telegraphen-Union*); and a major publishing house that owned four prominent newspapers and eighteen magazines (Scherl GmbH).[50] Yet, in the 1920s, with the intensification of Hugenberg's nationalism and antidemocratic sentiment, he departed company from even his Ruhr backers by being one of only three opponents on the most

---

[46] The following account of Hugenberg draws primarily from Leopold, *Alfred Hugenberg* (1977); Holzbach, *System Hugenberg* (1981); Daniel Gossel, *Medien und Politik in Deutschland und den USA: Kontrolle, Konflikt und Kooperation vom 18. bis zum frühen 20. Jahrhundert* (Stuttgart: Franz Steiner Verlag, 2010).

[47] These attributes fit perfectly a particular leadership style, identified by Ansell and Fish, "The Art of Being Indispensable: Noncharismatic Personalism and Contemporary Political Parties" (1999).

[48] For some recent interventions on the ADV in Weimar, in addition to the indispensible Jackisch, *Pan-German League* (2012), see Rainer Hering, *Konstruierte Nation: der Alldeutsche Verband, 1890 bis 1939* (Hamburg: Christians, 2003); Rainer Hering, "Realms of leadership and residues of social mobilization: The Pan-German League, 1918–1933," in *The German Right in the Weimar Republic*, ed. Larry Eugene Jones (New York: Berghahn Books, 2014), 108–33; and Bjorn Hofmeister, "Continuity and change on the German right: The Pan-German League and Nazism, 1918–1939," in *The German Right in the Weimar Republic*, ed. Larry Eugene Jones (New York: Berghahn Books, 2014), 134–64.

[49] Leopold, *Alfred Hugenberg* (1977), 5.

[50] This summary of Hugenberg's "three pillars" draws from the review essay by Karl-Heinz Janßen, "Who is Hugenberg? Ein verspätetes, aber immer noch aktuelles Porträt," *Die Zeit*, March 6, 1970.

important national industrial association, the League of German Industry, RDI (*Reichsverband der deutschen Industrie*) presidium to vote against supporting the Dawes Plan, which would benefit industry; he instead joined forces with the Pan-German League to advocate for changes in the DNVP itself.[51] The two men, Class and especially Hugenberg, were perfectly situated to operate within the ideologically fraught and organizationally permeable DNVP.[52]

The pair's overlapping organizational machinery was put to work from 1924 to 1927, while the moderate faction of the DNVP was still dominant, with the relatively modest goal of altering the party's course now that it was in government. Indeed, it was only after January 1927, in reaction to the DNVP's entry into the fourth Marx Cabinet, that a full-blown strategy of organizational takeover was implemented. Before then, initially without Hugenberg's direct aid, Class and his Pan-German League experimented with different techniques of pressuring the DNVP to alter their stances on key issues. For example, in October 1924, the Pan-German League's executive committee considered founding a new political party but instead decided to push for a "cleansing" of the party, focusing on "defeating leading figures of the party's moderate faction by undermining their support in the provinces."[53] This, it was argued, could be done via "naming names in public through published letters, newspaper articles, etc." that would add pressure to the DNVP parliamentary group.[54] The idea of influencing the party through the control of the candidate selection process was also broached for the first time. While the party lists for each of the thirty-six provincial election districts were de jure in the hands of party leaders, some scrambling in the fall of 1924 to secure favorable spots for local candidates loyal to Pan-German ideology suggests the beginning of a more coherent strategy. Because the December 1924 elections were around the corner, however, the effort had limited initial success.[55]

---

[51] Hugenberg's ideological roots were both nationalist and antisocialist. Before 1900, he had served as a civil servant as part of the Prussian Settlement Commission, a Prussian government effort to alter the ethnic balance by encouraging ethnic German farmers to buy up land from Poles in Posen and West Prussia. And, while working for Krupp after 1909, he was a strong advocate of loyal company unions, and enemy of Christian socialist and Social Democratic-leaning unions. Taken together, by 1909, Hugenberg was already a strong antidemocratic and antisocialist ideologue, laying the groundwork for his later political evolution. See Leopold, *Alfred Hugenberg* (1977), 1–5.

[52] Hugenberg's rise in the DNVP supports the main theoretical claims about the conditions under which noncharismatic personalistic leadership styles emerge; see Ansell and Fish, "The Art of Being Indispensible: Noncharismatic Personalism and Contemporary Political Parties" (1999). They assert political parties are wracked by intense ideological and territorial cleavages.

[53] The process of "cleansing" ("*Reinigung*") is used frequently in these descriptions. See original sources cited by Jackisch, *Pan-German League* (2012), 109.

[54] See archival sources cited by Jackisch, *Pan-German League* (2012), 110.

[55] There was one exception, which indicated that the cumulative crush of the radical pressure from the group was increasing in intensity. In the fall of 1924, after the passage of the Dawes Plan bill, Party Chairman Hergt received the resolution of eighteen local DNVP associations calling for his

This continued even under the new government in January 1925, with the DNVP in the cabinet under Chancellor Luther and as Foreign Minister Stresemann pushed for negotiations with the Allies. Class used press agitation and an informational campaign to discredit Stresemann and compel DNVP cabinet members to abandon their affiliation with the government's policies. The language was nearly always venomous, frequently calling Stresemann and his supporters "spineless" and "traitors."[56]

Again, however, the focus was less on replacing the leadership team than it was on altering the party's stance on issues and its support of the Weimar regime. As Jackisch describes it, the Pan-German League "launched an extensive public campaign... placing renewed pressure on the DNVP moderate leadership" with scathing condemnations in a series of dependable press outlets.[57] The goal, however, remained limited to thwarting the passage of the Locarno Treaties and, perhaps, convincing the DNVP to withdraw from the government. Each week, articles appeared in the *Deutsche Zeitung* criticizing Stresemann and the DNVP moderates. Indeed, the growing acrimony led party leaders to ban the newspapers' reporters, normally reliable advocates of the DNVP, from DNVP events altogether.[58]

In addition to informational campaigns, the Pan-German League also organized public rallies, including several large ones in Saxony, with the purpose of adding more coercive impetus on DNVP Reichstag members "from below." The Pan-German League overlapped at the local level with DNVP *Vereine*, leaning forcibly on those party leaders who aimed to carry out any transactional politics of compromise. The historian Hermann Beck describes the situation in the fall of 1925, as the new coalition government turned to the Locarno Treaties:

Never had the chasm between the German National Cabinet ministers, who favored acceptance of Locarno, and the party organization, which vehemently rejected it, been deeper. On 23 October 1925 the DNVP executive committee and chairmen of its Land Associations declared that Locarno Treaty was unacceptable. Resistance from the rank and file members... was enormous, and Land and Kreis associations were inundated with threats of irate party members to resign. By ratifying the Treaty, critics argued, the government acquiesced in the "robbery" of German territory.[59]

---

resignation, which took place on October 23, 1924. However, outright radical victory was elusive. Hergt remained prominent in the party (later serving as Minister in Marx's 1927 government); and his replacement as the chairman of the Reichstag group was announced to be Martin Schiele, who was regarded as being from the moderate grouping and affiliated with what then was a more pragmatic agricultural pressure group, the *Reichslandbund*. Schiele supported joining Chancellor Luther's government in January 1925 and would also serve as Cabinet minister in Marx's 1927 government. Despite being a founder member, Schiele would eventually exit the DNVP in 1930 once Hugenberg's domination of the party took its toll.

[56] See Jackisch, *Pan-German League* (2012), 118.
[57] Jackisch, *Pan-German League* (2012), 116.   [58] Jackisch, *Pan-German League* (2012), 122.
[59] Beck, *Fateful Alliance* (2008), 45.

The strategy began to bear fruit once the Pan-German League's campaign successfully drove the Reichstag delegation, against the wishes of the party leaders in the cabinet, to abandon the government. This move reduced the party's parliamentary leader, Martin Schiele, to a tearful public address in which he said his party's leadership had been "overwhelmed by a tidal wave" from the provincial associations.[60] On the other hand, despite the growing power of manufactured mobilization "from below," the impact of this strategy was in fact limited: the Locarno Treaties after all were signed by Germany despite the DNVP's withdrawal from government, and Germany joined the League of Nations against the radicals' wishes. All of this was implemented, like the Dawes Plan, but now *without* any DNVP role in the government to shape it. Jackisch notes the irony that "the DNVP gained nothing from its withdrawal from the government."[61] Indeed, the DNVP moderates were still in charge of the party.

Thus, in the wake of this strategy's failure, a new strategy evolved that included a full-scale assault on the DNVP's leadership coalition, though it did not emerge until 1926–1927. After Class's futile attempt in January 1926 to convince President von Hindenburg to support Hugenberg's appointment to chancellor, attention turned to a different approach: working from within to "take over" the DNVP.[62] The starting point for this was a pivotal meeting in January 1926 between Class and Hugenberg at a spa where Hugenberg was vacationing, during which the two came to an understanding that the Pan-German League would support Hugenberg's effort to dislodge Kuno von Westarp from the DNVP chairmanship.[63] This close alliance, which would culminate in Hugenberg's election to party chairman in October 1928, had begun.

Their first undertaking over the course of 1927 was to reintroduce the anti-moderate propaganda campaign in Pan-German press outlets (e.g., *Alldeutsche Blätter*) and the wider national press as well, though primarily targeting local and regional press given Germany's highly decentralized media market. Hugenberg's media conglomerate owned fourteen major newspapers, but this was a relatively small portion of the 3,000 newspapers printed in Germany in the mid-1920s.[64] More important was the fact that Hugenberg owned the

---

[60] See quote and source: Jackisch, *Pan-German League* (2012), 126–27.

[61] Jackisch continues, "The party lost its ability to affect the course of further foreign policy negotiation from within the government. Furthermore... the DNVP was again faced with an internal feud that threatened to divide it even further. By bowing to the radicals, the party went back over the opposition with very little to show for its roughly nine months in power." Jackisch, *Pan-German League* (2012), 127–28.

[62] The phrase "take over" is Class's own in a description of his plans with Hugenberg. See Jackisch (*Pan-German League*, 2012, 138–146) for the most thorough discussion of the flawed "Class Putsch." Critical for our purposes is that the putsch demonstrates that Class and Hugenberg came to the strategy of "party takeover" from within only after several alternatives had failed.

[63] Class's memoirs, cited by Jackisch, *Pan-German League* (2012), 135.

[64] Leopold, *Alfred Hugenberg* (1977), 13.

largest and only news agency, or wire service, in Germany, which was also the
semi-official wire service of the government. His *Telegraphen-Union* fed local
and regional newspapers with fully written news stories with a rightward slant
written by 250 correspondents at thirty branches spread across Germany and
the world.[65] Given the absence of a centralized DNVP newspaper (on the model
of the SPD's *Vorwärts*), Hugenberg's media empire became a major shaper of
public opinion throughout Germany.[66]

Second, beginning in the mid-1920s, Hugenberg leveraged his
indispensability as campaign contribution broker to the financially strapped
DNVP to shape the party.[67] He had thus fused his longstanding position as the
chief contact to the Ruhr industrialists with his new role as partner in the Pan-
German effort to transform the DNVP.[68] He could help finance local and
provincial party associations, which were short of revenue especially after the
early 1920s, and in turn could channel funds to individual candidates' districts
during campaign times. Hence, Hugenberg used his unusual position, in Class'
words, to "take over" the party.[69]

In 1928, for example, the year Hugenberg launched his pursuit of the party
chairmanship, the records of his media conglomerate, *Scherl GmbH*, include
evidence of an account containing 700,000 marks to be "freely... used to
patronize rightist movements of all kinds."[70] Additionally, Scherl GmbH had
a special election campaign fund of 300,000 marks to channel to candidates he
wanted to support.[71] Also, Hugenberg helped arrange multiple special election
funds for the DNVP, including one by Ruhr industrialists called "*Westliche
Gruppe*" that raised 487,000 marks for the May 1928 DNVP election
campaign and included donations from Thyssen and other economic
interests.[72] If we exclude the funds for "rightist movements of all kinds" and
simply add together Hugenberg's own election campaign contributions to the
DNVP in 1928 (300,000 marks) with those he arranged from others (487,000
marks), then what share of DNVP total campaign expenditures were under the
control of Hugenberg? Complete DNVP election spending data are not
available to get a sense of the relative importance of these funds to the
campaign. Hugenberg's contributions have always been shrouded in a great

[65] See Heidi Tworek, "Magic Connections: German News Agencies and Global News Networks,
1905–1945," *Enterprise & Society* 15, no. 4 (2014): 672–86.
[66] For an overview, see Ohnezeit, *Zwischen 'schärfster Opposition'* (2011), 83–87. See Holzbach,
System Hugenberg (1981).
[67] Until the early 1920s, the traditional prewar era vehicle for funding parties that furthered
industrial interests, the *Kommission zur Sammlung, Verwaltung und Verwendung des
Industriellen Wahlfonds* ("Commission for the Industrial Election Fund") aided a variety of
right-leaning parties, including the DNVP. But for all parties, the inflation devastated financing,
leaving figures like Hugenberg in an elevated position from the mid 1920s onwards.
[68] Holzbach, *System Hugenberg* (1981).   [69] Jackisch, *Pan-German League* (2012), 151.
[70] Leopold, *Alfred Hugenberg* (1977), 40.   [71] Leopold, *Alfred Hugenberg* (1977), 40.
[72] Ohnezeit, *Zwischen 'schärfster Opposition'* (2011), 81.

deal of mystery. However, we can try estimate the scale of Hugenberg's donations as we see that the largest German party, the SPD, reported in its transparent annual yearbook that its total party campaign expenditures – for both its central and local associations – were 2,569,612 M.[73] If we assume that the DNVP election budget was not larger than the SPD's – a safe assumption given the smaller size of the party – then the DNVP was reliant on a single individual for *at least 30 percent of its campaign costs!*[74]

The third and fourth strategies of party takeover consisted of colonizing the personnel of the DNVP's local and provincial associations with loyalists and then shaping candidate lists to create a grassroots base dedicated to Hugenberg and his aspirations to leadership. Since Class and Hugenberg knew the Pan-German position was weakest in the Reichstag, they instead sought the soft underbelly of the party's local associations; and, as the chairmen of the provincial associations played a significant role in the selection of party chairman, their efforts exerted there were not wasted.

Ohnezeit and Jackisch have both found examples of intervention in candidate selection and in local affairs that shaped who sat on the local party *Vereine*.[75] In May 1928, correspondence between party chairman von Westarp and Hugenberg, who, formally speaking, was only a single Reichstag delegate, indicates that Hugenberg threatened to withdraw his financial assistance entirely unless the party's candidate lists reflected his preferences.[76] While Westarp challenged Hugenberg's demands then, in a separate case in Saxony, Hugenberg insisted that his Pan-German ally Paul Bang be placed high on the 1928 DNVP electoral list in Eastern Saxony, in order to install an important ally and alter the profile of the Saxon party *Verein*.[77] Indeed, against the wishes of leading Saxon DNVP moderates such as Kurt Philipp, Bang was elected, provoking Philipp's resignation of chairman of the *Dresden-Bautzen* (East Saxony) Verein. Walter Rademacher, an ally of Philipp's, wrote a letter to von Westarp criticizing the "brutal snub" of the vast majority of Saxon industrialists, which was a "thinly veiled attempt to increase Pan-German influence in the party."[78]

The consequences of Hugenberg's pursuit of a loyal base began to pay off in a major showdown in July 1928. In the face of the electoral loss and the debate it

---

[73] *Jahrbuch der deutschen Sozialdemokratie*, 1929, 173 as cited by Pollock, *Money and Politics Abroad* (1932), 216.

[74] For an explanation of why this is a safe assumption, see Pollock, *Money and Politics Abroad* (1932), 213–17. John Leopold (1972, p. 17) also notes that Hugenberg negotiated exclusive rights to collect funds from the iron and coal industries (*Wahlfond des Berliner Kuratoriums*), putting himself in a critical position from which to pressure von Westarp.

[75] See, e.g., Jackisch, *Pan-German League* (2012), 152; Ohnezeit, *Zwischen 'schärfster Opposition'* (2011), 415–16.

[76] N. L. Westarp, Gaertringen (VN 67) "Hugenberg to Westarp" May 6, 1928; "Westarp to Hugenberg" May 8, 1928, as cited by Ohnezeit, *Zwischen 'schärfster Opposition'* (2011), 82.

[77] Jackisch, *Pan-German League* (2012), 152.   [78] Jackisch, *Pan-German League* (2012), 152.

sparked, in no small part fomented by Hugenberg-dominated local right-wing press, fifteen of the thirty-seven DNVP district organizations supported Hugenberg's effort to discredit von Westarp at the July *Parteivertretung* meeting; they all then dramatically resigned.[79] Following this, Hugenberg deftly raised a different issue entirely – "reform of the party organization" – publishing an article in his paper *Berliner Lokal-Anzeiger* entitled *"Block oder Brei?"* ("Party Bloc or Mush?"), in which he made the case for a reorganization and centralization of the party. This proposition appealed to local and provincial associations who felt ignored by the Reichstag group. The battle for the party chairmanship intensified, and a proposal that a triumvirate of leaders run the party was floated and rejected.

Finally, in October 1928, Hugenberg won over a sufficient number of provincial associations to be elected party chairman unopposed. Now, with the party leadership in the hands of a Pan-German leader, the profile of the DNVP transformed. Over the next two years, severe disunity followed as DNVP "pragmatists" abandoned or were forced out of the Reichstag delegation; previously loyal interest groups, like the agrarian *Reichslandbund*, began to look for party allies elsewhere; and election appeals sharpened. By 1930, the DNVP, once the largest party in the Reichstag and the largest non-socialist party in Germany, had dramatically shrunk, winning only 7 percent of the vote. The third and final phase of the party's evolution was underway.

THE SLIDE: FROM "RADICAL TAKEOVER" OF CONSERVATISM TO DEMOCRATIC BREAKDOWN

One might imagine that the radical takeover and subsequent disintegration of the strongest party of the electoral right could be "good news" for social democrats, opening space for a stable social democratic hegemony or, at the very least, an enduring non-conservative government. However, when center-right conservative political parties disappear, the results can be dangerous for democracy, as the trajectory of Germany's DNVP makes abundantly clear. Here, the absence of a robust center-right – when combined with severe economic downturn after 1929, flawed constitutional structures, and other factors cited in the last chapter – made the political system susceptible to what by 1928 was now an inexorable *slide* to democratic breakdown.

The death of German democracy proceeded in two stages: the first began in March 1930 with President Hindenburg's extreme concentration of executive power via the creation of Heinrich Brüning's "presidential cabinet." This subtle "suspensive coup from above" reduced the Reichstag to a nearly

---

[79] See Jones, "German Conservatism at the Crossroads" (2009): 153. For a listing of the districts loyal to Hugenberg, see Holzbach, *System Hugenberg* (1981), 243. For a listing of the districts loyal to Westarp, see Holzbach, *System Hugenberg* (1981), 242.

impotent body.[80] The second stage, of a different nature altogether, began in September 1930. Rather than coming from above, the challenge emerged via elections and was initiated with the NSDAP's Reichstag electoral breakthrough in September 1930, culminating in Adolf Hitler's appointment to Chancellor in January 1933.[81] The DNVP was a decisive factor in both periods, its own structural weakness leaving the regime more vulnerable to the disastrous political effects of economic crisis than it would have been otherwise.

THE STARTING POINT: DNVP ORGANIZATIONAL PURIFICATION AND SCHISM

A "proximate" precondition for democratic breakdown was the 1928 victory of Alfred Hugenberg over his competitors for control of the DNVP. The change in leadership prompted a radicalization of the party that resulted in organizational schism and breakdown. If moderates had retained control of the party in 1928, then the Weimar regime may have continued to "muddle through," as other democracies did through similar economic crises, and as it had done itself *until* 1928, despite possessing the same problematic constitutional structures since 1918 and 1919.[82]

However, following the triumph of Hugenberg's faction within the DNVP, history ran a starkly different course. Once Hugenberg became party chairman

---

[80] This stage displayed the hallmarks of a classic "suspensive coup" model of democratic breakdown (Capoccia, *Defending Democracy*, 2005), in this instance through quasi-constitutional means that were more subtle than an outright military coup but that nonetheless established a quasi-authoritarian, non-parliamentary regime without elections that restricted freedoms and fundamentally departed from previous constitutional practice. Some scholarly disagreement centers on whether Brüning was acting constitutionally and in fact was attempting to "save" German democracy from a period of intense economic and political crisis, e.g., Conze, "Brünings Politik unter dem Druck der großen Krise" (1964); Patch, *Heinrich Brüning* (1998). However, whatever the content of Brüning's intentions, the consequences of the regime's actions initiated a slide toward authoritarianism that became difficult to reverse.

[81] This second stage of democratic breakdown is often regarded as a paradigmatic instance of a "legal revolution" in which an anti-system political party utilizes formal electoral channels to dismantle democracy "from below" (Bracher, *Die Auflösung der Weimarer Republik*, 1955). This view severely understates the level of social violence involved with the Nazi ascension to power (Richard Evans, *The Coming of the Third Reich* (New York: Penguin Press, 2003); Beck, *Fateful Alliance* (2008)). However, intense violence coupled with an anti-system party's victories at the ballot box were the defining features of this stage of democratic breakdown.

[82] My account does not aim to exclude the importance of factors such as the extent of economic crisis and constitutional structures; my aim is more modest: to show that the same set of factors emphasized in my long-run account of democratization going back to the 1830s played out in the 1920s and 1930s in Germany as well. That said, the fact that other political systems with proportional representation (e.g., Sweden, Belgium) survived with their democracies intact does call into question the mechanistic view that certain formal political institutions fated democracy to die in some places but not in others.

of a captured conservative party, right-wing radicals sought, often with only a vague conception of the consequences for the political system as a whole, to consolidate their relatively insecure hold on power *within the party* through a series of ideological "purity tests," forcing out the remaining moderates. Rather than easily moving the whole party to the right to appeal to a different "right wing" voter, the internal policies pursued between 1928 and 1930 created deep organizational factionalism and splintering, shrinking the party, and undermining the political regime as a whole.[83]

To fully appreciate the link between the DNVP's internal radicalization and the collapse of democracy in Germany, we must elaborate how this process of organizational schism and disintegration unfolded. After four years of pragmatic rapprochement (1924–28) with the Weimar political regime, the DNVP radicalization followed a predictable pattern, given how political parties faced with waning enthusiasm tend to become preoccupied with "purifying" their ranks in order to renew organizational fervor.[84] Hugenberg consolidated his position in the DNVP via a dual strategy of organizational reform and internal "purification." Immediately, upon being elected in October 1928, for example, Hugenberg altered basic features of the party with the aim of bolstering his power.[85] In line with recommendations in his 1928 essay "Bloc oder Brei?" Hugenberg weakened the party executive (*Vorstand*) vis-à-vis the party leader and formally sidelined the Reichstag group from its central place in party decision-making. These party reforms disempowered prominent Reichstag leaders and former cabinet ministers, such as von Keudell and political representatives of the old "iron-rye" coalition from western Germany and eastern Prussia, who, despite real economic interests, were slowly coming to terms with the democratic political regime. Further, the party's executive committee was expanded to incorporate the "grassroots" by including chairmen of all forty-four district organizations, half of whom, not coincidentally, were replaced between 1928 and 1929 with Hugenberg loyalists.[86]

---

[83] As I will spell out below, those ejected moderates of the formerly dominant coalition exited to try to found their own party, but the collective-action problems of rapidly building a party "from scratch" were substantial, leaving chiefly organizational disarray on the right in its wake.

[84] The most important theoretical account of the issue of organizational schism is found in Christopher Ansell, *Between Solidarity and Schism* (Cambridge: Cambridge University Press, 2001). Ansell develops a general model that accords well with the DNVP. He argues that certain types of political parties are always more prone to organizational factionalism and schism in certain moments in their organizational development than others. He notes that when "groups held together by a sense of common identity" exit their period of founding and enter a period of routinization and moderation, they tend to confront internal resistance to the inevitable compromises made by the leadership, triggering schism motivated by ideological concerns and expressed via a "rhetoric of purity."

[85] Mergel, "Scheitern des deutschen Tory-Konservatismus" (2003): 346–47.

[86] Chanady, "Disintegration of the German National Peoples' Party" (1967): 84.

In addition to power-consolidating organizational reforms, Hugenberg sought to "purify" the party ideologically by ejecting experienced MPs who had cooperated with previous party leaders, and by taking polarizing public stances to force out all disloyal elements. In particular, between 1929 and 1931, Hugenberg orchestrated several intensely provocative public campaigns on divisive and symbolic issues, such as a national referendum on the Young Plan of 1929, which he co-organized with a nationalist committee (*Reichsausschuss*) of right-wing groups that included the NSDAP and the Steel Helmets.[87] His proposed law, the so-called "Freedom Law," would have required that any government official who supported repayment of reparations be arrested. By placing the item on the national agenda, the "Freedom Law" was intentionally inflammatory, seeking to mobilize the far right even as it failed to garner sufficient approval for passage.

Indeed, the goal was not merely to block passage of the Young Plan; it was intended also to push out internal opponents within the DNVP. Similarly, in 1931, this same collection of right-wing forces proposed another national referendum – that also was eventually defeated – to disband the Prussian state parliament simply because of the Social Democratic domination there. While the two national referendum proposals may have not garnered popular majorities in the broader electorate, they did successfully achieve their second purpose as ideological "purity tests" to dislodge moderates within the DNVP's own ranks.

As Hugenberg championed the "Freedom Law" in the fall of 1929, four leading DNVP moderates in the Reichstag – former Interior Minister Walter von Keudell, party manager Hans-Erdmann von Lindeiner-Wildau, Moritz Klönne, and Otto Hoetzsch – publicly announced their opposition to the extreme elements of the proposals, triggering a momentous intraparty fight.[88] When the bill came before the Reichstag, which it had to before passing on to the stage of national referendum, Kuno von Westarp, still chairman of the DNVP parliamentary group, tried to bridge the gap between the two groups, but his efforts failed. On November 30, 1929, the day of the Reichstag vote, thirteen DNVP Reichstag MPs, including the leading figure, Gottfried Reinhold Treviranus, challenged Hugenberg's leadership by not voting, and three MPs publicly attacked the party leadership on the issue. This prompted Hugenberg's call on December 3 for a DNVP executive committee meeting to initiate expulsion proceedings against his most vocal critics.[89]

By December 4, 1929, after vitriolic internal battles, the outcome was clear. Hoped-for grassroots opposition to Hugenberg failed to consolidate, and instead, twelve leading DNVP MPs, including Gottfried Treviranus, resigned from the party, and Kuno von Westarp resigned his leadership position of the

[87] Mergel, "Scheitern des deutschen Tory-Konservatismus" (2003): 350.
[88] Beck, *Fateful Alliance* (2008), 56.
[89] Jones, "German Conservatism at the Crossroads" (2009): 162–63.

parliamentary group.[90] The collection of secessionists, all relative moderates –
including, as Beck describes it, "senior civil servants, diplomats, and conservative
intellectuals, who were prepared to compromise with other parties in order to
have a voice in politics" – went on to form a new party led by Treviranus
in January 1930, which would become the Conservative People's Party
(*Konservative Volkspartei*, or KVP).[91] The fate of this group, as we will see
below, exposed the hazards of a fractured right for the stability of democracy.

A similar but even more extensive breach came in July 1930, four months after
Brüning's "cabinet without parties" came into power. While the SPD had good
reasons to be critical of Brüning's policies, which sought to balance budget deficits
in the midst of economic contraction, the DNVP joined the Nazi Party and the
KPD in adopting an intransigent line against Brüning's government. The aim was
the destruction of the political regime at all costs. After a series of contentious
face-offs between the DNVP and Brüning's conservative cabinet beginning
in April 1930, in July 1930 Hugenberg attempted to enforce the *Führerprinzip*
conception of leadership outlined in his "Bloc oder Brei?" manifesto onto the
DNVP by insisting his party embrace a no-confidence vote against the
government. In reaction, another twenty-five DNVP representatives, aligned
chiefly with agricultural interests that would benefit from Brüning's proposed
subsidies, revolted against the party for the final break, even prompting the nearly
always-conciliatory von Westarp to leave the party. Combined with
the November 1929 schism, this departure left the party a shell of its former self.

Hugenberg regarded both of these major fractures, in historian Larry Eugene
Jones's words, as "less a leadership crisis than a purge by which the DNVP had
cleansed itself of unreliable elements."[92] After the 1929 rupture, Paul Bang
summarized the pro-Hugenberg sentiment when he wrote to an ally, "Thank
God, they are now outside!"[93] And one sympathetic newspaper, the *Deutsche
Zeitung*, reported the "purification" of the party.[94] In 1930, the DNVP's main
leaders had been ousted and electoral support reduced to a mere 7 percent – the
National Socialists received over 17 percent, their first big breakthrough.
Hugenberg may have been the emperor of his party, *but it was now
a miniature kingdom that he ruled*. As the DNVP radicalized, it moved to the
right; but because of its organizational weakness, rather than resolving internal
conflicts, this move provoked a counter-reaction and an internal politics of
deeper schism, fragmentation, and eventually a complete folding of the party
itself. The DNVP had simply become a less viable player in parliamentary
politics, leaving a massive gap in the German political system.

---

[90] For more details, see citations in Jones, "German Conservatism at the Crossroads" (2009): 163–64.
[91] Beck, *Fateful Alliance* (2008), 58.
[92] Jones, "German Conservatism at the Crossroads" (2009): 165.
[93] Jackisch, *Pan-German League* (2012), 165.
[94] "Reinigung!" Deutsche Zeitung December 5, 1929, cited by Jackisch, *Pan-German League* (2012), 165.

SUSPENDING DEMOCRACY: FROM DNVP WEAKNESS
TO SEMIAUTHORITARIANISM "FROM ABOVE"

It is usually argued that the end of "normal" parliamentary politics in Weimar arrived three years before Hitler came to power, when the SPD-led coalition government collapsed in March 1930.[95] There is much to this perspective for the simple reason that normal parliamentary politics were thenceforth suspended and government cabinets no longer reflected parliamentary majorities. Instead President Hindenburg picked chancellor and cabinet members – dubbed "presidential cabinets" – with little regard for the distribution of votes in the Reichstag. The traditional account of the March 1930 collapse of the SPD-led grand coalition, which included the Center Party and the two liberal parties (the DDP and the DVP), emphasizes the irreconcilable internal differences as it faced the reverberations of the American stock market crash five months earlier.[96] While the economic crisis certainly intensified the government's weakness, the grand coalition did not fall on its own. It was pushed.[97] Further, it was no accident that it was replaced with a government without parliamentary support, a semiauthoritarian "presidential cabinet." The so-called "cabinet of experts" that replaced SPD Chancellor Hermann Müller's government was formed, in Richard Evans' words, quite explicitly "with the intention of bypassing the Reichstag through the use of Hindenburg's power to rule by emergency decree."[98]

What lay behind this shift in regime? There were several causes for the failure of the Müller government in March 1930, the formation of the subsequent temporary "presidential cabinet," and then the persistence of this government past the next Reichstag elections of September 1930. The economic crisis of the Great Depression undoubtedly amplified extremist voting, pressuring establishment conservatives and even high-ranking military opponents of Nazism to attempt to re-establish political order at all costs.[99] Also, the economic downturn sharpened the budgetary crisis, providing a rationale for "stronger leadership" to impose fiscal discipline.[100] Another factor is the "power vacuum" caused by the downfall of the SPD government and the absence of a clear-cut electoral alternative after the September 1930 elections,

---

[95] Evans, *The Coming of the Third Reich* (2003), 247.
[96] Mommsen, *Rise and Fall of Weimar Democracy* (1996), 287.
[97] The discussions of the formation of a presidential cabinet among Schleicher, Hindenburg, and others began long before Müller's government's fall. Further Müller's government only fell after Hindenburg denied Müller's request to deploy an emergency decree and out of plans hatched on the right. See Mommsen, *Rise and Fall of Weimar Democracy* (1996), 287–88.
[98] Evans, *The Coming of the Third Reich* (2003), 250.
[99] Conze, "Brünings Politik unter dem Druck der großen Krise" (1964). On military views, see Gordon Craig, *The Politics of the Prussian Army, 1640–1945* (London and New York: Oxford University Press, 1964), 436.
[100] Mommsen, *Rise and Fall of Weimar Democracy* (1996), 288.

arguably explaining the "need" for a strong presidential government.[101] And, finally, there is evidence that General von Schleicher, a close advisor to President Hindenburg in these years, had long harbored conspiratorial plans of toppling the SPD government and installing a right-leaning system "above" normal party politics if necessary.[102]

Yet, at the root of all of these alternative explanations for the endurance of the "cabinet government" was the dwindling size and radicalization of the DNVP. The weakness and extremism of the Hugenberg-led party triggered all of the other factors cited above, supporting my contention that if conservative forces believe that electoral politics will permanently exclude them from government, they are more likely to reject democracy outright.

Indeed, this logic mattered in two ways. First, let us consider the weakness of the DNVP. Indeed, even before the collapse of Müller's government in March 1930, key elements in the military hierarchy (*Reichswehrministerium*) and the German Employer Association (*Vereinigung der Deutschen Arbeitgeberverbände*) were anxiously opposed to the SPD and hoped that a right-oriented elected cabinet would serve as an alternative. The discontent of high-ranking officials in the Federal Ministry of War had a predictable source: it arose from their concerns over mounting pressures to cut military budgets and ambitions to rebuild German forces, as well as the apprehension of figures such as Minister of Defense Wilhelm Groener about the growing and "destructive" appeals of National Socialism.[103] Likewise, the German Employer Association and its chairman, Ernst von Borsig, had warned DVP Finance Minister Paul Moldenhauer of its unwillingness to increase employer contributions for rapidly growing unemployment costs, a fallout of the economic slowdown.[104] Facing these pressures, General Kurt von Schleicher, along with President Hindenburg's other close informal advisors, had begun to advocate, in a not entirely unexpected way, for a new "bourgeois Right" cabinet to alternate power with the SPD.

However, there was now no easy electoral solution to implement this alteration of government. With the decay and radicalization of the DNVP, a viable right-of-center majority coalition was no longer possible. Though Schleicher was clearly no democrat, one historian has observed that he did recognize "parliamentary politics as an inescapable fact of modern politics" and strategically had long sought a united right within the parliament to balance out the SPD.[105] However, the shrunken DNVP posed a fundamental barrier to this plan. In Hans Mommsen's words, "The radicalization of the DNVP under

[101] Bracher, *Die Auflösung der Weimarer Republik* (1955), 364–88.
[102] Peter Hayes, "'A Question Mark with Epaulettes'? Kurt von Schleicher and Weimar Politics," *The Journal of Modern History* 52, no. 1 (1980): 35–65.
[103] Craig, *The Politics of the Prussian Army, 1640–1945* (1964), 433.
[104] Mommsen, *Rise and Fall of Weimar Democracy* (1996), 288.
[105] Hayes, "'A Question Mark with Epaulettes'? Kurt von Schleicher and Weimar Politics" (1980): 40.

Hugenberg dealt a severe blow to [the] strategy that Schleicher had planned with such consummate care."[106]

Indeed, after 1928, no majority right party existed to create a counterweight to the SPD. With the DNVP gaining only 14 percent of the vote in 1928, a parliamentary path to a right-leaning or even center-right parliamentary government without the Social Democrats was impossible. The splintering of the DNVP prompted by Hugenberg's post-election "purification" efforts left the party even smaller, meaning the basic building blocks of a center-right coalition government, even in simple arithmetic terms, were rapidly vanishing.[107] The result was precisely the type of paralysis and stalemate that interwar critics of parliamentary government so often pointed to when decrying parliamentary "shop-talks."[108] A related problem was that in the wake of the Young Plan's passage, Hugenberg and his now "purer" Pan-German-dominated DNVP became vocal and vitriolic opponents of their former hero, President Hindenburg, who had "betrayed" them by signing the plan. This development was a clear indication that the DNVP had become, not unlike Prussian Conservatives before 1914, *plus royaliste que le roi*.[109] The DNVP had now moved to the right even of the arch-reactionary President von Hindenburg. Mommsen reports:

For the time being, there was no alternative but to write off the possibility of concentrating the various factions on the German Right into a united political front. In light of these developments, Schleicher now began to focus his attention on a new version of the *Bürgerblock* that would depend on the confidence of the Reich President.[110]

Kurt von Schleicher's vision of a president-centered government thus was a "substitute," filling in for the lack of a viable electoral right. But Schleicher had already conceived of the idea of using a president-appointed cabinet as a replacement for a weakened DNVP as far back as 1926. Historian Eberhard Kolb cites a memo of that same year in which Schleicher advised Hindenburg that if it proved impossible to form a right-wing coalition with the DNVP, he should "appoint a government in which he had confidence, without consulting the parties" and then "with the order of dissolution ready at hand, give the government every constitutional opportunity to get a majority in

---

[106] Mommsen, *Rise and Fall of Weimar Democracy* (1996), 282.
[107] For an account of the coalitional dynamics in Germany between 1924 and 1928, see Stürmer, *Koalition und Opposition in der Weimarer Republik 1924–1928* (1967).
[108] See Kennedy, *Constitutional Failure: Carl Schmitt in Weimar* (2004); John P. McCormick, *Carl Schmitt's Critique of Liberalism: Against Politics as Technology* (Cambridge and New York: Cambridge University Press, 1997); Peter C. Caldwell, *Popular Sovereignty and the Crisis of German Constitutional Law: The Theory and Practice of Weimar Constitutionalism* (Durham: Duke University Press, 1997).
[109] See Chapter 7 above; see Retallack, *The German Right* (2006).
[110] Mommsen, *Rise and Fall of Weimar Democracy* (1996), 283.

parliament."[111] In short, we see the outlines of a strategy: if a reasonable right could not be found, a quasi-authoritarian stand-in must be developed; and, second, if that path were followed, to re-establish parliamentary rule, a moderate right had to be created since it didn't already exist.

But, it was too late. The only way of restoring parliamentary rule after Brüning's quasi-authoritarian cabinet was formed, as Schleicher's own memo revealed, was for a new government "to get [or create] a majority in parliament." It is certainly true that the attitude of the presidential cabinet's supporters – including Schleicher, Groening, Brüning, and Treviranus – toward parliamentary rule in general remained, at best, unenthusiastic. However, Brüning's biographer has argued that he actively sought a right and non-socialist parliamentary-anchored cabinet throughout 1930.[112] Further, even President Hindenburg and Schleicher recognized the benefits of working with a parliamentary majority. Richard Evans insists on the strength of the constitutional consensus and notes that even in this period "any government which tried to change the constitution in an authoritarian direction without the legitimacy afforded by the backing of a majority in the legislature would run a risk of starting a civil war."[113]

Thus, whether or not Brüning was truly interested in reinstating parliamentary government, there were evidently only two possible ways to do this independent of social democratic government: either (1) to dislodge Hugenberg from his position atop the DNVP to make it a more "governmentalist" party, or (2) to encourage the formation of an entirely new and more conciliatory right political party altogether that could be the basis of a new parliamentary majority. Reflecting these two strategies, the new "presidential" cabinet of March 1930 included two former DNVP parliamentarians. The first, former DNVP parliamentary chairman Martin Schiele, was closely aligned with agricultural interests and opposed to Hugenberg though he had not yet left the party. The second, former DNVP parliamentarian Gottfried Treviranus, was founder of the *Volkskonservative Vereinigung* (renamed after Westarp joined the party in 1930), then viewed as a real alternative to the DNVP.[114]

Evidence of the first strategy – deposing Hugenberg from DNVP leadership to forge a more governmentalist party – is reported by historian Hans Mommsen, who notes that President Hindenburg's office "with support on its flanks from heavy industry did everything in its power to strengthen the anti-Hugenberg opposition within the DNVP in the unrealistic hope that it might

[111] Cited by Eberhard Kolb, *The Weimar Republic* (Boston: Unwin Hyman, 1988), 78.
[112] Patch also indicates Brüning's willingness to discuss and seek out collaborative ventures with the SPD in 1930. See Patch, *Heinrich Brüning* (1998), 89.
[113] Evans, *The Coming of the Third Reich* (2003), 302.
[114] On the founding of the *Volkskonservative Vereinung*, see Erasmus Jonas, *Die Volkskonservativen, 1928–1933* (Droste: Düsseldorf, 1965).

still be possible to have him replaced."[115] Once Brüning was in office, this chiefly consisted of making legislative budget proposals that included agricultural subsidies, debt relief, and protective tariffs with the hope of securing the backing of the remaining agriculturalists in the DNVP Reichstag group, thus putting pressure on Hugenberg, who might otherwise oppose the new government.[116] This worked in the short run: the DNVP split on an important tax bill, with Hugenberg's faction voting against it and the so-called "Westarp" group helping to pass it. Treviranus celebrated this as a sign that Hugenberg might soon vanish from the political stage.[117] But, such governmentalist optimism did not come to pass. As one historian puts it, though a "less determined man might have surrendered the chairmanship," Hugenberg was no such man.[118] Instead, Hugenberg stayed atop his party and deployed his still immense resources, even if it meant, as it did in June 1930, that twenty-five additional Reichstag delegates left the party. But, most critically, with this ever-shrinking party, Brüning's strategy of finding an ally in the DNVP to forge a parliamentary majority had failed.

Running parallel to this path, Treviranus, along with Brüning, also had high hopes that a new governmentalist right party formed "from scratch" in January 1930, the *Volksvereinigung*, might emerge as an alternative to Hugenberg's DNVP. This grouping was supported by the same type of senior civil servants and intellectuals previously associated with the Free Conservative Party, thus suggesting a party with a potentially deep historical legacy and promising future.[119] At the party's founding gathering in the Prussian *Herrenhaus* in January 1930, speakers emphasized many themes, but Otto Hoetzsch made the case that the new party should aim to create "*Tory-Demokratie*" for Germany.[120] Recognizing its need for a popular base, this elitist new party hoped to expand upon its ties to Walther Lambach's German National Shop Assistants' Association (*Deutschnationale Handlungsgehilfenverband*, or DHV), which had 400,000 members.[121] When the DNVP ruptured again in the summer of 1930, Westarp finally joined Treviranus' undertaking, but the popular base did not materialize, and it lost itself among the multiple groupings that sprang up in the wake of the DNVP's disintegration.[122] The barriers to party formation are always substantial, and the proportional representation system only exacerbated the problems of party system fragmentation at this time.

All of this meant that as Brüning dissolved the parliament, aided by President Hindenburg's invocation of his presidential emergency powers as stipulated in

[115] Mommsen, *Rise and Fall of Weimar Democracy* (1996), 282–83.
[116] Patch, *Heinrich Brüning* (1998), 80–81; Leopold, *Alfred Hugenberg* (1977), 74–75.
[117] Patch, *Heinrich Brüning* (1998), 80.   [118] Leopold, *Alfred Hugenberg* (1977), 75.
[119] Beck, *Fateful Alliance* (2008), 59.
[120] Erasmus Jonas, *Die Volkskonservativen, 1928–1933* (Düsseldorf: Droste, 1965), 59.
[121] Jonas, *Volkskonservativen* (1965), 80.   [122] Patch, *Heinrich Brüning* (1998), 99.

TABLE 9.1: *Reichstag Election Results, September 1930*

Party	Vote Share
Social Democratic Party (SPD)	24.5%
National Socialist Party (NSDAP)	18.25%
Communist Party (KPD)	13.3%
Center Party (Zentrum)	11.8%
German Nationalists (DNVP)	7%
German People's Party (DVP)	4.5%
Conservative People's Party (KVP)	0.8%

Article 48 of the constitution to push Brüning's budget bill through, efforts to find a solid *alternative* parliamentary majority in the September 1930 Reichstag elections failed. The results, as Table 9.1 reports, were a disaster for Brüning's attempt to construct a moderate right parliamentary majority. The National Socialist Party had a breakthrough, the Communists thrived, the SPD maintained its dominance, and the DNVP collapsed; but Treviranus' *Konservative Volkspartei* only won a meager four seats in the Reichstag.

As Richard Evans observes, "The centrist and right wing parties on which Brüning might possibly hope to build his government suffered catastrophic losses."[123] But, what about the hope that Treviranus's "Tory-Democratic" *Volkskonservative* Party might serve as the basis for a non-socialist parliamentary majority? Given the substantial and predictable problems of building a political party "from scratch," such a plan turned out to be wishful thinking; given the historical weakness of the electoral right, the room for maneuvering was shrinking.[124] The schism caused by the DNVP's embrace of radicalism – itself a product of the loosely coupled inheritance of German conservatism – left only organizational wreckage in its wake. When faced with economic crisis, this legacy first prompted a turn to non-parliamentary rule in March 1930, but, then – as the experience of Treviranus' ill-fated KVP teaches us – later prevented a *retreat* from it as well.[125]

---

[123] Evans, *The Coming of the Third Reich* (2003), 259; Capoccia, *Defending Democracy* (2005), 191. Capoccia adds this observation: "In Germany, after the elections of September 1930, none of the three coalition formulae previously tried could count on a majority." Indeed, with 289 seats necessary for a majority, the founding Weimar coalition had 231, the historic "bourgeois" coalition of the center right had only 250 seats, and the third option, the "Grand Coalition," could only muster 280.

[124] As a sign of the impossibility of forging the desired right parliamentary coalition, Brüning's government survived by relying on a "silent partner" – toleration and cooperation by the opposition SPD, which correctly understood the risks of Brüning's government failing. See Patch, *Heinrich Brüning* (1998), 103–17.

[125] According to Patch (*Heinrich Brüning* (1998), 112) one last effort to tame the DNVP after September 1930 occurred when Albert Vögler of United Steelworks "told the chancellor

THE CONSEQUENCE OF THE WEAK DNVP: OPENING SPACE
FOR THE RADICAL RIGHT

If the window was closing in September 1930 on the possibility of re-establishing parliamentary rule, the second stage of democratic breakdown also began then with the National Socialist Party's electoral breakthrough, ending ultimately with Adolf Hitler's appointment as chancellor in January 1933. The first stage of democratic breakdown had occurred with the soft coup "from above" through the concentration of executive power as an authoritarian "substitute" for a weak DNVP. Likewise, though the second stage transpired chiefly via elections and the resulting miscalculations of establishment politicians regarding the NSDAP, the shrinking and radicalizing DNVP once again played a pivotal role. Though the party was now small, its impact remained immense.

In this instance, the challenge came squarely from the anti-system Nazi Party's rise to power, which likely had "deep causes" in various features of German history, but its ascendance was facilitated via the more "proximate cause" of the radicalization, fragmentation, and demise of the DNVP. As a general rule, political scientists have observed that new or previously marginal political parties' electoral success reflects less their own strategies but more often the strategic choices of already existing mainstream political parties.[126] Thus, while dire socioeconomic and cultural conditions may explain diffuse fascist sentiments and movements in interwar Europe, more proximate factors – related to the strategies of mainstream political parties – are necessary for the translation of these sentiments and movements into electorally successful political parties. As in contemporary democracies, in interwar Europe, the blocking strategies of "border parties," adjacent to the anti-system right-wing parties, were decisive.[127] In particular, what mattered, as political Giovanni Capoccia has demonstrated, was whether the border parties could simultaneously channel the votes of potentially disgruntled voters and marginalize far-right parties through various delegitimizing *cordon sanitaire* measures. Weimar Germany is instructive as a negative case.

Because of the absence of a history of party institutionalization, the collapse and radicalization of the DNVP – in effect, the *absence of a moderate border*

---

that eight leading industrialists had corralled Hugenberg for a day-long discussion of the many ways in which the DNVP's intransigence aggravated the economic crisis. If Brüning would arrange another meeting with Hugenberg, Vögler predicated he would find the DNVP chairman amenable to reason." This foundered in the face-to-face meeting when Hugenberg insisted Brüning assist in dissolving the Prussian state government.

[126] For an elaboration of this insight, see Kitschelt, *The Radical Right in Western Europe: A Comparative Analysis* (1995). And more generally, see Bonnie Meguid, *Party Competition between Unequals: Strategies and Electoral Fortunes in Western Europe* (Cambridge and New York: Cambridge University Press, 2008).

[127] See Capoccia, *Defending Democracy* (2005); David Art, "The European radical right in comparative-historical perspective," in *Annual meeting of the American Political Science Association* (Philadelphia, PA: 2006).

party – generated the opposite dynamic, bolstering the Nationalist Socialist Party. This operated through two main mechanisms: (1) the DNVP's opening of electoral space in the electoral marketplace for a new radical-right party, and (2) the creation of a permissive institutional environment, as the respectability of the Nazi Party rose as a result of the DNVP's own desperate and miscalculated strategies to save itself. In both instances, the dynamic was simple: as the DNVP went down, it created new opportunities for the Nazi Party's ascendance.

The first mechanism, *altering the electoral marketplace*, opened enough electoral space for the far right to thrive. Between 1928 and 1930 the Nazi Party had its most significant electoral breakthrough. In 1928, the party received less than a million votes (810,127) and in 1930 its vote share grew to 6.4 million voters, a remarkable *seven-fold* explosion in two years. While the NSDAP continued to grow through 1933, the Nazi Party's single biggest percentage support came in the two-year window between 1928 and 1930. It was this threshold year, not the two elections of 1932, that marked a pivot in German elections. What explains this remarkable leap?

One traditional account points out that the party's 1930 threshold election was accompanied by an expansion in the total number of voters (i.e., higher voter turnout) between 1928 and 1930, leading to the hypothesis that new voters were integral to explaining the major spurt in Nazi Party popularity.[128] The most careful recent analyses – both aggregate as well as efforts to estimate individual-level voting patterns – challenge the idea that higher voter turnout was the primary factor. While between 1930 and 1932 there is a correlation between regions with growth in new voters and increase in Nazi vote share, analysis by political scientist Jürgen Falter demonstrates that this was not the case in the breakthrough years between 1928 and 1930.[129] In fact, Falter concludes it was in regions where the DNVP shrank the most that the NSDAP grew the most. Indeed, the negative correlation in vote share by electoral district between these two parties (1928 vs. 1930) was stronger than with any other pair across these two decisive elections. After the 1928 downfall of the DNVP group in parliament, formerly DNVP regions became strongholds of the Nazi Party in the 1930 elections.

But this is aggregate evidence which is ultimately inconclusive if we want to know whether the disintegration of the DNVP cleared the way for the NSDAP, an argument which stated in this way implies that *individual voters* who eventually voted for the Nazi Party in Reichstag 1930 disproportionately had voted for the DNVP in the past. Macro trends may conceal more important

[128] Reinhard Bendix, "Social Stratification and Political Power," *American Political Science Review* 46, no. 2 (1952): 357–75.
[129] Jürgen Falter, "The National Socialist Mobilization of New Voters, 1928–1933," in *The Formation of the Nazi Constituency, 1919–1933*, ed. Thomas Childers (London: Routledge, 1986), 202–30, 207

TABLE 9.2: *Percentage of 1928 Voters of Each Party That Cast Their Ballots for the Nazi Party (NSDAP) in 1930*

Party	Falter Estimate
National Socialist Party (NSDAP)	38%
German Nationalists (DNVP)	31%
Liberals (DVP and DDP)	26%
Non-Voters	14%
Social Democrats (SPD)	10%
Center Party (Zentrum)	10%
Communist Party (KPD)	5%

Notes: These data show that 38 percent of voters who cast their ballots for the NSDAP in 1928 did so again in 1930; 31 percent who voted for the DNVP in 1928 voted for the NSDAP in 1930; and 14 percent of nonvoters in 1928 voted for the NSDAP in 1930.
Data Source: Falter's estimates are reported Falter (1991), 111

individual-level fluctuations that are actually driving shifts in party support unless such trends are analyzed more carefully. Thus, drawing on research from Falter and others, we can summarize the best efforts to infer individual voter behavior from aggregate patterns.[130] Again, even here the evidence suggests that DNVP voters migrated disproportionately to the Nazi Party.

First, after Hugenberg's accession to party leader in 1928, DNVP voters fled the party in droves, which meant that in 1930 a greater share of Nazi Party's voters had migrated from the DNVP than from any other party. Falter estimates that 48 percent of 1930 Nazi Party voters in 1928 had been either DNVP voters (22 percent) or non-voters (24 percent), while Nazi Party voters came in less significant numbers from other parties.[131] Thus, the major groups behind the NSDAP's triumph in 1930 were a mix of new voters and disaffected conservatives. Additionally, while 24 percent of 1930 NSDAP voters had been non-voters in 1928, non-voters in fact flocked to all parties in 1930 in relatively high numbers.[132] As Table 9.2 shows, the share of those who had been non-voters in 1928 who then cast their ballots for the Nazi Party in 1930 was only 14 percent, substantially less than the 31 percent share of 1928 DNVP voters who supported the Nazi Party in 1930.

These findings reinforce the point that the DNVP was not only ideologically closer to the Nazi Party than other parties, but also that DNVP voters, unlike the Center Party and SPD voters in particular, were less embedded in real social structures, leaving DNVP voters more vulnerable to party switching. Thus, the

---

[130] See Jürgen Falter, *Hitlers Wähler* (Munich: Beck, 1991); Falter, "The National Socialist Mobilization of New Voters, 1928–1933" (1986).
[131] Falter, "The National Socialist Mobilization of New Voters, 1928–1933" (1986), 219.
[132] Ibid.

DNVP leadership crisis sparked a collapse of electoral support, thus freeing space on the far right for the Nazi Party to fill the void. Had the DNVP remained a viable electoral force with the capacity to retain voters like the Center Party, for example, it is possible that the NSDAP's vote share would have been reduced by at least a quarter in 1930.

In addition to opening up electoral space, a second mechanism linking the DNVP to the rise of the National Socialist Party was the DNVP's *creation of a permissive environment* via its increasingly cooperative if not outright supportive "alliance" with the Nazi Party, which bolstered the latter's respectability between 1929 and 1932. It is certainly correct, as historian Hermann Beck notes, that Conservatives and Nazis had at best an "uneasy alliance," one in which the DNVP leadership seriously underestimated and miscalculated the nature of their partner. After using DNVP assistance to gain power, the Nazi Party, an antibourgeois revolutionary force, quickly turned their "revolutionary fervor" against their former benefactors.[133] Like the Horse in Aesop's "The Horse, the Hunter, and the Stag," who was willing to put himself "under bit and spur" to capture the Stag but then found himself unable to escape the Hunter's control, the DNVP allowed itself to be harnessed by the Nationalist Socialist Party for its own purposes of transforming the regime and seizing power, but this alliance became a burden that could not be lifted.[134] First, when Hugenberg forged a united front in September 1929 against the Young Plan in the *Reichsausschuss*, he included the National Socialists and Hitler as equal partners. "With the help of Hugenberg's press," this had the effect of making Hitler's "name known throughout Germany."[135] As Richard Evans describes Hugenberg's inclusion of Hitler in his national anti–Young Plan referendum campaign,

Not only did the Nazis gain publicity from this campaign, they also won a degree of respectability on the mainstream right through the presence of Hitler on the organizing committee... The referendum itself was a failure... But the campaign had revealed to many supporters of the Nationalists how much more dynamic the brown-shirted and jackbooted Nazis were than the frock-coated and top-hatted leaders of their own party.[136]

---

[133] Beck, *Fateful Alliance* (2008), 288.
[134] Aeasop, *Aeasop's Fables*, trans. Laura Gibbs (Oxford: Oxford University Press, 2002). The fable "The Horse, the Stag, and the Hunter" is the following: "A quarrel had arisen between the Horse and the Stag, so the Horse came to a Hunter to ask his help to take revenge on the Stag. The Hunter agreed, but said: 'If you desire to conquer the Stag, you must permit me to place this piece of iron between your jaws, so that I may guide you with these reins, and allow this saddle to be placed upon your back so that I may keep steady upon you as we follow after the enemy.' The Horse agreed to the conditions, and the Hunter soon saddled and bridled him. Then with the aid of the Hunter the Horse soon overcame the Stag, and said to the Hunter: 'Now, get off, and remove those things from my mouth and back.' 'Not so fast, friend,' said the Hunter. 'I have now got you under bit and spur, and prefer to keep you as you are at present.'"
[135] Beck, *Fateful Alliance* (2008), 55.   [136] Evans, *The Coming of the Third Reich* (2003), 212.

This helped the NSDAP in the national Reichstag elections the next year, though it withdrew from the Referendum Committee in April 1930 after its primary goal of self-promotion had been achieved. But the diminishing strength of the DNVP, on full display after it gained a miserable 7 percent of the vote in September 1930, only convinced Hugenberg to double down on his strategy of collaboration with Hitler.[137] This time the alliance took the form of the Harzburg Rally, conceived of and initiated by Hugenberg himself, a meeting of the NSDAP and DNVP Reichstag groups planned for October 1931, before the opening of the Reichstag session. The intention was to issue, in typically provocative fashion, a joint condemnation of Brüning's government and a call for the government's transformation into a more right-wing formation.[138] The details of the rally were further complicated with the invitation of prominent Stahlhelm nationalists, the Pan-German League, and others, to the small town of Bad Harzburg in the state of Brunswick, where a Nazi-DNVP collaboration had been in place since earlier that year. The gathering, a kind of "shadow government" in the making, was held on the small and tree-lined cobblestone streets of the quiet resort town, which became a crowded scene filled with army officers in uniforms, Nazis both young and old in brown shirts, Pan-German and Stahlhelm members waving nationalist banners, and Hugenberg himself, standing out in his staid garb of suit and tie.

If Hugenberg's aim was to settle upon a common presidential candidate (i.e., himself) for a "united right," the rally was a failure: the evening before the event began, President Hindenburg invited Hitler to meet after realizing that of all those gathered at Bad Harzburg, Hitler's party was now the largest in the Reichstag. While President Hindenburg was reportedly unimpressed with Hitler, the conversation broached the topic of the conditions under which Hitler might accept the formation of a new cabinet, in Brüning's view mistakenly encouraging "many army officers and judges to regard the Nazi leader as a legitimate contender for power."[139] Likewise, for Hitler, with his own sense of self-importance undoubtedly elevated, "the presidential audience had transformed the normally ingratiating Hitler into 'a mixture of prima donna and Napoleon.'"[140] He left the meeting and proceeded to offend his Harzburg Front "allies" by arriving late and then leaving the event early, after the impressive appearance of his own 70,000 SA men but before the Stahlhelm

---

[137] The following account builds primarily on Leopold, *Alfred Hugenberg* (1977), 97–106; Bracher, *Die Auflösung der Weimarer Republik* (1955), 407–15; and Larry Eugene Jones, "Nationalists, Nazis, and the Assault against Weimar: Revisiting the Harzburg Rally of October 1931," *German Studies Review* 29, no. 3 (2006): 483–94.

[138] Jones, "Nationalists, Nazis, and the Assault against Weimar" (2006): 483.

[139] This is reported by Patch, *Heinrich Brüning* (1998), 195.

[140] The phrase "prima donna and Napoleon" was from Hugenberg's ally and DNVP leader, Otto Schmidt-Hannover, cited by Patch, *Heinrich Brüning* (1998), 194.

contingent marched past the VIP stands.[141] Again, Hugenberg was seeking in Hitler an ally to create a united front but in the process was only aiding a new rival.

We can see similar dynamics in February 1931 when the DNVP Reichstag group joined the NSDAP Reichstag group by dramatically walking out of the chambers in a joint protest of the government.[142] Again, we see this same story in the presidential elections of 1932, in which President Hindenburg ran for re-election at the end of his seven-year term. In the first round of the elections, Hugenberg endorsed the Stahlhelm candidate, Theodor Duesterberg, remarkably disavowing the incumbent and national hero President Hindenburg in a race that also included Hitler and the KPD candidate Ernst Thälmann. Even more extraordinarily, in the second round of balloting – between Thälmann, Hindenburg, and Hitler – Hugenberg endorsed no one, in effect providing a tacit endorsement of Hitler, given that the Pan-German League and other allies of the DNVP formally endorsed him.[143] This certainly contributed to the great electoral reversal between 1925 and 1932, in which former DNVP supporters of Hindenburg now voted for Hitler; just as former opponents of Hindenburg – such as the SPD, the Center Party, and the DDP – voted for Hindenburg.[144] Like the anti–Young Plan committee and the Harzburg Front, the presidential election of 1932 provided more momentum and respectability to Hitler's Nazi Party precisely as the DNVP was being marginalized.

It is correct that the apparently unrelenting electoral rise of Nazism appeared suddenly to stall in the November 1932 Reichstag elections. But, as the NSDAP appeared to falter, the dynamic emphasized here took hold again in the thirty days before Hitler's accession to power as Chancellor of Germany on January 30, 1933.[145] Once again, the willingness of a weak and declining conservative party to save itself by forming a coalition with an extremist party – despite its animosity to it – was a key facilitating condition.

In the wake of von Papen's demise, and as General von Schleicher's frantic negotiations to forge parliamentary support foundered, President Hindenburg and his entourage became convinced that Hitler, though weakened, provided the only way out; after all, the NSDAP remained the largest party in the

---

[141] For an account of this, see Jones, "Nationalists, Nazis, and the Assault against Weimar" (2006): 488.

[142] Beck, *Fateful Alliance* (2008), 71.

[143] For a subtle and rich reading of the 1932 campaign, see Anna von der Goltz, *Hindenburg: Power, Myth, and the Rise of the Nazis* (Oxford: Oxford University Press, 2009), 145–66; and Larry Eugene Jones, "Hindenburg and the Conservative Dilemma in the 1932 Presidential Elections," *German Studies Review* 20, no. 2 (1997): 235–59. The most recent work on this topic is Larry Eugene Jones, *Hitler versus Hindenburg: The 1932 Presidential Elections and the End of the Weimar Republic* (Cambridge: Cambridge University Press, 2015).

[144] See ecological data in Falter, *Hitlers Wähler* (1991).

[145] Henry Ashby Turner, *Hitler's Thirty Days to Power: January 1933* (Reading, MA: Addison-Wesley, 1996); Beck, *Fateful Alliance* (2008), 83–88.

Reichstag despite losing thirty-four seats in the November 1932 elections. The machinations and negotiations over this last month were devilishly complex, but several points are worth emphasizing. On the one hand, Hugenberg accurately regarded Hitler's movement as stalling. From Hugenberg's view, they needed his aid if a right-wing cabinet could be formed rather than what appeared to be the only alternative: a Schleicher–Hammerstein military coup to suppress the Communists and Nazis alike, which would destroy any chance of a Hugenberg-Hitler "united right."[146] As Bracher writes, the rumors of coups, at the last moment, "hurried along" the last act.[147] On the other hand, historians have also drawn on Hiller von Gaertingen's papers to argue that, given that Hitler now appeared the only feasible chancellor to lead a viable parliamentary majority, Hugenberg *feared* he would be left out entirely the moment that a Hitler-led cabinet could be formed.[148]

CONCLUSION

The demise of German democracy in the interwar years can always – in retrospect – be accounted for with deep structural and cultural factors; but the closer one gets to the frantic final days and hours of the regime, the less ironclad these factors appear to be. The uncertainty of what the main actors were actually intending to pursue, the multiple overlapping miscalculations and misjudgments, the apparent utter lack of awareness of the monumental stakes – all of this creates a dizzying disjuncture between what we think we know about the "big" forces at work and the "smallness" of the calculations of the actors at the precipice. There is a risk of analytical myopia if one focuses too closely on the last moments of a political regime.

Yet, the last stages of Weimar's political life are, when kept in proper perspective, still revealing. Hugenberg and his DNVP may have not then been the most important people in the room; indeed, John Leopold reports Hugenberg was sometimes not in the room at all as the details of the new cabinet were debated by President Hindenburg, von Papen, and other members of Hindenburg's entourage.[149] Yet, the DNVP mattered even here for two reasons: one immediate, the other reflecting the accumulation of decisions from the past.

First, most immediately, on January 30, 1933, it was evident that Hugenberg suddenly became a last veto point that could potentially derail the creation of a Hitler-led cabinet. With the swearing-in ceremony scheduled that day for 11:00 a.m., at first all details of the deal appeared to be sorted out: Hitler would be chancellor, Göring Minister of the Interior for Prussia, and Hugenberg Minister of

---

[146] Evans, *The Coming of the Third Reich* (2003), 306.
[147] Bracher, *Die Auflösung der Weimarer Republik* (1955), 724.
[148] Beck, *Fateful Alliance* (2008), 88.   [149] Leopold, *Alfred Hugenberg* (1977), 135.

the Economy and Agriculture. Yet, at the very last minute, the deal almost fell apart when Hugenberg learned that Hitler insisted to von Papen that new elections would be held *after* his appointment to chancellor – with the NSDAP now in charge of the state – to give Hitler a "freer hand."[150] The historian Beck writes,

When Hugenberg, now finally acquainted with Hitler's demand for new elections, got into an argument with the Chancellor-designate that put the formation of the new government in jeopardy... Papen, who had become fearful that his grand scheme might fall apart, indignantly confronted Hugenberg as to how he could possibly doubt the "the solemnly given word of a German man." But Hugenberg, whose acumen for once was not at fault, remained unyielding. It was only Meissner's breathless exhortation at 11:15 a.m. that Hindenburg could no longer be kept waiting that brought Hugenberg back into line. Less than half an hour later, Hitler was made Chancellor of the Reich.[151]

In effect, Hugenberg had become the last veto point, able to torpedo the agreement but in the end complying. And, indeed, even he realized the fateful weight of his decision. The very next day, Hugenberg infamously admitted to the conservative mayor of Leipzig, "I have just committed the greatest stupidity of my life; I have allied myself with the greatest demagogue in world history."[152] Though Hugenberg's sudden regret is fascinating, to attribute the decision to miscalculation alone effectively lets the culprits off the hook; there are other reasons why political actors make decisions that undermine their own power, including what sociologist Ivan Ermakoff calls "ideological collusion."[153] Put more simply, Hugenberg agreed to a Hitler-led chancellorship because that was what he had actually wanted since at least 1928.[154]

But if we step back from the last hours, we see that there is a second reason why Hugenberg and the DNVP mattered to these last moments of the regime's demise. In particular, that the political regime found itself in this crisis in the first place – with generals and former generals behind closed doors possessing the means and opportunity to negotiate the regime out of existence – was due to a gaping *absence*: the absence of a moderate right. The resulting dynamic brought on by the radicalization of the DNVP in 1928 made the political system vulnerable even before economic crisis had arrived. As the political

---

[150] See Bracher, *Die Auflösung der Weimarer Republik* (1955), 726–27; Beck, *Fateful Alliance* (2008), 86–87.

[151] Beck, *Fateful Alliance* (2008), 86–87. Beck's account draws on Turner, *Hitler's Thirty Days to Power: January 1933* (1996).

[152] Larry Eugene Jones, "'The Greatest Stupidity of My Life': Alfred Hugenberg and the Formation of the Hitler Cabinet, January 1933," *Journal of Contemporary History* 27, no. 1 (1992): 63–87. He also cites this confession, though does not attribute a source to it, asserting that it is possibly apocryphal. Beck (*Fateful Alliance*, 2008, 88), by contrast, cites Gerhard Ritter, *Carl Goerdeler und die deutsche Widerstandsbewegung* (Stuttgart: Deutsche Verlags-Anstalt, 1954), 65–66.

[153] Ivan Ermakoff, *Ruling Oneself Out: A Theory of Collective Self-Abdication* (Durham: Duke University Press, 2008), 131.

[154] Jones ("Greatest Stupidity of My Life," 1992) makes a similar argument, 79.

scientist Stanley Hoffmann once observed, paraphrasing Montesquieu, when states seem to collapse from one blow, there are deep reasons why that single blow was sufficient.[155] In what would turn out to be the most destructive instance of democratic collapse in the twentieth century, the fate of democracy in Germany was in the hands of conservatives; and the fundamental impetus driving events – in January 1933 – was not their strength, but rather their *weakness*.

---

[155] Stanley Hoffmann, "Hitler's Thirty Days to Power: January 1933," *Foreign Affairs* 76, no. 3 (1997): 135.

10

How Countries Democratize: Europe and Beyond

At the end of the Second World War, twelve years after Hitler's rise to power in January 1933, after more than a decade of war, violence, and destruction on an unprecedented scale, German Catholic and Protestant politicians began the grassroots work of overcoming a deep historical division to form by 1950 a new political party of the center right. The German Christian Democratic Union (CDU), a "spiritual dam" in Leo Schwering's phrase in 1945, played a key role in West Germany's postwar reconstruction under Konrad Adenauer's leadership and the watchful eye of Allied powers.[1] Transformed international conditions and the discrediting of the radical right had fundamentally reshuffled the possibilities of conservative party formation.[2] Our story of German and British democratization ends here with this remarkably successful case of center-right party-building in the form of the West German CDU because it coincided with the gradual and successful democratization of Germany between 1945 and 1989.[3] When the center-right finally made its peace with democracy, democracy could finally be achieved peacefully.

Strictly speaking this book's argument has made sense of political developments within Britain and Germany between the middle of the nineteenth and the middle of the twentieth centuries. But a second purpose, as promised in the introduction, was that the interpretation of these specific historical experiences has general implications for how to think about the

---

[1] Schwering's quote is found in Geoffrey Pridham, *Christian Democracy in Western Germany: The CDU/CSU in Government and Opposition, 1945–1976* (New York: St. Martin's Press, 1977), 14.

[2] As Charles Maier (p. 332) writes, "The major force preventing ideological polarization after World War II was neither the chastened left nor the tempered right but the new Christian Democratic Parties of the Center." See Charles S. Maier, "The Two Postwar Eras and the Conditions for Stability in Twentieth-Century Western Europe," *American Historical Review* 86, no. 2 (1981): 327–52.

[3] For an overview of this period in European history, see Tony Judt, *Postwar: A History of Europe since 1945* (New York: Penguin Press, 2005).

enduring impact of old-regime forces on democratization in other places and times. Is our understanding of the world in fact deepened when we widen our scope beyond the main cases we have studied? What more general implications can we draw?

SETTLED AND UNSETTLED DEMOCRATIZATION: DOES THE
ANALYSIS ILLUMINATE OTHER DEMOCRATIZATION EXPERIENCES?

Reanalyzing the "twenty-year crisis" between 1919 and 1939 in western Europe, during Weimar's rise and fall, but now with a focus on other countries provides an opportunity to reflect on these questions.[4] Though the interest in this book has been on long-run dynamics, this narrower period explored in a comparative framework casts into sharp relief the sources of Europe's long-run "crooked" and "straight" lines of democratization. Where democratization was chiefly a *settled* process over the century as a whole – in Belgium, the Netherlands, Britain, Sweden, and Denmark – mass democracy also survived after 1918. By contrast, where the long-run process was primarily *unsettled* – in Germany, Italy, Portugal, and Spain – mass democracy perished during these years of crisis.[5] Beyond Germany and Britain, can a focus on the organizational endowments of old regime parties and the electoral right help make sense of such diverse experiences?

As already noted, scholars have long emphasized a variety of factors, including different war experiences, economic crises, political institutions, political cultures, ideas, and the role of effective political leadership.[6] Some argue that enduringly powerful landed elites were the primary barriers to democracy; others that if Liberals were not electorally "dominant" before 1914, the possibilities of democratic survival were dramatically narrowed.[7]

As useful as this scholarship is in framing the debate, a comparative perspective shows that anomalies remain.[8] For example, while powerful

---

[4] The phrase "twenty year crisis" is from Edward Hallett Carr, *The Twenty Years' Crisis, 1919–1939: An Introduction to the Study of International Relations* (London: Macmillan & Co. Ltd, 1946).

[5] As we see below, France remains, in one analyst's useful phrase, a case of "ambiguous survival." See Michel Dobry, "France: An Ambiguous Survival," in *Conditions of Democracy in Europe, 1919–1939: Systematic Case Studies*, ed. Dirk Berg-Schlosser and Jeremy Mitchell (Basingstoke: Macmillan, 2000), 157–83. See discussion below.

[6] See discussion in Chapter 9. The relevant literature includes Berman, *The Social Democratic Moment: Ideas and Politics in the Making of Interwar Europe* (1998); Møller, Schmotz, and Skaaning, "Economic Crisis and Democratic Breakdown" (2015); Bernhard, *Institutions and the Fate of Democracy* (2005); Capoccia, *Defending Democracy* (2005).

[7] On the former idea, see Rueschemeyer, Stephens, and Stephens, *Capitalist Development and Democracy* (1992). On the latter, see Luebbert, *Liberalism, Fascism, or Social Democracy* (1991).

[8] See discussions in Herbert Kitschelt, "Political Regime Change: Structure and Process-Driven Explanations," *American Political Science Review* 86, no. 4 (1992): 1028–34; Thomas Ertman, "Democracy and Dictatorship in Interwar Western Europe Revisited," *World Politics* 50, no. 3

landed elites in Germany and Italy were no great friends of post-1918 democracy, the regions where fascism found most electoral support such as northwestern Germany and north-central Italy were dominated by small family farms.[9] Also, in neither Belgium nor the Netherlands was liberalism dominant before 1914, yet neither social democracy nor fascism triumphed there in the interwar years.[10] Proportional representation is sometimes blamed for the fractured political systems in these years, but it is worth noting that while democracy may have collapsed in some countries with proportional representation (e.g., Italy and Germany), it survived in others with variants of this same electoral system in place (e.g., Belgium and Sweden).[11] To untangle these anomalies, a focus on the role of conservative political parties and their organizational endowments provides a more comprehensive explanation. With their long pre-1914 political histories, these parties were a key factor in shaping interwar democratic experiences *beyond* Britain and Germany.

After 1918, the old predemocratic divide between European liberal and conservative parties was transformed by the rise of socialist parties, which altered the character of the left–right cleavage as well as what even counted as a political party "of the right." Table 10.1 provides a list of the major parties of the electoral right after 1918, noting which electoral right party had the greatest number of votes in the first postwar democratic elections, a score for the fragmentation of the right camp of parties in this period, and whether or not democracy survived the interwar years.

In the countries at the top of list – Sweden, Britain, Denmark, the Netherlands, and Belgium – old conservative parties, even if renamed, survived. In all of these cases, a single party largely dominated the right end of the party spectrum afterwards, with the exception of the Netherlands, which featured *two* highly institutionalized and closely allied Calvinist parties, founded before 1918.[12]

(1998): 475–505; James Mahoney, "Knowledge Accumulation in Comparative historical Research: the case of democracy and authoritarianism," in *Comparative Historical Analysis in the Social Sciences*, ed. James Mahoney and Dietrich Rueschemeyer (Cambridge: Cambridge University Press, 2003), 131–76.

[9] Luebbert, *Liberalism, Fascism, or Social Democracy* (1991), 308–09; Mahoney, "Knowledge Accumulation" (2003): 142.

[10] Kitschelt, "Political Regime Change: Structure and Process-Driven Explanations" (1992): 1029. See also Ertman, "Democracy and Dictatorship in Interwar Western Europe Revisited" (1998): 495–96. He observes that in Denmark and Norway, liberals were dominant before the First World War, yet social democracy was the interwar outcome.

[11] This argument about the negative impact of proportional electoral systems on democratic stability was originally formulated by Hermens, "Proportional Representation and the Breakdown of German Democracy" (1936).

[12] On the history of the CHU in this period, see Marcel ten Hooven and Ron de Jong, *Geschiedenis van de Christelijk-Historische Unie 1908–1980* (Meppel: Boom Distributie Centrum, 2008), 145–80.

TABLE 10.1: *Fragmentation of the Right in Interwar Europe and Democratic Breakdown*

Country	Largest Right Party at First Post-1918 Democratic Election	Index of Fragmentation of All Right Parties (Average of Period)[1]	Democratic Breakdown?
(1)	(2)	(3)	(4)
Sweden	Allmänna valmansförbundet	1.04	No
Great Britain	British Conservative Party	1.05	No
Denmark	Konservative Folkeparti	1.05	No
Belgium	Union Catholique Belge	1.47	No
Netherlands	Anti-Revolutionaire Partij	1.76	No
France	Fédération républicaine (Republican Union)	1.84	No[2]
Portugal	Partido Republicano Evolucionista	1.86	1926
Spain	Partido Republicano Radical	2.13	1936
Italy	Partido Popolare Italiano[3]	2.47	1922
Germany	Deutschnationale Volkspartei	2.81	1933

[1] I code which political parties are "right" parties (see Appendix C for coding decisions) and then measure the average "fragmentation of the right" by using a common measure of "effective number of parties" for right parties for each democratic election between 1918 and 1939 in a country calculated as $N = \frac{1}{\sum_{i=1}^{n} p_i^2}$ where n is the number of parties with at least one vote and p_i^2 the square of each party's portion of all votes. The measure is from Markku Laakso and Rein Taagepera, "'Effective' Number of Parties: A Measure with Application to West Europe," *Comparative Political Studies* 12, no. 1 (1979): 3–27. Data on Spanish parties from Angel Luis López Villaverde, *Cuenca durante la II República: elecciones, partidos y vida política, 1931–1936* (Cuenca: Universidad de Castilla-La Mancha, 1997), 231, 53, 70. Data on Italian parties from Christopher Seton-Watson, *Italy from Liberalism to Fascism, 1870–1925* (London: Methuen, 1981), 588. All remaining data from Nohlen and Stöver, *Elections in Europe: A Data Handbook* (2010).

[2] France is coded as a case of democratic survival though its survival, in the words of one analyst was "ambiguous." For more discussion, see below.

[3] Coding Italy's complex party system in 1919–1920 and identifying what "counts" as the right in this context is difficult, which bolsters the core claim of the disarray of the Italian right in this period. Nonetheless, of the parties present in 1919, I report the score if I code the PPI as a center-right party, following Kalyvas, *Rise of Christian Democracy* (1996). If the PPI is not included, Italy's fragmentation score is higher.

With their inheritance of conservative party organization and electoral success, the "legacy" parties of these pre-1918 parties performed quite well in first democratic elections. Despite the presence of proportional representation in nearly all of these countries, the right end of the political spectrum remained cohesive and was also frequently in power in the interwar years.[13] And, finally, democracy survived the interwar years in every one of these cases.

To be sure, the character of the electoral right among these countries varied in significant ways. The explicitly confessional or proto-Christian Democratic parties of religious self-defense in Belgium and the Netherlands emerged from a fusion of conservative and confessional groups, while more traditional secular parties prevailed in Britain, Sweden, Denmark, and France. These cohesive parties helped stabilize democracy in two ways.

First, by blocking fissures at the far end of the political spectrum, strong center-right parties provided a bulwark against the radical right. For example, once the Belgian economy collapsed in the early 1930s, the radical right-wing *Rexist Party* emerged as a genuine threat to democracy; however, it was sidelined by the mass organization conservative Catholic Party (*Union Catholique Belge*) which employed sophisticated strategies of exclusion and co-optation from a position of strength within the government.[14] The Catholic Party leadership resisted calls to form a coalition with *Rex* and took control of its own candidate lists in a way that distanced the party from extremism.[15] In this sense, a focus on center-right "party organization" allows us to identify the *conditions under which* political leaders behave in ways that protect democracy.[16]

There was a second mechanism by which a cohesive electoral right helped democratic consolidation: electoral success itself. Victory – or at least the plausible *prospect* of victory – helped turn ambivalent democrats into actors willing to comply with democratic institutions. This can be seen in the case of Swedish conservatives who only fully made their peace with democracy in this period.[17] It is sometimes thought that the Swedish right's orientation toward democratic was intrinsically unproblematic, but this is plainly incorrect. Recent

---

[13] In all five of these countries, the electoral right inherited robust party organization from the pre-First World War era, electoral fragmentation of the right was lower and the right more typically held power (Sweden, Denmark) during the mid-1920s or participated in governing cabinets during the Great Depression (Belgium, the Netherlands, Britain). The non-socialist confessional right served in *every* cabinet between 1918 and the onset of the Second World War in the Netherlands and Belgium. In France, Sweden, Britain, and Denmark, the electoral right was in power at least once. For election data, see Dieter Nohlen and Philip Stöver, *Elections in Europe: A Data Handbook* (Baden-Baden, Germany: Nomos, 2010).

[14] Capoccia, *Defending Democracy* (2005), 116–25.   [15] Ibid.

[16] This account therefore is consistent with, and is intended to supplement, Capoccia's (2005) important comparative insight into the impact of strategies of cooptation and exclusion not only by national parliamentarians but by national executives as well. For a discussion of the methodological issues involved with focusing on political leaders strategies, see Capoccia, *Defending Democracy* (2005), Chapter 8.

[17] For accounts of the opposition of increasingly marginal fringe groups at the radical right wing side of Swedish and British conservatism as late as the 1920s see Olsson, *Den svenska högerns anpassning till demokratin* (2000); Pugh, *Hurrah for the Blackshirts* (2006); Stevenson, "Conservatism and the Failure of Fascism in Britain" (1990). See, also Pugh, *Hurrah for the Blackshirts* (2006).

scholarship reveals continued ambivalence, if not outright opposition to, core features of democratic rule in the early 1920s among elite circles of the Swedish right.[18] Yet, organizational change and resulting election success sidelined radicals from within, transforming semi-loyalists into loyalists of democracy. Conservative access to power had the effect of marginalizing the anti-system radical right.

If these two mechanisms helped secure democracy, the cases where party fragmentation was high – where the right was split across *multiple* political parties – demonstrate the opposite. In Italy, Portugal, Spain, and Germany, the absence of a strongly organized pre-1918 conservative party meant that the interwar electoral right lacked organizational resources. In these cases, the organized center-right struggled to organize for the first time after 1918, while simultaneously facing the threat of socialist mobilization and mass democracy. These efforts were made more difficult by a mobilized radical right-wing during the interwar years.[19] This provoked, as we have seen in closer detail in Germany, spiraling polarization among political elites and ultimately democratic breakdown in all four cases. In sum, those center-right parties quickly cobbled together after 1918 were typically wracked with organizational schisms that left them unable to "defend democracy" against radical right-wing competition. In such a context, efforts to co-opt internal anti-parliamentary elements or to halt emerging radical far right parties were simply less viable.[20]

These cross-national patterns suggest a relationship, but all remains speculative unless our analysis of particular national cases also provides evidence consistent with plausible causal pathways linking historical conservative party organizational strength and democratic stability. By selecting cases well-predicted within the framework (i.e., on the "regression line"), evidence can emerge that either supports or undermines our theory.[21]

We begin by analyzing two "well-predicted" cases that appear to fit the framework: one where the right was relatively cohesive and democracy survived (Sweden), and one where it remained organizationally fractious and democracy ultimately collapsed (Spain). Finally, we analyze an ambiguous third case, France, which some regard as a case of democratic survival and others of democratic failure.[22] Only by analyzing developments within this case *over time*, can we assess how well the general theoretical framework illuminates even this difficult case.

[18] Olsson, *Den svenska högerns anpassning till demokratin* (2000).
[19] For a comparative view see Blinkhorn, ed., *Fascists and Conservatives* (1990).
[20] On the concept of "defending democracy," see Capoccia, *Defending Democracy* (2005).
[21] For an elaboration of this methodological point, see Evan Lieberman, "Nested Analysis as a Mixed-Method Strategy for Comparative Research," *American Political Science Review* 99, no. 3 (2005): 435–52.
[22] See Dobry, "France: An Ambiguous Survival" (2000).

SWEDEN

We turn first to Sweden, where the consolidation of the right before 1918 helped secure democracy during the crisis-ridden years of the 1920s and 1930s. The origins of this process lay in the early formation of a relatively robust conservative party before Sweden's 1918 transition to mass democracy. Without access to the instruments of electoral manipulation in the late nineteenth century, the competitive threat of *pre-democratic* electoral politics triggered a direct path of conservative party formation to defend establishment interests.[23]

The first organizational stirrings came with the "tariff dispute" of 1886–87, a battle between free traders, primarily drawn from cities and small farms, and protectionists, mainly the traditional landed elite.[24] While the salience of the tariff issue quickly receded, the cleavage dividing urban and rural interests remained. By the turn of the century this had evolved into a left–right political divide, pitting urban, free-trading Liberals and Social Democrats against protectionist conservatives in a conflict that increasingly centered on suffrage reform.[25] Liberals quickly gaining ground electorally with the help of vibrant civil society and free church movement while Social Democrats benefited from industrial growth, which lifted large numbers of workers into income categories providing them with voting rights.[26]

However, critical to the actual passage of suffrage reform was the far-sighted conservative Prime Minister Arvid Lindman. Like the British Conservative Benjamin Disraeli in 1867, Lindman turned the tables on his opponents and shepherded legislation ensuring suffrage reform (in this case, universal male suffrage) through parliament in 1907. Lindman's predecessor, the Liberal Karl Staaf had been elected in 1902 on the promise of suffrage reform, but – faced with strong opposition from an upper chamber still dominated by conservatives – he failed to enact changes and resigned. However, Lindman, well aware of the economic trends favoring Liberals and Social Democrats, aimed to resolve the suffrage issue while conservatives were still in control.

With the help of the influential conservative Lutheran Bishop Gottfrid Billing, who himself sat in the upper chamber, Lindman tied universal male suffrage in lower house elections to what Rustow calls the "tory guarantee" of

---

[23] For an account of how early bureaucratic reform and state autonomy eliminated opportunities for electoral manipulation, in eighteenth- and nineteenth-century Sweden, see Teorell, "Cleaning Up the Vote: The Case of Electoral Fraud in Sweden, 1719–1909."

[24] Rustow, *The Politics of Compromise: A Study of Parties and Cabinet Government in Sweden* (1955), 35–42.

[25] Lewin, *Ideology and Strategy: A Century of Swedish Politics* (1988), 34; Peter Esaiasson, "Svenska valkampanjer 1866–1988" (Allmänna förlaget, 1990), 83–85. See also Thermaenius, *Sveriges Politiska Partier* (1933), 19.

[26] Esaiasson, "Svenska valkampanjer 1866–1988" (1990), 85–86. See also, Lewin, *Ideology and Strategy: A Century of Swedish Politics* (1988), 70.

a shift from a majoritarian to a proportional electoral system.[27] Conservative electoral self-confidence in the face of suffrage reform had two sources. First, Lindman's reform restricted universal male suffrage to the lower house only. The upper chamber retained a strong legislative position and was indirectly elected via county councils where voting rights still depended on property and salary requirements. This would, it was hoped, continue to ensure conservative dominance and effective veto power.[28] Second, the early development of conservative party organization and the carefully crafted electoral system reforms of 1907–1909 appeared to guarantee significant conservative representation even if the right was unable to capture majorities in individual districts.[29] Hence, because of its electoral confidence and institutionalized veto power, the Swedish right *itself* passed significant democratizing reforms in 1907. These resources allowed conservatives a viable route of defending their interests within the new regime, which nonetheless fell far short of a fully democratic political system.[30]

Regardless of the progress made, countermajoritarian institutions – the "tory guarantees" – did not aid but rather ultimately blocked further democratization. As in Britain before the passage of the Parliament Act in 1911, pressure grew to reform the upper house in a democratic direction as well. How would the electoral right respond to these demands to eliminate such a key political crutch? The urgency grew as a dramatically expanding electorate put the electoral right on the defensive in lower chamber elections. Its share of the vote declined from 45 percent in 1905, prior to the reform, to 38 percent in 1908 and 31 percent in 1911. The Social Democrats jumped from under 10 to over 30 percent of the vote within the span of six years.[31] Thus, there was ample reason for wary conservatives to seek out new and non-democratic methods of self-defense.

But Lindman's conservative party, the General Electoral League (*Allmänna Valmansförbundet*, AVF), like the British Conservatives but unlike the Prussian

---

[27] Rustow, *The Politics of Compromise: A Study of Parties and Cabinet Government in Sweden* (1955), 72. For details on the passage of the reform, see Lewin, *Ideology and Strategy: A Century of Swedish Politics* (1988), 69ff.

[28] At first glance, then, this appears to support the notion that countermajoritarian institutions can bolster the chances of democratic transition. See Weingast, Alberts, and Warshaw, "Democratization and Countermajoritarian Institutions" (2012). A critique of this view follows below. For an account that reports on conservative expectations, see Olsson, *Den svenska högerns anpassning till demokratin* (2000), 49.

[29] Lewin, *Ideology and Strategy: A Century of Swedish Politics* (1988), 70.

[30] Universal suffrage to the lower chamber is sometimes taken as the indicator for the shift to a democratic regime in Sweden. More careful work persuasively argues that this should not be so for the Swedish case (see, e.g., Olsson, *Den svenska högerns anpassning till demokratin*, 2000, 48–50). Because the upper house retained its strong legislative position and voting requirements ensured conservative dominance, traditional interests and the right "retained [their] privileged position" (49). Further, full parliamentarization of the cabinet did not come until 1918.

[31] Nohlen and Stöver, *Elections in Europe: A Data Handbook* (2010), 1864.

Conservatives, had already begun successfully investing in party-building in the face of more competitive electoral politics. At the AVF's creation in 1904, its founders established only the basic infrastructure of a modern political party.[32] But, as in Britain, this organizational prehistory was critical because it provided groundwork for subsequent party-building before fuller democratization in 1918. The post-1907 shift to universal male suffrage and proportional representation had made campaigning without more robust party organization unfeasible, in the party's own official accounts of events.[33]

Thus, given the absence of parliamentary rule and the continued power of the undemocratic upper chamber, party-building on the right could occur *before* full democratization. In these years, campaigns were increasingly streamlined with centrally produced materials and nationally held trainings.[34] Like in Britain in an earlier era, the Swedish AVF's party organization was further bolstered with the addition of a cadre of full-time party administrators.[35] With a central party infrastructure in place to steer the process, efforts to forge links to business and industry provided resources to finance a larger party bureaucracy.[36] And, by 1912, many smaller right parties in the lower chamber that had retained their independence were incorporated into AVF.[37] Moreover, following the 1911 election, it was increasingly clear to AVF party leaders,

that [the AVF] had done best in districts where the electoral organization had been the most well-organized and where the "enlightenment" and agitation work had been the most focused and effective. Based on these experiences and lessons, the AVF concluded that further organizational development was desirable.[38]

After several decades of pre-democratic party building, the investment in party organization now began to pay off. The AVF made significant gains in 1914, proving itself as a viable competitor in more democratic lower house elections.

With the hardships imposed by the First World War, labor pressure for reform intensified.[39] By 1918 demands for more far-reaching democratization – i.e.,

[32] Edvard Thermænius, *Riksdagspartierna*, vol. 17 (Stockholm: Sveriges Riksdag, 1935), 174; Erik Nataneal Söderberg, *Allmnna valmansförbundet, 1904–1929: en tjugufemårskrönika* (Stockholm: Egnellska boktr., 1929); Axel Jäderin, *Allmänna valmansförbundet 1904–14. En krönika* (Stockholm: Allmänna valmansförbundet, 1914).
[33] Söderberg, *Allmänna valmansförbundet, 1904–1929: en tjugufemårskrönika* (1929), 100; Jäderin, *Allmänna valmansförbundet 1904–14. En krönika* (1914), 62–66.
[34] Jäderin, *Allmänna valmansförbundet 1904–14. En krönika* (1914), 81–82; 133–34. See also Söderberg, *Allmänna valmansförbundet, 1904–1929: en tjugufemårskrönika* (1929), 100–01.
[35] Ibid.
[36] Christer Ericsson, *Kapitalets politik och politikens kapital: högermän, industrimän och patriarker 1890–1985* (Stockholm: Santerus, 2008), 79.
[37] Söderberg, *Allämnna valmansförbundet, 1904–1929: en tjugufemårskrönika* (1929), 115–16.
[38] Ibid.,124–125.
[39] Sweden, of course, did not take part in the war. But the country suffered from severe food shortages and rationing. See Steven Koblik, "Wartime Diplomacy and the Democratization of Sweden in September–October 1917," *The Journal of Modern History* 41, no. 1 (1969): 29–45.

universal and direct suffrage in upper chamber elections – reached a peak. Revolutions in Russia and on the continent further upped the stakes by demonstrating how the violent overthrow of the status quo was a viable alternative to reform.[40] However, as we have seen in Germany before 1914, mere demand for democratic reform is not enough on its own. In December 1918, in the immediate wake of November's revolutionary events in Germany, the AVF party leadership's stance remained divided between Arvid Lindman in the lower chamber and the more conservative Ernst Trygger in the upper chamber. Both regarded the democratization of Sweden's upper chamber with initial skepticism, but Lindman ultimately pushed the party to accept the reform.[41]

Given that a countermajoritarian institution would be lost, what explains this acquiescence? First, Lindman convinced his upper chamber colleagues by arguing that the costs of the institutional change could be kept to a minimum. During the preceding decade, the AVF had proven itself to be electorally competitive in the democratic context of the lower house, which suggested it could also defend its interests in the upper chamber. Conservative leaders such Arvid Lindman believed that, in the words of one historian, "the right would do well within the new democratic system and that there was indeed no reason for despair."[42] Conservative newspapers argued that "there was much the right could do to win new voters," and following reform, the AVF resolved to expand and improve upon its own infrastructure.[43] Party organization for the electoral right had become its own safeguard; indeed, future events proved this to be a wise investment. Between 1920 and 1936, the AVF remained the second-strongest party in the Swedish parliament ahead of the agrarian Farmer's League and the Liberals and only trailing the Social Democrats.[44] It served in government in the late 1920s. And, even in the upper chamber, the AVF group, while smaller, remained the second-largest group after the Social Democrats.

In addition, mirroring British Conservative leader Stanley Baldwin's strategy in the different context of a majoritarian electoral system in Britain in the 1920s (see Chapter 5), Lindman behaved as a modern, strategic politician. By democratizing the upper chamber, he would dissolve the primary issue gluing the Liberals and Social Democrats together. This would give way, Lindman hoped, to contestation focused on the state's role in the economy, which might push the "bourgeois" liberals to the right.[45] Lindman himself hoped this carefully crafted strategy to "unite the anti-socialist bourgeois forces" would eventually forge a viable Liberal–Conservative governing

---

[40] Carl-Göran Andrae, "The Swedish Labor Movement and the 1917–1918 Revolution," in *Sweden's Development from Poverty to Affluence, 1750–1970*, ed. Steven Koblik (Minneapolis: University of Minnesota Press, 1975), 232–53.

[41] A key internal party vote occurred within the AVF leadership supporting the reform, passing 20–10. See Olsson, *Den svenska högerns anpassning till demokratin* (2000), 153.

[42] Olsson, *Den svenska högerns anpassning till demokratin* (2000), 178.   [43] Ibid., 176; 179.

[44] Nohlen and Stöver, *Elections in Europe: A Data Handbook* (2010), 1865–66.

[45] For evidence, see Olsson, *Den svenska högerns anpassning till demokratin* (2000), 178.

coalition.[46] Hence, the right's conviction that it could survive within a democratic political regime was bolstered by its own robust party organization and the prospects of a new anti-socialist coalition with the Liberals.

While certain elements had consistently opposed democratic reform during the first two decades of the twentieth century, the conservative right was loyal to democracy by the 1930s, which proved crucial for regime stability. Several extreme right movements entered Swedish electoral politics in the 1920s and 1930s, but the party leadership had the resources to distance themselves from all forms of authoritarianism. Not only did party leaders argue that democracy was the "Swedish form of government,"[47] with "deep" roots in the country's cultural and political traditions, but they also made the costly but path-shaping decision to break ties with their own 40,000-member-strong youth association (*Sveriges Nationella Ungdomsförbund*, SNU), which, especially after 1930, had steadily marched right-wards.[48] As a "youth" group – actually open to all ages – inspired by Italian fascism and Hitler's rise to power in January 1933, it pushed for the cause of stronger monarchy and aggressively agitated against the Social Democrats. The SNU's right-wing radicalism was a source of growing concern to the party leadership and it was ultimately expelled from AVF in 1933.[49] This new conservative commitment to democratic government, as well as the AVF's organizational ability to distance itself from its own radical grassroots, effectively shut out right-wing challengers during the troubled 1930s.

In sum, the Swedish right's accommodation to democracy in Sweden was important for regime stability in a period marked elsewhere by authoritarian reversals. Its commitment to democracy was, in turn, a relatively recent phenomenon, as conservatives opposed democratization throughout the first two decades of the 1900s. What made the right acquiesce, and eventually commit, to democracy was its growing stock of organizational resources, which allowed it to compete electorally and thus defend its interests within a democratic system as well as ability to sideline right-wing radicals within the party's own ranks.

SPAIN

Next, we turn to Spain. Unlike Sweden, interwar Spain exemplifies the effect of a legacy of extremely *weak* center-right political organization. In Spain there was a very different sequencing of full democratization and conservative party development than occurred in Sweden (and Britain). Spain's conservative

---

[46] Ibid.   [47] Olsson, *Den svenska högerns anpassning till demokratin* (2000), 240.
[48] Lena Berggren, "Swedish Fascism: Why Bother?" *Journal of Contemporary History* 37, no. 3 (2002): 395–417.
[49] Olsson, *Den svenska högerns anpassning till demokratin* (2000), 227; 43–54.

forces, like Germany's, had long thrived under a system of state intervention in elections and restricted competition during the nineteenth and early twentieth centuries. By the 1930s and the rise of the Second Republic, conservatives had still postponed party-building, despite the formal, early adoption of universal male suffrage in 1890. After 1931, they now faced *genuine* mass democratization for the first time, but were ill equipped to cope with the consequences of more fully democratic competition. As a result, Spain drifted toward democratic breakdown despite the best intentions of republican democratic reformers.

Why did Spain's party of the right fail to take the same path as Sweden's? To answer this question, we must return to at least the Restoration period (1874–1931). Unlike in Sweden, new forms of state-supported electoral manipulation were developed in the nineteenth century that compromised genuine electoral competition late into the modern era. Beginning in 1885 with an explicit bargain (*"el Pacto del Pardo"*) struck between Conservative Party leader Antonio Cánovas and Liberal Party leader Práxedes Mateo Sagasta to assure stability to the restored monarchy, Spain was characterized by *el turno* system. The two dynastic parties, the parliamentary groupings of Liberals (*Partido Liberal*) and the Conservatives (*Partido Conservador*, PC), carefully colluded by crafting alternations in power despite the presence of universal male suffrage.

The result was political stability achieved at the price of genuine electoral competition. Government control ensured that elections were no more than "a [hierarchical] mechanism of distributing power,"[50] a tool for reaching a predetermined outcome. Most importantly, the two parties made frequent pacts to ensure transitions occurred almost seamlessly. *Turnismo* depended on the deeply entrenched system of *caciquismo*, a pyramidal organization of power with only the loosest of political party structures. The Madrid-controlled system, whose prominent actors were landowners, professionals and prominent businessmen, divided the Spanish political territory into different *cacique*-controlled areas. The *caciquismo* system in turn was defined by well-developed and longstanding clientelistic networks.[51] The overall absence of political competition guaranteed that political party differentiation and organizational development occurred only sporadically.[52] In addition, the regional concentrations of power meant that political

---

[50] Mercedes Cabrera and Fernando del Rey, *El poder de los empresarios: política y economía en la España contemporánea, 1875–2010*, 1 ed. (Barcelona: RBA, 2011), 74.

[51] For an overview of the results of this system, region-by-region, see Varela Ortega, ed., *El poder de la influencia* (2001).

[52] Juan Linz, "The Party System of Spain: Past and Future," in *Party Systems and Voter Alignments: Cross-national Perspectives*, ed. Seymour Martin Lipset and Stein Rokkan (New York: Free Press, 1967), 208.

expression was most successful at the regional level, as the success of the conservative *Lliga Catalana* demonstrates.[53]

The restrictions on genuine electoral competition at the national level were no better under Primo de Rivera's dictatorship (1923–1931). Among other things, his government sought to replace *caciquismo* with a single, *apolitical* party; however, this only left the electoral right "weaker and more divided" than before.[54] During the last days of Primo de Rivera's rule, disarrayed members of the right were plagued with what Shlomo Ben-Ami calls "an incoherent conservatism."[55] Recognizing this problem, some prominent conservatives recognized the need for a single "Conservative Party of opinion on the English style."[56] Yet, schisms on the right endured.

In 1931, the abrupt end of the Spanish monarchy after the fall of Primo de Rivera's dictatorship and the subsequent formation of the Second Spanish Republic – a hopeful but ultimately transitory moment of democratic opening – had a major impact on the political landscape. Unlike Sweden and Britain where a single conservative political party had firmly established itself before the transition to full mass democracy, in Spain no significant conservative party survived the shift with its political organization intact.[57] Non-loyal (i.e., non-republican) forces took advantage of the gap, and more extreme and mobilized right-wing groups dominated Spanish right politics throughout the 1930s. Even the most noteworthy Tory-like group suffered from a "basic lack of organizational infrastructure."[58] The Liberal Republican Right (*Derecha Liberal Republicana*), founded by two prominent traditional elites, Niceto Alacalá-Zamora and Miguel Maura, was conceived as a conservative republican "defender of order" and "conservative classes," and a "barrier against

---

[53] The party was well organized, successful at the local level in both fighting *turnismo* and in defending the Catalan conservative bourgeoisie's interests. See Luis Arranz, Mercedes Cabrera, and Fernando del Rey, "The Assault of Liberalism, 1914–1923," in *Spanish History Since 1808*, ed. Alvarez Junco and Adrian Shubart (New York: Oxford University Press, 2000, 196) and in defending the Catalan conservative bourgeoisie's interests. See Joan Marcet, "La derecha en España: una aproximación histórica" (Barcelona, Spain: Institut de ciències polítiques i socials, Universitat Autonoma de Barcelona, 2012), 7.

[54] Alejandro Quiroga and Miguel Ángel del Arco Blanco, eds., *Soldados de dios y apóstoles de la patria: Las derechas españolas en la Europa de entreguerras* (Granada: Editorial Comares, 2010), xxi.

[55] Shlomo Ben-Ami, *The Origins of the Second Republic in Spain* (Oxford: Oxford University Press, 1978), 178.

[56] Ibid.

[57] The only "historical" republican party to make the transition with significant political power was the centrist Radical Republican Party. Stanley G. Payne, *Spain's First Democracy: The Second Republic, 1931–1936* (Madison: University of Wisconsin Press, 1993), 25.

[58] Mary Vincent, *Catholicism in the Second Spanish Republic: Religion and Politics in Salamanca, 1930–1936* (New York: Clarendon Press, 1996), 142.

Sovietism."[59] Yet, the party failed to take root, winning only 27 out of 427 parliamentary seats in the republic's inaugural 1931 election. The Liberal Republican Right was subject to internal schism and was superseded by other forces.[60]

After 1931, the half-century of constrained competition had ended, and conservatives, like all groupings, were faced with a radically different electoral environment. Unlike in Sweden, rightist forces in Spain were compelled to organize only *after* full democratization; indeed, many formed within weeks of the regime change. By 1933, the political atmosphere was already highly polarized.

This phenomenon of "postponed conservative party-building" made national party organization more difficult for the electoral right in two ways. First, long periods of electoral manipulation and periods of military rule had served as "substitutes" for electorally viable conservative parties. This delay meant that after 1931, the Spanish right had to deal with more than just a moderate opposition, as it would have in the era of restricted suffrage. Instead, it now faced a majority coalition of two parties, the Left Republicans and the Socialist Party, which had more ambitiously transformative socio-economic, anticlerical, and other institution-shaping goals. These included far-reaching land reform, an extensive program to separate church and state, and an effort to reform civil–military relations.[61] Further, after enduring forty years of manipulated elections and seven years of dictatorship, the political inclinations and strategies of the left had grown more extreme. During the de Rivera dictatorship, membership in the Socialist-affiliated union (*Unión General de Trabajadores*) grew, as did membership in the anarcho-syndicalist union (*Confederación Nacional de Trabajo*) and the Communist Party (*Partido Comunista de España*).

This led conservative social forces to seek out alternatives to party-building in order to survive.[62] As the unreconstructed rightist José Calvo Sotelo put it in 1936, "I think the Communist advance cannot be stopped by the instruments of a parliamentary democratic regime."[63] This resulted in a self-reinforcing negative vicious-circle: (1) postponed party-building for the right in Spain resulted in a conservative dependence on monarchy, manipulation, and military dictatorship; (2) in response, the left grew more active and radical; and (3) the right panicked and resorted to more extreme countermeasures,

[59] Ben-Ami, *The Origins of the Second Republic in Spain* (1978), 56. For a more general account of the *Derecha Republicana*, see José R. Montero, *La CEDA: el catolicismo social y político en la II República* (Madrid: Ediciones de la Revista de Trabajo, 1977), vol. 1, 223–43.
[60] Payne, *Spain's First Democracy: The Second Republic, 1931–1936* (1993), 50–51.
[61] For elaboration of the government's agenda, see Edward E. Malefakis, *Agrarian Reform and Peasant Revolution in Spain: Origins of the Civil War* (New Haven: Yale University Press, 1970).
[62] Gerard Alexander, *The Sources of Democratic Consolidation* (Ithaca: Cornell University Press, 2002), 111–13.
[63] Ibid., 108.

creating ideological schism on the right which complicated efforts to organize a moderate center-right party.

Delayed party-building also mattered for a second reason: an energetic and unruly national landscape of *right-wing* monarchist, Catholic and agrarian pressure groups and association, as well as right-wing youth associations, had already autonomously sprung up by the early 1930s, which made harnessing these fractious groups into a single party that much more difficult. Lacking the resources of a solid core at the start, party-builders were forced to contend with highly mobilized and anti-democratic forces. These fractious radical groups ultimately steered the organizational and ideological trajectory of Spain's late-developing conservative party.

After 1931, the right carved out a single party organization in the form of *Acción Nacional* – later renamed *Acción Popular* – and finally formed the umbrella organization *Confederación Española de Derechas Autónomas*, or Spanish Confederation of Autonomous Right-Wing Groups (*CEDA*) in 1933. But, as noted above, this project was constrained by a vibrant and ever-changing collection of right-wing pressure groups, press associations, and proto-parties, which also made the central party more vulnerable to radicalization. As Preston puts it, despite the absence of a single party, the privileged classes were not "entirely helpless."[64]

For example, one important group from this landscape was the ACNP (*Asociación Católica Nacional de Propagandistas*), a collection of five hundred Jesuit elites that self-identified as a "Catholic fifth column" with financial backing from a religious Basque banker.[65] Other prominent groups emerged from the provincial-level Catholic social infrastructure, aiming to stall or even halt the Republic's agrarian and anticlerical reforms. These included a mass-membership agrarian league of 500,000 members (*Confederación Nacional Católico-Agraria*), the more elite *Acción Castellana* in Salamanca and the *Bloque Agrario*. These groups ultimately formed the core of their national successor, *Acción Popular*. Other regional groups, typically founded by local notables, included *Derecha Regional Valencia* (founded by wealthy Valencian orange planters), *Acción Popular Agraria de Badajoz*, *Derecha Regional Agraria de Cáceres*, *Acción Agraria Manchega*, and *Acción Ciudadana y Agraria de Cuenca*.[66] All of these groups, developed outside the channels of traditional electoral politics, were intended to serve as "barricades" against the Republic – and acted as rivals for influence and power.

---

[64] Paul Preston, *The Coming of the Spanish Civil War: Reform, Reaction and Revolution in the Second Republic*, 2nd ed. (London: Routledge, 1994), 63.

[65] Vincent, *Catholicism in the Second Spanish Republic: Religion and Politics in Salamanca, 1930–1936* (1996), 118.

[66] Preston, *The Coming of the Spanish Civil War: Reform, Reaction and Revolution in the Second Republic* (1994), 46; 58.

In February 1933, nine months before the next national parliamentary elections, five hundred delegates representing forty-two of these groups attended a mass congress to form the single party of the right, *Confederación Española de Derechas Autónomas*, or Spanish Confederation of Autonomous Right-Wing Groups (CEDA).[67] Because CEDA was so quickly formed, in effect, from the "bottom-up" out of many autonomous regional entities it ended up being characterized by a loose confederative structure. The constitutive organizations generally fell into three categories: groups related to *Acción Popular*, agrarian associations, and rightist blocs.[68] And, while the task of governing this patchwork was formally in the hands of the party's General Assembly, in practice things ran very differently.[69] After the November elections, CEDA was largely subject to the direction of its *Jefe*, José-María Gil-Robles along with the party's National Council and the new CEDA parliamentary deputies themselves.[70] The massive achievement of its election campaign work, unparalleled in its thoroughness, was however carried out by autonomous groups such as the youth wing of the *Acción Popular*, leaving power in the hands of external groups. In addition to this, the weakness of the formal central organization was reflected in its effort to elevate the "charismatic" status of a single leader, Gil-Robles to unify the party, as well as its nebulous ideology ("defense of family and religion") and intentional ambiguity toward republicanism. One historian writes:

> The CEDA was, as its very name suggests, a loose confederation of autonomous right-wing groups held together only by the promise of power, which differed substantially from location to location and even within the same bodies ... The CEDA was home to fascists and conservatives, spanning the entire Spanish right; this made it populist and popular, all things to all right-wingers, but denied it internal cohesion and the ability to withstand defeat or crisis.[71]

Similarly, reflecting on the party's shortcomings, former *cedista* former minister, Jiménez Fernández, wrote, "The great defect of the CEDA was that in reality *it was never a party*."[72]

Despite its problems, CEDA's sprawling but decentralized organization enjoyed electoral success in the 1933 elections to the *Cortes Generales*, in which the republican and socialist left were replaced by a center-right government. But this electoral shift ironically highlights how lack of prior

---

[67] Ibid., 65.
[68] *Accion Popular*'s dominant influence can be seen in CEDA's early organizational makeup. In 1933, twenty-two of the thirty-eight organizations for which data are available fell into the first category. Montero, *La CEDA: el catolicismo social y político en la II República* (1977). Vol.1, 416–17
[69] Ibid., Vol. 2, 501; 506.   [70] Ibid., 471; 513.
[71] Sid Lowe, *Catholicism, War and the Foundation of Francoism: The Juventud de Acción Popular in Spain, 1931–1939* (Portland: Sussex Academic Press, 2010), 69.
[72] Ibid.

organization simultaneously created difficult choices for center-right republicans and opportunities for the far right. Prior to the 1933 elections, as socialist and republican cooperation foundered, republican parties took up the mission of building "the Republic of the Republicans" and attempted to cobble together a strong centrist bloc.[73] Unable to effectively work with any group left of center, the centrist Radicals (*Partido Republicano Radical*) turned to the right. And, lacking a viable conservative republican party, the Radicals became dependent on an explicitly non-republican conservative party, namely Jose Gil Robles' CEDA, and its anti-democratic Catholic mass network. Parliamentary arithmetic necessitated the decision.[74] The weakness of the conservative republicans forced centrist republicans to rely on an essentially anti-republican party for their coalition-building project.[75]

The 1933 electoral and consequential parliamentary alliance indeed only marked the beginning of a shift further to the right, which ultimately led three years later to the regime's collapse. Without a strong center-right option in the political system to oppose them, the organizationally powerful right wing of CEDA capitalized on the Radical's dependence and seized control of the conservative agenda. CEDA leveraged its dominant parliamentary position to push through policies that eliminated religious and labor legislation as well as comprehensive agrarian reform.[76] Further, the party influenced the government's heavy-handed response to strikes in Asturias and other parts of the country, suspending constitutional guarantees aimed at labor organizations.[77] CEDA obtained three key cabinet appointments in October 1934 (agriculture, labor, and justice) and increased that number to five the next year.

CEDA's rapid radicalization resulted from its loose, poorly institutionalized party structure. The party's confederative organization acted as a channel

---

[73] Nigel Townson, *The Crisis of Democracy in Spain: Centrist Policies Under the Second Republic (1931–1936)* (Portland: Sussex Academic Press, 2000), 186.

[74] Ibid. Alejandro Lerroux, Radical Party leader of the largest Republican contingent of the time, pointed to the infeasibility of a center left alliance due to the irreparable relations with the socialists and the dismal electoral prospects of the left republicans during a party address in Madrid on November 8, 1933.

[75] Ibid.

[76] Particular example of such legislation included an amnesty bill for the right-wing insurgents that participated in the failed August 10, 1932 coup; the restoration of the *hableres del clero* law which mandated that the state provide small-town priests with a salary; and the non-enforcement of the Law of Congregations which allowed religious schools to continue to function; Townson, *The Crisis of Democracy in Spain: Centrist Policies Under the Second Republic (1931–1936)* (2000), 186; 197; 223.

[77] According to a denunciation published by the Socialist movement's trade union organization, the UGT (*Unión General de Trabajadores*), the first 315 days of government after the election had been characterized by a "state of alarm" implying the suspension of constitutional guarantees, press censorship, seizures of newspapers, declaration of illegality for strikes, and the protection of fascist and monarchist groups. Cited in Townson, *The Crisis of Democracy in Spain: Centrist Policies Under the Second Republic (1931–1936)* (2000), 172.

through which the organization's more mobilized and radical elements could drive parliamentary behavior. This was nowhere more visible or consequential than with one of the core autonomous groups at the heart of CEDA, the Catholic youth group, *Juventudes de Acción Popular*, or JAP. Founded in 1932 as a youth wing of *Acción Popular* and then CEDA, by 1936 its membership reached 200,000 with 1,000 local organizations throughout Spain.[78] Like youth wings of rightist parties throughout Europe in the period, JAP incorporated strong elements of fascist ideology and style. It was conceived as a "paramilitary" organization with members marching in khaki uniforms and performing salutes. Its chief aim was to assure "purity" in the "parent party" – to prevent, in its own words, "suffocating asphyxiation in an atmosphere of cowardly caution." Its rejection of compromise served as a bridge between traditional conservatism and fascism.[79] Though called a "youth wing" and modeled after counterparts in the rest of Europe, the upper age limit for membership was thirty-five years. JAP was initially subordinate to CEDA, but the hierarchy was inverted over time. The internal radicalization within JAP pushed CEDA itself further and further to the right, contributing to Spain's democratic breakdown in 1936.

In an illuminating contrast to Sweden, where AVF party leaders had the leverage to expel their 40,000-member youth branch, CEDA's loose and recently built confederation structure had the opposite effect – it allowed JAP to become *more* autonomous and influential in the national party over time.[80] While certainly an opponent of democratic politics himself, Gil-Robles admitted that JAP's radicalization created "not inconsiderable problems" for him and that, in retrospect, the youth group "succeeded in imposing some of its identity upon CEDA."[81] Likewise, another CEDA deputy reported that "Gil Robles was obliged to grant the JAP a certain degree of freedom in order to keep the youth wing's allegiance."[82] And when the centrist government collapsed in 1936, President Niceto Alcalá-Zamora feared forming a new republican with Gil-Robles because "any attempt to make a moderate conservative power of the CEDA was doomed" and JAP "had begun to pull much of the wider party's rank and file with it."[83]

Though a mere constituent part of CEDA, JAP's leverage came from two sources: its ideological cohesion and the indispensable role it played in the party's campaign machinery. JAP was CEDA's "chief organizer" of elections across much of the country, preparing electoral rolls, holding political rallies, getting voters to the polls, and producing campaign materials.[84] During the

---

[78] Lowe, *Catholicism, War and the Foundation of Francoism: The Juventud de Acción Popular in Spain, 1931–1939* (2010), 101.

[79] Ibid., 81.

[80] Montero, *La CEDA: el catolicismo social y político en la II República* (1977). Vol 1, 595.

[81] Cited by Lowe, *Catholicism, War and the Foundation of Francoism: The Juventud de Acción Popular in Spain, 1931–1939* (2010), 66; 81.

[82] Ibid., 67.   [83] Ibid., 77; 78.   [84] Ibid.

Radical-CEDA government (1933–1935), while the parliamentary coalition worked on the issue of constitutional reform, JAP pushed CEDA to call for a stronger executive and dramatic limitations on the legislature.[85]

Once new elections were called for February 1936, JAP asserted itself even further. First, since the Spanish electoral system allowed for five deputies in each election district, JAP members announced they would no longer support moderate parliamentary candidates, vowing only to promote those with "*Juventud* [youthful] spirit."[86] Second, they filed formal complaints against CEDA's moderate-leaning candidates, prompting the party's General Secretary to write a letter to one association warning that "Despite your complaints we trust you will give the candidates the maximum support in the province."[87] Third, there was growing concern that JAP would intentionally sabotage CEDA by not distributing the correct candidate lists in provinces, a critical task that was remarkably in JAP's hands. And finally, after considering a rogue JAP-*Falange* (Fascist) slate in some places, JAP ran twenty-two of its own candidates.[88]

The loss of the election was devastating: With *Japistas* already flocking to monarchist groups and the still-small *Falange*, many of CEDA's regional offices were abandoned; Gil-Robles attempted to assert his leadership but failed to the prevent the party from disintegrating. A conspiracy was quickly plotted to use CEDA's money, social networks, and membership base to help organize a military coup.[89] While CEDA appeared stable until 1935, at the first sign of electoral weakness, the party's ideological base radicalized and shed its republican inclinations entirely. After Gil-Robles reportedly failed to convince the president to declare martial law immediately following the elections in 1936, former CEDA members officially began to associate themselves with fascist *Falange* to promote right-wing violence in the streets. Eventually, they participated in the planning of a military uprising that would spark civil war in July 1936 and lead to democracy's total collapse.[90]

In short, Spanish conservatives in the 1930s followed a particular historical trajectory – which we have seen also was mirrored in Germany, Portugal, and Italy – that proved to have profound implications for the Spanish Second Republic. Historically reliant on a pattern of electoral collusion and manipulation, the key parties of the right lacked autonomous national infrastructure and were fractured by intense confessional conflicts. Only when exposed to the arena of mass politics in 1931 did the center right attempt to

[85] Payne, *Spain's First Democracy: The Second Republic, 1931–1936* (1993), 241.
[86] Lowe, *Catholicism, War and the Foundation of Francoism: The Juventud de Acción Popular in Spain, 1931–1939* (2010), 97.
[87] Ibid., 100.   [88] Ibid., 96–100.
[89] On the army's own motivations in the July 1936 coup, Stanley G. Payne, *Politics and the Military in Modern Spain* (Stanford, CA: Stanford University Press, 1967), 214–40.
[90] Preston, *The Coming of the Spanish Civil War: Reform, Reaction and Revolution in the Second Republic* (1994), 256–59; 74.

organize at the national level, ultimately producing the initially successful but weakly institutionalized CEDA. When faced with the transformative agenda of the republican-socialist government, the party's impressive-looking but ultimately fragile structure succumbed to internal radical forces. Ultimately, all this left Spanish democracy profoundly vulnerable to eventual collapse.

FRANCE

Between the poles of settled and unsettled democratization, political events during the French interwar period illustrate the dynamics of a third, hybrid democratic outcome. While the Third Republic did not collapse outright, it is a mistake to exaggerate the regime's stability.[91] Indeed, it often teetered on the edge of collapse, especially in the 1930s; even periods of relative stability were punctuated by parliamentary crisis. Conservatives were strong enough to survive and remain political relevant, but they were not strong enough to contain the far right's fear of a growing left in France, especially after 1936. Therefore, they could not guarantee a robust, stable parliamentary regime.

In 1919, the National Bloc (*Bloc National*), a coalition of conservative forces accomplished what the right had rarely done since the 1870s: winning a governing parliamentary majority (417 seats) in the Chamber of Deputies.[92] Unlike the state-aided conservative majorities of the Bonapartist era, this victory was genuine. It was all the more remarkable because the right had long been split between Bourbon, Bonapartist, and Orléanist tendencies.[93] And while the National Bloc was now unified in its anti-socialism, the two mainstream conservative parties at the core of coalition, the Republican Federation (*Fédération républicaine*) and the Democratic Alliance (*Alliance démocratique*) – along with the Radical Party (*Parti radical*) – remained fractured across two historical fault-lines. First, religious tensions continued to smolder beneath the surface between

---

[91] Some have correctly regarded the creation of France's Third Republic (1871–1877) as a major and successful case of democratic transition (see, for example, Hanson, *Post-Imperial Democracies: Ideology and Party Formation in Third Republic France, Weimar Germany, and Post-Soviet Russia*, 2010). Others have rightly pointed out that, despite its success at preventing a formal return to pre-1871 instability, the "republican synthesis" at the core of the Third Republic was also a highly fragile equilibrium, especially by the 1930s (See, e.g., Hoffmann, *Decline or Renewal? France since the 1930s*, 1974; Kevin Passmore, *From Liberalism to Fascism: The Right in a French Province, 1928–1939*, Cambridge: Cambridge University Press, 1997). This ambiguity is precisely the outcome that requires explanation.

[92] The 1919 election returned the largest conservative majority since 1870. See Nohlen and Stöver, *Elections in Europe: A Data Handbook* (2010). Two other instances of when the right triumphed were from 1896 to 1898 when Jules Meline headed up a center-right majority and the so-called National Revival of 1911–1914. On the former, see Herman Lebovics, *The Alliance of Iron and Wheat in the Third French Republic, 1860–1914: Origins of the New Conservatism* (Baton Rouge: Louisiana State University Press, 1988). On the latter, see Eugen Weber, *The Nationalist Revival in France, 1905–1914* (Berkeley: University of California Press, 1959).

[93] Rémond, *Right Wing in France* (1969).

the anticlerical center-right, represented by the *Alliance démocratique* and Radicals at one end, and the more Catholic-minded *Fédération* on the other.[94] Second there was a socioeconomic fissure between large industrial interests (for example, electricity and chemicals), represented by the *Alliance*, and small producers, the traditional base of the Radicals.[95]

In 1919, the National Bloc appeared to overcome these divides hastily by cobbling together a powerful far-reaching anti-Socialist electoral alliance.[96] This was accomplished thanks to electoral reforms intended to stabilize the regime; a new party list system incentivized conservatives to muster the largest bloc possible in order to maximize representation because of a new party list system.[97] But, the oversized coalition came at a price: the challenge of accommodating a small but highly active set of far-right groups. While the alliance failed to yield dramatic gains for the extreme right, it revealed the incapacity of the modern French center-right to distance itself from the extreme right, as well as the shaky foundations of French parliamentary system as a whole.

By 1924, the tables quickly turned, and the Left Cartel (*Cartel des gauches*), a new alliance of socialists and Radicals, defeated the National Bloc to form a new left-of-center government. However, two short years later, in 1926, government proved unstable and collapsed due to fights over fiscal policy and monetary matters. Following this, Raymond Poincaré, elder statesmen and leader of the *Alliance démocratique*, formed an interim government of both the Left and the Right. The electorate appeared to endorse the new government's conservative economic program in the 1928 elections,[98] which aided the stabilization of the regime.

---

[94] For elaboration, see Kevin Passmore, *The Right in France from the Third Republic to Vichy* (Oxford: Oxford University Press, 2013), 219–24.

[95] Julian Jackson, *France: The Dark Years, 1940–1944* (Oxford: Oxford University Press, 2001), 67–68.

[96] The political process resulting in the *Bloc national* is telling. The idea of a national alliance of "Republicans" against Socialism was put into action in October 1919 – one month before the elections – and after internal strife over which groups were to be invited, a final permutation of conservative groups and a collective program emerged, calling for an "energetic opposition to Bolshevism." In terms of the specific composition, it is difficult to produce a complete and accurate list as the members varied across departments. In the department of the Seine, the Bloc included the Republican Federation, the Democratic Alliance, the Civic League, the Democratic League of Moral and Social Action, the Radicals, and, most notably, the National Socialist Party. To be clear, the Bloc did not invite groups that were outwardly anti-democratic, such as the Royalists; for a detailed account of the months leading to the November 1919 elections, see Maier, *Recasting Bourgeois Europe* (1975), 92–109.

[97] The July 12, 1919 electoral reform bill replaced the *scrutin d'arrondissement* system with a *scrutin de liste* system, or election by a general departmental ticket. The law and its nineteen articles are complex, but the most pertinent aspect of the law lies in the requirement that candidates are to be grouped on a party basis according to lists. For a review of the law and its mechanics see Kreuzer, *Institutions and Innovation* (2001), 65.

[98] Raymond Leslie Buell, *Contemporary French Politics* (New York: D. Appleton, 1920), 177–80; 87.

The 1924 election results and the rise of the *Cartel des gauches* seemed to challenge the old compromises between modernizing and traditional forces that had kept the Third Republic intact for so long.[99] This sparked a vigorous right-wing counter-reaction in what Robert Soucy has provocatively called the "first wave of organized fascism" in France. But, Poincaré's subsequent election success in 1928 "stole its thunder by defeating the cartel."[100] As Maier notes about the conservative election victories in this period, "Happy with the outcome of the elections, French business interests did not yet take refuge in corporatist efforts for bypassing the Assembly or authoritarian dreams of suppressing it."[101] Yet, new far-right groups known as *ligues* took root alongside the *Action française* (AF) movement, representing an attractive but pernicious force for many on the right. Indeed, with the rapid decline of the so-called "stalemate" compromise in the 1930s, the growing reliance of center-right political parties on far-right grassroots mobilizations shifted the balance of power between the two.

In February 1934, the Great Depression was well underway in France, and extreme institutional paralysis wracked the political system, which cycled through seven ministries in eighteen months. French conservatives began to grapple with the far right in earnest. The *Place de la Concorde* riots on February 6, 1934, were a violent showdown between various right-wing extra-parliamentary groups and police. Sixteen were killed and 2,000 injured virtually on the front steps of the National Assembly. These riots marked a watershed moment in which the anti-parliamentary far right burst into prominence, but this time enduringly, as they demonstrated what paramilitary organization and direction action could achieve.[102] Groups such as the *Action française*, the *Croix de feu*, and the *Jeunesses patriotes* adopted and refined these tactics as they grew in numbers.[103]

Even though the far right was growing in numbers and gaining influence, conservatives took little action to stem the tide.[104] Indeed, the largest party of the old right, *Fédération républicaine*, ambivalently viewed the new "Bonapartist" leagues as a potential electoral resource, but one that might come back to haunt the party. In the words of one *Fédération* MP, Philippe

---

[99] These compromises have been described as being at the heart of the "stalemate society," the interpretation of France's Third Republic, as described by Stanley Hoffmann, "The Effects of World War II on French Society and Politics," *French Historical Studies* 2, no. 1 (1961): 28–63.

[100] Robert Soucy, *French Fascism: The Second Wave, 1933–1939* (New Haven: Yale University Press, 1995), 27.

[101] Maier, *Recasting Bourgeois Europe* (1975), 109.

[102] Jackson, *France: The Dark Years, 1940–1944* (2001), 72.

[103] Sean Kennedy, *Reconciling France Against Democracy: The Croix de Feu and the Parti Social Français, 1927–1945* (Montreal: McGill-Queen's University Press, 2007a).

[104] At this point far right groups such as the *Croix de Feu* boasted memberships of up to 350,000. Moreover, they also benefited from the financial support of key French industrialists such as perfume magnate, Francois Coty; William L. Shirer, *The Collapse of the Third Republic: An Inquiry into the Fall of France in 1940* (New York: Simon and Schuster, 1969).

Henriot, the leagues were "a useful barrier of resolute men against the threatening violence of the revolutionary forces."[105] They were, in another party leader's phrase, "vigilant defenders of order."[106] Especially in the face of the Popular Front, the rise of communism, and the Radical Party's shift to the left in the mid-1930s, elitist parties were desperate for the support provided by mass-membership leagues such as the *Croix de feu* and the *Jeunesses patriotes*.

Because conservative parties were weak, they become increasingly dependent on anti-democratic mass membership groups. Indeed, overlapping leadership and membership triggered a familiar dynamic of capture: Federation party leaders ranging from Pierre Taittinger, Édouard Soulier, and Jean Ybarnégaray were also leading figures of the *Jeunesses patriotes*; five vice-presidents of the Federation also were members of the *Croix de feu*.[107] Overlapping membership at the local level and the absence of any genuine autonomous central party organization for the parliamentary parties gave the leagues tremendous leverage over party politicians. As a result, as Irvine summarizes,

The leagues... were not prepared to play the subordinate role that the *Fédération* had cast for them. As they grew in size, they demanded a more important role than that of serving as a praetorian guard for traditional conservative parties... It was at this time that the Croix-de-Feu adopted the slogan, 'One does not annex the Croix-de-Feu, one follows it.'[108]

All of this underscores the weakness of mainstream French conservatism, which tolerated and even accepted far-right intransigence in exchange for political support. Yet, by 1936, maintaining this relationship had become quite costly. Some far right ranks swelled to 700,000 and had garnered enough influence to directly challenge establishment conservatives electorally.[109] Fearing a coup d'etat after winning elections in 1936, the Popular Front legislated the dissolution of right-wing leagues in an attempt to diminish their influence. This only had the effect of further fracturing and agitating the right since many of the "new right" leagues transformed themselves into political parties, and now sought to compete in the electoral domain of the "old right."

The 1936 outbreak of civil war in neighboring Spain suggested ominous trends. Though France's Popular Front certainly had more modest ambitions than its Spain's counterpart, this did not prevent French conservatives from apocalyptically predicting Soviet-style revolution against bourgeois society. Just as boundaries between the extremist and parliamentary right began to blur, some fringe groups began accumulating arms caches, orchestrating terrorist

---

[105] William D. Irvine, "French Conservatives and the 'New Right' During the 1930s," *French Historical Studies* 8, no. 4 (1974): 542.
[106] Ibid., 539.   [107] Ibid., 545.   [108] Ibid., 545.
[109] Roger Austin, "The Conservative Right and the Far Right in France, 1934–1944," in *Fascists and Conservatives*, ed. Martin Blinkhorn (Abingdon: Routledge, 1990).

attacks, and trying to establish relations with the army.[110] To some, civil war seemed to be brewing, though ultimately reform under the Popular Front and later under Daladier suggested the possibility of democratic survival.

What prevented France from following Spain's self-destructive path? A key factor was that, unlike CEDA, the French parliamentary right never fully disintegrated after its electoral defeat of 1936. While radical right groups gained influence throughout the 1930s, the concerted effort of conservatives in France's Senate eventually defeated Léon Blum's Popular Front coalition government, prompting his departure. This left power in the hands of Édouard Daladier and his ideologically flexible Radical Party. With socialists now gone, the cabinet of 1938 included conservatives and Radicals but under Daladier's leadership tilted distinctively rightwards, attenuating the rebellious ambitions of the extremist right-wing fringe. Thus, as Julian Jackson argues, it is a mistake to draw a direct line between the weakness of French conservatism in the late 1930s and the "strange defeat" that followed Hitler's invasion of France. After all, despite the pernicious slogan that perhaps apocryphally circulated among French right-wing circles in 1936, "Better Hitler than Blum," it was not disaffection of the right from a republic but rather military and intelligence failures that led to France's military defeat.[111] As Jackson puts it, "The battle against the Popular Front had been won by 1938: conservatives did not need Hitler because they already had Daladier."[112]

Yet, even if the ultimate collapse of the regime following Germany's invasion of France in 1940 was not *directly* caused by conservative weakness, the radicalization of the French right was by no means irrelevant. After all, what happened *after* "the strange defeat" in May 1940 – the embrace of the authoritarian Vichy regime – was in fact intimately linked to domestic political vulnerabilities of the French Third Republic, including the nature of France's right. Unlike the military defeats in the Netherlands and Belgium, which prompted democratic governments to flee abroad to create "governments in exile," the French government was exceptional in staying put, simply converting itself into the authoritarian Vichy regime.[113] Aside from Charles de Gaulle, no major government figure went abroad. And the key parliamentary vote that occurred in the Grand Casino in Vichy on July 10, 1940, which granted Marshall Philippe Pétain his undemocratic powers was revealing: seventy-two of the eighty deputies who voted against the bill were on

---

[110] Jackson, *France: The Dark Years, 1940–1944* (2001), 77–79. For an account that emphasizes the military's own autonomous role in the establishment of Vichy, see Philip G. Nord, *France 1940: Defending the Republic* (New Haven: Yale University Press, 2015).

[111] See Ernest R. May, *Strange Victory: Hitler's Conquest of France* (New York: Hill and Wang, 2000); Julian Jackson, *The Fall of France: The Nazi Invasion of 1940* (Oxford: 2003b); Nord, *France 1940: Defending the Republic* (2015).

[112] Jackson, *France: The Dark Years, 1940–1944* (2001), 113.

[113] Nord, *France 1940: Defending the Republic* (2015), xvi–xvii.

the left, while only five deputies of the right were opposed.[114] The bill passed overwhelmingly 569–80. Thus, even if Germany's war was the initial impetus, key political continuities linked the 1930s and 1940s. Chief among them was the radicalization of former right-wing notables who became the founding "circle of Vichy conservatives" and regarded military defeat as an opportunity, a "divine surprise," to create a political regime they had long sought.[115]

In this sense, the French case sits uncomfortably between the two paradigmatic models of Britain and Germany: democracy certainly survived, but just barely. And, yet at another level, the case confirms the broader logic: French democracy's greatest domestic vulnerability was the weakness and fragmentation of its conservative forces, and their eventual capture by authoritarians.

LESSONS FROM BEYOND EUROPE'S HISTORICAL EXPERIENCE

Germany and Britain are exemplars of two patterns of long-run democratization in Europe where old-regime elites were incorporated into a new regime in different ways with profoundly important consequences. The fractured and weak electoral right in Portugal and Italy mirrored the German and Spanish experiences before 1914, and the resulting democracies were all exceedingly fragile in the interwar years. Denmark, Belgium, and the Netherlands are cases where the center-right either held power or was a viable contender throughout the 1920s and 1930s, mirroring Swedish and British experiences. In these latter cases, the descendants of "old-regime" opponents of democracy became willing participants in the democratic political process. And, while France fits uncomfortably between these two types, the fractured nature of its conservatism contributed to democracy's precarious state in France in the late 1930s.

Outside Europe, similar forces were at play both in the historical period we have been studying and beyond. A framework focused on old-regime forces helps us understand certain puzzling political outcomes even in different contexts. Political scientist Edward Gibson notes a clear pattern present in the sixteen countries of Latin America from the rise of mass suffrage until the end of the Cold War. In the four countries where conservative political

---

[114] Olivier Wieviorka, *Orphans of the Republic: The Nation's Legislators in Vichy France* (Cambridge, MA: Harvard University Press, 2009), 102–03. See also Ermakoff, *Ruling Oneself Out: A Theory of Collective Self-Abdication* (2008), 33–34.

[115] "Divine surprise" is the phrase of Charles Maurras (*Action française*); the term "Vichy circle of French conservatives" is from Hoffmann, *Decline or Renewal? France since the 1930s* (1974), 3. Who was this "circle" precisely? In his careful empirical analysis of voting patterns and statements in 1940, Ermakoff (2008, pp. 157–58) is able to identify at least one hundred conservative parliamentarians who explicitly "endorsed the prospect of a nondemocratic state."

parties emerged *before* mass suffrage – Chile Colombia, Costa Rica, and Uruguay – democratization even if predominately oligarchic at first, was on average more stable than in the rest of the region. By contrast, in the remaining twelve countries – Argentina, Brazil, Ecuador, Peru, and so on – where no conservative political party existed until *after* mass democratization, democracy was, on average, less durable.[116]

One revealing illustration is the chronic instability of Argentina in the first part of the twentieth century, which had deep roots in the historical weakness of its conservative party.[117] As in Europe in the same period, in Latin America's nineteenth-century oligarchic political systems – primarily dominated by landed elites and often bolstered by election manipulation and suffrage restrictions – all came under attack at the turn of the twentieth century. Unlike in Chile, however, Argentine landed elites were represented by an organizationally fragmented conservative party, the National Autonomist Party (*Partido Autonomist Nachional*, PAN).[118] As in Germany, the elites were habitually incapable of crafting a successful nationally encompassing party organization. Constrained by federalism, the structure of church–state conflict, and regional divides, strong parties of the right failed to materialize in Argentina.[119] Thus, as a result, when the Radical Civic Union (*Unión Cívica Radical*, UCR) emerged in the 1890s in Argentina as a mass-based challenge to the status quo old regime elites found themselves incapable of winning elections.

This ultimately led to the passage of the Sáenz Peña Law in 1912, which introduced universal, secret, and compulsory male suffrage for the first time in Argentine history. One analyst notes that "[the] PAN was not organized on a popular basis. Its leaders made little effort to recruit popular support . . . .[and] never developed a set of beliefs or ideas that could be identified as a partisan perspective."[120] As another writes, while PAN "was politically powerful and electorally unbeatable as long as male suffrage was not compulsory, voting was not secret, and free elections were only rare exceptions ... [o]nce the 1912

---

[116] Gibson, *Class and Conservative Parties* (1996), 26.

[117] A variant of this argument for Argentina is made by a range of authors including Di Tella, "La búsqueda de la fórmula política argentina" (1971/1972); Gibson, *Class and Conservative Parties* (1996); Atilio Borón, "Ruling Without a Party: Argentine Dominant Classes in the Twentieth Century," in *Conservative Parties, the Right, and Democracy in Latin America*, ed. Kevin J. Middlebrook (Baltimore: Johns Hopkins University Press, 2000), 139–63.

[118] On Chile, see Timothy Scully, *Rethinking the Center: Party Politics in Nineteenth- and Twentieth-Century Chile* (Stanford, CA: Stanford University Press, 1992).

[119] For an important account that emphasizes federalism and regional cleavages, see Gibson, *Class and Conservative Parties* (1996). For an account that highlights the impact of religious cleavages, see Middlebrook, ed., *Conservative Parties, the Right, and Democracy in Latin America* (2000).

[120] Karen L. Remmer, *Party Competition in Argentina and Chile: Political Recruitment and Public Policy, 1890–1930* (Lincoln: University of Nebraska Press, 1984), 30–31.

electoral reform was implemented, the PAN's extreme electoral weakness appeared in full force."[121]

After losing the presidency by a landslide to UCR candidate Hipólito Yrigoyen in 1916, the PAN quickly disbanded. In its place, traditional elites organized around provincial parties – perhaps most notably the Conservative Party of Buenos Aires – and a series of ill-fated national vehicles such as the Democratic Progressive Party (*Partido Demócrata Progresista*, PDP).[122] Given the disarray and failure of the counter-mobilization throughout the 1920s, dismayed and frightened traditional conservatives formed the core of a reactionary coup coalition in the 1920s. In September 1930, the armed forces overthrew Yrigoyen.

As Tourcato Di Tella and many others point out, the 1930 coup marked the beginning of a recurrent pattern in Argentine politics, in which electorally impotent conservatives, unable to build successful electoral organizations at the national level, retreat to a style of civil–military authoritarianism that precludes any hope of democratic stability in twentieth-century Argentina. Indeed, Argentina experienced coups in 1930, 1955, 1962, 1966 and 1976, "and was under direct military rule or some kind of military tutelage for most of the half-century between 1930 and 1983."[123] Thus, while sources of political instability may have been multiple, the weakness of political parties representing upper-class interests associated with the old regime was, in Di Tella's phrase, that country's original "Achilles heel," sabotaging democracy from the beginning of the twentieth century.[124]

Casting our view more widely, a common dynamic appears. The character of non-democratic political elites has profoundly shifted in the contemporary world; rather than landed elites of the nineteenth century, they are more likely to be ruling military officers of contemporary military regimes, apparatchiks of single-party regimes, and familial networks of power in neo-patrimonial regimes. Yet, everywhere, if an old elite has access to a particular type of robust and competitive party organization before full democratization, democratic changes are more likely to endure.

It is sometimes thought surprising that among the developmental states of Asia, the military regime of South Korea, the single party state of Taiwan, and the patrimonial authoritarian regime of Suharto's Indonesia democratized – in 1987, the early 1990s, and 1998, respectively – while much of the region has not. In all three contexts, democratization was achieved amid intense social

---

[121] Borón, "Ruling Without a Party: Argentine Dominant Classes in the Twentieth Century" (2000): 155.

[122] Gibson, *Class and Conservative Parties* (1996), 49–53.

[123] Loxton, "Authoritarian Inheritance and Conservative Party-Building in Latin America" (2014), 296.

[124] Di Tella, "La búsqueda de la fórmula política argentina" (1971/1972): 323.

unrest and contention. However, critical to each case were the political parties associated with the former old regime leaders (the Democratic Justice Party in South Korea, the Kuomintang (KMT) in Taiwan, and Golkar in Indonesia).[125] These groups calculated their pre-existing organizational resources allowed them, and their constituents, to thrive even faced with democratization.[126] Democracy emerged in part because incumbent elites expected to survive democratic transitions; and their confidence derived from their viable party organizations.

The unfolding of the 2011 Arab Spring, although in a very different setting, can also be interpreted through this lens. Everywhere, mass uprisings disrupted long-entrenched and imposing nondemocratic regimes. However, in Egypt, old regime forces associated with President Hosni Mubarak's pre-2011 regime lacked the party organization needed to compete electorally. In April 2011, an administrative court of the new regime dissolved Mubarak's old governing National Democratic Party (NDP), seized its assets, and wrote a ban into the constitution that prohibited former party leaders from running for office.[127] Because they lacked a strong, unified successor party, scrambling, infighting, and fragmentation occurred. And, in 2013, facing post-transition instability, old regime groups regarded a military coup as an attractive option.

By contrast, in neighboring Tunisia, while the new regime in March 2011 also dissolved the long-ruling party, *Rassemblement Constitutionnel Démocratique* (RCD), the new constitution did not prohibit former officials from running for elected office. As a result, a single secularist party, Nidaa Tounes, incorporated former supporters of ousted president Ben Ali into a broad coalition. The party was able to compete and achieved a sweeping electoral victory in 2014. Incorporating potential "spoilers" helped stabilize the beginning steps of Tunisian democracy.[128] Whether the pattern endures is an open question and can only, of course, be answered, in the long run.

From the old democracies of nineteenth-century Europe to new ones in contemporary Southeast Asia and North Africa, the point appears again and again: well-organized democratic opposition movements may be necessary to topple non-democratic regimes, and the impetus may come from a variety of sources, including shifting socioeconomic conditions or changing class relations. But, ultimately, *we cannot understand the course of a country's democratization trajectory without factoring in the role of democracy's adversaries.* Be it repression, democratic subversion, or democratization, the

---

[125] Slater and Wong, "Strength to Concede" (2013). [126] Ibid.
[127] Tarek E. Masoud, *Counting Islam: Religion, Class, and Elections in Egypt* (Cambridge: Cambridge University Press, 2014), 129.
[128] Ibid.

outcome hinges on the organizational resources of the incumbent elite at the moment they are challenged.

Thus, even strong democratic opposition does not always give rise to a democratic transition – let alone sustainable democratic consolidation. However, in instances where the opposition faces off against old regime elites who *are* able to overcome the substantial barriers to organizing effective and competitive political parties, a key precondition is met. Democratic transitions in such cases are both more likely to arrive and more likely to endure.

11

Conclusion

"If some important political forces have no chance to win," political scientist Adam Przeworski once noted, "those who expect to suffer continued deprivation under democratic institutions will turn against them."[1] This insight, which applies no matter if the major opponent of democracy is a traditional nineteenth-century landed elite or a modern-day autocratic tyrant, is powerful for several reasons. First, political economic elites of autocratic regimes are not characteristically the most convinced advocates of the self-evident virtues of democracy. Further, the costs of democracy for groups closely aligned with a predemocratic order offer powerful motives for rejecting or reversing democratic rule; they are likely to lose power, wealth, and status. And finally, no less important is that it is precisely these same groups who have the key potentially disruptive resources, including well-groomed access to the military and bureaucracy, which pose real barriers to democracy by effectively blocking or subverting it. Thus, if old-regime elites do not "buy in," a democratic political order is much harder to build and also much harder to sustain.

This book has argued that the relationship between a pre-existing concentration of social power, on the one hand, and inclusive political democracy, on the other, is inherently tension-ridden. However, the British and German historical experiences make clear that former opponents of democracy, holders of concentrated wealth and power, can be made to coexist with stable democracy. No matter the level of socioeconomic development or the formal constitutional structure of the state, the ability of old-regime elites to forge a robust and strong "conservative political party," a party that represents their interests in the new regime, is an essential factor in democratic development. When upper-class groups associated with any pre-

---

[1] Adam Przeworski, *Democracy and the Market: Political and Economic Reforms in Eastern Europe and Latin America* (Cambridge: Cambridge University Press, 1991), 32.

democratic *ancien régime* are able to build strong political parties, democracy evolves in a more settled fashion; when they cannot, democracy emerges, if at all, in a deeply unsettled way.

This argument departs in significant ways from how others have analyzed this issue. A central problem of democratization is how old-regime elements can be accommodated to newly inclusive political institutions to assure democratic institutions become self-enforcing.[2] But, *four* solutions to this dilemma, all of which are thought to tame the potentially voracious appetites of inclusive democratic political institutions vis-à-vis old elites, have gained most attention. Each offers alternative and possibly viable ways of either reducing the costs of democratization for important political and economic constituents of the former authoritarian regime or of providing incentives for these same actors to refrain from derailing democracy.

The first three focus on socioeconomic variables, anchored in the ameliorating effects of a modernizing economy; the fourth is an institutional argument that highlights how "constitutional engineering" can constrain the power of majorities. These factors are:

- Increased wealth: Increasing GDP per capita, classically associated with declining illiteracy and increasing education, makes the poor "less threatening," melting away the problems of allowing the "masses" to rule.[3]
- Declining economic inequality: Increasing GDP per capita is associated, over the long term, with declining income inequality. This reduces the redistributive threat of democracy by altering the median voter and reducing the cultural "distance" of the upper class from the lower class.[4]
- Increased capital or asset mobility: Increasing GDP per capita is associated, over the long term, with increased asset or capital mobility. By placing ever-growing portions of wealth beyond the "reach" of a stationary bandit state, this thereby reduces the threat of democracy.[5]
- Countermajoritarian constitutions: Formal political institutions that carve out special protections (e.g., independent judiciary, reserve rights for the military, upper chambers, federalism, unelected councils) provide "vertical constraints" against majorities. This makes democracy safer for pro-or post-authoritarian elites, helping generate "buy-in" that makes the

[2] For examples of this framing of the problem, see Weingast, Alberts, and Warshaw, "Democratization and Countermajoritarian Institutions" (2012); Acemoglu and Robinson, *Economic Origins of Dictatorship and Democracy* (2006); Boix, *Democracy and Redistribution* (2003); Lipset, "Some Social Requisites of Democracy" (1959).

[3] John Stuart Mill, *On Liberty* (London: John Parker, 1859); Lipset, "Some Social Requisites of Democracy" (1959).

[4] On the first mechanism, see Acemoglu and Robinson, *Economic Origins of Dictatorship and Democracy* (2006); Boix, *Democracy and Redistribution* (2003). On the second mechanism, see Lipset, "Some Social Requisites of Democracy" (1959).

[5] Boix, *Democracy and Redistribution* (2003).

new government, in political scientist Barry Weingast's terms, "self-enforcing."[6]

The relative presence or absence of each of these four factors is thought to reduce or augment the costs of democracy to old-regime elites, thereby possibly explaining why democracy emerges in a stable fashion in some places but not others. Empirical research lends some support to each view. But, these factors each have their own shortcomings, and most significantly, the list is not exhaustive. The first three variables – increased economic wealth, income inequality, and capital mobility – are correlated with democracy; yet, recent cross-national analyses have raised the notion that economic development and democratization themselves are both jointly determined by deeper historical causes.[7] Even the most recent comprehensive account of the economic sources of democratization notes that the relationship between national wealth and democracy through history has important caveats: (1) the strength of economic development's impact on democracy varies over time; (2) the relationship is nonlinear and subject to threshold effects; and (3) the relationship appears to be conditional on other factors and is mediated by historical institutional patterns of constraints on executives.[8]

Thus, while socioeconomic development may have large effects on average, for individual cases, other factors undoubtedly intervene to make democracy self-enforcing. Hence, we should not be surprised when we consider the immensely stark difference in regime outcomes among important European cases with diverse historical pathways of development – for example, between Britain, Belgium, Germany, and Sweden in the interwar period – and the often relatively small differences in their economic structures.

So, we turn to the fourth factor on the list, "countermajoritarian institutions," which also has arguably made democracy safer in many cases.[9] But the evidence supporting the idea that such institutions bring large returns to democracy, even in Western Europe, as we have noted, turns out to be surprisingly inconclusive. In some instances, constitutional safeguards appear to ease the way to democratic change; in others, they appear simply irrelevant.[10]

---

[6] Weingast, Alberts, and Warshaw, "Democratization and Countermajoritarian Institutions" (2012). See also O'Donnell, Schmitter, and Whitehead, eds., *Transitions from Authoritarian Rule: Comparative Perspectives* (1986). On the concept of "vertical constraints," see Dan Slater, "Democratic Careening" *World Politics* 65, no. 4 (2013): 729–63.

[7] Daron Acemoglu, Simon Johnson, James Robinson, and Pierre Yared, "Income and Democracy," *American Economic Review* 98, no. 3 (2008): 808–42.

[8] Boix, "Democracy, Development, and the International System" (2011).

[9] Weingast, Alberts, and Warshaw, "Democratization and Countermajoritarian Institutions" (2012).

[10] Consider for example the ambiguous impact of the Prussian House of Lords. See Spenkuch, *Das Preussische Herrenhaus: Adel und Bürgertum in der ersten Kammer des Landtags 1854–1918* (1998).

Furthermore, there are hidden costs to accommodating elites via countermajoritarian constitutional safeguards. First, since "constitutional safeguards" are by definition difficult to alter, the accumulation of countermajoritarian state institutions within a country (e.g., an unelected upper chamber, an insulated military malapportionment, a king) may make an elite more secure; but, as the case of Prussia before 1914 makes plainly evident, so too may it create a veto-filled "reform trap," blocking the possibility of implementing any democratic reforms at all, even in the face of massive social pressure.[11] If moments of constitutional "openness" are by chance stumbled into, democratic reforms burdened with incumbent-imposed "checks" on majoritarianism may result in a political system that is stable, but not democratically stable. Rather than "way-stations" on the path to fuller democracy, countermajoritarian institutions may simply be permanent detours. For example, as Albertus and Menaldo's analysis has demonstrated, if old elites are socioeconomically powerful at the moment of transition, they can design state structures that limit the inclusive qualities of democracy.[12] In short, countermajoritarian institutions may prove effective at achieving stability, but this may come at the expense of genuinely democratic stability in ways that should not be overlooked.

None of this is at all meant to suggest that it is unimportant whether or not elites feel self-confident vis-à-vis their fates under democracy.[13] Indeed, my central premise reinforces the basic insight that elite self-confidence is vital for democratic transition and consolidation.[14] However, given the evidence, we must not repeat the mistake of an earlier generation of political science that assumed that only hard or formal constitutional state institutions shape outcomes. Rather, political parties, viewed by an earlier generation of scholars with deep suspicion, can serve as "softer" political organizational buffers for old elites, offering an alternative way of making democracy safe and thus self-enforcing.[15] Put more generally, the evidence in this book suggests we should add a fifth variable to the list of factors cited above: strong

---

[11] On the idea that more veto-points make institutions harder to reform, see George Tsebelis, *Veto-Players* (Princeton: Princeton University Press, 2002). On the related notion of a "joint-decision trap," see Fritz Scharpf, "The Joint Decision Trap Revisited," *Journal of Common Market Studies* 44, no. 4 (2006): 845–64.

[12] Albertus and Menaldo, "Gaming Democracy: Elite Dominance During Transition and Prospects for Redistribution" (2014b). Albertus and Menaldo have also found that where incumbents have more weight in shaping the constitutions, they are less likely to be punished by exile or imprisonment by the new regime. See Michael Albertus and Victor Menaldo, "Dealing with Dictators: Negotiated Democratization and the Fate of Outgoing Autocrats," *International Studies Quarterly* 58, no. 3 (2014a): 550–65.

[13] This too is an insight of Rueschemeyer, Stephens, and Stephens, *Capitalist Development and Democracy* (1992).

[14] Fearon, "Self-enforcing Democracy" (2011); Weingast, Alberts, and Warshaw, "Democratization and Countermajoritarian Institutions" (2012).

[15] Ostrogorski, *Democracy and the Organization of Political Parties* (1902), 3.

conservative political party organizations may be an equally effective, if not *more* effective, means of reducing the costs of democracy to old-regime elites. What is more, unlike countermajoritarian institutions, "party organization" channels the counter-pressures to regime change in ways that *reinforce* democratization rather than undermine it.

Following this, I must highlight the caveat that there is an inherent contradiction between making elites "feel secure" and democratizing a political system. If we accept Przeworski's observation that democracy is premised on the "open-endedness" or "uncertainty" of inclusive political competition, where one side is willing to lose, we find that this runs at cross-purposes with elite security. As unavoidable as the tension is, however, the merit of a conservative party organizational buffer is its relative *superiority* in navigating this tension. State-centered formal or constitutionalized safeguards are countermajoritarian shortcuts that "hardwire" the reduction of electoral uncertainty precisely where uncertainty via democratic contestation *should* reign supreme. Absent the high-minded gloss that often begins by citing Montesquieu or James Madison as inspiration, the conceptual line is blurry between "respectable" countermajoritarian institutions in a democracy and the less appealing brute force of simple antimajoritarianism (i.e., authoritarianism), which has also been defined as "[tilting] the playing field" in favor of [former] incumbents."[16]

By contrast, a strong conservative political party acts as a safeguard that does not formally "hardwire" a reduction of the quality of democratic contestation into the structures of the political system itself. The opposite is the case; it arguably elevates the caliber of democratic competition. If old elites have the organization to compete, so too can democracy's proponents compete. Here is the main insight: a robust conservative political party organization can unleash a self-reinforcing virtuous cycle of electoral competition and open-endedness in electoral outcomes, prompting democracy's advocates to ratchet up their own mobilizational capacity to meet the challenge. This provides old elites with instruments to protect themselves *at least some of the time*. In short, a robust conservative political party may actually be a precondition for democracy.

In January 1885, the Liberal Unionist MP Joseph Chamberlain asked his audience at a rally of the Birmingham Artisan Association held at Birmingham's Town Hall, "What ransom will property pay for the security it enjoys?"[17] The self-evident answer to that question was "democracy." Our question here has been the logical corollary of Chamberlain's: *What ransom will advocates of democracy pay to property for its willingness to accommodate itself to democracy?* In simplest terms, this study has argued that the price that

---

[16] Steven Levitsky and Lucan Way, "The Rise of Competitive Authoritarianism," *Journal of Democracy* 13, no. 2 (2002): 51–65.

[17] Peter Marsh, *Joseph Chamberlain: Entrepreneur in Politics* (New Haven: Yale University Press, 1994), 186.

advocates of democracy must pay is that the propertied and powerful not only have a diffuse but disproportionate influence on society all the time, but also that it be protected by organizationally strong and well-endowed political parties that have the chance of winning elections at least some of the time.

Is this too high a price to pay? If the alternatives are either frequent and chronic regime oscillations between democracy and authoritarianism on the one hand, or a compromised democratic stability achieved with a citadel of hard-to-alter countermajoritarian institutional protections, on the other, a *viable and robust conservative political party* certainly appears to be a lower price than any of the alternatives. This is not a conclusion, I will admit, I thought I would reach when I began this study. I did not intend to present what may appear to be a "dismal science" conclusion, celebrating a compromised version of democracy. But this is where the evidence has led me.

APPENDIX A

The Professionalization of Political Party Organization in Britain, 1894

This appendix illustrates the degree of professionalization within the organizational apparatus of the British Conservative Party in the late nineteenth century. Two standard indicators of professionalization of an occupation are (a) the formalization of the accreditation criteria for membership, and (b) the value placed on "expertise" in that process. Below is an excerpt from a June 1894 issue of *The Tory*, the professional association publication for Conservative Party Agents (i.e., local campaign managers), which shows the professionalization of the Conservative Party by listing sample questions from a qualifying exam that professional party agents in the Conservative Party were *required* to pass to gain the status of "Associate."[1]

A Meeting of the Special Result Committee of the Board of Examiners was held at the office of the Yorkshire Union of Conservative Associations, Leeds on Friday May 11th, 1894, for the purpose of adjudicating on the examination papers of May 7th .... The following gentleman are the successful candidates and Associates' certificates will be forward to them in due time ...

List of Questions for the recent Examinations on May last. Parliamentary (County and Borough) County Electors and Municipal Registration

1. Who are entitled to be registered as voters—
   a) Elections for Parliament in Counties and Boroughs?
   b) Elections for Municipal County and Parish Councils?
2. Suppose a house destroyed by fire or lightning, state upon what condition the Occupier could retain his vote, and also state if the same conditions would apply to a Freeholder?
3. Can two or more persons (not partners) be registered for the occupation of one house and does its value make any difference?

---

[1] *The Tory, The Organ of the National Society of Conservative Agents*, June 1, 1894, No, 17, pp. 408–9 of microfilm.

4. State whether, in your opinion, a Freeholder can be registered in any other than a County Constituency, and if so, where and under what law?

5. For how long must a man be in possession of a Freehold, Copyhold, and Leasehold respectively to entitle him to be placed on the Ownership List of Voters?

6. Who may object to New Claims to be registered in respect of any qualification, and has notice of intention to object to be given to any one, if so, to whom?

7. Give a definition as to what constitutes a Lodger Qualification.

8. How many Committee Rooms, Clerks, and Messengers are allowed for a Parliamentary Election with an electorate of 5,100?

9. After the decision in the Walsall Petition, would Photographs of a Candidate for exhibition in windows come under the designation of distinguishing badge, cockade, etc.

10. Assume that a Riot takes in one of the polling districts of a County Constituency in the evening of the polling day, and that the ballot box and contents are burnt, what effect would this event have on the election return?

11. What would you consider the most successful method of organizing Ward Committees in a Borough constituency and how would you keep up the interest and enthusiasm of the workers from one election to another?

APPENDIX B

Regression Results for Figure 6.3

This appendix summarizes analysis in Chapter 6 and provides fuller statistical evidence that is the basis of Figure 6.3, which is based on Model 1, below.

Time Series Cross-Sectional Analysis of Electoral Fraud

Variable	Model 1	Model 2	Model 3	Model 4	Model 5
Electoral Fraud	DV	DV	DV	DV	DV
Rural Inequality (Gini)	2.092***	2.127***	2.182***	2.099***	2.198***
	(0.385)	(0.388)	(0.391)	(0.386)	(0.386)
Electoral Competitiveness					
Current Election	2.854***	2.900***	2.918***	2.858***	2.772***
	(0.259)	(0.262)	(0.264)	(0.259)	(0.261)
Religion					
% Catholics	−0.006***	−0.005***	−0.005***	−0.006***	−0.006**
	(0.002)	(0.002)	(0.002)	(0.002)	(0.002)
Mobilization	0.750**	0.464	0.419	0.698*	0.954***
(Voter Turnout)	(0.344)	(0.418)	(0.419)	(0.361)	(0.356)
Population	1.78	1.34	1.38	1.66	1.67
	(1.18)	(1.23)	(1.25)	(1.21)	(1.19)
Economic	0.007**	0.007**	0.006**	0.007**	0.007**
Modernization	(0.003)	(0.003)	(0.003)	(0.003)	(0.003)
(% Employment, Non-Agricultural Sector)					
Lagged DV	0.378***	0.372***	0.354***	0.377***	0.360***
	(0.095)	(0.095)	(0.96)	(0.095)	(0.096)

(*continued*)

(*continued*)

Variable	Model 1	Model 2	Model 3	Model 4	Model 5
Time		*0.005	*0.058***		
		(0.004)	(0.016)		
Time Quadratic			−0.001***		
			(0.000)		
Partisan "Center of Gravity" of Election Committee				0.054	
				(0.116)	
Neutral Election Committee Chair?					0.229***
					(0.085)
Constant	−3.231	−3.08	−3.504	−3.361	−3.487
	(0.446)	(0.459)	(0.475)	(0.536)	(0.460)
N	4272	4272	4272	4272	4272

Notes: *p-value < 0.1,**p-value < 0.05,***p-value < 0.01; robust standard errors in parentheses. Hypotheses are direction-specific; however, levels of significance reported are for 2-tailed test.

APPENDIX C

Parties of the Electoral Right by Country, 1918–1939[1]

Country	Parties of the Electoral Right
Belgium	• Catholic Party • Catholic Dissidents (DC) • Front Party (FP) • Rexist Party • Flemish National Alliance (VNV)
Denmark	• Conservative People's Party (KF) • Det nye Hojre • Vaelgerforeningen af 1918 • National Socialist Worker's Party (DNSAP) • National Cooperation (NS)
France	• Republican Union (UR) • "Cons./Mod" • Independent Radicals • Popular Democrats (DP)
Germany	• Center Party • German National People's Party (DNVP) • German People's Party (DVP) • German Hannoverian Party (DHP) • Bavarian People's Party (BVP) • National Socialist German Worker's Party (NDSAP) • Landbund (Land league) • Country-folk Party (LvP) • Business Party (WP) • Christian Social People's Service (CSVD) • Conservative People's Party (KonVP)

(continued)

---

[1] Based on Nohlen and Stöver, *Elections in Europe: A Data Handbook* (2010).

(*continued*)

Country	Parties of the Electoral Right
Italy	• Popular Party • Combatant's Party • Dissident Popular Party • Economic Party • Italian Fasci of Combat • National Blocs (Fascist Party, Liberals, Italian Nationalist Association) • Dissident Fascist • Liberal Party
Netherlands	• Anti-Revolution Party (ARP) • Christian Historical Union • Liberal State Party (LSP) • Reformed State Party (HGS) • Reformed Political Party (SGP) • Alliance for National Reconstruction (VNH) • General Dutch Fascist League (ANFB)
Portugal	• Evolutionists • Republican Union • Republican Liberal Party • Reconstitution • Monarchist Cause • Catholic Center Party • Nationalist Republican • Union of Economic Interests
Spain	• CEDA • Basque Nationalist Party (PNV) • Progressive Republican Party (PRP) • Liberal Democratic Republican Party (PRLD) • National Block (BN) • Agrarian Party (PA) • Falange • Carlist Party (PC) • Catalan League (LC) • Traditionalist Monarchists • Independent Right • Catholic Party ("*Mesocratas*")
Sweden	• General Association of Voters (H/M) • Swedish National Socialist Party (SNSP) • National League of Sweden (SNF) • National Socialist Workers' Party (NSAP/SSS)
United Kingdom	• Coalition Conservative • Conservative

Bibliography

(I) ARCHIVAL MATERIALS/UNPUBLISHED DOCUMENTS

Aretas Akers Douglas (1st Viscount Chilston) Papers, Kent County Archive,
    U564
    Salisbury to Akers Douglas, November 27, 1885, Kent County Archive,
        Aretas Akers Douglas Papers U564 A1226 c 18/4
British Library
Conservative Agents and Associations of the Counties and Boroughs of
    England and Wales (Westminster: Conservative Central Office, 1874)
Conservative Party Archive, Bodleian Libraries, Oxford University, NUA 2/1/1
    Minutes of Proceedings of First Conference of the National Union of
        Conservative Constitutional Associations, November 12, 1867, NUA
        2/1/1
    Minutes of Proceedings of First Conference of the National Union of
        Conservative Constitutional Associations, April 20, 1870, NUA 2/1/1
    Minutes of Proceedings of National Union of Conservative and
        Constitutional Associations held at Westminster Palace Hotel, July 1,
        1874 (8th annual meeting), NUA 2/1/1
    Minutes of Proceedings of National Union of Conservative and
        Constitutional Associations held at Brighton, June 19, 1875, NUA
        2/1/1
    George TC Bartley, "The Condition of the Conservative Party in the
        Midland Counties" National Union of Conservative and
        Constitutional Associations Convention, September 1883, NUA2/1/2
Correspondence of Richard Middleton, Oxford University, Special
    Collections, MSS Eng. C. 4833
    Northcote to Middleton, August 17, 1885, MS Eng C 4838
    Salisbury to Middleton, January 27, n.d. MS Eng C 4838,
    Nottingham Guardian, February 28, 1905, MS Eng Hist 1129

Salisbury Papers, Hatfield House, Hertfordshire
   Northcote to Salisbury, December 25, 1883
   Northcote to Salisbury, October 26, 1884
   Northcote to Salisbury, December 12, 1884
   Bartley Report to Salisbury/Northcote, October 25, 1884, Conservative
      Central Office, "Memorandum to the Marquess of Salisbury and Sir
      Stafford Northcote"
   Scottish Conservative Club, Edinburgh, Mackosh to Northcote,
      November 18, 1884
   Talbot to Northcote, November 18, 1884
   James Howler to Northcote, November 20, 1884
Conrad Freiherr von Wangenheim Papers, Bundesarchiv Berlin-Lichterfelde,
   N2323
   Briefwechsel Freiherr von Wangenheim/Dr. Roesicke im Jahre 1906,
      November 27, 1906, N 2323 Nr. 2
   Briefwechsel Freiherr von Wangenheim/Dr. Roesicke im Jahre 1908,
      July 31, 1908, N 2323 Nr. 3

Family Collection of the Private Papers of Gottfried Reinhold Treviranus, Bern,
Switzerland.

(2) PRINTED PRIMARY SOURCES

(a) Germany

Berliner Tageblatt, May 21, 1912
Berliner Tageblatt, July 31, 1907
Deutsche Konservative Partei, Stenographischer Bericht, December 8, 1892
Deutsche Konservative Partei, *Der Allgemeine Delegiertentag der Deutsch-
   Konservativen Partei. Stenographischer Bericht, 11 December 1909* (Berlin:
   Hauptverein der Deutch-Konservativen, 1909).
Deutscher Reichstag, Various years. *Stenographische Berichte über die
   Verhandlungen des Deutschen Reichstags.* (Berlin: Verlag der Buchdruckerei
   der Norddeutschen Allgemeinen Zeitung). [Online] www.reichstagsprotokolle
   .de/bundesarchiv.html
Grabowsky, Adolf, "Der Kulturkonservatismus und die Reichstagswahlen," *Der Tag*
   19, 22 (January 1911).
von Gerlach, Ernst Ludwig, "Die Bildung einer konservativen Partei und der Verein
   für König und Vaterland," *Neue Preußische Zeitung*, nr. 53 v. 31.8 1848, 2
   beilage.
Neue Preußische Zeitung, nr. 55, September 2, 1848, 1. Beil
Neue Preußische Zeitung, Nr 53, August 31, 1848, Zweite Beilage, p.333
Neue Preußische Kreuzzeitung, Nr. 321, July 12, 1906 (Abendausgabe), p.1
Korrespondenz des Bundes der Landwirte, "Stenographische Bericht über die 16
   General-Versammlung des Bundes der Landwirte," Nr. 15 February 23, 1909.

Preußen Haus der Abgeordneten. Various years *Stenographische Berichte über die Verhandlungen des Preußischen Hauses der Abgeordneten.* Berlin: Verlag des Preussischen Hauses der Abgeordneten.
Neue Preussische Zeitung, Number 603, December 24, 1892

(b) Britain

"Causes of Party Weakness," *The Economist,* November 26, 1904: 1887.
Cecil, Robert (Lord Salisbury), "The Budget and the Reform Bill," *Quarterly Review* 107 April (1860): 514–554).
Cecil, Robert (Lord Salisbury), "The Value of Redistribution: A Note on Electoral Statistics" *The National Review* October 20 1884, 145–164.
Chamberlain, Joseph, "The Caucus and a New Political Organization," *Federation Pamphlets* (1883).
"Conservative Associations," *Blackwood's Edinburgh Magazine* (July 1835), no. 237, v. 38, 1–15.
"A Conservative Caucus," *The Saturday Review* (May 17, 1884): 628–629;
"Conservative Reorganization," *Blackwoods Edinburgh Magazine* (June 1880): 804–811.
"Doctrine of Disorder," *The Economist,* August 17, 1912: 310.
Hopkins, T. M. 1897. "The Conservative Complexion of the English Church," *Westminster Review* 147: 324–34.
"Markets and Ulster," *The Times,* March 20, 1914: 21.
"The New Electioneering," *The Speaker,* February 16, 1895: 182.
"Out-Voters and How to Canvass Them," *The Tory,* 1894
"The Position in Stock Exchange Markets," *The Economist,* March 14, 1914: 651.
The Primrose League Gazette, 1881–1930
Schnadhorst, Francis. "The Caucus and Its Critics," *Federation Pamphlets* (1880).
"The Stock Exchange. Position," *The Economist,* February 14, 1914: 340.
"Stock Exchange: Improved Tone," *The Times,* March 23, 1914: 19.
"The Stock Markets," *The Economist,* March 21, 1914: 728.
"The Stock Markets," *The Economist,* March 28, 1914: 787.
"The Stock Markets," *The Economist,* June 27, 1914: 1575.
The Times of London, 12 May 1832.
"To Defend a Radical Objection Occupation," *The Tory,* 1894.

(3) STATISTICAL SOURCES

Census of England and Wales, *Ages, Conditions as to Marriage, Occupations, and Birth-Places of the People,* vol. III (Presented to both Houses of Parliament by Command of Her Majesty) (London, 1881).
Kollman, K., A., Hicken, D., Caramani, D., Backer, and D. Lublin. 2014. *Constituency-level elections archive* [data file and codebook]. Ann Arbor, MI: Center for Political Studies, University of Michigan [producer and distributor].
Global Financial Database www.globalfinancialdata.com/Databases/UKDatabase.html
Great Britain Historical GIS Project. 2012. *"Great Britain Historical GIS."* University of Portsmouth.

ICPSR (Inter-university Consortium for Political and Social Research). 1984. *"German Reichstag Election Data, 1871–1912."* [Online] http://id.thedata.org/hdl:1902.2 /00043.UNF:3:32:uKgmiCLL7UZgUTFS/jjxsQ==

Kaiserliches Statistisches Amt. 1898. *Statistik des Deutschen Reichs.* Bd. 112. Berlin: Verlag des Königlich Preussichen Statistischen Bureaus, pp. 351–413 [Table 9].

Handbuch über den königlichen Preussischen Hof und Staat für das Jahr 1892 (Berlin: 1891).

"The Roll of County and Borough Habitations," *The Primrose League Gazette*, Multiple Issues, 1886–1888, Oxford University.

Stenographische Berichte, July 13, 1909: 9462; March, 9, 1914: 7939.

Ziblatt, Daniel. 2010. "Landholding Inequality in Germany, at the Reichstag Constituency Level, and Prussian Chamber of Deputies Constituency Level, 1895," [Online] http://hdl.handle.net/1902.1/15023, Harvard Dataverse, V1.

Ziblatt, Daniel. 2011. "Replication data for: Shaping Democratic Practice (APSR)," [Online]: http://hdl.handle.net/1902.1/16066, Harvard Dataverse, V2.

Ziblatt, Daniel and Robert Arsenschek. 2010. "Complete Reichstag Election Dispute Dataset, 1871–1914." [Online] http://hdl.handle.net/1902.1/15015, Harvard Dataverse, V3.

Ziblatt, Daniel and Jeffrey Blossom. 2011. "Electoral District Boundaries, Germany, 1890–1912." Harvard University Geospatial Library [Online] http://calvert.hul.harvard.edu:8080/opengeoportal/openGeoPortalHome.jsp?BasicSearchTerm=La yerId:HARVARD.SDE2.GERMAN1895ELECTORALDISTRICTS.

(4) SECONDARY SOURCES

Abbott, Andrew Delano. 1988. *The System of Professions: An Essay on the Division of Expert Labor.* Chicago: University of Chicago Press.

Abraham, David. 1986. *The Collapse of the Weimar Republic: Political Economy and Crisis.* 2nd ed. ed. New York: Holmes & Meier.

Acemoglu, Daron, Simon Johnson, James Robinson, and Pierre Yared. 2008. "Income and Democracy." *American Economic Review* 98: 808–42.

Acemoglu, Daron, and James A. Robinson. 2006. *Economic Origins of Dictatorship and Democracy.* Cambridge: Cambridge University Press.

2000. "Why Did the West Extend the Franchise? Democracy, Inequality, and Growth in Historical Perspective." *The Quarterly Journal of Economics* 115: 1167–99.

Adams, R. J. Q. 1999. *Bonar Law.* Stanford: Stanford University Press.

Adcock, Robert, and David Collier. 2001. "Measurement Validity: A Shared Standard for Qualitative and Quantitative Research." *American Political Science Review* 95: 529–46.

Aeasop. 2002. *Aeasop's Fables.* Translated by Laura Gibbs. Oxford: Oxford University Press.

Ahmed, Amel. 2013. *Democracy and the Politics of Electoral System Choice: Engineering Electoral Dominance.* Cambridge: Cambridge University Press.

2010. "Reading History Forward: The Origins of Electoral Systems in European Democracies." *Comparative Political Studies* 43: 931–68.

Aidt, Toke, and Peter Jensen. 2014. "Workers of the World, Unite! Franchise Extensions and the Threat of Revolution in Europe, 1820–1938." *European Economic Review* 72: 52–75.

Albertus, Michael, and Victor Menaldo. 2014a. "Dealing with Dictators: Negotiated Democratization and the Fate of Outgoing Autocrats." *International Studies Quarterly* 58: 550–65.

2014b. "Gaming Democracy: Elite Dominance During Transition and Prospects for Redistribution." *British Journal of Political Science* 44: 575–603.

Aldrich, John. 1983. "A Downsian Spatial Model with Party Activism." *American Political Science Review* 77: 974–90.

1995. *Why Parties? The Origin and Formation of Party Politics in America*. Chicago: University of Chicago Press.

Aldrich, John, and David W. Rohde. 1998. "Measuring Conditional Party Government." Paper presented at the American Political Science Association Annual Convention, Chicago.

Alexander, Gerard. 2002. *The Sources of Democratic Consolidation*. Ithaca: Cornell University Press.

de Almeida, Pedro Tavares, and Antonio Costa Pinto. 2003. "Portuguese Ministers, 1851–1999: Social Background and Paths to Power." In *Who Governs Southern Europe? Regime Change and Ministerial Recruitment, 1850–2000*, eds. Pedro Tavares de Almeida, Antonio Costa Pinto and Nancy Bermeo. London: Frank Cass. 5–40.

Anderson, Margaret Lavinia. 2000. *Practicing Democracy: Elections and Political Culture in Imperial Germany*. Princeton, NJ: Princeton University Press.

1981. *Windhorst: A Political Biography*. Oxford: Clarendon Press.

Andrae, Carl-Göran. 1975. "The Swedish Labor Movement and the 1917–1918 Revolution." In *Sweden's Development from Poverty to Affluence, 1750–1970*, ed. Steven Koblik. Minneapolis: University of Minnesota Press. 232–53.

Angell, Norman. 1909. *The Great Illusion*.

Ansell, Ben, and David Samuels. 2014. *Inequality and Democratization: An Elite-Competition Approach*. Cambridge: Cambridge University Press.

Ansell, Christopher. 2001. *Between Solidarity and Schism*. Cambridge: Cambridge University Press.

Ansell, Christopher K., and M. Steven Fish. 1999. "The Art of Being Indispensible: Noncharismatic Personalism and Contemporary Political Parties." *Comparative Political Studies* 32: 283–312.

Arnold, Rollo. 1974. "The 'Revolt of the Field' in Kent, 1872–1879." *Past and Present* 64: 71–95.

Arranz, Luis, Mercedes Cabrera, and Fernando del Rey. 2000. "The Assault of Liberalism, 1914–1923." In *Spanish History since 1808*, eds. Alvarez Junco and Adrian Shubart. New York: Oxford University Press.

Arsenschek, Robert. 2003. *Die Kampf um die Wahlfreiheit im Kaiserreich. zur parlamentarischen Wahlprüfung und politischen Realität der Reichstagswahlen, 1871–1914*. Düsseldorf: Droste Verlag.

Art, David. 2006. "The European Radical Right in Comparative-Historical Perspective." Paper presented at the Annual meeting of the American Political Science Association, Philadelphia, Pennsylvania, 2006.

2011. *Inside the Radical Right: The Development of Anti-Immigrant Parties in Western Europe*. New York: Cambridge University Press.

Asquith, Herbert Henry. 1928. *Memories and Reflections: 1852–1927, Volume 1*. Edited by Alexander Mackintosh. Boston: Little, Brown, and Company.

Austin, Roger. 1990. "The Conservative Right and the Far Right in France, 1934–1944." In *Fascists and Conservatives*, ed. Martin Blinkhorn. Abingdon: Routledge.

Bachrach, Peter, and Morton Baratz. 1962. "Two Faces of Power." *American Political Science Review* 56: 947–52.

Bagehot, Walter. 1867. *The English Constitution*. London: Chapman and Hall.

Ball, Stuart. 2013. *The Conservative Party and British Politics, 1902–1951*. London: Routledge.

Ball, Stuart, and Anthony Seldon, eds. 2005. *Recovering Power: The Conservatives in Opposition since 1867*. Houndmills, Basingstoke, Hampshire: Palgrave Macmillan.

Bartolini, Stefano. 2000. *The Political Mobilization of the European Left, 1860–1980: The Class Cleavage*, Cambridge Studies in Comparative Politics. Cambridge, UK: Cambridge University Press.

Baumgartner, Frank, and Bryan Jones. 2009. *Agendas and Instability in American Politics*. Chicago and London: University of Chicago Press.

Bawn, Kathleen, Martin Cohen, David Karol, Seth Masket, Hans Noel, and John Zaller. 2012. "A Theory of Political Parties: Groups, Policy Demands and Nominations in American Politics." *Perspectives on Politics* 10: 571–97.

Beatty, Jack. 2012. *The Lost History of 1914: Reconsidering the Year the Great War Began*. New York: Bloomsbury Publishing.

Bebbington, David W. 1982. *The Nonconformist Conscience: Chapel and Politics, 1870–1914*. London: G. Allen & Unwin.

1984. "Nonconformity and Electoral Sociology, 1867–1918." *Historical Journal* 27: 633–56.

Beck, Hermann. 2008. *The Fateful Alliance: German Conservatives and Nazis in 1933. The Machtergreifung in a New Light*. Oxford and New York: Berghahn Press.

Beckert, Sven. 2002. "Democracy and Its Discontents: Contesting Suffrage Rights in Gilded Age New York." *Past and Present* 174: 116–57.

2000. "Die Kultur des Kapitals: Bürgerliche Kultur in New York und Hamburg im 19. Jahrhundert." In *Vorträge aus dem Warburg-Haus 4*, ed. Warburg Haus. Berlin: Akademie Verlag. 143–75.

2001. *The Monied Metropolis: New York City and the Consolidation of the American Bourgeoisie, 1850–1896*. Cambridge, UK, and New York: Cambridge University Press.

Beer, Samuel. 1956. "Pressure Groups and Parties in Britain." *American Political Science Review* 50: 1–23.

Beers, Laura. 2009. "Counter-Toryism: Labour's Response to Anti-Socialist Propaganda, 1918–1939." In *The Foundations of the Labour Party: Identities, Cultures and Perspectives*, ed. Matthew Worley. London: Ashgate. 231–68.

2010. *Your Britain: Media and the Making of the Labour Party*. Cambridge: Harvard University Press.

Ben-Ami, Shlomo. 1978. *The Origins of the Second Republic in Spain*. Oxford: Oxford University Press.

Bendix, Reinhard. 1952. "Social Stratification and Political Power." *American Political Science Review* 46: 357–75.

Benoit, Kenneth. 2007. "Electoral Laws as Political Consequences: Explaining the Origins and Change of Electoral Institutions." *Annual Review of Political Science* 10: 363–90.

Bentley, Michael. 2001. *Lord Salisbury's World: Conservative Environments in Late-Victorian Britain.* Cambridge: Cambridge University Press.

Berelson, Bernard R, Paul Lazarsfeld, and William McPhee. 1954. *Voting: A Study of Opinion Formation in a Presidential Campaign.* Chicago: University of Chicago Press.

Berggren, Lena. 2002. "Swedish Fascism: Why Bother?". *Journal of Contemporary History* 37: 395–417.

Berghahn, Volker 1987. *Modern Germany: Society, Economy, and Politics in the Twentieth Century.* 2nd ed. Cambridge: Cambridge University Press.

Bergsträsser, Ludwig. 1929. *Die Preussische Wahlrechtsfrage im Kriege und die Entstehung der Osterbotschaft.* Tübingen: Verlag von Mohr.

Berman, Sheri. 2006. *The Primacy of Politics: Social Democracy and the Making of Europe's Twentieth Century.* Cambridge: Cambridge University Press.

1998. *The Social Democratic Moment: Ideas and Politics in the Making of Interwar Europe.* Cambridge: Harvard University Press.

Bermeo, Nancy. 2010. "Interests, Inequality, and Illusion in the Choice for Fair Elections. (The Historical Turn in Democratization Studies)." *Comparative Political Studies* 43: 1119–47.

2003. *Ordinary People in Extraordinary Times: The Citizenry and the Breakdown of Democracy.* Princeton: Princeton University Press.

Bernhard, Michael. 2015. "Chronic Instability and the Limits of Path Dependence." *Perspectives on Politics* 13: 1–16.

Bernhard, Michael H. 2005. *Institutions and the Fate of Democracy: Germany and Poland in the Twentieth Century,* Pitt Series in Russian and East European Studies. Pittsburgh: University of Pittsburgh Press.

Bernstein, Eduard. 1906. *Der politische Massenstreik und die politische Lage der Sozialdemokratie in Deutschland: Vortrag gehalten im Sozialdemokratischen Verein.* Breslau: Verlag der Volkswacht.

Bessel, Richard. 1993. *Germany After the First World War.* Oxford: Oxford University Press.

Binkley, Robert C. 1935. *Realism and Nationalism, 1852–1871.* New York: Harper & Row.

Blackbourn, David. 1980. *Religion, and Local Politics in Wilhelmine Germany: The Centre Party in Württemberg Before 1914.* New Haven: Yale University Press.

Blackbourn, David, and Geoff Eley. 1984. *The Peculiarities of German History: Bourgeois Society and Politics in Nineteenth-Century Germany.* New York: Oxford University Press.

Blake, Robert. 1970. *The Conservative Party from Peel to Churchill.* London: Eyre & Spottiswoode.

1966. *Disraeli.* London: Eyre & Spottiswoode.

1956. *Unrepentant Tory: The Life and Times of Andrew Bonar Law, 1858–1923.* New York: St. Martins Press.

Blaxill, Luke, and Taym Saleh. 2016. "The Electoral Dynamics of Conservatism, 1885–1910: 'Negative Unionism' Reconsidered." *Historical Journal* 59: 417–45.

Blewett, Neal. 1965. "The Franchise in the United Kingdom, 1885–1918." *Past and Present* 32: 27–56.

Blinkhorn, Martin, ed. 1990. *Fascists and Conservatives*. Abingdon: Routledge.

Boemeke, Manfred F., Gerald D. Feldman, and Elisabeth Gläser. 1998. *The Treaty of Versailles: A Reassessment after 75 Years*. Washington, DC: German Historical Institute.

Boer, Remco. "The Anti-Revolutionary Vanguard: The Party Cadre of the Anti-Revolutionary Party in the Netherlands, 1869–1888." Leiden University, 2008.

Bohlmann, Joachim. "Die Deutschkonservative Partei am Ende des Kaiserreichs: Stillstand und Wandel einer untergehenden Organisation." Greifswald: Ernst-Moritz-Arndt-Universität, 2011.

Boix, Carles. 2003. *Democracy and Redistribution*, Cambridge Studies in Comparative Politics. Cambridge: Cambridge University Press.

2011. "Democracy, Development, and the International System." *American Political Science Review* 105: 809–28.

1999. "Setting the Rules of the Game: The Choice of Electoral Systems in Advanced Democracies." *The American Political Science Review* 93: 609–24.

Borón, Atilio. 2000. "Ruling without a Party: Argentine Dominant Classes in the Twentieth Century." In *Conservative Parties, the Right, and Democracy in Latin America*, ed. Kevin J. Middlebrook. Baltimore: Johns Hopins University Press. 139–63.

Bracher, Karl Dietrich. 1955. *Die Auflösung der Weimarer Republik*. Stuttgart: Ring-Verlag.

Bratt, James. 2013. *Abraham Kuyper: Modern Calvinist, Christian Democrat*. Grand Rapids, MI and Cambridge, UK: Eerdmans Publishing.

Brecht, Bertolt. 1960. "The Life of Galileo." In *Plays*, ed. Bertolt Brecht. Vol. I. London: Methuen.

Bridges, John. 1906. *Reminiscences of a Country Politician*. London: T. W. Laurie.

"British Political Party General Election Addresses, [1892–Ca. 1970] from the National Liberal Club Collection, Bristol University." 1986. ed. Library University of Bristol.

Broadberry, Stephen, Giovanni Federico, and Alexander Klein. 2010. "Sectoral Developments, 1870 – 1914." In *The Cambridge Economic History of Modern Europe: 1870 to the Present*, eds. Stephen Broadberry and Kevin H. O'Rourke. Cambridge: Cambridge University Press. 59–83.

Brock, Michael. 1973. *The Great Reform Act*. London: Hutchinson University Library.

Bronner, Laura. 2014. "Property and Power: Mps' Assets and Support for Democratization in the 1867 Reform Act." *Legislative Studies Quarterly* 39: 439–66.

Brown, Cyril. 1922. "Rathenau Is Buried as Martyr." *New York Times*, June 27.

Brown, Robert, and Stephen Easton. 1989. "Weak-Form Efficiency in the Nineteenth Century: A Study of Daily Prices in the London Market for 3 Per Cent Consols, 1821–1860." *Economica* 56: 61–70.

Bryce, James. 1908. *The American Commonwealth*. Vol. II. New York: The Commonwealth Publishing Company.

Bryce, James 1921. *Modern Democracies*. New York: The Macmillan Company.

Buell, Raymond Leslie. 1920. *Contemporary French Politics*. New York: D. Appleton.

Buggle, Johannes C. 2016. "Law and Social Capital: Evidence from the Code Napoleon in Germany." *European Economic Review* 87: 148–75.

Burness, Catriona. 2013. "The Making of Scottish Unionism, 1886–1914." In *Mass Conservatism: The Conservatives and the Public Sphere since the 1880s*, eds. Stuart Ball and Ian Holliday. London: Routledge. 16–35.

— 2003. *"Strange Associations": The Irish Question and the Making of Scottish Unionism, 1886–1918*. East Linton: Tuckwell Press.

Bussiek, Dagmar. 2002. *"Mit Gott Für König und Vaterland!" Die Neue Preussische Zeitung, 1848–1892*. Lit Verlag: Muenster.

Cabrera, Mercedes, and Fernando del Rey. 2011. *El Poder de los empresarios: Política y economía en la españa contemporánea, 1875–2010*. 1 ed. Barcelona: RBA.

Caldwell, Peter C. 1997. *Popular Sovereignty and the Crisis of German Constitutional Law: The Theory and Practice of Weimar Constitutionalism*. Durham: Duke University Press.

Cannadine, David. 1999. *The Decline and Fall of the British Aristocracy*. New York: Vintage.

— 1977. "The Landowner as Millionaire: The Finances of the Dukes of Devonshire, C.1800-C.1926." *The Agricultural History Review* 25: 77–97.

Cannon, John. 1973. *Parliamentary Reform, 1640–1832*. Cambridge: Cambridge University Press.

Capoccia, Giovanni. 2005. *Defending Democracy: Reactions to Extremism in Interwar Europe*. Baltimore: Johns Hopkins University Press.

Caramani, Danièle. 2003. "The End of Silent Elections: The Birth of Electoral Competition, 1832–1915." *Party Politics* 9: 411–43.

Caramani, Danièle. 2000. *Elections in Western Europe Since 1815: Electoral Results by Constituencies*, The Societies of Europe. London: Macmillan Reference.

Cardoza, Anthony L. 1997. *Aristocrats in Bourgeois Italy: The Piedmontese Nobility, 1861–1930*. New York: Cambridge University Press.

Carey, John M., and Matthew Soberg Shugart. 1995. "Incentives to Cultivate a Personal Vote: A Rank Ordering of Electoral Formulas." *Electoral Studies* 14: 417–39.

Carpenter, Dan. 2003. "The Petition as Tool of Recruitment." Harvard University.

Carr, Edward Hallett. 1946. *The Twenty Years' Crisis, 1919–1939: An Introduction to the Study of International Relations*. London: Macmillan & co. ltd.

Cawood, Ian. 2012. *The Liberal Unionist Party: A History*. London: I. B. Tauris.

Cecil, Lord Robert. 1860. "The Budget and the Reform Bill." *Quarterly Review* 214: 514–54.

Chadwick, Mary. 1976. "The Role of Redistribution in the Making of the Third Reform Act." *Historical Journal* 19: 665–83.

Chadwick, Owen. 1966. *The Victorian Church*. New York: Oxford University Press.

Chanady, Attila. 1967. "The Disintegration of the German National Peoples' Party 1924–1930." *The Journal of Modern History* 39: 65–91.

Charle, Christophe. 2010. "The Specificities of French Elites at the End of the Nineteenth Century: France Compared to Britain and Germany." *Historical Reflections* 36: 7–18.

Chickering, Roger. 2004. *Imperial Germany and the Great War, 1914–1918*. Cambridge: Cambridge University Press.

— 1984. *We Men Who Feel Most German: A Cultural Study of the Pan-German League, 1886–1914*. Boston: George Allen and Unwin.

Churchill, Winston. 1906. *Lord Randolph Churchill*. New York: The Macmillan company.

1958. *My Early Life*. New York: Charles Scribner's Sons.

Clark, Christopher. 2006. *Iron Kingdom: The Rise and Downfall of Prussia, 1600–1947*. Cambridge: Harvard University Press.

2013. *The Sleepwalkers: How Europe Went to War in 1914*: Penguin Press.

Clark, Samuel. 1984. "Nobility, Bourgeoisie and the Industrial Revolution in Belgium." *Past & Present*: 140–75.

1979. *Social Origins of the Irish Land War*. Princeton: Princeton University Press.

Clarke, Peter. 1992. *A Question of Leadership: Gladstone to Thatcher*. London: Penguin.

Coetzee, Frans. 1990. *For Party or Country: Nationalism and Dilemmas of Popular Conservatism in Edwardian England*. Oxford: Oxford University Press.

Collier, Ruth Berins. 1999. *Paths Towards Democracy: The Working Class and Elites in Western Europe and South America*. Cambridge: Cambridge University Press.

Colomer, Josep Maria. 2007. "On the Origins of Electoral Systems and Political Parties: The Role of Elections in Multi-Member Districts." *Electoral Studies* 26: 262–73.

Conrad, Sebastian, and Jürgen Osterhammel, eds. 2004. *Das Kaiserreich transnational: Deutschland in der Welt 1871–1914*. Goettingen: Vandenhoeck & Ruprecht.

Conservatives, Two. 1882. "The State of the Opposition." *Fortnightly Review* 32.

Conze, Werner. 1964. "Brünings Politik unter dem Druck der großen Krise." *Historische Zeitschrift* 199: 529–50.

Cornford, James. 1963. "The Transformation of Conservatism in the Late Nineteenth Century." *Victorian Studies* 7: 35–66.

Cowling, Maurice. 1967. *1867: Disraeli, Gladstone and Revolution: The Passing of the Second Reform Bill*. London: Cambridge University Press.

1971. *The Impact of Labour 1920–1924: The Beginning of Modern British Politics*. Cambridge: Cambridge University Press.

Cox, Gary. 1987. *The Efficient Secret: The Cabinet and the Development of Political Parties in Victorian England*, Political Economy of Institutions and Decisions. Cambridge: Cambridge University Press.

Cox, Jeffrey. 1982. *The English Churches in a Secular Society: Lambeth, 1870–1930*. New York: Oxford University Press.

Cragoe, Matthew. 2008. "The Great Reform Act and the Modernization of British Politics: The Impact of Conservative Associations, 1835–1841." *Journal of British Studies* 47: 581–603.

Craig, Fred W. S. 1976. *Electoral Facts, 1885–1975*. London: Macmillan Press.

Craig, Gordon. 1964. *The Politics of the Prussian Army, 1640–1945*. London and New York: Oxford University Press.

Craig, Gordon 1978. *Germany, 1866–1945*. New York: Oxford University Press.

Craigie, Major P. G. 1887. "The Size and Distribution of Agricultural Holdings in England and Abroad." *Journal of the Royal Statistical Society* 50: 86–149.

Cronin, James E. 1980. "Labor Insurgency and Class Formation: Comparative Perspectives on the Crisis of 1917–1920 in Europe." *Social Science History* 4: 125–52.

Crothers, George. 1941. *The German Elections of 1907*. New York: Columbia University Press.

Cusack, Thomas, Torben Iversen, and David Soskice. 2007. "Economic Interests and the Origins of Electoral System." *American Political Science Review* 101: 373–91.

Dahl, Robert. 1971. *Polyarchy: Participation and Opposition.* New Haven: Yale University Press.

Dangerfield, George. 1997. *The Strange Death of Liberal England.* Stanford: Stanford University Press.

Dasgupta, Aditya, and Daniel Ziblatt. 2015. "How Did Britain Democratize? A View from the Sovereign Bond Market." *Journal of Economic History* 57: 1–29.

Davidson, John Colin Campbell 1969. *Memoirs of a Conservative: J. C. C. Davidson's Memoirs and Papers, 1910–37.* London: Weidenfeld and Nicolson.

Di Tella, Torcuato S. 1971/1972. "La búsqueda de la fórmula política argentina." *Desarrollo Económico* 11: 317–25.

Diamond, Larry. 1999. *Developing Democracy: Toward Consolidation.* Baltimore: Johns Hopkins University Press.

Diehl, James M. 1985. "Von der 'Vaterlandspartei' zur 'Nationalen Revolution': Die Vereinigten vaterlaendischen Verbände Deutschlands (Vvvd) 1922–1932." *Vierteljahrshefte für Zeitgeschichte*: 617–39.

"Digest of Scottish Registration Cases, 1891–1893." 1894. *The Tory.*

Dobry, Michel. 2000. "France: An Ambiguous Survival." In *Conditions of Democracy in Europe, 1919–1939: Systematic Case Studies,* eds. Dirk Berg-Schlosser and Jeremy Mitchell. Basingstoke: Macmillan. 157–83.

Dörr, Manfred, ed. 1964. *Die Deutschnationale Volkspartei 1925 bis 1928.* Marburg: Philipps-University Marburg/Lahn.

Downs, Anthony. 1957. *An Economic Theory of Democracy.* New York: Harper.

Doyle, Barry. 2012. "A Crisis of Urban Conservatism? Politics and Organisation in Edwardian Norwich." *Parliamentary History* 31.

Dunbabin, J. P. D. 1963. "The 'Revolt of the Field': The Agricultural Labourers' Movement in the 1870s." *Past and Present* 26: 68–97.

   1994. "Some Implications of the 1885 British Shift Towards Single-Member Constituencies: A Note." *English Historical Review* 109: 89–100.

Dunk, Hermann von der. 1978. "Conservatism in the Netherlands." *Journal of Contemporary History* 13: 741–63.

Dutton, David 2005. "Conservatism in Crisis, 1910–1915." In *Recovering Power: The Conservatives in Opposition since 1867,* eds. Stuart Ball and Anthony Seldon. London: Palgrave. 113–33.

Duverger, Maurice. 1954. *Political Parties: Their Organization and Activity in the Modern State* London: Methuen.

Dybdahl, Vagn. 1969. *Partier og erhverv: Studier i partiorganisation og byerhvervenes politiske aktivitet ca. 1880–1913.* Aarhus: Universitetsforlaget i Aarhus.

Eastwood, David. 1997. "Contesting the Politics of Deference: The Rural Electorate, 1820–1860." In *Party, State, and Society: Electoral Behavior in Britain since 1820,* eds. Jon Lawrence and Miles Taylor. Aldershot, England: Scolar Press. 27–49.

Eckardt, Hans Wilhelm. 1980. *Privilegien und Parlament: Die Auseinandersetzungen um das Allgemeine und Gleiche Wahlrecht in Hamburg.* Hamburg: Landeszentrale für politische Bildung.

Eggers, Andrew, and Arthur Spirling. 2014. "Party Cohesion in Westminster Systems: Inducements, Replacement and Discipline in the House of Commons, 1836–1910." *British Journal of Political Science*: 1–23.

Eichengreen, Barry J. 2008. *Globalizing Capital: A History of the International Monetary System.* 2nd ed. Princeton: Princeton University Press.

Eifert, Christiane. 2003. *Paternalismus und Politik: Preussiche Landräte im 19. Jahrhundert*. Münster: Westfälisches Dampfboot.
Eley, Geoff. 1993. "Anti-Semitism, Agrarian Mobilization, and the Conservative Party: Radicalism and Containment in the Founding of the Agrarian League, 1890–189." In *Between Reform, Reaction, and Resistance: Studies in the History of German Conservatism from 1789 to 1945*, eds. Larry Eugene Jones and James Retallack. Oxford: Berg Publishers. 187–228.
2005. *A Crooked Line: From Cultural History to the History of Society*. Ann Arbor: University of Michigan Press.
2002. *Forging Democracy: The History of the Left in Europe, 1850–2000*. Oxford: Oxford University Press.
1980. *Reshaping the German Right: Radical Nationalism and Political Change after Bismarck* New Haven: Yale University Press.
Eliade, Mircea. 1959. *The Sacred and the Profane: The Nature of Religion*. 1st American ed. New York: Harcourt Brace.
Enos, Ryan D., and Eitan D. Hersh. 2015. "Party Activists as Campaign Advertisers: The Ground Campaign as a Principal-Agent Problem." 109: 252–78.
Epstein, Klaus. 1960. "Der Interfraktionelle Ausschuß und das Problem der Parlamentarisierung 1917–1918." *Historische Zeitschrift* 191: 562–84.
1966. *The Genesis of German Conservatism*. Princeton: Princeton University Press.
1959. *Matthias Erzberger and the Dilemma of German Democracy*. Princeton: Princeton University Press.
Ericsson, Christer. 2008. *Kapitalets politik och politikens kapital: Högermän, industrimän och patriarker 1890–1985*. Stockholm: Santerus.
Ermakoff, Ivan. 2008. *Ruling Oneself Out: A Theory of Collective Self-Abdication*. Durham: Duke University Press.
Ertman, Thomas. 1998. "Democracy and Dictatorship in Interwar Western Europe Revisited." *World Politics* 50: 475–505.
2010. "The Great Reform Act of 1832 and British Democratization." *Comparative Political Studies* 43: 1000–22.
2000. "Liberalization, Democratization, and the Origins of a 'Pillarized' Civil Society in Nineteenth Century Belgium and the Netherlands." In *Civil Society Before Democracy: Lessons from Nineteenth Century Europe*, eds. Nancy Bermeo and Philip Nord. Oxford: Rowman and Littlefield Publishers.
2009. "Western European Party Systems and the Religious Cleavage." In *Religion, Class Coalitions, and Welfare States*, eds. Kees van Kersbergen and Philip Manow. Cambridge: Cambridge University Press. 39–55.
Esaiasson, Peter. "Svenska valkampanjer 1866–1988." *Allmänna förlaget*, 1990.
Evans, Eric. 2000. *Parliamentary Reform in Britain, c. 1770–1918*. Abingdon: Routledge.
Evans, Richard. 2003. *The Coming of the Third Reich*. New York: Penguin Press.
1987a. *Death in Hamburg: Society and Politics in the Cholera Years, 1830–1910*. Oxford: Clarendon Press.
1979. "'Red Wednesday' in Hamburg: Social Democrats, Police and Lumpenproletariat in the Suffrage Disturbances of 17 January 1906." *Social History* 4: 1–31.
1987b. *Rethinking German History: Nineteenth Century Germany and the Origins of the Third Reich*. London: Allen and Unwin.

Fair, John D. 1991. "The Carnarvon Diaries and Royal Mediation in 1884." *English Historical Review* 106: 97–116.

1986. "From Liberal to Conservative: The Flight of the Liberal Unionists after 1886." *Victorian Studies* 29: 291–314.

1973. "Royal Mediation in 1884: A Reassessment." *English Historical Review* 88: 100–13.

Falter, Jürgen. 1991. *Hitlers Wähler*. Munich: Beck.

Falter, Jürgen 1986. "The National Socialist Mobilization of New Voters, 1928–1933." In *The Formation of the Nazi Constituency, 1919–1933*, ed. Thomas Childers. London: Routledge. 202–30.

Fawcett, Arthur William Potter. 1967. *Conservative Agent: A Study of the National Society of Conservative and Unionist Agents and Its Members*. Driffield (Yorks.): Published for the National Society of Conservative and Unionist Agents by East Yorkshire Printers.

Fearon, James. 2011. "Self-Enforcing Democracy." *The Quarterly Journal of Economics* 126: 1661–708.

Feis, Herbert. 1965. *Europe, the World's Banker, 1870–1914: An Account of European Foreign Investment and the Connection of World Finance with Dplomacy before World War I*. New York: W. W. Norton.

Feldman, Gerald D. 1966. *Army, Industry, and Labor in Germany, 1914–1918*. Princeton: Princeton University Press.

1971. "Big Business and the Kapp Putsch." *Central European History* 4: 99–130.

1997. *The Great Disorder: Politics, Economics, and Society in the German Inflation, 1914–1924*. New York: Oxford University Press.

Ferguson, Niall. 2002. *Paper and Iron: Hamburg Business and German Politics in the Era of Inflation, 1897–1927*. Oxford: Oxford University Press.

2006. "Political Risk and the International Bond Market Between the 1848 Revolution and the Outbreak of the First World War." *Economic History Review* 59: 70–112.

1994. "Public Finance and National Security: The Domestic Origins of the First World War Revisited." *Past and Present* 142: 141–68.

Feuchtwanger, E. J. 1959b. "The Conservative Party under the Impact of the Second Reform Act." *Victorian Studies* 2: 289–304.

1959a. "J. E. Gorst and the Central Organization of the Conservative Party, 1870–1882." *Bulletin of the Institute of Historical Research* 32: 192–208.

Fiorina, Morris. 1980. "The Decline of Collective Responsibility in American Politics." *Daedalus* 109: 25–45.

Fisch, Jörg. 2010. *Das Selbstbestimmungsrecht der Völker: Die Domestizierung einer Illusion*. München: Verlag C. H. Beck.

Fischer, Conan. 2006. "A Very German Revolution? The 1918–1920 Settlement Reconsidered." *German Historical Institute London Bulletin* 28: 6–32.

Fischer, Fritz. 1979. *Bündnis der Eliten: zur Kontinuität der Machtstrukturen in Deutschland 1871–1945*. Düsseldorf: Droste.

Fisman, Raymond. 2001. "Estimating the Value of Political Connections." *American Economic Review* 91: 1095–102.

Flora, Peter, and Jens Alber. 1981. "Modernization, Democratization, and the Development of Welfare States in Western Europe." In *The Development of*

Welfare States in Europe and America, eds. Peter Flora and Arnold J. Heidenheimer. New Brunswick, NJ: Transaction Books. 37–80.

Fontane, Theodore. 1995. *The Stechlin*. Columbia, South Carolina: Camden House.

Foster, Robert. 1981. *Lord Randolph Churchill: A Political Life*. Oxford: Oxford University Press.

Frauendienst, Werner. 1957. "Demokratisierung des deutschen Konstitutionalismus in der Zeit Wilhelms II." *Zeitschrift für die gesamte Staatswissenchaft* 113: 721–46.

Freiherr von Freytagh-Loringhoven, Axel. 1964. "Nicht grosse, sondern starke Rechte." In *Die Deutschnationale Volkspartei 1925 Bis 1928*, ed. Manfred Dörr. Marburg: Philipps-University Marburg/Lahn. Reprint, reprinted as Anlage Nr. 38.

Frieden, Jeffry A. 2006. *Global Capitalism: Its Fall and Rise in the Twentieth Century*. 1st ed. New York: Norton.

Friedman, Edward, and Joseph Wong, eds. 2008. *Political Transitions in Dominant Party Systems: Learning to Lose*. New York and London: Routledge.

Fukuyama, Francis. 2011. *The Origins of Political Order: From Prehuman Times to the French Revolution*: Farrar, Straus and Giroux.

Funck, Marcus. 2000. "Shock und Chance: Der preussische Militärsadel in der Weimarer Republik Zwischen Stand und Profession." *In Adel und Bürgertum in Deutschland*, ed. Heinz Reif. Berlin: Akademie. 127–71.

Garst, J. Daniel. 1998. "From Factor Endowments to Class Struggle: Pre World War I Germany and Rogowski's Theory of Trade and Political Cleavages." *Comparative Political Studies* 31: 22–44.

Gash, Norman. 1982. "The Organization of the Conservative Party, 1832–1846: Part I: The Parliamentary Organization." *Parliamentary History* 1: 137–60.

1983. "The Organization of the Conservative Party, 1832–1846: Part II: The Electoral Organization." *Parliamentary History* 2: 31–152.

1977. *Politics in the Age of Peel: A Study in the Technique of Parliamentary Representation, 1830–1850*. Hassocks, UK: Harvester Press.

Gerber, Alan, and Donald Green. 2008. *Get Out the Vote: How to Increase Voter Turnout*. Washington, DC: Brookings Institution Press.

Gerlach, Hellmut von. 1925. *Erinnerungen eines Junkers [Memoir of a Junker]*. Berlin: die Welt am Montag.

Gerring, John. 2007. *Case Study Research: Principles and Practices*. Cambridge: Cambridge University Press.

Gerring, John, Phillip J. Bond, William T. Barndt, and Carola Moreno. 2005. "Democracy and Economic Growth: A Historical Perspective." *World Politics* 57: 323–64.

Gerschenkron, Alexander. 1948. *Bread and Democracy in Germany*. Berkeley: University of California Press.

Gibson, Edward L. 2012. *Boundary Control: Subnational Authoritarianism in Federal Democracies*. Cambridge: Cambridge University Press.

1996. *Class and Conservative Parties: Argentina in Comparative Perspective*. Baltimore: Johns Hopkins University Press.

Goemans, Hein. 2000. *War and Punishment: The Causes of War Termination and the First World War*. Princeton: Princeton University Press.

Goltz, Anna von der. 2009. *Hindenburg: Power, Myth, and the Rise of the Nazis*. Oxford: Oxford University Press.

Gömmel, R. 1992. "Entstehung und Entwicklung der Effektenbörsen im 19. Jahrhundert bis 1914." In *Deutsche Börsengeschichte*, ed. H. Pohl. Frankfurt a. M.: Fritz Knapp Verlag. 133–207.

Gorst, Harold Edward. 1906. *The Fourth Party*. London: Smith Elder.

Gossel, Daniel. 2010. *Medien und Politik in Deutschland und den USA: Kontrolle, Konflikt und Kooperation vom 18. bis zum frühen 20. Jahrhundert*. Stuttgart: Franz Steiner Verlag.

Gould, Andrew. 1999. *Origins of Liberal Dominance: State, Church, and Party in Nineteenth Century Europe*, Interests, Identities, and Institutions in Comparative Politics. Ann Arbor: University of Michigan Press.

Granovetter, Mark. 1978. "Threshold Models of Collective Behavior." *American Journal of Sociology* 83: 1420–43.

Grathwol, Robert P. 1980. *Stresemann and the Dnvp: Reconciliation or Revenge in German Foreign Policy 1924–1928*. Lawrence: University Press of Kansas.

Green, E. H. H. 1995. *The Crisis of Conservatism: The Politics, Economics, and Ideology of the British Conservative Party, 1880–1914*. London: Routledge.

Grießmer, Axel. 2000. *Massenverbände und Massenparteien im Wilhelminischen Reich: zum Wandel der Wahlkultur 1903–1912*. Düsseldorf: Droste.

Grosser, Dieter. 1970. *Vom monarchischen Konstitutionalismus zur parlamentarischen Demokratie*. Hague: Martinus Nijhoff.

Grünthal, Günther. 1978. "Das preußische Dreiklassenwahlrecht: Ein Beitrag zur Genesis und Funktion des Wahlrechtsoktrois vom Mai 1849." *Historische Zeitschrift* 226: 17–66.

Grzymala Busse, Anna M. 2002. *Redeeming the Communist Past: The Regeneration of Communist Parties in East Central Europe*. Cambridge: Cambridge University Press.

Guizot, Francois. 1997. *The History of Civilization in Europe*. Translated by William Hazlitt. London: Penguin Books.

Guldi, Jo, and David Armitage. 2014. *The History Manifesto*. Cambridge: Cambridge University Press.

Haffner, Sebastian. 1969. *Die verratene Revolution: Deutschland 1918/1919*. Bern: Scherz Verlag.

Hagen, William. 2002. *Ordinary Prussians: Brandenburg Junkers and Villagers, 1500–1840*. Cambridge: Cambridge University Press.

Hagenlücke, Heinz. 1997. *Deutsche Vaterlandspartei: Die nationale Rechte am Ende des Kaiserreiches*. Düsseldorf: Droste.

Halperin, Samuel William. 1965. *Germany Tried Democracy: A Political History of the Reich from 1918 to 1933*. New York: W. W. Norton.

Hanham, H. J. 1959. *Elections and Party Management: Politics in the Time of Disraeli and Gladstone*. London: Longmans.

Hanson, Stephen E. 2010. *Post-Imperial Democracies: Ideology and Party Formation in Third Republic France, Weimar Germany, and Post-Soviet Russia*. Cambridge: Cambridge University Press.

Harling, Philip. 1996. *The Waning of "Old Corruption": The Politics of Economical Reform in Britain, 1779–1846*. Oxford: Clarendon Press.

Harris, James. 1992. "Rethinking the Categories of the German Revolution of 1848: The Emergence of Popular Conservatism in Bavaria." *Central European History* 25: 123–48.

Hayes, Peter. 1980. "'A Question Mark with Epaulettes'? Kurt Von Schleicher and Weimar Politics." *The Journal of Modern History* 52: 35–65.

Hayes, William. 1982. *The Background and Passage of the Third Reform Act.* New York: Garland Publishing.

Heckart, Beverly. 1974. *From Basserman to Bebel: The Grand Bloc's Quest for Reform in the Kaiserreich.* New Haven: Yale University Press.

Heinsohn, Kirsten. 2010. *Konservative Parteien in Deutschland 1912 bis 1933: Demokratisierung und Partizipation in Geschlechterhistorischer Perspektive.* Düsseldorf: Droste.

Henig, Ruth. 2002. *The Weimar Republic 1919–1933.* Hoboken: Taylor and Francis.

Herf, Jeffrey. 1984. *Reactionary Modernism: Technology, Culture, and Politics in Weimar and the Third Reich.* Cambridge: Cambridge University Press.

Hering, Rainer. 2003. *Konstruierte Nation: Der Alldeutsche Verband, 1890 bis 1939.* Hamburg: Christians.

Hering, Rainer 2014. "Realms of Leadership and Residues of Social Mobilization: The Pan-German League, 1918–1933." In *The German Right in the Weimar Republic,* ed. Larry Eugene Jones. New York: Berghahn Books. 108–33.

Hermens, Ferdinand A. 1936. "Proportional Representation and the Breakdown of German Democracy." *Social Research* 3: 411–33.

Herrick, Francis H. 1946. "Lord Randolph Churchill and the Popular Organization of the Conservative Party." *The Pacific Historical Review* 15: 178–91.

Herrigel, Gary. 1996. *Industrial Constructions: The Sources of German Industrial Power.* Cambridge: Cambridge University Press.

Hertzman, Lewis. 1963. *DNVP: Right-Wing Opposition in the Weimar Republic, 1918–1924.* Lincoln: University of Nebraska Press.

   1958. "The Founding of the German National People's Party (DNVP), November 1918–January 1919." *The Journal of Modern History* 30: 24–36.

Hewitson, Mark. 2001. "The Kaiserreich in Question: Constitutional Crisis in Germany before the First World War." *The Journal of Modern History* 73: 725–80.

Hicks-Beach, Lady Victoria. 1932. *Life of Sir Michael Hicks Beach.* London: Macmillan and Co.

Himmelfarb, Gertrude. 1966. "The Politics of Democracy: The English Reform Act of 1867." *Journal of British Studies* 6: 97–138.

Hirschman, Albert O. 1991. *The Rhetoric of Reaction: Perversity, Futility, and Jeopardy.* Cambridge, MA: Harvard University Press.

Hobsbawn, Eric J., and Terrence Ranger, eds. 1992. *The Invention of Tradition.* Cambridge: Cambridge University Press.

Hoffmann, Stanley. 1974. *Decline or Renewal? France Since the 1930s.* New York: Viking Press.

   1961. "The Effects of World War II on French Society and Politics." *French Historical Studies* 2: 28–63.

   1997. "Hitler's Thirty Days to Power: January 1933." *Foreign Affairs* 76: 135.

Hofmeister, Bjorn. 2014. "Continuity and Change on the German Right: The Pan-German League and Nazism, 1918–1939." In *The German Right in the Weimar Republic,* ed. Larry Eugene Jones. New York: Berghahn Books. 134–64.

Hofstadter, Richard. 1967. *The Paranoid Style in American Politics and Other Essays.* New York: Vintage Books.

Hohls, Rüdiger, and Hartmut Kaelble, eds. 1989. *Die regionale Erwerbsstruktur im deutschen Reich und in der Bundesrepublik 1895–1970*. St. Katharinen: Scripta Mercaturae Verlag.

Holzbach, Heidrun. 1981. *Das "System Hugenberg": Die Organisation bürgerlicher Sammlungspolitik vor dem Aufstieg der NSDAP*. Stuttgart: Deutsche Verlags-Anstalt.

Hooven, Marcel ten, and Ron de Jong. 2008. *Geschiedenis van de Christelijk-Historische Unie 1908–1980*. Meppel: Boom Distributie Centrum.

Hopkins, T. M. 1897. "The Conservative Complexion of the English Church." *Westminster Review* 147: 324–34.

Howard, Marc. 2003. *The Weakness of Civil Society in Postcommunist Europe*. Cambridge: Cambridge University Press.

Hunter, Archie. 2001. *A Life of Sir John Eldon Gorst: Disraeli's Awkward Disciple*. London: Frank Cass.

Huntington, Samuel. 1991. *The Third Wave: Democratization in the Late Twentieth Century*. Norman: University of Oklahoma Press.

Huntington, Samuel P. 1968. *Political Order in Changing Societies*. New Haven: Yale University Press.

Hurd, Madeleine. 2000. *Public Spheres, Public Mores, and Democracy: Hamburg and Stockholm, 1870–1914*. Ann Arbor: University of Michigan Press.

Hylén, Jan. 1991. *Fosterlandet främst? Konservatism och liberalism inom högerpartiet 1904–1985 Stockholm Studies in Politics*. Stockholm: Norstedts juridikförlag.

Irvine, William D. 1989. *The Boulanger Affair Reconsidered: Royalism, Boulangism, and the Origins of the Radical Right in France*. New York: Oxford University Press.

1974. "French Conservatives and the 'New Right' During the 1930s." *French Historical Studies* 8: 534–62.

Irwin, Galen A., and J. J. M. van Holsteyn. 1989. "Decline of the Structured Model of Electoral Competition." In *Politics in the Netherlands: How Much Change?*, eds. Hans Daalder and Galen A. Irwin. London: F. Cass. 21–41.

Iversen, Torben, and David Soskice. 2006. "Electoral Institutions and the Politics of Coalitions: Why Some Democracies Redistribute More Than Others." *American Political Science Review* 100: 165–81.

Jackisch, Barry A. 2012. *The Pan-German League and Radical Nationalist Politics in Interwar Germany, 1918–39*. Farnham: Ashgate Publishing Limited.

Jackson, Alvin. 2003a. *Home Rule: An Irish History, 1800–2000*. Oxford: Oxford University Press.

1993. "The Larne Gun Running of 1914." *History of Ireland* 1.

Jackson, Julian. 2003b. *The Fall of France: The Nazi Invasion of 1940*. Oxford.

2001. *France: The Dark Years, 1940–1944*. Oxford: Oxford University Press.

Jäderin, Axel. 1914. *Allmänna valmansförbundet 1904–14. En Krönika*. Stockholm: Allmänna valmansförbundet.

Jaggard, Edwin. 2008. "Managers and Agents: Conservative Party Organisation in the 1850s." *Parliamentary History* 27: 7–18.

Janos, Andrew C. 1989. "The Politics of Backwardness in Continental Europe, 1780–1945." *World Politics* 41: 325–58.

Janßen, Karl-Heinz. 1970. "Who Is Hugenberg? Ein Verspätetes, Aber Immer Noch Aktuelles Porträt." *Die Zeit* (March 6).

Jarvis, David. 1994. "Mrs Maggs and Betty: The Conservative Appeal to Women Voters in the 1920s." *Twentieth Century British History* 5: 129–52.

Jenkins, Jennifer. 2003. *Provincial Modernity: Local Culture and Liberal Politics in Fin-De-Siecle Hamburg.* Ithaca: Cornell University Press.

Jenkins, Roy. 1966. *Asquith: Portrait of a Man and an Era.* New York: E. P. Dutton.

Jonas, Erasmus. 1965. *Die Volkskonservativen, 1928–1933.* Düsseldorf: Droste.

Jones, Andrew. 1972. *The Politics of Reform 1884.* Cambridge: Cambridge University Press.

Jones, Larry Eugene. 2000. "Catholic Conservatives in the Weimar Republic: The Politics of the Rhenish-Westphalian Aristocracy, 1918–1933." *German History* 18: 60–85.

2009. "German Conservatism at the Crossroads: Count Kuno Von Westarp and the Struggle for Control of the DNVP, 1928–30." *Contemporary European History* 18: 147–77.

ed. 2014. *The German Right in the Weimar Republic: Studies in the History of German Conservatism, Nationalism, and Antisemitism from 1918 to 1933.* New York: Berghahn Books.

1992. "'The Greatest Stupidity of My Life': Alfred Hugenberg and the Formation of the Hitler Cabinet, January 1933." *Journal of Contemporary History* 27: 63–87.

1997. "Hindenburg and the Conservative Dilemma in the 1932 Presidential Elections." *German Studies Review* 20: 235–59.

2015. *Hitler Versus Hindenburg: The 1932 Presidential Elections and the End of the Weimar Republic.* Cambridge: Cambridge University Press.

1979. "Inflation, Revaluation, and the Crisis of Middle-Class Politics: A Study in the Dissolution of the German Party System, 1923–28." *Central European History* 12: 143–68.

2006. "Nationalists, Nazis, and the Assault against Weimar: Revisiting the Harzburg Rally of October 1931." *German Studies Review* 29: 483–94.

Jones, Mark, and Scott Mainwaring. 2003. "The Nationalization of Parties and Party Systems: An Empirical Measure and Application to the Americas." *Party Politics* 9: 139–66.

Judt, Tony. 2005. *Postwar: A History of Europe since 1945.* New York: Penguin Press.

Jusko, Karen Long. 2013. "Who Speaks for the Poor? Electoral Geography and the Political Representation of Low-Income and Working Class Citizens." Stanford University.

Kahan, Alan S. 2003. *Liberalism in Nineteenth-Century Europe: The Political Culture of Limited Suffrage.* New York: Palgrave Macmillan.

Kaiserliches Statistisches Amt, "Streiks und Aussperrung im Jahre 1909." 1910. In *Statistik des Deutschen Reichs.* Vol. 239. Berlin: Verlag von Puttkammer & Mühlbrecht.

Kalyvas, Stathis N. 1996. *The Rise of Christian Democracy in Europe.* Ithaca, NY: Cornell University Press.

Karol, David. 2009. *Party Position Change in American Politics: Coalition Management.* Cambridge: Cambridge University Press.

Katznelson, Ira. 2013. *Fear Itself: The New Deal and the Origins of Our Time.* New York: W. W. Norton.

Keiger, John F. V. 1997. *Raymond Poincaré.* Cambridge: Cambridge University Press.

Kennedy, Ellen. 2004. *Constitutional Failure: Carl Schmitt in Weimar*. Durham: Duke University Press.

Kennedy, Sean. 2007a. *Reconciling France against Democracy: The Croix De Feu and the Parti Social Français, 1927–1945*. Montreal: McGill-Queen's University Press.

Kennedy, Thomas. 2007b. "Troubled Tories: Dissent and Confusion Concerning the Party's Ulster Policy, 1910–1914." *Journal of British Studies* 46: 570–93.

Key, V. O. 1949. *Southern Politics in State and Nation*. New York: A. A. Knopf.

Keyssar, Alexander. 2000. *The Right to Vote: The Contested History of Democracy in the United States*. New York: Basic Books.

Kinnear, Michael. 1968. *The British Voter: An Atlas and Survey since 1885*. London: Batsford.

1973. *The Fall of Lloyd George: The Political Crisis of 1922*. London: Macmillan.

Kitschelt, Herbert. 1989. "The Internal Politics of Parties: The Law of Curvilinear Disparity Revisited." *Political Studies* 37: 400–21.

1992. "Political Regime Change: Structure and Process-Driven Explanations." *American Political Science Review* 86: 1028–34.

1995. *The Radical Right in Western Europe: A Comparative Analysis*. Ann Arbor: University of Michigan Press.

1994. *The Transformation of European Social Democracy*. Cambridge: Cambridge University Press.

Kitschelt, Herbert P., and Staf Hellmans. 1990. *Beyond the European Left: Ideology and Political Action in the Belgian Ecology Parties*. Durham: Duke University Press.

Klemperer, Klemens von. 1957. *Germany's New Conservatism, Its History and Dilemma in the 20th Century*. Princeton: Princeton University Press.

Kloppenberg, James T. 1986. *Uncertain Victory: Social Democracy and Progressivism in European and American Thought, 1870–1920*. New York: Oxford University Press.

Klovland, Jan T. 1994. "Pitfalls in the Estimation of the Yield on British Consols, 1850–1914." *The Journal of Economic History* 54: 164–87.

Koblik, Steven. 1969. "Wartime Diplomacy and the Democratization of Sweden in September-October 1917." *The Journal of Modern History* 41: 29–45.

Kolb, Eberhard. 1988. *The Weimar Republic*. Boston: Unwin Hyman.

Koss, Michael. 2013. "The Legitimate Secret: The Institutionalization of Parliamentary Agenda Control in the United Kingdom and Germany." Paper presented at the ECPR General Conference, Bordeaux.

Kousser, J. Morgan. 1974. *The Shaping of Southern Politics: Suffrage Restriction and the Establishment of the One-Party South, 1880–1910*. New Haven: Yale University Press.

Kreuzer, Marcus. 2001. *Institutions and Innovation: Voters, Interest Groups and Parties in the Consolidation of Democracy–France and Germany, 1870–1939*. Ann Arbor: University of Michigan Press.

2003. "Parliamentarization and the Question of German Exceptionalism: 1867–1918." *Central European History* 36: 327–57.

Kühne, Thomas. 2005. "Demokratisierung und Parlamentarisierung: Neue Forschungen zur Politischen Entwicklungsfähigkeit Deutschlands vor dem ersten Weltkrieg." *Geschichte und Gesellschaft* 31: 293–316.

1994. *Dreiklassenwahlrecht und Wahlkultur in Preussen 1867–1914: Landtagswahlen zwischen korporativer Tradition und politischem Massenmarkt,*

Beiträge zur Geschichte des Parlamentarismus und der politischen Parteien. Düsseldorf: Droste.

Kulczycki, John J. 1994. *The Foreign Worker and the German Labor Movement: Xenophobia and Solidarity in the Coal Fields of the Ruhr, 1871–1914.* Providence: Berg.

Kutz-Bauer, Helga. 1983. "Arbeiterschaft und Sozialdemokratie in Hamburg vom Gründerkrach bis zum Ende des Sozialistengesetzes." In *Arbeiter in Hamburg. Unterschichten, Arbeiter und Arbeiterbewegung seit dem Ausgehenden 18. Jahrhundert,* eds. Arno Herzig, Dieter Langewiesche, and Arnold Sywottek. Hamburg: Verlag Erziehung und Wissenschaft. 179–92.

Lambach, Walter. 1964. "Monarchismus." In *Die Deutschnationale Volkspartei 1925 bis 1928,* ed. Manfred Dörr. Marburg: Philipps-University Marburg/Lahn. 554–56.

Lamberti, Marjorie. 1968. "Lutheran Orthodoxy and the Beginning of Conservative Party Organization in Prussia." *Church History* 37: 439–53.

Lampedusa, Giuseppe Tomasi di. 2007. *Il Gattopardo [the Leopard].* New York: Pantheon.

Langewiesche, Dieter. 1978. "Die Anfänge der Deutschen Parteien. Partei, Fraktion und Verein in der Revolution von 1848/49." *Geschichte und Gesellschaft* 4: 324–61.

Lapp, Benjamin. 1997. *Revolution from the Right: Politics, Class, and the Rise of Nazism in Saxony, 1919–1933.* Atlantic Highlands, NJ: Humanities Press.

Lässig, Simone. 1996. *Wahlrechtskampf und Wahlreform in Sachsen, 1895–1909.* Weimar: Böhlau.

    1998. "Wahlrechtsreformen in den deutschen Einzelstaaten: Indikatoren für Modernisierungstendzen und Reformfähigkeit im Kaiserreich?" In *Modernisierung und Region im wilhelmischen Deutschland,* ed. Simone Lässig. Bielefeld: Verlag für Regionalgeschichte. 127–70.

Lawrence, Jon. 1993. "Class and Gender in the Making of Urban Toryism, 1880–1914." *English Historical Review* 108: 629–52.

Lawrence, Jon, and Jane Elliott. 1997. "Parliamentary Election Results Reconsidered: An Analysis of Borough Elections, 1885–1910." *Parliamentary History* 16: 18–28.

Layman, Geoffrey, Thomas Carsey, John Green, Richard Herrera, and Rosalyn Cooperman. 2010. "Activists and Conflict Extension in American Politics." *American Political Science Review* 104: 324–46.

Lebovics, Herman. 1988. *The Alliance of Iron and Wheat in the Third French Republic, 1860–1914: Origins of the New Conservatism.* Baton Rouge: Louisiana State University Press.

Lee, Robert. 2006. *Rural Society and the Anglican Clergy, 1815–1914: Encountering and Managing the Poor.* Woodbridge, UK: Boydell & Brewer Press.

Leicht, Johannes. 2012. *Heinrich Class, 1868–1953: Die politische Biografie eines Alldeutschen.* Paderborn: Ferdinand Schoeningh Verlag.

Leopold, John A. 1977. *Alfred Hugenberg: The Radical Nationalist Campaign against the Weimar Republic.* New Haven and London: Yale University Press.

Leslie, John. "Parties and Other Social Functions." Berkeley: University of California, 2002.

Levitsky, Steven, and Lucan Way. 2002. "The Rise of Competitive Authoritarianism." *Journal of Democracy* 13: 51–65.

Levy, Richard S. 1975. *The Downfall of the Anti-Semitic Political Parties in Imperial Germany.* New Haven: Yale University Press.

Lewin, Leif. 1988. *Ideology and Strategy: A Century of Swedish Politics*. Cambridge: Cambridge University Press.

Liebe, Werner. 1956. *Die Deutschnationale Volkspartei, 1918–1924*. Düsseldorf: Droste-Verlag.

Lieberman, Evan. 2005. "Nested Analysis as a Mixed-Method Strategy for Comparative Research." *American Political Science Review* 99: 435–52.

Linz, Juan. 1967. "The Party System of Spain: Past and Future." In *Party Systems and Voter Alignments: Cross-National Perspectives*, eds. Seymour Martin Lipset and Stein Rokkan. New York: Free Press.

Linz, Juan J., and Alfred C. Stepan. 1978. *The Breakdown of Democratic Regimes: Crisis, Breakdown and Reequilibration*. Baltimore: Johns Hopkins University Press.

Linz, Juan, Miguel Jerez, and Susana Corzo. 2002. "Ministers and Regimes in Spain: From the First to the Second Restoration, 1874–2002." *South European Society and Politics* 7: 41–116.

Lipset, Seymour Martin. 1983. "Radicalism or Reformism: The Sources of Working-Class Politics." *American Political Science Review* 77: 1–18.

  1959. "Some Social Requisites of Democracy: Economic Development and Political Legitimacy." *American Political Science Review* 53: 69–105.

Lipset, Seymour Martin, and Stein Rokkan. 1967. *Party Systems and Voter Alignments: Cross-National Perspectives*, International Yearbook of Political Behavior Research. New York: Free Press.

Lizzeri, Alessandro, and Nicola Persico. 2004. "Why Did the Elites Extend the Suffrage? Democracy and the Scope of Government, with an Application to Britain's Age of Reform." *The Quarterly Journal of Economics* 119: 707–65.

Llavador, Humberto, and Robert Oxoby. 2005. "Partisan Competition, Growth and the Franchise." *The Quarterly Journal of Economics* 120: 1155–89.

Lowe, Sid. 2010. *Catholicism, War and the Foundation of Francoism: The Juventud De Acción Popular in Spain, 1931–1939*. Portland: Sussex Academic Press.

Lowell, Lawrence A. 1912. *The Government of England*. New York: Macmillan.

Loxton, James "Authoritarian Inheritance and Conservative Party-Building in Latin America." Harvard University, 2014.

Lubenow, W. C. 1983. "Irish Home Rule and the Great Separation of the Liberal Party in 1886: The Dimensions of Parliamentary Liberalism." *Victorian Studies* 26: 161–80.

Luebbert, Gregory M. 1991. *Liberalism, Fascism, or Social Democracy: Social Classes and the Political Origins of Regimes in Interwar Europe*. New York: Oxford University Press.

Lustick, Ian. 1993. *Unsettled States, Disputed Lands: Britain and Ireland, France and Algeria, Israel and the West Bank-Gaza*. Ithaca: Cornell University Press.

Lynch, Patricia. 2003. *The Liberal Party in Rural England, 1885–1910: Radicalism and Community*, Oxford Historical Monographs. Oxford: Oxford University Press.

MacLaren, A. Allan. 1974. *Religion and Social Class: The Disruption Years in Aberdeen*. London: Routledge & K. Paul.

Maddison, Angus. 2007. *Contours of the World Economy* Oxford: Oxford University Press.

Mahoney, James. 2003. "Knowledge Accumulation in Comparative Historical Research: The Case of Democracy and Authoritarianism." In *Comparative*

Historical Analysis in the Social Sciences, eds. James Mahoney and Dietrich Rueschemeyer. Cambridge: Cambridge University Press. 131–76.

Maier, Charles S. 2000. "Consigning the Twentieth Century to History: Alternative Narratives for the Modern Era." *The American Historical Review* 105: 807–31.

    1975. *Recasting Bourgeois Europe: Stabilization in France, Germany and Italy in the Decade after World War I*. Princeton: Princeton University Press.

    1981. "The Two Postwar Eras and the Conditions for Stability in Twentieth-Century Western Europe." *American Historical Review* 86: 327–52.

Maine, Henry. 1886. *Popular Government*. London: John Murray.

Malefakis, Edward E. 1970. *Agrarian Reform and Peasant Revolution in Spain: Origins of the Civil War*. New Haven: Yale University Press.

Malinowski, Sebastian. 2003. *Vom König zum Führer. Sozialer Niedergang und politische Radikalisierung im Deutschen Adel Zwischen Kaiserreich und Ns-Staat* Berlin.

Manela, Erez. 2007. *The Wilsonian Moment: Self-Determination and the International Origins of Anticolonial Nationalism*. Oxford: Oxford University Press.

Manow, Philip, Valentin Schroeder, and Carsten Nickel. 2011. "Germany's 1918 Electoral Reform and the Reichstag's Efficient Secret." Paper presented at the Historical Democratization and Redistribution in Advanced Industrialized Democracies, Juan March Institute, Madrid, Spain, October 20–22.

Manow, Philip, and Daniel Ziblatt. 2015. "The Layered State: Patterns and Pathways of Modern Nation State Building." In *The Oxford Handbook of Transformations of the State*, eds. Stephan Leibfried, Evelyne Huber, Matthew Lange, Jonah D. Levy, and John D. Stephens. Oxford: Oxford University Press.

Marcet, Joan. 2012. "La derecha en España: una aproximación histórica." Barcelona, Spain: Institut de ciències polítiques i socials, Universitat Autonoma de Barcelona.

Mares, Isabela. 2015. *From Open Secrets to Secret Voting: Democratic Electoral Reforms and Voter Autonomy*. Cambridge: Cambridge University Press.

Margalit, Avishai. 2010. *On Compromise and Rotten Compromises*. Princeton: Princeton University Press.

Markoff, John. 1999. "Where and When Was Democracy Invented?" *Comparative Studies in Society and History* 41: 660–90.

Marks, Gary, Heather Mbaye, and Hyung-min Kim. 2009. "Radicalism or Reformism: Socialist Parties before World War I." *American Sociological Review* 74: 615–35.

Marsh, Peter. 1994. *Joseph Chamberlain: Entrepreneur in Politics*. New Haven: Yale University Press.

Marsh, Peter T. 1978. *The Discipline of Popular Government: Lord Salisbury's Domestic Statecraft, 1881–1902*. Hassocks, Sussex: Harvester Press.

Martin, Cathie Jo, and Duane Swank. 2012. *The Political Construction of Business Interests: Coordination, Growth, and Equality*. Cambridge: Cambridge University Press.

Marx, Karl. 1962. "The Elections in England–Tories and Whigs (New York Daily Tribune)." In *Karl Marx and Friedrich Engels on Britain*. Moscow: Foreign Languages Publishing House. 351–57.

Masket, Seth E. 2009. *No Middle Ground: How Informal Party Organizations Control Nominations and Polarize Legislatures*. Ann Arbor: University of Michigan Press.

Masoud, Tarek E. 2014. *Counting Islam: Religion, Class, and Elections in Egypt*. Cambridge: Cambridge University Press.

Massing, Paul. 1949. *Rehearsal for Destruction: A Study of Political Anti-Semitism in Imperial Germany*. New York: Harper.

Matthias, Erich, and Rudolf Morsey, eds. 1959. *Der Interfraktionelle Ausschuß 1917/ 18*. Düsseldorf: Droste.

May, Ernest R. 2000. *Strange Victory: Hitler's Conquest of France*. New York: Hill and Wang.

May, John D. 1973. "Opinion Structure of Political Parties: The Special Law of Curvilinear Disparity." *Political Studies* 21: 135–51.

Mayer, Arno J. 1981. *The Persistence of the Old Regime: Europe to the Great War*. New York: Pantheon Books.

McCarthy, John, and Mayer Zald. 1977. "Resource Mobilization and Social Movements: A Partial Theory." *American Journal of Sociology* 82: 1212–41.

McClosky, Herbert, Paul J. Hoffmann, and Rosemary O'Hara. 1960. "Issue Conflict and Consensus among Party Leaders and Followers." *The American Political Science Review* 54: 406–27.

McCormick, John P. 1997. *Carl Schmitt's Critique of Liberalism: Against Politics as Technology*. Cambridge, UK, and New York: Cambridge University Press.

McCrillis, Neal R. 1998. *The British Conservative Party in the Age of Universal Suffrage: Popular Conservatism, 1918–1929*. Columbus: Ohio State University Press.

McFaul, Michael. 2002. "The Fourth Wave of Democracy and Dictatorship: Noncooperative Transitions in the Postcommunist World." *World Politics* 54: 212–44.

McKenzie, Robert, and Allan Silver. 1968. *Angels in Marble: Working Class Conservatism in Urban England*. London: Heinemann.

McKenzie, Robert Trelford. 1955. *British Political Parties: The Distribution of Power within the Conservative and Labour Parties*. New York: St. Martin's Press.

McKibbin, Ross. 1974. *The Evolution of the Labour Party, 1910–1924*. London: Oxford University Press.

1990. *The Ideologies of Class: Social Relations in Britain, 1880–1950*. Oxford: Clarendon Press.

2010. *Parties and People, England, 1914–1951*. Oxford: Oxford University Press.

McLean, Iain. 2001. *Rational Choice and British Politics: An Analysis of Rhetoric and Manipulation from Peel to Blair*. Oxford: Oxford University Press.

2012. *What's Wrong with the British Constitution?* Oxford: Oxford University Press.

Meguid, Bonnie. 2008. *Party Competition between Unequals: Strategies and Electoral Fortunes in Western Europe*. Cambridge, UK, and New York: Cambridge University Press.

Mergel, Thomas. 2003. "Das Scheitern des Deutschen Tory-Konservatismus. Die Umformung der DNVP zu einer rechtsradikalen Partei 1928–1932." *Historische Zeitschrift* 276: 323–68.

Michels, Robert. 1915. *A Sociological Study of the Oligarchical Tendencies of Modern Democracy* New York: Hearsts International Library, Co.

Mickey, Robert G. 2015. *Paths out of Dixie: The Democratization of Authoritarian Enclaves in America's Deep South, 1944–1972*. Princeton: Princeton University Press.

Middlebrook, Kevin J., ed. 2000. *Conservative Parties, the Right, and Democracy in Latin America*. Baltimore: Johns Hopkins University Press.

Mill, John Stuart. 1859. *On Liberty*. London: John Parker.

Mitchell, B. R. 2003. *International Historical Statistics, Europe, 1750–2000*. 5 ed. New York: Palgrave Macmillan.

Moes, Jaap. 2012. *Onder aristocraten: over hegemonie, welstand en aanzien van adel, patriciaat en andere notabelen in Nederland, 1848–1914*. Hilvershum: Verloren.

Møller, Jørgen, Alexander Schmotz, and Svend-Erik Skaaning. 2015. "Economic Crisis and Democratic Breakdown in the Interwar Years: A Reassessment." *Historical Social Research* 40: 301–18.

Mommsen, Hans. 1996. *The Rise and Fall of Weimar Democracy*. Chapel Hill: University of North Carolina Press.

Montero, José R. 1977. *La CEDA: el catolicismo social y político en la II república*. Madrid: Ediciones de la Revista de Trabajo.

Moore, Barrington. 1966. *The Social Origins of Dictatorship and Democracy: Lord and Peasant in the Making of the Modern World*. Boston: Beacon Press.

Moore, David Cresap. 1976. *The Politics of Deference: A Study of the Mid-Nineteenth Century English Political System*. Hassocks: Harvester Press.

Moreno-Luzon, Javier. 2007. "Political Clientelism, Elites, and Caciquismo in Restoration Spain, 1875–1923." *European History Quarterly* 37: 417–41.

Morrison, Bruce. "Channeling the Restless Spirit of Innovation: Elite Concessions and Institutional Change in the British Reform Act of 1832." *World Politics* 63: 691–92.

Müller, Jan-Werner 2006. "Comprehending Conservatism: A New Framework for Analysis." *Journal of Political Ideologies* 11: 359–65.

Murphy, Richard. 1986. "Faction in the Conservative Party and the Home Rule Crisis, 1912–1914." *History* 71: 222–34.

Nasaw, David. 1993. *Going Out: The Rise and Fall of Public Amusements*. New York: Basic Books.

Neal, Larry. 1993. *The Rise of Financial Capitalism: International Capital Markets in the Age of Reason*. Cambridge: Cambridge University Press.

Nebelin, Manfred. 2010. *Ludendorff: Diktator im ersten Weltkrieg*. München: Siedler.

Neumann, Sigmund. 1930. *Die Stufen des Preussischen Konservatismus*. Berlin: E. Ebering.

  1956. *Modern Political Parties: Approaches to Comparative Politics*. Chicago: University of Chicago Press.

Nevill, Dorothy, and Ralph Nevill. 1906. *The Reminiscences of Lady Dorothy Nevill*. London: E. Arnold.

Nipperdey, Thomas. 1961. *Die Organisation der Deutschen Parteien vor 1918*. Düsseldorf: Droste Verlag.

Nohlen, Dieter. 1986. *Wahlrecht und Parteiensystem*. Leverkusen: Leske & Budrich.

Nohlen, Dieter, and Philip Stöver. 2010. *Elections in Europe: A Data Handbook*. Baden-Baden, Germany: Nomos.

Nolan, Mary. 1986. "Economic Crisis, State Policy and Working Class Formation in Germany, 1870–1900." In *Working Class Formation: Nineteenth Century Patterns in Western Europe and the United States*, eds. Ira Katznelson and Aristide Zolberg. Princeton: Princeton University Press. 352–96.

Nord, Philip G. 2015. *France 1940: Defending the Republic*. New Haven: Yale University Press.

Nordlinger, Eric. 1967. *The Working Class Tories: Authority, Deference, and Stable Democracy*. London: MacGibbon and Kee.

Norris, Pippa. 2005. *Radical Right: Voters and Parties in the Electoral Market.* New York: Cambridge University Press.

North, Douglas C., and Barry Weingast. 1989. "Constitutions and Commitment: The Evolution of Institutions Governing Public Choice in Seventeenth-Century England." *Journal of Economic History* XLIX: 803–32.

Norton, Philip. 2012. "Resisting the Inevitable? The Parliament Act of 1911." *Parliamentary History* 31: 444–59.

Nossiter, Thomas Johnson. 1974. *Influence, Opinion and Political Idioms in Reformed England: Case Studies from the North East 1832–1874.* New York: Barnes & Noble Books.

O'Donnell, Guillermo A., and Philippe C. Schmitter. 2013 [1986]. *Transitions from Authoritarian Rule. Tentative Conclusions About Uncertain Democracies.* Baltimore: Johns Hopkins University Press.

O'Donnell, Guillermo A., Philippe C. Schmitter, and Laurence Whitehead, eds. 1986. *Transitions from Authoritarian Rule: Comparative Perspectives.* Baltimore: Johns Hopkins University Press.

O'Rourke, Kevin H., and Jeffrey G. Williamson. 1999. *Globalization and History: The Evolution of a Nineteenth-Century Atlantic Economy.* Cambridge, Mass: MIT Press.

O'Brien, Paul. 2014. *A Question of Duty: The Curragh Incident 1914* Dublin: New Island.

O'Gorman, Frank. 1993. "The Electorate Before and After 1832." *Parliamentary History* 12: 171–83.

Offer, Avner. 1981. *Property and Politics, 1870–1914: Landownership, Law, Ideology, and Urban Development in England.* Cambridge: Cambridge University Press.

Ohnezeit, Maik. 2011. *Zwischen "Schärfster Opposition" und dem "Willen Zur Macht": die Deutschnationale Volkspartei (DNVP) in der Weimarer Republik 1918–1928.* Düsseldorf: Droste Verlag.

Olson, Mancur. 1965. *The Logic of Collective Action: Public Goods and the Theory of Groups.* Cambridge: Harvard University Press.

Olsson, Stefan. 2000. *Den Svenska högerns anpassning till demokratin.*

Orloff, Ann, and Theda Skocpol. 1984. "Why Not Equal Protection? Explaining the Politics of Public Social Spending in Britain, 1900–1911 and the United States, 1880s-1920." *American Sociological Review* 49: 726–50.

Orlow, Dietrich. 1986. *Weimar Prussia, 1918–1925: The Unlikely Rock of Democracy.* Pittsburgh: University of Pittsburgh Press.

Ostrogorski, Moisei. 1902. *Democracy and the Organization of Political Parties.* Vol. 1. London: Macmillan and Co.

Otte, Thomas G. 2013. "The Swing of the Pendulum at Home: By-Elections and Foreign Policy, 1865–1914." In *By-Elections in British Politics, 1832–1914,* eds. Thomas G. Otte and Paul Readman. Woodbridge: Boydell Press. 121–50.

Owen, Keith. "The Fourth Party and Conservative Evolution, 1880–1885." Texas Tech University, 2000.

Packer, Ian. 2011. "Contested Ground: Trends in British by-Elections, 1911–1914." *Contemporary British History* 25: 157–73.

Panebianco, Angelo. 1988. *Political Parties: Organization and Power* Cambridge: Cambridge University Press.

Parry, Jonathan. 1986. *Democracy and Religion: Gladstone and the Liberal Party, 1867–1875.* Cambridge: Cambridge University Press.

1993. *The Rise and Fall of Liberal Government in Victorian Britain.* New Haven: Yale University Press.

Partei, Deutsche Konservative, ed. 1909. *Der Allgemeine Delegiertentag der Deutsch-Konservativen Partei. Stenographischer Bericht, 11 December 1909.* Berlin: Hauptverin der Deutch-Konservativen.

Passmore, Kevin. 1997. *From Liberalism to Fascism: The Right in a French Province, 1928–1939.* Cambridge: Cambridge University Press.

2013. *The Right in France from the Third Republic to Vichy.* Oxford: Oxford University Press.

Patch, William. 1998. *Heinrich Brüning and the Dissolution of the Weimar Republic.* Cambridge: Cambridge University Press.

Payne, Stanley G. 1967. *Politics and the Military in Modern Spain.* Stanford, Calif.: Stanford University Press.

1993. *Spain's First Democracy: The Second Republic, 1931–1936.* Madison: University of Wisconsin Press.

Pelling, Henry. 1967. *Social Geography of British Elections, 1885–1910.* London: Macmillan.

Persson, Torsten, and Guido Tabellini. 2009. "Democratic Capital: The Nexus of Political and Economic Change." *American Economic Journal: Macroeconomics* 1: 88–126.

Petersen, Jens. 1990. "Der Italienische Adel von 1861 bis 1946." *Geschichte und Gesellschaft. Sonderheft* 13: 243–59.

Peukert, Detlev. 1993. *The Weimar Republic.* New York: Hill and Wang.

Phillips, Gregory. 1980. "Lord Willoughby De Broke and the Politics of Radical Toryism, 1909–1914." *Journal of British Studies* 20: 205–24.

Phillips, John A. 1992. *The Great Reform Bill in the Boroughs: English Electoral Behaviour, 1818–1841.* Oxford: Clarendon Press.

Phillips, John A., and Charles Wetherell. 1995. "The Great Reform Act of 1832 and the Political Modernization of England." *The American Historical Review* 100: 411–36.

Pierson, George. 1938. *Tocqueville and Beaumont in America.* New York: Oxford University Press.

Pierson, Paul. 2004. *Politics in Time: History, Institutions, and Social Analysis.* Princeton: Princeton University Press.

2015. "Power and Path Dependence." In *Advances in Comparative Historical Analysis*, eds. James Mahoney and Kathleen Thelen. Cambridge: Cambridge University Press.

Piketty, Thomas. 2014. *Capital in the Twenty-First Century.* Cambridge, MA: The Belknap Press of Harvard University Press.

Pincus, Steven 2009. *1688: The First Modern Revolution.* New Haven: Yale University Press.

Pincus, Steven, and James Robinson. 2011. "What Really Happened in the Glorious Revolution?" National Bureau of Economic Research.

Pollock, James. 1932. *Money and Politics Abroad.* Freeport: Books for Libraries Press.

Powell, Leigh Michael. 2000. "Sir Michael Hicks Beach and Conservative Politics." *Parliamentary History* 19: 377–404.

Preston, Paul. 1994. *The Coming of the Spanish Civil War: Reform, Reaction and Revolution in the Second Republic.* 2nd ed. London: Routledge.

Pridham, Geoffrey. 1977. *Christian Democracy in Western Germany: The Cdu/Csu in Government and Opposition, 1945–1976.* New York: St. Martin's Press.

Przeworski, Adam. 2008. "Conquered or Granted? A History of Suffrage Extension." *British Journal of Political Science* 39: 291–321.

   1991. *Democracy and the Market: Political and Economic Reforms in Eastern Europe and Latin America.* Cambridge: Cambridge University Press.

Przeworski, Adam, and John Sprague. 1986. *Paper Stones: A History of Electoral Socialism* Chicago: University of Chicago Press.

Pugh, Martin. 1978. *Electoral Reform in War and Peace, 1906–18.* London: Routledge & Kegan Paul.

   2006. *Hurrah for the Blackshirts! Fascists and Fascism in Britain between the Wars.* London: Pimlico.

   1985. *The Tories and the People, 1880–1935.* Oxford: B. Blackwell.

Puhle, Hans-Jürgen. 1967. *Agrarische Interessenpolitik und Preussischer Konservatismus im Wilhelminischen Reich, 1893–1914: ein Beitrag zur Analyse des Nationalismus in Deutschland am Beispiel des Bundes der Landwirte und der Deutsch-Konservativen Partei.* Hannover: Verlag für Literatur u. Zeitgeschehen

Pulzer, Peter G. J. 1972. *Political Representation and Elections in Britain,* Studies in Political Science. London: Allen and Unwin.

   1988. *The Rise of Political Antisemitism in Germany and Austria.* Cambridge: Harvard University Press.

Putnam, Robert. 2000. *Bowling Alone: The Collapse and Revival of American Community.* New York: Simon and Schuster.

Quinalt, R. E. 1979. "Lord Randolph Churchill and Tory Democracy, 1880–1885." *Historical Journal* 22: 141–65.

Quiroga, Alejandro, and Miguel Ángel del Arco Blanco, eds. 2010. *Soldados de dios y apóstoles de la patria: Las derechas Españolas en la Europa de entreguerras.* Granada: Editorial Comares.

Ramsden, John. 1978. *The Age of Balfour and Baldwin, 1902–1940.* London: Longman.

Rapport, Michael. 2009. *1848: Year of Revolution.* New York: Basic Books.

Rauh, Manfred. 1977. *Die Parlamentarisierung des Deutschen Reiches.* Düsseldorf: Droste Verlag.

Readman, Paul. 1999. "The 1895 General Election and Political Change in Late Victorian Britain." *Historical Journal* 42: 467–93.

   2001. "The Conservative Party, Patriotism, and British Politics: The Case of the General Election of 1900." *Journal of British Studies* 40: 107–45.

Reeves, Andrew. "To Power through Reform: The Development of Party through Electoral Reform in the Victorian House of Commons." Harvard University, 2008.

Reibel, Carl Wilhelm, ed. 2007. *Handbuch der Reichstagwahlen, 1890–1918: Bündnisse, Ergebnisse, Kandidaten.* Düsseldorf: Droste Verlag.

Remmer, Karen L. 1984. *Party Competition in Argentina and Chile: Political Recruitment and Public Policy, 1890–1930.* Lincoln: University of Nebraska Press.

Rémond, René. 1969. *The Right Wing in France from 1815 to De Gaulle.* Philadelphia: University of Pennsylvania Press.

Renard, Claude. 1966. *La Conquête du suffrage universel en Belgique.* Brussels Éditions de la Fondation J. Jacquemotte.

Renton, Tim. 2004. *Chief Whip: People, Power and Patronage in Westminster*. London: Politico's.

Retallack, James. 2006. *The German Right, 1860–1920: The Limits of the Authoritarian Imagination German and European Studies*. Toronto: University Press.

2012. "'Get Out the Vote!' Elections without Democracy in Imperial Germany." *Bulletin of the German Historical Institute* 51: 23–38.

Retallack, James N. 1988. *Notables of the Right: The Conservative Party and Political Mobilization in Germany, 1876–1918*. Boston: Unwin Hyman.

Riker, William H. 1986. *The Art of Political Manipulation*. New Haven: Yale University Press.

Ritter, Gerhard. 1954. *Carl Goerdeler und die deutsche Widerstandsbewegung*. Stuttgart: Deutsche Verlags-Anstalt.

Rix, Kathryn. "The Party Agent and English Electoral Culture, 1880–1906." Cambridge University, 2001.

Robb, Janet Henderson. 1942. *The Primrose League, 1883–1906*. Vol. 402, Columbia Studies in the Social Sciences. New York: Columbia University Press.

Roberts, Matthew. 2009. *Political Movements in Urban England, 1832–1914* London: Palgrave Macmillan.

2007. "Popular Conservatism in Britain, 1832–1914." *Parliamentary History* 26: 387–410.

2013. "A Terrific Outburst of Political Metereology: By-Elections and the Unionist Ascendancy in Late-Victorian England." In *By-Elections in British Politics, 1832–1914*, eds. Thomas G. Otte and Paul Readman. Woodbridge: Boydell Press. 177–200.

2006. "'Villa Toryism' and Popular Conservatism in Leeds, 1885–1902." *Historical Journal* 49: 217–46.

Roberts, Richard. 2014. *Saving the City: The Great Financial Crisis of 1914*. Oxford: Oxford University Press.

Rodden, Jonathan. 2010. "The Geographic Distribution of Political Preferences." *Annual Review of Political Science* 13: 321–40.

Rodgers, Daniel T. 1998. *Atlantic Crossings: Social Politics in a Progressive Age*. Cambridge, Mass: Belknap Press of Harvard University Press.

Rogowski, Ronald. 1989. *Commerce and Coalitions: How Trade Affects Domestic Political Alignments*. Princeton: Princeton University Press.

Röhl, John C. G. 1966. "Staatsstreichplan oder Staatsstreichbereitschaft? Bismarcks Politik in der Entlassungskrise." *Historische Zeitschrift* 203: 610–24.

Rokkan, Stein. 1970. *Citizens, Elections, Parties: Approaches to the Comparative Study of the Processes of Development*. New York: McKay.

1999. *State Formation, Nation-Building, and Mass Politics in Europe: The Theory of Stein Rokkan Based on His Collected Works*. Edited by Peter Flora, Stein Kuhnle and Derek W. Urwin. New York: Oxford University Press.

Rosanvallon, Pierre. 1992. *Le Sacre du citoyen: histoire du suffrage universel en France*. Paris: Gallimard.

Rose, Philip. 1859. "Election Notebook." Special Collections, Bodleian Library, Oxford.

Rosenberg, Arthur. 1931. *The Birth of the German Republic, 1871–1918*. New York: Oxford University Press.

1964. *Imperial Germany: The Birth of the German Republic 1871–1918*. Boston: Beacon Press.

Rosenblum, Nancy. 2008. *On the Side of the Angels: An Appreciation of Parties and Partisanship*. Princeton: Princeton University Press.

Rosenstone, Steven J., and John Mark Hansen. 1993. *Mobilization, Participation, and Democracy in America*, New Topics in Politics. New York: Macmillan.

Rubinstein, W. D. 1981. "New Men of Wealth and the Purchase of Land in Nineteenth-Century Britain." *Past & Present*: 125–47.

Rueschemeyer, Dietrich, Evelyne Huber Stephens, and John D. Stephens. 1992. *Capitalist Development and Democracy*. Chicago: University of Chicago Press.

Rush, Michael. 2001. *The Role of the Member of Parliament since 1868: From Gentlemen to Players*. New York: Oxford University Press.

Rustow, Dankwart A. 1955. *The Politics of Compromise: A Study of Parties and Cabinet Government in Sweden*. Princeton: Princeton University Press.

1970. "Transitions to Democracy: Toward a Dynamic Model." *Comparative Politics* 2: 337–63.

Sack, James J. 1993. *From Jacobite to Conservative: Reaction and Orthodoxy in Britain, 1760–1832*. New York: Cambridge University Press.

Salisbury, Lord 1884. "The Value of Redistribution: A Note on Electoral Statistics." *The National Review* (October 20).

Salmon, Philip. 2002. *Electoral Reform at Work: Local Politics and National Parties, 1832–1841*. London: Royal Historical Society.

Sanders, Robert. 1984. *Real Old Tory Politics: The Political Diaries of Sir Robert Sanders, Lord Bayford, 1910–35*. Edited by John Ramsden. London: The Historians' Press.

Saunders, Robert. 2011. *Democracy and the Vote in British Politics, 1848–1867: The Making of the Second Reform Act*. Farnham: Ashgate.

Schallert, Meike. "Why the Poor Organized and Lost Their Vote: Suffrage Robbery in Hamburg." Harvard University, 2008.

Scharpf, Fritz. 2006. "The Joint Decision Trap Revisited." *Journal of Common Market Studies* 44: 845–64.

1988. "The Joint-Decision Trap: Lessons from German Federalism and European Integration." *Public Administration* 66: 239–78.

Schattschneider, E. E. 1942. *Party Government*. New York: Farrar and Rinehart.

1960. *The Semi-Sovereign People: A Realist's View of Democracy in America*. New York: Holt, Rinehart, and Winston.

Scheck, Raffael. 2004. *Mothers of the Nation: Right-Wing Women in Weimar Germany*. Oxford: Berg.

Schelling, Thomas. 1971. "Dynamic Models of Segregation." *Journal of Mathematical Sociology* 1: 143–86.

Schijf, Huibert, Jaap Dronkers, and Jennifer van den Broeke-George. 2004. "Recruitment of Members of Dutch Noble and High Bourgeois Families to Elite Positions in the 20th Century." *Information sur les Sciences Sociales* 43: 435–75.

Schlesinger, Joseph. 1966. *Ambition and Politics: Political Careers in the United States* New York: Rand McNally.

Schlesinger, Joseph A. 1991. *Political Parties and the Winning of Office*. Ann Arbor: University of Michigan Press.

Schneider, Wolfgang. "Die Begrenzungen des Wahlrechts in Deutschland, Preußen und Hamburg (Im 19. Und 20. Jahrhundert)." Hamburg, 1955.

Schoenberger, Christoph. 2001. "Die überholte Parlamentarisierung: Einflussgewinn und fehlende Herrschaftsfähigkeit des Reichstags im sich demokratisierenden Kaiserreich." *Historische Zeitschrift* 272: 623–66.

Schorske, Carl E. 1955. *German Social Democracy 1905–1917: The Development of the Great Schism*. Cambridge: Harvard University Press.

Schremmer, D. E. 1989. "Taxation and Public Finance: Britain, France and Germany." In *The Cambridge Economic History of Europe. Volume Viii. The Industrial Economies: The Development of Economic and Social Policies*, eds. Peter Mathias and Sidney Pollard. Cambridge: Cambridge University Press. 315–494.

Schult, Richard. 1983. "Partei wider Willen: Kalküle und potentiale konservativer Parteigründer in Preußen zwischen erstem vereinigten Landtag und Nationalversammlung, 1847/1848." In *Deutscher Konservatismus im 19. und 20. Jahrhundert*, eds. Dirk Stegmann, Bernd-Jürgen Wendt and Peter-Christian Witt. Bonn: Verlag Neue Gesellschaft. 33–68.

Schwarz, Hans-Peter. 1995. *Konrad Adenauer: A German Politician and Statesman in a Period of War, Revolution, and Reconstruction*. Providence, RI: Berghahn Books.

Schwentker, Wolfgang. 1988. *Konservative Vereine und Revolution in Preussen, 1848/49: Die Konstituierung des Konservatismus als Partei*. Düsseldorf Droste.

Scott, James Brown. 1921. *Official Statements of War Aims and Peace Proposals, December 1916 to November 1918*. Washington, DC: Carnegie Endowment for International Peace.

Scully, Timothy. 1992. *Rethinking the Center: Party Politics in Nineteenth- and Twentieth-Century Chile*. Stanford, CA: Stanford University Press.

Searle, G. R. 2004. *A New England? Peace and War, 1886–1918*. Oxford: Clarendon Press.

Seidl, Klaus. 2014. *'Gesetzliche Revolution' im Schatten der Gewalt: die politische Kultur der Reichsverfassungskampagne in Bayern 1849*. Paderborn: Verlag Ferdinand Schöningh.

Selznick, Philip. 1952. *The Organizational Weapon: A Study of Bolshevik Strategy and Tactics*. Santa Monica: Rand Corporation.

Seymour, Charles. 1915. *Electoral Reform in England and Wales: The Development and Operation of the Parliamentary Franchise, 1832–1885*. Newton Abbot: David & Charles. Reprint, 1970.

Shannon, Richard. 1996. *The Age of Salisbury*. London and New York: Longman.

Sheets, Diane. "British Conservatism and the Primrose League: The Changing Character of Popular Politics." PhD, Columbia University, 1986.

Shepard, Walter. 1911. "Tendencies to Ministerial Responsibility in Germany." *American Political Science Review* 5: 57–69.

Shepsle, Kenneth A. 2003. "Losers in Politics (and How They Sometimes Become Winners): William Riker's Heresthetic." *Perspectives on Politics* 1: 307–15.

Shirer, William L. 1969. *The Collapse of the Third Republic: An Inquiry into the Fall of France in 1940*. New York: Simon and Schuster.

Simmons, Beth A. 1994. *Who Adjusts? Domestic Sources of Foreign Economic Policy During the Interwar Years*. Princeton: Princeton University Press.

Skocpol, Theda. 2003. *Diminished Democracy: From Membership to Management in American Civic Life*. Norman: University of Oklahoma Press.

Skowronek, Stephen, and Karen Orren. 2004. *The Search for American Political Development*. Cambridge Cambridge University Press.

Slater, Dan. 2013. "Democratic Careening". *World Politics* 65: 729–63.

Slater, Dan, and Erica Simmons. 2013. "Coping by Colluding: Political Uncertainty and Promiscuous Powersharing in Indonesia and Bolivia." *Comparative Political Studies* 46: 1366–93.

Slater, Dan, and Joseph Wong. 2013. "The Strength to Concede: Ruling Parties and Democratization in Development Asia." *Perspectives on Politics* 11: 717–33.

Smith, Francis Barrymore. 1966. *The Making of the Second Reform Bill*. Cambridge: Cambridge University Press.

Smith, Jeremy. 1993. "Bluff, Bluster and Brinkmanship: Andrew Bonar Law and the Third Home Rule Bill." *Historical Journal* 36: 161–78.

Smith, Paul, ed. 1972. *Lord Salisbury on Politics; a Selection from His Articles in the Quarterly Review, 1860–1883*. Cambridge: Cambridge University Press.

Söderberg, Erik Nataneal. 1929. *Allmänna Valmansförbundet, 1904–1929: En tjugufemårskrönika*. Stockholm: Egnellska boktr.

Soucy, Robert. 1995. *French Fascism: The Second Wave, 1933–1939*. New Haven: Yale University Press.

Spenkuch, Hartwin. 1998. *Das Preussische Herrenhaus: Adel und Bürgertum in der ersten Kammer des Landtags 1854–1918*. Düsseldorf: Droste Verlag.

Sperber, Jonathan. 1997. *The Kaiser's Voters: Electors and Elections in Imperial Germany*. Cambridge: Cambridge University Press.

Spring, David. 1980. "An Outsider's View: Alexis De Tocqueville on Aristocratic Society and Politics in 19th Century England." *Albion* 12: 122–31.

Stasavage, David. 2002. "Credible Commitment in Early Modern Europe: North and Weingast Revisited." *Journal of Law, Economics, and Organization* 18: 155–86.

2007. "Partisan Politics and Public Debt: The Importance of the Whig Supremacy for Britain's Financial Revolution." *European Review of Economic History* 11: 123–53.

Stegmann, Dirk. 1993. "Between Economic Interests and Radical Nationalism." In *Between Reform, Reaction, and Resistance: Studies in the History of German Conservatism from 1789 to 1845*, eds. Larry Eugene Jones and James Retallack. Providence, RI: Berg. 157–85.

1970. *Die Erben Bismarcks: Parteien und Verbände in der Spätphase des Wilhelminische Deutschlands*. Köln: Kipenheuer & Witsch.

Stenlas, Niklas. 2002. "Kampen om högern – Uppbyggnaden av Allmänna Valmansförbundet 1904–1922." In *Anfall Eller Forsvar?: Högern i Svensk Politik under 1900-Talet*, ed. Torbjorn Nilsson. Stockholm: Santeus.

Stephen, James. 1874. *Liberty, Equality and Fraternity*. London: Smith, Elder and Co.

Stephens, Gregory R, and John Leslie. 2011. "Parties, Organizational Capacities and External Change: New Zealand's National and Labour Parties, Candidate Selection and the Advent of Mmp." *Political Science* 63: 205–18.

Stern, Fritz. 1992. *The Failure of Illiberalism: Essays on the Political Culture of Modern Germany*. New York: Columbia University Press.

Stevenson, John. 1990. "Conservatism and the Failure of Fascism in Britain." In *Fascists and Conservatives: The Radical Right and the Establishment in Twentieth Century Europe*, ed. Martin Blinkhorn. Abingdon: Routledge.

Stewart, A. T. Q. 1967. *The Ulster Crisis*. London: Faber and Faber.

Stewart, Robert. 1978. *The Foundation of the Conservative Party, 1830–1867*. London: Longman.

Stigler, George. 1971. "The Theory of Economic Regulation." *Bell Journal of Economics and Management Science* 2: 3–21.

Stinchcombe, Arthur. 1968. *Constructing Social Theories*. New York: Harcourt Brace & World.

1965. "Social Structure and Organizations." In *Handbook of Organizations*, ed. James March. Chicago: Rand McNally & Co. 142–93.

"Storm Renewed in Reichstag: Cries of 'Revenge!' Interrupt Speeches on Rathenau Murder." 1922. *New York Times*, June 26.

Streeck, Wolfgang, and Kathleen Thelen. 2005. "Introduction: Institutional Change in Advanced Political Economies." In *Beyond Continuity*, eds. Kathleen Thelen and Wolfgang Streeck. Oxford: Oxford University Press. 1–39.

Stürmer, Michael. 1967. *Koalition und Opposition in der Weimarer Republik 1924–1928*. Düsseldorf: Droste Verlag.

Süle, Tibor. 1988. *Preussische Bürokratietradition: zur Entwicklung von Verwaltung und Beamtenschaft in Deutschland, 1871–1918*. Göttingen: Vandenhoeck & Ruprecht.

Suval, Stanley. 1985. *Electoral Politics in Wilhelmine Germany*. Chapel Hill: University of North Carolina Press.

Sykes, Alan. 1983. "The Radical Right and the Crisis of Conservatism before the First World War." *Historical Journal* 26: 661–76.

Tanner, Duncan. 1990. *Political Change and the Labour Party, 1900–1918*. Cambridge: Cambridge University Press.

Tavares de Almeida, Pedro. 1991. *Eleições e caciquismo no Portugal oitocentista (1868–1890), Memória E Sociedade*. Lisboa: Difel.

2006. "Materials for the History of Elections and Parliament in Portugal, 1820–1926." Lisbon: Biblioteca Nacional de Portugal.

2010. "Portugal." In *Elections in Europe: A Data Handbook*, ed. Dieter Nohlen. Oxford: Oxford University Press.

Taylor, Andrew J. 2005. "Stanley Baldwin, Heresthetics and the Realignment of British Politics." *British Journal of Political Science* 35: 429–63.

Taylor, Robert G. 1975. *Lord Salisbury*. London: Lane.

Teele, Dawn. 2014. "Ordinary Democratization: The Electoral Strategy That Won British Women the Vote." *Politics & Society* 42: 537–61.

Teorell, Jan. 2011. "Cleaning up the Vote: The Case of Electoral Fraud in Sweden, 1719–1909." Paper presented at the Juan March Institute, Madrid.

Thackeray, David. 2013. *Conservatism for the Democratic Age: Conservative Cultures and the Challenge of Mass Politics in Early Twentieth Century England*. Manchester: Manchester University Press.

Thelen, Kathleen. 2004. *How Institutions Evolve: The Political Economy of Skills in Germany, Britain, the United States, and Japan*, Cambridge Studies in Comparative Politics. Cambridge: Cambridge University Press.

Thermaenius, Edvard. 1933. *Sveriges politiska partier*. Stockholm: Hugo Gebers Förlag.

Thermænius, Edvard. 1935. *Riksdagspartierna*. Vol. 17. Stockholm: Sveriges Riksdag.

Thimme, Annelise. 1969. *Flucht in den Mythos: Die Deutschnationale Volkspartei und die Niederlage Von 1918*. Göttingen: Vandenhoeck and Ruprecht.

Tholfsen, Trygve. 1959. "The Origins of the Birmingham Caucus." *Historical Journal* 2: 161–84.

Thomas, John Alun. 1939. *The House of Commons, 1832–1901: An Analysis of Its Economic and Social Character*. Cardiff: University of Wales Press.

Thompson, Alastair. 2000. *Left Liberals, the State, and Popular Politics in Wilhelmine Germany*: Oxford University Press.

Thompson, E. P. 1963. *The Making of the English Working Class*. New York: Vintage Books.

Tilly, Charles. 2004. *Contention and Democracy in Europe, 1650–2000*. Cambridge: Cambridge University Press.

2007. *Democracy*. New York: Cambridge University Press.

Tirrell, Sarah. 1951. *German Agrarian Politics after Bismarck's Fall. The Formation of the Farmer's League*. New York: Columbia University.

Townson, Nigel. 2000. *The Crisis of Democracy in Spain: Centrist Policies under the Second Republic (1931–1936)*. Portland: Sussex Academic Press.

Trentmann, Frank. 2008. *Free Trade Nation: Commerce, Consumption, and Civil Society in Modern Britain*. Oxford: Oxford University Press.

Trippe, Christian F. 1995. *Konservative Verfassungspolitik 1918–1923: Die DNVP als Opposition in Reich und Ländern*. Düsseldorf: Droste.

Trollope, Anthony. 2008. *The Prime Minister*, Oxford World's Classics. Oxford: Oxford University Press.

Tsebelis, George. 2002. *Veto-Players*. Princeton: Princeton University Press.

Tuckwell, William. 1905. *Reminiscences of a Radical Parson*. London, Paris, New York and Melbourne: Cassell and Company.

Turner, Henry Ashby. 1985. *German Big Business and the Rise of Hitler*. New York: Oxford University Press.

1996. *Hitler's Thirty Days to Power: January 1933*. Reading, MA: Addison-Wesley.

Tworek, Heidi. 2014. "Magic Connections: German News Agencies and Global News Networks, 1905–1945." *Enterprise & Society* 15: 672–86.

Ulam, Adam B. 1981. *Russia's Failed Revolutions: From the Decembrists to the Dissidents*. New York: Basic Books.

Ur, Jason A. 2003. "Corona Satellite Photography and Ancient Road Networks: A Northern Mesopotamian Case Study." *Antiquity* 77: 102–15.

2013. "Spying on the Past: Declassified Intelligence Satellite Photographs and near Eastern Landscapes." *Near Eastern Archaeology* 76: 28–36.

Valenzuela, J. Samuel. 1985. *Democratización vía reforma: La expansión del sufragio en Chile*. Buenos Aires: Ediciones del IDES.

van Kersberger, Kees, and Philip Manow, eds. 2009. *Religion, Class Coalitions, and Welfare States*. Cambridge: Cambridge University Press.

Varela Ortega, José, ed. 2001. *El poder de la influencia: Geografía del caciquismo en España (1875–1923)*. Madrid: Centro de Estudios Politicos y Constitucionales.

1977. *Los amigos políticos: Partidos, elecciones y caciquismo en la restauración, 1875–1900*. Madrid: Alianza.

Vascik, Georg. 1993. "Agrarian Politics in Wilhelmine Germany: Diederich Hahn and the Agrarian League." In *Between Reform, Reaction, and Resistance. Studies in the History of German Conservatism*, eds. Larry Eugene Jones and James Retallack: Berg. 229–60.

Verba, Sindey, Henry Brady, and Kay Schlozman. 1995. *Voice and Equality: Civic Voluntarism in American Politics*. Cambridge: Harvard University Press.

Vernon, James. 1993. *Politics and the People: A Study in English Political Culture, 1815–1867*. New York: Cambridge University Press.

Vincent, John Russell, ed. 1984. *The Crawford Papers: The Journals of David Lindsay, Twenty-Seventh Earl of Crawford and Tenth Earl of Balcarres (1871–1940), During the Years 1892 to 1940*. Manchester: Manchester University Press.

Vincent, Mary. 1996. *Catholicism in the Second Spanish Republic: Religion and Politics in Salamanca, 1930–1936*. New York: Clarendon Press.

Volkov, Shulamit. 2012. *Walther Rathenau: The Life of Weimar's Fallen Statesman*. New Haven: Yale University Press.

Volkspartei, Deutschnationale. 1928. *Der Nationale Wille: Werden und Wirken der Deutschnationalen Volkspartei 1918–28*. Edited by Max Weiss. Essen: Deutsche Vertriebsstelle Rhein und Ruhr.

von Beyme, Klaus. 1984. *Parteien im westlichen Demokratien*. Munich: Piper.

von Westarp, Kuno Graf. 1928. *Die Regierung des Prinzen Max von Baden und die Konservative Partei 1918*. Berlin: Deutsche Verlagsgesellschaft für Politik und Geschichte.

von Winterfeldt, Joachim. 1942. *Jahreszeiten des Lebens*. Berlin: Propylän-Verlag.

Vössing, Konstantin. 2011. "Social Democratic Party Formation and National Variation in Labor Politics." *Comparative Politics* 43: 167–86.

Wagner, Patrick. 2005. *Bauern, Junker und Beamte: lokale Herrschaft und Partizipation im Ostelbien des 19. Jahrhunderts*. Vol. 9, Moderne Zeit. Göttingen: Wallstein.

Wald, Kenneth D. 1983. *Crosses on the Ballot: Patterns of British Voter Alignment since 1885*. Princeton, NJ: Princeton University Press.

Weber, Eugen. 1978. "Ambiguous Victories." *Journal of Contemporary History* 13: 819–27.

  1959. *The Nationalist Revival in France, 1905–1914*. Berkeley: University of California Press.

Weber, Max. 1984. "Das Preussische Wahlrecht." In *Zur Politik im Weltkrieg*, eds. Wolfgang Mommsen and Gangolf Huebinger. Tuebingen: JCB Mohr.

  1946. "Politics as a Vocation." In *From Max Weber: Essays in Sociology*, eds. H. H. Gerth and C. Wright Mills. New York: Oxford University Press. 77–128.

Weber, Reinhold. 2004. *Bürgerpartei und Bauernbund in Württemberg: Konservative Parteien im Kaiserreich und in Weimar (1895–1933)*. Düsseldorf: Droste.

Wehler, Hans-Ulrich. 1966. *Moderne Deutsche Sozialgeschichte*. Köln: Kiepenheur u. Witsch

Weingast, Barry, Susan Alberts, and Chris Warshaw. 2012. "Democratization and Countermajoritarian Institutions: The Role of Power and Constitutional Design in Self-Enforcing Democracy." In *Comparative Constitutional Design*, ed. Tom Ginsburg. New York: Cambridge University Press. 69–100.

Wendel-Hansen, Jens. 2013. "Landed Aristocracy and Danish Democratization, 1848–1940." Paper presented at the Seminar on the Historical Democratization of Northern Europe, Aarhus University, June 20, 2013.

Westarp, Graf. 1935. *Konservative Politik im letzen Jahrezent des Kaiserreichs*. Vol. 1. Berlin: Deutsche Verlagsgesellschaft.

Weston, Corinne. 1991. "Disunity on the Opposition Front Bench, 1884." *English Historical Review* 106: 80–96.

1967. "The Royal Mediation in 1884." *English Historical Review* 82: 296–322.

Weyland, Kurt. 2009. "The Diffusion of Revolution: '1848' in Europe and Latin America." *International Organization* 63: 391–423.

Wieviorka, Olivier. 2009. *Orphans of the Republic: The Nation's Legislators in Vichy France*. Cambridge, Mass.: Harvard University Press.

Wilensky, Harold L. 1964. "The Professionalization of Everyone?". *American Journal of Sociology* 70: 137–58.

Wilentz, Sean. 2005. *The Rise of American Democracy: Jefferson to Lincoln*. 1st ed. New York: Norton.

Willard, Kristen, Timothy Guinnane, and Harvey Rosen. 1996. "Turning Points in the Civil War: Views from the Greeback Market." *American Economic Review* 86: 1001–18.

Williamson, Philip. 2003. "The Conservative Party, 1900–1939: From Crisis to Ascendancy." In *A Companion to Early Twentieth-Century Britain*, ed. Chris Wrigley. London: Blackwell Publishing. 3–22.

ed. 1988. *The Modernisation of Conservative Politics: The Diaries and Letters of William Bridgeman 1904–1935*. London: Historians Press.

1992. *National Crisis and National Government: British Politics, the Economy and Empire, 1926–1932*. Cambridge: Cambridge University Press.

1999. *Stanley Baldwin: Conservative Leadership and National Values*. Cambridge: Cambridge University Press.

Windscheffel, Alex. 2007. *Popular Conservatism in Imperial London, 1868–1906*, Royal Historical Society Studies in History. Woodbridge, UK: Royal Historical Society.

Winkler, Heinrich August. 1985. *Der Schein der Normalität: Arbeiter und Arbeiterbewegung in der Weimarer Republik 1924 bis 1930*. Berlin: J. H. W. Dietz.

Wisseschaften, Berlin-Brandenburg Akademie der, ed. 1999. *Die Protokolle des Preussischen Staatsministeriums, 1817–1934/38*. 10 vols. Hildesheim: Olms Weidmann.

Witherell, Larry L. 1997. *Rebel on the Right: Henry Page Croft and the Crisis of British Conservatism, 1903–1914*. Newark: University of Delaware Press.

Witt, Peter-Christian. 1970. *Die Finanzpolitik des deutschen Reiches von 1903 bis 1913: eine Studie zur Innenpolitik des wilhelminischen Deutschland*. Lübeck: Matthiesen.

Wittenberg, Jason. 2006. *Crucibles of Political Loyalty: Church Institutions and Electoral Continuity in Hungary*, Cambridge Studies in Comparative Politics. New York: Cambridge University Press.

Wright, Jonathan. 2002. *Gustav Stresemann: Weimar's Greatest Statesman*. Oxford: Oxford University Press.

Zeldin, Theodore. 1958. *The Political System of Napoleon III*. New York: St. Martin's Press.

Ziblatt, Daniel. 2008. "Does Landholding Inequality Block Democratization?". *World Politics* 60: 610–41.

2006. "How Did Europe Democratize?". *World Politics* 58: 311–38.

2010. "Landholding Inequality in Germany, at the Reichstag Constituency Level, and Prussian Chamber of Deputies Constituency Level, 1895." 1 ed: Harvard Dataverse.

N. D. "Reluctant Democrats: Old Regime Conservative Parties in Democracy's First Wave." In *Life after Dictatorship: Authoritarian Successor Parties Worldwide*, eds. James Loxton and Scott Mainwaring.

2009. "Shaping Democratic Practice and the Causes of Electoral Fraud: The Case of Nineteenth-Century Germany." *American Political Science Review* 103: 1–21.

Index

weakness of, 206, 217, 219–20, 233n73, 314–15

Germany, 50–53, 373; anti-Semitic factions in, 194–97, 279n80, 282, 290–91; anti-socialist laws in, 185–86, 192, 228–29, 235; bond market volatility in, 63*t*; collapse of Hohenzollern empire in, 8–9, 260, 262, 266, 276–77; confessional divides in, 174, 177, 192, 210–13; conservative political parties in, 373; constitution of, 206–9, 216–17; democratic corporatism of, 268–69; disputed elections in, 181–82, 183*f*; East Prussian Junkers of, 18; election-time cross-party coalitions in, 187–90; embryonic conservative factions in, 32*t*; executive power in, 219–20; expansion of mass politics in, 17, 174–75, 185–86, 186nn52–53, 192, 206; failure of democratization efforts in, 215–58; federal Imperial system of, 20; Federal Ministry of War of, 320; fiscal federalism of, 235n78, 254; fragmentation of the right in, 186, 205–14, 259–60, 278–82, 337*t*, 339; geographic concentration of party seats in, 244–46; incomplete November 1918 Revolution in, 262–64, 278; industrialization in, 17, 51, 225–26; invasion of France in 1940 by, 357–58; landed wealth and inequality, 24–25, 52, 177, 178n23, 181–86, 216, 239, 252–53; National Liberal-Conservative coalition (Kartell) in, 185, 186, 192; organized interest groups in, 22–23, 175, 189–97, 203n131, 283; organized labor of, 18, 23, 52–53, 226–33, 255–58, 268–69; parliamentary sovereignty in, 10, 18; post-World War II democratization of, 334; Revolution of 1848 of, 22, 48, 220; right-wing media of, 170, 308–14; shifting relationship of conservatism to the state in, 193n80; single-member parliamentary districts of, 107n205, 187, 277; social unrest and mobilization in, 218, 225–33; state-based limits on suffrage in, 215–16, 220–24, 226–33, 233–42; suffrage retractions in, 255–58; trade protectionism in, 193, 198n105, 204, 225–26, 249; universal male suffrage in, 10, 18, 19, 22, 26, 27*t*, 45, 172, 176, 206, 217, 221*t*; volatility score for, 14, 15*f*; weak parliamentarization in, 27*t*, 206, 217, 219–20, 223, 233n73; women's suffrage in, 277; working and middle classes of, 51–52. *See also Prussia; Weimar Republic; World War I*

Gerschenkron, Alexander, 252
Gibson, Edward, 13n39, 30n28, 358, 359n119
Gierke, Anne von, 290n135
Gil-Robles, José María, 349–52
Gladstone, William, 56, 68n35, 83–84, 111–12, 142
Gladstonian coalitions, 266n27
Glagau, Otto, 194
Global Financial Database, 58n14
gold standard, 261, 262n7, 275, 288
Göring, Hermann, 331–32
Gorst, John, 72–73, 76–82, 84, 91–92, 94
Grabowsky, Adolf, 214, 247n112
Graefe-Godebee, Albrecht von, 290n134
Granovetter, Mark, 82
Grathwol, Robert P., 303
Great Britain. *See Britain*
Great Depression of 1929, 273, 276, 315n82, 319
The Great Illusion (Angell), 140
Great Reform Act of 1832 (Britain). *See Reform Act of 1832*
Green, E. H. H., 142
Grießmer, Axel, 197n101
Groener, Wilhelm, 263n13, 320, 322
Guizot, Francois, 6n16

habituation, 287n118
Haenisch, Konrad, 267–68
Haffner, Sebastian, 262, 263
Hahn, Diederich, 198, 199n113
Halperin, William, 265
Halsbury Club, 150n52
Hamburg (Germany), 221, 253–58; bourgeois merchant-class elite of, 254; governing structures of, 254; organized labor movement of, 254–58; retraction of political rights in, 256–58; universal male suffrage in, 255; weak political groups of, 257–58
Hammerstein, Wilhelm von, 194–95, 331
Harington, Lord, 135–36
Hassell, Ulrich von, 279n75
Hayes, William, 135
Helfferich, Karl, 282, 290
Helldorff-Bedra, Otto von, 194–95
Henning, Wilhelm, 290–91
Henriot, Philippe, 355–56
heresthetic strategies, 43–44, 46–48, 189; as BCP strategy, 44, 66, 99–100, 131–37; in Prussian suffrage votes, 236–38; religion and, 47–48, 99–100; in Weimar's governing

197–205, 246–51; poor parliamentary discipline of, 192, 283, 284*f*; radical takeover from within of, 297–333; reliance on outside funding of, 303, 304–5, 312–13; in Spain, 337*t*, 339, 344–53; vulnerability to radicalism of, 23, 175, 190–97, 205, 271–73, 299–306. *See also DNVP; German Conservative Party; organizational weakness of German conservative parties*

Weber, Max, 40, 71n52, 176n14, 223
Webster, Daniel, 6
Wehler, Hans-Ulrich, 252
Weigall, Archibald, 161
Weimar Republic, 1–2, 4, 17, 23, 259–96; Brüning's presidential cabinet of, 297n2, 314, 319–24; cabinet instability and minority governments of, 284–85; compromises with the old regime of, 262–64, 269; concentration of executive power in, 314–15, 318, 319–24; constitutional convention of, 268; democratic corporatism and, 268–69; DNVP's role in governments of, 273–76, 288–89, 292–95, 301, 305, 309, 310n55, 311; economic challenges of, 273, 276, 288, 315n82, 319; endgame and demise of, 23, 264, 297–333; enlargement of electoral districts in, 277n71; French occupation and the Dawes Plan, 282, 288, 291–94, 309; golden age of (1924–1928), 271, 273–75, 286–96; governing coalition of, 1–2, 52, 265–68, 271, 274*f*, 284–85, 287, 319–20, 324nn123–24; impact of the Versailles Treaty on, 259, 261–62, 291–93; Law for the Defense of the Republic of, 287; legacy of fragmented parties of, 259–60, 278–82; Nazi rise to power in, 325–33; new conservative party formations of, 260n2; proportional representation in, 277–78; right-wing coup attempts of, 284, 285–86, 289–90; right-wing political power in, 267–73; three stages of, 271, 273–75; traditional accounts of, 259, 261–64, 267; transitional moment of, 264–69; votes and seat share during, 274*f*, 284–85. *See also DNVP; Social Democratic Party*

Weingast, Barry, 365
Westarp, Graf von, 289, 293

Westarp, Kuno von, 237; in the DKP, 247n115, 249–50, 264n18, 278; as DNVP chairman, 311, 313–14; as parliamentary group leader, 317–18; resignation from DNVP by, 318; in the Volksvereinigung, 322–23
Weston, Corinne, 136n92
Whig Party (Britain), 64n22, 67, 83; interpretation of Britain's political development of, 111, 171; on monarchical power, 67n32; suffrage reform and, 109n91
Wilhelm II, Kaiser of Germany, 1
Williamson, Philip, 164, 171
Wilson, Henry, 155
Wilson, Woodrow, 260–61
Winterfeldt, Joachim von, 180
Winterfeldt, Karl Ulrich von, 178, 179–80
Wolff, Henry Drummond, 84, 92
Women's Unionist and Tariff Reform Association (WUTRA), 163
working-classes, 51–52; in Britain, 113–14, 118, 228*f*, 231; in Germany, 18, 23, 52–53, 226–33, 255–58, 268–69; in models of democratization, 16, 18, 23
Workmen's Compensation Act, 145n23
World War I: Britain's Liberal–Conservative coalition of, 164–67; collapse of empires following, 8–9, 260; cross-party political truce in Germany of, 265–66; democratic transitions following, 26, 260–61, 264–69, 270; German Inter-Party Committee of, 266; Great Schism on the left during, 231; impact on Britain's constitutional crisis of, 158–62; labor mobilizations following, 260, 262–63, 268–69; outbreak of, 153–54; peace negotiations and Versailles Treaty of, 259, 261–62, 291–93
Wulle, Reinhold, 290n134

Ybarnégaray, Jean, 356
Yeltsin, Boris, xii
Young Conservatives (Germany), 279n75
Yrigoyen, Hipólito, 360

"Zinoviev Letter," 169

Ton Notermans, *Money, Markets, and the State: Social Democratic Economic Policies since 1918*

Aníbal Pérez-Liñán, *Presidential Impeachment and the New Political Instability in Latin America*

Roger D. Petersen, *Understanding Ethnic Violence: Fear, Hatred, and Resentment in 20th Century Eastern Europe*

Roger D. Petersen, *Western Intervention in the Balkans: The Strategic Use of Emotion in Conflict*

Simona Piattoni, ed., *Clientelism, Interests, and Democratic Representation*

Paul Pierson, *Dismantling the Welfare State?: Reagan, Thatcher, and the Politics of Retrenchment*

Marino Regini, *Uncertain Boundaries: The Social and Political Construction of European Economies*

Kenneth M. Roberts, *Changing Course in Latin America: Party Systems in the Neoliberal Era*

Marc Howard Ross, *Cultural Contestation in Ethnic Conflict*

Roger Schoenman, *Networks and Institutions in Europe's Emerging Markets*

Ben Ross Schneider, *Hierarchical Capitalism in Latin America: Business, Labor, and the Challenges of Equitable Development*

Lyle Scruggs, *Sustaining Abundance: Environmental Performance in Industrial Democracies*

Jefferey M. Sellers, *Governing from Below: Urban Regions and the Global Economy*

Yossi Shain and Juan Linz, eds., *Interim Governments and Democratic Transitions*

Beverly Silver, *Forces of Labor: Workers' Movements and Globalization since 1870*

Theda Skocpol, *Social Revolutions in the Modern World*

Prerna Singh, *How Solidarity Works for Welfare: Subnationalism and Social Development in India*

Austin Smith et al, *Selected Works of Michael Wallerstein*

Regina Smyth, *Candidate Strategies and Electoral Competition in the Russian Federation: Democracy Without Foundation*

Richard Snyder, *Politics after Neoliberalism: Reregulation in Mexico*

David Stark and László Bruszt, *Postsocialist Pathways: Transforming Politics and Property in East Central Europe*

Sven Steinmo, *The Evolution of Modern States: Sweden, Japan, and the United States*

Sven Steinmo, Kathleen Thelen, and Frank Longstreth, eds., *Structuring Politics: Historical Institutionalism in Comparative Analysis*

Susan C. Stokes, *Mandates and Democracy: Neoliberalism by Surprise in Latin America*

Susan C. Stokes, ed., *Public Support for Market Reforms in New Democracies*

Susan C. Stokes, Thad Dunning, Marcelo Nazareno, and Valeria Brusco, *Brokers, Voters, and Clientelism: The Puzzle of Distributive Politics*

Milan W. Svolik, *The Politics of Authoritarian Rule*

CPSIA information can be obtained
at www.ICGtesting.com
Printed in the USA
BVHW031309170619
551210BV00001B/2/P